T0135246

Lecture Notes in Artificial Intelligence 13604

Subseries of Lecture Notes in Computer Science

Series Editors

Randy Goebel
University of Alberta, Edmonton, Canada

Wolfgang Wahlster
DFKI, Berlin, Germany

Zhi-Hua Zhou
Nanjing University, Nanjing, China

Founding Editor

Jörg Siekmann
DFKI and Saarland University, Saarbrücken, Germany

More information about this subseries at https://link.springer.com/bookseries/1244

Lu Fang · Daniel Povey · Guangtao Zhai ·
Tao Mei · Ruiping Wang (Eds.)

Artificial Intelligence

Second CAAI International Conference, CICAI 2022
Beijing, China, August 27–28, 2022
Revised Selected Papers, Part I

Springer

Editors
Lu Fang 🆔
Tsinghua University
Beijing, China

Daniel Povey 🆔
Xiaomi Inc.
Beijing, China

Guangtao Zhai 🆔
Shanghai Jiao Tong University
Shanghai, China

Tao Mei 🆔
JD Explore Academy
Beijing, China

Ruiping Wang 🆔
Chinese Academy of Sciences
Beijing, China

ISSN 0302-9743   ISSN 1611-3349 (electronic)
Lecture Notes in Artificial Intelligence
ISBN 978-3-031-20496-8   ISBN 978-3-031-20497-5 (eBook)
https://doi.org/10.1007/978-3-031-20497-5

LNCS Sublibrary: SL7 – Artificial Intelligence

This Springer imprint is published by the registered company Springer Nature Switzerland AG
The registered company address is: Gewerbestrasse 11, 6330 Cham, Switzerland

Preface

The present book includes extended and revised versions of papers selected from the second CAAI International Conference on Artificial Intelligence (CICAI 2022), held in Beijing, China, during August 27–28, 2022.

CICAI is a summit forum in the field of artificial intelligence and the 2022 forum was hosted by Chinese Association for Artificial Intelligence (CAAI). CICAI aims to establish a global platform for international academic exchange, promote advanced research in AI and its affiliated disciplines, and promote scientific exchanges among researchers, practitioners, scientists, students, and engineers in AI and its affiliated disciplines in order to provide interdisciplinary and regional opportunities for researchers around the world, enhance the depth and breadth of academic and industrial exchanges, inspire new ideas, cultivate new forces, implement new ideas, integrate into the new landscape, and join the new era. The conference program included invited talks delivered by two distinguished speakers, Qiang Yang and Dacheng Tao, as well as five theme tutorials with five talks for each theme, followed by an oral session of 18 papers, a poster session of 127 papers, and a demo exhibition of 19 papers. Those papers were selected from 521 submissions using a double-blind review process, and on average each submission received 3.2 reviews. The topics covered by these selected high-quality papers span the fields of machine learning, computer vision, natural language processing, and data mining, amongst others.

This three-volume series contains 164 papers selected and revised from the proceedings of CICAI 2022. We would like to thank the authors for contributing their novel ideas and visions that are recorded in this book.

The proceeding editors also wish to thank all reviewers for their contributions and Springer for their trust and for publishing the proceedings of CICAI 2022.

September 2022

Lu Fang
Daniel Povey
Guangtao Zhai
Tao Mei
Ruiping Wang

Organization

General Chairs

Lu Fang	Tsinghua University, China
Daniel Povey	Xiaomi, China
Guangtao Zhai	Shanghai Jiao Tong University, China

Honorary Program Chair

Lina J. Karam	Lebanese American University, Lebanon

Program Chairs

Tao Mei	JD Explore Academy, China
Ruiping Wang	Chinese Academy of Sciences, China

Publication Chairs

Hui Qiao	Tsinghua University, China
Adriana Tapus	Institut Polytechnique de Paris, France

Presentation Chairs

Mengqi Ji	Beihang University, Singapore
Zhou Zhao	Zhejiang University, China
Shan Luo	King's College London, UK

Demo Chairs

Kun Li	Tianjin University, China
Fu Zhang	University of Hong Kong, China

International Liaison Chair

Feng Yang	Google Research, USA

Advisory Committee

C. L. Philip Chen	University of Macau, China
Xilin Chen	Institute of Computing Technology, Chinese Academy of Sciences, China
Yike Guo	Imperial College London, UK
Ping Ji	The City University of New York, USA
Licheng Jiao	Xidian University, China
Ming Li	University of Waterloo, Canada
Chenglin Liu	Institute of Automation, Chinese Academy of Sciences, China
Derong Liu	University of Illinois at Chicago, USA
Hong Liu	Peking University, China
Hengtao Shen	University of Electronic Science and Technology of China, China
Yuanchun Shi	Tsinghua University, China
Yongduan Song	Chongqing University, China
Fuchun Sun	Tsinghua University, China
Jianhua Tao	Institute of Automation, Chinese Academy of Sciences, China
Guoyin Wang	Chongqing University of Posts and Telecommunications, China
Weining Wang	Beijing University of Posts and Telecommunications, China
Xiaokang Yang	Shanghai Jiao Tong University, China
Changshui Zhang	Tsinghua University, China
Lihua Zhang	Fudan University, China
Song-Chun Zhu	Peking University, China
Wenwu Zhu	Tsinghua University, China
Yueting Zhuang	Zhejiang University, China

Program Committee

Abdul Rehman	Bournemouth University, UK
Biao Jie	Anhui Normal University, China
Bing Cao	Tianjin University, China
Bo Xue	University of Science and Technology of China, China
Bo Wang	Dalian University of Technology, China
Bochen Guan	OPPO US Research Center, USA
Boyun Li	Sichuan University, China
Chang Yao	East China Normal University, China
Chao Bian	Nanjing University, China

Chao Wu	Zhejiang University, China
Chaokun Wang	Tsinghua University, China
Chengyang Ying	Tsinghua University, China
Chenping Fu	Dalian University of Technology, China
Chu Zhou	Peking University, China
Chun-Guang Li	Beijing University of Posts and Telecommunications, China
Dan Guo	Hefei University of Technology, China
Daoqiang Zhang	Nanjing University of Aeronautics and Astronautics, China
Dawei Zhou	Xidian University, China
Decheng Liu	Xidian University, China
Difei Gao	National University of Singapore, Singapore
Dong Liu	University of Science and Technology of China, China
Fan Li	Xi'an Jiaotong University, China
Fan Xu	Peng Cheng Laboratory, China
Fan-Ming Luo	Nanjing University, China
Feihong Liu	Northwest University, China
Feng Bao	University of California, USA
Gang Chen	Sun Yat-sen University, China
Gaosheng Liu	Tianjin University, China
Guangchi Fang	Sun Yat-sen University, China
Guofeng Zhang	Zhejiang University, China
Guorui Feng	Shanghai University, China
Guoxin Yu	Institute of Computing Technology, Chinese Academy of Sciences, China
Hailing Wang	Shanghai University of Engineering Science, China
Haiping Ma	Anhui University, China
Hanyun Wang	Information Engineering University, China
Hao Gao	Nanjing University of Posts and Telecommunications, China
Haozhe Jia	Research and Development Institute of Northwestern Polytechnical University in Shenzhen, China
Heyou Chang	Nanjing Xiaozhuang University, China
Hengfei Cui	Northwestern Polytechnical University, Canada
Hong Chang	Chinese Academy of Sciences, China
Hong Qian	East China Normal University, China
Hongjun Li	Beijing Forestry University, China
Hongke Zhao	Tianjin University, China
Hongwei Mo	Harbin Engineering University, China

Huan Yin	Hong Kong University of Science and Technology, China
Huanjing Yue	Tianjin University, China
Hui Chen	Tsinghua University, China
Huiyu Duan	Shanghai Jiao Tong University, China
Jiajun Deng	University of Science and Technology of China, China
Jian Zhao	Institute of North Electronic Equipment, China
Jianguo Sun	Harbin Engineering University, China
Jianhui Chang	Peking University, China
Jianing Sun	Dalian University of Technology, China
Jia-Wei Chen	Xidian University, China
Jimin Pi	Baidu, China
Jing Chen	Beijing Research Institute of Precise Mechatronics and Controls, China
Jingwen Guo	Peking University Shenzhen Graduate School, China
Jingyu Yang	Tianjin University, China
Jinjian Wu	Xidian University, China
Jinsong Zhang	Tianjin University, China
Jinyu Tian	University of Macau, China
Jinyuan Liu	Dalian University of Technology, China
Jun Wang	Shanghai University, China
Jupo Ma	Xidian University, China
Kai Hu	Xiangtan University, China
Kaiqin Hu	Xi'an Jiaotong University, China
Kan Guo	Beihang University, China
Ke Xue	Nanjing University, China
Keyang Wang	Chongqing University, China
Keyu Li	Xidian University, China
Kun Cheng	Xidian University, China
Kun Zhang	Hefei University of Technology, China
Le Wang	Xi'an Jiaotong University, China
Le Wu	Hefei University of Technology, China
Lei Wang	University of Wollongong, Australia
Lei Shi	Zhengzhou University, China
Leida Li	Xidian University, China
Liansheng Zhuang	University of Science and Technology of China, China
Liguo Zhang	Harbin Engineering University, China
Likang Wu	University of Science and Technology of China, China

Lili Zhao	University of Science and Technology of China, China
Lizhi Wang	Beijing Institute of Technology, China
Longguang Wang	National University of Defense Technology, China
Meiyu Huang	China Academy of Space Technology, China
Meng Wang	Hefei University of Technology, China
Mengting Xu	Nanjing University of Aeronautics and Astronautics, China
Mengxi Jia	Peking University Shenzhen Graduate School, China
Min Wang	Hefei Comprehensive National Science Center, China
Mingkui Tan	South China University of Technology, China
Mingrui Zhu	Xidian University, China
Min-Ling Zhang	Southeast University, China
Mouxing Yang	Sichuan University, China
Ningyu Zhang	Zhejiang University, China
Peijie Sun	Tsinghua University, China
Pengfei Zhang	National University of Defense Technology, China
Pengyang Shao	Hefei University of Technology, China
Pingping Zhang	Dalian University of Technology, China
Qi Liu	University of Science and Technology of China, China
Qian Ning	Xidian University, China
Qian Xu	CILAB
Qiao Feng	Tianjin University, China
Qing Li	Beijing Normal University, China
Qingbo Wu	University of Electronic Science and Technology of China, China
Qinglin Wang	National University of Defense Technology, China
Qun Liu	Chongqing University of Posts and Telecommunications, China
Richang Hong	Hefei University of Technology, China
Rongjun Ge	Southeast University, China
Ruiping Wang	Institute of Computing Technology, Chinese Academy of Sciences, China
Ruqi Huang	Tsinghua University, China
Sheng Shen	Tianjin University, China
Shishuai Hu	Northwestern Polytechnical University, China

Shuaifeng Zhi	National University of Defense Technology, China
Shuang Yang	Institute of Computing Technology, Chinese Academy of Sciences, China
Shuang Li	The Chinese University of Hong Kong, Shenzhen, China
Shulan Ruan	University of Science and Technology of China, China
Si Liu	Beihang University, China
Sida Peng	Zhejiang University, China
Sinuo Deng	Beijing University of Technology, China
Tan Guo	Chongqing University of Posts and Telecommunications, China
Tao Huang	Xidian University, China
Tao Yue	Nanjing University, China
Tao Zhang	Tsinghua University, China
Tao He	Tsinghua University, China
Ting Shu	Shenzhen Institute of Meteorological Innovation, China
Waikeung Wong	Hong Kong Polytechnic University, China
Wangmeng Zuo	Harbin Institute of Technology, China
Wei Cao	University of Science and Technology of China, China
Wei Jia	Heifei University of Technology, China
Wei Shen	Shanghai Jiao Tong University, China
Wei Sun	Shanghai Jiao Tong University, China
Wei Pang	Beijing Information Science and Technology University, China
Wei Hu	Peking University, China
Weicheng Xie	Shenzhen University, China
Weishi Zheng	Sun Yat-sen University, China
Wenbin Wang	Institute of Computing Technology, Chinese Academy of Sciences, China
Xi Li	Zhejiang University, China
Xia Wu	Beijing Normal University, China
Xiang Ao	Institute of Computing Technology, Chinese Academy of Sciences, China
Xiang Chen	Zhejiang University and AZFT Joint Lab for Knowledge Engine, China
Xiang Gao	Jihua Laboratory, China
Xiang Bai	Huazhong University of Science and Technology, China
Xiangjun Yin	Tianjin University, China

Xiangwei Kong	Zhejiang University, China
Xianwei Zheng	Foshan University, China
Xiaodan Liang	Sun Yat-sen University, China
Xiaopeng Hong	Xi'an Jiaotong University, China
Xiaoyan Luo	Beihang University, China
Xiaoyong Lu	Northwest Normal University, China
Xiaoyun Yuan	Tsinghua University, China
Xin Yang	Dalian University of Technology, China
Xin Yuan	Westlake University, China
Xin Geng	Southeast University, China
Xin Xu	JD.com, China
Xinggang Wang	Huazhong University of Science and Technology, China
Xinglong Zhang	National University of Defense Technology, China
Xinpeng Ding	The Hong Kong University of Science and Technology, China
Xiongkuo Min	Shanghai Jiao Tong University, China
Xiongzheng Li	Tianjin University, China
Xiushan Nie	Shandong Jianzhu University, China
Xiu-Shen Wei	Nanjing University of Science and Technology, China
Xueyuan Xu	Beijing Normal University, China
Xun Chen	University of Science and Technology of China, China
Xuran Pan	Tsinghua University, China
Yang Li	Tsinghua-Berkeley Shenzhen Institute, Tsinghua University, China
Yangang Wang	Southeast University, China
Yaping Zhao	The University of Hong Kong, China
Ye Tian	Harbin Engineering University, China
Yebin Liu	Tsinghua University, China
Yi Hao	Xidian University, China
Yi Zhang	Xidian University, China
Yicheng Wu	Monash University, Australia
Yifan Zhang	National University of Defense Technology, China
Yijie Lin	Sichuan University, China
Ying Fu	Beijing Institute of Technology, China
Yingqian Wang	National University of Defense Technology, China
Yiwen Ye	Northwestern Polytechnical University, Canada
Yonghui Yang	Hefei University of Technology, China

Yu Liu	Dalian University of Technology, China
Yu Wang	Beijing Technology and Business University, China
Yuanbiao Gou	Sichuan University, China
Yuanfang Guo	Beihang University, China
Yuanman Li	Shenzhen University, China
Yuchao Dai	Northwestern Polytechnical University, China
Yucheng Zhu	Shanghai Jiao Tong University, China
Yufei Gao	Zhengzhou University, China
Yulin Cai	Tsinghua University, China
Yulun Zhang	ETH Zurich, Switzerland
Yun Tie	Zhengzhou University, China
Yunfan Li	Sichuan University, China
Zhanxiang Feng	Sun Yat-sen University, China
Zhaobo Qi	University of Chinese Academy of Sciences, China
Zhaoxiang Zhang	Chinese Academy of Sciences, China
Zhaoxin Liu	Xidian University, China
Zheng-Jun Zha	University of Science and Technology of China, China
Zhengming Zhang	Southeast University, China
Zhengyi Wang	Tsinghua University, China
Zhenya Huang	University of Science and Technology of China, China
Zhenyu Huang	Sichuan University, China
Zhenzhen Hu	National University of Defense Technology, China
Zhibo Wang	Tsinghua University, China
Zhiheng Fu	University of Western Australia, Australia
Zhiying Jiang	Dalian University of Technology, China
Zhiyuan Zhu	Western University, Canada
Zhu Liu	Dalian University of Technology, China
Ziwei Zheng	Xi'an Jiaotong University, China
Zizhao Zhang	Tsinghua University, China
Zongzhang Zhang	Nanjing University, China
Zunlei Feng	Zhejiang University, China

Contents – Part I

Contents – Part II

Contents – Part III

Multi-agent Systems

Natural Language Processing

Optimization

Robotics

Other AI Related Topics

Demo

Computer Vision

Cross-Camera Deep Colorization

Yaping Zhao[1,2], Haitian Zheng[3], Mengqi Ji[4], and Ruqi Huang[1(✉)]

[1] Tsinghua-Berkeley Shenzhen Institute and Tsinghua Shenzhen International
Graduate School, Shenzhen, P.R. China
ruqihuang@sz.tsinghua.edu.cn
[2] Zhejiang Future Technology Institute (Jiaxing), Jiaxing, China
[3] University of Rochester, Rochester, USA
[4] Beihang University, Beijing, China

Abstract. In this paper, we consider the color-plus-mono dual-camera
system and propose an end-to-end convolutional neural network to align
and fuse images from it in an efficient and cost-effective way. Our method
takes cross-domain and cross-scale images as input, and consequently
synthesizes HR colorization results to facilitate the trade-off between
spatial-temporal resolution and color depth in the single-camera imaging
system. In contrast to the previous colorization methods, ours can adapt
to color and monochrome cameras with distinctive spatial-temporal resolutions, rendering the flexibility and robustness in practical applications.
The key ingredient of our method is a cross-camera alignment module
that generates multi-scale correspondences for cross-domain image alignment. Through extensive experiments on various datasets and multiple
settings, we validate the flexibility and effectiveness of our approach.
Remarkably, our method consistently achieves substantial improvements,
i.e., around 10dB PSNR gain, upon the state-of-the-art methods. Code
is at: https://github.com/THU-luvision.

Keywords: Image colorization · Image fusion · Computational
imaging

1 Introduction

Nowadays, it has become a common practice of leveraging fusion of multi-sensory
data from camera arrays to improve imaging quality [1,4,10,24,26,33,41,46,55,
59]. In this paper, we consider the color-plus-mono dual-camera system and propose a novel learning-based framework for data fusion. Such a setting enjoys the
advantages of photosensibility and high resolution of the monochrome camera,
and the color sensibility of the color camera simultaneously. More specifically,

This work is supported in part by the Shenzhen Science and Technology Research
and Development Funds (JCYJ20180507183706645), in part by the Provincial Key
R&D Program of Zhejiang (Serial No. 2021C01016), and the Shenzhen Key Laboratory of next generation interactive media innovative technolog (Funding No.
ZDSYS20210623092001004). The lab website is: http://www.luvision.net.

L. Fang et al. (Eds.): CICAI 2022, LNAI 13604, pp. 3–17, 2022.
https://doi.org/10.1007/978-3-031-20497-5_1

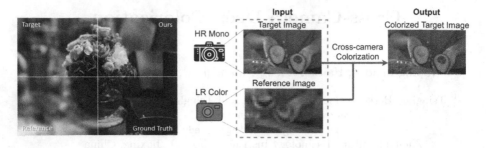

Fig. 1. Aiming at pursuing high-resolution and high color depth simultaneously, we proposed a general binocular imaging framework that performs cross-camera colorization. (Color figure online)

our pipeline takes as inputs a high-resolution (HR) grayscale image and a low-resolution (LR) color image, which are taken of the same scene by the respective cameras from similar viewpoints, as shown on the left of Fig. 1. After fusion, we obtain a HR color image illustrated on the right of Fig. 1, which to some extent facilitates the trade-off between spatial-temporal resolution and color depth in the single camera due to the space-bandwidth-product (SBP) [31].

In fact, the color-plus-mono dual camera has attracted an increasing amount of attention [11, 23, 29, 34, 38] recently. Most of the existing methods focus on addressing the cross-domain image color transfer. For example, traditional methods [3, 9, 14, 20, 30, 35, 40, 49] employ global color statistics or low-level feature correspondences while emerging learning-based approaches [17, 27] find high-level feature correspondences between images. Nevertheless, they commonly assume similar spatial resolution between data, and therefore can only deal with minor resolution gap, which is typically less than 2×.

On the other hand, it is naturally desirable to retain both high spatial-temporal resolution and high color depth. Thus methods assuming low-resolution gap have to either sacrifice resolution or require high-resolution input from *both* cameras, which can be costly and computationally heavy. Such discrepancy limits their practical applicability, for example, in using cameras with huge-resolution gaps to capture gigapixel video [54, 56], or in reducing the budget of a camera system [47].

In contrast, our method enables the imaging system to flexibly employ various cameras with different resolution gaps. The key ingredient of our method is a cross-camera alignment module that generates multi-scale correspondence for cross-domain image alignment. Without resorting to hand-crafted design on image registration or fusion [11, 23], we propose a novel neural network that leverages joint image alignment and fusion for cross-camera colorization. To improve the correspondence, we design visibility maps computation that explicitly computes and compensates warping errors. Finally, we utilize a warping regularization [42] to further improve the alignment quality.

Extensive experiments are performed to evaluate the proposed method under various settings, i.e., combinations of different resolution gaps, viewpoints, temporal steps, dynamic/static scenes. We test our method on various datasets, including the video dataset Vimeo90k [51], the light field dataset Flower [39], and the light field video dataset LFVideo [45]. Both the quantitative and qualitative experiments show the substantial improvements of our method over the state-of-the-art methods – remarkably, we achieve around 10dB gain in terms of PSNR in most of the test cases upon the best baseline.

Our main contributions are summarized as follows:

- A flexible and cost-effective imaging framework that is applicable to various color-plus-mono camera settings with multiple resolution gaps. In particular, our method can adapt to both spatial and temporal resolution gap more than 8×.
- A novel network design for cross-camera colorization: the cross-camera alignment generates dense correspondence for multi-scale feature alignment; the fusion module compensates alignment error via visibility map computation and performs synthesis; the warping regularization further improves the alignment.
- Extensive evaluation on a wide range of settings, i.e. different resolution gaps, combinations of viewpoints and temporal steps show the substantial improvements of our method, i.e., around 10dB PSNR gain over the state-of-the-art ones.

2 Related Work

2.1 Automatic Image Colorization

Most traditional methods perform colorization by optimization, e.g., Regression Tree Fields (RTFs) [22] and graph cuts [7]. With deep learning, some approaches [8,58] leverage large-scale color image data [37,63] to colorize grayscale images automatically. Yoo et al. [53] propose a colorization network augmented by external neural memory networks. Another line of works uses GANs [5,13,21,44] to colorize grayscale images by learning probability distributions.

However, automatic colorization is ill-conditioned since many potential colors can be assigned to the gray pixels of an input image. As a result, these methods tend to generate unnatural colorized images.

2.2 Reference-based Image Colorization

According to what is used as a reference, reference-based methods can be divided into strokes/palette-based ones and example-based ones.

Strokes/Palette-based Image Colorization. Strokes/palette-based image colorization methods [6,18,25,32,52] seek to reconstruct color images from the users-provided sparse stroke. However, these methods require intensive manual works. More importantly, scribbles and palettes provide insufficient color information for colorization, leading to unsatisfying results.

Example-based Image Colorization. To avoid the manual labor of scribbling or palette selection while facilitating controllable colorization, example-based methods are proposed to transfer the color of a reference image to the target image. The initial works [35,49] attempt to match color statistics globally. Targeting at more accurate color transfer, later works [3,9,14,20,30,40] utilize hand-crafted feature correspondences, *e.g.*, SIFT, Gabor wavelet to enforce local color consistency. Recently, He *et al.* [16] and Liao *et al.* [27] perform dense patch matching for color transfer. However, the patch-based correspondence [16,27] are inherently inefficient to compute. Furthermore, the inter-patch misalignment may hurt the image synthesis. Xiao *et al.* [50] propose a self-supervised approach that reconstructs a color image from its grayscale version and global color distribution coding. Although obtaining impressive results, the proposed approach does not utilize the spatial correspondence between two images for local colorization.

2.3   Flow-based or Non-rigid Correspondences

The cross-camera image colorization is also related to flow-based and non-rigid correspondence estimation. Specifically, back-warping reference images using estimated optical flow fields [19,28,60,61] can serve to align images from two viewpoints. In addition, HaCohen *et al.* [15] showcase the usage of estimating non-rigid dense correspondence for image enhancement. However, due to the domain and resolution gap between the two cameras, the above approaches fail in finding correct matching and result in poor performance under our cross-domain and cross-resolution setting.

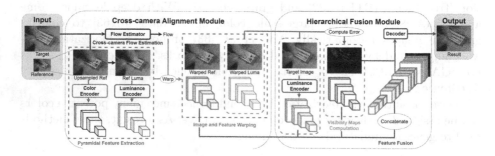

Fig. 2. Our network contains two modules: 1) the alignment module, which performs non-rigid transformation on the cross-camera image inputs and extracted features; 2) the fusion module, which performs features fusion and colorization synthesis.

3   Approach

Assume two images from different cameras capturing the same scene at similar viewpoints are given – an LR color image as the reference and an HR gray image as the target. We denote the target single-channel image as $I_1 \in \mathbb{R}^{sH \times sW \times 1}$ and the three-channel reference as $I_2 \in \mathbb{R}^{H \times W \times 3}$, where $s \geq 1$ is the scale factor representing the spatial-resolution gap in the dual camera, H and W are the horizontal and vertical spatial-resolution, respectively. Similarly, the ground-truth color image is denoted as $I_g \in \mathbb{R}^{sH \times sW \times 3}$, where I_g shares the same viewpoint with the target image I_1. Our goal is to generate an HR color image $I_c \in \mathbb{R}^{sH \times sW \times 3}$ as similar as possible to I_g.

To achieve this goal, we propose an end-to-end and fully convolutional deep neural network (see illustration in Fig. 2). Our network contains a cross-camera alignment module and a hierarchical fusion module: the former (Sect. 3.1) consists of a color encoder Net_E^c, a luminance encoder Net_E^l, and a flow estimator Net_{flow}; the latter (Sect. 3.2) consists of a decoder Net_D. On top of that, our network trains jointly the warping flow estimator and colorization neural networks by combining warping loss $\mathcal{L}_w$ and colorization loss $\mathcal{L}_c$ (Sect. 3.3).

3.1 Cross-camera Alignment Module

This module is designed to perform the temporal and spatial alignment. As shown on the left of Fig. 2, we first extract feature maps of input images and then utilize a flow estimator to generate the cross-camera correspondence at multiple scales. After flow estimation, we use cross-camera warping to perform the non-rigid transformation. In the following, we provide details of each part.

Pyramidal Feature Extraction. Considering the different resolutions of the input images, we first upsample the reference I_2 to the same resolution as I_1 via bicubic upsampling, denoted by $I_2^{\uparrow}$. I_1 and $I_2^{\uparrow}$ are of the same resolution but belong to different image modalities, thus we design two encoders to extract their pyramidal features respectively:

$$\{F_i^l\} = Net_E^l(I_1), \quad \{F_i^c\} = Net_E^c(I_2^{\uparrow}), \quad i = 1, 2, 3, 4, \tag{1}$$

where F_i^l (resp. F_i^c) is the feature map of target image I_1 (resp. I_2) at scale i.

To measure the image alignment across different modalities, we convert the upsampled reference image $I_2^{\uparrow}$ from RGB color space to YUV [43] color space. Thus, $I_2^{\uparrow}$ can be separated into a luminance component and two chrominance components. Discarding chrominance components, we retain the luminance components denoted as I_2^Y, which is a grayscale counterpart of the upsampled reference image $I_2^{\uparrow}$.

Then the luminance encoder is also used to extract multi-scale feature maps of I_2^Y, which is utilized latter in Sect. 3.2 to calculate warping errors on feature domain:

$$\{F_i^Y\} = Net_E^l(I_2^Y), \quad i = 1, 2, 3, 4. \tag{2}$$

Cross-camera Flow Estimation. For image alignment, we adopt the widely used FlowNetS [12] as our flow estimator, Net_{flow}, to generate the dense cross-camera correspondence at multiple scales. Tailored for our setting, we change the input channel number of the first convolutional layer of FlowNetS from 6 to 4, and obtain the following flow fields:

$$\{f_i\} = Net_{flow}(I_1, I_2^{\uparrow}), \quad i = 0, 1, 2, 3, 4, \tag{3}$$

where f_i is the estimated flow field at scale i.

Image and Features Warping. To perform the temporal and spatial alignment with the estimated flow fields, we utilize a warping operation similar to [62]. More specifically, our warping operation considers the cross-camera flow field f:

$$\tilde{I} = \mathcal{W}(I, f), \tag{4}$$

where $\mathcal{W}(I, f)$ denotes the result of warping the input I using the flow field f.

After flow estimation, we perform the warping operation on the reference image features F_i^c and corresponding luminance features F_i^Y. Using the multi-scale flow f_i in Eq. 3, we generate the temporally and spatially aligned features $\{\tilde{F}_i^c\}$ and $\{\tilde{F}_i^Y\}$:

$$\tilde{F}_i^c = \mathcal{W}(F_i^c, f_i), \quad \tilde{F}_i^Y = \mathcal{W}(F_i^Y, f_i), \quad i = 1, 2, 3, 4. \tag{5}$$

To measure image alignment latter in Sect. 3.2, we also perform the warping operation on the image domain. According to Eq. 4, we have:

$$\tilde{I}_2^Y = \mathcal{W}(I_2^Y, f_0), \tag{6}$$

where f_0 is the estimated flow field at scale 0 in Eq. 3, $\tilde{I}_2^Y$ is the warping result utilized latter in Sect. 3.2 to calculate warping errors on the image domain.

3.2 Hierarchical Fusion Module

Visibility Maps Computation. On the image domain, the warping error indicates the different light intensity between the target and the reference, *i.e.*, optical visibility. While on the feature domain, warping error represents the different activation value of the feature maps, *i.e.*, feature recognition. We combine the errors from both perspectives and define the multi-scale visibility maps $\{V_i\}$ as warping errors on both domains:

$$V_0 = \tilde{I}_2^Y - I_1, \quad V_i = \tilde{F}_i^Y - F_i^l, \quad i = 1, 2, 3, 4, \tag{7}$$

where V_i is the warping error at scale i.

To give an intuition of the visibility maps, we visualize it on the image domain in Fig. 3. There are lost details caused by the low-quality reference (*e.g.*, blurry words shown on the top of Fig. 3), motion blur caused by fast-moving objects (*e.g.*, waving hand shown on the bottom of Fig. 3), local occlusion caused by motion or parallax (*e.g.*, the garment occluded by the hand shown on the bottom of Fig. 3). The pixel-wise positive and negative values of visibility maps represent the invisible regions in the reference and the target image, respectively.

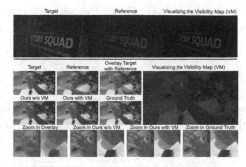

Fig. 3. Visualizing the visibility map on image domain. Red: invisible regions in the reference image; green: invisible regions in the target image. Zoom in to see details. (Color figure online)

Feature Fusion. In the end, we design a U-Net [36] like decoder to fuse feature maps and visibility maps, and synthesize the colorization result. As shown on the right of Fig. 2, the target features $\{F_i^l\}$, warped reference features $\{\widetilde{F}_i^c\}$ and visibility maps $\{V_i\}$ are concatenated as the input of fusion decoder. Finally we obtain the result I_c by:

$$I_c = Net_D(\{F_i^l\}, \{\widetilde{F}_i^c\}, \{V_j\}), \quad i = 1, 2, 3, 4, j = 0, 1, 2, 3, 4. \qquad (8)$$

3.3 Loss Function

We use two loss functions: warping loss and colorization loss. The former encourages the flow estimator to generate precise cross-camera correspondence for image alignment. The latter is responsible for the final synthesized image.

Warping Loss. Since the ground-truth flow is unavailable, it is difficult to train the flow estimator in an unsupervised fashion. To solve this problem, we adopt the warping loss from [42]. Specifically, since the input images capture the same scene, it is reasonable to require the warped-upsampled reference image owning a intensity distribution similar to the ground truth I_g as much as possible. Thus our warping loss is defined as:

$$\mathcal{L}_w = \frac{1}{2N} \sum_{i=1}^{N} \sum_{j} ||\widetilde{I}_2^{\uparrow (i)} - I_g^{(i)}||_2^2, \quad \widetilde{I}_2^{\uparrow} = \mathcal{W}(I_2^{\uparrow}, f_0), \qquad (9)$$

where N is the sample number, i iterates over training samples, f_0 is the estimated flow field at scale 0 in Eq. 3.

Colorization Loss. Given the network prediction $\widetilde{I_c}$ and the ground truth I_c, the colorization loss is defined as:

$$\mathcal{L}_c = \frac{1}{N} \sum_{i=1}^{N} \sum_j \rho(I_c^{(i)} - I_g^{(i)}), \tag{10}$$

where $\rho(x) = \sqrt{x^2 + 0.001^2}$ is the Charbonnier penalty function [2], $\widetilde{I_c}$ is obtained from Eq. 8, N is the sample number, i iterates over training samples.

Fig. 4. Colorization comparisons on Vimeo90K dataset under cross-scale $8\times$ settings.

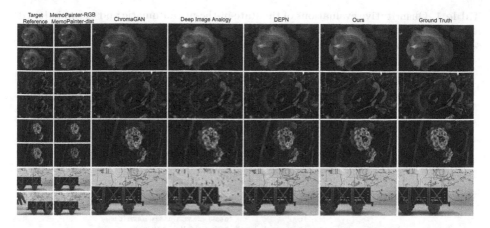

Fig. 5. Comparison under cross-scale 8× settings on Flower (the 1st, 2nd, 3rd rows) and LFVideo (the last row) dataset, respectively.

4 Experiments

4.1 Dataset

Video Dataset. The Vimeo90K [51] dataset consists of videos that cover a large variety of scenes and actions. Following [51], we selected $66, 178$ video sequences, each of which contains 7 frames with resolution of 448×256. To construct the training and testing datasets, we randomly divide it into $60, 000$ sequences for training and $6, 178$ sequences for testing. For training, we downsample the first frame at each video sequence as a reference image and randomly select the tth$(1 < t < 8)$ frame converted to the grayscale image as a target. For testing, reference images are sampled from the first video frame, while the target images are from the second and the last frame. See the supplementary material for training details.

Light-field Dataset. The Flower dataset [39] contains flowers and plants light-field images with the 376×541 spatial resolution, and 14×14 angular samples. Following [39], we extract the central 8×8 grid of angular sample, and randomly selected 343 samples for evaluations. The images at viewpoints $(1, 1)$ and $(7, 7)$ are converted to grayscale as target, and images at viewpoint $(0, 0)$ are downsampled as reference.

Light-field Video Dataset. The LFVideo dataset [45] contains real-scene light-field videos with the spatial resolution as 376×541, while the angular samples are 8×8. For evaluations, we randomly selected 270 video frames. The images of the tth$(t = 2, 9)$ frame at viewpoints $(i, i), i = 1, 7$ are converted to monochrome as target, and images of the first frame at viewpoint $(0, 0)$ are downsampled as reference.

Table 1. Quantitative evaluations of the state-of-the-art automatic and example-based algorithms on different datasets, in terms of NRMSE/PSNR/SSIM/LPIPS for different scale factors, frame gaps and parallax settings respectively.

Dataset	Frame	View	Scale	Methods	NRMSE	PSNR	SSIM	LPIPS	Runtime
Vimeo	2	-	N/A	MemoPainter-RGB [53]	0.3463	19.9920	0.7989	0.4206	0.5124
	2	-	N/A	MemoPainter-dist [53]	0.2352	22.5768	0.8751	0.3015	0.5620
	2	-	N/A	ChromaGAN [44]	0.2097	23.5276	0.8697	0.2917	2.6915
	2	-	4×	Deep Image Analogy [27]	0.1544	25.6775	0.7741	0.3184	219.5779
	2	-	4×	DEPN [50]	0.1313	27.5916	0.9313	0.1585	0.3425
	2	-	4×	Ours	**0.0227**	**43.2263**	**0.9884**	**0.0157**	**0.0838**
	2	-	8×	DEPN [50]	0.1316	27.5724	0.9310	0.1588	0.3525
	2	-	8×	Deep Image Analogy [27]	0.1951	23.5943	0.6954	0.4142	203.4619
	2	-	8×	Ours	**0.0275**	**41.6039**	**0.9845**	**0.0241**	**0.0847**
	7	-	N/A	MemoPainter-RGB [53]	0.3150	20.0014	0.7995	0.4201	0.5301
	7	-	N/A	MemoPainter-dist [53]	0.2326	22.4321	0.8738	0.3028	0.5483
	7	-	N/A	ChromaGAN [44]	0.2064	23.5428	0.8696	0.2909	2.7384
	7	-	4×	Deep Image Analogy [27]	0.2063	23.0956	0.7227	0.3529	214.3759
	7	-	4×	DEPN [50]	0.1306	27.5174	0.9313	0.1593	0.3548
	7	-	4×	Ours	**0.0380**	**39.5223**	**0.9823**	**0.0321**	**0.0846**
	7	-	8×	Deep Image Analogy [27]	0.2356	21.8671	0.66771	0.4260	220.8749
	7	-	8×	DEPN [50]	0.1309	27.4989	0.9311	0.1596	0.3478
	7	-	8×	Ours	**0.0408**	**38.6736**	**0.9796**	**0.0382**	**0.0891**
Flower	-	(1,1)	N/A	MemoPainter-RGB [53]	0.4172	22.0304	0.7508	0.3389	0.5623
	-	(1,1)	N/A	MemoPainter-dist [53]	0.3237	24.2114	0.8822	0.2668	0.6184
	-	(1,1)	N/A	ChromaGAN [44]	0.3046	24.4863	0.8407	0.3081	1.1562
	-	(1,1)	4×	Deep Image Analogy [27]	0.1874	28.6252	0.8065	0.2581	411.6000
	-	(1,1)	4×	DEPN [50]	0.1797	29.0692	0.9286	0.1711	0.4899
	-	(1,1)	4×	Ours	**0.0205**	**45.9354**	**0.9938**	**0.0041**	**0.1173**
	-	(1,1)	8×	Deep Image Analogy [27]	0.2620	25.6807	0.6976	0.4029	404.4650
	-	(1,1)	8×	DEPN [50]	0.1797	29.0730	0.9285	0.1710	0.4729
	-	(1,1)	8×	Ours	**0.0255**	**43.8623**	**0.9923**	**0.0077**	**0.1171**
	-	(7,7)	N/A	MemoPainter-RGB [53]	0.4216	21.9233	0.7525	0.3424	0.5912
	-	(7,7)	N/A	MemoPainter-dist [53]	0.3158	24.4801	0.8858	0.2617	0.6034
	-	(7,7)	N/A	ChromaGAN [44]	0.3065	24.4616	0.8404	0.3081	1.5492
	-	(7,7)	4×	Deep Image Analogy [27]	0.2532	25.9906	0.7100	0.2954	409.2839
	-	(7,7)	4×	DEPN [50]	0.1775	29.2156	0.9300	0.1663	0.4725
	-	(7,7)	4×	Ours	**0.0237**	**44.8138**	**0.9931**	**0.0060**	**0.1170**
	-	(7,7)	8×	Deep Image Analogy [27]	0.2903	24.7787	0.6703	0.4006	405.3829
	-	(7,7)	8×	DEPN [50]	0.1774	29.2186	0.9299	0.1663	0.4793
	-	(7,7)	8×	Ours	**0.0276**	**43.2567**	**0.9920**	**0.0092**	**0.1175**
LFVideo	2	(1,1)	N/A	MemoPainter-RGB [53]	0.4190	21.4680	0.7227	0.3470	0.6633
	2	(1,1)	N/A	MemoPainter-dist [53]	0.3317	23.7711	0.8565	0.2181	0.6927
	2	(1,1)	N/A	ChromaGAN [44]	0.1982	27.6557	0.8592	0.2120	0.5773
	2	(1,1)	4×	Deep Image Analogy [27]	0.3304	23.2553	0.6374	0.4040	755.4143
	2	(1,1)	4×	DEPN [50]	0.1129	32.7250	0.9668	0.0933	0.4824
	2	(1,1)	4×	Ours	**0.0459**	**41.0111**	**0.9857**	**0.0288**	**0.1173**
	2	(1,1)	8×	Deep Image Analogy [27]	0.3695	22.3074	0.5970	0.4944	748.9276
	2	(1,1)	8×	DEPN [50]	0.1129	32.7220	0.9669	0.0933	0.4793
	2	(1,1)	8×	Ours	**0.0492**	**40.3612**	**0.9849**	**0.0312**	**0.1167**
	2	(7,7)	N/A	MemoPainter-RGB [53]	0.4261	21.3552	0.7125	0.3527	0.6325
	2	(7,7)	N/A	MemoPainter-dist [53]	0.3058	24.4653	0.8662	0.2037	0.6429
	2	(7,7)	N/A	ChromaGAN [44]	0.1959	27.8429	0.8609	0.2097	0.5826
	2	(7,7)	4×	Deep Image Analogy [27]	0.3394	22.9054	0.6315	0.4041	751.4360
	2	(7,7)	4×	DEPN [50]	0.1104	32.9745	0.9679	0.0880	0.4529
	2	(7,7)	4×	Ours	**0.0448**	**41.0335**	**0.9859**	**0.0274**	**0.1185**
	2	(7,7)	8×	Deep Image Analogy [27]	0.3718	22.0710	0.5977	0.4920	753.5917
	2	(7,7)	8×	DEPN [50]	0.11070	32.9560	0.9680	0.0883	0.4826
	2	(7,7)	8×	Ours	**0.0480**	**40.4257**	**0.9853**	**0.0301**	**0.1179**
	9	(1,1)	N/A	MemoPainter-RGB [53]	0.4501	21.1598	0.6991	0.3608	0.6530
	9	(1,1)	N/A	MemoPainter-dist [53]	0.3290	23.7217	0.8582	0.2204	0.6498
	9	(1,1)	N/A	ChromaGAN [44]	0.2117	27.5192	0.8512	0.2244	0.5728
	9	(1,1)	4×	Deep Image Analogy [27]	0.3270	23.5479	0.6404	0.4102	749.7418
	9	(1,1)	4×	DEPN [50]	0.1165	32.5500	0.9670	0.0917	0.4692
	9	(1,1)	4×	Ours	**0.0508**	**40.7632**	**0.9853**	**0.0323**	**0.1169**
	9	(1,1)	8×	Deep Image Analogy [27]	0.3709	22.4716	0.5979	0.4954	747.7591
	9	(1,1)	8×	DEPN [50]	0.1166	32.5409	0.9671	0.0919	0.4792
	9	(1,1)	8×	Ours	**0.0538**	**40.1106**	**0.9845**	**0.0349**	**0.1167**
	9	(7,7)	N/A	MemoPainter-RGB [53]	0.4104	21.9786	0.7211	0.3464	0.6009
	9	(7,7)	N/A	MemoPainter-dist [53]	0.3271	23.9009	0.8628	0.2170	0.6947
	9	(7,7)	N/A	ChromaGAN [44]	0.2112	27.5598	0.8542	0.2248	0.5927
	9	(7,7)	4×	Deep Image Analogy [27]	0.3221	23.7166	0.6447	0.4058	747.9275
	9	(7,7)	4×	DEPN [50]	0.1130	32.7364	0.9676	0.0882	0.4865
	9	(7,7)	4×	Ours	**0.0492**	**40.8788**	**0.9858**	**0.0304**	**0.1420**
	9	(7,7)	8×	Deep Image Analogy [27]	0.3564	22.8959	0.6035	0.4921	750.8465
	9	(7,7)	8×	DEPN [50]	0.1132	32.7194	0.9678	0.0881	0.4539
	9	(7,7)	8×	Ours	**0.0518**	**40.3270**	**0.9851**	**0.0328**	**0.1453**

4.2   Comparison to State-of-the-Art Methods

Our method is compared against the state-of-the-art example-based colorization methods, namely Deep Image Analogy [27] and DEPN [50], and the recent automatic colorization approaches, including MemoPainter [53] and Chroma-GAN [44]. Following [53], we evaluated MemoPainter using RGB information and color distribution for color features, respectively. Both the quantitative evaluation in Table 1 and the qualitative results in Figs. 4 and 5 suggest that our performance is far beyond that of the baselines.

Our quantitative evaluation involves four image quality metrics: NRMSE, PSNR, SSIM [48], and LPIPS [57]. Table 1 shows quantitative comparisons, and it is evident that our method outperforms the baselines by a large margin in most of the settings, including combinations of different scale factors, frame gaps, and parallax. In general, our method achieves approximately 10dB gain of PSNR upon the baselines.

We provide qualitative comparisons in Figs. 4 and 5 respectively on the Vimeo90k, Flower, LFVideo datasets under the challenging scale 8×, largest parallax and largest frame gap setting. Firstly, benefiting from the reference image, the example-based approaches show better results than the automatic colorization approaches. Moreover, among the example-based approaches, our method generates the most coherent images with less color bleeding effects, showing the clear advantage of our algorithm.

4.3   Ablation Study

This section investigates the role of proposed visibility maps and warping loss by two variants of our pipeline, which respectively turn off one of the components while remaining others. In particular, we run our test on the Vimeo90k dataset, with resolution gaps being 4× and 8×. According to Fig. 6, disabling either component leads to a performance drop, suggesting the necessities of both.

Visibility Maps. When visibility maps are disabled, slight degradation in PSNR is observed in Fig. 6. Also, as shown in Fig. 3, artifacts are more evident without visibility maps, suggesting that visibility maps can reduce the wrong colorization due to inconsistent visibility between input images.

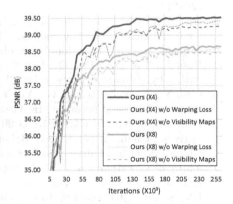

Fig. 6. The PSNR performance of the different variants with some of the components disabled during training on Vimeo90K dataset.

Warping Loss. From Fig. 6, the performance of our network drops if warping loss is remove. We speculate that it is because the colorization loss is for image synthesis and does not explicitly define terms for flow estimation. In contrast, the warping loss is necessary to regularize the flow estimator training and enable better convergence.

5 Conclusion

We propose a novel convolutional neural network to facilitate the trade-off between spatial-temporal resolution and color depth in the imaging system. Our method fuses data to obtain an HR color image given cross-domain and cross-scale input pairs captured by the color-plus-mono dual camera. In contrast to previous works, our method can adapt to color and monochrome cameras with the various spatial-temporal resolution; thus it enables more flexible and generalized imaging systems. The key ingredient of our method is a cross-camera alignment module that generates multi-scale corre-spondence for cross-domain image alignment. Experiments on several datasets demonstrate the superior performance of our method (around 10dB in PSNR) compared to state-of-the-art methods.

References

1. Brady, D.J., et al.: Multiscale gigapixel photography. Nature **486**(7403), 386–389 (2012)
2. Bruhn, A., Weickert, J., Schnörr, C.: Lucas/kanade meets horn/schunck: combining local and global optic flow methods. Int. J. Comput. Vis. **61**(3), 211–231 (2005)
3. Bugeau, A., et al.: Variational exemplar-based image colorization. IEEE TIP (2013)
4. Cao, X., Tong, X., Dai, Q., Lin, S.: High resolution multispectral video capture with a hybrid camera system. In: CVPR 2011, pp. 297–304. IEEE (2011)
5. Cao, Y., Zhou, Z., Zhang, W., Yu, Y.: Unsupervised diverse colorization via generative adversarial networks. In: Ceci, M., Hollmén, J., Todorovski, L., Vens, C., Džeroski, S. (eds.) ECML PKDD 2017. LNCS (LNAI), vol. 10534, pp. 151–166. Springer, Cham (2017). https://doi.org/10.1007/978-3-319-71249-9_10
6. Chang, H., et al.: Palette-based photo recoloring. ACM Trans, Graph (2015)
7. Charpiat, G., Hofmann, M., Schölkopf, B.: Automatic image colorization via multimodal predictions. In: Forsyth, D., Torr, P., Zisserman, A. (eds.) ECCV 2008. LNCS, vol. 5304, pp. 126–139. Springer, Heidelberg (2008). https://doi.org/10.1007/978-3-540-88690-7_10
8. Cheng, Z., Yang, Q., Sheng, B.: Deep colorization. In: ICCV, pp. 415–423 (2015)
9. Chia, A.Y.S., et al.: Semantic colorization with internet images. In: ACM TOG (2011)
10. Cossairt, O.S., et al.: Gigapixel computational imaging. In: ICCP. IEEE (2011)
11. Dong, X., Li, W.: Shoot high-quality color images using dual-lens system with monochrome and color cameras. Neurocomputing **352**, 22–32 (2019)
12. Dosovitskiy, A., et al.: Flownet: learning optical flow with conv networks. In: ICCV (2015)

13. Goodfellow, I., et al.: Generative adversarial nets. In: NeuIPS, pp. 2672–2680 (2014)
14. Gupta, R.K., et al.: Image colorization using similar images. In: ACM MM (2012)
15. HaCohen, Y., Shechtman, E., Goldman, D.B., Lischinski, D.: Non-rigid dense correspondence with applications for image enhancement. ACM TOG **30**(4), 1–10 (2011)
16. He, M., Liao, J., Yuan, L., Sander, P.V.: Neural color transfer between images. arXiv (2017)
17. He, M., et al.: Deep exemplar-based colorization. In: ACM TOG (2018)
18. Huang, Y.C., et al.: An adaptive edge detection based colorization algorithm and its applications. In: ACM MM (2005)
19. Ilg, E., et al.: Flownet 2.0: evolution of optical flow estimation with deep networks. In: CVPR, pp. 2462–2470 (2017)
20. Ironi, R., et al.: Colorization by example. In: Rendering Techniques. Citeseer (2005)
21. Isola, P., Zhu, J.Y., Zhou, T., Efros, A.A.: Image-to-image translation with conditional adversarial networks. In: CVPR, pp. 1125–1134 (2017)
22. Jancsary, J., Nowozin, S., Sharp, T., Rother, C.: Regression tree fields-an efficient, non-parametric approach to image labeling problems. In: CVPR, pp. 2376–2383. IEEE (2012)
23. Jeon, H.G., et al.: Stereo matching with color and monochrome cameras in low-light conditions. In: CVPR (2016)
24. Jin, D., et al.: All-in-depth via cross-baseline light field camera. In: ACM MM (2020)
25. Levin, A., et al.: Colorization using optimization. In: ACM SIGGRAPH 2004 Papers (2004)
26. Li, G., et al.: Zoom in to the details of human-centric videos. In: ICIP. IEEE (2020)
27. Liao, J., et al.: Visual attribute transfer through deep image analogy. arXiv (2017)
28. Liu, C., et al.: Sift flow: Dense correspondence across scenes and its applications. IEEE TPAMI (2010)
29. Liu, C., Shan, J., Liu, G.: High resolution array camera (Apr 19 2016), US Patent 9,319,585
30. Liu, X., et al.: Intrinsic colorization. In: ACM SIGGRAPH Asia 2008 papers, pp. 1–9 (2008)
31. Lohmann, et al.: Space-bandwidth product of optical signals and systems. JOSA A (1996)
32. Luan, Q., Wen, F., Cohen-Or, D., Liang, L., Xu, Y.Q., Shum, H.Y.: Natural image colorization. In: Eurographics Conference on Rendering Techniques, pp. 309–320 (2007)
33. Ma, C., Cao, X., Tong, X., Dai, Q., Lin, S.: Acquisition of high spatial and spectral resolution video with a hybrid camera system. IJCV **110**(2), 141–155 (2014)
34. Mantzel, W., et al.: Shift-and-match fusion of color and mono images (2017), US Patent
35. Reinhard, E., et al.: Color transfer between images. IEEE Comput. Graph. Appl. **21**(5), 34–41 (2001)
36. Ronneberger, O., Fischer, P., Brox, T.: U-Net: convolutional networks for biomedical image segmentation. In: Navab, N., Hornegger, J., Wells, W.M., Frangi, A.F. (eds.) MICCAI 2015. LNCS, vol. 9351, pp. 234–241. Springer, Cham (2015). https://doi.org/10.1007/978-3-319-24574-4_28
37. Russakovsky, O., et al.: ImageNet large scale visual recognition challenge. IJCV (2015)

38. Sharif, S., Jung, Y.J.: Deep color reconstruction for a sparse color sensor. Opt. Express **27**(17), 23661–23681 (2019)
39. Srinivasan, P.P., et al.: Learning to synthesize a 4D RGBD light field from a single image. In: ICCV, pp. 2243–2251 (2017)
40. Tai, Y.W., Jia, J., Tang, C.K.: Local color transfer via probabilistic segmentation by expectation-maximization. In: CVPR, vol. 1, pp. 747–754. IEEE (2005)
41. Tai, Y.W., et al.: Image/video deblurring using a hybrid camera. In: CVPR. IEEE (2008)
42. Tan, Y., et al.: Crossnet++: Cross-scale large-parallax warping for reference-based super-resolution. IEEE TPAMI (2020)
43. Union, I.T.: Encoding parameters of digital television for studios. CCIR Recommend. (1992)
44. Vitoria, P., Raad, L., Ballester, C.: Chromagan: An adversarial approach for picture colorization. arXiv preprint arXiv:1907.09837 (2019)
45. Wang, T.C., et al.: Light field video capture using a learning-based hybrid imaging system. ACM TOG (2017)
46. Wang, X., et al.: Panda: A gigapixel-level human-centric video dataset. In: CVPR (2020)
47. Wang, Y., Liu, Y., Heidrich, W., Dai, Q.: The light field attachment: Turning a DSLR into a light field camera using a low budget camera ring. IEEE TVCG **23**(10), 2357–2364 (2016)
48. Wang, Z., Bovik, A.C., Sheikh, H.R., Simoncelli, E.P.: Image quality assessment: from error visibility to structural similarity. IEEE TIP **13**(4), 600–612 (2004)
49. Welsh, T., Ashikhmin, M., Mueller, K.: Transferring color to greyscale images. In: Annual Conference on Computer Graphics and Interactive Techniques, pp. 277–280 (2002)
50. Xiao, C., Han, C., Zhang, Z., others, G., He, S.: Example-based colourization via dense encoding pyramids. In: Computer Graphics Forum. Wiley Online Library (2020)
51. Xue, T., et al.: Video enhancement with task-oriented flow. In: IJCV (2019)
52. Yatziv, L., Sapiro, G.: Fast image and video colorization using chrominance blending. IEEE Trans. Image Process. **15**(5), 1120–1129 (2006)
53. Yoo, S., Bahng, H., Chung, S., Lee, J., Chang, J., Choo, J.: Coloring with limited data: few-shot colorization via memory augmented networks. In: CVPR, pp. 11283–11292 (2019)
54. Yuan, X., Fang, L., Dai, Q., Brady, D.J., Liu, Y.: Multiscale gigapixel video: a cross resolution image matching and warping approach. In: ICCP, pp. 1–9. IEEE (2017)
55. Yuan, X., et al.: A modular hierarchical array camera. Science & Applications, Light (2021)
56. Zhang, J., Zhu, T., Zhang, A., et al.: Multiscale-VR: multiscale gigapixel 3D panoramic videography for virtual reality. In: ICCP, pp. 1–12. IEEE (2020)
57. Zhang, R., Isola, P., Efros, A.A., Shechtman, E., Wang, O.: The unreasonable effectiveness of deep features as a perceptual metric. In: CVPR, pp. 586–595 (2018)
58. Zhang, R., Isola, P., Efros, A.A.: Colorful image colorization. In: Leibe, B., Matas, J., Sebe, N., Welling, M. (eds.) ECCV 2016. LNCS, vol. 9907, pp. 649–666. Springer, Cham (2016). https://doi.org/10.1007/978-3-319-46487-9_40
59. Zhao, Y., Li, G., Wang, Z., Lam, E.Y.: Cross-camera human motion transfer by time series analysis. arXiv preprint arXiv:2109.14174 (2021)

60. Zhao, Y., et al.: EFENet: reference-based video super-resolution with enhanced flow estimation. In: CICAI, pp. 371–383. Springer (2021). https://doi.org/10.1007/978-3-030-93046-2_32
61. Zhao, Y., et al.: MANet: improving video denoising with a multi-alignment network. arXiv preprint arXiv:2202.09704 (2022)
62. Zheng, H., Ji, M., Wang, H., Liu, Y., Fang, L.: CrossNet: an end-to-end reference-based super resolution network using cross-scale warping. In: ECCV, pp. 88–104 (2018)
63. Zhou, B., et al.: Learning deep features for scene recognition using places database. In: NeuIPS, pp. 487–495 (2014)

Attentive Cascaded Pyramid Network for Online Video Stabilization

Yufei Xu[1], Qiming Zhang[1], Jing Zhang[1], and Dacheng Tao[2](✉)

[1] University of Sydney, Camperdown, Australia
{yuxu7116,qzha2506}@uni.sydney.edu.au, jing.zhang1@sydney.edu.au
[2] JD Explore Academy, Beijing, China
dacheng.tao@gmail.com

Abstract. Online video stabilization is important for hand-held camera shooting or remote robots control. Existing methods either need use the whole video to perform offline stabilization and result in long latency, or dismiss the nonuniform motion field in each frame and lead to large distortion. The non-uniform motion includes dynamic foreground motion and non-planar background motion. To better describe the shaky motion field online, we propose a novel attentive and multi-scale regression and refinement framework called ACP-Net. It exploits the idea of modeling camera motion on progressive levels, consisting of a flow-guided quiescent attention (FQA) module and a cascaded pyramid prediction (CPP) module. FQA module takes optical flow as an extra input and generates a soft mask to remedy the disturbance from dynamic foreground objects. Based on the attentive feature, the CPP module utilizes a multi-scale residual pyramid structure to do coarse to fine stabilization. Experimental results on public benchmarks show that our proposed method can achieve state-of-the-art performance both qualitatively and quantitatively, comparing to both online and offline methods.

1 Introduction

With the popularity of hand-held video capturing devices such as smartphones, there are massive amount of videos shot by amateurs. These videos always contain undesirable vibration caused by high-frequency camera shake. Video stabilization is such a process to compensate for the disturbing shake existing in the video and improve visual experience. With the aid of hardware-independent video stabilization algorithm, hand-held devices and robots become smaller, cheaper, and more popular since the reduction of external stabilizing devices [31].

Several digital video stabilization techniques have been proposed in the past decades. The majority of these methods adopt offline stabilization routine [6,11, 13,32]. They first estimate camera path based on the whole video. Then a new stable camera path is optimized by smoothing the estimated camera path. Final result is synthesized or re-projected based on the optimized camera path. Since the whole video is used for global optimization, offline stabilization methods

---

Y. Xu and Q. Zhang—Equal contribution.

L. Fang et al. (Eds.): CICAI 2022, LNAI 13604, pp. 18–29, 2022.
https://doi.org/10.1007/978-3-031-20497-5_2

can benefit from past and future motion information, obtaining small distortion and well stability in their results. Nevertheless, due to the requirement of future frames, these methods cannot be used in online situations like cameras on moving robots that require capturing and stabilizing simultaneously.

Recently, several deep learning based methods are proposed to do online video stabilization task [19,23–25]. Instead of modeling the stabilization task as a traditional three-step routine "estimation→optimization→reprojection" [11], online deep learning based approaches treat the task as an end-to-end ("unstable → stable") transformation matrix prediction problem without explicitly modeling whole camera path [19]. Specifically, given the historical stable frames and current unstable frame, the existing shake motion field between desired stable frame and current unstable frame is directly modeled by homography [23] or affine transformation [7], which is to inverse the vibration motion caused by shake and do stabilization by interpolation accordingly [7,19,23]. These methods achieve comparable online stabilization results on public test video sequences. However, they dismiss the fact that although vibration motion caused by camera shake is global, the local motions of dynamic foreground objects in the motion field will noise the prediction and introduce large distortion [14]. Besides, using a single homography transformation to describe the motion field is inaccurate when the background contains several non-planar motions due to depth variance.

To better model the motion field and enable nonuniform warping according to the motion's distribution, we propose a cascaded pyramid prediction (CPP) module to deal with local motion caused by depth variance and a flow-guided quiescent attention (FQA) module to alleviate the influence of dynamic foreground objects. The CPP module contains three cascaded branches: global prediction branch, transition branch, and refinement branch. The three-branch structure exploits the idea of progressive modeling the motion field as a combination of basic global motion and dynamic local motion. Taking the optical flow as guidance, FQA generates both a spatial and a channel co-attention mask to emphasize features related to global motion. In this way, it aids CPP to estimate more accurate global homography transformation. For the refinement branch, it uses the feature without attention to refining the local motion. Through the incorporation of these two modules, the network can model the global transformation and residual local transformation collaboratively, forming a progressive nonuniform stabilization framework, i.e., the ACP-Net.

In summary, the main contribution of the paper can be summarized as (1) we propose a novel online video stabilization framework named ACP-Net, which exploits the idea of modeling nonuniform motion field at progressive levels; (2) we propose a CPP module to do coarse to fine stabilization with the aid of a FQA module to alleviate the disturbance of dynamic objects; (3) we evaluate our model on public test videos and demonstrate that our model can achieve state-of-the-art performance.

2   Related Work

2.1   Traditional Offline 2D Video Stabilization

Generally, 2D stabilization methods describe the camera path as 2D motion and conduct path smoothing in 2D space [4,15,16,20]. Liu *et al.* organize feature trajectories into a matrix and perform smooth on the low-rank decomposed result [11]. Grundmann *et al.* smooth camera path using L1 norm optimization methods [6]. Liu *et al.* use bundled optimization for camera path smoothing [13]. Epipolar geometry [5] and geodesics optimization [32] are also used to do 2D stabilization. These 2D methods have low computation load and can stabilize the videos well. But they require that enough matching feature points can be tracked in a long duration to estimate camera path, which is hard due to occlusion, blur, *etc.* To relax the requirement of long trajectories, estimating motion profiles or local homography matrix on pixel and gird level is explored in [12,14,28]. Despite they can generally stabilize a video well, these methods may fail when camera shake is complex in 3D space and they need the whole video to do stabilization.

Our method also uses 2D transformation, *i.e.*, homography, to model the motion field and does 2D warping accordingly. In contrast to traditional 2D/3D methods, our method 1) exploits the idea of "decompose and approximate" that decomposes complex motion field into global motion and residual local motion and approximates them with simple 2D homography matrices; 2) can adapt to both background non-planar motion and dynamic foreground motion by leveraging a FQA module to emphasize features related to global motion.

2.2   CNN Based Video Stabilization

Some recent work seeks to use data driven methods to do stabilization based on convolution neural network (CNN). Yu *et al.* leverage CNN as an optimizer and train it with a single video to get stable results [29]. Choi *et al.* use neighboring frame interpolation to get smooth camera path [2]. Although they can achieve stable results, future frames are still needed. For online video stabilization, Wang *et al.* use a two branch Siamese network to regress grid-based homography matrices directly [19]. Xu *et al.* integrate adversarial training with several spatial transformer networks (STN) [8] to enhance stability [23]. However, they use global transformation to model the non-uniform motion field, ignoring the influence of background depth variance and dynamic foreground motions. PWStableNet [35] focuses on the pixel-level, which may be too hard for the network's learning. In contrast, we propose an online video stabilization framework that exploits the idea of modeling non-uniform motion field at progressive levels. Moreover, to remedy the influence of dynamic foreground motions, we propose a flow-guided quiescent attention module to emphasize features related to global motion. It should be noted [30] also adopts optical flow to guide the learning. However, it focus on the offline video stabilization, while ACPNet favors the online stabilization. Besides, it will be an interesting work to explore the usage of transformers [3,27,33,34] for video stabilization tasks, as demonstrated in lots of vision tasks [1,26]. We leave it as our future work Fig. 1.

3   Methods

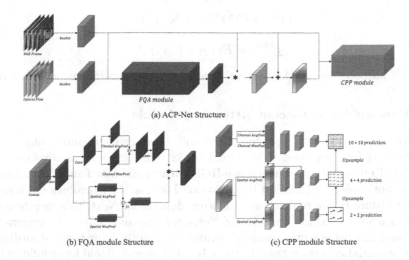

(a) ACP-Net Structure

(b) FQA module Structure   (c) CPP module Structure

Fig. 1. (a) Network structure of ACP-Net. ResNet-50 is used as encoder for both RGB branch and Optical Flow branch. (b) The FQA module predicts an attention map to alleviate the influence of dynamic objects, where the extracted features from RGB and Optical Flow are stacked as the input. (c) The CPP module employs a three-scale structure to predict non-uniform motion field progressively

3.1   RGB and Flow Feature Encoding

As shown in Fig. 3, there are two encoders for encoding both RGB and flow features in ACP-Net. For the RGB encoder, we use a large time interval to incorporate both long-term information and short-term temporal information. The set of historical stabilized frames is denoted as $\bar{S}_i = \{s_{i-32}, s_{i-16}, s_{i-8}, s_{i-4}, s_{i-2}, s_{i-1}\}$, where i is the current frame index. $\bar{S}_i$ is stacked with current unstable frame u_i to form the input to the RGB encoder (Enc_{RGB}), $i.e.$,

$$f_i^{RGB} = Enc_{RGB}\left([\bar{S}_i; u_i]\right), \tag{1}$$

where f_i^{RGB} denotes the encoded RGB feature.

Since the flow map contains rich motion information, we add a flow encoder to extract flow features. Specifically, the input of this branch is a set of adjacent historical stabilized frames $S_i = \{s_{i-7}, s_{i-6}, \cdots, s_{i-1}\}$ and the current frame u_i. We first use a pretrained PWC-Net [17] to extract optical flow between pairs: $\{s_{i-7}, s_{i-6}\}$, $\{s_{i-6}, s_{i-5}\}$, $\{s_{i-5}, s_{i-4}\}$, $\{s_{i-4}, s_{i-3}\}$, $\{s_{i-3}, s_{i-2}\}$, $\{s_{i-2}, s_{i-1}\}$ and $\{s_{i-1}, u_i\}$. The PWC-Net is fixed during training and testing. It is noteworthy that more advanced flow estimation methods, such as RAFT [18] and

GMFlow [22], can also be used to replace PWC-Net. Then, the extracted optical flow maps are stacked and taken as input to the flow encoder (Enc_{flow}), i.e.,

$$OF_i = PWCNet\left([S_i; u_i]\right),\tag{2}$$

$$f_i^{flow} = Enc_{flow}\left(OF_i\right),\tag{3}$$

where OF_i denotes the stacked optical flows, f_i^{flow} denotes the encoded features.

3.2 Flow-guided Quiescent Attention Module

We leverage optical flow to generate a soft mask, which guides our model to attend on features related to global background motion, as illustrated in Fig. 3(b). To this end, we concatenate RGB feature and flow feature as input to leverage both color and motion information. Then, a 1*1 convolutional layer is used for feature fusion and reducing feature dimension. Next, to generate a full attention map, we exploit the idea of "low-rank approximation" by generating spatial and channel attention maps separately and multiplying them accordingly.

In the spatial attention branch, there is a 3*3 convolutional layer followed by two separate global channel pooling layers based on max and average pooling. Then, the pooled features are concatenated together and fed into two subsequent convolutional layers for feature fusion. The last layer outputs a single channel map followed by a sigmoid activation function to generate the spatial soft mask. In the parallel channel attention branch, both global spatial max pooling and average pooling are used to obtain channel features. They are then concatenated together and fed into a fully connected layer with a sigmoid activation function to generate the channel soft mask. These two attention masks are multiplied together to generate the final full attention map, which is used to attend the RGB feature as follows:

$$f_i^{att} = f_i^{RGB} \times att_i + f_i^{RGB},\tag{4}$$

where att_i denote the full attention map. Note that we add a identity connect from the RGB feature to the attended feature to enforce a residual learning.

3.3 Cascaded Pyramid Prediction Module

We next construct the cascaded pyramid prediction module. We use the motion of grids' vertexes in the frame to represent the estimated transformation by following [19]. Specifically, the first two prediction branches receive the attentive feature f_i^{att} as input and use global spatial average pooling to reduce feature dimension. At the first (coarsest) level, there are three fully connected (FC) layers to transform the pooled feature into motion vector maps of size $3 * 3 * 2$, corresponding to the nine vertexes within 2*2 grids and a two-dimensional motion vector for each vertex. We describe this process as follows:

$$M_1 = \varphi_1\left(f_i^{att}\right),\tag{5}$$

where φ_1 denote the mapping function learned by the pooling and FC layers at the first level. At the second level, it has a similar structure of three FC layers and outputs motion vectors for 4*4 grids. In addition to the pooled feature, it also receives the embedded feature $(f_i^{\varphi_1})$ from the second FC layer in φ_1 as input. The process can be described as:

$$M_2 = \varphi_2 \left(\left[f_i^{att}; f_i^{\varphi_1} \right] \right) + M_1 \uparrow, \tag{6}$$

where φ_2 denotes the mapping function, "$\uparrow$" denotes bilinear upsampling.

As for the finest level, it is designed to capture both dynamic foreground local motions and background motion residuals that could not accurately be modeled by the first two levels. To this end, the original RGB feature f_i^{RGB} is used as input since it contains motion features from both foreground and background. Different from the first two levels, it uses both global channel max pooling and average pooling to obtain the pooled features. Meanwhile, it also receives the embedded feature $(f_i^{\varphi_2})$ from the second FC layer in φ_2 as input. Finally, it predicts a local motion vector for each vertex within 10*10 grids. The process can be described as:

$$M_3 = \varphi_3 \left(\left[f_i^{RGB}; f_i^{\varphi_2} \right] \right) + M_2 \uparrow, \tag{7}$$

Given the predicted motion vectors at each level, the homography matrix can be calculated for each grid and used by the Spatial Transformer Network to interpolate the stable result from the unstable frame u_i. The process can be described as:

$$\hat{s}_i^k = STN\left(M_k, u_i \right), k = 1, 2, 3 \tag{8}$$

where $\hat{s}_i^k$ denote the predicted stable frame from the kth level of CPP.

3.4   Training Objectives

In this paper, we use MSE loss, shape-preserving loss, and temporal consistency loss to supervise the training of ACP-Net. We also exploit the idea of deep supervision by adding MSE loss and shape-preserving loss on the predictions from each level of CPP. Specifically, the MSE loss is defined as:

$$L_{mse} = \sum_{k=1}^{3} \left\| \hat{s}_i^k - s_i \right\|^2, \tag{9}$$

where s_i and $\hat{s}_i^k$ represent the groundtruth stable frame and the stabilized frames generated by the network, as defined above. The shape-preserving loss consists of an intra-grid content preserving warping loss (L_k^{intra}) and an inter-grid line preserving loss (L_k^{inter}). It enforces a shape constraint on the transformation in different grids so that no large distortion is introduced by them due to inconsistent predictions. We followed [10,19] for the implementation. The shape-preserving loss is calculated as follows:

$$L_{shape} = \sum_{k=1}^{3} \left(L_k^{intra} + L_k^{inter} \right). \tag{10}$$

As for the temporal consistency loss, we warp the predicted stable frame to its next neighboring frame using the ground truth optical flow of stable frames. Then, we calculate the MSE loss between the warped one and the predicted stable frame to enforce temporal consistency, *i.e.*,

$$L_t = ||s_{i+1}^{\hat{k}} - \omega_{i \rightarrow i+1} \hat{s}_i^k||^2, k = 3, \tag{11}$$

where $\omega_{i \rightarrow i+1}$ represents the temporal warping operation from frame i to frame $i + 1$. Note that we only add the temporal consistency loss on the predictions from the finest level of CPP since it is used as our final prediction.

4   Experiments

We use public unstable video datasets from [13] to test our methods. We compare our method with representative state-of-the-art online and offline stabilization methods. Both quantitative evaluation and qualitative evaluation are presented to do a thorough comparison.

4.1   Implementation Details

We used the dataset proposed in [19] to train our model. The batch size during training was 10 and we used ADAM [9] for optimization with $\beta_1 = 0.9, \beta_2 = 0.99$. Initial learning rate was set to 2e–5 and decayed by 0.1 every 40,000 iterations. The model was first trained 1,000 iterations to learn an identity transformation where the unstable input frame also served as the output target. Then, it was trained for another 6,000 iterations without the temporal consistency loss. Finally, it was trained for a total of 100,000 iterations with all losses.

4.2   Quantitative Evaluation

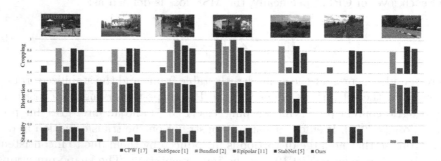

Fig. 2. Comparison between ACP-Net and state-of-the-art methods with respect to cropping ratio, distortion, and stability.

To perform the quantitative evaluation, we adopt the three metrics introduced in [12]: cropping rate, distortion and stability. The better a video is stabilized, the value is closer to 1.0, for all of the three metrics. We tested our method on seven public videos from [13] using the aforementioned metrics. The results were compared with the recent online deep learning based method [19] and several offline 2D methods [5,10,11,13]. The comparison videos were provided by authors or generated by their open source codes. The evaluation code was provided by [2] and same evaluation parameters were used for all videos and methods for a fair comparison. Note that, since the evaluation parameters are not publicly available in other literature, the evaluation results in this paper are a little different compared with theirs. The evaluation results are shown in Fig. 2. Regards the distortion metric, our method outperforms [19] for all videos, which shows the necessity of modeling motion field progressively. As for the stability metric, our method gets comparable scores with offline methods since the model gets a more precise global motion description from the FQA module and generates a better global coherent transformation. For the cropping ratio metric, our method performs large cropping as it tends to generate large transformation on the frame boundary, which reduces distortion but make the boundary irregular. The finer transformation causes less overlapping areas in the boundary region and leads to a decrease in cropping ratio.

4.3   Qualitative Evaluation

StabNet [5] result   Our result

Fig. 3. StabNet [19] results compared with ours results. The red and blue boxes are zoomed to do visual comparison, which shows that our method can produce less distortion on sharp edges and dynamic objects (Color figure online)

To intuitively validate the performance of our proposed methods, we visually compared our results with state-of-the-art online method [19] in Fig. 3. As indicated by the enlarged view of two local regions in two exemplar frames, our method introduces less distortion on sharp edges and dynamic objects. The results show that our method can retain more precise local details while keeping global coherence, thanks to the non-uniform motion field modeling ability.

4.4 Ablation Study

In this part, we study the effectiveness of the proposed FQA module and CPP module based on different model variants by including or excluding them in the ACP-Net structure.

For the CPP module, we carried out the ablation study on the choice of multiple branches. We first tested the baseline model (denoted Single-4) with only one single prediction branch that predicts motion vectors in 4*4 grids. Then, we added the coarsest level prediction branch which output motion vectors in 2*2 grids (Denoted Double-2&4). Finally, we included all the three branches (denoted Multi-2&4&10). In addition, we also constructed a variant by only using average pooling in the refinement branch (denoted Multi-Avg). The FQA module was not used in this study. The results are shown in Table 1.

Table 1. Ablation study of the CPP module

	Regular			Parallax			Zooming			QuickRoatation			Average		
	C	S	D	C	S	D	C	S	D	C	S	D	C	S	D
Single-4	0.7988	0.7303	0.8390	0.6824	0.7831	0.7258	0.8348	0.6513	0.7296	0.8259	0.8866	0.3379	0.7855	0.7628	0.6581
Double-2&4	0.8059	**0.7726**	0.8657	0.6881	**0.7996**	0.7380	0.8375	0.6486	0.7304	0.8245	0.9062	0.3821	0.7890	**0.7818**	0.6791
Multi-Avg	0.7807	0.7404	0.8180	0.6738	0.7753	0.7293	0.8309	**0.6677**	**0.7571**	0.8288	**0.9154**	0.3871	0.7786	0.7747	0.6729
Multi-2&4&10	0.8078	0.7437	**0.8773**	0.6835	0.7944	**0.7385**	0.8348	0.6638	0.7298	0.8255	0.9055	**0.4000**	0.7879	0.7769	**0.6864**

As indicated in Table 1, the baseline model with only one branch achieves the lowest stability and distortion scores. It is reasonable since it could not handle the non-uniform motion effectively with only a single branch. With the aid of 2*2 grids, Double-2&4 achieves an increase in both stability and distortion since 2*2 branch can better describe global motion and the origin 4*4 branch can focus on local regions to reduce distortion. While the Multi-2&4-&10 shows an increase in distortion while sacrificing a little stability. As the 10*10 branch provides transformation on a finer grid level and can model the nonuniform motion fields more precisely, the distortion value is increased. But more local motion information is embedded in the input feature of the three branches as the 10*10 branch needs to focus on local motion. More local motion information in global motion degrades the stability of the network. While for the Multi-Avg structure, stacked max pooling and average pooling can provide more local motion information than average pooling only. That's why there is a decrease in distortion when compare Multi-Avg with Multi-2&4-&10.

Then, we studied how to design the FQA module by testing two variants. One was the proposed structure illustrated in Fig. 3(b) with a parallel attention structure (denoted FQA-P). The other one had a cascaded attention structure by referring to CBAM [21] (denoted FQA-C). Note that we added the FQA module on the baseline model (Single-4). The results are summarized in Table 2. The FQA-R structure obtains an increase in both distortion and stability while the FQA-C version has a little decrease in these two metrics. It indicates that RGB feature only may not serve well as a denoiser for dynamic objects since it is a little hard for the RGB branch to pay attention to reconstruct the motion field from unstable to stable and recognize regions with dynamic objects together.

Table 2. Ablation Study of FQA module

	Regular			Parallax			Zooming			QuickRoatation			Average		
	C	S	D	C	S	D	C	S	D	C	S	D	C	S	D
FQA-C	0.8037	0.7033	0.8410	0.6823	0.7567	**0.7446**	0.8613	**0.6665**	0.6791	0.8094	**0.9063**	0.3254	0.7892	0.7582	0.6475
FQA-P	0.8232	**0.7477**	**0.8628**	0.6886	**0.8230**	0.7420	0.8361	0.6492	**0.7265**	0.8446	0.8972	**0.4055**	0.7981	**0.7793**	**0.6842**

4.5 User Study

Table 3. User study result

	Regular	Parallax	Crowd	QuickRot	Zoom	Run
Adobe Premiere	2.83	2.20	3.50	2.69	3.39	2.27
StabNet [19]	3.05	2.59	3.00	2.66	3.05	2.42
Our	3.42	3.06	3.07	2.80	3.53	2.91

We also carried out a user study to compare our model with the recent method StabNet [19] as well as a commercial stabilizer, *i.e.*, Adobe Premiere. Six categories of test videos in [13] were used, i.e., regular, crowd, parallax, quick rotation, running, and zooming. There were three videos randomly chosen from each category by following [23]. 22 subjects aged from 18–30 participated in this test. Each participant was asked to score the quality of the three stabilized videos, ranged from 0 to 5. The average score of each method is shown in Table 3. It can be observed that our method obtain the highest score except for the Crowd category, which contains lots of moving person and chaos flow field.

5   Conclusions

In this paper, we propose ACP-Net to deal with online video stabilization problem. It predicts the non-uniform motion field using a cascaded pyramid structure from coarse to fine. We show that the dynamic foreground motions have a side effect on estimating the global transformation, which should be eliminated. Therefore, we propose a flow-guided quiescent attention module which proves very effective. It guides the cascaded pyramid module focus on background regions where contain global motion clues. Both quantitative and subjective evaluation results suggest that ACP-Net can achieve comparable or better video stabilization results to/than state-of-the-art methods. Thereby, it can serve as a strong baseline for online video stabilization.

Acknowledgement. Mr Yufei Xu, Mr Qiming Zhang, and Dr Jing Zhang are supported in part by ARC FL-170100117 and IH-180100002.

References

1. Carion, N., Massa, F., Synnaeve, G., Usunier, N., Kirillov, A., Zagoruyko, S.: End-to-end object detection with transformers. In: Vedaldi, A., Bischof, H., Brox, T., Frahm, J.-M. (eds.) ECCV 2020. LNCS, vol. 12346, pp. 213–229. Springer, Cham (2020). https://doi.org/10.1007/978-3-030-58452-8_13
2. Choi, J., Kweon, I.S.: Deep iterative frame interpolation for full-frame video stabilization. ACM Trans. Graph. (TOG) 39(1), 1–9 (2020)
3. Dosovitskiy, A., et al.: An image is worth 16×16 words: transformers for image recognition at scale. arXiv preprint arXiv:2010.11929 (2020)
4. Gleicher, M.L., Liu, F.: Re-cinematography: Improving the camerawork of casual video. ACM Trans. Multimedia Comput. Commun. Appl. 5(1), 1–28 (2008)
5. Goldstein, A., Fattal, R.: Video stabilization using Epipolar geometry. ACM Trans. Graph. (TOG) 31(5), 1–10 (2012)
6. Grundmann, M., Kwatra, V., Essa, I.: Auto-directed video stabilization with robust L1 optimal camera paths. In: CVPR 2011, pp. 225–232. IEEE (2011)
7. Huang, C.H., Yin, H., Tai, Y.W., Tang, C.K.: Stablenet: semi-online, multi-scale deep video stabilization. arXiv preprint arXiv:1907.10283 (2019)
8. Jaderberg, M., Simonyan, K., Zisserman, A., et al.: Spatial transformer networks. In: Advances in Neural Information Processing Systems, pp. 2017–2025 (2015)
9. Kingma, D.P., Ba, J.: Adam: a method for stochastic optimization. arXiv preprint arXiv:1412.6980 (2014)
10. Liu, F., Gleicher, M., Jin, H., Agarwala, A.: Content-preserving warps for 3D video stabilization. ACM Trans. Graph. (TOG) 28(3), 1–9 (2009)
11. Liu, F., Gleicher, M., Wang, J., Jin, H., Agarwala, A.: Subspace video stabilization. ACM Trans. Graph. (TOG) 30(1), 1–10 (2011)
12. Liu, S., Tan, P., Yuan, L., Sun, J., Zeng, B.: MeshFlow: minimum latency online video stabilization. In: Leibe, B., Matas, J., Sebe, N., Welling, M. (eds.) ECCV 2016. LNCS, vol. 9910, pp. 800–815. Springer, Cham (2016). https://doi.org/10.1007/978-3-319-46466-4_48
13. Liu, S., Yuan, L., Tan, P., Sun, J.: Bundled camera paths for video stabilization. ACM Trans. Graph. (TOG) 32(4), 1–10 (2013)
14. Liu, S., Yuan, L., Tan, P., Sun, J.: SteadyFlow: spatially smooth optical flow for video stabilization. In: Proceedings of the IEEE Conference on Computer Vision and Pattern Recognition, pp. 4209–4216 (2014)
15. Matsushita, Y., Ofek, E., Ge, W., Tang, X., Shum, H.Y.: Full-frame video stabilization with motion inpainting. IEEE Trans. Pattern Anal. Mach. Intell. 28(7), 1150–1163 (2006)
16. Roberto e Souza, M., Maia, H.D.A., Pedrini, H.: Survey on digital video stabilization: concepts, methods, and challenges. ACM Comput. Surv. (CSUR) 55(3), 1–37 (2022)
17. Sun, D., Yang, X., Liu, M.Y., Kautz, J.: PWC-Net: CNNs for optical flow using pyramid, warping, and cost volume. In: Proceedings of the IEEE Conference on Computer Vision and Pattern Recognition, pp. 8934–8943 (2018)
18. Teed, Z., Deng, J.: RAFT: recurrent all-pairs field transforms for optical flow. In: Vedaldi, A., Bischof, H., Brox, T., Frahm, J.-M. (eds.) ECCV 2020. LNCS, vol. 12347, pp. 402–419. Springer, Cham (2020). https://doi.org/10.1007/978-3-030-58536-5_24
19. Wang, M., et al.: Deep online video stabilization with multi-grid warping transformation learning. IEEE Trans. Image Process. 28(5), 2283–2292 (2018)

20. Wang, Y.S., Liu, F., Hsu, P.S., Lee, T.Y.: Spatially and temporally optimized video stabilization. IEEE Trans. Vis. Comput. Graph. **19**(8), 1354–1361 (2013)
21. Woo, S., Park, J., Lee, J.Y., So Kweon, I.: CBAM: convolutional block attention module. In: Proceedings of the European Conference on Computer Vision (ECCV), pp. 3–19 (2018)
22. Xu, H., Zhang, J., Cai, J., Rezatofighi, H., Tao, D.: Gmflow: Learning optical flow via global matching. In: Proceedings of the IEEE/CVF Conference on Computer Vision and Pattern Recognition, pp. 8121–8130 (2022)
23. Xu, S.Z., Hu, J., Wang, M., Mu, T.J., Hu, S.M.: Deep video stabilization using adversarial networks. In: Computer Graphics Forum, vol. 37, pp. 267–276. Wiley Online Library (2018)
24. Xu, Y., Zhang, J., Maybank, S.J., Tao, D.: DUT: learning video stabilization by simply watching unstable videos. IEEE Trans. Image Process. **31**, 4306–4320 (2022)
25. Xu, Y., Zhang, J., Tao, D.: Out-of-boundary view synthesis towards full-frame video stabilization. In: Proceedings of the IEEE/CVF International Conference on Computer Vision, pp. 4842–4851 (2021)
26. Xu, Y., Zhang, J., Zhang, Q., Tao, D.: ViTPose: simple vision transformer baselines for human pose estimation. arXiv preprint arXiv:2204.12484 (2022)
27. Xu, Y., Zhang, Q., Zhang, J., Tao, D.: ViTAE: vision transformer advanced by exploring intrinsic inductive bias. In: Advances in Neural Information Processing Systems, vol. 34 (2021)
28. Yu, J., Ramamoorthi, R.: Selfie video stabilization. In: Proceedings of the European Conference on Computer Vision (ECCV), pp. 551–566 (2018)
29. Yu, J., Ramamoorthi, R.: Robust video stabilization by optimization in CNN weight space. In: Proceedings of the IEEE Conference on Computer Vision and Pattern Recognition, pp. 3800–3808 (2019)
30. Yu, J., Ramamoorthi, R.: Learning video stabilization using optical flow. In: Proceedings of the IEEE/CVF Conference on Computer Vision and Pattern Recognition, pp. 8159–8167 (2020)
31. Zhang, J., Tao, D.: Empowering things with intelligence: a survey of the progress, challenges, and opportunities in artificial intelligence of things. IEEE Internet Things J. **8**(10), 7789–7817 (2020)
32. Zhang, L., Chen, X.Q., Kong, X.Y., Huang, H.: Geodesic video stabilization in transformation space. IEEE Trans. Image Process. **26**(5), 2219–2229 (2017)
33. Zhang, Q., Xu, Y., Zhang, J., Tao, D.: ViTAEv2: vision transformer advanced by exploring inductive bias for image recognition and beyond. arXiv preprint arXiv:2202.10108 (2022)
34. Zhang, Q., Xu, Y., Zhang, J., Tao, D.: VSA: learning varied-size window attention in vision transformers. arXiv preprint arXiv:2204.08446 (2022)
35. Zhao, M., Ling, Q.: PWStableNet: learning pixel-wise warping maps for video stabilization. IEEE Trans. Image Process. **29**, 3582–3595 (2020)

Amodal Layout Completion in Complex Outdoor Scenes

Jingyu Wu[1], Zejian Li[1(✉)], Shengyuan Zhang[1], and Lingyun Sun[1,2]

[1] Alibaba-Zhejiang University Joint Institute of Frontier Technologies,
Zhejiang University, Hangzhou 310027, China
{wujingyu,zejianlee,zhangshengyuan,sunly}@zju.edu.cn
[2] Singapore Innovation and AI Joint Research Lab, Zhejiang, China

Abstract. A layout is a group of bounding boxes with labels annotating objects in complex scenes. However, manually labelled layouts often annotate only visible parts of objects (modal layout) instead of the whole body including both visible and invisible parts (amodal layout). Modal layouts are caused by occlusion in scenes, while amodal layouts contain more accurate information of objects' relative positions and sizes. In this paper, we investigate the influence of modal layout on the layout-to-image generation. Specifically, to recover an amodal layout from a modal layout and improve the generation quality, we propose Amodal Layout Completion Network (ALCN) regressing amodal bounding boxes from potential occluded boxes. Following a divide-and-conquer strategy, we divide the modal layout of a scene into occlusion groups of bounding boxes, which are processed by ALCN individually. Furthermore, we propose four challenging IoU variants to measure completion performances for different completion conditions. Experiment results show the ALCN achieves state-of-the-art layout completion performances in most cases and improves the layout-to-image generation performance.

Keywords: Amodal layout completion · Layout-to-image generation · IoU various indicators

1 Introduction

"Almost nothing is visible in its entirety, yet almost everything is perceived as a whole and complete" [1]. Human beings have the natural ability to perceive the complete shape of objects accurately, even under partial occlusion [2]. This ability is called *amodal perception*. There has been remarkable progress in amodal perception, such as repairing masks of obscured objects with new datasets [3–5].

A layout is a group of bounding boxes and labels used to label objects in complex scenes. It is fundamental in mainstream tasks like layout-to-image generation (**L2I generation** for short) which means synthesizing photo-realistic images from manually labelled layouts. Recently, remarkable progress has made in L2I generation [7–9]. However, the layouts that these models used only label the visible parts of objects, which lose intrinsic and overlap information.

L. Fang et al. (Eds.): CICAI 2022, LNAI 13604, pp. 30–41, 2022.
https://doi.org/10.1007/978-3-031-20497-5_3

Left: An illustration of the proposed method Right: Modal layout cause incomplete understanding in layout-to-image

Fig. 1. Left: The mainstream datasets mainly pay attention to modal layouts (the green and yellow boxes) but ignore the amodal layouts (the red boxes). To improve the performance on layout-to-image generation and complete the modal layout, the proposed ALCN takes the occluded bounding box and the recursively overlapped boxes as input (iii) and regresses an approximated box in blue close to the ground truth (GT) box in red (iv). Right: Bad example of modal layout on layout-to-image generation. (Color figure online)

We call the layout which only labels visible parts of objects as **modal layout**. On the contrary, an **amodal layout** is a layout that labels whole bodies of objects (including visible and invisible parts) (Fig. 1 (left)). An amodal layout contains more accurate relative position and size of objects than the modal layout does. The invisible parts are blocked by other objects with occlusion relationships. If they are ignored, the comprehension of the scene is incomplete.

Figure 1 (right) shows an example from COCO [10]. The advanced L2I model LostGANv2 [11] gets a fair performance given the original layout in the training set. However, the generative model considers each bounding box in the input layout as a complete object but pays no attention to the probability that the woman be occluded. Therefore, if we slightly change the input by decreasing the table height (−15 pixels), the model generates a lady standing on the table. Thus, we assume that the modal layouts decrease the quality of L2I generation.

We set pre-experiments to prove our assumption. Due to the mainstream L2I generation datasets [10,12] only have modal layout. We use an outdoor traffic dataset KINS [4] which annotates both modal and amodal layouts. By augmenting the KINS [4] dataset (Sect. 3.1), we train the famous L2I generation models [8,11] with modal and amodal layouts separately. The results show amodal layouts increase the quality and quantity scores notably (Sect. 3), which means that amodal layout does play an essential role in this task.

The recent works on amodal perception mainly focus on segmenting amodal layout/mask [13–16] or recovering amodal layout/mask [4,6,17,18] with real images. However, in L2I generation, we only have modal layouts as input, so it is inevitable to face the challenge that we need to get the amodal layout only using modal layouts without images.

We believe that the amodal bounding box of an object can be influenced by its attribute as well as the objects occluding it. Based on this assumption, we propose an Amodal Layout Completion Network (ALCN) to regress amodal bounding boxes from its occlusion group (Sect. 4). ALCN focuses on the relative spatial and category information in layouts rather than images' features. Using a divide-and-conquer strategy, ALCN reduces the irrelevant objects and divides a whole layout into disconnected occlusion groups (Sect. 4.1). For a modal bounding box in the group, ALCN predicts the potential amodal bounding box with the rest boxes and their categories in the group. This process is performed for each box one by one in each group, and finally, ALCN puts the completed bounding boxes to the corresponding positions in the original layout.

In addition, four challenging IoU variants are proposed to evaluate the task for different completion conditions. We evaluate previous methods and ALCN on both existing and new indicators. Experiments show that ALCN achieves state-of-the-art performance in the overall evaluation (Sect. 5.2). In the challenging cases where bounding boxes are tiny, ALCN also outperforms other methods (Sect. 5.4). Furthermore, we test the combination of ALCN and L2I generation (Sect. 5.3), and the results show generation performances are improved with completed layouts. We summarize our contributions as follows:

(1) We propose ALCN, which completes modal layouts to form amodal layouts. To be used on layout-to-image generation, it focuses on spatial information and is trained without images.
(2) We propose four challenging IoU variants indicators: $AIoU^{75L}$, $AIoU^{75S}$, $AIoU^{50L}$ and $AIoU^{50S}$ for evaluation in different completion conditions.
(3) The ALCN could improve the quality of generating images in layout-to-image generation and achieves state-of-the-art performance on each indicator.

2 Related Work

2.1 Amodal Perception

For years, standard benchmarks have focused on modal parts and ignored the world behind them (Fig. 1 (left)). Amodal perception aims to detect or segment the instance amodal layouts/masks or recover the instance modal layout/masks with ground truth images. Previous methods rely on ordering relationships and traditional algorithms, such as Euler Spiral [19] and cubic Bezier curves [20].

In recent years, with the development of the neural network, Kar et al. [13] first introduce two neural networks (class-specific and class agnostic) to regress from visible layout candidates and corresponding RGB images to amodal layout. Qi et al. [4] propose Multi-Level Coding (MLC) network with an occlusion classification branch to improve the amodal perception ability. Follmann et al. [15] propose Occlusion R-CNN to segment the amodal mask using Mask R-CNN [21] as the backbone. After that, SeGAN [14] and Yan et al. [17] are proposed to generate both amodal masks and images with the ground truth images.

Currently, a self-supervised scene de-occlusion framework is developed by Zhan et al. [6] for partial completion of occluded objects. Ke et al. [16] propose BCNet to detect the amodal layouts with images using overlapping bilayers. Qiao et al. [31] achieve amodal object estimation given only a single image of a scene. Liang et al. [32] propose ELA-Net which can learn a more discriminative image representation by localizing key vehicle parts. As for the amodal datasets, Zhu et al. [3] create two amodal datasets based on BSDS dataset [22] and COCO [10]. Due to the limitation of the number of the images in both datasets, Qi et al. [4] create KINS dataset from KITTI [23] for amodal instance segmentation.

2.2 Synthesize Image from Layout

Generative Adversarial Networks (GANs) [24] have achieved splendid success in conditional [25] image synthesis. Zhao et al. [7] introduce a task to generate complicated real-world images from layouts. Sun and Wu [8] propose LostGAN, which can improve the quality of generating images by ISLA-Norm. After that, they extend the ISLA-Norm and make a significant improvement on higher resolutions [11]. A current work [26] tries to train the L2I model and weakly supervised image semantic segmentation concurrently and gets compelling results. Other works [9] combine VQVAE [27] and transformer architecture to form VQGAN, which generates images on high resolutions.

However, previous works use the data from COCO [10] etc. which only have modal layouts. That leads to the possibility that the models assume that each bounding box is a complete object and overlook the case of occlusion. Li et al. [28] propose LAMA to adapt overlapped or nearby object masks in the generation, but the performance still needs to be improved. Our experiments (Sect. 5.3) provide another possible solution to this thorny problem using the amodal layout.

3 Pre-experiments

3.1 Data Augmentation

The mainstream datasets for L2I generation, such as VOC [12], COCO [10] only have modal layouts. We use an outdoor traffic dataset called KINS [4]. It annotates both modal and amodal layouts, which can be the training set for the discussed task. KINS [4] mainly focus on the real street scene and automatic driving is not suitable for training. Besides, images in the KINS dataset are in the resolution of 1200×400, and most objects are tiny.

Thus, we augment the images by dividing each image into three 400×400 sub-images in a horizontally equal manner. Besides, bounding boxes less than 0.02 of the augmented image size are removed as suggested by [8]. After augmentation, the number of training and valid images increased to 7,436 and 6,438, respectively. In addition, KINS only annotates eight categories of instance objects and does not contain stuff objects, resulting in numerous blank areas in both layouts and generated images. Therefore, we add a stuff annotation "background" to cover the blank areas. The augment KINS is only used on L2I generation.

Table 1. Pre-experiments reuslts on modal layout and ground truth amodal layout.

Models	Layout	Quantity scores			User study	
		FID↓	IS↑	DS↑	Visual fidelity	Layout alignment
LostGANv1	Modal	85.12	8.03 ± 0.24	0.41 ± 0.09	47.42%	44.52%
	Amodal	78.20	9.18 ± 0.12	0.47 ± 0.09	52.28%	55.48%
LostGANv2	Modal	79.69	8.56 ± 0.10	0.52 ± 0.08	45.44%	42.99%
	Amodal	**67.96**	**9.94 ± 0.14**	**0.56 ± 0.10**	54.56%	**57.01%**

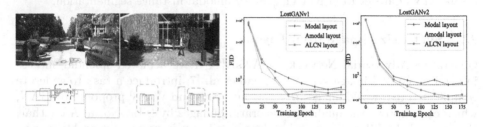

Fig. 2. Left: Example layouts in KINS. The KINS dataset has tiny bboxes or weak intra-connection groups which are difficult to regress. Right: FID values in the training of various layouts (modal, completed and amodal layouts).

3.2 Experiments and Evaluation

We train the famous L2I generation models LostGANv1 [8] and LostGANv2 [11] with modal and amodal layouts separately. Both methods have been trained for 125 epochs to give them equal opportunity to fit the training data and use images in the resolution of 128×128. We compare their performance on FID [29], Inception Score [30], Diversity Score [28]. We also set user studies (visual fidelity [28] and layout alignment [28]) to evaluate the generating performance. The results are shown in Table 1 and Fig. 2 (right).

In Fig. 2 (right), when trained with amodal layouts, the generative models converge faster and finally have lower FID values compared with those trained with modal layouts. All indicators in Table 1 demonstrate amodal layout has higher scores and better generate quality. The pre-experiments show that trained with the amodal layout, the models could learn faster and better.

4   Methodology

In this section, we introduce our proposed ALCN framework. The ALCN completes the given modal layout to the amodal layout. By giving the completed layout into L2I generation models, the performance of models improves notably.

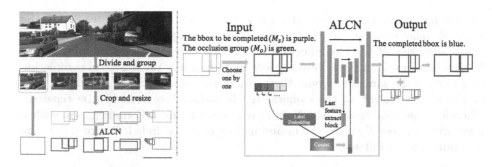

Fig. 3. ALCN use the divide-and-conquer strategy cluster layout to several occlusion groups and puts each group in the ALCN mainframe to regress the amodal layout. Left: The process of divide-and-conquer strategy. Right: The mainframe of ALCN. For each group, ALCN chooses a bounding box as M_s and others as M_o. ALCN transforms the layout into mask blocks and completes the bounding box.

4.1 Divide-and-Conquer Strategy

If a layout contains tiny bounding boxes ($\frac{Area(bbox_i^m)}{Area(I)} \leq 0.01$) which occupy a small part of an image (the blue area in Fig. 2 (left)), it is difficult for the model to regress the amodal layout precisely. This is because a slight change causes a large variation of IoU. Besides, a layout contains many bounding boxes, some of which do not have the occlusion relationship (the orange area in Fig. 2 (left)). If we use the whole modal layout as input directly, the model may learn irrelevant features from the bounding box that do not have an occlusion relationship. This will cause the performance to decrease as shown in the ablation study (Table 5).

To solve this problem, given a layout of an image, the ALCN uses a divide-and-conquer strategy to divide the bounding boxes into several occlusion groups instead of training with the original layout directly. G, H, W represents an occlusion group, image height and width respectively. If bounding boxes overlap or have edges adjacent to others, they will be grouped together. If not, we believe they are not occluded by each other and belong to different groups.

For a more accurate performance on tiny bounding boxes, we crop and resize each group G to the size of $H \times W$. Then we put G into the ALCN mainframe to complete bounding boxes. After completion, each G is resized to its original size and filled back into the original place. The process is shown in Fig. 3 (left).

4.2 ALCN Mainframe

In the training of an occlusion group G, ALCN chooses a modal bounding box in G as the source to be completed $bbox_s^m$ and other modal bounding boxes in G as the occlusion bounding boxes $bbox_o^m$. The l_s and l_o are the labels of $bbox_s^m$ and $bbox_o^m$. Both $bbox_s^m$ and $bbox_o^m$ are transformed to mask blocks M_s and M_o.

The input of ALCN is M_s, $M_o \in \{0, 1\}^{H \times W}$ and their labels $l_s, l_o \in C$. C represents the total category number. The backbone for ALCN is an encoder-decoder structure. For label embedding, we use a learnable $|C| \times d_e$ embedding matrix to obtain the vectorized representation for l_s, l_o. This results in the $m_g \times d_e$ label-to-vector matrix, where d_e is the embedding dimension and m_g is the max size of G. The embedding matrix is concatenated with the central hidden features. Hence, we have the loss $\mathcal{L}_1$ to consider the degree of completion and regress the amodal layout. However, in the case where M_s is the biggest or the object closest to the camera, the bounding box need not be repaired. Therefore, we discourage ALCN from over-completing a bounding box with a regularization loss $\mathcal{L}_2$ when the bounding box is not occluded. We formulate the loss functions as follows:

$$\mathcal{L}_1 = \frac{1}{N} \sum_{s,o} \mathcal{L}(F_{ALCN}(M_{s \backslash o}, M_o, l_s, l_o), M_t) \tag{1}$$

$$\mathcal{L}_2 = \frac{1}{N} \sum_{s,o} \mathcal{L}(F_{ALCN}(M_s, M_{o \backslash s}, l_s, l_o), M_t) \tag{2}$$

Here F_{ALCN} is completion network. $\mathcal{L}$ is a binary cross-entropy loss. M_t is the mask of the GT $bbox_s^a$. $M_{s \backslash o}$ is the difference set between M_s and M_o, namely $M_s - M_{s \cap o}$. Similarly, $M_{o \backslash s}$ is $M_o - M_{o \cap s}$. We formulate the final loss function as follows:

$$\mathcal{L}_{fin} = \alpha \mathcal{L}_1 + (1 - \alpha)\mathcal{L}_2 \tag{3}$$

where $\alpha \sim Bernoulli(\gamma)$ and γ is the probability of being repaired. The switching between two losses encourages the network to understand occlusion relationships between M_s and M_o and to determine whether to complete the bounding box. The entire process is visualized in Fig. 3 (right) and details of ALCN are in the supplementary materials.

4.3   New Indicators

The indicators mAP, AP^{50} and IoU evaluate the performance from a global view. We want to measure this task from multi-views and more comprehensively. In this way, we propose four challenging IoU variants indicators: AIoU^{75L}, AIoU^{75S}, AIoU^{50L} and AIoU^{50S} for evaluation in different completion conditions. The definitions of these indicators are as follows:

$$\text{AIoU}^{50S(50L)} = \frac{1}{N} \sum_{i=1}^{N} \text{IoU}(bbox_i^a, F_{ALCN}(bbox_i^m)),$$
$$\text{if IoU}(bbox_i^m, bbox_i^a) \leq 0.5(> 0.5) \tag{4}$$

AIoU^{75S} and AIoU^{75L} are defined similarly. AIoU^{50L} and AIoU^{75L} measure the performance of accuracy since the modal bounding box is close to the amodal bounding box. A slight change may cause the performance to decrease. AIoU^{50S} and AIoU^{75S} measure the performance of integrity as the overlap between the modal and amodal bounding box is low. AIoU^{75L} and AIoU^{50S} are more challenging than AIoU^{50L} and AIoU^{75S}. Our code is available at: https://github.com/JingyuWu-ZJU/Amodal-Layout-Completion-in-Complex-Outdoor-Scenes

5   Experiments

We test the ALCN performance on both amodal layout completion and the combination of ALCN and L2I generation models.

5.1   Datasets and Evaluation Metrics

Datasets. We conduct our amodal layout completion and L2I generation experiments on KINS [4] and the augment KINS (Sect. 3.1) datasets separately. KINS [4] is a large-scale dataset of complex outdoor scenes with annotated modal and amodal masks of all instances. The annotation contains seven categories. With the divide-and-conquer strategy, the layouts are clustered into 18,882 groups for training and 18,300 groups for testing. Each group has 2 to 24 bounding boxes and the average size of the occlusion group is 2.7 (STD = 3.2).

Evaluation Metrics. We evaluate the completion accuracy performance by mAP, AP^{50}, AP^{75} and four challenging IoU variants indicators: $AIoU^{75L}$, $AIoU^{75S}$, $AIoU^{50L}$ and $AIoU^{50S}$ (Sect. 4.3). Additionally, we also set two user study indicators: Layout Accuracy (LA) and Visual Performance (VP). Layout accuracy and visual performance aim to compare layout completion results with ground truth layouts and images separately. As for L2I generation, we use the common indicators: Frèchet Inception Distance (FID) [29], Diversity Score (DS) [28] and Inception Score (IS) [30].

Baseline. We evaluate the amodal layout completion performance on CSN [13], Occlusion-aware R-CNN [15], PCNets-M [6] and BCNets [16]. For L2I generation, we use the famous LostGANv1 [8] and LostGANv2 [11].

5.2   Experiments Results on Amodal Layout Completion

We evaluate the baseline models using the eight indicators above (Table 3). In addition, we evaluate the performance of each category in the appendix. The qualitative comparison are shown in Fig. 4 (left). Experiment results show that ALCN achieves state-of-the-art performance.

Table 2. User study on amodal layout completion.

	ALCN	PCNets-M	CSN
Layout Accuarcy↑	**68.72%**	21.01%	10.27%
Visual Performance↑	**82.90%**	10.06%	7.04%

Table 5 provides experimental results of ALCN and PCNets-M on tiny bounding boxes only. ALCN has a better performance in this challenging case. In addition, we conduct a user study to evaluate whether the refined bounding boxes find the perceptual size of objects precisely. ALCN gets the highest user preference scores comparing the other methods (Table 4). Specifically, the percentage that each worker favours ALCN is over 65% in all cases.

Table 3. Quantitative comparisons of eight indicators.

Model	mAP↑	AP^{50} ↑	AP^{75} ↑	IoU↑	$AIoU^{50S}$ ↑	$AIoU^{50L}$ ↑	$AIoU^{75S}$ ↑	$AIoU^{75L}$ ↑
GT modal	0.692	0.897	0.728	0.813	0.345	0.850	0.487	0.881
CSN	0.712	0.901	0.750	0.835	0.458	0.626	0.475	0.635
M-RCNN	0.466	0.627	0.522	0.540	–	0.577	0.015	0.621
OR-CNN	0.699	0.771	0.679	0.710	–	0.703	0.022	0.745
BCNets	0.733	0.932	0.793	0.850	–	0.801	0.530	0.849
PCNets-M	0.727	0.919	0.802	0.843	0.568	0.860	0.552	0.849
ALCN	**0.800**	**0.948**	**0.852**	**0.867**	**0.752**	**0.892**	**0.793**	**0.887**

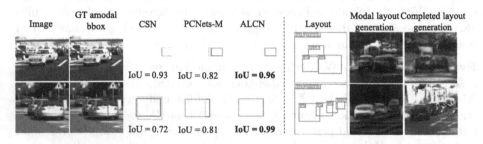

Fig. 4. Qualitative comparsios: amodal layout completion (left) and L2I (right).

5.3   Experiments Results on Layout-to-Image Generation

We test the combination ability of ALCN on L2I generation. Because the ALCN is a supervised learning model, it can not be trained on COCO [10]. We train ALCN on the augment KINS dataset and get the outputs of completed layouts.

We train the LostGANv1 and LostGANv2 with modal layout, completed layout and amodal layout. After training, we test the indicators above on each model (Table 4, Fig. 4). The results show that compared with the modal layout, the completed layout improves all the quantity indicators significantly. The qualitative results show training with modal layout tends to consider each bounding box as an independent complete object. Instead, training with amodal layout, consider more about occlusion cases. Thus, completing the modal layout as input could be an effective method to improve the performance of L2I models.

Table 4. Quantity results in the experiments of L2I generation.

Models	Layout	FID↓	IS↑	DS↑
LostGANv1	Modal	85.12	8.03 ± 0.24	0.41 ± 0.09
	Completed	80.21	8.97 ± 0.64	0.44 ± 0.10
LostGANv2	Modal	79.69	8.56 ± 0.10	0.52 ± 0.08
	Completed	**69.25**	**9.43 ± 0.14**	**0.55 ± 0.09**

5.4   Ablation Study

We compare ALCN with its variant trained with images and without clustering (Table 5). This is to test whether visual information is necessary and whether the divide-and-conquer strategy is beneficial. Results show that ALCN has a better generalization ability than its variant trained with images, indicating that relative spatial information is more important than visual information in the complete scenario. Besides, without clustering, ALCN has a decayed performance, especially for tiny bounding boxes, which take up 85.77% of all bounding boxes. Therefore, the clustering process in ALCN is important for completion. We also compare ALCN with other three variants, without l_s, without l_o and without l_s or l_o (Table 5). Results show the performance decays without any category.

Table 5. Ablation studies reuslts.

Model	Size	mAP↑		AP^{50} ↑	IoU↑		AIoU^{50S}	AIoU^{50L}
ALCN	Tiny	**0.783**		0.933	**0.862**		**0.724**	**0.878**
	Full	**0.800**		**0.948**	**0.867**		**0.752**	**0.892**
PCNets-M	Tiny	0.671		0.894	0.815		0.506	0.844
	Full	0.727		0.919	0.843		0.568	0.860
w/o Clustering	Tiny	(−0.061) 0.722		0.913	(−0.083) 0.779		0.503	0.817
	Full	(−0.034) 0.766		0.923	(−0.066) 0.801		0.528	0.832
w/o l_s or l_o	Full	(−0.040) 0.760		0.923	(−0.033) 0.834		0.857	0.730
w/o l_o	Full	(−0.034) 0.766		0.932	(−0.021) 0.846		0.870	0.764
w/o l_s	Full	(−0.008) 0.792		0.943	(−0.006) 0.861		0.879	0.778

6   Conclusion

This paper introduces ALCN for amodal layout completion. The ALCN regresses the amodal layout from a modal layout in order to improve the performance of the L2I generation task. State-of-the-art performance on amodal layout completion is obtained on KINS. Qualitative results and user preference demonstrate the proposed method is able to regress the amodal layout in most cases. In addition, ALCN consistently improves L2I generation performance. In the future work, we will further explore the amodal layout completion using self-supervised learning on different datasets to generalize this task.

Acknowledgement. This is paper is funded by National Key R&D Program of China (2018AAA0100703), and the National Natural Science Foundation of China (No. 62006208 and No. 62107035).

References

1. Palmer S.E.: Vision science: photons to phenomenology. MIT Press (1999)
2. Lehar, S.: Gestalt isomorphism and the quantification of spatial perception. Gestalt Theor. **21**, 122–139 (1999)
3. Zhu, Y., Tian, Y., Metaxas, D., Dollar, P.: Semantic amodal segmentation. In: Proceedings of the IEEE Conference on Computer Vision and Pattern Recognition (CVPR), pp. 1464–1472 (2017)
4. Qi, L., Jiang, L., Liu, S., Shen, X., Jia, J.: Amodal instance segmentation with KINS dataset. In: Proceedings of the IEEE/CVF Conference on Computer Vision and Pattern Recognition (CVPR), pp. 3014–3023 (2019)
5. Gupta, A., Dollar, P., Girshick, R.: LVIS: a dataset for large vocabulary instance segmentation. In: Proceedings of the IEEE/CVF Conference on Computer Vision and Pattern Recognition (CVPR), pp. 5356–5364 (2019)
6. Zhan, X., Pan, X., Dai, B., Liu, Z., Lin, D., Loy, C.C.: Self-supervised scene de-occlusion. In: 2020 IEEE/CVF Conference on Computer Vision and Pattern Recognition (CVPR), pp. 3783–3791 (2020)
7. Zhao, B., Meng, L., Yin, W., Sigal L.: Image generation from layout. In: Proceedings of the IEEE/CVF Conference on Computer Vision and Pattern Recognition (CVPR), pp. 8584–8593 (2019)
8. Sun, W., Wu, T.: Image synthesis from reconfigurable layout and style. In: Proceedings of the IEEE/CVF International Conference on Computer Vision (ICCV), pp. 10531–10540 (2019)
9. Esser, P., Rombach, R., Ommer, B.: Taming transformers for high-resolution image synthesis. In: Proceedings of the IEEE/CVF Conference on Computer Vision and Pattern Recognition (CVPR), pp. 12873–12883 (2021)
10. Lin, T.-Y., et al.: Microsoft COCO: common objects in context. In: Fleet, D., Pajdla, T., Schiele, B., Tuytelaars, T. (eds.) ECCV 2014. LNCS, vol. 8693, pp. 740–755. Springer, Cham (2014). https://doi.org/10.1007/978-3-319-10602-1_48
11. Sun, W., Wu, T.: Learning layout and style reconfigurable GANs for controllable image synthesis. TPAMI, pp. 5070–5087 (2022)
12. Everingham, M., Gool, L.V., Williams, C.K.I., Winn, J., Zisserman, A.: The pascal visual object classes (VOC) challenge. Int. J. Comput. Vis. **88**(2), 303–338 (2010)
13. Kar, A., Tulsiani, S., Carreira, J., Malik, J.: Amodal completion and size constancy in natural scenes. In: Proceedings of the IEEE International Conference on Computer Vision (ICCV), pp. 127–135 (2015)
14. Ehsani, K., Mottaghi, R., Farhadi, A.: Segan: segmenting and generating the invisible. In: Proceedings of the IEEE Conference on Computer Vision and Pattern Recognition (CVPR), pp. 6144–6453 (2018)
15. Follmann, P., König, R., Härtinger, P., Klostermann, M., Böttger, T.: Learning to see the invisible: end-to-end trainable amodal instance segmentation. In: 2019 IEEE Winter Conference on Applications of Computer Vision (WACV), pp. 1328–1336. IEEE (2019)
16. Ke, L., Tai, Y.-W., Tang, C.-K.: Deep occlusion-aware instance segmentation with overlapping bilayers. In: Proceedings of the IEEE/CVF Conference on Computer Vision and Pattern Recognition, pp. 4019–4028 (2021)
17. Yan, X., Wang, F., Liu, W., Yu, Y., He, S., Pan, J.: Visualizing the invisible: occluded vehicle segmentation and recovery. In: Proceedings of the IEEE/CVF International Conference on Computer Vision, pp. 7618–7627 (2019)

18. Bowen, R.S., Chang, H., Herrmann, C., Teterwak, P., Liu, C., Zabih, R.: OCONET: image extrapolation by object completion. In: Proceedings of the IEEE/CVF Conference on Computer Vision and Pattern Recognition, pp. 2307–2317 (2021)
19. Kimia, B.B., Frankel, I., Popescu, A.-M.: Euler spiral for shape completion. Int. J. Comput. Vis. **54**(1), 159–182 (2003)
20. Lin, H., Wang, Z., Feng, P., Lu, X., Yu, J.: A computational model of topological and geometric recovery for visual curve completion. Comput. Vis. Media **2**(4), 329–342 (2016). https://doi.org/10.1007/s41095-016-0055-3
21. He, K., Gkioxari, G., Dollár, P., Girshick, R.: Mask R-CNN. In: Proceedings of the IEEE International Conference on Computer Vision, pp. 2961–2969 (2017)
22. Arbelaez, P., Maire, M., Fowlkes, C., Malik, J.: Contour detection and hierarchical image segmentation. IEEE Trans. Pattern Anal. Mach. Intell. **33**(5), 898–916 (2010)
23. Geiger, A., Lenz, P., Urtasun, R.: Are we ready for autonomous driving? the KITTI vision benchmark suite. In: 2012 IEEE Conference on Computer Vision and Pattern Recognition, pp. 3354–3361 (2012)
24. Goodfellow, I., Pouget-Abadie, J., Mirza, M., Bing, X., Warde-Farley, D., Ozair, S., Courville, A., Bengio, Y.: Generative adversarial nets. Adv. Neural. Inf. Process. Syst. **27**, 2672–2680 (2014)
25. Odena, A., Olah, C., Shlens, J.: Conditional image synthesis with auxiliary classifier GANs. In: International Conference on Machine Learning, pp. 2642–2651. PMLR (2017)
26. Sun, W., Wu, T.: Deep consensus learning. arXiv preprint arXiv:2103.08475 (2021)
27. van den Oord, A., Vinyals, O., Kavukcuoglu, K.: Neural discrete representation learning. arXiv preprint arXiv:1711.00937 (2017)
28. Li, Z., Wu, J., Koh, I., Tang, Y., Sun, L.: Image synthesis from layout with locality-aware mask adaption. In: Proceedings of the IEEE/CVF International Conference on Computer Vision (ICCV), pp. 13819–13828 (2021)
29. Heusel, M., Ramsauer, H., Unterthiner, T., Nessler, B., Hochreiter, S.: GANs trained by a two time-scale update rule converge to a local nash equilibrium. In: Guyon, I., et al. eds, Advances in Neural Information Processing Systems, vol. 30, pp. 6626–6637. Curran Associates Inc. (2017)
30. Salimans, T., et al.: Improved techniques for training GANs. In: Lee, D., Sugiyama, M., Luxburg, U., Guyon, I., Garnett, R., eds, Advances in Neural Information Processing Systems, vol. 29. Curran Associates Inc. (2016)
31. Qiao, X., Hancke, G.P., Lau, R.W.H.: Learning object context for novel-view scene layout generation. In: Proceedings of the IEEE/CVF Conference on Computer Vision and Pattern Recognition, pp. 16990–16999 (2022)
32. Liang, L., Lang, C., Li, Z., Zhao, J., Wang, T., Feng, S.: Seeing crucial parts: vehicle model verification via a discriminative representation model, 18(1s), Jan (2022)

Exploring Hierarchical Prototypes
for Few-Shot Segmentation

Yaozong Chen and Wenming Cao[✉]

Shenzhen University, Shenzhen 518060, China
wmcao@szu.edu.cn

Abstract. Few-shot segmentation has recently attracted much attention due to its effectiveness in segmenting unseen object classes using a few annotated images. Many existing methods employ a global prototype generated by global average pooling (GAP) to preserve general support information. However, a single prototype inevitably creates ambiguity due to its limited representation capability. In order to alleviate this problem, we explore hierarchical prototypes for few-shot segmentation in this paper. Specifically, we propose feature interaction clustering (FIC) to extract local prototypes to contain detailed support information, fully mining the relationships among support features, prototypes, and query features. In addition, to compare query features with multiple prototypes, we propose a simple but effective prototype attention module (PAM) that fuses support information from different prototypes. Our method enhances the robustness of the prototypes and improves the utilization of support information. Extensive experiments on common datasets (PASCAL-5^i and COCO-20^i) demonstrate the effectiveness of our method.

Keywords: Few-shot segmentation · Hierarchical prototypes · Feature interaction clustering · Prototype attention

1 Introduction

With the rapid development of deep learning, semantic segmentation has progressed significantly [2,12,13,32]. However, to complete satisfactory performance, state-of-the-art semantic segmentation approaches require a large amount of annotated data, which is expensive to acquire. Their performance drops sharply without sufficient annotated data. Moreover, these methods are hard to deal with unseen class data.

In order to solve these problems, few-shot segmentation [17] is proposed to segment images with few annotated data. Due to prototype learning achieving remarkable performance in few-shot learning, many previous works [3,14,22,30,

This work is supported by National Natural Science Foundation of China, No.61771322, No.61971290 and Shenzhen foundation for basic research JCYJ20190808160815125.

L. Fang et al. (Eds.): CICAI 2022, LNAI 13604, pp. 42–53, 2022.
https://doi.org/10.1007/978-3-031-20497-5_4

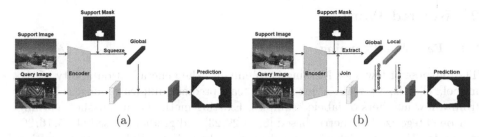

Fig. 1. Comparison between (a) common prototype framework and (b) our hierarchical prototypes framework.

31] introduce it into few-shot segmentation. As shown in Fig. 1(a), common prototype networks usually utilize global average pooling (GAP) to squeeze support features into a single prototype, which is compared with query features pixel by pixel. According to the research of SCL [29], even though the support image and the query image are the same, the existing methods cannot segment the query image accurately. Therefore, some works [1,9,21,24,27] implement novel frameworks without prototype learning, while other works [8,11,28,29] propose multi-prototype learning with different strategies for few-shot segmentation.

Inspired by previous works [8,22,28,30], we hope to extract prototypes containing support information of different levels and find a way to deal with multiple prototypes rationally. As shown in Fig. 1(b), in this paper, we build a framework with hierarchical prototypes. Hierarchical prototypes consist of one global prototype and many local prototypes. We utilize GAP to extract global prototype and dense comparison module (DCM) [30] to process it. In order to capture the detailed support information, we propose feature interaction clustering (FIC) to generate local prototypes. FIC fully explores the relationship among support features, prototypes, and query features to enhance the robustness of the prototypes. Besides, to fully use the detailed information provided by multiple prototypes, we propose a prototype attention module (PAM) to deal with local prototypes. PAM aims to leverage the relationship between prototypes and query features to control the fusion of support information in multiple prototypes.

Our contribution is summarized as follows:

- We design a hierarchical prototype framework for few-shot segmentation. In order to capture support information at different levels, we utilize GAP to generate the global prototype and propose feature interaction clustering (FIC) to generate local prototypes.
- We propose a prototype attention module (PAM) to compare query features and multiple prototypes, which leverages the relationship between them to fuse the support information of different prototypes.
- Experiments on PASCAL-5^i and COCO-20^i demonstrate the effectiveness of our method, especially in K-shot segmentation.

2   Related Work

2.1   Few-shot Learning

The purpose of few-shot learning is to enhance the generalization ability of the model, that is, to train a model that can predict samples of unseen classes from a few numbers of labeled samples. Existing methods for few-shot learning can be categorized as metric-based [5,19,20,23] and gradient-based [4,15,16,26] methods. The core idea of metric-based methods is to find a metric function to learn the relationship between support samples and query samples in the embedding space. Gradient-based methods aim at training a model that can fast adapt model parameters to novel tasks with only a few fine-tuning update. ProtoNet [19] is a metrics-based method that calculates the distance from the class-specific prototypes to the query sample in the metric space.

2.2   Few-shot Segmentation

Few-shot segmentation [3,7,8,18,21,28] can predict every pixel of the query image with only a few fully annotated support images. Inspired by few-shot learning, Shaban et al. [17] first propose the problem of few-shot segmentation. Compared with few-shot classification, few-shot segmentation is a more challenging task, which provides pixel-level prediction. Although prototype learning is a concise but effective way for few-shot segmentation, a single prototype inevitably leads to information loss. To alleviate this problem, some works [10,22,25] exploit the representation power of a single stereotype as much as possible, and some works [8,11,28,29] utilize multiple prototypes to capture the support information. PMMs [28] leverages the Expectation-Maximization (EM) algorithm to estimate multiple prototypes. SCL [29] implements a self-guided method that generates two complementary prototypes to mine the lost critical information. ASGNet [8] proposes a superpixel-guided clustering module to extract multiple prototypes and designs an adaptive guided prototype allocation (GPA) module to select the optimal prototype pixel by pixel to match the query features.

3   Method

3.1   Overview

Our method aims to enhance the representation capability of prototypes and improve the utilization of support information. As shown in Fig. 2, a shared CNN is used to extract support features $F_S \in R^{c \times h \times w}$ and query features $F_Q \in R^{c \times h \times w}$, where c, h and w represent the number of feature channels, height and width respectively. Subsequently, the masked F_S and F_Q are divided into samples by pixels. Our method extracts hierarchical prototypes, including a global prototype and multiple local prototypes that capture support information at different levels, and then utilizes different ways to treat them.

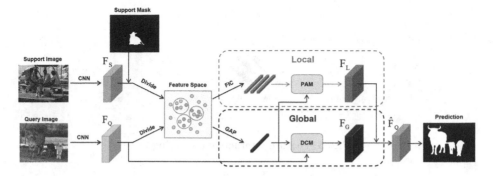

Fig. 2. Method overview. Our method utilizes global average pooling (GAP) and feature interaction clustering (FIC) to generate hierarchical prototypes. Subsequently, the dense comparison module (DCM) handles a single global prototype, while the prototype attention module (PAM) deals with multiple local prototypes.

For a single global prototype, we utilize the dense comparison module (DCM) to compare it with query features to output global features $F_G \in R^{c \times h \times w}$. Besides, we propose a prototype attention module (PAM) to compare query features with multiple local prototypes to output local features $F_L \in R^{c \times h \times w}$. F_G and F_L are fused to $\hat{F}_Q \in R^{c \times h \times w}$ by a convolution. Finally, a feature enrichment module (FEM) [22] decodes $\hat{F}_Q$ to the prediction of query image.

3.2   Hierarchical Prototypes

We denote all support samples and query samples as $V_S \in R^{c \times n}$ and $V_Q \in R^{c \times hw}$ respectively, where n represents the number of support samples, $v_s \in R^c$ and $v_q \in R^c$ represent single support sample and single query sample. While in K-shot segmentation, our method adds the support samples generated from K support images to the same V_S.

Global Prototype. Hierarchical prototypes contain a single global prototype and multiple local prototypes. The global prototype and the local prototypes complement each other. The local prototypes can supplement the detailed information lost by the global prototype, and the global prototype can provide the general information that the local prototypes lack. The global prototype p_0 is calculated by averaging all support samples, as

$$p_0 = \frac{\sum_{v_s \in V_S} v_s}{n}. \tag{1}$$

Local Prototypes. We propose feature interactive clustering (FIC) to estimate local prototypes. In contrast to the mechanisms of CRNet [10] and PANet [25], FIC interacts on features without additional training. As show in Fig. 3, FIC

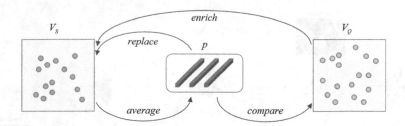

Fig. 3. Feature interactive clustering

exploits the relationship among the support samples, the local prototypes, and the query samples to enrich V_S, introducing additional samples during clustering to enhance the robustness of the local prototypes. Before clustering, FIC first set up the iteration times T and then randomly selects m cluster centers $p = \{p_1, p_2, ..., p_m\}$ from V_S, where $p \in R^{c \times m}$ and $p_i \in R^c$. In addition, the threshold α are set to control the interaction between support features and query features.

In each iteration, FIC divides V_S into m subsets $\{V_1, V_2, ..., V_m\}$ and recalculates the cluster centers p. For every $v_s \in V_S$, the index of the nearest center is calculated as

$$i' = \arg\min_{i \in 1,...,m}\{\|v_s - p_i\|_2\}, \tag{2}$$

so that v_s is divided into $V_{i'}$. After dividing all samples in V_S, the cluster center p_i is recalculated as

$$p_i = \frac{\sum_{v_s \in V_i} v_s}{|V_i|}, \tag{3}$$

where $|V_i|$ means the number of samples in subset V_i.

In order to enrich the support samples V_S, FIC computes the cosine similarity between query samples V_Q and clustering centers p to add more relevant query samples to V_S. For every query sample $v_q \in V_Q$, FIC calculates the similarities between v_q and all cluster centers p and then takes the maximum value as the similarity value

$$r_q = \max_{i \in 1,...,m} \{\frac{v_q \cdot p_i}{\|v_q\| \|p_i\|}\}. \tag{4}$$

If r_q is greater than α, v_q is selected as one of additional samples. Finally, local prototypes p are generated by iterating over updated support samples V_S. In this way, we use the local prototypes as a bridge to interact with the support features and query features during clustering, which effectively enhances the representation capability of the local prototypes.

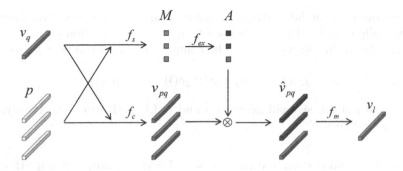

Fig. 4. Prototype attention module

3.3 Prototype Attention Module

Since CANet [30] proposed the dense comparison module (DCM), many subsequent works have adopted this way to deal with a single prototype. The DCM uses convolution to efficiently compare the query features with a single prototype but cannot directly deal with multiple prototypes. Naturally, we need a way to effectively leverage the support information in multiple local prototypes. Different from the Guided Prototype Allocation (GPA) of ASGNet [8], we expect to fuse information from all prototypes. Inspired by the DCM, we propose the prototype attention module (PAM) to compare query features with multiple prototypes and improve the information utilization of local prototypes.

As shown in Fig. 4, PAM inputs a query sample $v_q \in R^c$ and multiple prototypes $p \in R^{c \times m}$, and outputs a local feature $v_l \in R^c$ that incorporates low level support information. PAM assigns different attention to different prototypes by calculating the correlation between the query sample and multiple prototypes, and then fuses the comparison results. PAM is divided into three parts: comparison, compression, and fusion.

Comparison. PAM first compares a query sample v_q and every prototype $p_i \in p$. Consistent with DCM, PAM concatenates v_q with every p_i, and then uses a comparison function f_c (convolution), to activate feature channels related to foreground. Intermediate features $v_{pq} \in R^{c \times m}$ are generated by comparing the query sample v_q with all prototypes p, as

$$v_{pq} = f_c(v_q' \oplus p), \tag{5}$$

where v_q' means to copy v_q m times.

Compression. At the same time, PAM directly calculates the similarity between the query feature v_q and the prototypes p, and maps the similarity to the attention of the different prototypes. Specifically, the distance function f_s (Euclidean distance) is used to compute the distance map $M \in R^m$ and compress the relevant information between v_p and p. The excitation function f_{ex} (two fully connected layers) is used to map M to attention map $A \in R^m$, exerting different influences on v_{pq}. The compression stage can be expressed as

$$A = f_{ex}(f_s(v_q, p)) = \sigma(W_2 \delta(W_1 \| v_q' - p \|_2)), \tag{6}$$

where σ and δ mean sigmoid activation and ReLU activation respectively, W_1 and W_2 are weights.

Fusion. After comparison and compression, PAM allocates different attention to v_{pq} and merges the partial results. In the fusion stage, attention map A is treated as weighting factors multiplied by v_{pq}, activating features that are more relevant to local prototypes. Finally, the merge function f_m (convolution with a kernel size of $1 \times m$) is used to fuse the support information of different prototypes and output local feature $v_l \in R^c$ for segmentation, as

$$v_l = f_m(A \otimes v_{pq}), \tag{7}$$

where $\otimes$ means broadcast multiplication.

4   Experiments

4.1   Experimental Settings

Datasets and Metric. We evaluate our method on two public datasets for few-shot segmentation, i.e., the PASCAL-5^i and COCO-20^i. The PASCAL-5^i [17] contains 20 categories, and the COCO-20^i [14] contains 80 categories. They divide all categories into four splits, three splits for training and the remaining for evaluation. Following [8,17,28], we use the mean Intersection-over-Union (mIoU), widely recognized in image segmentation, as the metric for performance evolution.

Implementation Details. We implement PFENet [22] as baseline model, which utilizes ResNet-50 and ResNet-101 [6] as backbone. PFENet is a typical single prototype network, our method replaces the single prototype with hierarchical prototypes and add PAM to process local prototypes. We train our model with a SGD optimizer with momentum 0.9 and weight decay 1e-4. During training, we set the initial learning rate as 0.0025 with batch size 4 on Pascal-5^i for 200 epochs and 0.002 with batch size 8 on COCO-20^i for 50 epochs. The number of iterations for FIC is set to 5, and the number of local prototypes is set to 4. We implement our model using PyTorch and run experiments on Nvidia RTX 3090.

Table 1. Performance of 1-way 1-shot and 5-shot segmentation on PASCAL-5^i.

Method	Backbone	1-shot					5-shot					Params
		s-0	s-1	s-2	s-3	Mean	s-0	s-1	s-2	s-3	Mean	
CANet [30]	ResNet-50	52.5	65.9	51.3	51.9	55.4	55.5	67.8	51.9	53.2	57.1	36.4M
RPMMs [28]		55.2	66.9	52.6	50.7	56.3	56.3	67.3	54.5	51.0	57.3	-
CRNet [10]		-	-	-	-	55.7	-	-	-	-	58.8	-
PFENet [22]		61.7	69.5	55.4	56.3	60.8	63.1	70.7	55.8	57.9	61.9	10.8M
ASGNet [8]		58.8	67.9	**56.8**	53.7	59.3	63.7	70.6	**64.3**	57.4	63.9	10.4M
SCL [29]		63.0	70.0	56.5	57.7	61.8	64.5	70.9	57.3	58.7	62.9	-
Ours		**63.7**	**70.9**	55.7	**58.2**	**62.1**	**66.9**	**72.1**	58.9	**63.3**	**65.3**	10.7M
FWB [14]	ResNet-101	51.3	64.5	**56.7**	52.2	56.2	54.8	67.4	62.2	55.3	59.9	43.0M
PFENet [22]		60.5	69.4	54.4	55.9	60.1	62.8	70.4	54.9	57.6	61.4	10.8M
ASGNet [8]		59.8	67.4	55.6	54.4	59.3	64.6	71.3	**64.2**	57.3	64.4	10.4M
Ours		**63.9**	**71.3**	54.4	**56.5**	**61.5**	**69.1**	**73.1**	59.9	**63.3**	**66.3**	10.7M

Table 2. Performance of 1-way 1-shot and 5-shot segmentation on COCO-20^i.

Method	Backbone	1-shot					5-shot					Params
		s-0	s-1	s-2	s-3	Mean	s-0	s-1	s-2	s-3	Mean	
PANet [25]	ResNet-50	31.5	22.6	21.5	16.2	23.0	45.9	29.2	30.6	29.6	33.8	23.5M
PPNet [11]		36.5	26.5	26.0	19.7	27.2	48.9	31.4	36.0	36.7	31.5	31.5M
RPMMs [28]		29.5	36.8	28.9	27.0	30.5	33.8	41.9	32.9	33.3	35.5	-
FWB [14]	ResNet-101	19.9	18.0	21.0	28.9	21.2	19.1	21.5	23.9	30.1	23.7	43.0M
PFENet [22]		34.3	33.0	32.3	30.1	32.4	38.5	38.6	38.2	34.3	37.4	10.8M
SCL [29]		36.4	38.6	37.5	35.4	37.0	38.9	40.5	41.5	**38.7**	39.9	-
Ours	ResNet-50	**37.4**	**39.4**	**37.8**	**36.3**	**37.7**	**41.7**	**46.1**	**43.4**	37.6	**42.2**	10.7M

4.2 Performance Comparison

Comparisons to prior related works on the PASCAL-5^i are shown in Table 1. It can be seen that, with comparable parameters, our method significantly outperforms other methods in 1-shot and 5-shot settings. Specifically, our method surpasses baseline in 1-shot setting by 1.3% and 1.4% with ResNet-50 and ResNet-101, competitive with other methods. In particular, our method achieves significant improvement in 5-shot setting, exceeding the baseline by 3.4% and 4.9% with the two backbones, superior to other methods.

Figure 5 shows some representative segmentation examples. It can be seen that the segmentation example of our method has excellent quality, especially in the complex and detailed areas (in the yellow box). The hierarchical prototypes capture both global and local support information, making segmentation results more accurate in details.

Table 2 shows the performance comparison between our method and other methods of mean IoU on COCO-20^i, a more challenging dataset with abundant samples and diverse categories. As can be seen, our method improves the

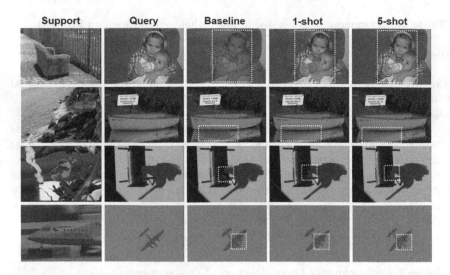

Fig. 5. Segmentation examples.

Table 3. Ablation study of hierarchical prototypes on PASCAL-5^i for 1-shot segmentation.

Global	Local(m)	s-0	s-1	s-2	s-3	mIoU(%)
1	0	60.2	70.2	**57.9**	55.8	61.0
0	4	63.0	70.6	54.8	56.9	61.3
1	1	60.9	69.4	56.7	55.2	60.6
1	2	62.5	69.6	55.7	57.7	61.3
1	3	62.6	70.7	56.8	57.5	61.9
1	4	**63.7**	**70.9**	55.6	**58.2**	**62.1**

baseline by 5.3% and 4.8% in 1-shot setting and 5-shot setting respectively, which demonstrates the effectiveness of our method in such complex scenarios.

4.3   Ablation Study

Hierarchical Prototypes. We first conduct an ablation study on level and number of hierarchical prototypes in Table 3. It is shown that using hierarchical prototypes to capture support information is better than using global prototype or local prototypes alone. In addition, multiple local prototypes perform better than a single global prototype. As for the effect of the number m of local prototypes, as can be seen, when m equals 4, our method achieves the best performance. When m goes from 1 to 4, our method has a significant performance improvement, which validates the effectiveness of local prototypes.

FIC utilizes the threshold α to control the interaction between support features and query features. Table 4 shows the performance of different α for

Table 4. Ablation results (mIoU%) of different threshold α on PASCAL-5^i and COCO-20^i for 1-shot segmentation.

α	1	0.9	0.8	0.7
PASCAL-5^i	61.5	**62.1**	61.7	61.4
COCO-20^i	37.0	**37.7**	37.6	37.4

Table 5. Ablation study of PAM with different components on PASCAL-5^i for 1-shot segmentation.

Component					mIoU(%)
Concatenate	Weight	Average	GPA	Convolution	
	✓	✓			61.6
	✓		✓		61.4
✓				✓	61.8
	✓			✓	**62.1**

few-shot segmentation. When α equals 1, there is no interaction between the support features and the query features. As we can see that, with the appropriate threshold, FIC can effectively screen out related features, improving the robustness of the prototypes.

Prototype Attention Module. Table 5 shows the ablation studies on PAM with different components. PAM treats the attention map A as weights to control features with local support information. As a comparison, we design a contrast experiment that concatenates the attention map A with the features. Furthermore, PAM utilizes a merge function f_m (convolution) to fuse support information of different prototypes. We implement the other two merge functions, average and GPA, for comparison. GPA is proposed in ASGNet, which is a method to find the most similar prototype to compare with query features. As can be seen, weight and convolution collocation is a simple but effective method to combine the support information of different prototypes, while other methods will inevitably lose some support information, resulting in performance degradation.

5 Conclusion

In this paper, we propose a novel framework with the feature interactive clustering (FIC) and the prototype attention module (PAM) to explore hierarchical prototypes for few-shot segmentation. FIC extracts local prototypes containing detailed information by fully exploiting the relationships among support features, prototypes, and query features. On the other hand, PAM implements the comparison of query features and multiple prototypes in a simple but efficient way. Extensive experiments and ablation studies demonstrate the effectiveness of our method.

References

1. Boudiaf, M., Kervadec, H., Masud, Z.I., Piantanida, P., Ben Ayed, I., Dolz, J.: Few-shot segmentation without meta-learning: a good transductive inference is all you need? In: Proceedings of the IEEE/CVF Conference on Computer Vision and Pattern Recognition, pp. 13979–13988 (2021)
2. Chen, L.C., Zhu, Y., Papandreou, G., Schroff, F., Adam, H.: Encoder-decoder with atrous separable convolution for semantic image segmentation. In: Proceedings of the European Conference on Computer Vision (ECCV), pp. 801–818 (2018)
3. Dong, N., Xing, E.P.: Few-shot semantic segmentation with prototype learning. In: BMVC, vol. 3 (2018)
4. Finn, C., Abbeel, P., Levine, S.: Model-agnostic meta-learning for fast adaptation of deep networks. In: International conference on machine learning, pp. 1126–1135. PMLR (2017)
5. Garcia, V., Bruna, J.: Few-shot learning with graph neural networks. arXiv preprint arXiv:1711.04043 (2017)
6. He, K., Zhang, X., Ren, S., Sun, J.: Deep residual learning for image recognition. In: Proceedings of the IEEE Conference on Computer Vision and Pattern Recognition, pp. 770–778 (2016)
7. Hu, T., Yang, P., Zhang, C., Yu, G., Mu, Y., Snoek, C.G.: Attention-based multi-context guiding for few-shot semantic segmentation. In: Proceedings of the AAAI Conference on Artificial Intelligence, vol. 33, pp. 8441–8448 (2019)
8. Li, G., Jampani, V., Sevilla-Lara, L., Sun, D., Kim, J., Kim, J.: Adaptive prototype learning and allocation for few-shot segmentation. In: Proceedings of the IEEE/CVF Conference on Computer Vision and Pattern Recognition, pp. 8334–8343 (2021)
9. Liu, B., Jiao, J., Ye, Q.: Harmonic feature activation for few-shot semantic segmentation. IEEE Trans. Image Process. **30**, 3142–3153 (2021)
10. Liu, W., Zhang, C., Lin, G., Liu, F.: CRNet: cross-reference networks for few-shot segmentation. In: Proceedings of the IEEE/CVF Conference on Computer Vision and Pattern Recognition, pp. 4165–4173 (2020)
11. Liu, Y., Zhang, X., Zhang, S., He, X.: Part-aware prototype network for few-shot semantic segmentation. In: Vedaldi, A., Bischof, H., Brox, T., Frahm, J.-M. (eds.) ECCV 2020. LNCS, vol. 12354, pp. 142–158. Springer, Cham (2020). https://doi.org/10.1007/978-3-030-58545-7_9
12. Long, J., Shelhamer, E., Darrell, T.: Fully convolutional networks for semantic segmentation. In: Proceedings of the IEEE Conference on Computer Vision and Pattern Recognition, pp. 3431–3440 (2015)
13. Mehta, S., Rastegari, M., Caspi, A., Shapiro, L., Hajishirzi, H.: ESPNet: efficient spatial pyramid of dilated convolutions for semantic segmentation. In: Proceedings of the European Conference on Computer Vision (ECCV), pp. 552–568 (2018)
14. Nguyen, K., Todorovic, S.: Feature weighting and boosting for few-shot segmentation. In: Proceedings of the IEEE/CVF International Conference on Computer Vision, pp. 622–631 (2019)
15. Ravi, S., Larochelle, H.: Optimization as a model for few-shot learning (2016)
16. Rusu, A.A., et al.: Meta-learning with latent embedding optimization. arXiv preprint arXiv:1807.05960 (2018)
17. Shaban, A., Bansal, S., Liu, Z., Essa, I., Boots, B.: One-shot learning for semantic segmentation. arXiv preprint arXiv:1709.03410 (2017)

18. Siam, M., Oreshkin, B.N., Jagersand, M.: AMP: adaptive masked proxies for few-shot segmentation. In: Proceedings of the IEEE/CVF International Conference on Computer Vision, pp. 5249–5258 (2019)
19. Snell, J., Swersky, K., Zemel, R.: Prototypical networks for few-shot learning. In: Advances in Neural Information Processing Systems, vol. 30 (2017)
20. Sung, F., Yang, Y., Zhang, L., Xiang, T., Torr, P.H., Hospedales, T.M.: Learning to compare: relation network for few-shot learning. In: Proceedings of the IEEE Conference on Computer Vision and Pattern Recognition, pp. 1199–1208 (2018)
21. Tavera, A., Cermelli, F., Masone, C., Caputo, B.: Pixel-by-pixel cross-domain alignment for few-shot semantic segmentation. In: Proceedings of the IEEE/CVF Winter Conference on Applications of Computer Vision, pp. 1626–1635 (2022)
22. Tian, Z., Zhao, H., Shu, M., Yang, Z., Li, R., Jia, J.: Prior guided feature enrichment network for few-shot segmentation. IEEE Trans. Pattern Anal. Mach. Intell. **44**, 1050–1065 (2020)
23. Vinyals, O., et al.: Matching networks for one shot learning. In: Advances in Neural Information Processing Systems, vol. 29 (2016)
24. Wang, H., Zhang, X., Hu, Y., Yang, Y., Cao, X., Zhen, X.: Few-shot semantic segmentation with democratic attention networks. In: Vedaldi, A., Bischof, H., Brox, T., Frahm, J.-M. (eds.) ECCV 2020. LNCS, vol. 12358, pp. 730–746. Springer, Cham (2020). https://doi.org/10.1007/978-3-030-58601-0_43
25. Wang, K., Liew, J.H., Zou, Y., Zhou, D., Feng, J.: PANet: few-shot image semantic segmentation with prototype alignment. In: Proceedings of the IEEE/CVF International Conference on Computer Vision, pp. 9197–9206 (2019)
26. Wang, Y.-X., Hebert, M.: Learning to learn: model regression networks for easy small sample learning. In: Leibe, B., Matas, J., Sebe, N., Welling, M. (eds.) ECCV 2016. LNCS, vol. 9910, pp. 616–634. Springer, Cham (2016). https://doi.org/10.1007/978-3-319-46466-4_37
27. Wu, Z., Shi, X., Lin, G., Cai, J.: Learning meta-class memory for few-shot semantic segmentation. In: Proceedings of the IEEE/CVF International Conference on Computer Vision, pp. 517–526 (2021)
28. Yang, B., Liu, C., Li, B., Jiao, J., Ye, Q.: Prototype mixture models for few-shot semantic segmentation. In: Vedaldi, A., Bischof, H., Brox, T., Frahm, J.-M. (eds.) ECCV 2020. LNCS, vol. 12353, pp. 763–778. Springer, Cham (2020). https://doi.org/10.1007/978-3-030-58598-3_45
29. Zhang, B., Xiao, J., Qin, T.: Self-guided and cross-guided learning for few-shot segmentation. In: Proceedings of the IEEE/CVF Conference on Computer Vision and Pattern Recognition, pp. 8312–8321 (2021)
30. Zhang, C., Lin, G., Liu, F., Yao, R., Shen, C.: CANet: class-agnostic segmentation networks with iterative refinement and attentive few-shot learning. In: Proceedings of the IEEE/CVF Conference on Computer Vision and Pattern Recognition, pp. 5217–5226 (2019)
31. Zhang, X., Wei, Y., Yang, Y., Huang, T.S.: SG-one: similarity guidance network for one-shot semantic segmentation. IEEE Trans. Cybern. **50**(9), 3855–3865 (2020)
32. Zhao, H., Shi, J., Qi, X., Wang, X., Jia, J.: Pyramid scene parsing network. In: Proceedings of the IEEE Conference on Computer Vision and Pattern Recognition, pp. 2881–2890 (2017)

BSAM: Bidirectional Scene-Aware Mixup for Unsupervised Domain Adaptation in Semantic Segmentation

Congying Xing, Gao Li, and Lefei Zhang[(✉)]

School of Computer Science, Wuhan University, Wuhan, China
{xingcongying,gaoli1218,zhanglefei}@whu.edu.cn

Abstract. Unsupervised domain adaptation for semantic segmentation aims to transfer the knowledge from the labeled source domain to the unlabeled target domain. Existing mixup methods usually paste parts of the source domain images onto the target domain images. However, they often neglect the scene consistency of the generated images, which will result in wrong semantic relationships. To address this issue, we propose a Bidirectional Scene-Aware Mixup (BSAM) method in this paper. BSAM adopts a bi-directional pasting strategy to ensure scene awareness between the two domains, and takes the correctness of semantic relationships into account. Specifically, BSAM selects some contextually related classes from each domain to another domain, and generates bidirectional fused images for training. BSAM ensures the correct scene layout, facilitating the model to adapt to the different scenario characteristics. Extensive experiments on two benchmarks (GTA5 to Cityscapes and SYNTHIA to Cityscapes) demonstrate that BSAM achieves state-of-the-art performance.

Keywords: Domain adaption · Unsupervised learning · Semantic segmentation

1 Introduction

Semantic segmentation is a crucial task for computer vision, which aims to assign pixel-level labels to the images. Extensive and accurate semantic labels are indispensable for training a high-performance segmentation model. However, building such large-scale datasets is time-consuming and laborious since every pixel in every image needs to be annotated manually. An alternative approach is to train on datasets with simply-acquired labels, such as computer-synthesized datasets. However, while computers can generate images of scenes similar to the real world, they actually have very different data distributions. Such domain gap between two domains can incur severe performance degradation of the segmentation model.

Unsupervised Domain Adaptation (UDA) methods are proposed to tackle this problem, which can effectively eliminate the domain discrepancy through adversarial training [8,9,18,19], maximum mean discrepancy [15], self-training [24,25], etc. Recently, mixup methods [7,17] have emerged as a simple

L. Fang et al. (Eds.): CICAI 2022, LNAI 13604, pp. 54–66, 2022.
https://doi.org/10.1007/978-3-031-20497-5_5

yet competitive approach in UDA tasks. This kind of method usually selects parts of the source images and fuses them with target images for data augmentation, implicitly encouraging domain alignment by injecting pseudo-labels with ground-truth semantic maps. Lately, transformer structures [22] have produced impressive results in computer vision, for example, DAFormer [10] proposes to sample source images with rare classes more often than frequent classes to learn them better and earlier. Though effective, they suffer from inconsistent appearance, inappropriate contextual relationships, and misplaced spatial layout issues caused by naive pasting.

In this paper, we further propose a Bidirectional Scene-Aware Mixup (BSAM) method, which can create bidirectional scene-aware mixed images for unsupervised domain adaptation semantic segmentation. Specifically, BSAM first adopts an image-to-image translation algorithm ProCST [4] to transfer the style of source images to the target-like style, which facilitates the subsequent mixing process to remain consistent in appearance. Then we propose a bidirectional mixing strategy to generate fused images with both domains, ensuring the mutual scene-awareness. With a rare-classes priority sampling principle, some classes in the source domain images are pasted onto the target domain images with their corresponding ground-truth labels. Mixing from source to target leads to the pseudo-labels always having a part of the ground truth, ensuring fast convergence of the network. The reverse mixing selects semantically related classes from target images to the source images, enabling the bidirectional scene-awareness and improving the generalization ability of the model.

Our main contributions can be summarized as follows:

- We propose a Bidirectional Scene-Aware Mixup (BSAM) method for unsupervised domain adaptation semantic segmentation. BSAM mixes two domain images in both directions while ensuring correct semantic relationships, which allows two domains to be mutually scene-aware.
- We conduct extensive comparison experiments on two challenging tasks to verify the superiority of BSAM when compared with state-of-the-art methods. Ablation studies are also conducted to demonstrate the effectiveness of each module.

2   Methods

2.1   Preliminaries

For the study, we denote $S = \{(x_i^s, y_i^s)\}_{i=1}^{N_S}$ as the source domain, where each sample $x_s \in \mathbb{R}^{H \times W \times 3}$ is a colored RGB image, with corresponding $y_s \in \mathbb{R}^{H \times W \times C}$ as the associated ground-truth segmentation maps. Similarly, let $T = \{(x_i^s)\}_{i=1}^{N_T}$ as the target domain without ground truth semantic labels. N_S, N_T are the the number of images in the respective dataset. We train our model in both S and T, looking for accurate semantic labels on unlabelled target domain T. To this issue, we present a novel Bidirectional Scene-Aware Mixup (BSAM) for domain adaption to transfer cross-domain contexts.

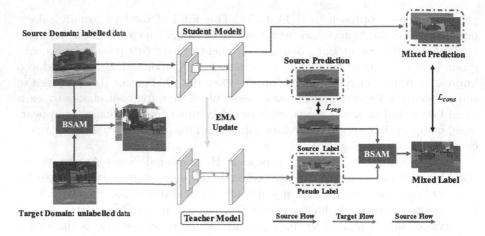

Fig. 1. Overview of the proposed method under mean-teacher framework. Source flow is drawn in red, target flow is drawn in blue and mix flow is drawn in purple. The source images and mixed images are fed into the student network and the target images are fed into the teacher network to generate pseudo labels. The parameters of the teacher network are the EMA of the student network parameters and we make prediction on target domain using teacher network in the end. Best viewed in color. (Color figure online)

As depicted in Fig. 1, our method is deployed under the mean teacher framework [16] containing two networks with the same structure. The parameters of the teacher model are updated as an exponential moving average (EMA) of the student model weights, and then the student model is guided by the teacher model to learn the aggregated knowledge.

2.2 Stylized Source Domain

The gap between the source domain and the target domain is reflected in various aspects such as appearance, texture, style, etc., leading to different difficulties for a network to learn domain-invariant features without any adaption. To address this issue, we introduce a stylized source domain by image-to-image translation. In this paper, we utilize ProCST [4], an image-to-image translation framework, to generator intermediate domain.

It is worth noting that the focus of our work is introducing an intermediate domain that holds the content of the source domain and the style of the target domain, i.e., the stylized source domain (ST), without caring about how to achieve it. Let denote the image Generator from [4] as G_f, and obtain the stylized source domain image:

$$x_{ST} = G_f(x_s) \tag{1}$$

where $x_{ST} \in \mathbb{R}^{H \times W \times 3}$ denotes transferred image from the source domain to the target domain with the same shape as source images.

Then, we can define stylized source domain $ST = \{(x_i^{st}, y_i^s)\}_{i=1}^{N_S}$, which shares the same labels as the source domain. In the following training, we take this domain as the source domain, on which we perform the domain adaptation method.

2.3   Bidirectional Scene-Aware Mixup

Unlike pasting part of the source mage directly to the target image or pasting part of the target image to the source image, we propose a bi-directional mixing algorithm that intends to learn different domain invariant information.

Source to Target Mixing. In the previous mixup method, some classes are randomly selected from the source image and pasted into the target image. But compared with some classes that appear more frequently and account for a larger proportion, (e.g., Road, Sky), some classes appear very infrequently, which we call long-tail classes. Nevertheless, we discover that the common classes usually correspond to the stuff classes [1](amorphous background regions) and long-tail classes correspond to thing classes [1](objects with definite shapes) through statistics. To address the problem that thing classes will be more difficult to learn due to requiring detailed annotations in the target domain, we will give priority to these classes when randomly selecting categories.

Specifically, given the images from source domain S, we first calculate the frequency distribution of their classes as $\{p_1, p_2, p_3, \ldots, p_C\}$, thus we can calculate the probability of each class p_c:

$$p_c = \frac{\sum_{i=1}^{N} \sum_{j=1}^{HW} \left[y_S^{(i,j,c)} \right]}{N * H * W} \tag{2}$$

where N indicates the total number of images in S, $\left[y_S^{(i,j,c)} \right]$ indicates whether the $j-th$ pixel of the $i-th$ image belongs to class c. We observe that the lowest frequent eight classes are all thing classes. Naturally, we define these categories as the things classes in this paper. For training, we choose x_{ST} and x_T from each of ST and T and randomly select half of the categories from x_{ST} as our base classes. In addition, for the thing classes that exist on x_{ST}, we further select R classes from them to add to the base classes. The corresponding mask M_{st} is generated according to the final selected classes. The mixed source image x_{st} can be obtained by:

$$x_{st} = M_{st} \odot x_{ST} + (1 - M_{st}) \odot x_T \tag{3}$$

Target to Source Mixing. Most of the existing mixup methods only select parts of pixels from the source images and paste them into the target images, although such an approach can learn cross-domain information, the target domain unable to sense the source domain information. To address this issue, we propose a bidirectional mixup(BSAM) strategy. By adding a reverse paste direction from the target to source, not only the source domain can perceive the distribution of the target domain, but also the source domain scene distribution can be perceived by target domain via pasting. In this way, both domains can perceive semantic relationships from the other and learn domain invariant features.

Despite the vast disparity between the two domains, we find that both the two domains have similar contextual information, i.e., the sky is always at the top of the image and the road is always at the bottom, traffic signs and signals usually appear together, riders are on bicycles, cars and trucks are always on the road, etc. With this in mind, we take these scene layout relations when perceiving information. This information will be fully considered in the paste without breaking the semantic consistency. We consider that the semantic information of different domains has a similar consistency. Therefore, this information is taken into account when pasting without destroying the semantic consistency of the image.

To be specific, we divided the categories into several groups l based on scene layout integrity. After randomly selecting half of the categories, we will incorporate relevant classes according to l. The overall implementation of the Target-to-Source Mixing is shown in the Algorithm1. Accordingly, we can also get a mask M_{ts} and obtain a new mixed image x_{ts} contains semantic information about the scene:

$$x_{ts} = M_{ts} \odot x_T + (1 - M_{ts}) \odot x_{ST} \tag{4}$$

The pseudo label $\hat{y}_T$ of the target image x_T can be obtained by the teacher network. Thus, we can calculate the labels for x_{st} and x_{ts} respectively:

$$
\begin{aligned}
y_{st} &= M_{st} \odot y_S + (1 - M_{st}) \odot \hat{y}_T \\
y_{ts} &= M_{ts} \odot \hat{y}_T + (1 - M_{ts}) \odot y_S
\end{aligned}
\tag{5}
$$

Overall, the generated bidirectional fused images are used to train the student network along with the source domain images.

2.4   Self-training Under Mean-Teacher Framework

Self-training is an effective means for unsupervised domain adaptation, where the student network f_θ is trained on augmented target data, and the teacher $f_{\theta'}$ network generates the pseudo-labels [11] for non-augmented target data. The whole training process is illustrated in Algorithm 1.

For stylized source images x_{ST} with labels y_S, we can directly calculate the segmentation loss $\mathcal{L}_{seg}$:

$$\mathcal{L}_{\mathbf{seg}}(x_{ST}) = -\sum_{h,w} \sum_{c \in C} y_S^{(h,w,c)} \log p_{ST}^{(h,w,c)} \tag{6}$$

where p_{ST} represents predict semantic map obtained from student network.

Algorithm 1. Bidirectional Scene-Aware Mixup

Input: Stylized source images x_{ST}, labels y_T target image x_T, a style-aware list l, student model f_θ, teacher model $f_{\theta'}$

1: $C \leftarrow$ Set of the classes present in $\hat{Y}_T$
2: $c \leftarrow$ Randomly select $|C|/2$ classes in C
3: **if** Source to Target Mixup **then**
4:     $TC \leftarrow$ Set of the thing classes present in y_T
5:     $r \leftarrow$ Randomly select $|R|$ classes present in TC
6:     $c.append(r)$
7: **end if**
8: **if** Target to Source Mixup **then**
9:     $\hat{Y}_T \leftarrow \arg max_{c'} \hat{F}_{\theta'} \left(i, j, c' \right)$
10:     **for** k in c **do**
11:         **if** $k \in cand k \in l$ **then**
12:             $\tilde{k} \leftarrow$ the semantic-related classes of k
13:             **if** $\tilde{k} \in C$ **then**
14:                 $c.append\left(\tilde{k} \right)$
15:             **end if**
16:         **end if**
17:     **end for**
18: **end if**
19: **for** each i, j **do**
20:     $M(i,j) = \begin{cases} 1, if\ \hat{Y}_T(i,j) \in c \\ 0,\ otherwise \end{cases}$
21: **end for**
22: **Return** M

For the same image but under different perturbations, the predictions between them gained by student and teacher network should be invariant, consequently we adopt the consistency loss $\mathcal{L}_{cons}$ to train the network:

$$\mathcal{L}_{cons} = -\sum_{h,w}\sum_{c\in C} \hat{y}_{st}^{(h,w,c)} \log p_{st}^{(h,w,c)} - \sum_{h,w}\sum_{c\in C} \hat{y}_{ts}^{(h,w,c)} \log p_{ts}^{(h,w,c)} \qquad (7)$$

where y_{st} and y_{ts} denote pseudo labels for the images x_{st} and x_{ts} generated by our BSAM, part of which is predicted by the teacher network, while p_{st} and p_{ts} are the corresponding predict semantic maps predicted by student network.

Finally, the overall loss function for the training of the whole network is a weighted average of the two losses.

$$\mathcal{L} = \mathcal{L}_{seg} + \lambda_{cons}\mathcal{L}_{cons} \qquad (8)$$

where λ_{cons} is a hyper-parameter that determines the impact of the $\mathcal{L}_{cons}$ on the total loss during training. λ_{cons} is set to 1 by default.

In such a way, the parameters of the student network θ_t are optimized by $\mathcal{L}$ via gradient back-propagation, while the parameters of the teacher network θ'_t are updated using EMA:

$$\theta_t^{'} = \alpha\theta_{t-1}^{'} + (1 - \alpha)\theta_t \qquad (9)$$

3　Experiments

In this section, we present and discuss our experimental results. We first introduce the used datasets as well as the training set. Then, in order to validate the proposed BSAM algorithm, qualitative experimental results are presented and compared to the state-of-the-art methods under two popular datasets for UDA.

3.1　Implementation Details

Datasets. Following the previous UDA protocols, we present results for semantic segmentation of two synthetic-to-real benchmarks namely GTA5 → Cityscapes and SYNTHIA → Cityscapes. For the target domain, the Cityscapes dataset [2] contains 2975 training images and 500 validation images with a resolution of $2,048 \times 1,024$. For the source domain, GTA5 [13] and SYNTHIA [14] contain 24,966 and 9,400 synthetic images for training, respectively. 500 validation images are used to evaluate the performance of the model with the mean Intersection over Union (mIoU) over all classes, and the Intersection over Union (IoU) over each class in both set-ups.

Network Architecture. In the implementation, our model is based on DAFormer [10], which adopts MiT-B5 [21] as encoder to extract multi-level feature maps and design a context-aware feature fusion decoder to make semantic predictions. The encoder is pre-trained on ImageNet [3]. All experiments are implemented using PyTorch on a single NVIDIA GeForce RTX 3090 GPU with 24 GB memory.

Training. Following [10], we use AdamW [12] as the optimizer. q The initial learning rate is set to 6×10^{-5} for encoder with $\beta_1 = 0.9$, $\beta_2 = 0.99$ respectively. The weight decay is 0.01. We use a linear learning rate warmup for 1,500 iterations with a factor of 1.0 by default. During training, we resize Cityscapes, GTA5, and SYNTHIA to $1,024 \times 512$, $1,280 \times 720$, and $1,280 \times 760$ respectively, and set crop size to 512×512. The same data argumentation methods as [17] are applied. The model is trained for 80k iterations with a batch size of 2. The training starts with generating the stylized intermediate domain ST, and then reducing the domain gap between ST and T according to the proposed BSAM algorithm.

3.2　Comparison with State-of-the-Art Methods

In this section, we evaluate our proposed method on two challenging tasks: GTA5 → Cityscapes and SYNTHIA → Cityscapes respectively and present the comparison results with several UDA methods. Our model achieves State-of-the-art

Table 1. Results of different domain adaptation methods for the GTA5 → Cityscapes task and SYNTHIA → Cityscapes task.

GTA5 → Cityscapes

Methods	Road	S.walk	Build.	Wall	Fence	Pole	Tr.Light	Sign	Veget.	Terrain	Sky	Person	Rider	Car	Truck	Bus	Train	M.bike	Bike	mIoU
CBST [24]	91.8	53.5	80.5	32.7	21.0	34.0	28.9	20.4	83.9	34.2	80.9	53.1	24	82.7	30.3	35.9	16	25.9	42.8	45.9
DACS [17]	89.9	39.7	87.9	30.7	39.5	38.5	46.4	52.8	88	44.0	88.8	67.2	35.8	84.5	45.7	50.2	0.0	27.3	34	52.1
CroDA [20]	94.7	63.1	87.6	30.7	40.6	40.2	47.8	51.6	87.6	47	89.7	66.7	35.9	90.2	48.9	57.5	0.0	39.8	56.0	56.6
ProDA [23]	87.8	56	79.7	46.3	44.8	45.6	53.5	53.5	88.6	45.2	82.1	70.7	39.2	88.8	45.5	59.4	1.0	48.9	56.4	57.5
ProCST [4]	95.4	68.2	**89.8**	**55.1**	46.4	**50.4**	56.4	**63.4**	90.4	49.9	92.3	72.4	45.3	92.6	**78.4**	81.2	70.6	**56.8**	**63.6**	69.4
DAFormer [10]	**95.7**	**70.2**	89.4	53.5	48.1	49.6	55.8	59.4	89.9	47.9	**92.5**	72.2	44.7	92.3	74.5	78.2	65.1	55.9	61.8	68.3
Ours	95.3	68.7	89.7	54.1	**48.6**	47.9	**59.6**	62.9	**89.9**	**51.1**	91.9	**75.2**	**47.5**	**92.6**	74.4	**84.4**	**75.6**	55.7	57.8	**69.6**

Synthia → Cityscapes

Methods	Road	S.walk	Build.	Wall	Fence	Pole	Tr.Light	Sign	Veget.	Terrain	Sky	Person	Rider	Car	Truck	Bus	Train	M.bike	Bike	mIoU
CBST [24]	68.0	29.9	76.3	10.8	1.4	33.9	22.8	29.5	77.6	-	78.3	60.6	28.3	81.6	-	23.5	-	18.8	39.8	42.6
DACS [17]	80.6	25.1	81.9	21.5	2.9	37.2	22.7	24.0	83.7	-	90.8	67.6	38.3	82.9	-	38.9	-	28.5	47.6	48.3
CroDA [20]	93.3	61.6	85.3	19.6	5.1	37.8	36.6	42.8	84.9	-	90.4	69.7	41.8	85.6	-	38.4	-	32.6	53.9	55.0
ProDA [23]	87.8	45.7	84.6	37.1	0.6	44.0	54.6	37.0	88.1	-*	84.4	74.2	24.3	88.2	-	51.1	-	40.5	45.6	55.5
ProCST [4]	84.5	40.7	**88.4**	**41.5**	6.5	50.0	55.0	54.6	86.0	-	89.8	73.2	48.2	87.2	-	53.2	-	53.9	61.7	60.9
DAFormer [10]	84.8	39.5	88.2	40.2	**7.3**	51.1	56.3	55.1	86.5	-	89.8	74.6	48.4	86.5	-	58.6	-	**55.6**	62.9	61.6
Ours	**85.3**	**43.3**	87.6	25.7	4.2	**54.1**	**59.6**	**59.1**	87.6	-	**94.0**	74.2	**50.2**	**88.7**	-	**61.6**	-	52.7	**63.1**	**61.9**

in both UDA benchmarks. As revealed in Table 1, our proposed BSAM outperforms the previous State-of-the-art methods by 0.2% and 0.3% in mIoU on two datasets, respectively. Take a closer look at the results of the pre-category in Table 1, our BSAM is even highly effective at learning tough categories, such as fence, rider, trains, buses, and traffic light, which cannot be well handled by previous methods, and achieves the best IoU. This demonstrates these classes can be adequately learned when executeing bidirectional mixing. As for the SYNTHIA to Cityscapes task over 16 classes, in addition to the tough classes mentioned above, categories such as road and vegetation also achieve the best performance, demonstrating that both thing classes with fine segmentation details and stuff classes benefit from our BSAM. Moreover, some semantically relevant classes exceed the previous best results, including road and sidewalk, rider and bike, traffic light, and traffic sign. This phenomenon reveals the importance of considering the complete semantic information of the image when mixing for learning domain invariant information.

3.3   Parameter Analysis and Ablation Study

In this section, we are going to analyze the contributions of the various components of the proposed approach. The ablation studies on GTA5 → Cityscapes task are reported in Table 2. "MT" means Mean Teacher framework [16] with a 68.3% mIoU. "S → T" means mixing from the source domain to the target domain taking into account the thing classes, it improves the performance from 68.3 to 68.5% mIoU. "T → S" means just the opposite. "ST" denotes using stylized source domain ST as the source domain, the use of ST successfully brings 1.1% improvements. The inverse mixup method from target domain to source domain is designed to capture complete scene information. On top of that,

"T → S" brings another 0.2% mIoU improvements. By contrast, our BSAM method with the introduction of the stylized domain ST outperforms the baseline model by 1.3% mIoU.

Table 2. Alation study of proposed BSAM. S → T denotes mixing from the source domain to target domain taking into account the thing classes. T → S denotes mixing from the target domain to source domain.

MT	S → T	Stylized domain	T → S	mIoU(%)	Gain(%)
✓				68.3	–
✓	✓			69.5	+0.2
✓	✓	✓		69.4	+1.1
✓	✓	✓	✓	**69.6**	**+1.3**

Table 3 displays the impact of the settings of hyper-parameter R on the experimental results, where R means using the different number of thing classes. It can be observed that as R gradually increases, the mIoU increases and the performance peaks when $R = 2$. However, the continued increment of R leads to a decrease in performance, which is 0.9% 1.7% worse than the peak. We speculate that this phenomenon may be caused by the possible overfitting of the network to the source domain when too many categories are chosen.

Table 3. Hyper-parameter study of the number of Thing classes R.

GTA5 → Cityscapes						
R	0	1	2	3	4	5
mIoU(%)	68.7	69.5	**69.6**	68.7	68.6	66.9

To investigate the superiority of our proposed BSAM algorithm, we conduct a series of comparisons with the existing mixup algorithm on GTA5 → Cityscapes, results are shown in Table 4. MT refers to Mean Teacher architecture [16]. Both CowMix [5] and CutMix [6] randomly select some pixels in the image without considering their class relationship, which tends to result in class conflation. Only 53.2% and 54.0% of mIoU are obtained respectively. DACS [17] chooses pixels based on category and achieves 68.3% mIoU. We observe a further improvement to 69.6% mIoU by using our BSAM, showing that leveraging scene relevance to facilitate domain adaptation can prevent category confusion to a large extent.

Table 4. Comparisons with existing domain mixup methods.

Method	mIoU(%)	Gain(%)
MT + CutMix [6]	53.2	–
MT + CowMix [5]	54.0	+0.8
MT + DACS [17]	68.3	+15.1
MT + BAWM	**69.6**	**+16.4**

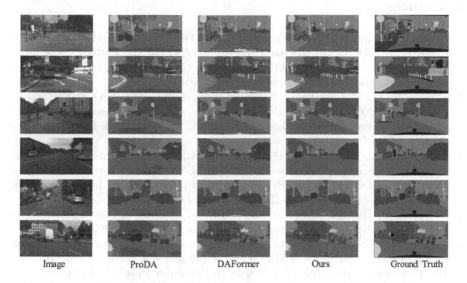

Image   ProDA   DAFormer   Ours   Ground Truth

Fig. 2. Qualitative segmentation results on GTA5 → Cityscapes.

Figure 2 displays some segmentation results on the GTA5 → Cityscapes task. The five columns plot (a) RGB input images, (b) ProDA [23] outputs, (c) DAFormer [10] outputs, (d) the predictions of BSAM and (e) ground truth. The first row demonstrates that the BSAM avoids a typical error case: misclassification of riders and bicycles. The second, third, fourth, and fifth rows show a better recognition for train, sidewalk, bus, and truck, respectively. The sixth row is an example showing a better recognition of cars as opposed to trucks. In general, the proposed BSAM has the capability to generate high confidence predictions on both thing classes and stuff classes.

4   Conclusion

In this paper, we proposed a novel Bidirectional Scene-Aware Mixup (BSAM) method for unsupervised domain adaptation in semantic segmentation. We first leverage image translation to narrow the gap between the two domains at the input level. To guarantee scene awareness between the two domains, we introduce a bidirectional mixup algorithm, i.e., paste from the source and target domain images to each other separately. Besides, to fully perceive the scene-aware semantic information and ensure the correct layout of the scene during the pasting, we select the classes with strong scene relationships. Furthermore, we perform an evaluation of BSAM for two popular domain adaptation benchmarks, where it outperforms existing methods and pushes the state of the art in domain adaptive semantic segmentation.

References

1. Caesar, H., Uijlings, J.R.R., Ferrari, V.: COCO-Stuff: thing and stuff classes in context. In: 2018 IEEE Conference on Computer Vision and Pattern Recognition, CVPR 2018, Salt Lake City, UT, USA, June 18–22, 2018, pp. 1209–1218. Computer Vision Foundation/IEEE Computer Society (2018)
2. Cordts, M., et al.: The cityscapes dataset for semantic urban scene understanding. In: 2016 IEEE Conference on Computer Vision and Pattern Recognition, CVPR 2016, Las Vegas, NV, USA, June 27–30, 2016, pp. 3213–3223. IEEE Computer Society (2016)
3. Deng, J., Dong, W., Socher, R., Li, L., Li, K., Fei-Fei, L.: ImageNet: a large-scale hierarchical image database. In: 2009 IEEE Computer Society Conference on Computer Vision and Pattern Recognition (CVPR 2009), 20–25 June 2009, Miami, Florida, USA, pp. 248–255. IEEE Computer Society (2009)
4. Ettedgui, S., Hussein, S.A., Giryes, R.: Procst: boosting semantic segmentation using progressive cyclic style-transfer. CoRR abs/2204.11891 (2022)
5. French, G., Oliver, A., Salimans, T.: Milking cowmask for semi-supervised image classification. In: Farinella, G.M., Radeva, P., Bouatouch, K. (eds.) Proceedings of the 17th International Joint Conference on Computer Vision, Imaging and Computer Graphics Theory and Applications, VISIGRAPP 2022, Volume 5: VISAPP, Online Streaming, February 6–8, 2022, pp. 75–84. SCITEPRESS (2022)
6. French, G., Laine, S., Aila, T., Mackiewicz, M., On, G.D.F.: Semi-supervised semantic segmentation needs strong, varied perturbations. In: 31st British Machine Vision Conference 2020, BMVC 2020, Virtual Event, UK, September 7–10, 2020. BMVA Press (2020)
7. Gao, L., Zhang, J., Zhang, L., Tao, D.: DSP: dual soft-paste for unsupervised domain adaptive semantic segmentation. In: Shen, H.T., et al. (eds.) MM '21: ACM Multimedia Conference, Virtual Event, China, October 20–24, 2021, pp. 2825–2833. ACM (2021)
8. Hoffman, J., et al.: Cycada: cycle-consistent adversarial domain adaptation. CoRR abs/1711.03213 (2017)
9. Hoffman, J., Wang, D., Yu, F., Darrell, T.: FCNs in the wild: pixel-level adversarial and constraint-based adaptation. CoRR abs/1612.02649 (2016)
10. Hoyer, L., Dai, D., Gool, L.V.: Daformer: improving network architectures and training strategies for domain-adaptive semantic segmentation. CoRR abs/2111.14887 (2021)
11. Lee, D.H., et al.: Pseudo-label: the simple and efficient semi-supervised learning method for deep neural networks. In: Workshop on challenges in representation learning, ICML. vol. 3, p. 896 (2013)

12. Loshchilov, I., Hutter, F.: Decoupled weight decay regularization. In: 7th International Conference on Learning Representations, ICLR 2019, New Orleans, LA, USA, May 6–9, 2019. OpenReview.net (2019)

13. Richter, S.R., Vineet, V., Roth, S., Koltun, V.: Playing for data: ground truth from computer games. In: Leibe, B., Matas, J., Sebe, N., Welling, M. (eds.) ECCV 2016. LNCS, vol. 9906, pp. 102–118. Springer, Cham (2016). https://doi.org/10.1007/978-3-319-46475-6_7

14. Ros, G., Sellart, L., Materzynska, J., Vázquez, D., López, A.M.: The SYNTHIA dataset: a large collection of synthetic images for semantic segmentation of urban scenes. In: 2016 IEEE Conference on Computer Vision and Pattern Recognition, CVPR 2016, Las Vegas, NV, USA, June 27–30, 2016, pp. 3234–3243. IEEE Computer Society (2016)

15. Saito, K., Watanabe, K., Ushiku, Y., Harada, T.: Maximum classifier discrepancy for unsupervised domain adaptation. In: 2018 IEEE Conference on Computer Vision and Pattern Recognition, CVPR 2018, Salt Lake City, UT, USA, June 18–22, 2018, pp. 3723–3732. Computer Vision Foundation/IEEE Computer Society (2018)

16. Tarvainen, A., Valpola, H.: Mean teachers are better role models: weight-averaged consistency targets improve semi-supervised deep learning results. In: 5th International Conference on Learning Representations, ICLR 2017, Toulon, France, April 24–26, 2017, Workshop Track Proceedings. OpenReview.net (2017)

17. Tranheden, W., Olsson, V., Pinto, J., Svensson, L.: DACS: domain adaptation via cross-domain mixed sampling. CoRR abs/2007.08702 (2020)

18. Tsai, Y., Hung, W., Schulter, S., Sohn, K., Yang, M., Chandraker, M.: Learning to adapt structured output space for semantic segmentation. In: 2018 IEEE Conference on Computer Vision and Pattern Recognition, CVPR 2018, Salt Lake City, UT, USA, June 18–22, 2018, pp. 7472–7481. Computer Vision Foundation/IEEE Computer Society (2018)

19. Vu, T., Jain, H., Bucher, M., Cord, M., Pérez, P.: ADVENT: adversarial entropy minimization for domain adaptation in semantic segmentation. In: IEEE Conference on Computer Vision and Pattern Recognition, CVPR 2019, Long Beach, CA, USA, June 16–20, 2019, pp. 2517–2526. Computer Vision Foundation/IEEE (2019)

20. Wang, Q., Dai, D., Hoyer, L., Gool, L.V., Fink, O.: Domain adaptive semantic segmentation with self-supervised depth estimation. In: 2021 IEEE/CVF International Conference on Computer Vision, ICCV 2021, Montreal, QC, Canada, October 10–17, 2021, pp. 8495–8505. IEEE (2021)

21. Xie, E., Wang, W., Yu, Z., Anandkumar, A., Alvarez, J.M., Luo, P.: Segformer: simple and efficient design for semantic segmentation with transformers. In: Ranzato, M., Beygelzimer, A., Dauphin, Y.N., Liang, P., Vaughan, J.W. (eds.) Advances in Neural Information Processing Systems 34: Annual Conference on Neural Information Processing Systems 2021, NeurIPS 2021, December 6–14, 2021, virtual, pp. 12077–12090 (2021)

22. Xu, Y., et al.: Multi-task learning with multi-query transformer for dense prediction. arXiv (2022). https://doi.org/10.48550/ARXIV.2205.14354

23. Zhang, P., Zhang, B., Zhang, T., Chen, D., Wang, Y., Wen, F.: Prototypical pseudo label denoising and target structure learning for domain adaptive semantic segmentation. In: IEEE Conference on Computer Vision and Pattern Recognition, CVPR 2021, virtual, June 19–25, 2021, pp. 12414–12424. Computer Vision Foundation/IEEE (2021)

24. Zou, Y., Yu, Z., Kumar, B.V.K.V., Wang, J.: Domain adaptation for semantic segmentation via class-balanced self-training. CoRR abs/1810.07911 (2018)
25. Zou, Y., Yu, Z., Liu, X., Kumar, B.V.K.V., Wang, J.: Confidence regularized self-training. In: 2019 IEEE/CVF International Conference on Computer Vision, ICCV 2019, Seoul, Korea (South), October 27 - November 2, 2019, pp. 5981–5990. IEEE (2019)

Triple GNN: A Pedestrian-Scene-Object Joint Model for Pedestrian Trajectory Prediction

Xinshengzi Huang, Qiong Liu, and You Yang[✉]

School of Electronic Information and Communications, Huazhong University
of Science and Technology, Wuhan, China
yangyou@hust.edu.cn

Abstract. Pedestrian trajectory prediction is an amazing but challenging task for vision guided applications, including autonomous driving, intelligent surveillance system, etc. Practically, the trajectory is a result of interaction among pedestrian's surrounding people, scenes and related objects, which can be represented by a triple. In previous works, limited interactions have been exploited, such as pedestrian-pedestrian and pedestrian-object. These works are facing challenges when comprehensive interactions in natural scenes are involved. In this paper, we propose a triple graph neural network (Triple GNN) where interactions among pedestrians, scenes and objects are all taken into the prediction of pedestrian trajectory. Based on that, spatial relation is exploited to describe the mutual interaction among triple elements, and a two-stage optimization scheme is proposed on weights of the interaction aggregation for better relation exploitation and prediction. Furthermore, temporal relation is also exploited for compact representation and effective computation of future trajectories based on the spatial relation. Our method is verified via ETH and UCY datasets and achieves the state-of-the-art performance.

Keywords: Trajectory prediction · Graph neural network · Interaction modeling

1 Introduction

Doctor Strange is able to see through the time with magic from Time Stone in Marvel's Avengers, and this capability is amazing and attractive to all ordinary people and intelligent machines [1]. Therefore, in recent years, action or event prediction has witnessed a rapid development in the community of computer vision, and pedestrian trajectory prediction (PTP) is among these hot topics [2,10,12–14,18,21,24]. The advantage taken by PTP is crucial in many vision based applications for safety reasons, especially for those unmanned vehicle,

This work was supported in part by the National Key Research and Development Program of China under Grant 2020YFB2103501, in part by the National Natural Science Foundation of China under Grant 61971203.

surveillance system, service robots and other kinds of intelligent bodies [4,23,30]. Different from the magic of Time Stone, PTP in computer vision is a task with complex processes, including actions of pedestrian, spatio-temporal relations of surroundings, and so on. Therefore, in order to have a better prediction result, challenges arise from how to model the relations among pedestrians and their surroundings.

The research on PTP, sometimes it is also named as pedestrian path prediction, is a real hard-exploration through these years. Generally, there are three sub-topics that should be involved to solve the task, including *what should be modeled, how to model,* and *how to compute*. Actually, human behavior is profoundly influenced by the interactions, and the interaction is a social action where many semantic objects and relations can be involved, and all of these can be hardly used while modeling. Originally, researchers used hand-crafted approaches to capture the interactions between pedestrians for PTP. For example, Social Forces proposed by Helbing and Molnar [9] laid the foundation for using interaction among pedestrians to predict trajectories. Later, Social Forces has been constantly used and improved [7,15,16,19,29]. After that, hand-crafted features are replaced by learning based tools [3,8,20,26,31]. For example, Alahi *et al.* [3] used a pooling mechanism to aggregate the influence of neighborhood. Gupta *et al.* [8] adopted adversarial training for a better modeling of the interactions among pedestrians. Mohamed *et al.* [20] adopted a reverse of Euclidean distance to model the impacts between pedestrians. All of these works try to model the pedestrian-pedestrian interactions via some kinds of features. However, human behavior in natural scenes is profoundly influenced by his/her surroundings, including other objects, and even the scene besides pedestrians. New attempts have been tried by taking the scene element into modeling. For example, Sadeghian *et al.* [25] adopted convolutional neural networks(CNN) to capture the pedestrian-scene interaction and used generative adversarial networks (GAN) to predict the trajectories. These attempts consider both the pedestrian-scene interaction and the pedestrian-pedestrian interaction by apparent features, which are facing challenges in natural scenes due to a lack of semantic information. It is believed that the complex interaction is benefit from the object semantic features extracted by semantic segmentation models. Based on that, the comprehensive interaction in natural scenes is better modeled by the triple interactions among pedestrians, scenes and objects.

After the problem of *what should be modeled, how to model* becomes a new topic. Relation mining benefits from learning based tools, and the researches of PTP are booming after various of deep learning tools are introduced. For example, Alahi *et al.* [3] applied a recurrent neural network (RNN) with a social pooling strategy to simulate the influence of nearby pedestrians. Gupta *et al.* [8] utilized GAN on Social-LSTM to generate possible trajectory coordinates. Recently, graph neural networks (GNN) showed its capability in relation mining. Different from typical graphs such as social networks, the applications in computer vision need to consider how to construct the graph for the reason that images are not typical graphs. Some researches [11,20,28] in the application of pedestrian trajectory prediction uses GNN to predict the future trajectories and achieve remarkable results. The above work turn out that GNN is promising for modeling the comprehensive interaction, but challenges exist in the graph construction and aggregation.

When it turns to *how to compute*, some research adopted GNN to solve this problem. Mohamed *et al.* [20] modeled pedestrian interaction as a graph. Nodes and edges represented pedestrians and the interaction between pedestrians respectively. The strength of interaction is measured by the distance between pedestrians. Huang *et al.* [11] exploited a graph attention mechanism to capture the spatial interaction among pedestrians at each time step. Wang *et al.* [28] modeled spatial interactions as social graphs and proposed a graph attention network based on edge features to capture pedestrian interactions. The above research has made some progress in PTP, but there are still some challenges in the graph modeling of pedestrian interaction when the interactions are multiple or the scenario is dense with pedestrians. Recently, temporal convolutional networks (TCN) [5] have attracted much attention for the inspiring fact that it overcomes the above difficulties of RNN in the field of sequence prediction. The convolution operation in the temporal dimension can better capture the time dependency and greatly improve the efficiency for it can process in parallel.

Inspired by the above discussions and analysis, we propose a Triple GNN to properly solve the above three tasks. The triple elements (i.e., pedestrians, scenes and objects) are extracted for the exploitation of mutual relations between each pair of these elements. Based on that, a two-stage optimization strategy with GNN is utilized to aggregate the spatial interaction among the triple elements and optimize the interaction weight from coarse to fine in the spatial dimension. Besides, we design a compact temporal convolutional networks with dilated convolution and residual connections to capture the temporal dependence and predict the final trajectory coordinates in temporal dimension. Based on these modules, Triple GNN is suitable for complex scenarios where interactions among pedestrians, scenes and objects are all taken into the PTP.

Our contribution can be summarized by two-fold:

- A pedestrian-scene-object joint model, i.e., Triple GNN, is proposed to solve the problem of pedestrian trajectory prediction. The relation of pedestrian-scene-object is described as a triple, and all subsequent processes are proposed on these data representation.
- We propose a two-stage scheme with attention mechanism to optimize the interaction weight in the Triple GNN from coarse to fine. In this way, more interaction information is considered effectively.

2 The Proposed Pedestrian-Scene-Object Joint Model for Pedestrian Trajectory Prediction

2.1 Problem Statements and the Framework of Our Work

We suppose that there are $N \in \mathbb{N}$ pedestrians in the observed video sequence with length $T_{obs} \in \mathbb{N}$, and pedestrian and frame is denoted as p_i and f_t

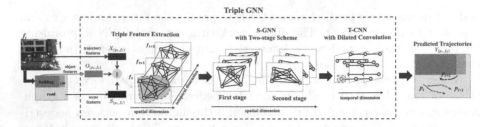

Fig. 1. The proposed pedestrian-scene-object joint model for pedestrian trajectory prediction.

respectively, where $i \in \{1, \ldots, N\}$ and $t \in \{1, \ldots, T_{obs}\}$. The presentation of p_i consists of trajectory features $X_{(p_i, f_t)}$, surrounding scene features $S_{(p_i, f_t)}$ and object features $O_{(p_i, f_t)}$. Our goal is to predict the future trajectory $Y_{(p_i, f_{\tilde{t}})}$, where $\tilde{t} \in \{T_{obs} + 1, \ldots, T_{obs} + T_{pred}\}$ for all p_i in future frame $f_{\tilde{t}}$, where T_{pred} is the length of prediction. It can be generally assumed that $Y_{(p_i, f_{\tilde{t}})}$ follows the bivariate Gaussian distribution parameterized by mean $\mu_i^{\tilde{t}}$, standard deviation $\sigma_i^{\tilde{t}}$, and correlation coefficient $\rho_i^{\tilde{t}}$, such that $Y_i^{\tilde{t}} \sim \mathcal{N}(\mu_i^{\tilde{t}}, \sigma_i^{\tilde{t}}, \rho_i^{\tilde{t}})$. The task of pedestrian trajectory prediction can be thus modeled as:

$$(\mu_i^{\tilde{t}}, \sigma_i^{\tilde{t}}, \rho_i^{\tilde{t}}) = f(X_{(p_j, f_t)}||S_{(p_j, f_t)}||O_{(p_j, f_t)}), \tag{1}$$

where $j \in \{1, \ldots, N\}$ and $||$ is the concatenation operation. How can $\mu_i^{\tilde{t}}$, $\sigma_i^{\tilde{t}}$, and $\rho_i^{\tilde{t}}$ be properly estimated is the pre-request in handling the prediction of $Y_i^{\tilde{t}} \sim \mathcal{N}(\mu_i^{\tilde{t}}, \sigma_i^{\tilde{t}}, \rho_i^{\tilde{t}})$.

In order to solve the problem modeled by Eq. 1, a Triple GNN is proposed in our work, and the framework of this network is given by Fig. 1. As depicted by this framework, our Triple GNN consists of three modules, including *Triple Feature Extraction*, *S-GNN with Two-stage Scheme* and *T-CNN with Dilated Convolution*. Next we will introduce these modules in detail.

2.2   Triple Feature Extraction

This module aims to extract each pedestrian's presentation including trajectory features as well as scene and object features. Figure 2 shows the process of feature extraction in details. The three features are concatenated as this pedestrian's property after the triple features are extracted.

Scene and Object Features. Pedestrian paths are usually influenced by those surrounding scenes and objects. The effect of conducting feature extraction on a whole frame is inferior because pedestrian path can be influenced by only a limited range of scenes and objects. Based on this common sense, we extract the features of $\Omega(p_i) \in f_t$ to represent the interaction between p_i and its surroundings, where $\Omega(p_i)$ is the neighborhood of p_i. In the first step, the pre-trained scene segmentation model proposed in [6] is used on f_t to extract scene feature map (i.e., M_s). We then use a convolutional layer to resize the M_s to $[h, w, dim]$, where h and w are the horizontal and vertical number of grids respectively, and each grid is assigned with features of segmentation, and dim is the length of each grid's features. After that, we can build up a relation between each p_i and one specific grid, and this grid is regarded as $\Omega(p_i)$. And in the second step, scene and object features are extracted from the M_s. In other words, if one pedestrian p_i is inside the grid where $h = 1$ and $w = 1$, his scene and/or object features are $M_s[1, 1, dim]$. For more specifically, the size of scene features $S_{(p_i, f_t)}$ in the observed frames is $[D_1, T_{obs}, N]$ and the size of object features $O_{(p_i, f_t)}$ is $[D_2, T_{obs}, N]$, where D_1 and D_2 are both equal to dim. Then we concatenate these two features to get the scene and/or object features of size $[D_e, T_{obs}, N]$, where D_e is a hyper parameter mentioned above to make sure these features have equal weight. After these steps, the interaction between pedestrians and their surroundings is properly represented by the extracted scene and object features.

Trajectory Features. By processing the captured video, we can get the 2D trajectory coordinates of each p_i from time 1 to T_{obs}. The total size of the trajectory coordinates for all pedestrians in the observed frames is $[D_3, T_{obs}, N]$. Specified for features of 2D trajectory, $D_3 = 2$ because 2D coordinates are used. In order to get more contextual information from the historical trajectory, a convolutional layer can be used to embed the 2D coordinates into deeper dimensions as $[D_e, T_{obs}, N]$, where D_e is the embed feature which can be regarded as a hyper parameter which will be discussed later. In this way, trajectory features $X_{(p_i, f_t)}$ are obtained with rich information.

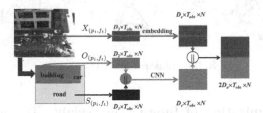

Fig. 2. The process of feature extraction and relation construction.

2.3 S-GNN with Two-stage Scheme

In this part, the S-GNN is introduced in two aspects: the construction of the graph and the two-stage interaction weight optimization. We use a graph model to represent this triple interaction for three reasons. First of all, the flexible construction of nodes and edges of graph is suitable to represent the multiple relationship of pedestrians-scenes-object. Besides of that, the way information is passed and updated between a pair of nodes represent the process of interaction. Finally, the graph construction is flexible as it can naturally handle arbitrary number of surround pedestrians without pooling compared with RNN or CNN.

Graph Construction. The construction of the graph is modeled in three parts, including connections of the spatio-temporal graph, nodes and edges' attributes. In the proposed Triple GNN, the graph is organized in both spatial and temporal dimensions. This spatio-temporal graph is denoted as $\mathscr{G}_{\text{Triple}} = \{G_t | t \in \{1, \ldots, T_{obs}\}\}$. We construct a spatial graph $G_t = (V_t, E_t, W_t)$ in every time step t to model the spatial interaction between pedestrians, scenes and objects. Inside this graph, $V_t = \{v_{t|i} | i \in \{1, \ldots, N\}\}$ is a set of vertices that corresponds to p_i in time step t. The pedestrian feature extracted in Sec. 2.2 is the attribute of $V_{t|i}$. In this way, the interaction between the pedestrian and its surrounding objects and scenes is involved in G_t as the attribute of the nodes. In G_t, $E_t = \{e_{t|ij} | i, j \in \{1, \ldots, N\}\}$ is the set of edges which corresponds to the interaction between p_i and p_j in time step t. In G_t, each $v_{t|i}$ is connected to $v_{t|j \neq i}$ to build up relations between each pair of pedestrians. Different from those previous works where only the influence of the nearby pedestrians is considered, G_t takes all pedestrians in the f_t into account, whether nearby or not. Finally, W_t is a weight matrix with size $N \times N$ that defined on E_t, and each $w_{t|ij} \in [0, 1] \subset \mathbb{R}$ describes the interaction weight (i.e., the strength of interaction) for corresponding e_{ij}. The details of operations on initialization and update for W_t will be discussed in the subsequent section. In this way, $\mathscr{G}_{\text{Triple}}$ can handle complex scenarios where the interactions are multiple. In the construction of $\mathscr{G}_{\text{Triple}}$, $v_{t|i}$ is connected to both $v_{t-1|i}$ and $v_{t+1|i}$ in G_{t-1} and G_{t+1} respectively to build up the relation in time dimension for each p_i. Therefore, the construction of $\mathscr{G}_{\text{Triple}}$ is able to capture interactions of both spatial and temporal dimensions for all p_i.

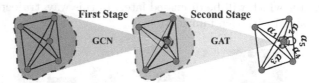

Fig. 3. The illustration of the S-GNN.

Two-stage Optimization of Interaction Weight. Through the construction of $\mathscr{G}_{\text{Triple}}$, the triple interaction will be involved compared to previous works which limited interactions are concerned. In this case, attention mechanism is basically required to handle the W_t of $\mathscr{G}_{\text{Triple}}$ to adaptively increase the weight of the discriminative features. In order to solve this problem, a two-stage optimization model is proposed for W_t, and the workflow of this model is depicted by Fig. 3. As can be found in this figure, in the first stage, Euclidean distance between p_i and p_j is adopted to initialize the strength of interaction, and then be updated by graph convolutional network (GCN). Intermediate vertex attributes can be obtained after this stage, and these features are only updated by distance. It is believed that distance updated features are not enough to model the interactions in the scenarios, and thus further optimizations should be implement in the second stage. Therefore, a graph attention network (GAT) is adopted to tune the triple interaction and update W_t. More interaction factors, i.e., surrounding scenes and objects is considered to optimize the global optimal solution and model the triple interaction more effectively. It is believed that our two-stage strategy is able to capture the interaction from coarse to fine when comparing to those one-stage strategies. Moreover, the two-stage model eliminate the negative effects from unnecessary features effectively. Details of our two-stage optimization model are discussed below.

In the first stage, each $w_{t|ij}$ in W_t is initialized to represents the strength of interaction between p_i and p_j. We assume that the strength of interaction is an inverse relation to distance between p_i and p_j. In this way, $w_{t|ij}$ can be defined as

$$w_{t|ij} = \begin{cases} 1/||v_{t|i} - v_{t|j}||_2, & i \neq j \\ 0, & i = j, \end{cases} \tag{2}$$

where $||v_{t|i} - v_{t|j}||_2$ is the Euclidean distance between the bounding box centers of p_i and p_j, and it is measured by pixels. In this way, higher value of $w_{t|ij} \in [0, 1]$ corresponds to higher strength of interaction.

Based on the initialization of W_t, we use the following GCN operation of Eq. 3 to aggregate the feature of adjacent nodes.

$$\mathscr{F}(V_t) = \sigma(\Lambda_t^{-\frac{1}{2}}(W_t + I)\Lambda_t^{-\frac{1}{2}} V_t \mathbf{W}_{\mathrm{GCN}}). \tag{3}$$

where Λ_t is the diagonal matrix of node degrees matrix $W_t + I$, where I is an unit matrix. $\Lambda_t^{-\frac{1}{2}}(A^t+I)\Lambda_t^{-\frac{1}{2}}$ is the normalized Laplacian matrix. $\mathbf{W}_{\mathrm{GCN}}$ is the weight matrix of a learned linear transformation. $\sigma(\cdot)$ is the activation function. After $\mathscr{F}(\cdot)$ has been applied over all V_l ($t-1, \cdots, T_{obs}$), all features of $v_{t|ij}$ in $\mathscr{G}$ are optimized by Euclidean distance, and we call these features as intermediate vertex features.

It should be noted that the intermediate vertex attribute obtained by GCN only measures the spatial interaction by Euclidean distance. This kind of features are not enough to deal with complex scenarios if more factors should be involved into consideration. Therefore, an attention mechanism is necessary to figure out these factors and their contributions to features of vertex. In order to solve this problem, in the second stage, we use GAT proposed in [27] to figure out the deeper interaction between pedestrians based on the prior knowledge from GCN. According to GAT, the weight $\alpha_{t|ij}$ passed from $v_{t|j}$ to $v_{t|i}$ can be obtained as below if they are adjacent,

$$\alpha_{t|ij} = \frac{\exp(LeakyReLU(\mathbf{a}[\mathbf{W}_{\mathrm{GAT}}v_{t|i}||\mathbf{W}_{\mathrm{GAT}}v_{t|j}]))}{\Sigma_{k \in \mathcal{N}_i} \exp(LeakyReLU(\mathbf{a}[\mathbf{W}_{\mathrm{GAT}}v_{t|i}||\mathbf{W}_{\mathrm{GAT}}v_{t|k}]))} \tag{4}$$

where $\mathbf{W}_{\mathrm{GAT}}$ is a shared weight matrix of a learned linear transformation, $\mathbf{a}$ is the weight vector to perform self-attention, $||$ is the concatenation operation, and $\mathcal{N}_i$ is the set of adjacent vertices for $v_{t|i}$. Through GAT, the contribution can be figured out from other factors except distance to vertex features, and then the final aggregated features for $v_{t|i}$ can be obtained where fully spatial interactions are captured.

2.4   T-CNN with Dilated Convolution

After the aggregated spatial features have been obtained on triple interactions, temporal dependencies should be considered and properly used for the subsequent trajectory prediction. In order to do that, we propose a model of T-CNN. This module contains three steps. In the first step, the obtained aggregated spatial features in each G_t are concatenated, and a CNN module is used to change the size of the concatenated feature to $5 \times T_{obs} \times N$. The purpose of this size change is for the calculation of $\rho_i^{\tilde{t}}$, $\mu_i^{\tilde{t}}$ and $\sigma_i^{\tilde{t}}$ in $X - Y$ coordinates for subsequent operations. In the second step, another CNN module is used to change the size of concatenated feature from $5 \times T_{obs} \times N$ to $5 \times T_{pred} \times N$. Therefore, the remaining task is to figure out $\rho_i^{\tilde{t}}$, $\mu_i^{\tilde{t}}$ and $\sigma_i^{\tilde{t}}$ for $\tilde{t} \in \{T_{obs} + 1, \cdots, T_{obs} + T_{pred}\}$. In order to figure out these parameters, in the third step, a three-layer CNN is designed to model the temporal dependence. In this step, the white circles are the padding part and the orange circles are concatenated features in different time steps. The input and output feature are denoted as h_{in} and h_{out}, respectively. The three skip connections in yellow arrows on the right side are designed to enhance the capability of representation and reasoning for higher layers in the networks. Operations of dilated causal convolution, weighted normalization, activation, dropout and residual connection are involved in each layer. Specially, the dilated causal convolution operation makes the output feature in time step t aggregate the input feature from time 1 to $t - 1$. Between two neighboring layers, three circles spaced one by one in the lower layer point to the orange circle in the higher layer through the orange arrow, which means that the kernel size is 3 and the dilation size is 1. In this way, we expand the receptive field with less network layers and parameters and get the compact features in the temporal dimension accurately.

3   Experiments, Results and Discussions

3.1   Experimental Settings

Datasets and Evaluation Metrics. Our Triple GNN is evaluated and compared by two public datasets for pedestrian trajectory prediction, including ETH [22] and UCY [17]. We use *Leave-one-scene-out* data split to evaluate our model. We follow the evaluation metrics proposed in [3,20] for better comparison, and metrics of average displacement error (ADE) and final displacement error (FDE) are used. Specifically, ADE is an average L_2 distance between the ground truth and prediction of the primary pedestrian over all predicted time steps. FDE is the L_2 distance between the final ground truth coordinates and the final prediction coordinates of the primary pedestrian. For both of these two metrics, lower value of them corresponds to better prediction accuracy.

Implementation Details. The proposed Triple GNN is trained with stochastic gradient descent optimizer. The initial learning rate is set as 0.035 and changed to 0.0175 after 150 epochs. The batch size is 32 and the total epochs are 250. We use PReLU and ReLU in our model. Specified in two-stage optimization for S-GNN, the GAT module comprises 8 attention heads.

3.2 Overall Results

Our method is compared to baseline and state-of-the-art methods, including STGAT [11], Social-STGCNN [20], Social-LSTM [3], Social-GAN [8], Sophie [25]. The result of Social-STGCNN [20] and STGAT [11] in Table 1 are trained with the same datasets as ours for fair comparison because the initial video of some datasets is not available.

The overall results are organized in Table 1. Results are organized in *ADE/FDE* format in this table, and *Avg.* stands for the average results of each row in the table. As can be found through these results, our method performs superior than all the other methods in average ADE and FDE. Our method improves the average FDE by at least 11% and at most 40% when comparing to other methods, and we believe this result is meaningful for destination prediction for pedestrian in practical scenarios.

Table 1. The overall results of our Triple GNN compared to baseline approaches.

Method	ETH	HOTEL	UNIV	ZARA1	ZARA2	Avg.
Sophie [25]	**0.70**/1.43	0.76/1.67	**0.54**/1.24	**0.30**/0.63	0.38/0.78	0.54/1.15
Social-LSTM [3]	1.09/2.35	0.79/1.76	0.67/1.40	0.47/1.00	0.56/1.17	0.72/1.54
Social-GAN [8]	0.81/1.52	0.72/1.61	0.60/1.26	0.34/0.69	0.42/0.84	0.58/1.18
STGAT [11]	0.82/1.51	0.51/1.11	0.63/1.35	0.36/0.76	**0.31**/0.67	0.53/1.08
Social-STGCNN [20]	**0.70**/1.24	0.62/1.17	0.55/**1.02**	0.41/0.63	0.33/**0.49**	0.52/0.91
Our method	0.77/**1.19**	**0.50/0.78**	0.61/1.05	0.37/**0.59**	**0.31**/0.50	**0.51/0.82**

3.3 Ablation Experiments

Effectiveness of Pedestrian-Scene and Pedestrian-Object Interactions: We investigate the contribution of pedestrian-scene and pedestrian-object interactions by removing the two kinds of interactions in Triple GNN. The results are shown in the third row of Table 2. We found that the average of the ADE and FDE metrics of our triple interaction model are significantly better than only pedestrian-pedestrian interaction. This result shows that the interaction of pedestrians and surroundings has a positive influence on the trajectory prediction. We reach the conclusion that the appropriate introduction of triple interaction between pedestrians, scenes and objects indeed improves the accuracy of pedestrian trajectory prediction.

Table 2. The results of ablation experiments.

Method	ETH	HOTEL	UNIV	ZARA1	ZARA2	Avg.
Our full model	**0.77/1.19**	**0.50/0.78**	0.61/1.05	0.37/0.59	0.31/0.50	**0.51/0.82**
No triple interaction	0.80/1.45	0.83/1.47	0.60/1.08	0.45/0.79	0.35/0.54	0.61/1.07
No GAT	1.18/2.13	0.80/1.42	0.68/**1.02**	0.57/0.86	0.49/0.79	0.74/1.24
No GCN	0.79/1.25	0.52/0.85	**0.59**/1.04	0.41/0.71	**0.32/0.49**	0.53/0.87

Effectiveness of Two-Stage Attention Mechanism: In the fifth and sixth row of Table 2, we remove the GCN and GAT module separately to evaluate the effect of two-stage attention mechanism. Results show the benefit of our two-stage mechanism.

3.4 Qualitative Evaluation

The visualization Results show the following cases: one meeting the other two persons, and one merging with a group of people. The green line represents the observed trajectory. The yellow line represents ground truth. The red dashed line represents the predicted.

One Meeting the Other Two Persons: As shown in Fig. 4 (a) and (b), a person is walking towards two other people. If they don't change their trajectory, there will be a collision. It is easy to find that the predict trajectory of the person in the opposite direction of Social-STGCNN totally deviate from the ground truth. The prediction of Triple GNN not only predicts the change in trajectory direction, but also very close to the ground truth.

One Merging with a Group of People: As shown in Fig. 5 (a) and (b), a group of people are moving in the same direction at a consistent speed, and another person is walking towards them. Triple GNN suggests that this person will go through this group of people, but in the process adjusting his trajectory to avoid collisions. However, the prediction of Social-STGCNN of this person is quite different from the ground truth.

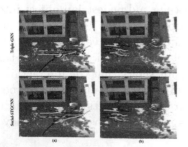

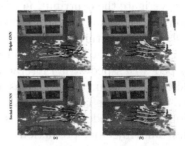

Fig. 4. One meeting the other two persons.

Fig. 5. One merging with a group of people.

4   Conclusions

PTP is an amazing but challenging task for vision guided applications. Practically, the trajectory is a result of interaction among pedestrian's surrounding people, scenes and related objects, which can be represented by a triple. In this paper, we propose a triple graph neural network (Triple GNN) where interactions among pedestrians, scenes and objects are all taken into the prediction of pedestrian trajectory. Based on that, spatial relation is exploited to describe the mutual interaction among triple elements, and a two-stage optimization scheme is proposed on weights of the interaction aggregation for better relation exploitation and prediction. Furthermore, temporal relation is also exploited for compact representation and effective computation of future trajectories based on the spatial relation. Our work is verified and compared to the state-of-art models, and superiority can be found on ADE and FDE metrics. Specifically, Our method improves the average FDE by at least 11% and at most 40% when comparing to other methods. It can be seen that the Triple GNN is helpful to PTP.

References

1. Doctor   strange.   https://marvelcinematicuniverse.fandom.com/wiki/Doctor_Strange_(film)
2. Al-Mallah, R., Quintero, A., Farooq, B.: Prediction of traffic flow via connected vehicles. IEEE Trans. Mobile Comput. **21**, 264–277 (2020). https://doi.org/10.1109/TMC.2020.3006713
3. Alahi, A., Goel, K., Ramanathan, V., Robicquet, A., Fei-Fei, L., Savarese, S.: Social LSTM: human trajectory prediction in crowded spaces. In: IEEE Conference on Computer Vision and Pattern Recognition, pp. 961–971 (2016)
4. Bai, H., Cai, S., Ye, N., Hsu, D., Lee, W.S.: Intention-aware online POMDP planning for autonomous driving in a crowd. In: IEEE International Conference on Robotics and Automation, pp. 454–460. IEEE (2015)
5. Bai, S., Kolter, J.Z., Koltun, V.: An empirical evaluation of generic convolutional and recurrent networks for sequence modeling. arXiv preprint arXiv:1803.01271 (2018)
6. Chen, L.C., Zhu, Y., Papandreou, G., Schroff, F., Adam, H.: Encoder-decoder with atrous separable convolution for semantic image segmentation. In: European Conference on Computer Vision, pp. 801–818 (2018)
7. Choi, W., Savarese, S.: Understanding collective activities of people from videos. IEEE Trans. Pattern Anal. Mach. Intell. **36**(6), 1242–1257 (2013)
8. Gupta, A., Johnson, J., Fei-Fei, L., Savarese, S., Alahi, A.: Social GAN: socially acceptable trajectories with generative adversarial networks. In: IEEE Conference on Computer Vision and Pattern Recognition, pp. 2255–2264 (2018)
9. Helbing, D., Molnar, P.: Social force model for pedestrian dynamics. Phys. Rev. E **51**(5), 4282 (1995)
10. Hou, J., Wu, X., Wang, R., Luo, J., Jia, Y.: Confidence-guided self refinement for action prediction in untrimmed videos. IEEE Trans. Image Process. **29**, 6017–6031 (2020)
11. Huang, Y., Bi, H., Li, Z., Mao, T., Wang, Z.: STGAT: modeling spatial-temporal interactions for human trajectory prediction. In: IEEE International Conference on Computer Vision, pp. 6272–6281 (2019)

12. Ke, Q., Bennamoun, M., Rahmani, H., An, S., Sohel, F., Boussaid, F.: Learning latent global network for skeleton-based action prediction. IEEE Trans. Image Process. **29**, 959–970 (2020)
13. Keller, C.G., Gavrila, D.M.: Will the pedestrian cross? a study on pedestrian path prediction. IEEE Trans. Intell. Transp. Syst. **15**(2), 494–506 (2014)
14. Kong, Y., Tao, Z., Fu, Y.: Adversarial action prediction networks. IEEE Trans. Pattern Anal. Mach. Intell. **42**(3), 539–553 (2020)
15. Leal-Taixé, L., Fenzi, M., Kuznetsova, A., Rosenhahn, B., Savarese, S.: Learning an image-based motion context for multiple people tracking. In: IEEE Conference on Computer Vision and Pattern Recognition, pp. 3542–3549 (2014)
16. Leal-Taixé, L., Pons-Moll, G., Rosenhahn, B.: Everybody needs somebody: modeling social and grouping behavior on a linear programming multiple people tracker. In: IEEE International Conference on Computer Vision Workshops, pp. 120–127. IEEE (2011)
17. Lerner, A., Chrysanthou, Y., Lischinski, D.: Crowds by example. In: Computer Graphics Forum, vol. 26, pp. 655–664. Wiley Online Library (2007)
18. Li, B., Tian, J., Zhang, Z., Feng, H., Li, X.: Multitask non-autoregressive model for human motion prediction. IEEE Trans. Image Process. **30**, 2562–2574 (2021)
19. Mehran, R., Oyama, A., Shah, M.: Abnormal crowd behavior detection using social force model. In: IEEE Conference on Computer Vision and Pattern Recognition, pp. 935–942. IEEE (2009)
20. Mohamed, A., Qian, K., Elhoseiny, M., Claudel, C.: Social-STGCNN: a social spatio-temporal graph convolutional neural network for human trajectory prediction. In: IEEE Conference on Computer Vision and Pattern Recognition, pp. 14424–14432 (2020)
21. Ng, Y.B., Fernando, B.: Forecasting future action sequences with attention: a new approach to weakly supervised action forecasting. IEEE Trans. Image Process. **29**, 8880–8891 (2020)
22. Pellegrini, S., Ess, A., Van Gool, L.: Improving data association by joint modeling of pedestrian trajectories and groupings. In: Daniilidis, K., Maragos, P., Paragios, N. (eds.) ECCV 2010. LNCS, vol. 6311, pp. 452–465. Springer, Heidelberg (2010). https://doi.org/10.1007/978-3-642-15549-9_33
23. Raksincharoensak, P., Hasegawa, T., Nagai, M.: Motion planning and control of autonomous driving intelligence system based on risk potential optimization framework. Int. J. Autom. Eng. **7**(AVEC14), 53–60 (2016)
24. Riofrıo-Luzcando, D., Ramırez, J., Berrocal-Lobo, M.: Predicting student actions in a procedural training environment. IEEE Trans. Learn. Technol. **10**(4), 463–474 (2017)
25. Sadeghian, A., Kosaraju, V., Sadeghian, A., Hirose, N., Rezatofighi, H., Savarese, S.: Sophie: an attentive GAN for predicting paths compliant to social and physical constraints. In: IEEE Conference on Computer Vision and Pattern Recognition, pp. 1349–1358 (2019)
26. Salzmann, T., Ivanovic, B., Chakravarty, P., Pavone, M.: Trajectron++: Dynamically-Feasible Trajectory Forecasting with Heterogeneous Data. In: Vedaldi, A., Bischof, H., Brox, T., Frahm, J.-M. (eds.) ECCV 2020. LNCS, vol. 12363, pp. 683–700. Springer, Cham (2020). https://doi.org/10.1007/978-3-030-58523-5_40
27. Veličković, P., Cucurull, G., Casanova, A., Romero, A., Lio, P., Bengio, Y.: Graph attention networks. arXiv preprint arXiv:1710.10903 (2017)

28. Wang, C., Cai, S., Tan, G.: GraphTCN: spatio-temporal interaction modeling for human trajectory prediction. In: Proceedings of the IEEE/CVF Winter Conference on Applications of Computer Vision, pp. 3450–3459 (2021)
29. Yamaguchi, K., Berg, A.C., Ortiz, L.E., Berg, T.L.: Who are you with and where are you going? In: IEEE Conference on Computer Vision and Pattern Recognition, pp. 1345–1352. IEEE (2011)
30. Yasuno, M., Yasuda, N., Aoki, M.: Pedestrian detection and tracking in far infrared images. In: IEEE Conference on Computer Vision and Pattern Recognition Workshop, p. 125. IEEE (2004)
31. Yu, C., Ma, X., Ren, J., Zhao, H., Yi, S.: Spatio-temporal graph transformer networks for pedestrian trajectory prediction. In: Vedaldi, A., Bischof, H., Brox, T., Frahm, J.-M. (eds.) ECCV 2020. LNCS, vol. 12357, pp. 507–523. Springer, Cham (2020). https://doi.org/10.1007/978-3-030-58610-2_30

Cross-domain Trajectory Prediction with CTP-Net

Pingxuan Huang[1], Zhenhua Cui[2], Jing Li[3], Shenghua Gao[3], Bo Hu[2], and Yanyan Fang[2(✉)]

[1] University of Michigan, Ann Arbor, USA
`pxuanh@umich.edu`
[2] Fudan University, Shanghai, China
{`19110720030,bohu,yyfang`}`@fudan.edu.cn`
[3] ShanghaiTech University, Shanghai, China
{`lijing1,gaoshh`}`@shanghaitech.edu.cn`

Abstract. Most pedestrian trajectory prediction methods rely on a huge amount of trajectories annotation, which is time-consuming and expensive. Moreover, a well-trained model may not effectively generalize to a new scenario captured by another camera. Therefore, it is desirable to adapt the model trained on an annotated source domain to the target domain. To achieve domain adaptation for trajectory prediction, we propose a Cross-domain Trajectory Prediction Network (CTP-Net). In this framework, encoders are used in both domains to encode the observed trajectories, then their features are aligned by a cross-domain feature discriminator. Further, considering the consistency between the observed and the predicted trajectories, a target domain offset discriminator is utilized to adversarially regularize the future trajectory predictions to be in line with the observed trajectories. Extensive experiments demonstrate the effectiveness of our method on domain adaptation for pedestrian trajectory prediction.

Keywords: Trajectory prediction · Domain adaptation · Cross-domain feature discriminator

1 Introduction

Pedestrian trajectory prediction is attracting increasing attention these years due to its promising application prospects, such as autonomous driving [7], safety monitoring [6], socially-aware robots [18], *etc.* However, existing deep learning based trajectory prediction methods [25,31,33,35] usually need huge amounts of annotated data. When these methods are applied to a new scenario with different data distribution, the model trained on the original scenario may not generalize well and the performance degrades [20]. Moreover, annotating the future trajectories for the new scenario is time-consuming and expensive. Therefore, in this paper, we introduce a cross-domain trajectory prediction task, where both observed trajectories and annotated future trajectories are available in the existing scenario (*i.e.*, source domain), but only the observed trajectories is available

L. Fang et al. (Eds.): CICAI 2022, LNAI 13604, pp. 80–92, 2022.
https://doi.org/10.1007/978-3-031-20497-5_7

in the new scenario (*i.e.*, target domain). Furthermore, the trajectories distribution varies between the source and the target domain. Accordingly, we aim to improve the model performance in the target domain, without any annotated future trajectory in the target domain. To the best of our knowledge, this is the first work to consider domain adaptation for trajectory prediction task.

To perform domain adaptation in trajectory prediction, the Cross-domain Trajectory Prediction Network (CTP-Net) is proposed, which consists of two domain adaptation parts: the feature-level cross-domain alignment, and the target domain trajectory alignment. In detail, the feature-level cross-domain adaptation aims to align the features from the source domain and the target domain, while the target domain trajectory alignment is in charge of regularizing the consistency between the predicted future trajectories and the observed trajectories on the target domain.

We first pre-train a source domain encoder-decoder to predict the future trajectories with supervision, under a standard training pipeline. Observed trajectories are encoded into a latent feature space, then the encoded feature is decoded to predict offsets of the future time-steps. Thereafter, the parameters of the source encoder-decoder are fixed in further training. The next step is to implement the feature-level cross-domain alignment by training a target encoder and a cross-domain feature discriminator. The discriminator aims to estimate the distribution distance between the source encoder features and the target encoder features. Then, the adversarial objective of the target encoder is to mitigate the distribution distance between source and target encoder features. Consequently, the target features are adversarially aligned with the source features.

After training the target encoder, the target domain trajectory alignment is conducted by training a target decoder and a target domain offset discriminator. The purpose of the target domain offset discriminator is to estimate the distribution distance between the target domain observed trajectories offsets and the predicted offsets. As to the target decoder, it is composed of the fixed source decoder and a trainable coordinate offset adaptor aiming at transforming the source decoder prediction to the target domain. Especially, the offset adaptor is adversarially trained to mitigate the distribution distance between the predicted offsets and the target observed offsets. Therefore, the predicted future offsets are regularized to be consistent with that of the target domain observed trajectories.

The main contributions of this paper are summarized as follows: i.) the domain adaptation is first introduced into trajectory prediction; ii.) a Cross-domain Trajectory Prediction Network (CTP-Net) is proposed to adapt the model from the annotated source domain to the target domain by both feature-level cross-domain alignment and the target domain trajectory alignment; iii.) extensive experiments demonstrate the effectiveness of our method on domain adaptation for trajectory prediction.

2   Related Work

Recent works on deep-learning-based trajectory prediction and domain adaptation are introduced briefly.

Trajectory Prediction. With the development of deep learning, many methods have been proposed in trajectory prediction area [5,8,14,23,29,31,35]. Early works [19,32] model person motions independently. Gradually, researchers [1,34] introduced the modeling of human-human interactions. Recently, there are a variety of perspectives to consider trajectory prediction, such as Imitative Decision Learning (IDL) [15], Inverse Reinforcement Learning (IRL) [24], Social Interpretable Tree (SIT) [28], Constant Velocity method [26], and Graph-based methods [13,36], *etc.* Different from existing works, we introduce a cross-domain trajectory prediction network (CTP-Net), which utilizes feature-level cross-domain alignment and observation-future consistency to adapt the model from the labeled source domain to the unlabeled target domain.

Domain Adaptation. Domain adaptation is one of the research focuses on Transfer Learning [9]. Its main task is to enhance models' performance on test (target) data by minimizing the marginal distribution difference between the training (source) data space and the test data space [37]. Traditional methods, including the TCA [21] and JDA [16] tend to minimize a distribution distance metric. After the success of deep learning, neural networks are introduced to assist future extraction and automatic future adaptation. Many representative works, such as the DDC [30], and DAN [17] are proposed. Recently, with the development of Generative Adversarial Networks (GAN), such as the Wasserstein-GAN [2], adversarial domain adaptation is becoming increasingly popular. Many classical structures, such as the DANN [10], DSN [4] have justified the rationality of their back stone idea: to minimize the difference between the source and target domain until the adversary domain discriminator could not distinguish them. Inspired by the achievement of domain adaptation, we proposed a task-oriented Cross-domain Trajectory Prediction Network (CTP-Net) to conduct trajectory prediction. To the best of our knowledge, our work is the first to successfully use domain adaptation in trajectory prediction.

3   Method

3.1   Problem Formulation

In our scenario, data comes from 2 domains: the Source domain($\mathbb{S}$), which has ground truth, and the Target domain($\mathbb{T}$), which is unlabeled. Under this setting, our goal is to predict the future trajectory of target domain data ($\mathbb{F}_t \in \mathbb{R}^{lf \times 2}$) with the target domain observation data ($\mathbb{O}_t \in \mathbb{R}^{lo \times 2}$).

Previous trajectory prediction models are firstly trained on the source domain ($\mathbb{O}_s$ & $\mathbb{F}_s$). Afterward, they will be directly applied to the target domain, which might miss the abundant information from the target domain. However, in our task, with the assistance of the encoder-decoder structure, as well as the domain

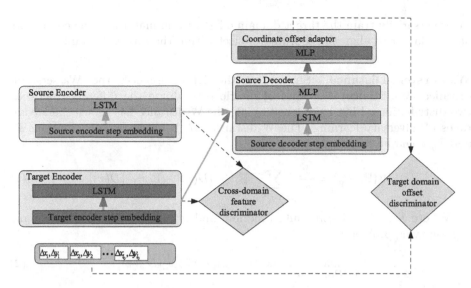

Fig. 1. Structure of the CTP-Net module for Cross-domain Trajectory Prediction. Where *green* represents source-related components; *red* represents target-related components; *gray* represents adaptation-related components; *solid lines* represent data/feature flow for trajectory prediction; *dashed lines* represent feature flow for domain adaptation. (Color figure online)

adaptation method, we hope to construct a network that could successfully map the target data into the source trajectory feature domain ($\mathbb{M}_s$), then project the prediction trajectory back to the target domain. Specifically, instead of predicting absolute coordinate, we set the coordinate offset($\mathbb{C}$), which is the changing values between two consecutive coordinates, as our predicting stuff.

3.2 Cross-domain Trajectory Prediction Network

The Cross-domain Trajectory Prediction Network (CTP-Net) contains two domain adaptation steps: the first is to align the cross-domain feature space, and the second is to align the coordinate offset space within the target domain. The whole pipeline of CTP-Net architecture is illustrated in Fig. 1. Roughly speaking, CTP-Net is composed of 3 components: 1. The source encoder-decoder; 2. The Cross-domain feature discriminator and the target encoder; 3. The coordinate offset adaptor, and the target domain offset discriminator.

In this framework, we first pre-train the source encoder-decoder with a standard training pipeline on the source domain to predict the future trajectories. Afterward, we fix the source encoder-decoder parameters. Then we use the cross-domain feature discriminator and the target encoder to achieve feature-level cross-domain alignment. The purpose of this discriminator is to estimate the distribution distance between the source and the target feature domain. Finally, we adversarially train the target domain offset discriminator and the coordinate offset adaptor to align the coordinate offset within the target domain.

Wasserstein-Distance. Similar to the KL-divergence, the Wasserstein-distance (W-distance) is a kind of metric to evaluate the difference between two distributions. First introduced by [2], the W-distance has shown the advantages of adversary learning. The W-distance [27] between two distributions $\mathbb{P}_r$ and $\mathbb{P}_g$ could be calculated by:

$$W(\mathbb{P}_r, \mathbb{P}_g) = \frac{1}{K} \sum_{||D||_L \leq K} \mathbb{E}_{x \sim \mathbb{P}_r}[D(x)] - \mathbb{E}_{x \sim \mathbb{P}_g}[D(x)] \tag{1}$$

Where $D(x)$ is a K-Lipschitz function, and it can be estimated by solving the following problem:

$$\max_{w:||D_w||_L \leq K} \mathbb{E}_{x \sim \mathbb{P}_r}[D_w(x)] - \mathbb{E}_{x \sim \mathbb{P}_g}[D_w(x)] \tag{2}$$

Source Domain Training. This step is aimed to construct a trajectory prediction model on the source domain, which has an Encoder-Decoder structure.

When it comes to our method, we construct both the source and the target encoder as the combination of a step embedding (SEB) and an LSTM ($k \in [1 : lo]$), where θ_{se} is the source encoder parameter to be learned:

$$h_{sk}, out_{sk} = LSTM(h_{s(k-1)}, SEB(o_{sk}); \theta_{se}) \tag{3}$$

The final hidden state of the encoder i.e. h_{slo}, is defined as the trajectory feature(m_s). The decoder part is composed of a step embedding, an LSTM, and an MLP(ψ). Specially, both the input and output of decoder are coordinate offsets ($\delta o_s / \delta f_s$, $k \in [lo + 1 : lo + lf]$):

$$h_{sk}, out_{sk} = LSTM(h_{s(k-1)}, SEB(\delta o_{s(k-1)} / \delta f_{s(k-1)}); \theta_{sd})$$
$$\delta f_{s(k)} = \psi(out_{sk}; \theta_{sd}) \tag{4}$$

Trajectory Feature Domain Adaptation. The purpose of this step is to map the trajectory feature from the target domain into the source domain. Therefore, we adapt it to a Domain Adaptation task, which means the task of this step is to minimize the data distribution difference between $\mathbb{M}_s$ and $\mathbb{M}_t$. Accordingly, with the target decoder, we could estimate $Pr(m_s | o_t)$.

To achieve this goal, we employ the W-distance-based Adversarial Domain Adaptation. Specifically, this step needs to train the target encoder with parameter θ_{te}, and the cross-domain feature discriminator with parameter θ_{dA}. According to Eq. (1): denoting the data distribution on $\mathbb{M}_s$ and $\mathbb{M}_t$ as $\mathbb{P}_{ms}$ and $\mathbb{P}_{mt}$, the W-distance between $\mathbb{P}_{ms}$ and $\mathbb{P}_{mt}$ could be estimated by:

$$W(\mathbb{P}_{ms}, \mathbb{P}_{mt}) \approx \mathbb{E}_{x \sim \mathbb{P}_{ms}}[\hat{D}_w(x)] - \mathbb{E}_{x \sim \mathbb{P}_{mt}}[\hat{D}_w(x)] \tag{5}$$

where $\hat{D}_w(x)$, could be estimated by solving the problem:

$$\min_{w:||D_w||_L \leq 1} L_{wd} = \mathbb{E}_{x \sim \mathbb{P}_{mt}}[D_w(x)] - \mathbb{E}_{x \sim \mathbb{P}_{ms}}[D_w(x)] \tag{6}$$

To enforce the constraint of the Lipschitz Function, the Gradient Penalty [11] is used, and the following problem is obtained:

$$L_{gp} = \mathbb{E}_{\hat{x} \sim \mathbb{P}_{\hat{x}}}[(||\nabla_{\hat{x}} D(\hat{x})||_2 - 1)^2] \tag{7}$$

$\mathbb{P}_{\hat{x}}$ is uniformly distributed on the straight line between pairs of points sampled from $\mathbb{P}_{ms}$ and $\mathbb{P}_{mt}$. Eventually, we should solve the problem:

$$\min_{D(x;\theta_{dA})} L_{wd} - \lambda L_{gp} \tag{8}$$

After getting the estimation of the distribution distance, the task of the target encoder is to minimize the distribution difference between $\mathbb{M}_s$ and $\mathbb{M}_t$, i.e.

$$\min_{\theta_{te}}(-\mathbb{E}_{x \sim \mathbb{P}_{o_t}}[\hat{D}(TE_{\theta_{te}}(x))]) \tag{9}$$

Where $\mathbb{P}_{o_t}$ is the data distribution of $\mathbb{O}_t$, TE is target encoder. The detailed algorithm to train the cross-domain feature discriminator $(D_{\theta_{dA}})$, and the target encoder is shown as Algorithm 1. In our network, the structure of the target encoder is the same as that of the source encoder, and the input of the Cross-domain feature discriminator is the concatenation of the m_s/m_t.

Algorithm 1: CTP-Net cross-domain feature alignment algorithm

---

Input: The learning rate of cross-domain feature discriminator, and target encoder: α, β; The gradient penalty coefficient λ; batch size m; adversarial training epoch N, domain critic training iteration n.

1 Fix θ_{se};
2 **for** $T = 1,2 \ldots N$ **do**
3   **for** $t = 1,2 \ldots n$ **do**
4          $L \leftarrow 0$;
5   **for** $i = 1,2 \ldots m$ **do**
6   Sample o_s from $\mathbb{O}_s$, sample o_t from $\mathbb{O}_t$, generate random number $\gamma \sim U[0,1]$;
7              $m_s \leftarrow$ Source Encoder(o_s);
8              $m_t \leftarrow$ Target Encoder(o_t);
9              $m_m \leftarrow \gamma m_s + (1 - \gamma)m_t$;
10             $L \leftarrow L + D_{\theta_{dA}}(m_t) - D_{\theta_{dA}}(m_s) + \lambda(||\nabla_{m_m} D_{\theta_{dA}}(m_m)||_2 - 1)^2$;
11         $\theta_{dA} \leftarrow RMSprop(\nabla_{\theta_{dA}} \frac{1}{m}L; \alpha)$;
12   Sample $\{o_t\}_{i=1}^{m}$ from $\mathbb{O}_t$;
13     $\theta_{te} \leftarrow RMSprop(\nabla_{\theta_{te}} \frac{1}{m} \sum_{k=1}^{m} -D_{\theta_{dA}}(\text{Target Encoder}(o_t)); \theta_{te}, \beta)$;

Coordinate Offset Domain Adaptation. The purpose of the Coordinate offset Adaptor (CA) is to project the coordinate offset from the source domain to the target domain, which is a part of Domain Adaptation, and a similar structure of the previous part is employed. Instead of the absolute pedestrian coordinate, we select the coordinate offset as the input and the output of both the decoder and the CA. Both the theoretical and the experimental analysis demonstrate the rationality of this setting. To be specific, in most circumstances, it is reasonable to assume that the distribution of the coordinate offset is a symmetric distribution with mean zero. Because pedestrians could go both up/down, and right/left freely. On the contrary, the variation of starting coordinates will significantly enlarge the sample space and complicate the absolute coordinate distribution. Accordingly, coordinate offset space is more suitable for domain adaptation tasks. Furthermore, the ablation experiment also justifies this setting.

Since the lo is usually different from lf (in our experiment, $lo = 8$, $lf = 12$), given the requirement of training the target domain offset discriminator, the input frame length of CA might not be 12. In our model, we set the CA input as the concatenation of 6 consecutive frames.

Inference. Previous sections show the details to construct a CTP-Net that could map the trajectory feature from the target domain to the source domain, as well as project the coordinate offset from the source domain to the target domain. When finishing training, the inference procedure on the target domain is: Target Encoder → Source Decoder → Coordinate Offset Adaptor.

4   Experiments

4.1   Datasets and Evaluation Metrics

Datasets: We evaluate proposed model on the following public datasets: **ETH** [22] and **UCY** [12]. The ETH dataset contains two scenes named ETH-univ and ETH-hotel, while the UCY dataset contains three scenes named UCY-zara01, UCY-zara02, and UCY-univ. Especially, we conduct experiments on the following 4 datasets: ETH-univ, ETH-hotel, UCY-zara02, and UCY-univ. Figure 2 presents the X/Y coordinates distribution for each dataset.

Evaluation Metrics: Following previous works [1,22], we adopt two common metrics for testing. (1) *Average Displacement Error (ADE)*: is the mean squared error (MSE) between the ground truth and the prediction over all estimated time steps. (2) *Final Displacement Error (FDE)*: is the Euclidean distance between the prediction and the ground truth at the final prediction. They are defined as:

$$ADE = \frac{\sum_{i=1}^{N}\sum_{t=lo}^{lo+lf-1}||\hat{F}_{t+1}^{i} - F_{t+1}^{i}||_2}{N * lf}$$

$$FDE = \frac{\sum_{i=1}^{N}||\hat{F}_{lo+lf}^{i} - F_{lo+lf}^{i}||_2}{N} \tag{10}$$

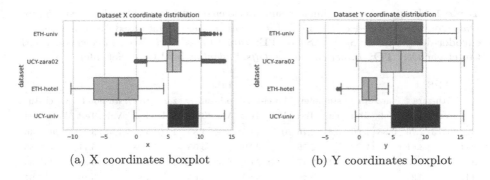

Fig. 2. Trajectories coordinates distribution

Where N is the sample size, lf is the number of predicted frames, lo is the number of observed frames, $\hat{F}^i_{t+1}$ is the predicted trajectory coordinates of the ith pedestrian at time $t+1$, and F^i_{t+1} is the corresponding ground truth.

4.2   Experimental Setup

According to Fig. 2, the coordinates distribution of ETH-univ is similar to that of UCY-zara02, but the coordinates distribution of ETH-hotel is much different from that of UCY-univ. Therefore, we construct 4 groups of experiments, so that to test our method under **both the similar and dissimilar** distribution.

1. Source: UCY-zara02, Target: ETH-univ.
2. Source: ETH-univ; Target: UCY-zara02.
3. Source: UCY-univ; Target: ETH-hotel.
4. Source: ETH-hotel; Target: UCY-univ.

For each source domain dataset, we separate the *training : validation* as 8 : 2; For each target domain dataset, we separate the *training : test* as 4 : 6. Therefore, models are trained on the source training and the target training set, validated on the validation set, and tested on the test set. Following the common setting [1], we set the observation frame length as 8 (3.2 s), and the prediction frame length as 12 (4.8 s).

4.3   Implementation Details

In our experiments, we set the step embedding size as 32, the LSTM hidden size as 512, and the layer amount of the source decoder MLP as 3. Moreover, all the offset adaptor, the target domain offset discriminator, and the cross-domain feature discriminator are constructed by MLP with ReLU functions, and the layer amounts for them are 2, 10, and 5.

Table 1. Comparative experiment results between our model and baselines. **SO**: *Source Only*, source encoder-decoder; **F-T**: *Fine-Tuning*, fine-tuning based on trained source encoder-decoder; **S-L**: *Social-LSTM*; **TE**: *Target Encoder*, replace source encoder with target encoder; **TO**: *Target encoder + Offset adaptor*, final CTP-Net inference path.

	ADE								FDE							
	eth-zara		zara-eth		stu-hotel		hotel-stu		eth-zara		zara-eth		stu-hotel		hotel-stu	
	Val	Test	Val	Test	Val	Test	Val	Test	Val	Test	Val	Test	Val	Test	Val	Test
SO	1.73	2.76	0.88	2.90	0.81	2.76	0.74	4.63	3.06	4.89	1.46	5.28	1.55	5.14	1.26	8.46
F-T		3.61		2.98		2.56		2.50		5.55		5.08		5.11		3.85
S-L	4.01	**1.27**	0.92	3.65	1.17	2.17	1.00	2.01	6.32	**1.83**	1.47	6.10	2.07	3.86	1.52	3.30
TE		3.34		2.60		2.79		3.89		5.65		4.85		5.19		7.07
TO		1.42		**2.40**		**1.59**		**1.61**		2.73		**4.35**		**2.79**		**2.93**

4.4 Results

We compared the performance with 2 models, the results[1] are shown in Table 1:

- Social-LSTM [1]: With the assistance of pooling layer, the Social-LSTM vectorizes and utilizes the interaction between pedestrians.
- Fine-tuning: This model is fine-tuned on the target training set. Specifically, based on the trained source encoder-decoder, this model takes the first 4 frames from the target observation as input and predicts the next 4 frames.

For both the Source-Only model and the Social-LSTM, in most comparison settings, there is a significant performance gap between Test (target) and Validation (source) set, which justifies the necessity of domain adaptation. Moreover, our schema is able to outperform the baselines in most cases, which is especially true when the source and target distributions are dissimilar to each other.

4.5 Ablation and Visulazation

In the ablation experiments, we examined the efficacy of the 2 adaptation stages and compared the performance of using offset or coordinate as the prediction objective, results are shown in Table 2. Although 2-stage adaptation (TO) significantly boosts performance, only the first adaptation stage (TE) has little or even negative effect. Moreover, the result demonstrates the coordinate offset is more appropriate than the absolute coordinate for adaptation.

To intuitively verify the efficacy of CTP-Net, we visualized the distribution of target sample cumulative offsets in Fig. 3a. To be specific, we subtract each step of predicted trajectories/ground truth by their last observation step, which is equal to moving the start prediction point to $(0, 0)$, then we draw the *Kernel Distribution Estimate-plot*[2] for each model. Based on the visualization result,

---

[1] For the convenience of reading, we refer to the dataset with its corresponding abbreviation: *eth*: ETH-univ; *hotel*: ETH-hotel; *zara*: UCY-zara02; *stu*: UCY-univ.

[2] https://seaborn.pydata.org/generated/seaborn.kdeplot.html.

Table 2. Ablation experiment results. **SO**: *Source Only*; **TE**: *Target Encoder*; **TO**: *Target encoder + Offset adaptor*; **CO**: *COordinate*; **OF**: *OFfsets*.

	ADE								FDE							
	eth-zara		zara-eth		stu-hotel		hotel-stu		eth-zara		zara-eth		stu-hotel		hotel-stu	
	CO	OF	CO	OF	CO	OF	CO	OF	CO	OF	CO	OF	CO	OF	CO	OF
Val	2.32	1.73	1.18	0.88	0.79	0.81	1.20	0.74	2.90	3.06	1.36	1.46	1.41	1.55	1.51	1.26
SO	3.90	2.76	3.24	2.90	3.90	2.76	10.39	4.63	5.65	4.89	4.63	5.28	4.72	5.13	10.37	8.46
TE	4.12	3.34	3.36	2.61	4.01	2.79	11.02	3.89	5.70	5.65	4.45	4.85	4.44	5.19	12.48	7.06
TO	4.52	**1.42**	3.68	**2.40**	3.47	**1.59**	4.66	**1.61**	4.83	**2.73**	**4.32**	4.35	3.90	**2.79**	5.55	**2.93**

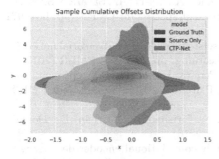
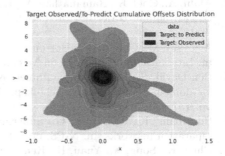

(a) Target sample cumulative offsets distributions of the ground truth, source-only, and CTP-Net prediction.

(b) Target-train observation and to-predict data cumulative offsets distributions

Fig. 3. Cumulative offsets distributions

compared with the Source-Only model, after adaptation, our prediction distribution is much closer to the target ground truth, which is especially true in the region of $y \leq 0$ and $x \geq 0$. To further understand the adaptation result, we additionally visualized the cumulative offsets distribution of the target-train to-predict and observation data, which is used in the second adaptation stage. The result is shown in Fig. 3b, which is equal to moving the start observation point of each trajectory to $(0,0)$ and then drawing their distribution plots. We figured out that the observation cumulative offsets distribution is closer (has more overlap) with the source-only cumulative offsets distribution in the $y \leq 0$ and $x \geq 0$ region. Since the adaptation is with a higher probability of success [3] when the two regions are similar, the CTP-Net has the potential to achieve better performance in these 2 areas.

5 Conclusion

In this work, we introduce domain adaptation task into pedestrian trajectory prediction, where the source domain is fully annotated, but the target domain is unlabeled. In order to adapt the model from the source domain to the target domain, Cross-domain Trajectory Prediction Network (CTP-Net) is proposed.

In the CTP-Net, two parts of adaptations are conducted: To align the target encoder features with the source encoder features distribution, the feature-level cross-domain alignment is performed; To make the predicted future trajectories consistent with the observed trajectories on the target domain, the target domain trajectory alignment is further implemented in the CTP-Net. Experiments justify the CTP-Net on domain adaptation for pedestrian trajectory prediction.

References

1. Alahi, A., Goel, K., Ramanathan, V., Robicquet, A., Fei-Fei, L., Savarese, S.: Social LSTM: human trajectory prediction in crowded spaces. In: CVPR, pp. 961–971 (2016)
2. Arjovsky, M., Chintala, S., Bottou, L.: Wasserstein generative adversarial networks. In: International Conference on Machine Learning, pp. 214–223. PMLR (2017)
3. Ben-David, S., Blitzer, J., Crammer, K., Pereira, F.: Analysis of representations for domain adaptation. In: Schölkopf, B., Platt, J.C., Hofmann, T. (eds.) NIPS, pp. 137–144. MIT Press (2006)
4. Bousmalis, K., Trigeorgis, G., Silberman, N., Krishnan, D., Erhan, D.: Domain separation networks. In: NIPS, pp. 343–351 (2016)
5. Chen, K., Song, X., Yuan, H., Ren, X.: Fully convolutional encoder-decoder with an attention mechanism for practical pedestrian trajectory prediction. IEEE Trans. Intell. Transp. Syst. (2022)
6. Corbetta, M., Banerjee, P., Okolo, W., Gorospe, G., Luchinsky, D.G.: Real-time UAV trajectory prediction for safety monitoring in low-altitude airspace, p. 3514 (2019). https://doi.org/10.2514/6.2019-3514
7. Cui, H., et al.: Multimodal trajectory predictions for autonomous driving using deep convolutional networks. In: ICRA, pp. 2090–2096 (2019)
8. Fang, L., Jiang, Q., Shi, J., Zhou, B.: TPNet: trajectory proposal network for motion prediction. In: CVPR, pp. 6796–6805 (2020)
9. Farahani, A., Voghoei, S., Rasheed, K., Arabnia, H.R.: A brief review of domain adaptation. In: Stahlbock, R., Weiss, G.M., Abou-Nasr, M., Yang, C.-Y., Arabnia, H.R., Deligiannidis, L. (eds.) Advances in Data Science and Information Engineering. TCSCI, pp. 877–894. Springer, Cham (2021). https://doi.org/10.1007/978-3-030-71704-9_65
10. Ghifary, M., Kleijn, W.B., Zhang, M.: Domain adaptive neural networks for object recognition. In: Pham, D.-N., Park, S.-B. (eds.) PRICAI 2014. LNCS (LNAI), vol. 8862, pp. 898–904. Springer, Cham (2014). https://doi.org/10.1007/978-3-319-13560-1_76
11. Gulrajani, I., Ahmed, F., Arjovsky, M., Dumoulin, V., Courville, A.C.: Improved training of wasserstein GANs. In: Guyon, I., et al. (eds.) Advances in Neural Information Processing Systems, vol. 30. Curran Associates, Inc. (2017). https://proceedings.neurips.cc/paper/2017/file/892c3b1c6dccd52936e27cbd0ff683d6-Paper.pdf
12. Lerner, A., Chrysanthou, Y., Lischinski, D.: Crowds by example. In: Computer Graphics Forum, vol. 26, pp. 655–664. Wiley Online Library (2007)
13. Li, L., Pagnucco, M., Song, Y.: Graph-based spatial transformer with memory replay for multi-future pedestrian trajectory prediction. In: CVPR, pp. 2231–2241 (2022)

14. Li, Y., Liang, R., Wei, W., Wang, W., Zhou, J., Li, X.: Temporal pyramid network with spatial-temporal attention for pedestrian trajectory prediction. TNSE (2021)
15. Li, Y.: Which way are you going? imitative decision learning for path forecasting in dynamic scenes. In: Proceedings of the IEEE Conference on Computer Vision and Pattern Recognition, pp. 294–303 (2019)
16. Long, M., Wang, J., Ding, G., Sun, J., Yu, P.S.: Transfer feature learning with joint distribution adaptation. In: ICCV, pp. 2200–2207 (2013)
17. Long, M., Cao, Y., Wang, J., Jordan, M.: Learning transferable features with deep adaptation networks. In: ICML, pp. 97–105. PMLR (07–09 Jul 2015)
18. Luber, M., Stork, J.A., Tipaldi, G.D., Arras, K.O.: People tracking with human motion predictions from social forces. In: ICRA, pp. 464–469 (2010)
19. Ma, W., Huang, D., Lee, N., Kitani, K.M.: Forecasting interactive dynamics of pedestrians with fictitious play. In: CVPR, pp. 4636–4644 (2017)
20. Minoofam, S.A.H., Bastanfard, A., Keyvanpour, M.R.: Trcla: a transfer learning approach to reduce negative transfer for cellular learning automata. IEEE Trans. Neural Netw. Learn. Syst., pp. 1–10 (2021). https://doi.org/10.1109/TNNLS.2021. 3106705
21. Pan, S.J., Tsang, I.W., Kwok, J.T., Yang, Q.: Domain adaptation via transfer component analysis. In: Boutilier, C. (ed.) IJCAI 2009, Proceedings of the 21st International Joint Conference on Artificial Intelligence, Pasadena, California, USA, July 11–17, 2009, pp. 1187–1192 (2009)
22. Pellegrini, S., Ess, A., Schindler, K., Van Gool, L.: You'll never walk alone: modeling social behavior for multi-target tracking. In: ICCV, pp. 261–268. IEEE (2009)
23. Quan, R., Zhu, L., Wu, Y., Yang, Y.: Holistic LSTM for pedestrian trajectory prediction. IIP **30**, 3229–3239 (2021)
24. Rhinehart, N., Mcallister, R., Kitani, K., Levine, S.: Precog: prediction conditioned on goals in visual multi-agent settings. In: ICCV, pp. 2821–2830 (2019)
25. Sadeghian, A., Kosaraju, V., Sadeghian, A., Hirose, N., Rezatofighi, H., Savarese, S.: Sophie: an attentive GAN for predicting paths compliant to social and physical constraints. In: CVPR, pp. 1349–1358 (2019)
26. Schöller, C., Aravantinos, V., Lay, F., Knoll, A.: What the constant velocity model can teach us about pedestrian motion prediction. IEEE Robot. Autom. Lett. **5**(2), 1696–1703 (2020)
27. Shen, J., Qu, Y., Zhang, W., Yu, Y.: Wasserstein distance guided representation learning for domain adaptation. arXiv e-prints arXiv:1707.01217 (2017)
28. Shi, L., et al.: Social interpretable tree for pedestrian trajectory prediction. CoRR (2022). https://doi.org/10.48550/arXiv.2205.13296
29. Tang, H., Wei, P., Li, J., Zheng, N.: EvoSTGAT: evolving spatiotemporal graph attention networks for pedestrian trajectory prediction. Neurocomputing **491**, 333–342 (2022)
30. Tzeng, E., Hoffman, J., Zhang, N., Saenko, K., Darrell, T.: Deep domain confusion: maximizing for domain invariance. arXiv preprint arXiv:1412.3474 (2014)
31. Xu, Y., Piao, Z., Gao, S.: Encoding crowd interaction with deep neural network for pedestrian trajectory prediction. In: CVPR, pp. 5275–5284 (2018)
32. Yagi, T., Mangalam, K., Yonetani, R., Sato, Y.: Future person localization in first-person videos. In: CVPR, pp. 7593–7602 (2018)
33. Yi, S., Li, H., Wang, X.: Pedestrian behavior modeling from stationary crowds with applications to intelligent surveillance. TIP **25**(9), 4354–4368 (2016)

34. Yi, S., Li, H., Wang, X.: Pedestrian behavior understanding and prediction with deep neural networks. In: Leibe, B., Matas, J., Sebe, N., Welling, M. (eds.) ECCV 2016. LNCS, vol. 9905, pp. 263–279. Springer, Cham (2016). https://doi.org/10.1007/978-3-319-46448-0_16
35. Zhang, P., Ouyang, W., Zhang, P., Xue, J., Zheng, N.: SR-LSTM: state refinement for LSTM towards pedestrian trajectory prediction. In: CVPR, pp. 12085–12094 (2019)
36. Zhou, H., Ren, D., Xia, H., Fan, M., Yang, X., Huang, H.: AST-GNN: an attention-based spatio-temporal graph neural network for interaction-aware pedestrian trajectory prediction. Neurocomputing **445**, 298–308 (2021)
37. Zhou, K., Liu, Z., Qiao, Y., Xiang, T., Loy, C.C.: Domain generalization: a survey. IEEE Trans. Pattern Anal. Mach. Intell. (2022)

Spatial-Aware GAN for Instance-Guided Cross-Spectral Face Hallucination

Wenpeng Xiao[1], Cheng Xu[1], Huaidong Zhang[1(✉)], and Xuemiao Xu[1,2,3,4(✉)]

[1] South China University of Technology, Guangzhou, China
`huaidongzhang49@gmail.com, xuemx@scut.edu.cn`
[2] State Key Laboratory of Subtropical Building Science, Guangzhou, China
[3] Ministry of Education Key Laboratory of Big Data and Intelligent Robot,
Guangzhou, China
[4] Guangdong Provincial Key Lab of Computational Intelligence and Cyberspace
Information,Guangzhou, China

Abstract. An efficient strategy to solve the Heterogeneous Face Recognition (HFR) is to translate the probes to the same spectrum domain of the galleries using generative models. However, without or with only globally-pooled appearance representation from a reference, the low-quality generated images restrict the recognition accuracy. The intuition of our paper is the spatially-distributed appearance contains details beneficial to higher-quality image synthesis. Particularly, we propose a semantic spatial adaptive alignment module to solve the inevitable misalignment between the content from the near-infrared (NIR) image and the appearance from the visible (VIS) reference. In this way, arbitrary VIS reference can provide appearance with sufficient details to assist the NIR-to-VIS translation. Based on this, we propose an unsupervised spatial-aware instance-guided cross-spectral facial hallucination network (SICFH) for visual-pleasing and identity-preserved VIS image translation. Qualitative and quantitative experiments on three challenging NIR-VIS datasets demonstrate the synthesized VIS images address the HFR problem effectively and achieve state-of-the-art recognition accuracy.

Keywords: Cross-spectral face synthesis · Heterogeneous face recognition · Generative adversarial network

1 Introduction

Near infrared (NIR) face recognition is a popular biometric imaging application which has received much attention over the past decades for the high robustness to illumination changes and low-cost acquisition solution of NIR face imagery. Nevertheless, due to the huge domain gap between the NIR and visible (VIS) images, the existing VIS face recognition systems suffer from severe performance degradation when directly applied to NIR data.

The work was supported by Key-Area Research and Development Program of Guangdong Province, China (2020B010166003, 2020B010165004).

L. Fang et al. (Eds.): CICAI 2022, LNAI 13604, pp. 93–105, 2022.
https://doi.org/10.1007/978-3-031-20497-5_8

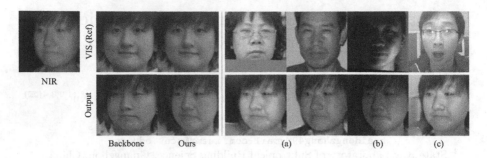

Fig. 1. Left: our method takes the whole VIS image as the reference with spatially-detailed appearance information and yields a visual-pleasing visible image of the input NIR face compared to the backbone. Right: our model trained on CASIA NIR-VIS-2.0 [18] can take arbitrary referred visual images from (a) NIR-VIS-2.0 [18], (b) BUAA-VisNir [11], and (c) Oulu-CASIA NIR-VIS [1] datasets to generate visual-pleasing images.

To tackle the problem of NIR face recognition, substaintial efforts have been devoted to narrowing the gap between NIR and VIS data. The existing methods can be generally divided into three categories [3]. The first category aims to remove domain-irrelevant information and extract the domain-invariant features for robust NIR face recognition [2,8,17,19,20]. Another typical solution is to project NIR and VIS images into a common latent space to enable relevance measurement between embeddings from two domains [5,9,13,30,31]. With the prevalence of "recognition via generation" paradigm [3,10], many works adopt image synthesis strategy to translate NIR images into the VIS domain [3,4,15, 26,33]. In this way, high-performance VIS face recognition system can be directly applied to the translated NIR images. This not only bypasses the data deficiency issue, but also significantly boosts the recognition rates of NIR images.

Current image synthesis based methods fail to generate high-quality VIS image from the NIR input with limited reference guidance, thus the synthesized results are less accurately recognized by a VIS face recognition network. Particularly, previous works either adopt cyclic constraints for unsupervised learning [25] or exploit pixel-level correspondence supervision by performing image warping [3,33], which ignores the highly ill-posed fashion of synthesizing VIS counterparts from NIR images only. Recently, cropped facial skin patch [3] or global pooled appearance representation [27,32] are applied to boost the translation between NIR and VIS domains by mitigating the learning ambiguity. To sufficiently utilize the appearance from the referred VIS image, thus yielding visually pleasant and identity-discriminative results, we propose to adaptively introduce the spatial appearance representation with rich facial details. To this end, we propose an *Spatial-aware Instance-guided Cross-spectral Face Hallucination Network* (SICFH), to achieve identity-preserved NIR-to-VIS face image translation by using arbitrary image in target domain as guidance. Given an input NIR image and another arbitrary VIS as guidance, SICFH synthesizes a

VIS image with the appearance of the guidance while preserving the face content of the input NIR image (see Fig. 1). Specifically, to cope with the spatial misalignment between the input NIR face and the guided VIS face, we propose *Fine-grained Spatially Adaptive Alignment* (FSAA) to adaptively align the appearance from the VIS reference to the content of the NIR image in feature space. The aligned appearance representation is then injected to the content via a *Fine-grained Aligned Spatially Adaptive Normalization* (FASAN) module for a visual-pleasing and identity-preserved VIS image synthesis. In addition, we propose a gradient-aware face structure loss to preserve the face structure consistency between the output VIS and the input NIR images, which effectively elevate the synthesis quality and improve the face recognition performance.

In summary, our main contributions are as follows:

- We propose an unsupervised Spatial-aware Instance-guided Cross-spectral Face Hallucination network (SICFH) to synthesize visual-pleasing and identity-preserved VIS face image for heterogeneous face recognition.
- We delve into the spatial misalignment problem between the NIR image and VIS reference and propose a novel Fine-grained Aligned Spatially Adaptive Normalization (FASAN) to adaptively align the spatial distribution of the VIS appearance representation to the NIR content.
- Extensive quantitative and qualitative experiments on three challenging NIR-VIS datasets demonstrate our proposed performs favorably against the state-of-the-art methods in generating visually pleasant VIS images with well-preserved identity.

2   Method

We aim to translate a NIR image to its VIS counterpart, given a VIS reference as guidance. In this way, the challenging Heterogeneous Face Recognition (HFR) problem can be simplified into a homogeneous one. To this end, we propose an unsupervised Spatial-aware Instance-guided Cross-spectral Face Hallucination (SICFH). Our framework consists of two parts. As shown in Fig. 2, the first part of SICFH contains two encoders with a proposed Fine-grained Spatially Adaptive Alignment Module (FSAA), which aims to adapt the spatial distribution of the encoded VIS appearance features refer to the encoded NIR content. The second part is a decoder equipped with stacked Fine-grained Aligned Spatially Adaptive Normalization (FASAN) blocks to transfer the VIS style information to the NIR features for VIS image synthesis. In the following, we only elaborate on the translation from NIR to VIS, as the inverse mapping is defined similarly.

2.1   Spatial-aware Instance-guided Cross-spectral Face Hallucination

The overview of our proposed SICFH for the mapping of NIR-to-VIS is shown as Fig. 2. Given a source NIR image $\mathcal{I}_{nir}^{(1)}$ and an arbitrary reference VIS image $\mathcal{I}_{vis}^{(2)}$, the content representation $f_{nir}^{(1)}$ and the appearance representation $f_{vis}^{(2)}$ are

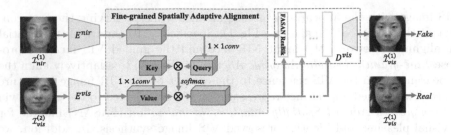

Fig. 2. Overview of the proposed SICFH.

extracted by the NIR content encoder E_c^{nir} and the VIS appearance encoder E_a^{vis} respectively. The two feature maps are fed into the proposed FSAA module $\mathcal{A}$ to align the spatial distribution of the appearance embeddings. The output of FSAA, *i.e.*, the aligned appearance representation is then fed into the decoder D^{vis} for synthesizing the final visual image $\hat{\mathcal{I}}_{vis}^{(1)}$. The overall process can be formulated as

$$\hat{\mathcal{I}}_{vis}^{(1)} = \mathcal{G}^{vis}\left(\mathcal{I}_{nir}^{(1)}, \mathcal{I}_{vis}^{(2)}\right) = D^{vis}\left(E_c^{nir}\left(\mathcal{I}_{nir}^{(1)}\right), \mathcal{A}_{vis}\right), \qquad (1)$$

$$\mathcal{A}_{vis} = \mathcal{A}\left(E_c^{nir}\left(\mathcal{I}_{nir}^{(1)}\right), E_a^{vis}\left(\mathcal{I}_{vis}^{(2)}\right)\right). \qquad (2)$$

Note that the input NIR and VIS images can be of different identities. The synthesized visual image by the generator $\mathcal{G}^{vis}$ and a real one with arbitrary identity are fed to the discriminator $\mathcal{D}^{vis}$ for adversarial learning.

2.2 Fine-grained Aligned Spatially Adaptive Normalization

Our method aims to transfer visual appearance from arbitrary references to an NIR image, thus spatial misalignment naturally exists between the appearance representation and the content representation. In order to address this mismatching problem while sufficiently utilizing the appearance information with discriminative details, we propose Fine-grained Spatially Adaptive Alignment (FSAA) equipped with Fine-grained Aligned Spatially Adaptive Normalization (FASAN). Particularly, we extend AdaIN to point-wise adaptive modulation for style injection, following a non-local alignment for the re-arrangement of appearance embeddings.

Fine-grained Spatially Adaptive Alignment. As shown in Fig. 2, a query Q and a key K are obtained by separately performing individual 1×1 convolutions on the encoded content $f_{nir}^{(1)}$ and the encoded appearance $f_{vis}^{(2)}$. The appearance embeddings are then re-arranged along the spatial distribution of the content by considering the inner correlations between every two pixels, which can be described as

$$\hat{f}_{vis}^{(2)} = \mathcal{A}_{vis} = \text{softmax}\left(Q^T K\right) \cdot f_{vis}^{(2)}, \qquad (3)$$

In this way, the processed appearance embeddings are expected to match the facial content distribution indicated by the NIR face.

Fine-grained Aligned Spatially Adaptive Normalization. SPADE [22] has demonstrated that spatially adaptive normalization achieves pleasant image generation with various spatial details. However, they predict style representation from paired semantic maps, which differs from our adaptively aligned appearance. As shown in Fig. 3(a), two 1×1 convolutions on $\hat{f}_{vis}^{(2)}$ are used to calculate the modulation parameters Γ and B of the same size as $f_{nir}^{(1)}$. The aligned appearance representation is then injected to the normalized content in the way shown as Eq. 4,

$$f_{mod}^{(1)} = \Gamma \odot \frac{f_{nir}^{(1)} - \mu_{nir}^{(1)}}{\sigma_{nir}^{(1)}} + B, \tag{4}$$

where $\mu_{nir}^{(1)}$ and $\sigma_{nir}^{(1)}$ are the channel-wise mean and standard variance of $f_{nir}^{(1)}$ respectively, and $\odot$ represents element-wise multiplication. Furthermore, we propose FASAN residual block to incorporate FASAN for sufficient transferring of the appearance as shown in Fig. 3 (b).

2.3 Training Objective

We formulate the NIR-to-VIS problem as an unsupervised instance-guided image-to-image translation task and design the full framework as a cyclic translation scheme as described in [34]. To boost the training, we apply 4 objective functions, namely, adversarial loss, cycle consistency loss, identity-preserving loss, and a novel gradient-aware structure consistency loss.

Adversarial Loss. In generative adversarial networks [6], the discriminator is trained to distinguish real samples from synthesized samples while the generator attempts to generate fake samples as indistinguishable as possible to foolish the discriminator. The inter min-max game between them will finally make the generator able to synthesis natural samples with high quality. Specially, the adversarial loss is defined as follows,

$$\mathcal{L}_{adv} = \mathbb{E}_{\mathcal{I}_{nir}^{(i)} \sim \mathcal{N}, \mathcal{I}_{vis}^{(j)} \sim \mathcal{V}} \left[\log \mathcal{D}_{vis} \left(\mathcal{I}_{vis}^{(j)} \right) + \log \left[1 - \mathcal{D}_{vis} \left(\mathcal{G}^{vis} \left(\mathcal{I}_{nir}^{(i)}, \mathcal{I}_{vis}^{(j)} \right) \right) \right] \right.$$
$$\left. + \log \mathcal{D}_{nir} \left(\mathcal{I}_{nir}^{(i)} \right) + \log \left[1 - \mathcal{D}_{nir} \left(\mathcal{G}^{nir} \left(\mathcal{I}_{vis}^{(j)}, \mathcal{I}_{nir}^{(i)} \right) \right) \right] \right], \tag{5}$$

where $\mathcal{N}$ and $\mathcal{V}$ represent the NIR domain and VIS domain, respectively.

Cycle Consistency Loss. The cycle consistency loss helps reduce the learning ambiguity in unsupervised image-to-image translation. In particular, the synthesized image should be able to generate the original input content image through the inverse mapping when given the original content image for appearance guidance. Hence, the cycle consistency loss can be described as Eq. 6

$$\mathcal{L}_{cyc} = \parallel \mathcal{I}_{nir}^{(i)} - \mathcal{G}^{nir}\left(\mathcal{G}^{vis}\left(\mathcal{I}_{nir}^{(i)}, \mathcal{I}_{vis}^{(j)}\right), \mathcal{I}_{nir}^{(i)}\right) \parallel_1$$
$$+ \parallel \mathcal{I}_{vis}^{(j)} - \mathcal{G}^{vis}\left(\mathcal{G}^{nir}\left(\mathcal{I}_{vis}^{(j)}, \mathcal{I}_{nir}^{(i)}\right), \mathcal{I}_{vis}^{(j)}\right) \parallel_1 . \quad (6)$$

Identity-Preserving Loss. We expect the synthesized VIS image keeps the same identity to the NIR image. Specially, we randomly select one of the VIS image of the same identity from $\mathcal{V}$, and note it as $\mathcal{I}_{vis}^{(i)}$. A pretrained face recognition network Φ, such as LightCNN [28], is used to extract identity-discriminative embedding for each image. Intuitively, the two embeddings are expected to be similar, following which we define the identity-preserving loss as Eq. 7

$$\mathcal{L}_{idt} = \parallel \Phi(\mathcal{I}_{vis}^{(i)}) - \Phi(\hat{\mathcal{I}}_{vis}^{(i)}) \parallel_1 + \parallel \Phi(\mathcal{I}_{nir}^{(j)}) - \Phi(\hat{\mathcal{I}}_{nir}^{(j)}) \parallel_1 . \quad (7)$$

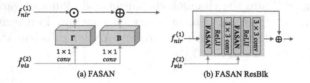

Fig. 3. (a) The structure of the semantic aligned spatially adaptive normalization. The mean B and the vairance Γ are adaptively predicted based on the aligned appearance $\hat{f}_{vis}^{(2)}$ using two distinct 1×1 convolutions. Γ and B are then used to modulate $f_{nir}^{(1)}$ as 4. (b) The structure of a single FASAN residual block containing two FASAN blocks for feature normalization, where the arrow from $\hat{f}_{vis}^{(2)}$ are reduced for simplification.

Gradient-aware Structure Loss. To further retain the identity and to eliminate the distortion artifacts, we constrain the structure to unchange after the translation. We argue that the luminance consistency loss in [33] introduce spectrum information of different modalities, which impedes the translation capacity. Instead, we adopt Laplacian operator lap to extract the boundaries of the images followed by ReLU to subtract the negative values for a sparser structure map. Let $*$ represent convolution operation, the gradient-aware structure loss is defined as Eq. 8

$$\mathcal{L}_{str} = \parallel \text{ReLU}\left(lap * \mathcal{I}_{nir}^{(i)}\right) - \text{ReLU}\left(lap * \hat{\mathcal{I}}_{vis}^{(i)}\right) \parallel_1$$
$$+ \parallel \text{ReLU}\left(lap * \mathcal{I}_{vis}^{(j)}\right) - \text{ReLU}\left(lap * \hat{\mathcal{I}}_{nir}^{(j)}\right) \parallel_1 . \quad (8)$$

Total Objective. The final loss to train our models is a weighted sum of the above losses as described as Eq. 9

$$\min_{\mathcal{G}^{vis}, \mathcal{G}^{nir}} \max_{\mathcal{D}^{vis}, \mathcal{D}^{nir}} \mathcal{L}_{total} = \mathcal{L}_{adv} + \lambda_{cyc}\mathcal{L}_{cyc} + \lambda_{idt}\mathcal{L}_{idt} + \lambda_{str}\mathcal{L}_{str}, \quad (9)$$

where $\lambda_{cyc}, \lambda_{idt}, \lambda_{str}$ are weighting parameters to balance each objective item.

Table 1. Comparisons with other state-of-the-art methods on the first fold of the CASIA NIR-VIS 2.0 dataset.

	$Rank-1$	$VR@FAR = 1\%$	$VR@FAR = 0.1\%$
LightCNN [28]	96.84	99.10	94.68
Pixel2Pixel [14]	22.13	39.22	14.45
CycleGAN [34]	87.23	93.92	79.41
PCFH [33]	98.50	99.58	97.32
PACH [3]	99.00	99.61	98.51
LAMP-HQ [32]	99.10	99.70	98.10
EGCH [27]	98.76	99.71	98.23
Ours w/o FSAA	98.97	99.84	98.56
Ours w/o $\mathcal{L}_{str}$	98.79	99.82	98.73
Ours ($\mathcal{L}_Y$)	98.97	99.86	98.53
Ours	**99.42**	**99.85**	**99.24**

3 Experiments

In this section, we conduct extensive quantitative and qualitative experiments on three widely-used datasets to demonstrate the effectiveness of our proposed model, which includes the CASIA NIR-VIS 2.0 [18], the Oulu-CASIA NIR-VIS [1], and the BUAA-VisNir [11] datasets. We follow the data-spilt settings in DVR [29] to conduct the experiments. All images are aligned to 144×144 and center cropped to 128×128. Specifically, during training, both the identities of the input pair of a NIR and VIS image for NIR-to-VIS translation, and the identities of the real and synthesized images for adversarial learning, are unnecessary to be the same. In reference, each VIS image in the gallery are used as the appearance guidance for the synthesis of the visual counterpart, after which the identity similarity between the translated and the VIS images are calculated. Specially, for quantitative comparisons and ablations, the Rank-1 accuracy, $VR@FAR = 1\%$ and $VR@FAR = 0.1\%$ are reported.

Network Architecture. The content encoder comprises two downsampling layers followed by 8 residual blocks. For the appearance encoders, we adopt the style encoder in [21] to merge multi-scale appearance representations. The decoders consist of 8 FASAN residual blocks and 2 upsampling blocks. Furthermore, multi-scale discriminators are applied in the adversarial learning, and 3 and 5 downsampling blocks are used for local and global discriminative representation extraction. Specially, $\mathcal{G}^{vis}$ and $\mathcal{G}^{nir}$ are trained individually to ensure sufficient translation capacity for each mapping direction.

Implementation Details. We implement our method on the Pytorch framework [24] and conduct all the experiments on a NVIDIA RTX 3090 GPU with

Table 2. Comparisons with other state-of-the-art methods on the 10-fold of the CASIA NIR-VIS 2.0 dataset.

	$Rank-1$	$VR@FAR=1\%$	$VR@FAR=0.1\%$
VGG [23]	62.1 ± 1.88	71.0 ± 1.25	39.7 ± 2.85
TRIVET [20]	95.7 ± 0.52	98.1 ± 0.31	91.0 ± 1.26
LightCNN [28]	96.7 ± 0.23	98.5 ± 0.64	94.8 ± 0.43
IDR [7]	97.3 ± 0.43	98.9 ± 0.29	95.7 ± 0.73
ADFL [25]	98.2 ± 0.34	99.1 ± 0.14	97.2 ± 0.48
PCFH [33]	98.8 ± 0.26	99.6 ± 0.08	97.7 ± 0.26
PACH [3]	98.9 ± 0.19	99.6 ± 0.10	98.3 ± 0.21
LAMP-HQ [32]	99.2 ± 0.04	99.7 ± 0.01	98.2 ± 0.19
EGCH [27]	98.8 ± 0.18	99.64 ± 0.01	97.7 ± 0.16
Ours	$\mathbf{99.6\pm0.19}$	$\mathbf{99.9\pm0.00}$	$\mathbf{99.6\pm0.00}$

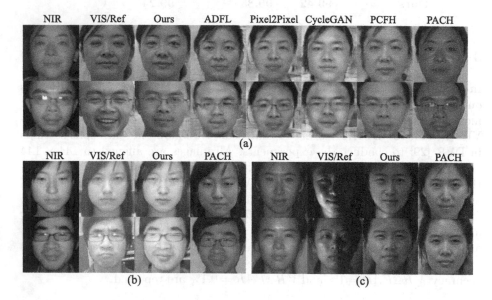

Fig. 4. Qualitative comparisons of our method to the state-of-the-arts on (a) the first fold of the CASIA NIR-VIS 2.0 dataset, (b) the Oulu-CASIA NIR-VIS dataset, and (c) the BUAA-VisNir dataset.

24 GB memory. The balancing weights λ_{cyc}, λ_{idt}, and λ_{str} for the loss items are set to 10, 0.5, and 1, respectively. We use the Adam optimizer [16] with a batch size of 1 and the learning rate is initialized to 1e-4 and linearly decayed to zero after the first half of the training.

Table 3. Comparison on the Oulu-CASIA NIR-VIS and BUAA-VisNir.

	Oulu-CASIA NIR-VIS			BUAA-VisNir		
	$Rank - 1$	$VR@1\%$	$VR@0.1\%$	$Rank - 1$	$VR@1\%$	$VR@0.1\%$
KDSR [12]	66.9	56.1	31.9	83.0	86.8	69.5
TRIVET [20]	92.2	67.9	33.6	93.9	93.0	80.9
IDR [7]	94.3	73.4	46.2	94.3	93.4	84.7
ADFL [25]	95.5	83.0	60.7	95.2	95.3	88.0
LightCNN [28]	96.7	92.4	65.1	96.5	95.4	86.7
PCFH [33]	100	97.7	86.6	98.4	97.9	92.4
PACH [3]	100	97.9	88.2	98.6	98.0	93.5
LAMP-HQ [32]	100	97.7	89.0	98.9	98.3	93.4
EGCH [27]	100	98.0	89.5	98.5	98.1	92.7
Ours	**100**	**98.2**	**95.39**	**100**	**99.9**	**98.4**

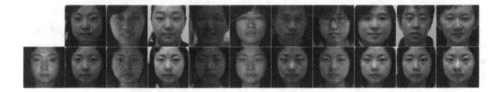

Fig. 5. Multi-modal translation by applying different VIS reference.

3.1 Quantitative Evaluations

Evaluation on the CASIA NIR-VIS 2.0 Dataset. We firstly compare our method to the state-of-the-arts on the CASIA NIR-VIS 2.0 dataset. The statistics are reported in Tab. 1 and Tab. 2, and the visual comparisons are shown as Fig. 4(a). Our full method achieves the highest recognition accuracy in all the metrics and all the folds. Especially, the large margin with respect to $VR@FAR=0.1\%$ indicates our superiority to explore and preserve the identity in the NIR image, which results in a much larger similarity to the target VIS image than to the others in the metric space.

Evaluation on the Oulu-CASIA NIR-VIS Dataset. We apply the model trained on the 1-fold of the CASIA NIR-VIS 2.0 dataset to conduct the evaluation. Statistics and synthesized images are listed in Tab. 3 and Fig. 4(b) respectively. Our method outperforms all the compared state-of-the-arts even without any finetuning on this new dataset.

Evaluation on the BUAA-VisNir Dataset. We use the model trained on the 10-fold of the CASIA NIR-VIS 2.0 dataset for evaluating on the BUAA-VisNir dataset. As shown in Tab. 3, our method achieves the best accuracy, especially

Fig. 6. Qualitative comparisons to (a) PACH [3] and (b) EGCH [27] on high-resolution image-to-image translation (256 × 256).

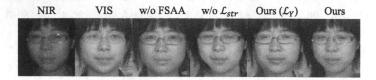

Fig. 7. Qualitative comparisons of our method to its variants on the first fold of the CASIA NIR-VIS 2.0 dataset.

obtaining a large margin in VR@FAR=0.1%. Moreover, as shwon in Fig. 4(c), our method can preserve the extreme illuminations from the reference VIS images, which indicates that spatial appearance representation contains richer guidance for cross spectral face image translation.

3.2   Qualitative Evaluations

We propose visual comparisons in Fig. 4. Specifically, Pixel2Pixel [14], Cycle-GAN [34], ADFL [25] and PCFH [33] tend to synthesis visual images with similar average skin colors and illuminations as they discard the one-to-many mapping in NIR-to-VIS translation (e.g., the fourth to seventh columns in Fig. 4)(a). PACH [3] inject a patch of skin from an arbitrary VIS image as reference, which provides very limited even misleading appearance guidance. For example, dark skin is yielded as shown as the last column in Fig. 4(a).

A more impressive example in Fig. 5 demonstrates the disentanglement of content and appearance in our model. Our method successfully transfers the facial appearance (e.g., the skin color and the illumination) from various VIS images to the same NIR image while preserves the original identity and content well. Finally, we compare to different methods on high-resolution image translation, i.e., 256 × 256, in Fig. 6. Our methods synthesis sharper faces with more realistic facial textures than PACH [3] and EGCH [27], which attributes to the reference on spatial-wise appearance representation rather than a local facial skin patch or a globally-pooled embedding (Fig. 7).

3.3   Ablation Studies

In this section, we conduct both quantitative and qualitative comparisons of our method to its variants. In particular, "w/o FSAA" means the omittion of the proposed FSAA, *i.e.*, to replace $\hat{f}_{vis}^{(2)}$ with $f_{vis}^{(2)}$. Quantitative results are reported in Table 1. Both the alignment of the appearance embeddings and the gradient-based structure constraint facilitate the homogeneous recognition accuracy. This is because FSAA adaptively selects corresponding appearance embeddings for different contents discarding the original identity- and pose-aware spatial localization, while sufficient appearance information helps synthesize more realistic VIS images. On the other hand, the sparse structure naturally describes the identity information better, which accounts for more improvement on recognition accuracy than a dense luminance (Ours ($\mathcal{L}_Y$)).

4 Conclusion

In this paper, we propose a novel cyclic method for unsupervised Spatial-aware Instance-guided Cross-spectral Face Hallucination to translate the NIR image to its VIS counterpart referenced by a VIS image. Specifically, we propose fin-grained spatially adaptive alignment to align the localization of the appearance embeddings to address the misalignment between the NIR-VIS pair. A fine-grained aligned spatially adaptive normalization is further proposed to inject such an aligned spatial appearance representation, which is further incorporated in the FASAN residual block in the generator. Extensive experimental evaluations on three widely used heterogeneous face datasets demonstrate that the superiority of our method and the generalization capacity to diverse galleries.

References

1. Chen, J., Yi, D., Yang, J., Zhao, G., Li, S.Z., Pietikainen, M.: Learning mappings for face synthesis from near infrared to visual light images. In: CVPR, pp. 156–163. IEEE (2009)
2. Cho, M., Kim, T., Kim, I.J., Lee, K., Lee, S.: Relational deep feature learning for heterogeneous face recognition. IEEE Trans. Inf. Forensics Secur. **16**, 376–388 (2020)
3. Duan, B., Fu, C., Li, Y., Song, X., He, R.: Cross-spectral face hallucination via disentangling independent factors. In: CVPR, pp. 7930–7938 (2020)
4. Fu, C., Wu, X., Hu, Y., Huang, H., He, R.: Dual variational generation for low-shot heterogeneous face recognition. arXiv preprint arXiv:1903.10203 (2019)
5. Fu, C., Wu, X., Hu, Y., Huang, H., He, R.: Dvg-face: dual variational generation for heterogeneous face recognition. IEEE Trans. Pattern Anal. Mach. Intell. **44**, 2938–2952 (2021)
6. Goodfellow, I., et al.: Generative adversarial nets. In: NeurIPS, vol. 27 (2014)
7. He, R., Wu, X., Sun, Z., Tan, T.: Learning invariant deep representation for nir-vis face recognition. In: AAAI (2017)
8. He, R., Wu, X., Sun, Z., Tan, T.: Wasserstein cnn: learning invariant features for nir-vis face recognition. IEEE Trans. Pattern Anal. Mach. Intell. **41**(7), 1761–1773 (2018)
9. Hou, C.A., Yang, M.C., Wang, Y.C.F.: Domain adaptive self-taught learning for heterogeneous face recognition. In: ICPR, pp. 3068–3073. IEEE (2014)

10. Hu, Y., Wu, X., Yu, B., He, R., Sun, Z.: Pose-guided photorealistic face rotation. In: CVPR, pp. 8398–8406 (2018)
11. Huang, D., Sun, J., Wang, Y.: The buaa-visnir face database instructions. School Comput. Sci. Eng., Beihang Univ., Beijing, China, Technical Report IRIP-TR-12-FR-001 3 (2012)
12. Huang, X., Lei, Z., Fan, M., Wang, X., Li, S.Z.: Regularized discriminative spectral regression method for heterogeneous face matching. IEEE Trans. Image Process. **22**(1), 353–362 (2012)
13. Huo, J., Gao, Y., Shi, Y., Yang, W., Yin, H.: Heterogeneous face recognition by margin-based cross-modality metric learning. IEEE Trans. Cybern. **48**(6), 1814–1826 (2017)
14. Isola, P., Zhu, J.Y., Zhou, T., Efros, A.A.: Image-to-image translation with conditional adversarial networks. In: CVPR, pp. 1125–1134 (2017)
15. Juefei-Xu, F., Pal, D.K., Savvides, M.: Nir-vis heterogeneous face recognition via cross-spectral joint dictionary learning and reconstruction. In: CVPR Workshops, pp. 141–150 (2015)
16. Kingma, D.P., Ba, J.: Adam: a method for stochastic optimization. arXiv preprint arXiv:1412.6980 (2014)
17. Klare, B., Li, Z., Jain, A.K.: Matching forensic sketches to mug shot photos. IEEE Trans. Pattern Anal. Mach. Intell. **33**(3), 639–646 (2010)
18. Li, S., Yi, D., Lei, Z., Liao, S.: The casia nir-vis 2.0 face database. In: CVPR Workshops, pp. 348–353 (2013)
19. Liao, S., Yi, D., Lei, Z., Qin, R., Li, S.Z.: Heterogeneous face recognition from local structures of normalized appearance. In: Tistarelli, M., Nixon, M.S. (eds.) ICB 2009. LNCS, vol. 5558, pp. 209–218. Springer, Heidelberg (2009). https://doi.org/10.1007/978-3-642-01793-3_22
20. Liu, X., Song, L., Wu, X., Tan, T.: Transferring deep representation for nir-vis heterogeneous face recognition. In: International Conference on Biometrics, pp. 1–8. IEEE (2016)
21. Men, Y., Mao, Y., Jiang, Y., Ma, W.Y., Lian, Z.: Controllable person image synthesis with attribute-decomposed gan. In: CVPR, pp. 5084–5093 (2020)
22. Park, T., Liu, M.Y., Wang, T.C., Zhu, J.Y.: Semantic image synthesis with spatially-adaptive normalization. In: CVPR, pp. 2337–2346 (2019)
23. Parkhi, O.M., Vedaldi, A., Zisserman, A.: Deep face recognition (2015)
24. Paszke, A., et al.: Pytorch: an imperative style, high-performance deep learning library. In: NeurIPS (2019)
25. Song, L., Zhang, M., Wu, X., He, R.: Adversarial discriminative heterogeneous face recognition. In: AAAI, vol. 32 (2018)
26. Wang, K., He, R., Wang, L., Wang, W., Tan, T.: Joint feature selection and subspace learning for cross-modal retrieval. IEEE Trans. Pattern Anal. Mach. Intell. **38**(10), 2010–2023 (2015)
27. Wu, H., Huang, H., Yu, A., Cao, J., Lei, Z., He, R.: Exemplar guided cross-spectral face hallucination via mutual information disentanglement. In: ICPR, pp. 4206–4212. IEEE (2021)
28. Wu, X., He, R., Sun, Z., Tan, T.: A light cnn for deep face representation with noisy labels. IEEE Trans. Inf. Forensics Secur. **13**(11), 2884–2896 (2018)
29. Wu, X., Huang, H., Patel, V.M., He, R., Sun, Z.: Disentangled variational representation for heterogeneous face recognition. In: AAAI, vol. 33, pp. 9005–9012 (2019)
30. Wu, X., Song, L., He, R., Tan, T.: Coupled deep learning for heterogeneous face recognition. In: AAAI (2018)

31. Yi, D., Lei, Z., Li, S.Z.: Shared representation learning for heterogenous face recognition. In: Proceedings of IEEE Conference on Automatic Face and Gesture Recognition, vol. 1, pp. 1–7. IEEE (2015)
32. Yu, A., Wu, H., Huang, H., Lei, Z., He, R.: Lamp-hq: a large-scale multi-pose high-quality database and benchmark for nir-vis face recognition. Int. J. Comput. Vision **129**(5), 1467–1483 (2021)
33. Yu, J., Cao, J., Li, Y., Jia, X., He, R.: Pose-preserving cross spectral face hallucination. In: IJCAI, pp. 1018–1024 (2019)
34. Zhu, J.Y., Park, T., Isola, P., Efros, A.A.: Unpaired image-to-image translation using cycle-consistent adversarial networks. In: ICCV, pp. 2223–2232 (2017)

Lightweight Image Compression Based on Deep Learning

Mengyao Li[1], Zhengyong Wang[1], Liquan Shen[1(✉)], Qing Ding[2], Liangwei Yu[1], and Xuhao Jiang[3]

[1] Shanghai university, Shanghai, China
sdlmy@shu.edu.cn jsslq@163.com
[2] Beihang university, Beijing, China
[3] Fudan university, Shanghai, China

Abstract. Deep learning based image compression (DLIC) algorithms have achieved higher compression gain than conventional algorithms. However, the large parameters and float-point operations (FLOPs) of DLIC severely limit their application on mobile devices. To reduce the parameters and FLOPs while maintaining the superior compression gain, this paper proposes lightweight algorithms especially for the feature analysis, synthesis, and fusion modules in DLIC networks. Firstly, based on the observation that there are highly correlated pairing convolution kernels in the analysis/synthesis modules, a new Dynamic Concatenated Convolution (DCC) is proposed to discard half of pairing convolution kernels, which are then restored by the affine transformation of the remaining convolution kernels. Secondly, a novel Depthwise Separable Residual Block (DSRB), utilizing improved depthwise separable convolutions and skipped connections, is proposed to simplify the stacks of residual blocks in feature fusion modules, significantly reducing parameters and FLOPs. Extensive experimental results demonstrate that the proposed lightweight algorithms have fewer parameters/FLOPs and better image compression gain compared with the existing state-of-the-art lightweight algorithms.

Keywords: Image compression · Lightweight network · Depthwise separable convolution

1 Introduction

As the core technique of image transmission and storage, image compression aims to preserve image fidelity as much as possible with the constrained bit-rate. Recently, deep learning based image compression (DLIC) algorithms [1–5] have achieved higher compression gain than conventional algorithms such as JPEG [6], JPEG2000 [7], and BPG (intra coding from HEVC) [8]. The general framework of DLIC networks consist of three modules, including feature analysis module, feature synthesis module, and feature fusion module, as shown in Fig. 1.

© The Author(s), under exclusive license to Springer Nature Switzerland AG 2022
L. Fang et al. (Eds.): CICAI 2022, LNAI 13604, pp. 106–116, 2022.
https://doi.org/10.1007/978-3-031-20497-5_9

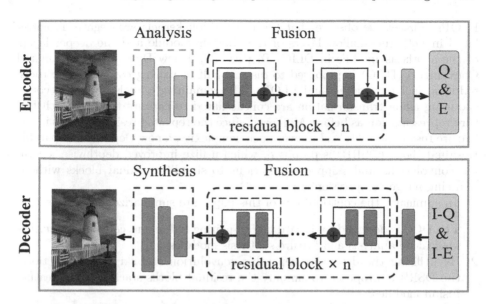

Fig. 1. The general structure of the DLIC network. Q and I-Q, denote quantization and inverse quantization, respectively. E and I-E denote entropy encoding and entropy decoding, respectively.

The structures of feature analysis and synthesis modules are symmetrical, which conduct upsampling and downsampling respectively. The feature fusion modules adopt repeated residual blocks [9] to form deeper networks [4,5] or enlarge receptive field size [10], significantly improving the image compression performance. However, the repeated stack of residual blocks brings millions of parameters and billions of float-point operations (FLOPs). Consequently, it is difficult to apply these superior DLIC networks on resource-limited mobile devices and embedded platforms.

To reduce the network parameters and FLOPs, pruning [11,12] and lightweight architecture design [13–19] are mainstream resolutions. The pruning cuts off the convolution kernels with low contributions to a slim deep network. The lightweight methods design lightweight architecture with fewer parameters and FLOPs to replace the corresponding structure in the original deep network. Specifically, the design of lightweight architecture can be divided into two categories. One is based on the depthwise separable convolution [14–17], which achieves fewer parameters and computation cost through dividing a standard convolution into depthwise (Dwise) and 1×1 pointwise convolution. The other is to explore the combination of convolution kernels with different kernel sizes [18,19]. Although there have been lots of lightweight architectures for high-level computer vision tasks such as object detection [18] and classification [19], none of them is designed for DLIC, one low-level computer vision task.

In this paper, lightweight algorithms are especially proposed for DLIC networks to achieve undegraded compression gain with fewer parameters and

FLOPs. Firstly, we observe that the convolution kernels are negatively corre-lated in both the shallow layers of the analysis module and the deeper layers of the synthesis module in DLIC. To this end, a new Dynamic Concatenated Convolution (DCC) is proposed to discard half of pairing convolution kernels, reducing half parameters and FLOPs. The remaining kernels and their corre-sponding affine transformation are concatenated to capture the same rich fea-ture representation as before. Moreover, since the repeated residual blocks in the feature fusion modules lead to overmuch complexity, a new Depthwise Separable Residual Block (DSRB) is proposed, which utilize improved depthwise separa-ble convolutions and skipped connections to simplify residual blocks without reducing image compression gain.

In summary, the contributions of this paper are summarized as follows:

1. The DCC is designed to discard half of pairing redundant convolution kernels for feature analysis and feature synthesis modules.
2. By utilizing the depthwise separable convolution and skipped connections, the DSRB is proposed to simplify the residual blocks stacked in the feature fusion modules.
3. Integrating our lightweight approaches into various DLIC networks, the parameters and FLOPs of these DLIC networks are reduced significantly while their superior image compression gain is maintained.

2   The Proposed Methods

2.1   Dynamic Concatenated Convolution (DCC)

In this section, we observe that there are pairing convolution kernels with high cosine similarity in feature analysis and synthesis modules. Based on this obser-vation, the DCC is proposed to reduce half of these redundant convolution ker-nels.

Cosine similarity (CS) is a method of similarity measurement between two vectors by measuring the cosine of the angle between the two vectors, which is very common used in many fields such as information retrieval, pattern matching, and so on. In [20], the CS of two convolution kernels is calculated to evaluate the similarity of two kernels. When the CS equals to -1, the two convolution kernels are strictly negatively correlated; otherwise, the value of CS is 0, which indicates that these two convolution kernels are completely uncorrelated. Assuming the i/j-th kernel in a convolution layer is defined by φ_i/φ_j, the CS between φ_i and φ_j is calculated by:

$$\mu_{ij} = \frac{\varphi_i \times \varphi_j}{\|\varphi_i\| \times \|\varphi_j\|} \tag{1}$$

The pairing convolution kernel of φ_i is defined as $\bar{\varphi}_i$, which is described in the following equation,

$$\bar{\varphi}_i = \arg \min_{\varphi_j} \mu_{ij} \tag{2}$$

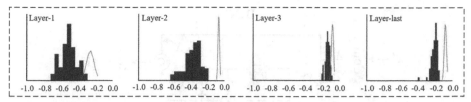

(a) First three layers and the last layer in the analysis module

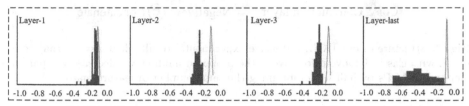

(b) First three layers and the last layer in the synthesis module.

Fig. 2. Histograms of pairing kernels' CS in different convolution layers. Blue/yellow represents the CS distribution between the pairing kernels in the analysis/synthesis module. The red curve represents the CS distribution of the random and uncorrelated Gaussian convolution kernels. The CS distribution is more close −1, and then the correlation is higher. (Color figure online)

When the negative correlation between pairing convolution kernels is high (i.e., CS closes to −1), one convolution kernel can be discarded and obtained by the other one's negative value to reduce parameters and FLOPs of networks.

The histograms of pairing kernels' CS in different convolution layers are plotted in Fig. 2. For comparison, the CS of random and uncorrelated Gaussian kernels is represented by the red line. Figure 2(a) shows that the CS of pairing kernels of the shallow layers (e.g., Layer-1) is closer to −1, and that of deep layers (e.g., Layer-last) is close to 0 (i.e., uncorrelated Gaussian distribution) in the feature analysis module. This implies that the shallow layers' kernels are more correlated than those of deep layers in the analysis module. In contrast, the phenomenon in the feature synthesis module is opposite to that in the feature analysis module. Figure 2(b) shows the CS of the pairing convolution kernels in the first three layers and the last layer in the synthesis module. It can be observed that the CS of shallow layers (e.g., Layer-1) is close to 0. However, when the layer gradually deepens, the CS is closer to −1. Thus, it can be concluded that the deep layers' kernels are more correlated than that of shallow layers in the synthesis module.

Therefore, half of pairing convolution kernels in shallow layers of analysis modules and deep layers of synthesis modules can be discarded to save the network's parameters and FLOPs. Specifically, in our experiments, the first/last two layers of the analysis/synthesis modules perform the above operations. Considering the CS distributions in Fig. 2 are not entirely equal to −1, the convolution kernels are not strictly negatively correlated. To make their correlation close

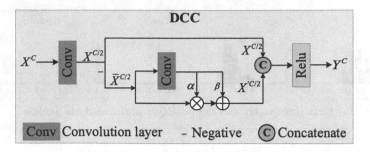

Fig. 3. Structure of our DCC. Extensive experimental results demonstrate that compared with classical convolution layers, the proposed module can decrease the parameters and FLOPs by half when obtaining the same number of feature maps.

to –1, the DCC is proposed to recalibrate their distribution through an affine transformation. The operation of DCC can be formulated as:

$$Y^c = Relu\left\{Concat[(-X^{c/2}) \times \alpha + \beta, X^{c/2}]\right\} \tag{3}$$

where Y^c is the DCC output of c channels, and $X^{c/2}$ denotes the output of $c/2$ convolution kernels. α is scale and β is bias, which are introduced to recalibrate the CS distribution close to –1.

Figure 3 shows the structure of the proposed DCC. Firstly, $c/2$ convolution kernels are used to generate $X^{c/2}$. Then the negative $X^{c/2}$, denoted as $\bar{X}^{c/2}$, perform an affine transformation by multiplying α and adding β to get $X'^{c/2}$. Lastly, $X^{c/2}$ and $X'^{c/2}$ are concatenated and undergone the non-linear activation Relu. After the above operation, the proposed DCC can reduce nearly half parameters and FLOPs compared with the classic convolution layer when generating the same number of feature maps.

2.2 Depthwise Separable Residual Block (DSRB)

In order to achieve higher image compression gain, many residual blocks are stacked in the feature fusion module of DLIC to deepen the network. However, it leads to a huge increase in the network parameters and FLOPs. To address this issue, we propose an efficient and lightweight residual block DSRB to build a deep network with fewer parameters and FLOPs.

The structure of our DSRB is shown in Fig. 4(f). The classic residual block (RB) consists of two convolutions [9], as shown in Fig. 4(a). Compared with standard convolution, depthwise separable convolution (DS) has fewer parameters, because the DS divides a standard convolution into two separate layers [15], as shown in Fig. 4(c). The first layer is depthwise convolution (Dwise), which performs filtering on each input channel by applying a single channel convolution kernel. The second layer is a 1 × 1 convolution. Our DSRB improves the structure of classic residual block and depthwise separable convolution and finally combines them. Specifically, the following improvements are performed in our DSRB.

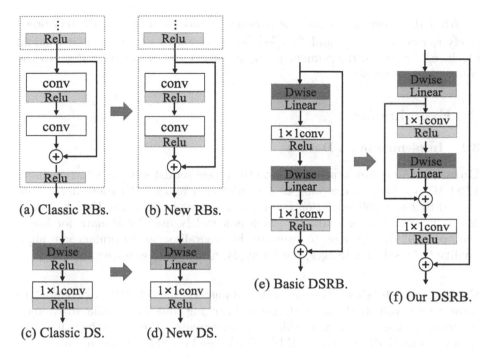

Fig. 4. Different residual blocks.

Improvement of the Classic RB. The Relu behind residual in classic RB is adjusted to the front of the residual in new RB, as shown in Fig. 4(b). Since the outputs of Relu for negative inputs are 0, there are many 0 values in its outputs to make network sparsity, reducing overfitting [21]. The output of convolution does not possess this characteristic. In classic RB, the residual output is the sum of the Relu's output and the convolution's output, which destroys the network sparsity. To handle this issue, we adjust the position of Relu. The adjustment of the position of Relu causes the output of residual to be the sum of the Relus' output to make network sparsity, reducing overfitting.

Improvement of the Classic DS. The Relu behind Dwise in classic DS is replaced with linear activation function in the new DS, as shown in Fig. 4(d). The non-linear activation (e.g., Relu) is beneficial to deep feature spaces, while the shallow feature maps are destroyed by Relu, resulting in information loss [14]. Since the Dwise is a 1-channel shallow convolution space, its output can be captured by linear layers instead of non-linear activation layers.

Combination of New RB and New DS. Replacing the convolution in new RBs with new DS can get the basic DSRB, as shown in Fig. 4(e). Then we add a shortcut between two Dwise convolutions in addition to the shortcut between the input and output of the classic RB, as shown in Fig. 4(f). It helps to interchange shallow information while having more gradient backwards, solving the vanishing-gradient problem and accelerating training convergence [9].

After the above operations, the parameters and FLOPs of our DSRB respectively reduce by $\frac{1}{cc'} + \frac{1}{k^2}$ and $\frac{2c(c'+k^2)-(c+c')}{2cc'k^2-c'}$ compared with the classic residual block. c/c' refers to the number of input/output channels, and k denotes the convolution kernel size.

3 Experiments

3.1 Implementation Details

Datasets. All networks are trained on the ImageNet dataset [22], which includes 1,281,167 training images and 49,998 validation images. All these images are resized to 256×256 resolution for training and evaluation. The Kodak dataset [23] is used as the test dataset, which is a widely used benchmark for image compression. Furthermore, to evaluate the generalization performance on high-quality full resolution images, the B100 [24] dataset is also tested.

Evaluation Metrics. The network parameters and FLOPs are counted to respectively evaluate the network size and running time. Meanwhile, to evaluate the image compression gain, the bit per pixel increase (Δbpp) and the multi-scale structural similarity increase (ΔMS-SSIM) based on the baseline are applied.

3.2 Lightweight Ability Evaluation

To evaluate the lightweight ability of the proposed algorithms, we compare our methods with three other state-of-the-art lightweight algorithms on Mentzer's DLIC network [4]. Among the three comparison algorithms, MixConv [18] explores the combination of convolution kernels with different kernel sizes. ShuffleNet [17] and MobileNet [15] are based on depthwise separable convolution. Experimental results are shown in Table 1.

As shown in Table 1, our approaches achieve the best result in terms of parameter reduction. The parameters reduce to 1.56 M by our lightweight algorithms,

Table 1. Comparative Parameters (M), FLOPs (G), Δbpp (%) and ΔMS-SSIM (dB) on Kodak. The best and the second best results are marked red and blue respectively.

Methods	Parameters ↓	FLOPs ↓	Δbpp ↓	ΔMS-SSIM ↑
Mentzer [4] (Baseline)	40.16	3754.6	/	/
MixConv [18]	2.01	95.3	+12.4	−0.361
ShuffleNet [17]	1.61	183.9	+21.6	−1.905
MobileNet [15]	1.72	111.6	+6.8	−0.016
Proposed Method	1.56	102.9	+5.4	+0.033

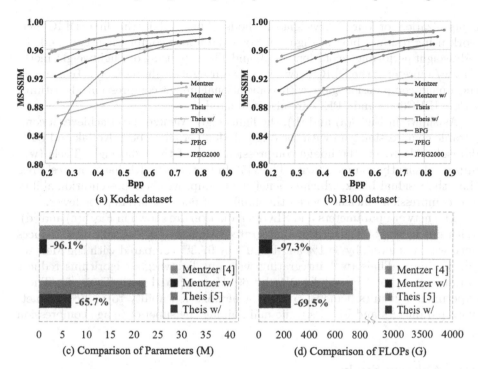

Fig. 5. Image compression and lightweight performance on different test datasets and DLIC networks. Mentzer [4] and Theis [5] refer to two DLIC networks, and w/ denotes the DLIC network using our lightweight algorithms.

which is 22.4% better than that of MinConv (2.01 M), 3.1% better than that of ShuffleNet (1.61 M) and 9.3% better than that of MobileNet (1.72 M). For the FLOPs reduction, our approaches achieve the second best result (102.9 G). Since our algorithms utilize lots of residuals, which are not adopted in MixConv [18], our FLOPs (102.9 G) is 7.9% more than that of MixConv [18] (95.3 G). However, our approaches achieve better results in terms of Δbpp and ΔMS-SSIM. Specifically, our algorithms achieve less bpp increment of 5.4% and more MS-SSIM increment of 0.033 dB among the comparative lightweight algorithms.

It should be noted that the purpose of lightweight algorithms is to lighten networks without degrading the performance. Even though MixConv [18] has the fewest FLOPs, its MS-SSIM drops by 0.361 dB and bpp increases by 12.4%, which is unacceptable. Considering both the complexity reduction and the image compression performance, our lightweight algorithms have better lightweight ability than all compared lightweight algorithms.

3.3   Generalization Ability Evaluation

In addition to the DLIC network of Mentzer [4], our lightweight methods are additionally integrated into the DLIC network of Theis [5] to verify the generalization of our lightweight methods. Theis [5] is the first DLIC network using residual blocks. Figure 5 shows the image compression gain and the lightweight performance of Mentzer [4] and Theis [5] using our lightweight methods. w/ represents the DLIC network using our lightweight methods. To compare the image compression gain with conventional image compression algorithms, BPG, JPEG2000 and JPEG are also evaluated.

As shown in Fig. 5(a) and (b), the lightweight Mentzer (w/) achieves a comparable compression gain with the original Mentzer [4] on both Kodak and B100 datasets. Moreover, the image compression gain of the lightweight Theis (w/) improved slightly compared with Theis [5]. In fact, our DSRB has more residuals than the residual block, which is beneficial to improve the representation ability and compression efficiency when the number of network layers [5] is fewer.

The network parameters and FLOPs reduction are shown in Fig. 5(c) and (d). With our lightweight algorithms integrated, Mentzer (w/) significantly reduces network parameters by 96.1% and FLOPs by 97.3% compared with the Mentzer [4]. Similarly, Theis (w/) integrating with our lightweight algorithms reduces parameters by 65.7% and FLOPs by 69.5% compared with Theis [5]. These experimental results demonstrate our generalization ability to reduce the network parameters and FLOPs while maintaining the superior image compression gain.

3.4   Ablation Study

Two sets of ablation studies are conducted to validate the lightweight performance of the proposed DCC and DSRB. Consistent with the previous experiment of lightweight ability evaluation, Mentzer [4] is selected as the baseline. Firstly, the repeated residual blocks of feature fusion modules in [4] are replaced with our DSRBs.Then, the first/last two convolution layers of analysis/synthesis modules are replaced with our DCCs. The experimental results at 0.4 bpp are presented in Table 2. It can be observed that the parameters and FLOPs of the baseline without DCC and DSRB are 40.16M and 3754.6G. After using the DSRBs, the parameters and FLOPs respectively reduce to 1.76M and 147.1G. As the parameters and FLOPs reduce significantly, the MS-SSIM decreases slightly

Table 2. Lightweight performance and image compression gain of DCC and DSRB over Mentzer [4] on Kodak, BPP = 0.4

Ablation Models	MS-SSIM	Parameters(M)	FLOPs(G)
Baseline	0.9735	40.16	3754.6
Baseline + DSRB	0.9724	1.76	147.1
Baseline + DSRB + DCC (Ours)	0.9737	1.56	102.9

from 0.9735 to 0.9724. This demonstrates the DSRB's superior lightweight performance with minor loss for image compression efficiency. The best result is achieved with both DCC and DSRB, which indicates the effectiveness of the combination of our DCC and DSRB.

4 Conclusion

In this paper, we propose lightweight algorithms especially for DLIC networks, including feature analysis, synthesis and fusion modules. The DCC is proposed to remove half of the pairing kernels observed in the shallow/deep layers of feature analysis/synthesis modules. As for the repeated residual blocks stacked in the feature fusion modules, the DSRB is proposed to simplify these blocks using the improved residual block and depthwise separable convolution. Experimental results show that the proposed lightweight algorithms have achieved more advanced lightweight performance and better image compression gain for the DLIC network compared to other lightweight algorithms. In our future work, we plan to focus on lightening the DLIC networks while improving image compression performance.

References

1. Hu, Y., Yang, W., Ma, Z., Liu, J.: Learning end-to-end lossy image compression: a benchmark. IEEE Trans. Pattern Anal. Mach. Intell. **44**(8), 4194–4211 (2022)
2. Ma, Y., Zhai, Y.Q., Yang, J.Y., Yang, C.H., Wang, R.G.: AFEC: adaptive feature extraction modules for learned image compression. In: ACM International Conference on Multimedia, pp. 5436–5444 (2021)
3. Yang, F., Herranz, L., Weijer, J.V.D., Zhao, J.A.I., López, A.M., Mozerov, M.G.: Variable rate deep image compression with modulated autoencoder. IEEE Signal Process. Lett. **27**(2), 331–335 (2020)
4. Mentzer, F., Agustsson, E., Tschannen, M., Timofte, R., Gool, L.V.: Conditional probability models for deep image compression. In: Proceedings of IEEE/CVF Conference Computer Vision and Pattern Recognition (CVPR), pp. 4394–4402 (2018)
5. Theis, L., Shi, W., Cunningham, A., Huszár, F.: Lossy image compression with compressive autoencoders (2017). arXiv preprint arXiv:1703.00395
6. Wallace, G.K.: The jpeg still picture compression standard. Commun. Acm **38**(1), xviii–xxxiv (1992)
7. Christopoulos, C., Skodras, A., Ebrahimi, T.: The JPEG2000 still image coding system: an overview. IEEE Trans. Cons. Electron. **46**(4), 1103–1127 (2000)
8. Bellard, F.: Bpg image format, vol. 1 (2015). https://bellard.org/bpg
9. He, K., Zhang, X., Ren, S., Sun, J.: Deep residual learning for image recognition. In: Proceedings of IEEE/CVF Conference Computer Vision and Pattern Recognition (CVPR), pp. 770–778 (2016)
10. Cheng, Z., Sun, H., Takeuchi, M., Katto, J.: Deep residual learning for image compression. In: Proceedings of CVPR Workshops (2019)
11. Yu, R., et al.: Nisp: pruning networks using neuron importance score propagation. In: Proceedings of IEEE/CVF Conference Computer Vision and Pattern Recognition (CVPR), pp. 9194–9203 (2018)

12. He, Y., Dong, X., Kang, G., Fu, Y., Yan, C., Yang, Y.: Asymptotic soft kernel pruning for deep convolutional neural networks. IEEE Trans. Cybern. **50**(8), 3594–3604 (2020)
13. Tian, G., Chen, J., Zeng, X., Liu, Y.: Pruning by training: a novel deep neural network compression framework for image processing. IEEE Signal Process. Lett. (2021). https://doi.org/10.1109/LSP.2021.3054315
14. Chollet, F.: Xception: deep learning with depthwise separable convolutions. In: Proceedings of IEEE/CVF Conference Computer Vision and Pattern Recognition (CVPR), pp. 1800–1807 (2017)
15. Howard, A.G., et al.: Mobilenets: efficient convolutional neural networks for mobile vision applications (2017). arXiv preprint arXiv:1704.04861
16. Zhang, X., Zhou, X., Lin, M., Sun, J.: Shufflenet: an extremely mefficient convolutional neural network for mobile devices. In: Proceedings of IEEE/CVF Conference Computer Vision and Pattern Recognition (CVPR), pp. 6848–6856 (2018)
17. Ma, N., Zhang, X., Zheng, H.-T., Sun, J.: Shufflenet v2: practical guidelines for efficient cnn architecture design. In: Proceedings of the European Conference on Computer Vision (ECCV), pp. 116–131 (2018)
18. Tan, M., Le, Q.V.: Mixconv: mixed depthwise convolutional kernels. arXiv preprint arXiv:1907.09595 (2019)
19. Daquan, Z., Hou, Q., Chen, Y., Feng, J., Yan, S.: Rethinking bottleneck structure for efficient mobile network design. arXiv preprint arXiv:2007.02269 (2020)
20. Shang, W., Sohn, K., Almeida, D., Lee, H.: Understanding and improving convolutional neural networks via concatenated rectified linear units. In: Proceedings of International conference on machine learning (ICML), pp. 2217–2225 (2016)
21. Sandler, M., Howard, A.G., Zhu, M., Zhmoginov, A., Chen, L.C.: MobileNetV2: inverted residuals and linear bottlenecks. In: Proceedings of IEEE/CVF Conference Computer Vision and Pattern Recognition (CVPR), pp. 4510–4520 (2018)
22. Russakovsky, O., et al.: Imagenet large scale visual recognition challenge. Int. J. Comput. Vision **115**(3), 211–252 (2015)
23. Kodak, E.: The kodak photocd dataset. http://r0k.us/graphics/kodak/.6
24. Timofte, R., De Smet, V., Van Gool, L.: A+: adjusted anchored neighborhood regression for fast super-resolution. In: Cremers, D., Reid, I., Saito, H., Yang, M.-H. (eds.) ACCV 2014. LNCS, vol. 9006, pp. 111–126. Springer, Cham (2015). https://doi.org/10.1007/978-3-319-16817-3_8

DGMLP: Deformable Gating MLP Sharing for Multi-Task Learning

Yangyang Xu and Lefei Zhang[✉]

School of Computer Science, Wuhan University, Wuhan, China
{yangyangxu,zhanglefei}@whu.edu.cn

Abstract. With the development of deep learning, many dense prediction tasks have been significantly improved. In this work, we introduce a DGMLP model that jointly learns multiple dense prediction tasks in a unified multi-task learning architecture that is trained end-to-end. Specifically, the DGMLP consists of (i) a spatial deformable MLP to capture the valuable spatial information for different tasks and (ii) a spatial gating MLP to learn the shared feature across all the tasks. Deformable MLP can adaptively adjust the receptive field and sample valuable locations in this approach. In addition, the Gating MLP is adopted to learn task-relevant features for each task. We take advantage of the spatial deformable MLP and spatial gating MLP to build a new MLP-like architecture that is especially simple and effective for multiple visual dense prediction tasks. We provide extensive experiments and evaluations to verify the advantages of our approach, and the extensive experiments demonstrate the superiority of the proposed framework over state-of-the-art methods.

Keywords: Scene understanding · Multi-task learning · Dense prediction

1 Introduction

In most computer vision models, a model usually executes only one vision task. In contrast, the multi-task learning (MTL) model for dense image prediction in this manner: require multiple visual information as input, and train a general model to execute simultaneously multiple visual tasks such as classification, object detection, semantic segmentation, and depth estimation, *etc.*

Generally, based on the criteria proposed by [23], we distinguish between two MTL models: encoder-based and decoder-based architectures. This depends on where the task interactions take place. The Encoder-based architectures learn a shared feature in the encoder for different tasks and then decode each task using separate task-specific heads. NDDR-CNN [9] model first concatenates task-specific features with the same spatial resolution from different tasks, then dimensionality reduction techniques are used to learn a discriminative feature embedding for each task, which also satisfies input sizes of the following layers. MTAN [13] is a similar method of [9] using the shared features to learn a global

© The Author(s), under exclusive license to Springer Nature Switzerland AG 2022
L. Fang et al. (Eds.): CICAI 2022, LNAI 13604, pp. 117–128, 2022.
https://doi.org/10.1007/978-3-031-20497-5_10

feature pool containing features across all tasks. Then the soft-attention module is designed for each task. Since decoder-based architectures directly use a learned feature to perform predictions for all tasks, they cannot capture the commonalities and differences among tasks. Several algorithms [4,11,13,15,16,30] have been proposed to explore the relationship between different tasks. The decoder-based architectures leverage task-specific features to exchange information between tasks to capture the task interaction information. The PSD [11] model is proposed to mine and propagate the relationships from task-specific and task-across features. ATRC [4] employs scaled dot-product attention technology to find the most efficient interaction process through contextual source task features, then refines each task pixel-wise prediction. The core of these models is to enable adequate interaction of features between tasks and extract meaningful information across tasks to improve performance further.

Our goal in this work is to design a model to produce a shared visual representation for different tasks that are simpler and more efficient. We propose an MLP-liked architecture named DGMLP. To the best of our knowledge, this is the first MTL work combining MLP-liked models. In this paper, we introduce a novel MLP-like model that leverages the spatial deformable MLP, spatial gating MLP, and the shared visual representation. For that, we first design the spatial deformable MLP, which adopts the deformable convolutions and channel linear to capture the spatial information and interaction information for different tasks. Deformable convolution [36,37] increases the sampling position of the convolution with additional offsets and learns the offsets from the target task. In addition, the receptive field and the sampling locations adaptively adjust to the size and shape of the object. Deformable convolution operations are performed along with the image feature height and width, respectively. The trainable spatial gating MLP is proposed to be shared across all the tasks. The spatial gating MLP is very flexible that can learn to share features between tasks. Within this framework, we take advantage of the spatial deformable MLP and spatial gating MLP to build a new MLP-like architecture that is especially simple and effective for dense image predictions.

The main contributions of this work are as follows:

- We propose a new MLT framework built upon MLP-like architecture, named DGMLP, which is then enabled for end-to-end training/predicting. DGMLP captures the task-specific features of the whole image feature while being able to model the multiple task interactions.
- Through deformable convolution and gating mechanisms, our model automatically adjusts parameterization between modeling shared vision features and task-specific information.
- We conduct extensive experiments on the NYUD-v2 and PASCAL-Context datasets and demonstrate that the proposed DGMLP method is able to achieve promising results in multiple tasks.

2 Related Work

Convolutional Neural Networks (CNNs) for MTL. Recently, the application of CNNs [18,31] in MTL has shown promising results in a wide range of computer vision tasks, from image to video vision for scene understanding. A key factor for success in MTL is the ability of neural network models to learn shared and task-specific representations. CNN-based architectures for dense prediction tasks [2,24]. SFGs [2] probabilistically groups convolutional kernels, thus defining the connectivity of features in CNN, and subsequently, the network generates task-specific and generalist features. In [20], the model exploits the combination of multiple dilation convolutions and the DenseNet architecture to enable multi-resolution information exchange in most layers while avoiding the confounding problem that occurs when we merge dilation convolutions in DenseNet.

Transformer for MTL. With excellent performance, transformer and attention mechanism models were first employed in NLP tasks. The self-attention mechanism is adopted in many fields [14,26,32]. Recently, transformer structures [10,25,34] have also produced impressive results in computer vision. The images are divided into a constant number of patches, which are embedded as input into the Transformer network. Following the Transformer computation paradigm will project the patches into the feature space and are defined as queries, keys, and values. Currently there are various transformer variants such as Deformable DETR [37], FP-DETR [26], PVT [27] and Swin-Transformer [14]. Vision Transformer (ViT) [8], and Swin Transformer [14] claim that the transformer-based model outperforms the CNN-based model in terms of accuracy for image detection, classification, and segmentation tasks. Swin Transformer improves self-attention computation efficiency via non-overlapping local windows and cross-window connections. Recent MTL models [1,30] employ the transformer for Multi-task dense prediction.

Neural Architecture Search (NAS) for MTL. NAS has received increasing attention, aiming to design high-performing deep neural network models that perform well in an automated approach. NAS [4,33] and knowledge distillation techniques are used to find valuable complementary information by searching for relevant task-sharing information. For example, [19] is designed to identify effective feature sharing across tasks. In addition, [4] developed an Adaptive Task-Relationship Context (ATRC) module that exploits inter and intra-task relationships. The multimodal distillation module explicitly considers task relationships while using scaled dot-product attention to enrich the features of the target task.

Multi-layer Perceptrons (MLPs). Transformer-based models following ViT [8] abandoned the convolution operation and adopted the self-attention operation, which outperformed CNN-based or even higher accuracy in vision tasks.

Recently, MLP-like models [6,12,21,22,28] propose an architecture containing only MLP layers, thus abandoning convolution and self-attention operations. The MLP-like architecture consisting of two Linear function layers and a nonlinear activation function has received much attention from researchers. gMLP [12] is the first variants of MLP-Mixer [22] to be presented. In [12], gMLP designs a spatial gating unit to enable cross-token interactions and achieves strong results on ImageNet. WaveMLP [21] considers that different tokens contain diverse semantic contents. They aggregate tokens by dynamically estimating the phase. Wave-MLP architecture is built through stacking the token mixing and channel-mixing MLP. CycleMLP [6] and Wave-MLP [21] also obtain better performance on the dense prediction tasks such as semantic segmentation and object detection.

3   Method

In this section, we introduce the proposed DGMLP for vision multiple tasks. First, we describe the overall architecture concisely. Then, we present the detailed feature extractor, spatial deformable MLP, and spatial gating MLP in the DGMLP model. Finally, we present the loss function.

3.1   Overview

The architectural foundation for our network design is simple. As shown in Fig. 1, the network architecture forms three sections that resemble the process of a classical representation method: feature extractor, the proposed DGMLP model, and dense prediction. The DGMLP consists of a sequence of spatial deformable MLP and spatial gating MLP and can process images of any input dimensions (see Fig. 2). We remark that our MLP-like model is not only architecturally simple to construct but also shows strong experiment results on several MTL datasets.

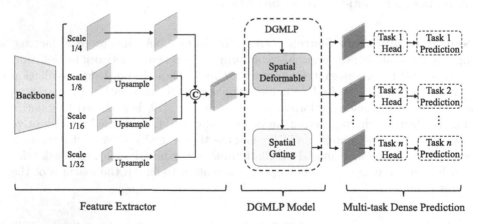

Fig. 1. An overview of the DGMLP model. It comprises a feature extractor, the DGMLP model, and multi-task dense prediction. The backbone output four scale image features. The symbol 'C' indicates concatenation operation in the feature extractor. The DGMLP represents an MLP-like model and performs joint multi-task learning.

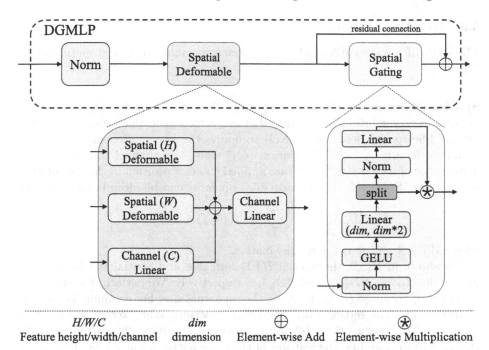

H/W/C	dim	$\oplus$	$\circledast$
Feature height/width/channel	dimension	Element-wise Add	Element-wise Multiplication

Fig. 2. Illustration of the DGMLP model. Similar to classical MLP domain methods, this architecture mainly includes two modules: spatial deformable MLP and spatial gating MLP. "Spatial (H) Deformable" means that we perform deformable convolution calculation along the H side of the image feature, and the similarly for in "Spatial (W) Deformable." The image feature is split into two image features along the channel in the spatial gating module.

3.2 Feature Extractor

We developed a simple feature extractor to generate image features. We use HRNet [18] as the CNN backbone and Swin Transformer [14] as the transformer backbone for the feature extractor. HRNet and Swin Transformer can generate multi-scale image features for dense prediction tasks such as detection and semantic segmentation.

As shown in Fig. 1, the backbone outputs four-scale of image features. We upsample the scale 1/8, scale 1/16, and scale 1/32 features to match the resolution of the scale 1/4 feature, as shown in Fig. 1 (Feature extractor). After the upsample operation, the four scale image features have the same resolution. They are concatenated along the channel dimension to obtain an image feature. The image feature of one scale output by the feature extractor can be denoted as $X \in \mathbb{R}^{H \times W \times C}$, where H, W, and C are the height, width, and channel of the image feature, respectively. The image feature $X_{(i,j,c)}$ ((i,j) is spatial position on the c-th channel) is served as the input to the downstream DGMLP model.

3.3 DGMLP Method

The DGMLP consists of Norm layers, spatial deformable MLP, and spatial gating MLP.

Spatial Deformable Module. In [36,37], the experiment has shown that the deformable convolution can achieve better performance than standard convolution. The spatial deformable (SD) computes the convolution matrix applied to image feature X at each position (i, j) along the channel dimension. The deformable offsets $\Delta \in \mathbb{R}^{H \times W \times 2}$ are applied for each position in the convolution kernel. The "Spatial(H/W) Deformable" operator can be formulated as below:

$$SD(X_{i,j,c}) = \sum W_1 \cdot X((i, j) + \Delta_{(i,j)}, c), \tag{1}$$

where $W_1 \in \mathbb{R}^{C \times C_{out}}$ is the weight matrix.

As shown in Fig. 2, the Spatial(H) Deformable and Spatial(W) Deformable can be denoted as $SD(\cdot)_H$ and $SD(\cdot)_W$, respectively. We perform the computation of $SD(\cdot)_H$ and $SD(\cdot)_W$ by using the set kernel size. For example, kernel size $(1, 3)or(1, 7)$ is the setting value of $SD(\cdot)_H$ function. When kernel size is set to $(3, 1)or(7, 1)$, it means that $SD(\cdot)_W$ is executed. To efficiently capture valuable spatial features, we fuse the features of the three paths in the spatial deformable module. This process is defined as below:

$$\hat{\mathbf{X}} = SD(\mathbf{X})_H + SD(\mathbf{X})_W + \mathbf{W_2}(\mathbf{X}), \tag{2}$$

where W_2 is a weight parameter. $SD(\mathbf{X})_H$ denotes the deformable convolution calculation along with the height (H) on the feature X. $SD(\mathbf{X})_W$ performs the same operation along the width (W).

Channel Linear. The channel linear allows information transfer between channels to complete channel information interaction in feature spatial. Thus, a channel linear can be written as follows:

$$\hat{\mathbf{X}}_{i,j} = \mathbf{W_3}(\hat{\mathbf{X}})_{i,j}, \text{ for } (i, j) = 1 \dots HW, \tag{3}$$

where W_3 is a weight parameter.

Spatial Gating MLP. In this spatial gating MLP, a gating network for different tasks can capture task relationships. The spatial gating MLP ensembles the results from channel mixing features. Before splitting $\hat{X}$, we use a linear function to expand the feature channel dimension. This operation could be written as:

$$\hat{\mathbf{X}} = \mathbf{W_4}\sigma\left(\text{Norm}(\hat{\mathbf{X}}_{i,j})\right), \tag{4}$$

where $\sigma(\cdot)$ is the non-linearity function; $\mathbf{W_4} \in \mathbb{R}^{C \times 2C}$. Thus, we split the image feature $\hat{\mathbf{X}}$ into two features X_1 and X_2 $(X_1, X_2 \in \mathbb{R}^{H \times W \times C})$ along the channel dimension. In this work, we use a sample linear gating and a residual connection. The spatial gating is formulated as:

$$\hat{\mathbf{X}} = \hat{\mathbf{X}}_{i,j} + \mathbf{X_1} * (\mathbf{W_5} \, \mathrm{Norm}(\mathbf{X_2}) + \mathbf{b}), \tag{5}$$

where $*$ denotes element-wise multiplication. b refers to the learnable bias of this function of shape $(\mathbb{R}^C)$. The $\hat{\mathbf{X}}_{i,j}$ is a residual connection unit. We also normalize the x_2, which empirically improves the stability of the feature transmission. The spatial gating MLP is trained to optimize each task.

3.4   Loss Function

We should construct a total scaled loss $\mathcal{L}_{total}$ so that the network parameters can arrive at one consolidated result with Stochastic Gradient Descent (SGD) optimizer. In addition, We empirically set the balancing factors for different task losses. We then form a total loss for multi-task as follows:

$$\mathcal{L}_{total} = \sum_{t=1}^{T} \lambda_t \mathcal{L}_t, \tag{6}$$

where λ_t is a balancing factor. T denotes the total number of tasks ($t \in [1, T]$).

4   Experiments

In this section, the proposed DGMLP has been compared to recent contributions in the multi-task area. Our DGMLP model is extensively experimented on the standard public NYUD-v2 [17] and PASCAL-Context [7] datasets. Ablation studies and visualizations are shown on two datasets to provide a more comprehensive and intuitive understanding of our approach.

Datasets. NYUD-V2 consists of video sequences of various indoor visual scenes recorded by RGB and depth cameras. NYUD-V2 has 1449 densely labeled pairs of aligned RGB and depth images, with 464 new scenes taken from 3 cities, which are 795 training and 654 testing. NYUD-V2 is mainly used for semantic segmentation ('SemSeg'), depth estimation ('Depth'), surface normal estimation ('Normal'), and boundary detection ('Bound') tasks. PASCAL-Context has a total of 459 annotations containing 10103 images, of which 4998 are used in the training set and 5105 in the validation set. PASCAL-Context is labeled for semantic segmentation, human parts segmentation ('PartSeg'), saliency estimation ('Sal'), surface normal estimation, and boundary detection.

Backbone. Our experiments are based on CNN and vision Transformers, namely HRNet [18] and Swin Transformer [14]. We use CNN-based and Transformer-based models as the backbone to extract the pyramidal features and prove that the DGMLP method is robust. We use HRNet pre-trained on ImageNet as the backbone of our network architecture. The Swin-Tiny (Swin-T), Swin-Small (Swin-S), Swin-Base (Swin-B), and HRNet18 are employed as a shared backbone for all tasks.

Table 1. Comparison results on NYUD-v2 dataset. The notation '↓': lower is better. The notation '↑': higher is better. Parm denotes parameters. The table is an extended version from [4].

Model	Backbone	Parm (M)	SemSeg (mIoU)↑	Depth (rmse)↓	Normals (mErr)↓	Bound (odsF)↑
multi-task baseline	HRNet18	4.52	36.35	0.6284	21.02	76.36
multi-task baseline	Swin-T	38.05	37.78	0.6322	21.09	75.60
multi-task baseline	Swin-S	59.37	47.90	0.6053	21.17	76.90
Cross-Stitch[15]	HRNet18	4.52	36.34	0.6290	20.88	76.38
Pad-Net[29]	HRNet18	5.02	36.70	0.6264	20.85	76.50
PAP[35]	HRNet18	4.54	36.72	0.6178	20.82	76.42
PSD[11]	HRNet18	4.71	36.69	0.6246	20.87	76.42
NDDR-CNN[9]	HRNet18	4.59	36.72	0.6288	20.85	76.38
ATRC[4]	HRNet18	5.06	38.90	0.6010	20.48	76.34
ATRC[4]	HRNet48	73.58	46.27	0.5495	20.20	77.60
DGMLP (ours)	HRNet18	7.3	39.01	0.6019	20.43	76.50
DGMLP (ours)	Swin-T	37.5	42.53	0.5851	20.84	76.10
DGMLP (ours)	Swin-S	58.3	46.66	0.5664	20.14	76.80

Evaluation Metric. We adopt four evaluation metrics to evaluate the performance of the multi-task models. (1) The mean Intersection over Union (mIoU) is used to evaluate the semantic segmentation and human part segmentation tasks. (2) The root mean square error (rmse) is used to evaluate the depth estimation task. (3) The mean Error (mErr) is used to evaluate the surface normals task. (4) The optimal dataset scale F-measure (odsF) is used to evaluate the edge detection task. (5) The maximum F-measure (maxF) is used to evaluate the saliency estimation task.

4.1 Comparisons with State-of-the-art Models

Performance Analysis on NYUD-v2. In Table 1, it is clear that DGMLP outperforms all the competitive efficient multi-task models by large margins. For example, with the same HRNet18 backbone, it is about 2 points higher than SemSeg for the multi-task baseline, and DGMLP has improved performance on all four tasks compared to baseline. In addition, our model using different backbones also achieves strong performances on other tasks. It is worth noting that the DGMLP performs best on the transformer-based backbone, which has uniformly higher metrics on all tasks than the best existing models. While our best-performing DGMLP model uses Swin-S as the backbone, using less than 58.3 parameters retains a performance of 46.66 on the SemSeg task.

Table 2. Results on the PASCAL-Context dataset. '↓': lower is better. '↑': higher is better. The table is an extended version from [4].

Model	Backbone	SemSeg	PartSeg	Sal	Normals	Bound
		(mIoU)↑	(mIoU)↑	(maxF)↑	(mErr)↓	(odsF)↑
multi-task baseline	HRNet18	51.09	57.12	83.19	14.40	69.7
multi-task baseline	Swin-T	64.74	53.25	76.88	15.86	69.0
multi-task baseline	Swin-S	68.10	56.20	80.64	16.09	70.2
ATRC [4]	HRNet18	57.89	57.33	83.77	13.99	69.74
ASPP [5]	ResNet50	62.70	59.98	83.81	14.34	71.28
BMTAS [3]	ResNet50	56.37	62.54	79.91	14.60	72.83
ATRC [4]	ResNet50	62.99	59.79	82.25	14.67	71.20
DGMLP (ours)	HRNet18	58.12	58.11	83.90	14.02	69.8
DGMLP (ours)	Swin-T	68.69	55.72	82.58	14.61	71.0
DGMLP (ours)	Swin-S	71.15	59.36	83.29	14.56	71.6

Table 3. Ablation studies and analysis on NYUD-v2 dataset using a Swin-T backbone. Spatial deformable MLP (SDM) and spatial gating MLP (SGM) are part of our model. The notation '↓': lower is better. The notation '↑': higher is better. The ✓ indicates **"using"**. The w/ means **"with"**.

Model	SDM	SGM	SemSeg(mIoU) ↑	Depth(rmse)↓	Normals(mErr) ↓	Bound(odsF)↑
Baseline			37.78	0.6322	21.09	75.6
w/SDM	✓		40.78	0.6482	21.96	75.7
w/SGM		✓	39.03	0.6459	22.42	75.7
Ours	✓	✓	42.53	0.5851	20.84	76.1

Performance Analysis on PASCAL-Context. HRNet18, Swin-T, and Swin-S are implemented as backbones. We compare DGMLP against some state-of-the-art methods in MTL in Table 2. Across all tasks evaluated, DGMLP significantly improves performance compared to a multi-task baseline. For example, our DGMLP using the Swin-S backbone achieves a 12.95% (71.15 vs. 62.99 (ATRC)) higher than the best performance in the SemSeg task. This reveals that task-relevant information can be adequately captured at a single scale, as long as the backbone can effectively extract and fuse multi-scale information.

4.2 Ablation Study

Effectiveness of Components. The comparison results are reported in Table 3. The proposed DGMLP consists of spatial deformable MLP and spatial gating MLP. To better understand the effectiveness of the components of DGMLP, a series of elaborate ablation studies were conducted in Table 3. We consider three variants as well: (i) the baseline; (ii) only using spatial deformable

Fig. 3. Visualization results. Visualization results (a) are from the NYUD-v2 dataset. Visualization results (b) come from the PASCAL-Context dataset.

MLP; (iii) only using spatial gating MLP. Using spatial deformable MLP, which allows spatial information exchange along with image feature height and width, can bring an additional 3 points (baseline (37.78) vs. SDM (40.78)) improvement in SemSeg. The spatial deformable MLP captures valuable spatial information for different tasks. We show the distribution of the spatial gating MLP of the DGMLP in Table 3. When only spatial gating is applied, it achieves about 1.25 points higher than the baseline in the SemSeg task. In the ablation experiments, the results indicate that the features are updated by each of the two components and passed to the downstream, making the features learn better. The spatial gating MLP learns a shared feature across all the tasks.

4.3 Visualization

In Fig. 3, we show the results of our DGMLP (using Swin-t as the backbone) visualization on different tasks. We sample the prediction figure results from NYUD-v2 and PASCAL-Context. It can be seen that our approach effectively focuses on the features of different tasks such as semantic segmentation, depth estimation, surface normal estimation, and boundary detection. In Fig. 3(a), we can observe that our model focuses on different tasks' features and obtains good dense prediction results. Figure 3(b) also illustrates the strong visualization results obtained on the most miniature DGMLP model. In addition, the last row of Fig. 3(b) shows nothing on the 'Human Parts' task, which shows that DGMLP can accurately recognize the human in the images.

5 Conclusion

In this paper, we propose a simple and efficient deformable and gating MLP (DGMLP) model to perform MTL dense prediction tasks. We first propose a spatial deformable MLP to capture valuable spatial information for different tasks. Then, the spatial gating MLP is present to learn the shared feature across all the tasks. Extensive experiments and visualization on the dense prediction benchmark NYUD-v2 and PASCAL-Context demonstrate the effectiveness of our proposed DGMLP method while achieving state-of-the-art performance.

References

1. Bhattacharjee, D., Zhang, T., Süsstrunk, S., Salzmann, M.: Mult: an end-to-end multitask learning transformer. In: CVPR (2022)
2. Bragman, F.J., Tanno, R., Ourselin, S., Alexander, D.C., Cardoso, J.: Stochastic filter groups for multi-task cnns: learning specialist and generalist convolution kernels. In: ICCV (2019)
3. Bruggemann, D., Kanakis, M., Georgoulis, S., Van Gool, L.: Automated search for resource-efficient branched multi-task networks. In: BMVC (2020)
4. Bruggemann, D., Kanakis, M., Obukhov, A., Georgoulis, S., Gool., L.V.: Exploring relational context for multi-task dense prediction. In: ICCV (2021)
5. Chen, L.C., Zhu, Y., Papandreou, G., Schroff, F., Adam, H.: Encoder-decoder with atrous separable convolution for semantic image segmentation. In: ECCV (2018)
6. Chen, S., Xie, E., GE, C., Chen, R., Liang, D., Luo, P.: CycleMLP: a MLP-like architecture for dense prediction. In: ICLR (2022)
7. Chen, X., Mottaghi, R., Liu, X., Fidler, S., Urtasun, R., Yuille, A.: Detect what you can: detecting and representing objects using holistic models and body parts. In: CVPR (2014)
8. Dosovitskiy, A., et al.: An image is worth 16×16 words: transformers for image recognition at scale. In: ICLR (2021)
9. Gao, Y., Ma, J., Zhao, M., Liu, W., Yuille, A.L.: Nddr-cnn: layerwise feature fusing in multi-task cnns by neural discriminative dimensionality reduction. In: CVPR (2019)
10. Lan, M., Zhang, J., He, F., Zhang, L.: Siamese network with interactive transformer for video object segmentation. In: AAAI (2022)
11. Ling, Z., et al.: Pattern-structure diffusion for multi-task learning. In: CVPR (2020)
12. Liu, H., Dai, Z., So, D., Le, Q.V.: Pay attention to mlps. In: NeurIPS (2021)
13. Liu, S., Johns, E., Davison, A.J.: End-to-end multi-task learning with attention. In: CVPR (2019)
14. Liu, Z., et al.: Swin transformer: hierarchical vision transformer using shifted windows. In: ICCV (2021)
15. Misra, I., Shrivastava, A., Gupta, A., Hebert, M.: Cross-stitch networks for multitask learning. In: CVPR (2016)
16. Ru, L., Du, B., Zhan, Y., Wu, C.: Weakly-supervised semantic segmentation with visual words learning and hybrid pooling. IJCV **130**(4), 1127–1144 (2022)

17. Silberman, N., Hoiem, D., Kohli, P., Fergus, R.: Indoor segmentation and support inference from rgbd images. In: ECCV (2012)
18. Sun, K., Xiao, B., Liu, D., Wang, J.: Deep high-resolution representation learning for human pose estimation. In: CVPR (2019)
19. Sun, X., Panda, R., Feris, R., Saenko, K.: Adashare: learning what to share for efficient deep multi-task learning. NeurIPS (2020)
20. Takahashi, N., Mitsufuji, Y.: Densely connected multi-dilated convolutional networks for dense prediction tasks. In: CVPR (2021)
21. Tang, Y., et al.: An image patch is a wave: phase-aware vision MLP. In: CVPR (2022)
22. Tolstikhin, I.O., et al.: Mlp-mixer: an all-mlp architecture for vision. arXiv (2021). https://arxiv.org/abs/2105.01601
23. Vandenhende, S., Georgoulis, S., Gansbeke, W.V., Proesmans, M., Dai, D., Gool, L.V.: Multi-task learning for dense prediction tasks: a survey. IEEE TPAMI **44**, 3641–3633 (2021)
24. Vandenhende, S., Georgoulis, S., Van Gool, L.: MTI-Net: multi-scale task interaction networks for multi-task learning. In: Vedaldi, A., Bischof, H., Brox, T., Frahm, J.-M. (eds.) ECCV 2020. LNCS, vol. 12349, pp. 527–543. Springer, Cham (2020). https://doi.org/10.1007/978-3-030-58548-8_31
25. Wang, W., et al.: Exploring sequence feature alignment for domain adaptive detection transformers. In: ACM MM (2021)
26. Wang, W., Cao, Y., Zhang, J., Tao, D.: FP-DETR: detection transformer advanced by fully pre-training. In: ICLR (2022)
27. Wang, W., et al.: Pyramid vision transformer: a versatile backbone for dense prediction without convolutions. In: ICCV (2021)
28. Wei, G., Zhang, Z., Lan, C., Lu, Y., Chen, Z.: Activemlp: an mlp-like architecture with active token mixer. arXiv (2022). https://doi.org/10.48550/arXiv.2203.06108
29. Xu, D., Ouyang, W., Wang, X., Sebe, N.: Pad-net: multi-tasks guided prediction-and-distillation network for simultaneous depth estimation and scene parsing. In: CVPR (2018)
30. Xu, Y., et al.: Multi-task learning with multi-query transformer for dense prediction. arXiv (2022). https://doi.org/10.48550/ARXIV.2205.14354
31. Xu, Y., Li, X., Li, J., Wang, C., Gao, R., Yu, Y.: SSSER: spatiotemporal sequential and social embedding rank for successive point-of-interest recommendation. IEEE Access **7**, 156804–156823 (2019)
32. Xu, Y., Wang, Z., Shang, J.S.: Paenl: personalized attraction enhanced network learning for recommendation. Neural Comput. Appl., 1–11 (2021)
33. Yang, Y., You, S., Li, H., Wang, F., Qian, C., Lin, Z.: Towards improving the consistency, efficiency, and flexibility of differentiable neural architecture search. In: CVPR (2021)
34. Yuan, H., et al.: Polyphonicformer: unified query learning for depth-aware video panoptic segmentation. In: ECCV (2022)
35. Zhang, Z., Cui, Z., Xu, C., Yan, Y., Sebe, N., Yang, J.: Pattern-affinitive propagation across depth, surface normal and semantic segmentation. In: CVPR (2019)
36. Zhu, X., Hu, H., Lin, S., Dai, J.: Deformable convnets v2: more deformable, better results. In: CVPR (2019)
37. Zhu, X., Su, W., Lu, L., Li, B., Wang, X., Dai, J.: Deformable DETR: deformable transformers for end-to-end object detection. In: ICLR (2021)

Monocular 3D Face Reconstruction with Joint 2D and 3D Constraints

Huili Cui[1], Jing Yang[1], Yu-Kun Lai[2], and Kun Li[1(✉)]

[1] College of Intelligence and Computing, Tianjin University, Tianjin 300350, China
{huilicui_1,jingyang,lik}@tju.edu.cn
[2] School of Computer Science and Informatics, Cardiff University,
Cardiff CF24 3AA, UK
LaiY4@cardiff.ac.uk

Abstract. 3D face reconstruction from a single image is a challenging problem, especially under partial occlusions and extreme poses. This is because the uncertainty of the estimated 2D landmarks will affect the quality of face reconstruction. In this paper, we propose a novel joint 2D and 3D optimization method to adaptively reconstruct 3D face shapes from a single image, which combines the depths of 3D landmarks to solve the uncertain detections of invisible landmarks. The strategy of our method involves two aspects: a coarse-to-fine pose estimation using both 2D and 3D landmarks, and an adaptive 2D and 3D re-weighting based on the refined pose parameters to recover accurate 3D faces. Experimental results on multiple datasets demonstrate that our method can generate high-quality reconstruction from a single color image and is robust for self-occlusions and large poses.

Keywords: Face reconstruction · Occlusion · Joint 2D and 3D · Coarse-to-fine · Re-weighting

1 Introduction

Human reconstruction from images, especially for faces, is an important and challenging problem, which has drawn much attention from both academia and industry [15,24] . Although existing face reconstruction methods based on multiple images have achieved promising results, it is still a tough problem for a single input image, especially under partial occlusions and extreme poses.

3D Morphable Model (3DMM) [6,14] is a popular and simple linear parametric face model. Some methods [1,32,33] achieve 3D face reconstruction from a single image using convolutional neural networks (CNN). To fit 3DMM to a facial image with self-occlusions or large poses, Zhu *et al.*[37] and Yi *et al.*[34] take a 3D solution to reconstruct the face with 3D landmarks. However, these methods ignore the effect of 2D landmarks for visible parts which are more accurate. Moreover, lack of

---

Supplementary Information The online version contains supplementary material available at https://doi.org/10.1007/978-3-031-20497-5_11.

L. Fang et al. (Eds.): CICAI 2022, LNAI 13604, pp. 129–141, 2022.
https://doi.org/10.1007/978-3-031-20497-5_11

enough 3D face datasets with ground-truth for training limits the performance of these learning-based methods. By contrast, traditional optimization-based methods [18,20,29] are more flexible to fit the 3DMM model. But these methods heavily depend on accurate 2D landmark detection, and tend to generate poor or incorrect face reconstruction for facial images with occlusions. To address the occlusion problem, Lee *et al.*[23] and Qu *et al.*[26] discard the occluded landmarks, but their methods lack constraints of complete landmarks. To fix 2D landmark correspondence errors caused by face orientation or hair occlusion, Zhu *et al.*[36] and Luo *et al.*[20] propose landmark marching methods to update silhouette vertices. However, they need to manually label 68 landmark vertices, which is laborious and time consuming. Due to the lack of depth information, these traditional methods are still hard to correctly reconstruct invisible areas, and hence difficult to deal with extreme poses, *e.g.*, 90° side faces.

Inspired by recent work on 3D landmark detection, we use the depth information of 3D landmarks together with 2D landmarks to resolve the inherent depth ambiguities of the re-projection constraint during 3D face reconstruction by joint 2D and 3D optimization. 2D landmarks give the pixel positions of facial silhouettes based on the input image, while 3D landmarks give the depth positions of the facial silhouettes. It is hard

Fig. 1. 3D face reconstruction results from single images using our method.

to decide which detected landmarks are more believable. In order to effectively combine 2D and 3D landmarks, we propose a 2D and 3D re-weighting method to adaptively adjust the weights of 2D and 3D landmarks. In addition, instead of solving pose parameters directly, we design a coarse-to-fine method for accurate face pose estimation. Our method does not need manual intervention, and is robust to extreme poses and partial occlusions. Experimental results demonstrate that our method outperforms the state-of-the-art methods on AFLW2000 [37] and MICC [4] datasets, especially for non-frontal images. Figure 1 shows some 3D face reconstruction results using our method.

Our main contributions are summarized as follows:

- **Joint 2D and 3D optimization**. We formulate the 3D face reconstruction problem in a unified joint 2D and 3D optimization framework. To our best knowledge, our method is the first optimization method using both 2D and 3D information for face reconstruction. Our method is fully automatic and robust to extreme poses and partial occlusions.
- **Coarse-to-fine pose estimation**. To obtain accurate pose parameters for face reconstruction, we propose a coarse-to-fine scheme using both 2D and 3D landmarks. We generate a coarse pose estimation by fitting the 3DMM model with the silhouettes of 2D landmarks and obtain a refined pose estimation by replacing the invisible 2D landmarks with the corresponding 3D silhouettes.

– **Adaptive 2D and 3D re-weighting.** We propose an adaptive 2D and 3D re-weighting scheme to adaptively adjust the weights of 2D and 3D landmarks according to the acquired pose estimation. Among them, 2D landmarks are sufficiently accurate for visible areas, and the depth information of 3D landmarks will improve the detection accuracy for invisible areas. For example, the weights of 2D landmarks should be increased under small poses while the weights of 3D landmarks should be increased under large poses. To achieve this, we provide two adaptive weight adjustment schemes to deal with small-pose and large-pose, respectively.

2   Related Work

Over the years, many methods solve the face reconstruction problem caused by self-occlusions or head rotations with multiple images. Although these methods achieve promising results, the requirement of multiple inputs limits their practical applications. It is more prospective and challenging to reconstruct a 3D face from a single image. In this section, we review the related work on 3D face reconstruction from a single image.

2D and 3D Face Alignment. Most of early face alignment methods can only roughly detect the 2D face landmarks, until the emergence of new techniques based on cascaded regression [9,13,37]. This kind of methods largely improves the accuracy of 2D face alignment methods and performs well on the LFPW [5] and 300-W [28] datasets. With the development of convolutional neural networks (CNNs), Sun et al.[30] propose to acquire 68 facial landmarks by a CNN cascade method. Multi-task learning and attribute classification are combined with CNN to obtain better results [35]. However, these methods are mainly effective for near-frontal faces. Some methods are proposed to solve 3D face alignment [21, 37] that works better on large poses. Bouaziz et al.[7] propose an algorithm of 2D/3D registration based on RGB-D devices. Yi et al.[10] take an image and 2D landmarks as inputs and use a 2D-to-3D network to learn the corresponding 3D landmarks, which can detect both the 2D landmarks and 3D landmarks.

Single-View 3DMM-Based Face Reconstruction. 3D Morphable Model (3DMM) is first proposed by Blanz and Vetter [6], and improved to have expression parameters by using 3D FaceWarehouse [11]. 3DMM has a wide range of applications due to its flexibility and convenience by adjusting parameters to present different face shapes and expressions. Given a single color image, optimization-based methods [19,23] estimate the 3DMM face by constraining the data similarities of facial landmarks, lighting or edges. Recently, learning-based approaches [31] have been proposed to deal with the single-image reconstruction problem. Tran et al.[33] propose a regression-based method to refine the 3DMM parameters, and Kim et al.[22] design deeper networks to obtain more discriminative results. Yi et al.[34] propose an end-to-end method including a volumetric sub-network and a parametric sub-network to reconstruct a face model, which separates the identity and expression parameters. However, lack of enough 3D face datasets with ground-truth for training limits the performance of these learning-based methods.

Landmark Updating Method. To fix the landmark fitting error caused by large poses and self-occlusions, Lee [23] and Qu et al.[26] propose to discard invisible landmarks, but these methods cannot make full use of landmark constraints. Asthana et al.[3] propose a look-up table containing 3D landmark configurations for each pose, but this method depends on pose estimation and need to build a large table in unconstrained environment. Zhu et al.[36] first propose a landmark marching method which intends to move the 3D landmarks along the surface to rebuild the correspondence of 2D silhouette automatically. Zhang et al.[20] update the silhouette landmark vertices by constructing a set of horizontal lines and choosing among them a set of vertices to represent the updated silhouette. A common disadvantage of their approaches is that they need to manually label many landmarks, which takes a lot of time and effort. Moreover, when the deflection angle becomes larger, the detected 2D landmarks of the invisible face part will be less accurate. Even if the silhouette is updated, the methods do not work well for large-pose images with a deflection angle larger than 60°.

In this paper, we propose a novel automatic 3DMM-based face reconstruction method from a single image by joint 2D and 3D optimization, which is robust to extreme poses and self-occlusions.

3   Method

It is difficult to accurately detect 2D landmarks along the face silhouette under large poses or partial occlusions, but 3D depth information of the face provides strong constraints even for invisible landmarks. Therefore, our method solves the face reconstruction problem under large poses or partial occlusions by joint 2D and 3D optimization. Figure 2 illustrates the pipeline of our method. Our method reconstructs a 3D face model from a single image based on 3DMM [6]. For an input image, we first detect the 2D and 3D positions of the 68 landmarks using an efficient detection method [10] that provides both 2D and 3D landmarks for the same image.

Traditional pose estimation methods are difficult to accurately obtain the face pose due to the errors in detection of 2D landmarks in the occluded regions. We propose a coarse-to-fine pose estimation scheme using both 2D and 3D landmarks. In the coarse step, we estimate Euler angles using the left and right silhouette landmarks respectively, and then choose the maximum value as the initial pose. In the refined step, 68 landmarks are updated by replacing the 2D landmarks of the invisible silhouette landmarks with the corresponding 3D landmarks. In order to make full use of 3D depth information and 2D position information, we propose to automatically adjust 2D and 3D weights with an adaptive re-weighting scheme. We regard the pose estimation and adaptive re-weighting as a bundle to reconstruct the 3D face geometry.

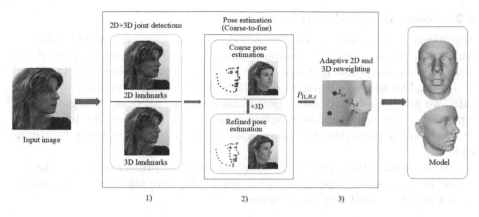

Fig. 2. The pipeline of our method: 1) 2D and 3D landmark detection; 2) Coarse-to-fine pose estimation: Coarse pose estimation includes 68 2D landmarks (the occluded silhouette landmarks are shown in green and the estimated coarse pose with mean face is shown in the input image), and the pose is refined by combining them with the estimated 3D silhouette landmarks (the occluded 3D silhouette landmarks are shown in green and the estimated refined pose with mean face is shown in the input image); 3) Adaptive 2D and 3D re-weighting: λ_{2d} and λ_{3d} are 2D and 3D weights, respectively. 2) and 3) are regarded as a bundle to achieve 3D face reconstruction. (Color figure online)

3.1 3D Morphable Model

3D Morphable Model is a 3D face statistical model, which is proposed to solve the problem of 3D face reconstruction from 2D images. In this work, we merge the Basel Face Model (BFM) [25] and the Face Warehouse [12] with non-rigid ICP [2] to construct our 3DMM. It is a linear model based on Principal Components Analysis (PCA) which describes the 3D face space as

$$M = \bar{m} + \Gamma_{sha}\alpha + \Gamma_{\exp}\beta, \tag{1}$$

where M represents a 3D face, $\bar{m}$ is the mean shape, Γ_{sha} is the principal axes corresponding to face shapes coming from BFM [25] and α is the shape parameter. $\Gamma_{\exp}$ is the principal axes corresponding to face expressions coming from Face Warehouse [12] and β is the expression parameter. The collection of pose parameters is $P_{\Pi,R,t}$, where R is a 3×3 rotation matrix constructed from rotation angles (*pitch, yaw, roll*) and t is a 3×1 translation vector. The projection matrix Π is formulated as

$$\Pi = s \begin{bmatrix} 1 & 0 & 0 \\ 0 & 1 & 0 \end{bmatrix}, \tag{2}$$

where s is the scale factor. The 2D projection of the 3D face model with weak perspective projection [8] is represented as

$$l_{2d}(\alpha, \beta) = \Pi R \left(\bar{m} + \Gamma_{sha}\alpha + \Gamma_{\exp}\beta \right) + t. \tag{3}$$

3.2   Joint 2D and 3D Optimization

Traditional face reconstruction methods depend on the detected 2D landmarks which have low accuracy for non-frontal images, especially for very large poses. In order to solve the problem of inaccurate detection of 2D silhouette landmarks in non-frontal images, we propose a joint 2D and 3D optimization method. Specifically, we propose a coarse-to-fine pose estimation method using both 2D and 3D landmarks, and then iteratively optimize them with the projected 3D vertices. In order to handle various rotation angles, we propose an adaptive reweighting method.

We solve the fitting process by joint 2D and 3D optimization and take the shape and expression prior terms into a hybrid objective function. We formulate it as a nonlinear least squares problem:

$$E_{fit}\left(\alpha, \beta, P_{\Pi,R,t}\right) = \lambda_{2d}E_{2d}\left(\alpha, \beta, P_{\Pi,R,t}\right)$$
$$+\lambda_{3d}E_{3d}\left(\alpha, \beta, P_{\Pi,R,t}\right) + E_p\left(\alpha, \beta\right), \tag{4}$$

where λ_{2d} and λ_{3d} are 2D and 3D weights, respectively. $E_{2d}\left(\alpha, \beta, P_{\Pi,R,t}\right)$ and $E_{3d}\left(\alpha, \beta, P_{\Pi,R,t}\right)$ are the alignment energies based on regressed 2D and 3D landmarks, respectively, which will be elaborated in Sect. 3.2. $E_p\left(\alpha, \beta\right)$ is a prior term of both shape and expression, which will be explained in Sect. 3.2.

We first initialize the shape parameter α and expression parameter β with zeros, and then use our coarse-to-fine pose estimation method to estimate a coarse pose and a refined pose. Based on the pose estimation, we finally solve the optimization problem to obtain shape and expression parameters iteratively. After each iteration, we get a new model with the updated shape and expression parameters, and then re-estimate pose parameters. This process iterates four times in our experiments, which is sufficient to converge in practice.

Coarse Pose Estimation. We estimate a coarse pose P_c by computing Euler angles using the 2D landmarks of the left or right silhouettes and the rest 51 landmarks respectively. There are 17 detected 2D face silhouette landmarks, which are divided into three parts according to the locations: left (1 to 9), middle (10), and right (11 to 17). If the Euler angle calculated by the left silhouette P_l is greater than that by the right silhouette P_r, it means that the head orientation is to the left, and vice versa. We regard the max value $P_c = P_l$ or $P_c = P_r$ as the final face pose direction on the Y axis.

Refined Pose Estimation. To resolve the inevitable depth ambiguities of 2D re-projection constraint, we add 3D constraint to improve the accuracy of pose estimation. First, we project the mean face model onto the image plane to accurately capture the invisible 2D silhouette landmarks. Then, we replace the invisible 2D silhouette landmarks with the corresponding estimated 3D landmarks by the method [10]. Finally, we update the 68 landmarks and fit the parametric face model with our input image to get the refined pose parameters P_{ref}. We regard the refined pose estimation as the initial value for the optimization, and in the next iteration, we will update pose parameters as $P_{\Pi,R,t}$.

2D and 3D Fitting with Adaptive Re-weighting. For each input image, we detect the 2D and 3D landmarks $\{L_{2d,i} \in \mathbb{R}^2\}_{1 \leq i \leq 68}$ and $\{L_{3d,i} \in \mathbb{R}^3\}_{1 \leq i \leq 68}$ using an efficient detection method [10]. The 2D fitting constraint E_{2d} is defined as

$$E_{2d}\left(\alpha, \beta, P_{\Pi,R,t}\right) = \sum_{i=1}^{68} \|l_{2d,i}(\alpha, \beta) - L_{2d,i}\|_2^2, \tag{5}$$

where $l_{2d,i}(\alpha, \beta)$ is the 2D projection coordinates of the i-th vertex of the 3D face model, as defined in Sect. 3.1. $L_{2d,i}$ is the i-th detected 2D landmark. We solve the 3DMM parameters by minimizing the Euclidean distances between the detected landmarks and the 2D projections of 3D points. We further incorporate the 3D depth information into the optimization to solve the ambiguities of invisible face area, by proposing a 3D alignment term as follows:

$$E_{3d}\left(\alpha, \beta, P_{\Pi,R,t}\right) = \sum_{i=1}^{68} \|l_{3d,i}(\alpha, \beta) - (L_{3d,i} + t')\|_2^2, \tag{6}$$

where $l_{3d,i}(\alpha, \beta)$ is the 3D position of the i-th face landmark, and $L_{3d,i}$ is the i-th detected 3D landmark. $t' \in \mathbb{R}^3$ is an auxiliary variable that transforms the $L_{3d,i}$ to the global coordinate system. The pose parameters and the optimization method are the same as E_{2d}. In order to effectively combine the 2D and 3D landmarks, we propose an adaptive weighting method:

$$W_\lambda = \begin{cases} 1 & \frac{2|yaw|}{\pi} \geq \varepsilon \\ 0 & \text{otherwise,} \end{cases} \tag{7}$$

where ε is set to 0.5, which means that we regard a 45° angle as the boundary of head rotation for large pose and small pose. $W_\lambda = 1$ means large pose, and in that case, the 3D weight and the 2D weight are calculated as

$$\lambda_{3d} = \frac{2|yaw|}{\pi}, \lambda_{2d} = \left(1 - \frac{2|yaw|}{\pi}\right) \cdot w, \tag{8}$$

where w is set to 0.5. Otherwise, if $W_\lambda = 0$, which means that the pose angle is less than 45°, the 3D weight and the 2D weight are calculated as

$$\lambda_{3d} = \frac{2|yaw|}{\pi} \cdot w, \lambda_{2d} = 1 - \frac{2|yaw|}{\pi}. \tag{9}$$

The pose estimation and adaptive re-weighting are regarded as a bundle to achieve 3D face reconstruction.

Shape and Expression Priors. We expect that each of the shape and expression parameters follows a normal distribution with zero mean and unit variance. The shape and expression prior terms are defined as

$$E_p\left(\alpha, \beta\right) = \lambda_\alpha E_{prior}\left(\alpha\right) + \lambda_\beta E_{prior}\left(\beta\right), \tag{10}$$

where $E_{prior}(\alpha)$ and $E_{prior}(\beta)$ are shape and expression priors, respectively. λ_α and λ_β are their corresponding weights. The shape prior is calculated as

$$E_{prior}(\alpha) = (\lambda_{2d} + \lambda_{3d}) \sum_{i=1}^{N_\alpha} \left(\frac{\alpha_i}{\sqrt{\delta_{\alpha_i}}} \right)^2, \tag{11}$$

where N_α is the number of shape parameters, α_i is the i-th shape principal component, and δ_{α_i} is the eigenvalue corresponding to the principal component. The expression prior is similarly defined as

$$E_{prior}(\beta) = (\lambda_{2d} + \lambda_{3d}) \sum_{i=1}^{N_\beta} \left(\frac{\beta_i}{\sqrt{\delta_{\beta_i}}} \right)^2. \tag{12}$$

4   Experimental Results

In this section, we first introduce the datasets and metrics in Sect. 4.1. Then, we perform an ablation study to analyze the effects of different components of our approach in Sect. 4.2. Finally, we compare our method with several state-of-the-art methods quantitatively and qualitatively in Sect. 4.3. More results can be found in the supplementary material.

4.1   Datasets and Metrics

We conduct our qualitative experiments on AFLW2000 [37] dataset, which is a large-scale face database including multiple poses and perspectives. The MICC dataset [4] contains 53 videos with various resolutions, conditions and zoom levels for each subject. In order to demonstrate the effectiveness for partial occlusions and extreme poses, in ablation study, we select 106 non-frontal images with left or right view direction (53 images per case) in the Indoor-Cooperative videos for each subject to demonstrate the effectiveness of our each component quantitatively and qualitatively. During the comparison, the reconstructed face is aligned with its corresponding ground-truth model using the Iterative Closest Point (ICP) method [27], and we calculate the reconstruction errors for the face part by cropping the model at a radius of 85 mm around the tip of nose. 3D Root Mean Square Error (3DRMSE) is used to measure the model quality:

$$\sqrt{\sum_i (\mathbf{X} - \mathbf{X}^*)^2 / N}, \tag{13}$$

where $\mathbf{X}$ is the reconstructed face (after cropping), $\mathbf{X}^*$ is the ground truth, and N is the number of vertices of the 3D model cropped from the reconstructed face.

4.2   Ablation Study

To prove the performance improvement of our method for partial occlusions and extreme poses, we select 106 non-frontal images with left or right view direction (53 images per case) for each subject from the MICC dataset [4] as our test dataset in this section. The visual results of different variants are shown in Fig. 3. The reconstruction errors are color-coded on the reconstructed model for visual inspection, and the average error is given below each case. It can be seen that it is difficult to recover an accurate model with only 2D landmarks due to lack of the depth information. Combining 3D landmarks with the corresponding 2D landmarks can largely improve the reconstruction accuracy. Adaptive re-weighting further improves the performance. The most satisfactory result is achieved by adding the coarse-to-fine pose estimation method.

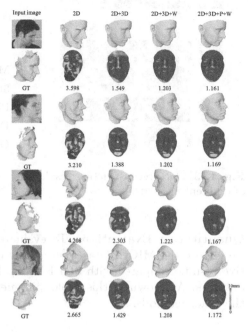

Fig. 3. Qualitative results on the MICC dataset [4]. 2D: 2D fitting method, 2D+3D: joint 2D and 3D fitting method, W: adaptive re-weighting, P: pose refinement.

4.3   Comparison

Qualitative Evaluation. In order to prove the reliability of our method, we compare our method with four state-of-the-art face reconstruction approaches, 3DDFA [37], PRN [17], MMFace [34] and DECA [16], on the AFLW2000 [37], 300VW-3D [10] and MICC [4] datasets. Because MMface [34] does not publish the code, we only make a qualitative comparison with this method by using the images provided in their paper. Figure 4 illustrates the qualitative evaluation results compared with these methods. In order to show the reconstruction results consistent with MMface [34], we reduce the transparency of the model to overlay on the image, which can better observe the correctness of the eyes, mouth, nose, and face shape of the model compared with the input image. It can be seen that 3DDFA [37] can reconstruct fine models but the results are all similar to the mean face and lack the consistency with the image. PRN [17] can estimate accurate face orientation but fails to reconstruct fine facial geometry. MMFace [34] cannot recover the contour well, *e.g.*, the third image. DECA [16] has the same problems as MMFace [34], *e.g.*, the first image. Our method estimates better poses and reconstructs more accurate face models, benefitting from our coarse-to-fine pose estimation and joint 2D and 3D optimization with adaptive re-weighting.

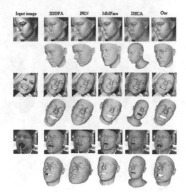

Fig. 4. 3D face reconstruction results of different methods.

Table 1. Comparison of 3D face reconstruction on MICC dataset [4].

Method	Frontal	Non-frontal
3DDFA [37]	2.244	2.379
PRN [17]	2.086	1.934
DECA [16]	2.996	3.017
Ours	**1.819**	**1.770**

Quantitative Evaluation. To evaluate the performance on different cases, we choose the MICC dataset [4] as our test datasets. Table 1 shows quantitative results compared with 3DDFA [37], PRN [17] and DECA [16] on the test datasets. As shown in this table, our method achieves smaller 3DRMSE than the other methods.

5   Conclusion and Discussion

In this paper, we propose a novel method to solve the challenges of face reconstruction from a single image under partial occlusions and large poses. First, we propose a coarse-to-fine pose estimation method, which divides pose estimation into two steps to improve the accuracy. Second, we propose a novel joint 2D and 3D optimization method with adaptive re-

Fig. 5. Examples of failure cases.

weighting. Our pose estimation and the 2D and 3D weight adaptation are considered as a bundle, and solved by a joint optimization algorithm. Experimental results on public datasets demonstrate that our method can reconstruct more accurate face geometry consistent with the images even for occlusions or extreme poses, compared with the state-of-the-art methods.

Figure 5 shows some failure examples using our method due to wrong estimation of 2D and 3D landmarks for occlusion cases. In the future work, we will try to improve the accuracy of landmark detection with the help of face reconstruction iteratively. Also, we will try to combine our optimization method with learning-based prior or representation.

Acknowledgements. This work was supported in part by the National Natural Science Foundation of China (62171317 and 62122058).

References

1. Amberg, B., Knothe, R., Vetter, T.: Expression invariant 3D face recognition with a morphable model. In: Proceedings of IEEE International Conference on Automatic Face and Gesture Recognition, pp. 1–6. IEEE (2008)
2. Amberg, B., Romdhani, S., Vetter, T.: Optimal step nonrigid ICP algorithms for surface registration. In: Proceedings of IEEE Conference on Computer Vision and Pattern Recognition, pp. 1–8. IEEE (2007)
3. Asthana, A., Zafeiriou, S., Cheng, S., Pantic, M.: Robust discriminative response map fitting with constrained local models. In: Proceedings of IEEE Conference on Computer Vision and Pattern Recognition, pp. 3444–3451 (2013)
4. Bagdanov, A.D., Del Bimbo, A., Masi, I.: Florence faces: a dataset supporting 2D/3D face recognition. In: Proceedings of International Symposium on Communications, Control and Signal Processing, pp. 1–6. IEEE (2012)
5. Belhumeur, P.N., Jacobs, D.W., Kriegman, D.J., Kumar, N.: Localizing parts of faces using a consensus of exemplars. IEEE Trans. Pattern Anal. Mach. Intell. **35**(12), 2930–2940 (2013)
6. Blanz, V., Vetter, T.: A morphable model for the synthesis of 3D faces. In: Proceedings of Computer Graphics and Interactive Techniques, pp. 187–194 (1999)
7. Bouaziz, S., Tagliasacchi, A., Pauly, M.: Dynamic 2D/3D registration. In: Eurographics (Tutorials), p. 7 (2014)
8. Bruckstein, A.M., Holt, R.J., Huang, T.S., Netravali, A.N.: Optimum fiducials under weak perspective projection. Int. J. Comput. Vision **35**(3), 223–244 (1999)
9. Bulat, A., Tzimiropoulos, G.: Convolutional aggregation of local evidence for large pose face alignment. In: Proceedings of British Machine Vision Conference (2016)
10. Bulat, A., Tzimiropoulos, G.: How far are we from solving the 2D & 3D face alignment problem?(and a dataset of 230,000 3D facial landmarks). In: Proceedings of IEEE International Conference on Computer Vision, pp. 1021–1030 (2017)
11. Cao, C., Weng, Y., Zhou, S., Tong, Y., Zhou, K.: Facewarehouse: a 3D facial expression database for visual computing. IEEE Trans. Visualization Comput. Graph. **20**(3), 413–425 (2013)
12. Cao, C., Weng, Y., Zhou, S., Tong, Y., Zhou, K.: Facewarehouse: a 3D facial expression database for visual computing. IEEE Trans. Visualization Comput. Graph. **20**(3), 413–425 (2014)
13. Cao, X., Wei, Y., Wen, F., Sun, J.: Face alignment by explicit shape regression. Int. J. Comput. Vision **107**(2), 177–190 (2014)
14. Egger, B., et al.: 3D morphable face models-past, present and future. ACM Trans. Graph. (TOG) (2019)
15. Fang, Y., Li, Y., Tu, X., Tan, T., Wang, X.: Face completion with hybrid dilated convolution. Signal Process. Image Commun. **80**, 115664 (2020)
16. Feng, Y., Feng, H., Black, M.J., Bolkart, T.: Learning an animatable detailed 3D face model from in-the-wild images, vol. 40. ACM (2021)
17. Feng, Y., Wu, F., Shao, X., Wang, Y., Zhou, X.: Joint 3D face reconstruction and dense alignment with position map regression network. In: Proceedings of European Conference on Computer Vision, pp. 534–551 (2018)

18. Garrido, P., Zollhöfer, M., Dan, C., Valgaerts, L., Varanasi, K., Pérez, P., Theobalt, C.: Reconstruction of personalized 3D face rigs from monocular video. ACM Trans. Graph. **35**(3), 1–15 (2016)
19. Huber, P., Hu, G., Tena, R., Mortazavian, P., Kittler, J.: A multiresolution 3D morphable face model and fitting framework. In: Proceedings of Computer Vision, Imaging and Computer Graphics Theory and Applications (2016)
20. Jiang, L., Zhang, J., Deng, B., Li, H., Liu, L.: 3D face reconstruction with geometry details from a single image. IEEE Trans. Image Process. **27**(10), 4756–4770 (2018)
21. Jourabloo, A., Liu, X.: Large-pose face alignment via CNN-based dense 3D model fitting. In: Proceedings of IEEE Conference on Computer Vision and Pattern Recognition (2016)
22. Kim, H., Zollhöfer, M., Tewari, A., Thies, J., Richardt, C., Theobalt, C.: Inverse-facenet: deep monocular inverse face rendering. In: Proceedings of IEEE Conference on Computer Vision and Pattern Recognition (2018)
23. Lee, Y.J.: Single view-based 3D face reconstruction robust to self-occlusion. Eurasip J. Adv. Signal Process. **2012**(1), 176 (2012)
24. Liang, Y., Zhang, Y., Zeng, X.X.: Pose-invariant 3D face recognition using half face. Signal Process. Image Commun. **57**, 84–90 (2017)
25. Paysan, P., Knothe, R., Amberg, B., Romdhani, S., Vetter, T.: A 3D face model for pose and illumination invariant face recognition. In: Proceedings of IEEE International Conference on Advanced Video and Signal Based Surveillance, pp. 296–301. IEEE (2009)
26. Qu, C., Monari, E., Schuchert, T., Beyerer, J.: Fast, robust and automatic 3D face model reconstruction from videos. In: Proceedings of Advanced Video and Signal Based Surveillance, pp. 113–118. IEEE (2014)
27. Rusinkiewicz, S., Levoy, M.: Efficient variants of the icp algorithm. In: Proceedings of Conference on 3-D Digital Imaging and Modeling, pp. 145–152. IEEE (2001)
28. Sagonas, C., Tzimiropoulos, G., Zafeiriou, S., Pantic, M.: A semi-automatic methodology for facial landmark annotation. In: Proceedings of IEEE Conference on Computer Vision and Pattern Recognition, pp. 896–903 (2013)
29. Saito, S., Li, T., Li, H.: Real-time facial segmentation and performance capture from RGB input. In: Leibe, B., Matas, J., Sebe, N., Welling, M. (eds.) ECCV 2016. LNCS, vol. 9912, pp. 244–261. Springer, Cham (2016). https://doi.org/10.1007/978-3-319-46484-8_15
30. Sun, Y., Wang, X., Tang, X.: Deep convolutional network cascade for facial point detection. In: Proceedings of IEEE Conference on Computer Vision and Pattern Recognition, pp. 3476–3483 (2013)
31. Thies, J., Zollhöfer, M., Stamminger, M., Theobalt, C., Nießner, M.: Demo of face2face: real-time face capture and reenactment of rgb videos. In: Proceedings of SIGGRAPH 2016, pp. 1–2 (2016)
32. Tran, L., Liu, X.: Nonlinear 3D face morphable model. In: Proceedings of IEEE Conference on Computer Vision and Pattern Recognition, pp. 7346–7355 (2018)
33. Tuan Tran, A., Hassner, T., Masi, I., Medioni, G.: Regressing robust and discriminative 3D morphable models with a very deep neural network. In: Proceedings of IEEE Conference on Computer Vision and Pattern Recognition, pp. 5163–5172 (2016)
34. Yi, H., et al.: MMFace: a multi-metric regression network for unconstrained face reconstruction. In: Proceedings of IEEE Conference on Computer Vision and Pattern Recognition, pp. 7663–7672 (2019)

35. Zhang, Z., Luo, P., Loy, C.C., Tang, X.: Facial landmark detection by deep multi-task learning. In: Fleet, D., Pajdla, T., Schiele, B., Tuytelaars, T. (eds.) ECCV 2014. LNCS, vol. 8694, pp. 94–108. Springer, Cham (2014). https://doi.org/10.1007/978-3-319-10599-4_7
36. Zhu, X., Lei, Z., Yan, J., Yi, D., Li, S.Z.: High-fidelity pose and expression normalization for face recognition in the wild. In: Proceedings of IEEE Conference on Computer Vision and Pattern Recognition, pp. 787–796 (2015)
37. Zhu, X., Zhen, L., Liu, X., Shi, H., Li, S.Z.: Face alignment across large poses: a 3D solution. In: Proceedings of IEEE Conference on Computer Vision and Pattern Recognition (2016)

Scene Text Recognition with Single-Point Decoding Network

Lei Chen⬤, Haibo Qin⬤, Shi-Xue Zhang⬤, Chun Yang$^{(\boxtimes)}$⬤, and Xucheng Yin⬤

University of Science and Technology Beijing, Beijing, China
{chunyang,xuchengyin}@ustb.edu.cn

Abstract. In recent years, attention-based scene text recognition methods have been very popular and attracted the interest of many researchers. Attention-based methods can adaptively focus attention on a small area or even single point during decoding, in which the attention matrix is nearly one-hot distribution. Furthermore, the whole feature maps will be weighted and summed by all attention matrices during inference, causing huge redundant computations. In this paper, we propose an efficient attention-free Single-Point Decoding Network (dubbed SPDN) for scene text recognition, which can replace the traditional attention-based decoding network. Specifically, we propose Single-Point Sampling Module (SPSM) to efficiently sample one key point on the feature map for decoding one character. In this way, our method can not only precisely locate the key point of each character but also remove redundant computations. Based on SPSM, we design an efficient and novel single-point decoding network to replace the attention-based decoding network. Extensive experiments on publicly available benchmarks verify that our SPDN can greatly improve decoding efficiency without sacrificing performance.

Keywords: Single-point · Attention · Scene text recognition

1 Introduction

Scene text widely appears on streets, billboards, and product packaging, which contains abundant valuable information. Recently, scene text recognition has drawn much attention from researchers and practitioners, because it can be used in various applications, such as image search, intelligent inspection, and visual question answering. Although optical character recognition in scanned documents is well-developed, scene text recognition is still a challenging task due to complexity of background, diversity, variability of text, irregular arrangement, lighting and occlusion.

The development of scene text recognition can be divided into three periods. In the first period, the text recognition methods are mainly based on character segmentation [28], handcrafted features [19], or automatic features [10].

L. Fang et al. (Eds.): CICAI 2022, LNAI 13604, pp. 142–153, 2022.
https://doi.org/10.1007/978-3-031-20497-5_12

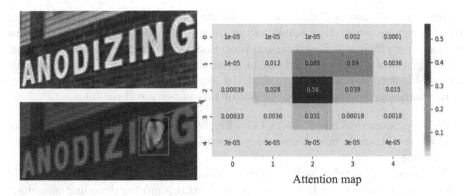

Attention map

Fig. 1. Demonstration of the attention map when decoding the eighth character "N". The weights of the attention map just focus on a very small area or even one point.

However, the performance of character segmentation suffers from various factors in natural scenes, such as complex background, various text styles, and irregular arrangement. In the second period, the connectionist temporal classification (CTC) based methods [24] regard text recognition as sequence recognition and use the CTC algorithm [5] to predict symbols. However, CTC-based methods still have some limitations. One problem is that the computational cost of long text is very huge due to the complexity of the underlying implementation of the CTC algorithm. The other is that it is not easy for CTC-based methods to solve the two-dimensional text recognition problems. In the third period, benefiting from attention mechanism [1], attention-based methods have been widely popularized and achieved excellent performance.

Attention mechanism has been applied in various tasks benefiting from its excellent performance in sequence model, which can model the relationship between any two objects without considering their distance in the input or output sequences [1,13]. However, there are still some intrinsic defects in existing attention-based methods. In IFA [30], Wang *et al.* have mathematically proved that the attention map nearly tends to a one-hot distribution in the attention mechanism. As shown in Fig. 1, we can find that the weights of the attention map just focus on a very small area or even one point, which are much larger than the weights of the unfocused area. Obviously, the acquisition of attention maps will bring unnecessary computational cost and storage cost.

To address the above problems, in this paper, we propose an innovative and efficient **Single-Point Decoding Network** for scene text recognition, named **SPDN**, which adopts an efficient decoding network with a single point to perform decoding instead of a complex decoding network based on attention from traditional scene text recognition methods. Specifically, we proposed a **Single-Point Sampling Module (SPSM)**, which can directly locate and sample one key point on the feature map for decoding one character. A position constraint loss, which is based on the priori information that the difference in character width is small, is used to improve the accuracy of sampling point positions.

In this way, our method can not only locate the key point of each character but also remove redundant computation during decoding and greatly improve the decoding efficiency. Based on the proposed SPSM, we design a single-point decoding network, which can greatly improve the decoding efficiency and achieve comparable decoding accuracy against the attention-based decoding network.

In summary, the main contributions of this paper are three-fold:

1) We propose a novel Single-Point Decoding Network for scene text recognition, which adopts an efficient decoding network with a single point to perform decoding.
2) We propose a Single-Point Sampling Module (SPSM), which can directly locate and sample one key point on the feature map for decoding one character.
3) Extensive experiments on public benchmarks demonstrate that our method can not only improve decoding efficiency but also achieve promising performance.

2   Related Work

Deep learning technology is widely used in many fields [7,33–38]. As a hot topic, scene text recognition is mainly divided into segmentation-based methods and sequence-based methods, and the current mainstream is the latter. The sequence-based methods predict the entire text directly from the original image without processing a single character. In sequence-based methods, the encoder-decoder framework is adopted widely. According to the structure of decoders, the sequence-based methods can be roughly divided into two categories: Connectionist Temporal Classification based (CTC-based) methods and Attention-based methods.

CTC-based methods [24] adopt CTC loss to train the model without any alignment between the input sequence and the output sequence. Methods of this type usually adopt convolutional neural network (CNN) to extract visual features and employ recurrent neural network (RNN) to model the contextual information. However, CTC has a large amount of computation on the long text and is difficult to be applied to two-dimensional prediction.

Attention-based methods [2,14] employ attention mechanism to learn the mapping between sequence features and target text sequence, which has achieved great success in text recognition. Lee *et al.* [14] used recursive CNN to obtain long contextual information, and adopted an attention-based decoder to generate target sequence. To solve the problem of irregular text recognition, Shi *et al.* [26] proposed a spatial transformation network (STN) [9] to rectify the irregular text into horizontal text, and then recognized the optical character sequences in them by an attention-based recognition network. Lee *et al.* [15] proposed the self-attention mechanism to describe the 2D spatial dependence of characters for recognizing irregular text. However, the accuracy of these methods based on the inherent decoding mechanism with attention suffers from attention drift. To solve this problem, Cheng *et al.* [2] proposed Focus Attention Network (FAN), consisting of an attention network (AN) and a focusing network (FN), in which FN is used to adjust attention by evaluating whether AN can accurately focus on the target area. Despite their popularity and excellent performance, attention-based methods still suffer from redundant computations. In this paper, we propose a single-point decoding network to reduce computation while maintaining performance.

3   Method

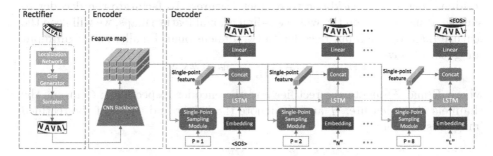

Fig. 2. The overall framework of our SPDN. The pipeline of our method includes three components: a rectifier for rectifying irregular text, an encoder for extracting visual features from the rectified images, and a single-point decoder for decoding recurrently.

As shown in Fig. 2, The SPDN is composed of three parts, a rectifier for rectifying irregular text, an encoder for extracting visual features from the rectified images, and a single-point decoder for decoding recurrently and generating the final output. The rectifier consists of the localization network, the grid generator, and the sampler. After the input image is rectified by the rectification network, the encoder extracts the feature from the rectified image. Then the decoder uses LSTM to recurrently decode according to the feature. In the decoder, a single-point sampling module is designed to sample the feature of a single point on the feature map based on the priori knowledge.

3.1   Rectifier

Due to the superior performance of Thin Plate Spline (TPS) [31] in processing curved and perspective text, we use the STN with TPS as the framework of the rectification network. The rectification network, which is generally similar to the STN of ASTER [26], aims to adaptively rectify irregular text from the input image and convert it into a new image.

3.2   Encoder

In main text recognition methods [25, 26], the text recognition is regarded as the task of sequence recognition, where the visual features will be converted into sequence features. However, some important information will be lost when the encoder transforms two-dimensional visual features into one-dimensional sequence features. To solve this problem, our encoder extracts the two-dimensional features and directly feeds the two-dimensional features into the decoder. The single-point sample module in our decoder can enhance the encoder's capacity to extract discriminative features. Our decoder only uses the single point in the feature map to decode one character, which will force the feature corresponding to each character must be sufficiently concentrated at a single point.

As shown in Fig. 2, our encoder uses a stack of convolutional layers with residual connects as backbone to extract features. To facilitate the decoder to sample a single point on the wide two-dimensional feature maps, we will keep the feature maps of the input decoder to two-dimensional. Finally, for origin input image x, we have:

$$F = \mathcal{F}(\mathcal{R}(x)), F \in \mathbb{R}^{C \times \frac{H}{8} \times \frac{W}{8}}, \tag{1}$$

where $\mathcal{R}$ and $\mathcal{F}$ denote the rectifier and the encoder respectively; C means the channels of the feature; H and W denote the height and width of the rectified image respectively.

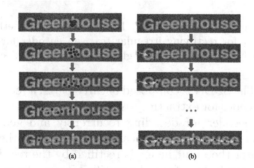

Fig. 3. (a) Parallel sampling strategy. (b) Serial sampling strategy.

3.3 Decoder

As shown in Fig. 2, our singe-point decoding network adopts a recurrent structure with LSTM as the decoding unit and a single-point sampling module as the core role. The LSTM unit takes the hidden state at the previous moment and the embedding of the last output character as input, and generates output. As shown in Fig. 3, We design two strategies for sampling the single-point feature. The parallel sampling strategy generates T points initially, in which each point corresponds to a symbol. These points rely on weak constraints to learn to align the symbols, such as position embedding. The serial sampling strategy generates sampling points step by step under distance loss. From the ablation experiments in Sect. 4.4, we verify that the serial sampling strategy has higher performance, thus we adopt the serial sampling strategy as our sampling method.

Single-Point Mechanism. In this subsection, we will introduce the general attention mechanism and theoretically analyze its essence and elaborate on the principle of our single-point mechanism.

Usually, an attention sequence-to-sequence model is a unidirectional recurrent network which iteratively works T steps to produce T symbols including all characters in the dictionary and an end-of-sequence symbol (EOS), denoted by $(\boldsymbol{y_1}, \boldsymbol{y_1}, ..., \boldsymbol{y_T})$. At step t, we first calculate the attention weight map through the softmax function, as shown in the following two formulas:

$$e_{t,i} = \mathbf{W}_e \tanh(\mathbf{W}_s \mathbf{s}_{t-1} + \mathbf{W}_h \mathbf{h}_i + b), \tag{2}$$

$$\alpha_{t,i} = \frac{\exp(e_{t,i})}{\sum_{j=1}^{T} \exp(e_{t,j})}, \tag{3}$$

where $\mathbf{W}_e, \mathbf{W}_s, \mathbf{W}_h$ are trainable weights. $\mathbf{s}_{t-1}$ is the hidden state in the LSTM decoder at step t-1 and $\mathbf{h}_i$ is the i_{th} vector of the encoder output $\mathbf{H}$. Then the decoder takes the attention weight map as the coefficients to calculate the context vector:

$$\mathbf{c}_t = \sum_{i=1}^{T} \alpha_{t,i} \mathbf{h}_i. \tag{4}$$

The context vector is fed into the recurrent cell of the decoder to generate an output vector and a new hidden state:

$$\mathbf{x}_t, \mathbf{s}_t = LSTM(\mathbf{s}_{t-1}, concat(\mathbf{c}_t, emb(y_{t-1}))), \tag{5}$$

where y_{t-1} is the $t-1$ step output symbol and $concat(\mathbf{c}_t, emb(y_{t-1}))$ is the concatenation of c_t and the embedding of y_{t-1}. At last, $\mathbf{x}_t$ is taken to the last classifier $\mathbb{C}$ for predicting the t step symbol:

$$y_t = \mathbb{C}(\mathbf{x}_t) = \mathbf{W}_o \mathbf{x}_t + b_o. \tag{6}$$

According to the formulas above, we simplify the expression of y_t to:

$$y_t = \mathbb{C}(RNN(\sum_{i=1}^{T} \alpha_{t,i} \mathbf{h}_i)) = \mathbf{W} \sum_{i=1}^{T} \alpha_{t,i} \mathbf{h}_i, \tag{7}$$

where $\mathbf{W}$ is the learnable weights. Since the attention map is nearly one-hot distribution, we have:

$$y_t = \mathbf{W} \sum_{i=1}^{T} \alpha_{t,i} \mathbf{h}_i \approx \mathbf{W} \alpha_{t,i'} \mathbf{h}_{i'} \approx \mathbf{W} \mathbf{h}_{i'}, \tag{8}$$

where $i' = argmax(\alpha_{t,i})$, representing the attention center at t step. Similarly, on the two-dimensional feature, we have the following expression:

$$y_t = \mathbf{W} \sum_{i=1}^{h} \sum_{j=1}^{w} \alpha_{t,i,j} \mathbf{F}_{i,j} \approx \mathbf{W} \alpha_{t,i',j'} \mathbf{F}_{i',j'} \approx \mathbf{W} \mathbf{F}_{i',j'}, \qquad (9)$$

where $\mathbf{F}$ denotes the two-dimensional feature map, $i', j' = argmax(\alpha_{t,i,j})$, representing the attention center on the two-dimensional feature map at t step.

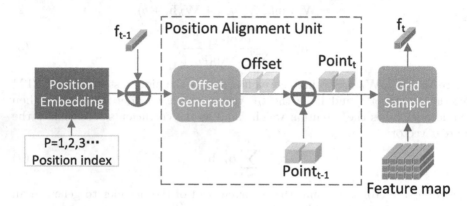

Fig. 4. The illustration of the single-point sampling module.

Single-Point Sampling Module. As shown in Fig. 2, the single-point sampling module plays an important role in the decoder. The sampling module determines whether the single character feature of the current step can be accurately collected, which will affect the performance of the decoder.

The structure of the single-point sampling module is shown in Fig. 4. The single-point sampling module is composed of a position embedding layer, a position alignment unit (PAU), and a grid sampler. The character position index will be encoded by the position embedding layer. The embedding vector of the position index will be concatenated with the single-point feature of the previous moment into the PAU. The PAU contains an offset generator for generating the offset of the current sampling point from the previous sampling point. The offset generator consists of some linear layers.

3.4   Loss Function

In order to sample a single point more accurately, we calculate the L_1 loss between the current sampling point and the previous sampling point. The final objective function of the proposed method can be formulated as:

$$\mathcal{L} = \mathcal{L}_{rec} + \lambda \mathcal{L}_{dist}, \qquad (10)$$

where $\mathcal{L}_{rec}$ is the cross entropy loss between predicted symbols and groundtruth, $\mathcal{L}_{dist}$ is the L_1 loss between two adjacent sample points, and λ is the balanced factor. Empirically, we set λ to 1.

4 Experiments

4.1 Datasets

Our SPDN is trained on two publicly available synthetic datasets (Synth90K [8] and SynthText [6]) without finetuning on other datasets. We evaluate the recognition performance on six standard benchmarks, including three regular text datasets, e.g., ICDAR 2015 (IC15) [11], Street View Text (SVT) [27], ICDAR 2013 (IC13) [12], and three irregular text datasets, e.g., ICDAR 2015 (IC15) [11], Street View Text Perspective (SVTP) [20], and CUTE80 (CUTE) [22].

4.2 Implementation Details

We adopt ADADELTA as the optimizer with a batch size of 100 to minimize the objective function. The initial learning rate is set to 1, then is adjusted to 0.1 and 0.01 at the end of the 5th and 7th epochs. Our experiments are mainly carried out on 4 NVIDIA GeForce GTX 1080Ti GPUs with 11 GB memory.

Table 1. Results of our SPDN and SOTA methods. The second group of rows in the table denotes the comparison of our SPDN and ASTER. Numbers in bold represent best performance.

Methods	IIT5K	SVT	IC13	IC15	SVTP	CUTE	FLOPs (G)	Speed (ms/image)
CRNN [24]	81.2	82.7	89.6	–	–	–	–	–
RARE [25]	81.9	81.9	88.6	–	71.8	59.2	–	–
R²AM [14]	78.4	80.7	90.0	–	–	–	–	–
AON [3]	87.0	82.8	–	68.2	73.0	76.8	–	–
NRTR [23]	90.1	91.5	95.8	–	–	–	29.50	10.52
SAR [16]	91.5	84.5	91.0	69.2	76.4	83.3	32.15	3.43
CA-FCN [17]	91.9	86.4	91.5	–	–	79.9	–	–
DAN [29]	93.3	88.4	94.2	71.8	76.8	80.6	3.77	1.15
RobustScanner [32]	95.3	88.1	94.8	77.1	79.5	**90.3**	15.27	2.38
SEED [21]	93.8	89.6	92.8	80.0	81.4	83.6	1.44	1.50
SATRN [15]	92.8	91.3	94.1	79.0	86.5	87.8	38.63	10.22
MASTER [18]	95.0	90.6	95.3	79.4	84.5	87.5	14.87	7.91
ABINet [4]	**96.3**	**93.0**	**97.0**	**85.0**	**88.5**	89.2	5.93	2.13
ASTER [26]	93.4	89.5	91.8	76.1	78.5	79.5	1.11	1.07
SPDN (ours)	94.1	89.9	91.7	77.9	79.8	81.6	**1.04**	**0.65**

4.3   Comparisons with State-of-the-Arts

We compare our method with the state-of-the-art (SOTA) methods on 6 benchmarks in Table 1. The second group of rows in the table denotes the comparison of our SPDN and ASTER. Our baseline model is based on ASTER. The encoder of our SPDN is similar to the encoder of ASTER. The decoder of our method is shown in Fig. 2, which contains a single-point sampling module differently. Compared with ASTER, our SPDN not only surpasses it in performance, but also have faster speed. SPDN has an improvement of 0.7%, 0.4%, 1.8%, 1.3%, and 1.1% on IIIT5K, SVT, IC15, SVTP, and CUTE respectively, which shows that our model has a significant improvement especially on irregular datasets. There is a gap between our method and the recent SOTA methods on performance, because our method is based on a relatively lightweight backbone and only uses LSTM for semantic modeling, while the recent SOTA methods mostly adopt heavy backbone networks like ResNet with FPN, and strong semantic modeling methods such as BCN language model. However, it is worth noting that compared to all recent sota method, our model has a significant advantage in speed. Specially, our method is nearly two times faster than DAN and 16 times faster than NRTR. Notably, our SPDN is efficient and can replace traditional attention-based decoding network to greatly improve the decoding efficiency.

4.4   Ablation Study

Single-point Sampling Strategy. We conduct experiments to explore the impact of two sampling strategies on performance. The performance comparison of the two sampling strategies is listed in Table 2. According to Table 2 we can find that serial decoding outperforms parallel decoding in performance, which is because the parallel decoding does not utilize any priori information in text sequence. Our experiments are based on serial strategies.

Table 2. The performance of the two sampling strategies.

Sampling strategy	IIIT5K	SVT	IC13	IC15	SVTP	CUTE
Parallel sampling	93.6	87.4	89.4	76.2	76.7	79.9
Serial sampling	94.1	89.9	91.7	77.9	79.8	81.6

Impact of the Number of Key Points on Performance. In this subsection, we conduct experiments to explore the influence of the number of key points on performance. As shown in Table 3, with the increase of the number of key points, the recognition performance increases slowly, but the decoding speed decrease significantly. It is experimentally shown that the feature of each character can be fully expressed by only one key point.

Table 3. Impact of the number of key points on performance. "#" means the number of key points acquired by the single-point sampling module.

Key points	IIIT5K	SVT	IC13	IC15	SVTP	CUTE	Speed (ms/image)
1	94.1	89.9	91.7	77.9	79.8	81.6	0.65
2	94.2	89.9	91.8	77.8	79.4	81.9	0.74
3	94.4	90.1	92.0	78.0	79.6	81.8	0.81
4	94.5	89.8	92.1	78.5	79.7	81.9	0.88

Fig. 5. Visual examples of the single-point decoding process.

4.5 Visual Illustrations

Figure 5 shows the visualization of single-point decoding, the first row shows short words that are less than four in length; the second row shows medium words of length 4–6; the third row shows long words that are more than six in length; the last row shows the curved text. According to Fig. 5, we can find that our single-point sampling module can adaptively locate the position of the key points on the text with any length and shape.

5   Conclusion

In this paper, we propose a novel scene text recognition network, named single-point decoding network (SPDN), which can use a single-point feature to decode one character. In addition, we propose a single-point sampling module, which can use the priori information to accurately and adaptively locate key points on the text with any length and shape. Our SPDN can greatly improve decoding efficiency and achieve comparable performance.

Acknowledgment. The research is partly supported by the National Key Research and Development Program of China (2020AAA0109701), The National Science Fund for Distinguished Young Scholars (62125601), and the National Natural Science Foundation of China (62006018, 62076024).

References

1. Bahdanau, D., Cho, K., Bengio, Y.: Neural machine translation by jointly learning to align and translate. arXiv:1409.0473 (2014)
2. Cheng, Z., Bai, F., Xu, Y., Zheng, G., Pu, S., Zhou, S.: Focusing attention: towards accurate text recognition in natural images. In: ICCV, pp. 5076–5084 (2017)
3. Cheng, Z., Xu, Y., Bai, F., Niu, Y., Pu, S., Zhou, S.: Aon: towards arbitrarily-oriented text recognition. In: CVPR, pp. 5571–5579 (2018)
4. Fang, S., Xie, H., Wang, Y., Mao, Z., Zhang, Y.: Read like humans: autonomous, bidirectional and iterative language modeling for scene text recognition. In: CVPR, pp. 7098–7107 (2021)
5. Graves, A., Fernández, S., Gomez, F., Schmidhuber, J.: Connectionist temporal classification: labelling unsegmented sequence data with recurrent neural networks. In: ICML, pp. 369–376 (2006)
6. Gupta, A., Vedaldi, A., Zisserman, A.: Synthetic data for text localisation in natural images. In: CVPR, pp. 2315–2324 (2016)
7. Hou, J.B., et al.: Detecting text in scene and traffic guide panels with attention anchor mechanism. TITS 22(11), 6890–6899 (2020)
8. Jaderberg, M., Simonyan, K., Vedaldi, A., Zisserman, A.: Synthetic data and artificial neural networks for natural scene text recognition. arXiv:1406.2227 (2014)
9. Jaderberg, M., Simonyan, K., Zisserman, A., et al.: Spatial transformer networks. NIPS 28, 2017–2025 (2015)
10. Jaderberg, M., Vedaldi, A., Zisserman, A.: Deep features for text spotting. In: ECCV, pp. 512–528 (2014)
11. Karatzas, D., et al.: Icdar 2015 competition on robust reading. In: ICDAR, pp. 1156–1160 (2015)
12. Karatzas, D., et al.: Icdar 2013 robust reading competition. In: ICDAR, pp. 1484–1493 (2013)
13. Kim, Y., Denton, C., Hoang, L., Rush, A.M.: Structured attention networks. arXiv:1702.00887 (2017)
14. Lee, C.Y., Osindero, S.: Recursive recurrent nets with attention modeling for ocr in the wild. In: CVPR, pp. 2231–2239 (2016)
15. Lee, J., Park, S., Baek, J., Oh, S.J., Kim, S., Lee, H.: On recognizing texts of arbitrary shapes with 2D self-attention. In: CVPR Workshops, pp. 546–547 (2020)
16. Li, H., Wang, P., Shen, C., Zhang, G.: Show, attend and read: a simple and strong baseline for irregular text recognition. In: AAAI, vol. 33, pp. 8610–8617 (2019)
17. Liao, M., et al.: Scene text recognition from two-dimensional perspective. In: AAAI, vol. 33, pp. 8714–8721 (2019)
18. Lu, N., et al.: Master: multi-aspect non-local network for scene text recognition. Pattern Recogn. 117, 107980 (2021)
19. Neumann, L., Matas, J.: Real-time scene text localization and recognition. In: CVPR, pp. 3538–3545 (2012)
20. Phan, T.Q., Shivakumara, P., Tian, S., Tan, C.L.: Recognizing text with perspective distortion in natural scenes. In: ICCV, pp. 569–576 (2013)
21. Qiao, Z., Zhou, Y., Yang, D., Zhou, Y., Wang, W.: Seed: semantics enhanced encoder-decoder framework for scene text recognition. In: CVPR, pp. 13528–13537 (2020)
22. Risnumawan, A., Shivakumara, P., Chan, C.S., Tan, C.L.: A robust arbitrary text detection system for natural scene images. Expert Syst. Appl. 41(18), 8027–8048 (2014)

23. Sheng, F., Chen, Z., Xu, B.: Nrtr: a no-recurrence sequence-to-sequence model for scene text recognition. In: ICDAR, pp. 781–786. IEEE (2019)
24. Shi, B., Bai, X., Yao, C.: An end-to-end trainable neural network for image-based sequence recognition and its application to scene text recognition. TPAMI **39**(11), 2298–2304 (2016)
25. Shi, B., Wang, X., Lyu, P., Yao, C., Bai, X.: Robust scene text recognition with automatic rectification. In: CVPR, pp. 4168–4176 (2016)
26. Shi, B., Yang, M., Wang, X., Lyu, P., Yao, C., Bai, X.: Aster: an attentional scene text recognizer with flexible rectification. TPAMI **41**(9), 2035–2048 (2018)
27. Wang, K., Babenko, B., Belongie, S.: End-to-end scene text recognition. In: ICCV, pp. 1457–1464. IEEE (2011)
28. Wang, K., Belongie, S.: Word spotting in the wild. In: ECCV, pp. 591–604 (2010)
29. Wang, T., et al.: Decoupled attention network for text recognition. In: AAAI, vol. 34, pp. 12216–12224 (2020)
30. Wang, T., et al.: Implicit feature alignment: learn to convert text recognizer to text spotter. In: CVPR, pp. 5973–5982 (2021)
31. Warps, F.L.B.P.: Thin-plate splines and the decompositions of deformations. TPAMI **11**(6) (1989)
32. Yue, X., Kuang, Z., Lin, C., Sun, H., Zhang, W.: RobustScanner: dynamically enhancing positional clues for robust text recognition. In: Vedaldi, A., Bischof, H., Brox, T., Frahm, J.-M. (eds.) ECCV 2020. LNCS, vol. 12364, pp. 135–151. Springer, Cham (2020). https://doi.org/10.1007/978-3-030-58529-7_9
33. Zhang, S.X., Zhu, X., Chen, L., Hou, J.B., Yin, X.C.: Arbitrary shape text detection via segmentation with probability maps. TPAMI (2022)
34. Zhang, S.X., et al.: Deep relational reasoning graph network for arbitrary shape text detection. In: CVPR, pp. 9699–9708 (2020)
35. Zhang, S.X., Zhu, X., Yang, C., Wang, H., Yin, X.C.: Adaptive boundary proposal network for arbitrary shape text detection. In: ICCV, pp. 1305–1314 (2021)
36. Zhu, X., Li, Z., Li, X., Li, S., Dai, F.: Attention-aware perceptual enhancement nets for low-resolution image classification. Inf. Sci. **515**, 233–247 (2020)
37. Zhu, X., Li, Z., Lou, J., Shen, Q.: Video super-resolution based on a spatio-temporal matching network. Pattern Recogn. **110**, 107619 (2021)
38. Zhu, X., Li, Z., Zhang, X.Y., Li, C., Liu, Y., Xue, Z.: Residual invertible spatio-temporal network for video super-resolution. In: AAAI, vol. 33, pp. 5981–5988 (2019)

Unsupervised Domain Adaptation for Semantic Segmentation with Global and Local Consistency

Xiangxuan Shan⬤, Zijin Yin⬤, Jiayi Gao⬤, Kongming Liang(✉)⬤,
Zhanyu Ma⬤, and Jun Guo

School of Artificial Intelligence, Beijing University of Posts and Telecommunications,
Beijing 100876, China
{samsxx,yinzijin2017,gaojiayi,liangkongming,mazhanyu,
guojun}@bupt.edu.cn

Abstract. Unsupervised domain adaptation(UDA) for semantic segmentation aims to learn from labeled synthetic data to segment the unlabeled real data. Many recent methods use generative networks to acquire real-like images for mitigating domain shift. However, these methods only ensure global style consistency between two domains and fail to impose pixel-wise constraint which is also referred to as local content consistency. To address the above problem, we propose a global and local consistency network to reduce the domain gap in unsupervised domain adaptation for semantic segmentation. To this end, we first constrain global style consistency through a generative adversarial network to acquire real-like latent domain images. Then we enhance local content consistency based on pixelwise entropy minimization. Experimental results show that our method has superiority over other competitive methods on GTA5 → Cityscapes.

Keywords: Unsupervised domain adaptation · Semantic segmentation · Style transfer

1 Introduction

Semantic Segmentation is a challenging task of computer vision that aims to conduct the pixel-level semantic prediction. It is widely applied in Autonomous vehicles [21], medical diagnoses [27], and other complex application scenarios. Nowadays, deep neural network based methods [11,24] have achieved admirable performance in supervised semantic segmentation [13]. However, training these methods requires a large number of pixel-wise manual labels, which are very time-consuming and laborious to annotate. An appealing resolution is to utilize the synthetic datasets collected by game engines, such as Grand Theft Auto V(GTA5) [17] and SYNTHIA [18], which have similar semantic information to real-world datasets like Cityscapes [5]. Nevertheless, due to the appearance difference, a model trained on the source synthetic domain behaves poorly in the real-world target domain, which is the so-called domain gap.

© The Author(s), under exclusive license to Springer Nature Switzerland AG 2022
L. Fang et al. (Eds.): CICAI 2022, LNAI 13604, pp. 154–165, 2022.
https://doi.org/10.1007/978-3-031-20497-5_13

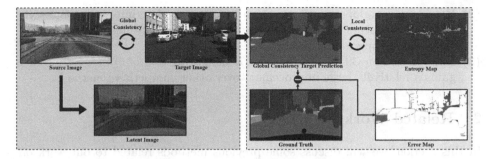

Fig. 1. Visualization results from only ensuring global consistency. Through the image translation method, we can generate a latent image that has a similar appearance to the target image. But the prediction still maintains inaccuracy mainly around object boundaries just as the Error Map illustrates. The color region of the Error Map indicates the wrong pixels of the prediction map. Meanwhile, we find that the entropy of the prediction map is higher (indicated as yellow) around these areas. Therefore, minimizing entropy can improve the prediction accuracy of boundaries and ensure local consistency. (Color figure online)

In recent years, a series of unsupervised domain adaptation(UDA) methods [21,25,31] have been proposed to reduce the domain gap. They try to use labeled source domain and unsupervised target domain to train a segmentation network that has satisfactory performance on the target test set during the evaluation procedure. Most of the existing UDA methods tackle the domain shift problem through adversarial training or auxiliary image translation networks. Style transfer [6], as a common practice in UDA, generates latent domain images that retain the semantic content of the source domain but the appearance style such as color and texture of the target domain, reduces the domain gap, and hence facilitates domain alignment learning. However, as the images from two domains are captured from different scenes, they can only be transferred in an unpaired manner. This will cause the insufficiency of structural constraint, and result in the distortion of the object boundaries and hence severe performance, as illustrated in the Error Map of Fig. 1.

To address the above issue, we propose a global and local consistency method that transfers the global style at the image level and the local content at the boundary level. To be specific, we first use a phase consistency image translation network to generate latent domain images through global style alignment. The phase restriction is imposed to ensure semantic invariance. After that, from the view of information theory, we find that the entropy on object boundaries is much higher than in the interior. And the boundaries of the prediction are much worse as shown in Fig. 1. So the entropy map of the prediction can be used as a constraint to promote the boundary consistency of the object. Therefore, we adopt adversarial entropy minimization to achieve local content alignment. The contributions of our proposed method can be concluded as follows:

(1) We find that the common style transfer methods can only align global style but fail to constrain the data distribution difference of local content around boundaries where the entropy is higher than interior pixels.

(2) We propose a global and local consistency method to improve global style transfer and local content alignment simultaneously through image translation and entropy minimization.

(3) Experiments on GTA5 → Cityscapes demonstrate that our proposed method gains a relatively large improvement over other competitive methods.

2   Related Work

In this section, we will discuss some previous methods related to our work on semantic segmentation and unsupervised domain adaptation.

2.1   Semantic Segmentation

Semantic Segmentation is one of the most popular tasks in computer vision. The main character of it is to make the pixel-level classification. [13] is the first work that uses deep learning and Fully Convolutional Network (FCN) in semantic segmentation. Recently, some works find that mainstream efforts overlook the importance of the semantic category boundaries, which are more challenging to segment precisely, as the receptive field of boundary pixel contains pixels from different classes and ambiguous semantic information. Based on this consensus, [1,22,23,30] concentrate on class boundaries and have achieved new state-of-the-art results. However, most semantic segmentation methods need numerous real-world images with pixel-level annotations which must be labeled manually. An effective solution is to use photo-realistic synthetic data.

2.2   Unsupervised Domain Adaptation

To tackle the problem of insufficient pixel-level annotated images, many synthetic datasets have been released [17,18]. As a sub-task of transfer learning, unsupervised domain adaptation aims to decrease the large domain gap between labeled source synthetic data and unlabeled target real-world data. A variety of methods have been presented, and generative networks and feature adaptation are two main methods to tackle this problem.

Generative Networks. One way to achieve cross-domain uniformity is to align the global style of two domains, which is known as image translation. [31] uses two pairs of generative adversarial networks to transform the synthetic images of the source domain to the style information of the target images via cycle consistency. [26] swaps the low-frequency spectrum of the source image with the target one so that the image style information can be transferred. [25] finds that semantic content is mainly carried by the phase component of the Fourier Transform. So they introduce phase consistency in the CycleGAN Network.

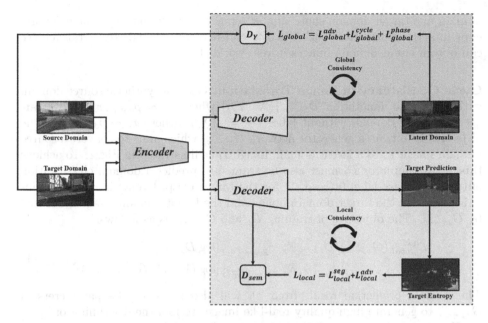

$$L_{global} = L_{global}^{adv} + L_{global}^{cycle} + L_{global}^{phase}$$

$$L_{local} = L_{local}^{seg} + L_{local}^{adv}$$

Fig. 2. The overall architecture of our global and local consistency method. Our network contains two parts: (1) global consistency, which reduces the domain gap in image-level to align style, such as color and texture. This part contains two pairs of GAN and constrains adversarial loss $\mathcal{L}_{global}^{adv}$, cycle consistency loss $\mathcal{L}_{global}^{cycle}$, and phase consistency loss $\mathcal{L}_{global}^{phase}$ to the network. The figure in this part is simplified. (2) local consistency, which aligns the content of two domains at boundary level through entropy minimization. Segmentation loss $\mathcal{L}_{local}^{seg}$ and entropy adversarial loss $\mathcal{L}_{local}^{adv}$ are applied to the network.

Feature Adaptation. A different approach is to seek a distribution alignment of network latent embeddings. Following the emphasis on category boundaries in semantic segmentation, [2] tries to adapt shallow features of the network by predicting boundary maps as the domain gap of shallow features between two domains is small. [28] adapts prototypes of two domains. The prototypes of the domain are computed by features.

3   Methods

In this section, we present the global and local consistency approaches. The global consistency is about style information, which aims to align the appearance of the two domains. And the local consistency is through adversarial entropy minimization to align the boundary content. The whole architecture is illustrated in Fig. 2.

3.1   Global Consistency

To achieve consistency at the image level, we follow the work in [25] to apply phase consistency in CycleGAN [31] for common style transfer. As the source domain and target domain share similar semantic layouts but have huge domain gaps in style information, such as color and texture, through style transfer, we can obtain latent domain images in real-world style.

Cycle Consistency in Image Translation. Given a synthetic source domain with pixel-wise annotation $\mathcal{D}_S = \{(X_s, Y_s)\}$ where $x_s \sim p_{\text{data}}(x_s)$ and a target real-world domain without label $\mathcal{D}_T = \{(X_t)\}$ where $x_t \sim p_{\text{data}}(x_t)$, The objective is to train a generator network $G_{x_s \rightarrow x_t}$ which aims to convert a source domain image x_s to a latent domain image x_l as illustrated in Fig. 1. To achieve this, a discriminator D_t must also be trained to predict a domain classification output $i.e.$, class label 0 (resp. 1) for the target (resp. latent) image to distinguish between the target domain image and the latent domain image generated by $G_{x_s \rightarrow x_t}$. The objective of training D_t and $G_{x_s \rightarrow x_t}$ is as follows:

$$\mathcal{L}_{global}^{adv}(G_{x_s \rightarrow x_t}, D_t) = \mathbb{E}_{x_t \sim p_{\text{data}}(x_t)}[\log D_t(x_t)] \\ + \mathbb{E}_{x_s \sim p_{\text{data}}(x_s)}[\log(1 - D_t(G_{x_s \rightarrow x_t}(x_s)))] \tag{1}$$

The domain prediction result from D_t will also influence the parameters of $G_{x_s \rightarrow x_t}$ to generate high-quality real-like images to fool the discriminator.

However, only one pair of the generative adversarial network can not guarantee correct image translation, as the insufficiency of supervision information may lead to a condition that source images will map to the same latent image and the semantic information can not be preserved [31]. So followed the method in [31], another pair of generative adversarial networks $G_{x_t \rightarrow x_s}$ and D_s should be introduced to translate latent images $x_l = G_{x_s \rightarrow x_t}(x_s)$ back to the source domain so that to force the cycle translated image $x'_s = G_{x_t \rightarrow x_s}(x_l)$ to be consistent with the original source image x_s, $i.e.$, $x_s \rightarrow G_{x_s \rightarrow x_t}(x_s) \rightarrow G_{x_t \rightarrow x_s}(G_{x_s \rightarrow x_t}(x_s)) \approx x_s$. To achieve this, the optimization objective of $G_{x_t \rightarrow x_s}$ and D_t are similar to $G_{x_s \rightarrow x_t}$ and D_s. And the cycle consistency loss is as follows:

$$\mathcal{L}_{global}^{cycle}(G_{x_s \rightarrow x_t}) = \mathbb{E}_{x_s \sim p_{\text{data}}(x_s)}[\|G_{x_t \rightarrow x_s}(G_{x_s \rightarrow x_t}(x_s)) - x_s\|_1] \tag{2}$$

where $|\cdot|_1$ is the L1 norm. Through cycle consistency and reconstructed image matching, the generator $G_{x_s \rightarrow x_t}$ we used can generate relatively precise latent images.

Phase Consistency. Although applying the method above can achieve the style information consistency to obtain latent images, we observe that the semantic categories of latent images can not align with the classes in source images precisely due to the non-supervision of semantic information. This problem will lead to semantic mistakes. For example, the sky may be aligned with trees. To tackle this problem, we follow the work in [25] to force phase consistency in the network as the phase of the spectrum of an image contains its semantic information:

$$\mathcal{L}_{global}^{phase}(G_{x_s \rightarrow x_t}) = -\sum_c \frac{\langle \mathcal{F}(x_s)_c, \mathcal{F}(G_{x_s \rightarrow x_t}(x_s))_c \rangle}{\|\mathcal{F}(x_s)_c\|_2 \cdot \|\mathcal{F}(G_{x_s \rightarrow x_t}(x_s))_c\|_2} \tag{3}$$

where c is the class number, $\mathcal{F} : \mathbb{R}^{H \times W} \to \mathbb{R}^{H \times W \times 2}$ is the Fourier Transform, $\langle , \rangle$ is the dot-product, and $\| \cdot \|_2$ is the L2 norm. Through the phase consistency constraint, the semantic information of the source domain and latent domain should be aligned as Fig. 1 shows.

3.2 Local Consistency

Following Sect. 3.1, after the first stage transfer at the global style, the latent domain $\mathcal{D}_\mathcal{L} = \{(X_l, Y_l)\}$ which has $Y_l = Y_s$ is obtained. As a result, the latent domain, as the intermediate level between the two domains, has a smaller domain gap with the target domain. However, a segmentation network trained on the latent domain is still difficult to obtain precise predictions on the target domain, as the insufficiency of structural constraint just as Fig. 1 illustrates. From the view of Information Theory we know that, along the object borders, the entropy is higher than the internal pixels of objects. So adversarial entropy minimization can align the boundary data distribution to reduce the domain gap and achieve consistency at the boundary level.

Latent Domain Supervised Segmentation. First, our semantic segmentation network G_{local} is trained through supervised standard cross-entropy loss on the labeled latent domain $\mathcal{D}_\mathcal{L} = \{(X_l, Y_l)\}$ where $x_l \sim p_{\text{data}}(x_l)$:

$$\mathcal{L}_{local}^{seg}(G_{local}) = \mathbb{E}_{x_l \sim p_{\text{data}}(x_l)} [\log G_{local}] \tag{4}$$

G_{local} is the basic segmentation part of the network. And the target images will be segmented by it in the evaluation procedure.

Adversarial Entropy Minimization. For the unlabeled target domain, as we do not have pixel-level annotations, so the segmentation can not be supervised by Eq. 4. And due to the insufficiency of structural constraint, a segmentation model trained on the latent domain can not generate precise predictions around boundaries in the target domain, as illustrated in Fig. 1. So we need to ensure local content consistency around boundaries. The achievement of Shannon Entropy [19] has proved that a signal with high uncertainty will have high entropy. Due to the boundary misalignment and noise, the segmentation network is uncertain about the boundary prediction, which causes the prediction inaccurate and entropy high. So we use the method in [21] to minimize the entropy of the prediction. The entropy map of a target image $E_{x_t} \in [0, 1]^{H \times W}$ is defined as follows:

$$E_{x_t}^{(h,w)} = \frac{-1}{\log(C)} \mathbb{E}_{x_t \sim p_{\text{data}}(x_t)} [\log G_{local}] \tag{5}$$

However, minimizing the entropy map of the target image directly will overlook the difference in structure information between the two domains. Therefore, we follow the work in [21] and apply an entropy adversarial learning network to ensure local content consistency.

To be specific, for a pixel prediction $P_{x_t}^{(h,w,c)}$, where h and w are the sizes of the prediction map and c is the class number, its Shannon entropy is $E_{x_t}^{(h,w)} = E_{x_t \sim p_{\text{data}} (x_t)}(I_{x_t}^{(h,w)})$, where $I_{x_t}^{(h,w)} = -P_{x_t}^{(h,w)} \cdot \log P_{x_t}^{(h,w)}$ is the self-information vector.

As a result, the discriminator network D_{local} takes the weighted self-information map I_{x_l} and I_{x_t} as input, which is computed from the prediction of the segmentation network G_{local}. And the discriminator network D_{local} will be trained with supervision to predict domain classification outputs. Apart from this, for the sake of fooling the discriminator, the segmentation network G_{local} should also be trained to generate entropy maps of the target domain predictions to be similar to the latent domain:

$$
\begin{aligned}
\mathcal{L}_{local}^{adv}(G_{local}, D_{local}) &= \mathbb{E}_{x_t \sim p_{\text{data}} (x_t)} \left[\log D_{local}(I_{x_t}) \right] \\
&+ \mathbb{E}_{x_l \sim p_{\text{data}} (x_l)} \left[\log \left(1 - D_{local}(I_{x_l}) \right) \right]
\end{aligned}
\tag{6}
$$

where class label 0 (resp. 1) for the target (resp. latent) weighted self-information map of the prediction. Through indirectly adversarial entropy minimization, the method we used in this section achieves local content consistency successfully.

3.3   Overall Training Loss

Our method is a global and local consistency network. For the global consistency mentioned in Sect. 3.1, the overall loss is as follows:

$$
\begin{aligned}
\mathcal{L}_{global} &= \mathcal{L}_{global}^{adv}(G_{x_s \to x_t}, D_t) + \lambda_{global}^{cycle} \mathcal{L}_{global}^{cycle}(G_{x_s \to x_t}) \\
&+ \lambda_{global}^{phase} \mathcal{L}_{global}^{phase}(G_{x_s \to x_t})
\end{aligned}
\tag{7}
$$

And the objective for the local consistency mentioned in Sect. 3.2 is as follows:

$$
\mathcal{L}_{local} = \mathcal{L}_{local}^{seg}(G_{local}) + \lambda_{local}^{adv} \mathcal{L}_{local}^{adv}(G_{local}, D_{local})
\tag{8}
$$

where all the λ mentioned before are hyperparameters, whose values will be discussed in Sect. 4. And the segmentation loss and adversarial loss will be trained simultaneously. Following the global and local consistency, our method minimizes the domain gap between the two domains.

4   Experiments

In this section, we will introduce the experiments with our method. We will first discuss the datasets we used and the implementation details of our network. Then the performance comparison and visualization will be presented.

4.1 Datasets

Cityscapes is the high-quality real-world dataset we used as the unlabeled target domain [5]. It includes 3975 images with pixel-level manual annotation. The resolution of each image is 2048×1024 and the categories of the dataset are 19, including road, sidewalk, car, and so on. The dataset has 2975 images for training and 500 for validation. Following the previous works [2,12,21], we only utilize the training set without labels for training and the validation set for evaluation.

GTA5 is the large synthetic dataset we used as the labeled source domain [17]. Captured automatically in a same name computer game, GTA5 contains 24966 labeled images. And the resolution of it is 1914×1052. This dataset shares the same categories as Cityscapes and all the data are used in our training procedure. GTA5 dataset has the same scene and semantic information as Cityscapes, as they are all presented in the urban scene.

4.2 Implementation Details

In this section, we will introduce the structure of the network we used and details of the network. All the experiments are implemented with Pytorch on a single NVIDIA 2080TI GPU with 11 GB memory. To save the GPU memory, the training procedure of the global and local consistency is separated. The prediction result of the first stage transfer will be fed to the second stage.

Following the setting in [21,25], for ensuring global consistency, we adopt the architecture from [10] for the generator and 70 × 70 PatchGANs [9] for the discriminator. While for local consistency, Deeplab-V2 [3] is used as the segmentation network and DCGAN [16] as the discriminator. The batch size is set to 1 and the data of the target dataset is chosen randomly as the source dataset is much larger than the target dataset. ResNet is used as the backbone. For the optimizer, we use an Adam solver and set the dynamic learning rate with the polynomial annealing procedure. Apart from this, due to the limitation of GPU memory, in the training procedure, the images from the source domain are resized to 1280×720, and from the target domain are resized to 1024×512.

As for the hyperparameters, for the overall loss Eq. 7, $\lambda_{global}^{cycle} = 10$ and $\lambda_{global}^{phase} = 5$. For the loss Eq. 8, $\lambda_{local}^{adv} = 0.001$.

4.3 Results

In this section, we will discuss the experiment performance of the method we used compared to other advanced methods. For the sake of fairness, ResNet-101 is used as the backbone for all methods. And we choose mean per-class Intersection-Over-Union (mIoU) as the evaluation criteria. Our global and local consistency method achieves a relatively large promotion compared to other methods.

Table 1. The semantic segmentation result of the evaluation procedure by adapting from GTA5 to Cityscapes in the 19 categories. The best results are highlighted in bold.

Models	Road	Sidewalk	Building	Wall	Fence	Pole	Light	Sign	Veg	Terrain	Sky	Person	Rider	Car	Truck	Bus	Train	Mbike	Bike	mIoU
ADVENT [21]	88.9	25.4	78.5	22.5	20.9	28.9	35.9	17.9	83.7	30.6	72.4	56.8	13.6	83.6	30.2	39.2	0.02	19.6	5.8	42.1
DLOW [7]	87.1	33.5	80.5	24.5	13.2	29.8	29.5	26.6	82.6	26.7	81.8	55.9	25.3	78.0	33.5	38.7	0.0	22.9	34.5	42.3
Adapt-SegMap [20]	86.5	36.0	79.9	23.4	23.3	23.9	35.2	14.8	83.4	33.3	75.6	58.5	27.6	73.7	32.5	35.4	3.9	30.1	28.1	42.4
CyCADA [8]	86.7	35.6	80.1	19.8	17.5	**38.0**	**39.9**	**41.5**	82.7	27.9	73.6	**64.9**	19.0	65.0	12.0	28.6	4.5	31.1	42.0	42.7
CLAN [14]	87.0	27.1	79.6	27.3	23.3	28.3	35.5	24.2	83.6	27.4	74.2	58.6	28.0	76.2	33.1	36.7	6.7	31.9	31.4	43.2
MaxSquare [4]	88.1	27.7	80.8	28.7	19.8	24.9	34.0	17.8	83.6	34.7	76.0	58.6	28.6	84.1	**37.8**	43.1	**7.2**	**32.2**	34.5	44.3
ESSL [15]	85.3	35.6	81.7	29.9	20.2	35.5	36.6	35.9	83.2	28.1	81.8	63.8	**29.2**	81.8	23.4	24.6	4.7	31.0	47.3	45.2
TTDA [29]	**91.5**	**42.4**	**84.6**	29.2	**23.9**	29.5	32.5	36.4	83.0	37.1	80.8	58.4	25.3	82.7	27.7	46.1	0	26.3	29.6	45.6
Source Only	64.6	27.3	76.9	19.1	21.1	27.0	32.1	18.5	81.2	14.5	72.4	55.4	21.6	62.9	29.4	8.4	2.4	24.2	35.0	36.5
Ours(Global Only)	88.2	41.3	83.2	28.8	21.9	31.7	35.2	28.2	83.0	26.2	**83.2**	57.6	27.0	77.1	27.5	34.6	2.5	28.3	**36.1**	44.3
Ours(Global+Local)	90.4	39.2	82.2	**32.4**	22.5	32.8	36.4	20.6	**84.8**	34.8	81.2	59.2	22.7	**85.8**	36.3	**49.2**	0.08	30.2	4.3	**46.0**

Performance Comparison. Table 1 introduces the semantic segmentation results in the adaptation from GTA5 to Cityscapes. Through the quantitive consequence, we can see, compared with Source Only, which means the method without any transfer, our method improves by 9.5% mIoU. Compared with other methods proposed in recent years, our method still has satisfactory results. Some methods also use entropy to constrain semantic segmentation networks, like ADVENT and MaxSquare. Our approach has a significant improvement compared with them. DLOW, ESSL, and TTDA use image translation to reduce domain gaps, but they fail to ensure local content consistency. So our method shows improvement in almost all classes. Adversarial training is applied in most of the methods, like Adapt-SegMap, CyCADA, CLAN, and ADVENT. Our method is also based on it, and we have achieved the best mIoU among them.

Visualization Result. Figure 3 shows the visualization results of our method. Source Only shows the prediction results without any transfer. We can see that the prediction is noisy, which indicates the inconsistency of data distribution between the synthetic source domain and the real-world target domain. From the results of Global Only, which means only ensuring global consistency, we can find that, with the adaptation of the global style, the domain gap is reduced as the performance is much better and clearer. However, distortion still exists, especially around object boundaries and small objects whose interior pixels are very few, as the yellow square illustrates. It proves that global style consistency can not guarantee local content alignment. This problem is solved by our Global+Local as the predictions of boundaries around the sidewalk and person in the yellow squares are much similar to the Ground Truth. Through local content consistency, the shape of prediction objects is more integral. And small objects can be segmented better. The visualization of Global+Local shows the effect of our method.

Ablation Study. At the bottom of Table 1, we perform the ablation study results of the method we used. From the table, we can see that the model trained only in the source domain without domain adaptation results in 36.5% mIoU which shows that the source domain and target domain has a huge domain

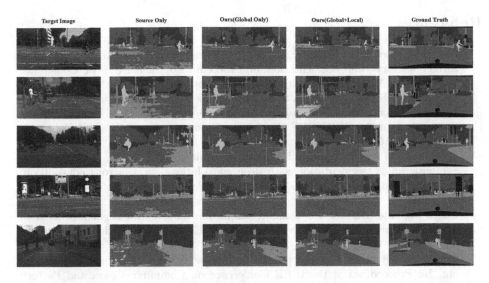

Fig. 3. Visualization results from different methods. Compared to Source Only, our Global Only method yields better prediction but fails to ensure local content consistency around object boundaries which is addressed to some extent by our global and local consistency as the yellow square indicates. (Color figure online)

gap. The Global Only method gains an improvement of 7.8% mIoU. This result indicates that our global consistency can align the two domains to some extent. However, after our global and local consistency, we achieve an improvement of 9.5% mIoU compared to Source Only. This result proves the fact that local content consistency around boundaries through adversarial entropy minimization can further reduce the domain gap. This group of data shows the effect of every component of our model and proves the superiority of our method.

5   Conclusion

In this paper, we present an unsupervised domain adaptation method that uses global and local consistency to jointly reduce the domain gap between source and target domain. Specially, we use phase to constrain the style transfer network to align two domains in appearance for global consistency. And an entropy minimization adversarial network is further adapted to reduce the domain gap through boundary data distribution alignment for the local consistency. The experimental results demonstrate that both global and local consistency are essential for unsupervised domain adaptation for semantic segmentation. Overall, our proposed method can achieve an improvement over other competitive methods.

Acknowledgements. This work was supported in part by National Natural Science Foundation of China (NSFC) No. 61922015, 62106022, U19B2036, 62225601, and in part by Beijing Natural Science Foundation Project No. Z200002.

References

1. Borse, S., Wang, Y., Zhang, Y., Porikli, F.: Inverseform: A loss function for structured boundary-aware segmentation. In: Proceedings of the IEEE/CVF Conference on Computer Vision and Pattern Recognition, pp. 5901–5911 (2021)
2. Cardace, A., Ramirez, P.Z., Salti, S., Di Stefano, L.: Shallow features guide unsupervised domain adaptation for semantic segmentation at class boundaries. In: Proceedings of the IEEE/CVF Winter Conference on Applications of Computer Vision, pp. 1160–1170 (2022)
3. Chen, L.C., Papandreou, G., Kokkinos, I., Murphy, K., Yuille, A.L.: Deeplab: Semantic image segmentation with deep convolutional nets, atrous convolution, and fully connected crfs. IEEE Trans. Pattern Analysis Mach. Intell. **40**(4), 834–848 (2017)
4. Chen, M., Xue, H., Cai, D.: Domain adaptation for semantic segmentation with maximum squares loss. In: Proceedings of the IEEE/CVF International Conference on Computer Vision, pp. 2090–2099 (2019)
5. Cordts, M., et al.: The cityscapes dataset for semantic urban scene understanding. In: Proceedings of the IEEE Conference on Computer Vision and Pattern Recognition, pp. 3213–3223 (2016)
6. Fang, Y., Deng, W., Du, J., Hu, J.: Identity-aware cyclegan for face photo-sketch synthesis and recognition. Pattern Recogn. **102**, 107249 (2020)
7. Gong, R., Li, W., Chen, Y., Gool, L.V.: Dlow: domain flow for adaptation and generalization. In: Proceedings of the IEEE/CVF Conference on Computer Vision and Pattern Recognition, pp. 2477–2486 (2019)
8. Hoffman, J., et al.: Cycada: cycle-consistent adversarial domain adaptation. In: International Conference on Machine Learning, pp. 1989–1998. PMLR (2018)
9. Isola, P., Zhu, J.Y., Zhou, T., Efros, A.A.: Image-to-image translation with conditional adversarial networks. In: Proceedings of the IEEE Conference on Computer Vision and Pattern Recognition, pp. 1125–1134 (2017)
10. Johnson, J., Alahi, A., Fei-Fei, L.: Perceptual losses for real-time style transfer and super-resolution. In: Leibe, B., Matas, J., Sebe, N., Welling, M. (eds.) ECCV 2016. LNCS, vol. 9906, pp. 694–711. Springer, Cham (2016). https://doi.org/10.1007/978-3-319-46475-6_43
11. Li, Q., Du, J., Song, F., Wang, C., Liu, H., Lu, C.: Region-based multi-focus image fusion using the local spatial frequency. In: 2013 25th Chinese Control and Decision Conference (CCDC), pp. 3792–3796. IEEE (2013)
12. Liu, Y., Deng, J., Gao, X., Li, W., Duan, L.: Bapa-net: boundary adaptation and prototype alignment for cross-domain semantic segmentation. In: Proceedings of the IEEE/CVF International Conference on Computer Vision, pp. 8801–8811 (2021)
13. Long, J., Shelhamer, E., Darrell, T.: Fully convolutional networks for semantic segmentation. In: Proceedings of the IEEE Conference on Computer Vision and Pattern Recognition, pp. 3431–3440 (2015)
14. Luo, Y., Zheng, L., Guan, T., Yu, J., Yang, Y.: Taking a closer look at domain shift: category-level adversaries for semantics consistent domain adaptation. In: Proceedings of the IEEE/CVF Conference on Computer Vision and Pattern Recognition, pp. 2507–2516 (2019)
15. Piva, F.J., Dubbelman, G.: Exploiting image translations via ensemble self-supervised learning for unsupervised domain adaptation. arXiv preprint arXiv:2107.06235 (2021)

16. Radford, A., Metz, L., Chintala, S.: Unsupervised representation learning with deep convolutional generative adversarial networks. arXiv preprint arXiv:1511.06434 (2015)
17. Richter, S.R., Vineet, V., Roth, S., Koltun, V.: Playing for data: ground truth from computer games. In: Leibe, B., Matas, J., Sebe, N., Welling, M. (eds.) ECCV 2016. LNCS, vol. 9906, pp. 102–118. Springer, Cham (2016). https://doi.org/10.1007/978-3-319-46475-6_7
18. Ros, G., Sellart, L., Materzynska, J., Vazquez, D., Lopez, A.M.: The synthia dataset: a large collection of synthetic images for semantic segmentation of urban scenes. In: Proceedings of the IEEE Conference on Computer Vision and Pattern Recognition, pp. 3234–3243 (2016)
19. Shannon, C.E.: A mathematical theory of communication. Bell Syst. Technol. J **27**(3), 379–423 (1948)
20. Tsai, Y.H., Hung, W.C., Schulter, S., Sohn, K., Yang, M.H., Chandraker, M.: Learning to adapt structured output space for semantic segmentation. In: Proceedings of the IEEE Conference on Computer Vision and Pattern Recognition, pp. 7472–7481 (2018)
21. Vu, T.H., Jain, H., Bucher, M., Cord, M., Pérez, P.: Advent: adversarial entropy minimization for domain adaptation in semantic segmentation. In: Proceedings of the IEEE/CVF Conference on Computer Vision and Pattern Recognition, pp. 2517–2526 (2019)
22. Wang, C., et al.: Active boundary loss for semantic segmentation. arXiv preprint arXiv:2102.02696 (2021)
23. Wang, Z., Li, Y., Wang, S.: Noisy boundaries: lemon or lemonade for semi-supervised instance segmentation? arXiv preprint arXiv:2203.13427 (2022)
24. Xu, L., Du, J., Li, Q.: Image fusion based on nonsubsampled contourlet transform and saliency-motivated pulse coupled neural networks. Math. Prob. Eng. **2013** (2013)
25. Yang, Y., Lao, D., Sundaramoorthi, G., Soatto, S.: Phase consistent ecological domain adaptation. In: Proceedings of the IEEE/CVF Conference on Computer Vision and Pattern Recognition, pp. 9011–9020 (2020)
26. Yang, Y., Soatto, S.: FDA: fourier domain adaptation for semantic segmentation. In: Proceedings of the IEEE/CVF Conference on Computer Vision and Pattern Recognition, pp. 4085–4095 (2020)
27. Yin, Z., Liang, K., Ma, Z., Guo, J.: Duplex contextual relation network for polyp segmentation. In: 2022 IEEE 19th International Symposium on Biomedical Imaging (ISBI), pp. 1–5. IEEE (2022)
28. Zhang, P., Zhang, B., Zhang, T., Chen, D., Wang, Y., Wen, F.: Prototypical pseudo label denoising and target structure learning for domain adaptive semantic segmentation. In: Proceedings of the IEEE/CVF Conference on Computer Vision and Pattern Recognition, pp. 12414–12424 (2021)
29. Zhang, X., Zhang, H., Lu, J., Shao, L., Yang, J.: Target-targeted domain adaptation for unsupervised semantic segmentation. In: 2021 IEEE International Conference on Robotics and Automation (ICRA), pp. 13560–13566. IEEE (2021)
30. Zhu, C., Zhang, X., Li, Y., Qiu, L., Han, K., Han, X.: Sharpcontour: a contour-based boundary refinement approach for efficient and accurate instance segmentation. arXiv preprint arXiv:2203.13312 (2022)
31. Zhu, J.Y., Park, T., Isola, P., Efros, A.A.: Unpaired image-to-image translation using cycle-consistent adversarial networks. In: Proceedings of the IEEE International Conference on Computer Vision, pp. 2223–2232 (2017)

Research on Multi-temporal Cloud Removal Using D-S Evidence Theory and Cloud Segmentation Model

Xinwei Wang[1], Kailai Sun[1], Qianchuan Zhao[1(✉)], and Jianhong Zou[2,3]

[1] Center for Intelligent and Networked Systems, Department of Automation, BNRist, Tsinghua University, Beijing 100084, China
{wxw21,skl18}@mails.tsinghua.edu.cn, zhaoqc@tsinghua.edu.cn
[2] Technology Development Department, Fujian Big Data Co., LTD., Fuzhou, China
[3] Fujian Nebula Big Data Application Service Co., LTD., Fuzhou, China

Abstract. Satellite remote sensing technology is widely applied for real-time drawing maps, forecasting weather, and predicting natural disasters. However, many remote sensing satellite images contain cloud noise, resulting in difficulties in practical applications. Existing cloud removal methods are limited when an image contains lots of clouds or thick clouds. Besides, most methods need a cloudless image as a reference. Our study proposes an advanced algorithm to remove cloud noise (especially thick clouds) in remote sensing images, including a cloud segmentation model, prior knowledge refinement, and Dempster-Shafer (D-S) evidence theory. Firstly, we trained a Cloud-net model to segment cloud regions. RGB and Near Infrared (NIR) images are fed into the Cloud-net model. Then it outputs coarse segmentation images. Secondly, we introduced the prior knowledge to refine and recover segmentation results. Finally, we designed cloud removal rules based on D-S evidence theory to fuse muti-temporal remote sensing images. Our method achieves a surprising performance on GaoFen-4 (GF-4) satellite images, reducing the average percentage of cloud noise from 30%–40% to 2%–8% per image.

Keywords: Satellite remote sensing image · D-S evidence theory · Cloud segmentation model · Multi-temporal denoising

1 Introduction

Remote sensing is an essential tool for acquiring environmental information and natural resources. It perceives distant information about an object. Our study focuses on satellite remote sensing, which could be used for real-time mapping, weather forecasting, and natural disasters warning (e.g., typhoons and tsunamis). However, various kinds of noise will appear in remote sensing processes. How to denoise is a challenging and meaningful issue.

X. Wang and K. Sun—These authors contributed equally to this work.

L. Fang et al. (Eds.): CICAI 2022, LNAI 13604, pp. 166–178, 2022.
https://doi.org/10.1007/978-3-031-20497-5_14

There are three main types of noise: impulsive noise caused by cosmic high-energy particle radiation; Gaussian noise generated by the transmission medium or the equipment; cloud noise caused by ground surface clouds and fog. Our study focuses on how to remove cloud noise. So far, there are more than 700 remote sensing satellites all over the world that have captured a large number of images. However, lots of images cannot be directly used because of the heavy cloud noise. Removing the cloud noise can significantly increase the quality of existing remote sensing images.

Existing cloud removal studies can be divided into two categories: thin and thick cloud removal. These studies apply frequency domain filtering method, wavelet filtering method, etc., on a single image to remove thin clouds [1–6]. These methods rely on ground surface information but cannot work when thick clouds completely cover ground surface. Thick cloud removal studies can be divided into two categories: many methods are based on cloudless reference image [7–9]; and other methods fuse multi-temporal images [10–12]. The former methods select a cloudless image as the reference to reconstruct the target image. The target and the reference images are captured at the same location but at different times by the same satellite. The latter methods take multiple cloudy images, then repairs the target image by finding cloudless patches (or pixels) in reference images. These reference images are also captured at the same location but at different times, but they all contain clouds. These methods provide the possibility of removing thick clouds. However, the reference-based method needs cloudless images, which are hard to be obtained in practice. Besides, many of the mentioned methods are based on virtual synthetic cloudy images or few-cloud images, causing difficulties in practical applications.

To overcome these issues, we propose an accurate multi-temporal cloud removal method based on Cloud-net [13] and D-S evidence theory. Our approach is applied to natural satellite remote sensing image sequences. It performs well on natural heavy-cloudy images, not depending on cloudless images. It uses Cloud-net to conduct preliminary cloud segmentation on remote sensing images, then introduces color prior knowledge to refine and complement the segmentation maps, and finally applies the D-S evidence theory to fuse them.

To our best knowledge, previous cloud removal studies on natural images with a high percentage of cloud noise are rare. Our work has the following contributions: ① We trained Cloud-net and introduced color prior knowledge to improve cloud detection performance. ② Based on the D-S evidence theory, we designed a cloud removal rule that can effectively fuse multi-temporal remote sensing images. ③ We applied our method to real satellite remote sensing images and achieved a significant cloud removal performance. Compared with previous cloud removal methods, our method has the following advantages: ① we do not need cloudless images as the reference; ② we can apply our method to real remote sensing images containing thick clouds with excellent performance; ③ our method can deal with images with a high percentage of cloud noise.

2   Related Work

2.1   Cloud Removal Methods

For the thin cloud removal methods, thin cloud regions are treated as a combination of ground surface and clouds. The thin clouds are removed by frequency domain filtering [1]. Authors [2] segment cloud regions using Poisson matting, then remove cloud noise using wavelet filtering. Other methods [3–6] treat clouds as signals with specific characteristics and remove them through different filtering methods. These methods focus on processing a single thin cloudy image and cannot remove thick clouds.

The thick cloud removal methods [7–12] are developed from earlier research on blank pixel repairment of remote sensing images [14,15]. For the thick cloud removal methods, study [7] uses cloudless images of the same region as a reference, guiding the Markov random field (MRF) model to estimate the pixels in the target image. Studies [8,9] perform sparse decomposition of the cloudless image to obtain a dictionary with sparse coefficients to remove clouds. Authors [10] use a linear spectral decomposition method to recognize cloudy patches. Next, they use cloudless patches in different temporal images to fill the cloudy area. Study [11] is based on a global optimization process. When it detects a cloudy patch, it finds cloudless patches in different temporal images and then performs cloud removal using the two-dimensional gradient of cloudless regions. Study [12] performs cloud detection to extract cloudy patches. The cloudy and cloudless patches in different temporal images are fed into a deep convolutional network. At last, the network outputs cloud removal results. However, they have many limitations. Studies [7–9] use cloudless images as the reference. But in practice, it is hard to get them. Studies [7–9,12] use virtual synthetic cloudy images for training and testing, which is unreliable in practice. Study [10] uses an unreliable cloud detection method. The effect of cloud removal becomes poor when facing a large cloud coverage. Study [11] requires manual annotation of cloudy regions.

2.2   Cloud Detection Methods

Cloud detection methods are an essential part of our multi-temporal cloud removal method. They are mainly divided into three categories: ① Threshold methods [16]. ② Pattern recognition methods based on artificial neural networks [13,17–20]. ③ Spatial variation analysis methods and texture feature methods [21,22]. The threshold method sets a threshold to classify cloud and ground surface pixels by the difference in brightness and chromaticity. The spatial variation analysis and texture characterization methods are used to analyze the edge of the cloud to achieve more accurate and robust cloud detection. The primary neural network model for cloud detection is a semantic segmentation network based on U-net or its variants [23]. It can theoretically segment a single image's cloud targets at the pixel level. Other network structures also exist for cloud detection models, such as Cloud-net [13] and MSCN [19].

3   Methods

The aim of our study is to remove clouds on multi-temporal images, then reconstruct the true ground surface. Our method has four parts: ① Cloud-net for cloud segmentation. ② Color prior knowledge for refining segmentation results. ③ D-S evidence theory for combining multi-temporal segmentation results. ④ Evidence fusion method to reconstruct ground surface.

3.1   Cloud-net

We employee the convolutional neural segmentation network named Cloud-net [18], whose structure is shown in Fig. 1. The network is divided into two parts. The upper part extracts deeper features step by step. The lower part extracts multi-scale cloud information by concatenating the upper part features. It detects cloud regions accurately through its complex convolution module, not relying on pre-processing methods. The **contr_arm** module combines the original input with the output of the first and second convolution layers to produce a multi-scale feature map. Compared to the **contr_arm** module, **imprv_contr_arm** adds the third convolution layer; the **bridge** module adds a dropout layer; the **improve_ff_block** module concatenates the upper layer output with the lower layer output and obtains multi-scale feature information. At last, the network outputs cloud confidence when the feature map is resized to the original size.

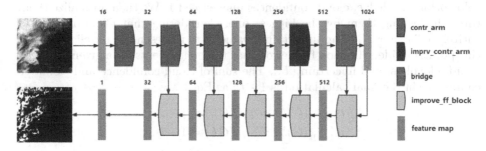

Fig. 1. Structure of the Cloud-net model

3.2   Color Prior Knowledge

There is a clear difference in satellite images covering large areas: images in cloud areas are whiter and brighter; images at ground surface/sea areas are bluer/darker. Based on this fact, to obtain better segmentation results of cloud areas, we convert the RGB image into the gray image [24] and then conduct Eq. 1 on the cloud confidence map generated by Cloud-net.

$$Conf'(i,j) = Conf(i,j) + J[Gray(i,j), L] \times Bias,$$

$$J[Gray(i,j), L] = \begin{cases} 1, & Gray(i,j) > L \\ 0, & Gray(i,j) \leq L, \end{cases} \tag{1}$$

where $Conf(i,j)$ is the cloud confidence value at location (i,j) output by Cloud-net model. $Conf'(i,j)$ is the refined confidence value. $Gray(i,j)$ is the gray value at location (i,j). J is a function to classify pixels in the gray image. L is a fixed classification threshold in J. $Bias$ is a fixed correction value for pixels that are classified bright by J. Here, $Conf'(i,j)$ may exceed 1. We will talk about how to handle this in Sect. 3.3

This prior knowledge effectively classifies cloud regions on large-scale remote sensing images. For small-scale objects (e.g., white buildings) that may bring errors, our method increases same confidence for these objects and clouds. In this situation, their classification results only rely on cloud-net. Thus in the worst case, the performance with the method is no worse than without it.

3.3   D-S Evidence Theory

The D-S evidence theory originated in the 1960s s and was proposed by A.P. Dempster and his students [25]. The theory is based on uncertain evidence and performs information fusion to produce reliable results.

We apply the theory of migration to the cloud removal problem with the following definitions: at the time t, the cloud-net outputs cloud confidence 0.86 in the location (i,j), then:

$$m_{(i,j)t}(C) = 0.86, \tag{2}$$

where m means the mass function. C means event 'cloud'. The Cloud-net outputs cloud confidence for each location, which is the mass function value. Due to color prior knowledge, cloud confidences may exceed 1. We then normalize them through dividing them by the biggest one. Considering that Cloud-net is not entirely reliable, we add an uncertainty value U to represent its unreliability. At this point, our identification framework has three judgments for a given location: cloud, cloudless, and uncertain (U). The sum of cloud confidence and cloudless confidence in the final calculation is 1 - U, as Eq. 3.

$$m_{(i,j)t}(C) + m_{(i,j)t}(CL) = 1,$$
$$m'_{(i,j)t}(C) + m'_{(i,j)t}(CL) = 1 - U, \tag{3}$$

where CL represent event 'cloudless'. m' means mass function value after introducing U. Because there are only two assertions: the overall multi-temporal information is cloudy (OC) or cloudless (OCL). Our study only used the plausibility function in D-S evidence theory to calculate the final confidence based on multi-temporal confidence information as in Eq. 4.

$$Pla(OC) = \frac{1}{K} \sum_{A_1 \cap A_2 \dots \cap A_q = C} m_1(A_1) m_2(A_2) \dots m_q(A_q),$$
$$Pla(OCL) = \frac{1}{K} \sum_{A_1 \cap A_2 \dots \cap A_q = CL} m_1(A_1) m_2(A_2) \dots m_q(A_q), \tag{4}$$

where Pla represents the value of the plausibility function supporting a particular assertion. K is the normalization factor. A_t represents possible events (cloudy, cloudless, and uncertain) at time t. $m_t(A)$ represents mass function value of event A at time t. The representation of location (i,j) is omitted for brevity.

Here, we specifically define that:

$$C \cap U = C, \quad CL \cap U = CL, \quad C \cap CL = \emptyset. \tag{5}$$

To get an assertion, we use this rule to perform evidence fusion on multi-temporal cloud confidence maps. Then we use the assertion and multi-temporal images to implement cloud removal.

3.4 Evidence Fusion Method

After obtaining the refined confidence map and fusing the results using D-S evidence theory, we fuse the data based on the following rules.

If the D-S evidence theory fusion result in the location (i,j) is OCL, then:

Step1. Takes the RGB values of pixels $P_1, P_2...P_m$ in time series 1,2,...m at location (i,j) for clustering.

Step2. If there exists a pixel clustering center C of which grayscale value is less than the brightness threshold L, and the number of pixels belonging to C exceeds threshold N_1, we select C as the fusion result. If there is no such clustering center, go to Step3.

Step3. Select the top N_2 pixels with the lowest cloud confidence, then take their mean value as the fusion result.

If the fusion result is OC, reduce N_1 and N_2. Then conduct the above steps.

N_1 and N_2 are defined based on the length of time series. We design this rule based on the assumption that these multi-temporal images have slight ground surface variation. Cloud differs sea/ground significantly. Therefore if there are multiple dark pixels with similar RGB values at the same location, these pixels could represent the true ground surface better. If there are no such pixels, we can only trust the Cloud-net and the prior knowledge, then take the mean value of the top N_2 pixels with the lowest cloud confidence as output.

4 Experiment

First, we trained Cloud-net in Sect. 4.1 to figure out whether it can perform well on OOD (Out of Distribution) dataset. Second, we designed an experiment to prove that color prior knowledge can refine segmentation results of the Cloud-net in Sect. 4.2. Third, we show that our method can effectively remove the cloud and reconstruct the ground surface in Sect. 4.3. Then. we designed ablation experiment to discuss the effects of the prior knowledge and the D-S evidence theory in Sect. 4.4. Finally, we demonstrate that our method is superior to other existing cloud-removal methods in Sect. 4.5. The experiment was run in the following environment: software environment: Python 3.6, Tensorflow 1.12.0, Keras 2.2.4, Scikit-image 0.15.0, windows 10; hardware environment: RTX3090, AMD EPYC 7702 processor.

4.1   Training Cloud-net

We selected the dataset and pre-trained network weights provided by [13]. The dataset contains 8400 images (resolution: 384 × 384) from the Landsat 8 satellite. After removing the images whose blank areas are more than 10%, it remains 4382 images with four channels (RGB and NIR). We use a transfer learning strategy to fine-tune the pre-trained weights. In our study, we choose 10^{-5} as the learning rate, 20% of the total dataset as the validation set, 80% as the training set, 16 as batchsize, and other parameters are set to default values. The loss function is defined as shown in Eq. 6.

$$loss = 1 - \frac{sum(\boldsymbol{y_{pred}} \odot \boldsymbol{y_{gt}}) + \varepsilon}{sum(\boldsymbol{y_{pred}} + \boldsymbol{y_{gt}}) - sum(\boldsymbol{y_{pred}} \odot \boldsymbol{y_{gt}}) + \varepsilon}, \tag{6}$$

where $\boldsymbol{y_{pred}}$ is the predicted 384 × 384 matrix, $\boldsymbol{y_{gt}}$ is the labeled matrix. $\odot$ is the Hadamard product. $sum()$ is matrix summation function. ε is a small value that is larger than 0 (we choose 10^{-7} in the experiment). The loss function value approaches convergence quickly. The test images are part of the data taken by GF-4. There are 34 images spread over six locations, each containing 4 to 7 images at different times. Part of the test images and corresponding cloud segmentation results are shown in Fig. 2. The network has an adequate cloud detection performance but demonstrates poor performance when facing OOD data from the training set shown in Fig. 2. So we use the color prior knowledge to refine and complement segmentation results.

4.2   Experiments with Color Prior Knowledge

To make the segmentation results more accurate, we introduce the color prior knowledge module in Sect. 3.2. Experimental results are shown in Fig. 2. The color prior knowledge module effectively improves the segmentation results when facing OOD data. Using manually annotated cloud pixels as ground truth, the color prior knowledge can increase the segmentation accuracy defined from an average of 30% to over 90%. Segmentation accuracy (SA) is calculated by $SA = AN/TN$, where AN is the number of accurately classified cloud pixels, TN is the number of total cloud pixels.

4.3   Multi-temporal Remote Sensing Cloud Removal Experiments

To verify the effectiveness of our cloud removal method, we took multi-temporal images captured by the GF-4 satellite as test data. Part of the experimental results is shown in Fig. 3. As our method tends to select darker pixels and the image itself is not very bright, we conducted a gamma transform on reconstructed images to make them clearer. As we can see, the final output image of the algorithm contains very few clouds. To measure its performance quantitatively, we manually annotate the cloud areas in test images. We calculate the cloud rate in each input image and corresponding reconstructed results. The cloud rate (CR) is calculated by this: $CR = C_n/T_n$, where C_n is the number of cloud

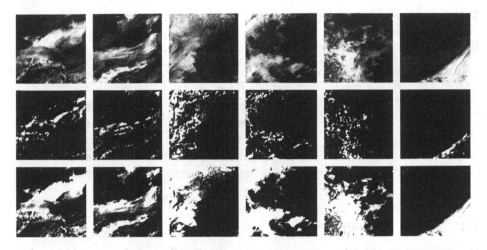

Fig. 2. Comparison of input against the output of the Cloud-net with the color prior knowledge. Row 1: test images captured by GF-4 satellite. Row 2: segmentation results of Cloud-net, and the white part are cloud regions classified by cloud-net. Row 3: refined segmentation results by color prior knowledge.

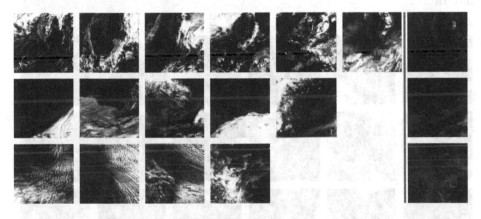

Fig. 3. Results of our cloud removal method. The last column is the final cloud removal results, and the other columns are the multi-temporal remote sensing images.

pixels, T_n is the number of total pixels. As shown in Table 1 and Fig. 3, our method removes most clouds. However, few cloud areas still exist after cloud removal. The main reason is that the areas are always covered with clouds in an image sequence. Therefore, there is no true ground surface information available for reconstruction. On the other hand, the above results show that more images captured at the same location and more complementary cloudless areas will lead to better cloud removal results.

Table 1. Estimated cloud rates before and after cloud removal. Minimum and Maximum means the smallest and biggest cloud rates in these areas. WLR, STS-CNN and PSTCR will be introduced in Sect. 4.5

Area/Cloud rate	Minimum	Maximum	WLR	STS-CNN	PSTCR	Our method
1	26.65%	41.96%	22.51%	23.07%	20.49%	**2.55%**
2	16.30%	44.31%	33.90%	15.44%	24.59%	**2.66%**
3	30.12%	49.02%	28.35%	26.89%	22.76%	**2.14%**
4	40.65%	46.23%	33.86%	24.74%	29.79%	**7.37%**
5	21.31%	48.68%	31.13%	26.75%	25.85%	**2.67%**
6	24.34%	50.31%	31.79%	29.32%	17.51%	**1.76%**

4.4   Ablation Experiment

We designed an ablation experiment to verify the effect of the prior knowledge and the D-S evidence theory. To remove the D-S evidence theory, we simply output the pixel with the lowest cloud confidence. We did not remove Cloud-net because it is essential. The results of ablation experiment are shown in Fig. 4 and Table 2.

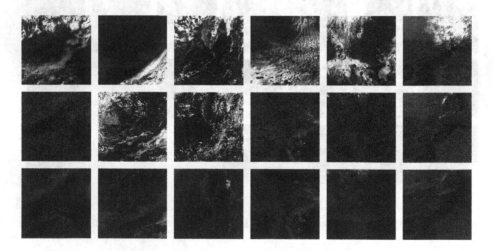

Fig. 4. Row 1: outputs without the prior knowledge. Row 2: outputs without the D-S evidence theory. Row 3: outputs with all components.

We can see from Fig. 4 and Table 2: outputs of W/O_P still contain lots of clouds, which means the prior knowledge can significantly refine the results of cloud segmentation. Outputs of W/O_D-S contain less cloud than W/O_P overall, but more cloud than ALL. Also, we found that the outputs of W/O_D-S contain many cloud pixels which are similar to salt noise. Obviously, the D-S evidence theory can make outputs more smooth.

Table 2. Cloud rates in ablation experiment. W/O_P means our method without the prior knowledge. W/O_D-S means without our method the D-S evidence theory. ALL means our method with all components.

Area/Ablation	W/O_P	W/O_D-S	ALL
1	28.46%	19.81%	**2.55%**
2	15.69%	33.20%	**2.66%**
3	24.31%	31.38%	**2.14%**
4	39.65%	20.80%	**7.37%**
5	33.11%	19.27%	**2.67%**
6	19.27%	14.73%	**1.76%**

4.5 Comparison Against Other Cloud Removal Methods

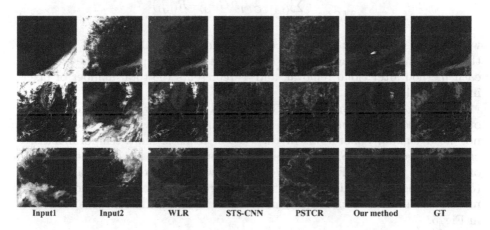

Input1   Input2   WLR   STS-CNN   PSTCR   Our method   GT

Fig. 5. Column 1 and column 2: inputs. Column 3: outputs of WLR. Column 4: outputs of STS-CNN. Column 5: outputs of PSTCR, which can only process grayscale image. Column 6: outputs of our method. Column7: ground truth (combination of cloudless parts from two inputs).

For previous thick cloud removal methods, we choose WLR [14], STS-CNN [15], and PSTCR [12] for comparison. WLR and STS-CNN take cloudy target images, cloudless reference images, and cloud segmentation maps as input. Then they use the reference images to fill the target images. PSTCR can only process grayscale images, selects multiple cloudy images with cloud segmentation maps as input, and supplements the images with a convolutional neural network. After obtaining the codes corresponding to the above methods, we followed its original hyper-parameters and experimented with manually labeled cloudy images as inputs. To quantify the cloud-removal effect, we fused their inputs by combining their cloudless regions to obtain the complementary image gt. The red regions in gt mean both regions in two inputs are cloudy. Subsequently, the MSE(Mean

Table 3. Comparison of MSE against different cloud removal methods on test images

Area/Methods	WLR	STS-CNN	PSTCR	Our method
1	0.0552	0.0931	0.0844	**0.0501**
2	0.1152	0.0200	0.1204	**0.0191**
3	1.066	0.8268	0.9092	**0.7813**
4	0.1484	0.0886	0.2025	**0.0335**
5	1.115	0.7198	0.8202	**0.6664**
6	0.0832	0.1190	0.0416	**0.0348**

Square Error) was calculated for the cloudless part of gt and the corresponding part of the output images processed by different methods, defined as in Eq. 7.

$$MSE = \frac{\sum_{(i,j)\in CFR} \left(G_{(i,j)} - R_{(i,j)}\right)^2}{T}, \tag{7}$$

where $(i,j) \in CFR$ represents the coordinates of the cloudless part, G represents the complementary image after pixel normalization, R represents the output of each method after cloud removal, and T represents the total number of pixels in the cloudless region.

As can be seen from Table 1, Table 3 and Fig. 5, our method outperforms other methods. These methods use manual annotations, while our method does not need manual annotation. In the case of realistic multi-temporal massive cloudy images, the MSE values output by our method are lower than those of the other methods. Furthermore, because we use the original image's pixels (or clustering centers) directly for filling, our restored images are smoother and more realistic without producing many blank regions and mutations, as shown in Fig. 5.

5   Conclusion

Our study presents a multi-temporal thick cloud removal method, applying cloud segmentation networks, prior knowledge, and D-S evidence theory. Our method does not require cloudless images as the reference. Reconstructed images are close to the true ground surface. Our method significantly reduces the cloud rate on GF-4 satellite remote sensing images. Theoretically, our method can achieve complete cloud removal when thick clouds cover not all the regions at the same location. However, our study still has limitations: Our study does not consider dealing with the shadows from cloud occlusion now. Thin clouds are not easily recognized in our study. Our method is based on the assumption that the true ground surfaces in different images differ very little. If the overall brightness or true ground surface changes significantly, they may lead to wrong fusion results. These problems need to be addressed in future research.

Acknowledgement. This work is supported by Key R&D Project of Chinaunder Grant No.2017YFC0704100, 2016YFB0901900, National Natural Science Foundation of China under Grant No. 61425024, the 111 International Collaboration Program of China under Grant No. BP2018006, 2019 Major Science and Technology Program for the Strategic Emerging Industries of Fuzhou under Grant No.2019-Z-1, and in part by the BNRist Program under Grant No.BNR2019TD01009.

References

1. Liu, J.: Thin cloud removal from single satellite images. Opt. Express **22**(1), 618–632 (2014)
2. Wang, Z., Jin, J., Liang, J., Yan, K., Peng, Q.: A new cloud removal algorithm for multi-spectral images. In: MIPPR 2005: SAR and Multispectral Image Processing, vol. 6043, p. 60430W. International Society for Optics and Photonics (2005)
3. Xu, M., Pickering, M., Plaza, A.J., Jia, X.: Thin cloud removal based on signal transmission principles and spectral mixture analysis. IEEE Trans. Geosci. Remote Sens. **54**(3), 1659–1669 (2015)
4. Li, J., Wu, Z., Hu, Z., Zhang, J., Li, M., Mo, L., Molinier, M.: Thin cloud removal in optical remote sensing images based on generative adversarial networks and physical model of cloud distortion. ISPRS J. Photogram. Remote Sens. **166**, 373–389 (2020)
5. Chun, F., Jian-wen, M., Qin, D., Xue, C.: An improved method for cloud removal in aster data change detection. In: IGARSS 2004. 2004 IEEE International Geoscience and Remote Sensing Symposium, vol. 5, pp. 3387–3389. IEEE (2004)
6. Tarel, J.P., Hautiere, N.: Fast visibility restoration from a single color or gray level image. In: 2009 IEEE 12th International Conference on Computer Vision, pp. 2201–2208. IEEE (2009)
7. Cheng, Q., Shen, H., Zhang, L., Yuan, Q., Zeng, C.: Cloud removal for remotely sensed images by similar pixel replacement guided with a spatio-temporal mrf model. ISPRS J. Photogram. Remote Sens. **92**, 54–68 (2014)
8. Xu, M., Jia, X., Pickering, M., Plaza, A.J.: Cloud removal based on sparse representation via multitemporal dictionary learning. IEEE Trans. Geosci. Remote Sens. **54**(5), 2998–3006 (2016)
9. Li, X., Wang, L., Cheng, Q., Wu, P., Gan, W., Fang, L.: Cloud removal in remote sensing images using nonnegative matrix factorization and error correction. ISPRS J. Photogram. Remote Sens. **148**, 103–113 (2019)
10. Tseng, D.C., Tseng, H.T., Chien, C.L.: Automatic cloud removal from multitemporal spot images. Appl. Math. Comput. **205**(2), 584–600 (2008)
11. Lin, C.H., Tsai, P.H., Lai, K.H., Chen, J.Y.: Cloud removal from multitemporal satellite images using information cloning. IEEE Trans. Geosci. Remote Sens. **51**(1), 232–241 (2012)
12. Zhang, Q., Yuan, Q., Li, J., Li, Z., Shen, H., Zhang, L.: Thick cloud and cloud shadow removal in multitemporal imagery using progressively spatio-temporal patch group deep learning. ISPRS J. Photogram. Remote Sens. **162**, 148–160 (2020)
13. Mohajerani, S., Saeedi, P.: Cloud-net: an end-to-end cloud detection algorithm for landsat 8 imagery. In: IGARSS 2019–2019 IEEE International Geoscience and Remote Sensing Symposium, pp. 1029–1032. IEEE (2019)

14. Zeng, C., Shen, H., Zhang, L.: Recovering missing pixels for landsat etm+ slc-off imagery using multi-temporal regression analysis and a regularization method. Remote Sens. Environ. **131**, 182–194 (2013)
15. Zhang, Q., Yuan, Q., Zeng, C., Li, X., Wei, Y.: Missing data reconstruction in remote sensing image with a unified spatial-temporal-spectral deep convolutional neural network. IEEE Trans. Geosci. Remote Sens. **56**(8), 4274–4288 (2018)
16. Derrien, M., et al.: Automatic cloud detection applied to noaa-11/avhrr imagery. Remote Sens. Environ. **46**(3), 246–267 (1993)
17. Jang, J.D., Viau, A.A., Anctil, F., Bartholomé, E.: Neural network application for cloud detection in spot vegetation images. Int. J. Remote Sens. **27**(4), 719–736 (2006)
18. Mohajerani, S., Krammer, T.A., Saeedi, P.: Cloud detection algorithm for remote sensing images using fully convolutional neural networks. arXiv preprint arXiv:1810.05782 (2018)
19. Li, Z., Shen, H., Wei, Y., Cheng, Q., Yuan, Q.: Cloud detection by fusing multi-scale convolutional features. ISPRS Ann. Photogramm. Remote Sens. Spat. Inf. Sci **4**, 149–152 (2018)
20. Ma, N., Sun, L., Wang, Q., Yu, Z., Liu, S.: Improved cloud detection for landsat 8 images using a combined neural network model. Remote Sens. Lett. **11**(3), 274–282 (2020)
21. Solvsteen, C.: Correlation-based cloud detection and an examination of the split-window method. In: Global Process Monitoring and Remote Sensing of the Ocean and Sea Ice, vol. 2586, pp. 86–97. SPIE (1995)
22. Peng, C., Rong, Z., Lu, Z.: Feature extraction in remote sensing image cloud map recognition. J. Univ. Sci. Technol. China **5**, 234–241 (2009)
23. Ronneberger, O., Fischer, P., Brox, T.: U-Net: convolutional networks for biomedical image segmentation. In: Navab, N., Hornegger, J., Wells, W.M., Frangi, A.F. (eds.) MICCAI 2015. LNCS, vol. 9351, pp. 234–241. Springer, Cham (2015). https://doi.org/10.1007/978-3-319-24574-4_28
24. Kumar, T., Verma, K.: A theory based on conversion of rgb image to gray image. International Journal of Computer Applications **7**(2), 7–10 (2010)
25. Yager, R.R.: On the dempster-shafer framework and new combination rules. Inf. Sci. **41**(2), 93–137 (1987)

SASD: A Shape-Aware Saliency Object Detection Approach for RGB-D Images

Lingling Zi and Xin Cong(✉)

College of Computer and Information Science, Chongqing Normal University,
Chongqing 401331, China
chongzi610@163.com

Abstract. Saliency object detection is a fundamental problem in the field of computer vision. With the commercial success of consumer-grade depth sensors such as Microsoft Kinect, the captured RGB-D images provide users with a higher viewing experience, but also pose a higher challenge to the current saliency detection technology. In this paper, we propose a shape-aware saliency object detection approach SASD, manifesting in two aspects: 1) obtaining high quality saliency maps, especially the salient details; 2) displaying irregular salient regions, such as circles, ellipses, and splines. The proposed SASD approach consists of three steps. First, the initial saliency map is obtained by combing depth information and edge details. On this basis, the rules for the dominant factors of saliency detection are designed and the method of enhanced saliency map calculation is proposed. Finally, an irregular shape display method is demonstrated, the purpose of which is to fit the obtained saliency map to different shapes. The experiment demonstrates the effectiveness of our approach in subjective and objective aspects.

Keywords: Saliency detection · RGB-D images · Irregular shapes · Depth information

1 Introduction

With the commercial success of consumer-grade depth sensors, the captured RGB-D images pose a higher challenge to the current saliency object detection [1–3]. Compared with existing RGB images, adding depth maps can enrich the image information and provide useful cues for visual attention [4–6]. However, the quality of the obtained depth maps is not very good, and there are defects such as loss of depth data and strange data [7,8]. This will affect saliency object detection to a certain extent. Therefore, reasonable utilization of depth data is very important to improve the accuracy of saliency detection. In addition, the quality of the saliency maps plays an important role in the actual applications. However, we find that the existing methods ignore the detailed display of the

This work is supported by the Doctoral Research Foundation of Chongqing Normal University (No.21XLB029, No.21XLB030).

generated saliency maps, so how to preserve fine details in the resulting maps is a key issue that should be solved. Based on the above analysis, we need to conduct special research on RGB-D images to improve the accuracy of saliency detection and the clarity of saliency regions.

Moreover, the rapid development of virtual reality technology and LED display technology has put forward the demand for displaying images or videos on display devices with irregular shapes, such as pentagonal LED displays, circular water curtains, and heart-shaped photo frames, etc. Nevertheless, the existing methods either display the rectangular attention regions or obtain saliency objects, ignoring the display of irregular shapes, thereby affecting the viewer's experience. Therefore, how to display a salient region with an irregular shape has become another important issue currently.

To solve the above problems, we propose a shape-aware saliency object detection approach SASD, which is driven by the dual goals of salient content preservation and shape requirements, and mainly completes the following two tasks. One is to obtain detailed high-quality saliency maps through color features, depth information and the relationship between them. The other is to use shape information to display irregular salient regions. Specifically, the main contributions of SASD are as follows.

(1) From a novel perspective, a shape-aware RGB-D saliency detection framework is constructed to achieve high-quality display of irregular salient regions. The framework uses multiple types of information, including color, depth, edge, and shape.
(2) To improve the accuracy of saliency detection, a coarse-to-fine saliency map calculation method is proposed, including the initial saliency map using the deep-supervised short connection network and the enhanced saliency map based on the relationship between details and edges. Furthermore, adaptive manifold filtering is adopted to add the details of the salient map, saliency detection rules are designed to determine the dominant saliency factors, and then different calculation methods are performed.
(3) Combining the shape parameters, an irregular shape display method is proposed to fit the obtained salient regions. It can achieve the display of irregular shapes such as circles, ellipses, and splines, and its implementation mainly includes the key point detection, parametric equation construction, driving force calculation and parametric update.

2   Related Work

Saliency Detection. Currently, computer vision has a wide range of applications [9–12], and saliency detection is the basis of many applications. The essence of saliency detection is to find the most significant region or object in the image. According to the research object, it can be divided into RGB image and RGB-D image. RGB saliency detection methods have been extensively studied. In particular, the deeply supervised salient object detection with short connections [13] preforms better than the other methods. But in the real environment, the human visual attention mechanism needs to be applied to the three-dimensional scene, and the depth information plays an important role in the process of detecting objects. However, it is a neglected factor in the RGB saliency detection methods, so RGB-D methods are proposed. Cheng et al. [14] used the depth characteristics of feature contrast and spatial bias to develop an enhanced saliency detection method, which demonstrates that the depth information is necessary for detecting objects in complex scenes. Peng et al. [15] proposed a novel salient object detection method, which is a classic method. Ren et al. [16] proposed the use of a global prior method for RGB-D saliency detection. Although these methods have achieved the task of 3D saliency detection, there are still problems of inaccurate detection and low quality of saliency maps.

Geometric Shape Model. How to display the obtained salient region in an irregular shape to meet the requirements of different display devices is a key problem. For this problem, we consider that the shape of the salient region to be displayed can be described in a geometric form, and then use irregular shapes to fit as much as possible. In view of the time and efficiency factors, we found that the solution to this problem is to fit geometric shapes to the image data, using the active geometric model [17]. The model uses a force field to fit a geometric shape in the image, which detects and segments the object region described by the geometric shape without training data. Therefore, we try to introduce this model into the proposed SASD to complete the task of displaying irregular shapes. In this paper, we explore simple irregular shapes, such as circles, ellipses, and splines.

3 The Proposed SASD Approach

The problem to be solved in this paper is how to display the salient regions of RGB-D images with irregular shapes. We can divide it into two sub-problems: one is to obtain the saliency map of the RGB-D image, and the other is to display the saliency region in irregular shapes. The proposed SASD can solve the above problems. Its framework is shown in Fig. 1, including initial saliency map computation, enhanced saliency map calculation and irregular shape display.

The mathematical description is as follows. Given a RGB-D image, it is decomposed into color channel IR and depth channel ID. The saliency map ESM and display result ISD under the condition of irregular shape RS are:

$$
\begin{aligned}
Ini(IR, ID) &\rightarrow IDSM, IESM \\
Enh(ISM) &\rightarrow ESM \\
Display(ESM, RS) &\rightarrow ISD
\end{aligned}
\tag{1}
$$

In Eq. 1, function $Ini()$ represents the process of calculating initial saliency map according to IR and ID, the result ISM is obtained, including detail saliency map $IDSM$ and edge saliency map $IESM$. On this basis, function

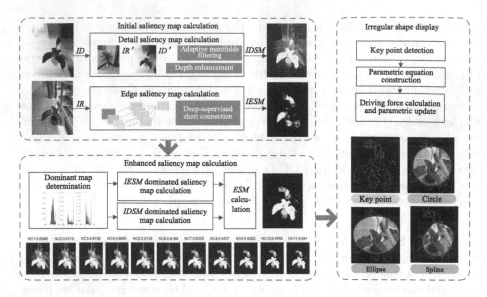

Fig. 1. The SASD framework.

$Enh()$ is performed and ESM can be acquired. Finally, function $Display()$ is performed under the specified shape RS to get salient region in the form of an irregular shape. Next, we will elaborate the details of $SASD$ in each step.

3.1 Initial Saliency Map Calculation

We calculate the initial saliency map from two perspectives, detail saliency map and edge saliency map. The former fully exerts the role of depth information to preserve the details of the salient map. The latter emphasizes the role of color information, highlighting the edges of the saliency map.

Detail Saliency Map Calculation. We compute the detail saliency map using a two-stage process and this process can be expressed as:

$$IDSM' \leftarrow Filter(IR, ID)$$
$$IDSM \leftarrow Integr(IDSM') \tag{2}$$

In Eq. 2, $IDSM'$ includes IR' and ID', in which IR' denotes a color detail map and ID' denotes a depth smoothing map. $Filter()$ emphasizes the color contrast and reduces the influence of defected depth data. And $Integr()$ preforms integration operation to compute detail saliency map.

Adaptive manifold filtering [18] provides a way for improving fine details and we apply it to compute $IDSM'$, which consists of IR' corresponding to IR and ID' corresponding to ID. On this basis, detail saliency map can be calculated from the sum of three parts, color detail $SR_c(IR_{Rj})$, depth detail

$SR_d(ID_{Rj})$ and depth enhancement $SR_b(ID_{Rj})$. The first two parts adopt the cues of obtained details to compute integration contrast, shown as follows.

$$SR_c(IR_{Rj}) = \sum_{j=1}^{num} \frac{\sigma_j}{N} \exp^{-d(IR_{Rj}, IR_{Rv})/\varepsilon^2} ||CIR_{Rj} - CIR_{Rv}|| \qquad (3)$$

$$SR_d(ID_{Rj}) = \sum_{j=1}^{num} \frac{\sigma_j}{N} \exp^{-d(ID_{Rj}, ID_{Rv})/\varepsilon^2} (CID_{Rj} - CID_{Rv}) \qquad (4)$$

where σ_j and N denote the number of pixels in IR_{Rj} and IR', respectively. In which IR_{Rj} denotes the divided region in IR. $d(IR_{Rj}, IR_{Rv})$ is defined as the distance function between IR_{Rj} and IR_{Rv}, and ϵ is the intensity parameter. The last part enhances depth saliency [19]. The difference from [19] is that the calculation of DOF, which uses a difference method to define the average depth of the pixel in ID' within the nearest and farthest depth range.

Edge Saliency Map Calculation. In view of the great success of the RGB images in full convolutional neural networks, we adopt a deep-supervised significant object detection network with short connections [13] to enhance the edge information of the salient map. The foundation of this network architecture is Caffe library, FCN, VGGNet, and Holistically-Nested Edge Detector (HED). The architecture includes saliency locating and detail refinement in function, which can work better for RGB images, especially single objects and high-contrast environments. We directly use the pre-trained well model [13] as the test model, without retraining the model. Its input is IR and its output is $IESM$. In the experiment, we found that although we only input RGB information, we can still get good results, which shows that color details are very important for RGB-D image processing.

3.2   Enhanced Saliency Map Calculation

We propose the dominant map method to compute the enhanced saliency map ESM. The process can be expressed as:

$$DF \leftarrow Deter(IR, ID, IDSM)$$
$$ESM \leftarrow ESC(DF, IDSM, IESM) \qquad (5)$$

where $Deter()$ denotes the dominant function, indicating whether the dominant map is $IDSM$ or $IESM$. According to the dominant map, $ESC()$ is executed to obtain ESM. To determine the dominant map, we design the following rules.

Rule 1: Under the condition of valid depth maps, when the depth similarity of ID is high but the color contrast of IR is not high, the depth cue is the dominant factor and the detail saliency map is used as the dominant map. In order to quantify the depth similarity, depth similarity score $dscore$ is defined, shown as follows.

$$dscore = cos(H_1, H_2) \tag{6}$$

where H_1 is the histogram of $IDSM$ or $IESM$, and H_2 is the histogram of inverted ID. Similarly, the RGB histogram variance σ_{RGB} is used to measure color contrast. Inspired by the structural score [20], we define saliency similarity score $sscore$ for assessment of saliency independent standards.

$$sscore = \frac{2\overline{P}_s\overline{P}_r}{(\overline{P}_s)^2+(\overline{P}_r)^2} \cdot \frac{2\sigma_{P_s}\sigma_{P_r}}{\sigma_{P_s}^2+\sigma_{P_r}^2} \cdot \frac{\sigma_{P_s P_r}}{\sigma_{P_s}\sigma_{P_r}} \tag{7}$$

In Eq. 7, P_s denotes $IDSM$ or $IESM$, P_r denotes the reference map. $\overline{P}_s$ and $\overline{P}_r$ denote the mean of P_s and P_r. σ_{P_s} and σ_{P_r} denote the standard deviations of P_s and P_r. And $\sigma_{P_s P_r}$ is the covariance between the two. The calculation of P_r contains two steps. First, reverse ID to ID_{re}, and then use the closer pixels as the salient pixels. In our implementation, we chose pixels with $ID_{re}(i,j) > 180$ and $ID_{re}(i,j) < 256$, putting the map NGT. Then we design the following rule.

Rule 2: When the saliency similarity score of detail saliency map is comparably high, and its depth similarity score is also high, the depth cue is the dominant factor and the detail saliency map is used as the dominant map.

IESM Dominated Saliency Map Calculation. This idea is to take advantage of the edge saliency map to obtain accurate edges, while combining with the detail saliency map to preserve details, thereby improving the quality of the saliency map. The calculation process is shown below.

Step 1: Calculate the contour guide map IE_{Mask}.
Step 2: Calculate the enhanced map I_{ESM} using $I_{ESM} = I_{IDSM} \cdot * IE_{Mask}$. In which, I_{IDSM} denotes the $IDSM$ map. Figure 2 shows the obtained result ESM. From left to right, $IR, IESM, IDSM, IE_{Mask}$ and ESM are listed. From this figure, we can see the clear details of ESM.

Fig. 2. The obtained result using $IESM$ dominated saliency map.

IDSM Dominated Saliency Map Calculation. Its core is to compute adaptively the structural similarity guide map to find the map with the highest saliency similarity score. The mainly process is as follows.

Step 1: Initialize $Mask_i(i = 1 \cdots 11)$ and calculate NGT.

Step 2: Calculate the initial saliency map C, which is the sum of $IESM$ and $IDSM$.

Step 3: Set the threshold A_i corresponding to $Mask_i$ using $A_i = 100 + 10 * (i-1)$, in which $i = 1 \cdots 11$.

Step 4: For each pixel in C, if its value is more than A_i, then the pixel value of $Mask_i$ is set to 1.

Step 5: Calculate the structural similarity guide map NC_i which is $NC_i = I_{IDSM} * Mask_i$.

Step 6: Calculate the saliency similarity score of NC_i, and select NC_i with the maximum similarity score as ESM.

3.3   Irregular Shape Display

The idea of irregular shape display is to model the saliency object in ESM using geometric shape, and then associate each parameter of the geometric shape to establish a parametric equation, which is described as the integral of the force field along the contour. This process contains three parts: key point detection, parametric equation construction, driving force calculation and parametric update.

For key point detection, we consider how to fit the geometric shape to the saliency map of the image. To solve this problem, we detect ESM described by geometric shapes without using training data. For ESM description, we use model-based image analysis, especially geometric modelling provide an effective way. However, we want to fit the saliency map as much as possible, rather than the entire image. Therefore, a feasible method is to extract important information from ESM. In view of the good performance of the Canny operator, we use it to extract the positions of important points in ESM, donated as (p_x, p_y), as the key points for irregular display.

Next, we construct parametric equation. We use parametric equations to describe the circle, including radius r and center coordinates (px_c, py_c). Then the coordinates of the pixel px_i and py_i are:

$$px_i = px_c + r \cos \theta_i, py_i = py_c + r \sin \theta_i \tag{8}$$

where θ_i denotes the corresponding value of each pixel on the circle of ESM, $\theta_i \in [0, 2\pi]$. Ellipse parameters include semi-major axis length a, semi-minor axis length b, center coordinate (px_c, py_c) and orientation ϕ:

$$\begin{aligned} px_i &= px_c + a \cos \theta_i cos\phi - bsin\theta_i \sin \phi \\ py_i &= py_c + a \cos \theta_i \sin \phi + bsin\theta_i \cos \phi \end{aligned} \tag{9}$$

The spline curve is more complex, which embodies a freer shape. Assuming that the center of the shape is also (px_c, py_c), for any pixel in this shape (px_c, py_c), its orientation is ℓ_1, the distance to the center is D_i, then the coordinates of this pixel are:

$$px_i = px_c + D_i \cos \ell_i, py_i = py_c + D_i \sin \ell_i \qquad (10)$$

The force field is used to calculate the driving force of irregular shapes [18]. Through numerical iteration, driving force will push the key point in *ESM* to move to a more suitable position. We adopt gradient vector flow $\mathbf{DF}(p_x, p_y) = [m(p_x, p_y), n(p_x, p_y)]$ as the force field of pixel $P(p_x, p_y)$.The driving force setting and parameter update rules for irregular shapes are the same as [17]. The difference from [17] is that we add subtle adjustment values in the last iteration.

4   Experiments and Discussion

In this section, we will evaluate the proposed SASD from subjective and objective perspectives. We conduct experiments using the MATLAB platform. Our data are from the NLPR database [15], which consists 1000 images from indoor and outdoor scenes.

Figure 3 shows the obtained visual results of saliency detection, in which a single saliency object exits in the scene. We compare four methods, including the deep learning method based on short connection(DL) [13], the deep enhancement method(DES) [14], the classic RGB-D method(CSD) [15] and global prior method(Global) [16]. In this figure, color images, depth maps, results by DL, results by DES, results by CSD, results by Global, our results and the ground truth are shown from left to right. We can see that saliency results using our method are clearer than those of other methods. In particular, our results have more details.

Fig. 3. Visual results of saliency detection. From left to right, IR, ID, DL, DES, CSD, Global, SASD and the ground truth.

Figure 4 shows the obtained visual results of saliency detection in a complex background. The results using our method are also better than those of others. In addition, the last row shows visual effects of multiple salient objects in the scene. By adopting the proposed method, the details of resulting saliency maps are exhibited clearly.

Fig. 4. Visual results of saliency detection. From left to right, IR, ID, DL, DES, CSD, Global, SASD and the ground truth.

Figure 5 demonstrate the results of irregular shapes marked with red lines in the same image, including circles, ellipses, and splines. It can be seen that our method uses irregular shapes to display important regions reasonably. All the shapes contain saliency contents, which can lay the foundation for irregular shape resizing applications.

Fig. 5. Irregular shape display.

Since high-quality saliency results are the basis for irregular shape display, we evaluate the quality of saliency maps. Mean Absolute Error (MAE) and F-measure are traditional evaluation metrics. Our method is compared with four saliency detection methods, including DL, DES, CSD and Global method. Figure 6 shows the comparison results of average MAE and average F-measure, respectively. From this figure, we can see our MAE values are always lower than the comparison methods, while F-measure values are higher. This indicates our results are closer to the ground truth.

We can also apply our method to achieve depth-of-field effect, which combines irregular shape display and the depth-based selective blurring method [21]. Figure 7 shows the depth-of-field effect using circles, ellipses, and splines from

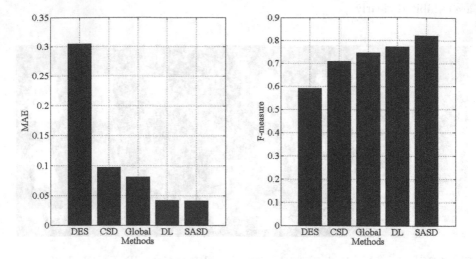

Fig. 6. Comparison results.

Fig. 7. Depth-of-field effect using by our method.

top to bottom. We can see clear and important content in irregular shapes and blurred backgrounds, which obtains interesting effects.

5   Conclusion

We propose the SASD method to calculate the saliency regions of irregular shapes to meet the requirements of the multi-shape development of the display. SASD mainly consists of two parts: coarse-to-fine saliency map calculation and an irregular shape display. The former applies adaptive manifold filtering to enhance details of the salient map, and designs saliency detection rules to improve the performance of saliency detection. The latter combines the active geometric shape model to fit the saliency region to the specified shape. The proposed SASD not only provides good detection results, but also shows better details. In the future, we will expand the SASD method to display more shapes, such as hearts, stars, etc. In addition, we will further study the evaluation of SASD to provide better evaluation standards.

References

1. Zhou, T., Fan, D.P., Cheng, M.M., et al.: RGB-D salient object detection: a survey. Comput. Visual Media **7**(1), 37–69 (2021)
2. Venek, V., Kremser, W.: Towards a live feedback training system: interchangeability of orbbec persee and microsoft kinect for exercise monitoring. Designs **5** (2021)
3. Maharaj, A.V., Gutierrez, A., Cueto, C., et al.: Automated measurement of repetitive behavior using the Microsoft Kinect: a proof of concept. Behav. Intervent. **35**(4), 488–497 (2020)
4. Ahmed, A., Jalal, A., Kim, K.: RGB-D images for object segmentation, localization and recognition in indoor scenes using feature descriptor and Hough voting. In: 17th International Bhurban Conference on Applied Sciences and Technology (IBCAST), pp. 290–295. IEEE (2019)
5. Zhang, Y., Sidib, D., Morel, O., et al.: Incorporating depth information into few-shot semantic segmentation. In: 2020 25th International Conference on Pattern Recognition(ICPR), pp. 3582–3588. IEEE (2021)
6. Wei, X., Du, J., Liang, M., et al.: Boosting deep attribute learning via support vector regression for fast moving crowd counting. Pattern Recogn. Lett. **119**, 12–23 (2019)
7. Shi, C., Han, X., Song, L., et al.: Deep collaborative filtering with multi-aspect information in heterogeneous networks. IEEE Trans. Knowl. Data Eng. **33**(4), 1413–1425 (2019)
8. Li, W., Jia, Y., Du, J.: Resilient filtering for nonlinear complex networks with multiplicative noise. IEEE Trans. Autom. Control **64**(6), 2522–2528 (2018)
9. Fang, Y., Deng, W., Du, J., et al.: Identity-aware CycleGAN for face photo-sketch synthesis and recognition. Pattern Recogn. **102**, 107249 (2020)
10. Cao, J., Mao, D., Cai, Q., et al.: A review of object representation based on local features. J. Zhejiang Univ. Sci. **14**(7), 495–504 (2013)

11. Li, J., Du, J.: Study on panoramic image stitching algorithm. In: 2010 Second Pacific-Asia Conference on Circuits, Communications and System, pp. 417–420. IEEE (2010)

12. Hu, W., Gao, J., Li, B., et al.: Anomaly detection using local kernel density estimation and context-based regression. IEEE Trans. Knowl. Data Eng. **32**(2), 218–233 (2018)

13. Hou, Q., Cheng, M.M., Hu, X., et al.: Deeply supervised salient object detection with short connections. In: IEEE Conference on Computer Vision and Pattern Recognition, pp. 3203–3212. IEEE (2017)

14. Cheng, Y., Fu, H., Wei, X., et al.: Depth enhanced saliency detection method. In: International Conference on Internet Multimedia Computing and Service, pp. 23–27. ACM (2012)

15. Peng, H., Li, B., Xiong, W., Hu, W., Ji, R.: RGBD salient object detection: a benchmark and algorithms. In: Fleet, D., Pajdla, T., Schiele, B., Tuytelaars, T. (eds.) ECCV 2014. LNCS, vol. 8691, pp. 92–109. Springer, Cham (2014). https://doi.org/10.1007/978-3-319-10578-9_7

16. Ren, J., Gong, X., Yu, L., et al.: Exploiting global priors for RGB-D saliency detection. In: IEEE Conference on Computer Vision and Pattern Recognition workshops, pp. 25–32. IEEE (2015)

17. Wang, Q., Boyer, K.L.: The active geometric shape model: a new robust deformable shape model and its applications. Comput. Vision Image Underst. **116**(12), 1178–1194 (2012)

18. Gastal, E.S., Oliveira, M.M.: Adaptive manifolds for real-time high-dimensional filtering. ACM Trans. Graph. (TOG) **31**(4), 1–11 (2012)

19. Feng, D., Barnes, N., You, S., et al.: Local background enclosure for RGB-D salient object detection. In: IEEE Conference on Computer Vision and Pattern Recognition, pp. 2343–2350. IEEE (2016)

20. Fan, D.P., Cheng, M.M., Liu, Y., et al.:Structure-measure: a new way to evaluate foreground maps. In: IEEE International Conference on Computer Vision, pp. 4548–4557. IEEE (2017)

21. Mukherjee, S., Guddeti, R.: Depth-based selective blurring in stereo images using accelerated framework. 3D Res. **5**(3), 1–21(2014)

Dual Windows Are Significant: Learning from Mediastinal Window and Focusing on Lung Window

Qiuli Wang[1], Xin Tan[2(✉)], Lizhuang Ma[3], and Chen Liu[4]

[1] Chongqing University, Chongqing, China
[2] East China Normal University, Shanghai, China
xtan@cs.ecnu.edu.cn
[3] Shanghai Jiao Tong University, Shanghai, China
[4] The First Affiliated Hospital of Army Medical University, Chongqing, China
liuchen@aifmri.com

Abstract. Since the pandemic of COVID-19, several deep learning methods were proposed to analyze the chest Computed Tomography (CT) for diagnosis. In the current situation, the disease course classification is significant for medical personnel to decide the treatment. Most previous deep-learning-based methods extract features observed from the lung window. However, it has been proved that some appearances related to diagnosis can be observed better from the mediastinal window rather than the lung window, e.g., the pulmonary consolidation happens more in severe symptoms. In this paper, we propose a novel Dual Window RCNN Network (DWR-Net), which mainly learns the distinctive features from the successive mediastinal window. Regarding the features extracted from the lung window, we introduce the *Lung Window Attention Block* (LWA Block) to pay additional attention to them for enhancing the mediastinal-window features. Moreover, instead of picking up specific slices from the whole CT slices, we use a Recurrent CNN and analyze successive slices as videos. Experimental results show that the fused and representative features improve the predictions of disease course by reaching the accuracy of 90.57%, against the baseline with an accuracy of 84.86%. Ablation studies demonstrate that combined dual window features are more efficient than lung-window features alone, while paying attention to lung-window features can improve the model's stability.

Keywords: Chest computed tomography · COVID-19 · Mediastinal window

1 Introduction

COVID-19, which is resulted from the novel coronavirus, has been out-breaking, and the number of infected persons is reaching a new peak everyday. According to the World Health Organization (WHO) report, there are 240 million confirmed cases and 4.8 million confirmed deaths by the end of October 22, 2021 [28]. The

© The Author(s), under exclusive license to Springer Nature Switzerland AG 2022
L. Fang et al. (Eds.): CICAI 2022, LNAI 13604, pp. 191–203, 2022.
https://doi.org/10.1007/978-3-031-20497-5_16

rapid spread of COVID-19 undoubtedly has long-range effects on the world and puts tremendous pressure on the current medical systems of every country. To relieve the docotors' workloads and speed up the treatment, the fast diagnose of COVID-19 and the decisions of its courses are strongly required.

Since the development of deep neural networks and the accumulation of lung Computed Tomography (CT) images infected by COVID-19, many CNN-based models are proposed to diagnose the COVID-19 automatically, such as [24, 26]. Although these methods have achieved some success to a certain extent for community-acquired pneumonia, few studies have pay attention to the disease course prediction, which plays a crucial role in CAD systems for COVID-19. The difficulty of disease course prediction is that, as the successive step of COVID-19 diagnosis, it has to deal with the cases which have obvious symptoms caused by COVID-19.

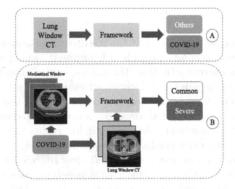

Fig. 1. A: Conventional methods learn lung window CT directly. B: DWRNet uses the mediastinal window as the main image window, and adds lung window features with Lung Window Attention Block.

Conventional methods usually analyze CT slices with single-channel window, as shown in Fig. 1.A. However, based on the official *Diagnosis and Treatment Protocol for COVID-19 Patients* [5] provided by the China National Health Commission, Ground-Glass Opacity (GGO) is commonly observed in the common cases of COVID-19, and consolidation may occur in the chest of severe cases. Generally speaking, the lung window is the appropriate CT window for the observation of GGO [17]. Meanwhile, the consolidations can be better observed with the mediastinal window, which is a more stable method in the aspect of the inter-reader agreement [2], and show better performance in measuring the solid tissues [30, 31]. The effect of CT image windows is shown in Fig. 2. It is obvious that GGO can be seen with a lung window setting but disappears when using the mediastinal window setting. However, with the mediastinal window setting, solid pulmonary consolidation can be clearly seen and avoid the influences caused by other symptoms.

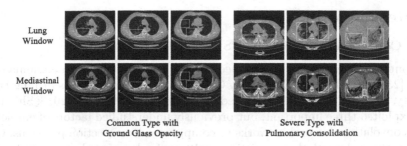

Fig. 2. Comparison between the lung window and mediastinal window. We can see that the common cases with GGO have apparent visual features with the lung window but are difficult to be diagnosed with the mediastinal window (red blocks). The severe cases show severe lung pathological changes when using the lung window. When changed to the mediastinal window, pulmonary consolidation can be clearly seen (yellow blocks). (Color figure online)

A straightforward solution to solve the above issue is to add another stream to learn useful features from the mediastinal window and combine two kinds of features, *i.e.*, lung-window features, and mediastinal-window features. However, there are high chances that both kinds of features have some repeated information since they are just extracted from the same CT HU values.

In this paper, we propose a Dual Window RCNN Network (DWRNet) based on a mediastinal window image. It also adds additional lung window features to the framework by attention mechanism. The overflow of DWRNet is shown in Fig. 1.B. Previous works learn most information from the lung window. Unlike these studies, our framework learns the main features from the mediastinal window, then just uses lung window features as the attention map by designing a Lung Window Attention Block (LWA Block). Moreover, instead of picking up specific CT images, the proposed DWRNet analyzes two successive CT windows as videos and learns the discriminative features from the whole slices. Experiments show that using the mediastinal as the main CT window can significantly improve the overall performances, and an additional attention map from the lung window makes the framework have better performances and more stable.

In summary, this paper has the following contributions:

- To our best knowledge, this is the first work to emphasize the importance of features observed from the mediastinal window for disease course diagnosis of COVID-19, which is able to obviously improve the diagnosis accuracy.
- We propose a dual window RCNN network to predict the courses of COVID-19 by dual windows. Dual window features are adaptively fused by the Lung Window Attention Block, and treated as successive video frames, which reduce the information redundancy.
- Experimental results show that the proposed model achieves high accuracy in courses prediction. Moreover, it demonstrates that learning from the mediastinal window and focusing on the lung window is an ideal way to reach competitive results, meanwhile improve stability.

2 Related Works

2.1 Computer-Aid Diagnosis Systems for Pneumonia

Computed Tomography (CT) has been widely used for clinical pneumonia diagnosis [23,29]. Unlike X-Ray images, CT can provide more details of lung tissue density, and avoid the shallows caused by ribs or other tissues. In 2016, Shin *et al.* [19] exploited three important, but previously understudied factors of employing deep convolutional neural networks to computer-aided detection problems: CNN architectures, dataset characteristics, and transfer learning. Later in 2018, Gao *et al.* [7] presented a method to classify interstitial lung disease imaging patterns on CT images and introduced normal lung rescale, high attenuation rescale, and low attenuation rescale. In 2020, the study in [25] further fused demographic information with multi-window CT images. In a word, deep learning methods have been widely adopted for the analysis of chest CT.

Recently, COVID-19 has been a global pandemic and threatening all over the world. Chest CT, especially high-resolution CT, has been recommended as a major clinical diagnosis tool in the hard-hit region such as Hubei, China [34]. In 2020, Kang *et al.* [13] proposed a unified latent representation to explore multiple features describing CT images from different views fully for COVID-19. Fan *et al.* [6] proposed a novel COVID-19 Lung Infection Segmentation Deep Network (Inf-Net) automatically identifies infected regions from chest CT slices. Xinggang Wang *et al.* [27] further proposed a weakly-supervised framework based on 3D CT volumes. However, existing methods seldom analyze the effect of different image window settings on deep learning methods for COVID-19. There are two main difficulties for CT-based frameworks: First, some abnormal regions are not salient enough in the early stage and may be ignored. Second, in the severe stage, the abnormal regions may look similar to some community-acquired pneumonia, which also results in some wrong diagnoses.

Invoked by the studies [7], we design a framework that can make the most of lung and mediastinal windows for diagnosing the COVID-19 disease course. In our study, we use the mediastinal window as the main observation window and use the lung window as the enhancement for detecting severe symptoms such as pulmonary consolidation. Generally speaking, two image window inputs usually require two branches of CNN, such as study [20]. In our study, two image windows are treated as video frames and analyzed by a 2D ResNet. Both CT windows share the same pre-trained ResNet-50 [10] as a feature extractor so that we can significantly reduce the burden of calculation.

2.2 Attention Mechanisms

Attention mechanisms help guide the networks to focus on some important and discriminative features to improve the performances for multiple computer vision tasks, such as image captioning [9,32], semantic segmentation [4,22], crowd counting [12], saliency detection [16], image super-resolution [33], mirror detection [21], and so on. Attention mechanisms are becoming one of the most popular approaches for learning some important and useful information. There are mainly two directions of using attention including channel-wise attention and spatial attention. Channel-wise attention [4] is to learn different weights by multi-channels to emphasize on some special features, while spatial attention [3,8] is to learn different weights by different spatial information in a map.

Regarding the diagnosis of COVID-19, there are also some attention-related networks proposed to highlight the important area for making clinical decisions. For example, Ouyang et al. [18] designed a dual-sampling attention network, with uniform sampling and size-balanced sampling, to ensure that the network can make decisions based on highlighted infection regions. Fan et al. [6] utilized edge-attention to enhance the representations. Li et al. [14] tried to take the attention heatmap to illustrate the abnormal regions. Similar to these studies, we also take the attention methods to recognize the important regions which are having effects on decisions. Moreover, to our best knowledge, we are the first to propose using lung-window features as the attention map, while learning most information from the mediastinal window.

3 Methods

3.1 Dual Window Network

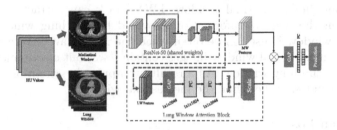

Fig. 3. Architecture of the DWRNet. The input HU values will be transformed into the lung window images and the mediastinal window images with thresholding methods. 'GAP' indicates Global Average Pooling layers. FC indicates a fully-connected layer. The lung window (LW) features will be fed into the Lung Window Attention Block and rescaled.

The architecture of the DWRNet is shown in Fig. 3. Before being fed into the framework, the original HU values will be transformed into two CT image windows: lung window X_L (HU$[-1000, 400]$), and mediastinal window X_M (HU$[-160, 240]$). Unlike the conventional two-stream method, our two image windows share the same ResNet-50 model as a visual feature extractor. This design allows us to build a deeper framework with low memory cost. To boost the training speed, we use the ResNet-50 pre-trained on ImageNet.

More specifically, the X_L and X_M are fed into the ResNet separately and get two separate feature vectors F_L and F_W with $ResNet(X_L, X_M)$.

Because the mediastinal window can provide more discriminative features for the diagnosis of severe cases, we treat it as the main CT window. To enhance the visual features fed into the decision-making process, we use a Lung Window Attention Block (LWA Block), which is invoked by the study [11], to learn the attention map from the lung window feature channels, and then add this attention information to the mediastinal window features as a guideline: $FV_M \otimes LWA(V_L)$.

3.2 Lung Window Attention Block

The architecture of LWA Block is also shown in Fig. 3. The lung window features and mediastinal window features come from ResNet-50 without fully-connected layers, which have a shape of $8 \times 8 \times 2048$. Then we use Global Average Pooling (GAP) [15] to transform lung window features into 1×2048, which will be fed into two fully-connected layers with shapes of 1×1024, and 1×2048. After two fully-connected layers, the learned weights will be fused with corresponding channels in the mediastinal window features. This block can help to reduce redundant information from the lung window, and highlight the different symptom appearances between two CT image windows.

We fuse attention features directly to the mediastinal window features for two reasons: 1. The lung window is the most common CT window used in clinical practice, which means the lung window can provide more but unnecessary visual features than the mediastinal window. LWA Block can extract more critical features from the massive information provided by the lung window. 2. The mediastinal window is used more often when the lungs have severe symptoms. It means the mediastinal window images contain fewer but discriminative visual features than the lung window. As a result, we apply the attention mechanism to the lung window rather than the mediastinal window.

3.3 Overall Loss

After fusing the lung window attention features and the mediastinal window features, the fused information will be fed into a GAP layer and two fully-connected layers. The prediction results will be given after the final Softmax layer: $Pred = Softmax(F(V_M \otimes SE(V_L)))$.

The disease course diagnosis is actually a binary classification task, so we use the cross-entropy function as the loss function:

$$\arg\min_{W} -\frac{1}{Q} \sum_{q=1}^{Q} \frac{1}{N} \sum_{X_n \in \chi} (y_n^q = q) log(Pred(y_n^q = q | X_n; W)) \qquad (1)$$

$\chi = \{X_n\}_{n=1}^{N}$ denotes the training set, X_n represents n-th case of training set. y^q is the label vector. In this study, the class labels are used in a back-propagation procedure to update the network weights in the convolutional, and learn the most relevant features in the fully-connected layers. W denotes the trainable parameters of the proposed framework. Q is equal to 2, which indicates two classes in our study.

4   Experiments

4.1   Evaluation Dataset and Experimental Settings

In this paper, we analyze 235 adult cases of COVID-19 cases from Hubei province collected by the First Affiliated Hospital of Army Medical University, which contain more than 161 thousand COVID-19 CT slices. All cases were labeled by the radiologists into two categories: common cases (163) and severe cases (72). We only keep the slices with the largest number and the smallest slice-thickness. Then we transform all CT images into HU values to keep unified standards. Before training, we further transform all HU values into the lung window image and the mediastinal window image.

We randomly select 165 cases (70%) as the training set, and the rest cases are used as the testing set. The training set and testing set have the same data distribution. There are 163 common type samples, including 114 samples for training and 49 for testing. There are 72 severe type samples, including 51 for training and 21 for testing. Our framework is built on the Tensorflow 1.4 [1], and runs on a Tesla-V100 GPU. The learning rate is set to 5×10^{-4}, and drops 50% each 800 steps. The whole framework will be trained 12 epochs.

4.2   Experimental Analyse

In this section, we will discuss the experimental performances of the proposed framework. We build five models: Recurrent CNN with original HU images (RCNN-HU), Recurrent CNN with lung window images (RCNN-LW), Recurrent CNN with mediastinal window images (RCNN-MW), DWRNet with mediastinal window attention (DWRNet-M), and DWRNet with lung window attention (DWRNet-L), which is final design of our framework. It should be noted that DWRNet-M uses lung window images as its main image window, and on the contrary, DWRNet-L uses mediastinal window images as its main image window.

Experimental results are listed in Table 1. We test all models five times and calculate the average sensitivity, specificity, and accuracy for comprehensive comparisons. The sensitivity indicates the ability to classify positive severe COVID-19 cases; the specificity indicates the ability to classify negative common COVID-19 cases.

We can see that RCNN-HU and RCNN-LW have similar accuracy, but RCNN-LW has higher sensitivity. RCNN-MW has an accuracy of 88.29%, which is higher than RCNN-HU and RCNN-LW, it means the mediastinal window is more suitable for the classification of disease courses. Our DWRNet-L has the highest performances in all accuracy, sensitivity, and specificity. DWRNet-M has a lower accuracy than RCNN-MW, but higher than RCNN-LW.

Effect of CT Image Window Settings. In this section, we discuss the influences of CT image windows. The baseline Recurrent CNN is trained with HU images, which are directly sampled from CT. The sensitivity, specificity, and

Table 1. Experimental Results. Five models are tested: Recurrent CNN with original HU images (RCNN-HU), Recurrent CNN with lung window images (RCNN-LW), Recurrent CNN with mediastinal window images (RCNN-MW), DWRNet with mediastinal window attention (DWRNet-M), and DWRNet with lung window attention (DWRNet-L). ACC, SPE and SEN indicate accuracy, specificity, and sensitivity.

Data	EVA	Test1	Test2	Test3	Test4	Test5	Ave
RCNN-HU	SEN	0.5714	0.5714	0.6190	0.5714	0.5714	0.5810
	SPE	0.9388	0.9796	0.9796	0.9592	0.9592	0.9633
	ACC	0.8286	0.8571	0.8714	0.8429	0.8429	0.8486
RCNN-LW	SEN	0.5714	0.5714	0.6667	0.6667	0.6667	0.6667
	SPE	0.9184	0.9592	0.9592	0.9592	0.9184	0.9429
	ACC	0.8143	0.8429	0.8714	0.8714	0.8429	0.8486
RCNN-MW	SEN	0.7143	0.6667	0.7619	0.6667	0.6667	0.6952
	SPE	0.9592	0.9592	0.9796	0.9388	0.9796	0.9633
	ACC	0.8857	0.8714	0.9143	0.8571	0.8857	0.8829
DWRNet-M	SEN	0.6667	0.6667	0.6667	0.7143	0.6667	0.6762
	SPE	0.9592	0.9388	0.9592	0.9592	0.9388	0.9510
	ACC	0.8714	0.8714	0.8714	0.8857	0.8571	0.8714
DWRNet-L	SEN	0.7619	0.7143	0.7619	0.7143	0.7143	**0.7333**
	SPE	0.9796	0.9796	0.9796	0.9796	0.9796	**0.9796**
	ACC	0.9143	0.9000	0.9143	0.9000	0.9000	**0.9057**

accuracy of the baseline are 58.10%, 96.33%, and 84.86%. As can be seen, this model tends to predict cases as common cases. When the CT image is adjusted to the lung window, the performance of sensitivity improves by 8.57%. However, the accuracy of RCNN-LW is still 84.86%. When we use the mediastinal window as inputs, the sensitivity is improved to 69.52%, and the accuracy is improved to 88.29%.

It is a very interesting phenomenon since most of the existing studies mainly focus on analyzing CT with the lung window. According to our experiments, the mediastinal window is more suitable for classifying common/severe cases. We believe it is because severe COVID-19 cases contain more severe symptoms that may lead to density changes, such as pulmonary consolidation, and the mediastinal window has its unique advantage in observing soft tissues. As a result, we use the mediastinal window as the main image window in our DWRNet.

Effect of Different Main Image Window. In this section, we will compare two versions of DWRNet: DWRNet-M, DWRNet-L. DWRNet-M takes the lung window as its main image window and uses the mediastinal window to guide the framework using the attention mechanism. On the contrary, DWRNet-L takes the mediastinal window as its main image window and uses the lung window as its guideline.

As can be seen in the Table 1, DWRNet-M achieves higher accuracy than RCNN-LW, but lower than RCNN-MW. DWRNet-L achieves the highest sensitivity, specificity, and accuracy among all models, which reflect the effect of the mediastinal window and the attention map from the lung window.

Moreover, the proposed DWRNet also shows better stability. We calculate the standard deviations of each model in five tests, which are listed in Table.2. As can be seen, both versions of DWRNets have better stability than RCNN with a single image window. DWRNet-M has the lowest standard deviation in specificity, and DWRNet-L has the lowest standard deviations in both specificity and accuracy. It means the attention information of additional CT image windows can improve the performances of the proposed framework and improve the stability.

According to our experimental results, a few conclusions can be summarized: 1. The mediastinal window is more suitable for the diagnosis of COVID-19 disease course since it can provide more discriminative visual features for severe cases. 2. The additional attention map provided by LWA Block can improve the performances and stability of the framework.

Table 2. Standard Deviations of Sensitivity, Specificity, and Accuracy. Four models are tested: Recurrent CNN with lung window images (RCNN-LW), Recurrent CNN with mediastinal window images (RCNN-MW), DWRNet with mediastinal window attention (DWRNet-M), and DWRNet with lung window attention (DWRNet-L).

Model	RCNN-LW	RCNN-MW	DWRNet-M	DWRNet-L
SEN	0.0494	0.0399	**0.0195**	0.0240
SPE	0.0205	0.0156	0.0101	**0.0**
ACC	0.0220	0.0194	0.0091	**0.0071**

Effectiveness of LWA Block. To further demonstrate the effectiveness of the LWA Block, we show activation maps of DWRNet-M and DWRNet-L in Fig. 4 and Fig. 5. As shown in both figures, the activation maps with LWA Block concentrate more on the areas of lungs, which means the LWA Block with additional CT windows can help the DWRNet focus on the important areas as our design. In Sect. 4.2, we observe that the DWRNet-L has better performance than DWRNet-W, which can also be explained by Fig. 5: the mediastinal window images can help the framework better focus on the areas of the lungs, which can significantly provide better receptive fields for neural networks. Moreover, the DWRNet-L can correct the focus with the help of LWA Block and achieve better and more stable performances.

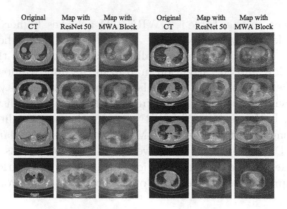

Fig. 4. Feature Maps of DWRNet-M. Eight slices of COVID-19 CT are shown. For each slice, we show the original CT, activation maps of ResNet, and activation maps of our framework.

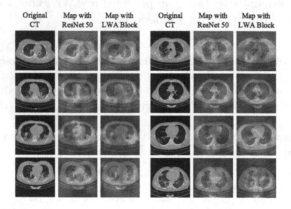

Fig. 5. Feature Maps of DWRNet-L.This framework uses mediastinal window as its main image window, and the LWA Block learns attention features from the lung window.

5   Discussion

As can be seen, the highest sensitivity is still lower than 80%, which may limit the clinical practice of DWRNet. We look into the *Diagnosis and Treatment Protocol for COVID-19 Patients* [5] and find some facts that can explain why the sensitivity is low.

According to the [5], the diagnosis of severe cases need to consider four facts: 1) Whether the respiration rate is higher than 30 times per minute; 2) Whether the oxygen saturation is lower than 93% at rest; z) Arterial oxygen partial pressure (PaO2)/Inspired oxygen concentration (FiO2) is lower than 300 mmHg; and 4) Progressive aggravation of clinical symptoms by observing lung images. In other words, CT is not the only discriminative information that can be used for classifying common/severe cases. The only solution to improving the sensitivity or detecting severe cases is to fuse multiple information resources, such as respiration rate, oxygen saturation, et al. However, collecting such information is a time-consuming task, and the deep learning framework needs to be updated for learning more information. We are collecting more data and our future work will focus on this task.

6 Conclusions

This paper proposes a novel Dual Window RCNN Network (DWRNet), which treats the mediastinal window as the main visual information resource, and uses an attenuation map from the lung window to improve the overall performances. In this paper, instead of picking up specific slices for a deep learning framework, CT slices are treated as videos and analyzed by RCNN, which can keep 3D information and reduce calculation burden at the same time. A Lung Window Attention (LWA Block) is introduced to fuse lung window features into mediastinal window features as guidance. Our experiments show that the mediastinal window is more suitable for the diagnosis of disease course. Moreover, the fused and representative features can improve the stability of the DWRNet, and improve the accuracy by 4% compared to the baseline.

References

1. Abadi, M., Agarwal, A., Barham, P., Brevdo, E., Chen, Z., Citro, C., et al.: Tensorflow: large-scale machine learning on heterogeneous distributed systems (2016)
2. Ahn, H., et al.: Effect of computed tomography window settings and reconstruction plane on 8th edition t-stage classification in patients with lung adenocarcinoma manifesting as a subsolid nodule. Eur. J. Radiol. 98, 130 (2018)
3. Chen, L.C., Yang, Y., Wang, J., Xu, W., Yuille, A.: Attention to scale: scale-aware semantic image segmentation. In: IEEE/CVF Conference on Computer Vision and Pattern Recognition (CVPR), pp. 3640–3649 (2016)
4. Chen, L., et al.: Sca-cnn: spatial and channel-wise attention in convolutional networks for image captioning. In: IEEE/CVF Conference on Computer Vision and Pattern Recognition (CVPR) (2017)
5. N.H.C. of the People's Republic of China: Diagnosis and treatment protocol for covid-19 patients (tentative 8th edition). http://en.nhc.gov.cn/2020-09/07/c_81565.htm
6. Fan, D.: Inf-net: automatic covid-19 lung infection segmentation from ct images. IEEE Trans. Med. Imaging 39(8), 2626–2637 (2020)
7. Gao, M., et al.: Holistic classification of ct attenuation patterns for interstitial lung diseases via deep convolutional neural networks. Comput. Methods Biomech. Biomed. Eng. Imaging Vis. 6(1), 1–6 (2018)
8. Gregor, K., Danihelka, I., Graves, A., Rezende, D.J., Wierstra, D.: Draw: a recurrent neural network for image generation. In: International Conference on Machine Learning (ICML), pp. 1462–1471 (2015)
9. Guo, L., Liu, J., Zhu, X., Yao, P., Lu, S., Lu, H.: Normalized and geometry-aware self-attention network for image captioning. In: IEEE/CVF Conference on Computer Vision and Pattern Recognition (CVPR) (2020)

10. He, K., Zhang, X., Ren, S., Sun, J.: Deep residual learning for image recognition (2015)
11. Hu, J., Shen, L., Albanie, S., Sun, G., Wu, E.: Squeeze-and-excitation networks. IEEE Trans. Pattern Anal. Mach. Intell. (2017)
12. Jiang, X., et al.: Attention scaling for crowd counting. In: IEEE/CVF Conference on Computer Vision and Pattern Recognition (CVPR) (2020)
13. Kang, H.: Diagnosis of coronavirus disease 2019 (covid-19) with structured latent multi-view representation learning. IEEE Trans. Med. Imaging **39**(8), 2606–2614 (2020)
14. Li, L., et al.: Artificial intelligence distinguishes covid-19 from community acquired pneumonia on chest ct. Radiology (2020)
15. Lin, M., Chen, Q., Yan, S.: Network in network (2014)
16. Liu, N., Han, J., Yang, M.H.: Picanet: learning pixel-wise contextual attention for saliency detection. In: IEEE/CVF Conference on Computer Vision and Pattern Recognition (CVPR), pp. 3089–3098 (2018)
17. Macmahon, H., et al.: Guidelines for management of incidental pulmonary nodules detected on ct images: from the fleischner society 2017. Radiology **284**(1), 228–243 (2017)
18. Ouyang, X., et al.: Dual-sampling attention network for diagnosis of covid-19 from community acquired pneumonia. IEEE Trans. Med. Imaging **39**(8), 2595–2605 (2020)
19. Shin, H.C., et al.: Deep convolutional neural networks for computer-aided detection: CNN architectures, dataset characteristics and transfer learning. IEEE Trans. Med. Imaging **35**(5), 1285–1298 (2016)
20. Simonyan, K., Zisserman, A.: Two-stream convolutional networks for action recognition in videos (2014)
21. Tan, X., Lin, J., Xu, K., Pan, C., Ma, L., Lau, R.W.H.: Mirror detection with the visual chirality cue. IEEE Trans. Pattern Anal. Mach. Intell. (2022). https://doi.org/10.1109/TPAMI.2022.3181030
22. Tan, X., Xu, K., Cao, Y., Zhang, Y., Ma, L., Lau, R.W.H.: Night-time scene parsing with a large real dataset. IEEE Trans. Image Process. **30**, 9085–9098 (2021). https://doi.org/10.1109/TIP.2021.3122004
23. Upchurch, C.P., et al.: Community-acquired pneumonia visualized on ct scans but not chest radiographs: pathogens, severity, and clinical outcomes. Chest **153**(3) (2017)
24. Wang, J., Bao, Y., Wen, Y., Lu, H., Qian, D.: Prior-attention residual learning for more discriminative covid-19 screening in ct images. IEEE Trans. Med. Imaging (2020)
25. Wang, Q., Yang, D., Li, Z., Zhang, X., Liu, C.: Deep regression via multi-channel multi-modal learning for pneumonia screening. IEEE Access **8**, 78530–78541 (2020)
26. Wang, S.H., Govindaraj, V.V., Górriz, J.M., Zhang, X., Zhang, Y.D.: Covid-19 classification by fgcnet with deep feature fusion from graph convolutional network and convolutional neural network. Inf. Fusion (2020). https://doi.org/10.1016/j.inffus.2020.10.004
27. Wang, X., et al.: A weakly-supervised framework for covid-19 classification and lesion localization from chest ct. IEEE Trans. Med. Imaging **39**(8), 2615–2625 (2020)
28. (WHO), W.H.O.: Weekly operational update on covid-19. https://www.who.int/emergencies/diseases/novel-coronavirus-2019/situation-reports

29. Xie, Y., Zhang, J., Xia, Y., Fulham, M., Zhang, Y.: Fusing texture, shape and deep model-learned information at decision level for automated classification of lung nodules on chest ct. Inf. Fusion **42**, 102–110 (2018). https://doi.org/10.1016/j.inffus.2017.10.005

30. Yanagawa, M., Kusumoto, M., Johkoh, T., Noguchi, M., Tomiyama, N.: Radiologic-pathologic correlation of solid portions on thin-section ct images in lung adenocarcinoma: a multicenter study. Clin. Lung Cancer **19**(3) (2018)

31. Yao, G.: Value of window technique in diagnosis of the ground glass opacities in patients with non-small cell pulmonary cancer. Oncol. Lett. **12**(5), 3933–3935 (2016)

32. You, Q., Jin, H., Wang, Z., Fang, C., Luo, J.: Image captioning with semantic attention. In: IEEE/CVF Conference on Computer Vision and Pattern Recognition (CVPR), pp. 4651–4659 (2016)

33. Zhang, Y., Li, K., Li, K., Wang, L., Zhong, B., Fu, Y.: Image super-resolution using very deep residual channel attention networks. In: Proceedings of the European Conference on Computer Vision (ECCV), pp. 286–301 (2018)

34. Zu, Z.Y., et al.: Coronavirus disease 2019 (covid-19): a perspective from china. Radiology, 200490–200490 (2020)

CDNeRF: A Multi-modal Feature Guided Neural Radiance Fields

Qi Zhang[✉], Qiaoqiao Liu, and Hang Zou

Beijing Research Institute, China Telecom Corporation Limited, Beijing, China
{zhangq75,liuqq11,zouh3}@chinatelecom.cn

Abstract. We present CDNeRF, a simple yet powerful learning framework that creates novel view synthesis by reconstructing neural radiance fields from a single view RGB image. Novel view synthesis by neural radiance fields has achieved great improvement with the development of deep learning. However, how to make the method generic across scenes has always been a challenging task. A good idea is to introduce 2D image features as prior knowledge for adaptive modeling, yet RGB features (**C**) lack geometry and 3D spacial information. To compensate, we introduce depth features into the model. Our method uses a variant depth estimation network to extract depth features (**D**) without the need for additional input. In addition, we also introduce the transformer module to effectively fuse the multi-modal features of RGB and depth. Extensive experiments are carried out on two categories specific benchmarks (i.e., Chair, Car) and two category agnostic benchmarks (i.e., ShapeNet, DTU). The results demonstrate that our CDNeRF outperforms the previous methods, and achieves state-of-the-art neural rendering performance.

Keywords: Neural rendering · Novel view synthesis · Vision transformer · 3D implicit reconstruction

1 Introduction

Novel view synthesis in computer vision and graphics is a long-standing challenging task. This research direction is very promising and has important applications in fields such as meta-verse, holographic communication, digital twins, etc. Recently, due to emerging of neural implicit representations or neural radiance fields (NeRF), this long-standing problem has made progress. NeRF can create photorealistic novel views, however, it has a number of drawbacks: i) it sometimes lacks access to the dense views it strictly needs; ii) it takes a long time to infer because of the lengthy optimization process; iii) it is frequently impracticable due to lack of generality, necessitating a time-consuming per-scene optimization.

To address these issues, more and more improved methods for NeRF have been proposed. Among them, a number of works are researching generality to solve the vanilla NeRF of modeling only a single scene. It was found that for

© The Author(s), under exclusive license to Springer Nature Switzerland AG 2022
L. Fang et al. (Eds.): CICAI 2022, LNAI 13604, pp. 204–215, 2022.
https://doi.org/10.1007/978-3-031-20497-5_17

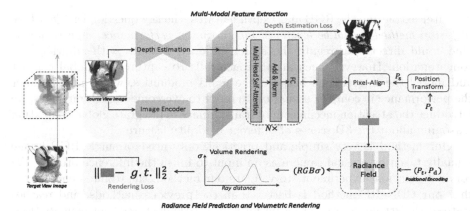

Fig. 1. The framework of CDNeRF. Given the source view image and target view position, we predict the $RGB\sigma$ values on a set of 3D positions. The RGB feature of the source image is extracted by a pre-trained image encoder. Meanwhile, the source image is fed into a depth estimation network to extract the depth feature. Then the two features will be entered into the transformer module to get the fused global feature. The target view position will be transformed to the source view position so as to index the pixel-aligned feature of the global feature. This, together with the matching position and direction, will then be input into the NeRF network for the prediction of the final RGB. The volume rendering is conducted finally to get novel views.

a network to be general, the model should not only have the ability to distinguish between different scenarios but also know what a particular scene "looks like" [2–4]. In order to make the reconstructed scene more in line with the real structure, rather than some meaningless pixel stacking, it requires the model to introduce high semantic features. RGB features undoubtedly encoded high semantic features e.g. outlines, textures, and even categories, and many previous methods (e.g. pixelNeRF [2], IBRNet [4], Grf [3]) have introduced RGB visual features as a condition signal for 3D implicit reconstruction. But these methods are prone to spacial confusion due to the lack of 3D spatial features and stereoscopic geometric features, which are very important for recovering the geometric and spatial information of a 3D scene.

Specifically, we expect the model can incorporate the relative position, size, distance, and other spatial relative features of the objects in the scene. Therefore, we explicitly introduce the depth feature besides the RGB feature into our model, and these two features complement each other to encode more comprehensive features, which helps the model obtain 3D semantic information easily.

There are also many methods (e.g. [19,20,22]) introduce depth information in order to improve the effect of NeRF. Specifically, they use the depth estimated value as strong supervision, which makes the network converge faster and the render results better, but they are still single-scenario models. Unlike these methods, we extract the features of the depth map as the condition signal. This guarantees the generality of the model and maintains high semantic information.

After extracting the RGB and Depth features, the key question is: *What kind of fusion method should be leveraged for maximum performance improvements?* One could directly aggregate the aforementioned features with addition and concatenation. However, such an approach fails to capture the global context and model the interactions between the multi modalities, which may hamper the performance in complex scenarios. In order to overcome these limitations, we introduce the attention mechanism of transformers to integrate global contextual reasoning about the 3D scenes of different modality features.

Our method is very simple and practical, only needs a single RGB image casually taken by a usual camera as an input to finish the inference process. We conduct sufficient experiments to validate our method, the results demonstrate that our CDNeRF method is better than the previous methods, and reaches state-of-the-art neural rendering performance. Briefly stated, our contributions are:

- We present a new general-purpose NeRF model called CDNeRF that enables single-view image-based rendering, and CDNeRF outperforms existing view synthesis methods on novel scenes.
- We extract the depth feature and RGB feature of a query point from only a single image as input. These two complementary features capture more comprehensive high-semantic and spatial information to guide nerf to be generalized.
- We introduce the transformer module to efficiently fuse the two modal features, to further make the two features play maximum performance improvements.

2   Related Work

2.1   Neural Radiance Field with Generality

A significant advancement in the field of novel vision synthesis is neural radiance fields (NeRF) [5]. NeRF implicitly represents a 3D scene with a fully connected neural network and then renders it through the differential volumetric rendering algorithms. Due to the entire framework of NeRF being physically interpretable and its rendering results being photorealism, there has been an explosion of NeRF-based approaches for novel view synthesis as this topic has drawn increasing scientific interest.

The prevalence of NeRF can be divided into two tracks: 1) The first track is to train a model particular to the scene in order to produce novel views on the scenario (i.e. [18,23–26]). These approaches cannot generalize to new settings despite synthesizing high-fidelity novel views and necessitating a lengthy optimization phase. 2) The second track makes an effort to learn to generalize the neural radiance fields across various scenarios (i.e. [2–4,27,28]). Take pixelNeRF [2] as an example, it introduces 2D image visual features as part of the input to NeRF network and learns adaptive features to reconstruct different scenes. pixelNeRF has taken a big step forward in both performance and generality. However, only the RGB features may lack 3D spacial features and leading to implausible geometries and blurry results. We introduced depth features, making the network simpler while retaining spatial features, and using the transformer to get the efficiently fused features.

2.2   Depth Prior to NeRF

A few recent works have also introduced depth information into NeRF. NerfingMVS [20] overfits a depth predictor to the scene using depth from MVS. The NeRF sampling is guided by the derived depth prior. DONeRF [18] suggested directly sampling a NeRF density function's surface when training a depth oracle to increase rendering speed. [22] improves color and depth quality greatly by applying depth completion to structure-from-motion (SFM) sparse depth estimation and by using a depth loss to supervise the geometry recovered by NeRF. In order to guarantee that the rendered rays termination distribution respects the surface priors provided by each key point, [19] additionally employs extra supervision from depth retrieved from 3D point clouds computed from executing SFM.

Unlike these methods, we extract the features of the depth map as the condition signal, which not only remains high semantic information but also ensures the generality of the model. As far as I know, we are the first to propose a model that introduces depth features while maintaining model generality.

3   Methods

Overview. In our research, we found how to get better features is the key to recovering the 3D information of scenes. To this end, we weighed the two factors of simplicity and comprehensiveness and proposed CDNeRF, a novel 3D implicit reconstruction and rendering framework based on multi-modal vision features. Specifically, we incorporate both RGB features and depth features into the NeRF model. The overall process is illustrated as Fig. 1, which consists of three stages: feature extraction, nerf network training, and novel view rendering.

Given a single source image as input, there are two branches in the feature extraction stage. In the first branch, the source image will be fed into the depth estimation network for dense depth estimation. Then a pre-trained depth estimation network is used to extract the depth feature. In the second branch, the source image will be fed into a pre-train network to extract RGB features. Subsequently, the depth feature and the RGB feature are effectively fused by the transformer module. The bilinear interpolate operation will be adopted subsequently to get the pixel-aligned features of the corresponding position. The feature finally was input to the neural radiation field networks together with the position encoding of position and direction respectively to predict the color and density values of the points in the space. As a result, we can get novel view images by volumetric rendering.

3.1   Multi-modal Feature Extraction

RGB Features. Given source image $\mathbf{I} \in [0,1]^{H \times W \times 3}$ as input, we first introduce a pre-trained image encoder (e.g., ResNet) to extract feature map $\mathbf{Fc} \in \mathbb{R}^{H \times W \times k_c}$ from image I.

Depth Features. Although RGB Features capture semantic information of a scene, the image encoder is pre-trained in ImageNet, which is designed for object classification and lacks fine-grained geometric information. Therefore, we leverage depth features that capture fine details of geometric appearance to complement RGB features for radiance field learning. Specifically, given source image $\mathbf{I}$ as input, we first employ a well pre-trained Convolutional Spatial Propagation Network (CSPN) to extract depth features $\mathbf{Fd} \in \mathbb{R}^{H \times W \times k_d}$.

Multi-modal Fusion. The fundamental idea of our approach is to investigate the self-attention mechanism of the transformer to incorporate the global context for RGB and Depth modalities gave their complementary nature. We stack the RGB features $\mathbf{F_c}$ and Depth features $\mathbf{F_d}$ together to form a multi-modal feature $\mathbf{F_m} \in \mathbb{R}^{D_f \times (2*H*W)}$. To enable the network to capture the spatial connections between various tokens, we extend transformers by including a learnable position embedding.

A set of queries, keys, and values are computed by the transformer using linear projections,

$$\mathbf{Q} = \mathbf{F}_m \mathbf{W}^q, \mathbf{K} = \mathbf{F}_m \mathbf{W}^k, \mathbf{V} = \mathbf{F}_m \mathbf{W}^v \tag{1}$$

where $\mathbf{W}^q \in \mathbb{R}^{D_f \times D_q}$, $\mathbf{W}^k \in \mathbb{R}^{D_f \times D_k}$ and $\mathbf{W}^v \in \mathbb{R}^{D_f \times D_k}$ are matrices parameters. The attention weights, calculated by scaled dot products between $\mathbf{Q}$ and $\mathbf{K}$, is introduced to aggregate the values $\mathbf{V}$,

$$\mathbf{Z} = \text{softmax}\left(\frac{\mathbf{Q}\mathbf{K}^{\mathbf{T}}}{\sqrt{D_k}}\right)\mathbf{V} \tag{2}$$

At last, the output features are obtained as follows:

$$\mathbf{F} = \mathbf{MLP}(\mathbf{Z}) + \mathbf{F}_m \tag{3}$$

Pixel-Aligned Feature. Following pixelNeRF, we conduct a bilinear interpolation operation (denoted as Map) on feature map $\mathbf{F}$ to obtain the pixel-aligned feature. Specifically, We transform the target view position P_t in world coordinate to the pixel coordinate of source image P_s by the camera intrinsic and extrinsic parameters, following $m(\mathbf{F}) = Map(l^c \times f + c, F) \in \mathbb{R}^k$. Here l^c, f and c denote points in the camera coordinate, camera focal and camera center respectively.

3.2 Radiance Field Prediction and Volumetric Rendering

We use an MLP f as Eq. (4) to create the radiance field of an input single-view image I by regressing the volume density and view-dependent radiance r from the 3D coordinates of a query point X, a viewing direction d, and the related pixel-aligned features.

$$\sigma, \mathbf{r} = f\left(\gamma_m(\mathbf{X}), \gamma_n(\mathbf{d}); m(\mathbf{F})\right) \tag{4}$$

where γ_m and γ_n are position encoding functions that are applied to X, d respectively. This method reduces the positional bias present in Cartesian coordinates without compromising their disagreement between them. Specifically, γ is a function that converts Cartesian coordinates from $\mathbb{R}$ into the high-dimensional space $\mathbb{R}^{2L}$.

$$\gamma_L(\mathbf{p}) = \left(\sin\left(2^0\pi\mathbf{p}\right), \cos\left(2^0\pi\mathbf{p}\right)\right.$$
$$\left. \ldots, \sin\left(2^{L-1}\pi\mathbf{p}\right), \cos\left(2^{L-1}\pi\mathbf{p}\right)\right) \tag{5}$$

Volumetric rendering is a process of integrating along each point l on a ray r. Specifically, given a voxel representation of a 3D scene, rays are projected into this 3D space. If the image to be rendered has a shape of (H, W), $H \times W$ rays are generated according to the corresponding position. Integrating along each line results in the RGB value of each pixel. Since computational hardware barely handles continuous integration operations, we simplify it to a discrete summation operation by sampling following [5]. Hierarchical volume sampling was leveraged to get coarse and fine rendering results respectively (sampling uniformly first, and then adopting the importance of sampling near points with larger density values).

The RGB and density value of each point along the ray are integrated according to the following rules presented in (7). $\hat{C}(\mathbf{r})$ is the output color of 2D plane alone the ray $\mathbf{r}$, $\mathbf{c}$, σ denote the RGB and density value of a 3D point respectively, δ is the distance between adjacent samples. The transmittance $T(t)$ is calculated by (6), and $\hat{C}(\mathbf{r})$ is calculated in (7).

$$T_i = \exp\left(-\sum_{j=1}^{i-1} \sigma_j\delta_j\right) \tag{6}$$

$$\hat{C}(\mathbf{r}) = \sum_{i=1}^{N} T_i\left(1 - \exp\left(-\sigma_i\delta_i\right)\right)\mathbf{c}_i \tag{7}$$

3.3 Optimization Functions

The network parameters θ are optimized using a loss function $\mathcal{L}_\theta$ made up of a Mean Squared Error (MSE) term $\mathcal{L}_{\text{color}}$ and a Gaussian Negative Log-Likelihood (GNLL) term $\mathcal{L}_{\text{depth}}$:

$$\mathcal{L}_\theta = \sum_{r \in R} \left(\mathcal{L}_{\text{color}}\left(\mathbf{r}\right) + \lambda \mathcal{L}_{\text{depth}}\left(\mathbf{r}\right) \right) \tag{8}$$

Depth Estimation Loss. We introduce a sparse depth map by running the struct-from-motion(SFM) algorithm, which performs as the ground truth of this pre-trained dense depth estimation network. Then the depth estimation network can be fine-tuned according to our task.

During the training process, the depth estimation loss is calculated as Eq. (9).

$$\mathcal{L}_{depth} = \frac{1}{n} \sum_{j=1}^{n} \left(\log\left(s_j^2\right) + \frac{\left(z_j - z_{\text{sparse},j}\right)^2}{s_j^2} \right) \tag{9}$$

where n is the number of valid pixels in the dense depth map, z_j and s_j are the predicted depth and standard deviation of pixel j, respectively, and $z_{sparse,j}$ is the value of the sparse depth at j.

Rendering Loss. After rendering, the L2 loss between the ground-truth image and rendered target image can be calculated as Eq. (10).

$$\mathcal{L}_{\text{color}} = \sum_{r \in \mathcal{R}(\mathbf{P})} \|\hat{\mathbf{C}}(\mathbf{r}) - \mathbf{C}(\mathbf{r})\|_2^2 \tag{10}$$

4   Experiments

4.1   Datasets and Evaluation

Datasets. We perform comprehensive experiments on 2 category-specific benchmarks (i.e., Car and Chair using the protocol and dataset introduced in [8]), and 2 category agnostic benchmarks (i.e., ShapeNet [15] and DTU [9]), where DTU is real-world data, while the rest are synthetic data.

- **Car and Chair.** The Car dataset contains 2457 training scenes, 351 validate scenes, and 704 test scenes. The Chair dataset contains 4612 training scenes, 662 validation scenes, and 1317 test scenes. In both datasets, each training scene contains 50 images, each test and validate scene contains 251 images and the size of the images in the dataset is 128×128.
- **ShapeNet.** There are 13 scenes in ShapeNet and each scene is a separate dataset with its training and testing set divisions, and we put these scenarios together in our experiment.
- **DTU.** The dataset consists of 128 scanned scenes, and each scene has 49 posed images with the size of 64×64. This dataset contains a wide variety of scenarios (houses, walls, toys, etc.). In our experiment, 88 scenes were used for training, 15 scenes were used for validation and the rest were used for testing.

Evaluation Metrics. For each evaluation, we include the standard picture quality measures PSNR and SSIM [14]. We also incorporate LPIPS [13], which is a better representation of human vision. In order to maintain consistency with earlier studies [1,3,6,7], we strictly adhere to the SRN [8] protocol in this setting.

4.2 Implementation Details

We implement the image feature extraction network using ResNet34 [17] which is pre-trained on ImageNet for our experiments. We implement the CSPN [30] network for depth map estimation, and for depth feature extraction, we remove the last layer and use the penultimate layer to extract the depth feature. For feature fusion, we set a 3-layer transformer encoder and each of them has 8-head attention. We train 8 linear layers for the final $RGB\sigma$ value prediction.

We train for 400k iterations for the Car and Chair dataset, 800k iterations for the ShapeNet dataset, and 600k iterations for the DTU dataset. We set the learning rate to be 10^{-4} over all experiments and it is decreased with cosine decay. We employ a batch size of 4 instances, each with 128 rays. The λ in loss function is set to 0.5 in all experiments.

4.3 Results

Table 1. Experiments on Car and Chair benchmark.

		TCO [1]	WRL [21]	dGQN [6]	SRN [8]	pixelNeRF [2]	**Ours***
Cars	PSNR	18.15	16.89	18.19	20.72	23.17	**23.85**
	SSIM	0.79	0.77	0.78	0.85	0.90	**0.91**
Chairs	PSNR	21.27	22.11	21.59	22.89	23.72	**24.66**
	SSIM	0.88	0.90	0.87	0.89	0.91	**0.92**

In category specific datasets Car and Chair, we report our results in comparison with state-of-the-art methods TCO [1], dGQN [6], ENR [7] and GRF [3] in Table 1. The results show that our method consistently outperforms all methods in single-view experiments. We train a single model on 13-category ShapeNet. As can be seen in Table 2, we achieve significant performance improvements on the strong baseline pixelNeRF [2], SRN [8], and DVR [10]. It shows our method performs better in almost the same experimental setup and further confirms our model generalizes well to novel scenes.

As can be seen in Table 3, our approach also performs well in more complex and diverse real-world scenarios. Given a single input view, separate NeRFs are trained per scene while pixelNeRF and ours require only a single model. This experimental result shows that our method not only performs well in the synthesis of novel images but also maintains robustness in more complex real-world scenarios (Fig. 2).

Table 2. Experiments on ShapeNet benchmark.

		plane	bench	cbnt.	car	chair	disp.	lamp	spkr.	rifle	sofa	table	phone	boat	mean
↑ PSNR	DVR	25.29	22.64	24.47	23.95	19.91	20.86	23.27	20.78	23.44	23.35	21.53	24.18	25.09	22.70
	SRN	26.62	22.20	23.42	24.40	21.85	19.07	22.17	21.04	24.95	23.65	22.45	20.87	25.86	23.28
	pixelNeRF	29.76	26.35	27.72	27.58	23.84	24.22	28.58	24.44	30.60	26.94	25.59	**27.13**	29.18	26.80
	Ours	**31.15**	**27.28**	**28.41**	**28.20**	**24.38**	**24.66**	**28.78**	**24.53**	**30.81**	**27.46**	**26.63**	27.12	**29.47**	**26.95**
↑ SSIM	DVR	0.905	0.866	0.877	0.909	0.787	0.814	0.849	0.798	0.916	0.868	0.840	0.892	0.902	0.860
	SRN	0.901	0.837	0.831	0.897	0.814	0.744	0.801	0.779	0.913	0.851	0.828	0.811	0.898	0.849
	pixelNeRF	0.947	0.911	0.910	0.942	0.858	0.867	0.913	0.855	**0.968**	0.908	0.898	0.922	0.939	0.910
	Ours	**0.950**	**0.917**	**0.915**	**0.947**	**0.869**	**0.870**	**0.917**	**0.861**	0.966	**0.913**	**0.901**	**0.922**	**0.944**	**0.918**
↓ LPIPS	DVR	0.095	0.129	0.125	0.098	0.173	0.150	0.172	0.170	0.094	0.119	0.139	0.110	0.116	0.130
	SRN	0.111	0.150	0.147	0.115	0.152	0.197	0.210	0.178	0.111	0.129	0.135	0.165	0.134	0.139
	pixelNeRF	0.084	0.116	0.105	0.095	0.146	0.129	0.114	0.141	0.066	0.116	0.098	0.097	0.111	0.108
	Ours	**0.080**	**0.115**	**0.103**	**0.093**	**0.141**	**0.127**	**0.112**	**0.139**	**0.061**	**0.115**	**0.096**	**0.094**	**0.108**	**0.106**

Fig. 2. The visualization results on the car and chair datasets. Compared to SRN and pixelNeRF, our approach greatly reduced the blurring of the picture and achieves better qualitative results.

4.4 Ablation and Analysis

We conduct ablation studies to investigate the individual contributions of the RGB feature and depth feature respectively. We conduct experiments on the Chair and Car dataset and test the performance of the network after removing the source image feature (C) and the depth feature (D) respectively. The experimental results are recorded in Table 4(a). We find that only remaining the depth feature will result in a discount in network performance, and in the case of both two features retained can achieve the optimal result. It is worth mentioning that to exclude the influence of other factors, we only used the cleanest element-wise add for fusion. Our experiments prove that both the depth feature and the source image feature can contribute to enhancing the network's efficiency.

Table 3. Experiment on DTU benchmark.

		PSNR	SSIM	LPIPS
Ours	Mean	**15.63**	**0.539**	**0.531**
	SD	1.85	0.098	0.065
pixelNeRF	Mean	15.55	0.537	0.535
	SD	1.87	0.127	0.081
NeRF	Mean	8.00	0.286	0.703
	SD	3.20	0.093	0.055

Table 4. Ablation studies. We conduct experiments on the Chair and Car dataset.

	Feature	PSNR	SSIM			PSNR	SSIM
Car	C	23.17	0.90	Car	Trans.	**23.85**↑	**0.91** ↑
	D	21.92↓	0.87↓		Conc.	23.51	0.90
	C&D(Add)	**23.45** ↑	0.90		Add	23.45	0.90
Chair	C	23.72	0.91	Chair	Trans.	**24.66**↑	**0.92** ↑
	D	22.15↓	0.88 ↓		Conc.	24.17	0.91
	C&D(Add)	**24.19** ↑	0.91		Add	24.19	0.91

We also explore the role of the transformer in the model. When fusing RGB features and depth features, we test the effect of using Trans., Conc., and Add respectively. The result is shown on the right side of Table 4. Specifically, 'Trans'. is our transformer module, 'Add' is directly an element-wise addition, and Conc. is to concatenate the two features first and then add a learnable MLP for fusion.

We find that the transformer works best, further proof of the effectiveness of the transformer can learn the relationship between features of different modalities, and thus can get better feature representation.

To conclude, after incorporating the depth feature, the feature will always be better than the source map feature alone. The state-of-the-art result will be achieved if the transformer is further used for feature fusion.

5   Conclusion

We present a novel 3D implicit reconstruction framework, in which we carefully incorporate the depth feature besides the RGB feature in the neural rendering framework and further design a transformer module to fuse them to make them play maximum performance improvements. We conduct elaborate experiments to validate that our method brings considerable improvements and achieves state-of-the-art results in Car, Chair, ShapeNet, and DTU benchmarks.

References

1. Tatarchenko, M., Dosovitskiy, A., Brox, T.: Single-view to multi-view: reconstructing unseen views with a convolutional network. CoRR abs/1511.06702 **1**(2), 2 (2015)
2. Yu, A., Ye, V., Tancik, M., Kanazawa, A.: pixelNeRF: neural radiance fields from one or few images. In: Proceedings of the IEEE/CVF Conference on Computer Vision and Pattern Recognition, pp. 4578–4587 (2021)
3. Trevithick, A., Yang, B.: GRF: learning a general radiance field for 3D representation and rendering. arXiv preprint arXiv:2010.04595 (2020)
4. Wang, Q., et al.: IBRNet: learning multi-view image-based rendering. In: Proceedings of the IEEE/CVF Conference on Computer Vision and Pattern Recognition, pp. 4690–4699 (2021)
5. Mildenhall, B., Srinivasan, P.P., Tancik, M., Barron, J.T., Ramamoorthi, R., Ng, R.: NeRF: representing scenes as neural radiance fields for view synthesis. In: Vedaldi, A., Bischof, H., Brox, T., Frahm, J.-M. (eds.) ECCV 2020. LNCS, vol. 12346, pp. 405–421. Springer, Cham (2020). https://doi.org/10.1007/978-3-030-58452-8_24
6. Eslami, S.A., et al.: Neural scene representation and rendering. Science **360**(6394), 1204–1210 (2018)
7. Dupont, E., Martin, M.B., Colburn, A., Sankar, A., Susskind, J., Shan, Q.: Equivariant neural rendering. In: International Conference on Machine Learning, pp. 2761–2770. PMLR, November 2020
8. Sitzmann, V., Zollhöfer, M., Wetzstein, G.: Scene representation networks: continuous 3D-structure-aware neural scene representations. In: Advances in Neural Information Processing Systems, vol. 32 (2019)
9. Jensen, R., Dahl, A., Vogiatzis, G., Tola, E., Aanæs, H.: Large scale multi-view stereopsis evaluation. In: Proceedings of the IEEE Conference on Computer Vision and Pattern Recognition, pp. 406–413 (2014)
10. Niemeyer, M., Mescheder, L., Oechsle, M., Geiger, A.: Differentiable volumetric rendering: learning implicit 3D representations without 3D supervision. In: Proceedings of the IEEE/CVF Conference on Computer Vision and Pattern Recognition, pp. 3504–3515 (2020)
11. Vaswani, A., et al.: Attention is all you need. In: Advances in Neural Information Processing Systems, vol. 30 (2017)
12. Dosovitskiy, A., et al.: An image is worth 16×16 words: transformers for image recognition at scale. arXiv preprint arXiv:2010.11929 (2020)
13. Richard, Z., Phillip, I., Alexei, A.E., Eli, S., Oliver, W.: The unreasonable effectiveness of deep features as a perceptual metric. In: CVPR (2018)
14. Wang, Z., Bovik, A.C., Sheikh, H.R., et al.: Image quality assessment: from error visibility to structural similarity. IEEE Trans. Image Process. **13**(4), 600–612 (2004)
15. Chang, A.X., et al.: ShapeNet: an information-rich 3D model repository. arXiv preprint arXiv:1512.03012 (2015)
16. Kajiya, J.T., Von Herzen, B.P.: Ray tracing volume densities. ACM SIGGRAPH Comput. Graph. **18**(3), 165–174 (1984)
17. He, K., Zhang, X., Ren, S., Sun, J.: Deep residual learning for image recognition. In: Proceedings of the IEEE Conference on Computer Vision and Pattern Recognition 2016, pp. 770–778 (2016)

18. Neff, T., et al.: DONeRF: towards real-time rendering of compact neural radiance fields using depth oracle networks. In: Computer Graphics Forum, vol. 40, no. 4, pp. 45–59, July 2021

19. Deng, K., Liu, A., Zhu, J.Y., Ramanan, D.: Depth-supervised nerf: fewer views and faster training for free. In: Proceedings of the IEEE/CVF Conference on Computer Vision and Pattern Recognition, pp. 12882–12891 (2022)

20. Wei, Y., Liu, S., Rao, Y., Zhao, W., Lu, J., Zhou, J.: NerfingMVS: guided optimization of neural radiance fields for indoor multi-view stereo. In: Proceedings of the IEEE/CVF International Conference on Computer Vision, pp. 5610–5619 (2021)

21. Worrall, D.E., Garbin, S.J., Turmukhambetov, D., Brostow, G.J.: Interpretable transformations with encoder-decoder networks. In: Proceedings of the IEEE International Conference on Computer Vision, pp. 5726–5735 (2017)

22. Roessle, B., Barron, J.T., Mildenhall, B., Srinivasan, P.P., Nießner, M.: Dense depth priors for neural radiance fields from sparse input views. In: Proceedings of the IEEE/CVF Conference on Computer Vision and Pattern Recognition, pp. 12892–12901 (2022)

23. Liu, L., Gu, J., Zaw Lin, K., Chua, T.S., Theobalt, C.: Neural sparse voxel fields. In: Advances in Neural Information Processing Systems, vol. 33, pp. 15651–15663 (2020)

24. Martin-Brualla, R., Radwan, N., Sajjadi, M.S., Barron, J.T., Dosovitskiy, A., Duckworth, D.: NeRF in the wild: neural radiance fields for unconstrained photo collections. In: Proceedings of the IEEE/CVF Conference on Computer Vision and Pattern Recognition, pp. 7210–7219 (2021)

25. Park, K., et al.: Nerfies: deformable neural radiance fields. In: Proceedings of the IEEE/CVF International Conference on Computer Vision, pp. 5865–5874 (2021)

26. Tretschk, E., Tewari, A., Golyanik, V., Zollhöfer, M., Lassner, C., Theobalt, C.: Non-rigid neural radiance fields: reconstruction and novel view synthesis of a dynamic scene from monocular video. In: Proceedings of the IEEE/CVF International Conference on Computer Vision, pp. 12959–12970 (2021)

27. Chen, A., et al.: MVSNeRF: fast generalizable radiance field reconstruction from multi-view stereo. In: Proceedings of the IEEE/CVF International Conference on Computer Vision, pp. 14124–14133 (2021)

28. Chibane, J., Bansal, A., Lazova, V., Pons-Moll, G.: Stereo radiance fields (SRF): learning view synthesis for sparse views of novel scenes. In: Proceedings of the IEEE/CVF Conference on Computer Vision and Pattern Recognition, pp. 7911–7920 (2021)

29. Yu, X., et al.: PVSeRF: joint pixel-, voxel-and surface-aligned radiance field for single-image novel view synthesis. arXiv preprint arXiv:2202.04879 (2022)

30. Cheng, X., Wang, P., Yang, R.: Learning depth with convolutional spatial propagation network. IEEE Trans. Pattern Anal. Mach. Intell. 42(10), 2361–2379 (2019)

MHPro: Multi-hypothesis Probabilistic Modeling for Human Mesh Recovery

Haibiao Xuan, Jinsong Zhang, and Kun Li[(✉)]

College of Intelligence and Computing, Tianjin University, Tianjin, China
{hbxuan,jinszhang,lik}@tju.edu.cn

Abstract. Recovering 3D human meshes from monocular images is an inherently ambiguous and challenging task due to depth ambiguity, joint occlusion and truncation. However, most recent works avoid modeling uncertainty, typically obtaining a single reconstruction for a given input. In contrast, this paper presents the ambiguity of reception reconstruction and considers the problem as an inverse problem for which multiple feasible solutions exist. Our method, **MHPro**, first constructs a probability distribution and obtains a set of feasible recovery results (*i.e.* multi-hypotheses), from monocular images. Intra-hypothesis refinement is then performed to achieve independent feature enhancement. Finally, the multi-hypothesis features are aggregated by inter-hypothesis communication to recover the final 3D human mesh. The effectiveness of our method is validated on two benchmark datasets, Human3.6M and 3DPW, where experimental results show that our method achieves state-of-the-art performance and recovers more accurate human meshes. Our results validate the importance of intra-hypothesis refinement and inter-hypothesis communication in probabilistic modeling and show optimal performance across a variety of settings. Our source code will be available at http://cic.tju.edu.cn/faculty/likun/projects/MHPro.

Keywords: Human mesh recovery · Monocular images · Multi-hypothesis · Probabilistic modeling

1 Introduction

3D human mesh recovery from a single color image is a widely-studied problem in computer vision, as well as a vision task with a wide range of application scenarios, such as action recognition [1], human-computer interaction [2] and AR/VR [3]. However, human mesh recovery from a single image remains a challenging task and an inherently ill-posed problem due to depth ambiguity, joint occlusion and truncation.

Given a single image, recent literature for 3D human mesh recovery typically returns a single deterministic 3D mesh output [4,13,19,21]. These efforts mainly consider that systems returning a single deterministic output, tend to be sufficiently convenient and make comparisons on benchmarks straightforward and

© The Author(s), under exclusive license to Springer Nature Switzerland AG 2022
L. Fang et al. (Eds.): CICAI 2022, LNAI 13604, pp. 216–228, 2022.
https://doi.org/10.1007/978-3-031-20497-5_18

fairly. But this often leads to unsatisfactory results, especially for challenging input images. On the other hand, some scholars accept the ill-poseness from 2D to 3D and the uncertainty from ambiguity and occlusion, and successively propose to estimate probability distributions or generate multi-hypotheses [26–29]. Although these works have shown interesting potentials, they often rely on one-to-many mappings by adding multiple output heads to the existing architectures, which leads to potentially unscalable and poorly expressive multi-hypothesis output. Also, they suffer from an important shortcoming in failing to establish the relationship between the different hypothesis features, because it is essential to improve the expressiveness and performance of the model.

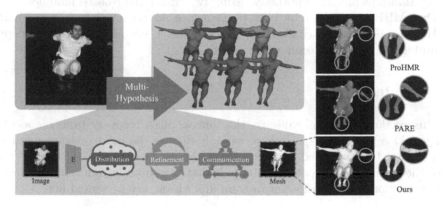

Fig. 1. We propose a multi-hypothesis method to recovering 3D human meshes from monocular images. Right: recovery results of the probabilistic method ProHMR [27], SOTA method PARE [21] and our method for a challenging image.

Our method aims to generate multi-hypotheses from the input monocular image and construct their relationships to enrich the diversity of features and obtain more accurate final results. To achieve this, we propose MHPro, which has many desirable properties missed in recent work. We first use a probabilistic model based on normalizing flow to regress a feasible pose distribution and generate multiple initial human mesh hypotheses, as depicted in Fig. 1. Then, we propose two transformer-based modules, the *Intra-hypothesis refinement* module and the *Inter-hypothesis communication* module, to construct hypothetical relationships and enhance feature representations. The former module focuses on refining the features of each single hypothesis, which models each hypothesis feature separately and enhances the information transfer within each hypothesis. In addition, for all the hypotheses to share their respective enhancements, a single fusion representation is converged from multi-hypotheses, and is then divided into several divergent hypotheses. But the relationship between different hypotheses is not sufficient. To address this, the latter module captures relationships and passes information among hypotheses. Finally, multi-hypotheses are aggregated to regress the final human mesh.

We conduct extensive experiments to demonstrate the validity of our proposed MHPro and the importance of refining and communicating the hypotheses. Experimental results demonstrate our ability to represent features and generate more accurate human mesh recovery results, especially for monocular image inputs including depth ambiguity, joint occlusion and truncation. Our contributions can be summarized as follows:

– We propose MHPro for human mesh recovery from monocular images. Our model can efficiently and adequately learn the feature representation of multi-hypotheses.
– We achieve a better representation of image features and establish strong relationships among hypotheses, using two transformer-based modules.
– Our MHPro achieves the best performance on the large-scale benchmark Human3.6M and the challenging 3DPW dataset, even for the cases of depth ambiguity, joint occlusion and truncation.

2   Related Work

In this section, we mainly discuss the human mesh recovery from monocular images. Due to limited space, here we only discuss the most relevant methods and suggest the interested readers refer to the recent surveys [5,6]. Apart from this, the recent multi-hypothesis methods that have been introduced into human reconstruction, and transformer in computer vision, are presented here.

2.1   Human Mesh Recovery from Monocular Images

Recovering 3D human meshes from monocular images is quite challenging due to the inherent ambiguity in lifting 2D observations into 3D space, flexible body structures and insufficient annotated 3D data.

Previous methods proposed to use a parametric human model and estimate the pose and shape coefficients for human mesh recovery. SMPL [7] is one of the widely used parametric human models, which is also used in this work. Bogo *et al.* [8] proposed SMPLify to estimate 3D human mesh by fitting the SMPL model to the predicted 2D keypoints and minimizing the re-projection error. Lassner *et al.* [9] used silhouettes and 2D keypoints in the optimization procedure to capture the overall information from a simple 2D input. In turn, Song *et al.* [10] utilized the learning gradient descent method in the optimization process. These optimization-based methods are fragile and inefficient, require additional data, and struggle with time-consuming inference on image inputs. In contrast, regression-based methods [11–21] trained deep neural networks for regressing SMPL parameters directly from pixels and enhanced the robustness and plausibility of the results. For example, HMR [11], a regressor from 2D joints to SMPL parameters, used a discriminator of unpaired 3D data to encourage plausible poses. SPIN [13] revisited reconstruction methods that work with neural networks and extended SMPLify [8] to provide more supervision in the training loop. Unlike previous work, PARE [21] focused on predicting body-part-guided attention masks and achieved a degree of robustness to occlusion.

Although these methods have produced encouraging results and the issue of occlusion has been focused on, they are still not robust enough and produce only approximate single reconstructions. In this work, we generate multiple plausible hypotheses from monocular images with the help of probabilistic models, and further improve the model's recovery accuracy in cases of depth ambiguity, joint occlusion and truncation through refinement and communication.

2.2 Multi-hypothesis Methods

Multiple hypothesis methods have been gradually introduced into 3D human pose estimation and human mesh reconstruction, to deal with the inherent ambiguities of the reconstructions described earlier, such as depth ambiguity, joint occlusion or truncation. Several recent works generated different hypotheses for this problem and demonstrated significant performance gains relative to a single solution [22–29]. For example, Li *et al.* [22] proposed multi-modal hybrid density networks to generate multiple feasible 3D pose hypotheses. Oikarinen *et al.* [27] followed conditional normalizing flows to model the conditional probability distribution, which makes for a more powerful and expressive model. Li *et al.* [29] proposed a multi-hypothesis transformer to learn the spatio-temporal representation of multiple plausible pose hypotheses and modeled multi-hypothesis features for accurate 3D human pose estimation from monocular videos. Unlike their work, we attempt not just to generating plausible human pose and shape, but to establish strong relationships between hypothesis features and achieve effective modeling of different features through intra-hypothesis refinement and inter-hypothesis communication.

2.3 Transformer in Computer Vision

Transformer [30], an encoder-decoder model, is first proposed in NLP field. Inspired by its achievements, the transformer, equipped with a powerful multi-head self-attention mechanism, has received increasing research attention in the computer vision community. Vision Transformer (ViT) [31] considered an image as a 16×16 patch sequence, and trained a standard transformer architecture for image classification. METRO [32] achieved progressive dimensionality reduction using a multi-level transformer for pose estimation. In addition, transformer has also achieved impressive results in many downstream tasks, including image generation [33], denoising [34], object detection [35], video inpainting [36], *etc.*

3   Method

Our aim is to achieve higher performance in human mesh recovery from monocular images. Figure 2 shows the framework of our method. In our method, we extract image features from a given input image, establish a pose distribution,

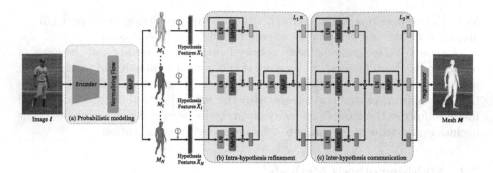

Fig. 2. Overview of the proposed method. Given an input monocular image **I**, we perform probabilistic modeling (a) with normalizing flows to extract image features, predict a pose distribution and generate multiple initial human mesh hypotheses (N indicates the number of hypotheses), input these multi-hypotheses into *Intra-hypothesis refinement* module (b) for independent refinement and feature enhancement, use *Inter-hypothesis communication* module (c) to implement their mutual communication and finally regress to obtain the recovered human mesh **M**.

construct hypothetical relationships, enhance feature representations, and finally output accurate recovery results. Our method consists of three steps: 1) probabilistic modeling and initial hypothesis generation (Sect. 3.2); 2) Intra-hypothesis Refinement (Sect. 3.3); 3) Inter-hypothesis Communication (Sect. 3.4).

3.1   Preliminary

SMPL Model. SMPL [7] provides a differentiable function $\mathcal{M}(\theta, \beta)$ which takes body pose parameters $\theta \in \mathbb{R}^{72}$ and shape parameters $\beta \in \mathbb{R}^{10}$ as inputs and outputs the body mesh $M \in \mathbb{R}^{6890 \times 3}$. While θ represents the global body rotation and the relative rotation of 23 joints in axis-angle format, β represents the first 10 coefficients of a PCA shape space, controlling the shape of the body. Given the mesh M, 3D joint locations can be obtained using a linear regressor, $\mathbf{J}^{3D} = JM$, where $J \in \mathbb{R}^{L \times 6890}$ is a regression matrix for L joints.

Transformer. Our refinement and communication of multi-hypotheses are based on the transformer architecture, as it performs well in feature representation and information stabilisation in propagation. Here we briefly describe Multi-Head Self-Attention (MHSA) and Multi-Layer Perceptron (MLP).

MHSA. In the MHSA, the inputs $X \in \mathbb{R}^{n \times d}$ are linearly mapped to queries $Q \in \mathbb{R}^{n \times d}$, keys $K \in \mathbb{R}^{n \times d}$, and values $V \in \mathbb{R}^{n \times d}$, where n is the sequence length and d is the dimension. Then, Q, K, and V, are split into h different subspaces, so that self-attention can be performed on them independently. Finally, the outputs from the different subspaces are concatenated to form the final result $Y \in \mathbb{R}^{n \times d}$. The scaled dot-product attention can be expressed as:

$$\text{Attention}(Q, K, V) = \text{softmax}\left(\frac{QK^T}{\sqrt{d}}\right)V. \tag{1}$$

MLP. The MLP consists of two linear layers, which are used for non-linearity and feature transformation:

$$\text{MLP}(X) = \sigma\left(XW_1 + b_1\right)W_2 + b_2, \tag{2}$$

where σ is activation function, $W_1 \in \mathbb{R}^{d \times d_m}$ and $W_2 \in \mathbb{R}^{d_m \times d}$ are the weights of the two linear layers respectively, and $b_1 \in \mathbb{R}^{d_m}$ and $b_2 \in \mathbb{R}^d$ are the bias terms.

3.2 Probabilistic Modeling

Given a monocular RGB image $\mathbf{I}$ as input, we attempt to learn a distribution of plausible poses conditional on $\mathbf{I}$ to obtain initial multiple plausible hypotheses. Inspired by ProHMR [27], we first encode the input image $\mathbf{I}$ using a CNN g to obtain image features $f_{\mathbf{I}}$. Subsequently, the probability distribution of the human pose $p_{\Theta|\mathbf{I}}(\theta \mid f_{\mathbf{I}} = g(\mathbf{I}))$ is modeled using Conditional Normalizing Flows. Unlike ProHMR, we adopt probabilistic modeling only to obtain feasible initial multiple hypotheses, rather than focusing on one-to-many mappings.

Normalizing Flow models are used to transform arbitrary complex distributions into a simple base distribution $p_Z(z)$ by constructing a series of reversible transformations. Each building block f_i consists of 3 basic transformations:

$$f_i = f_{\text{AC}} \circ f_{\text{LT}} \circ f_{\text{IN}}, \tag{3}$$

where $f_{\text{IN}}(\mathbf{z}) = \mathbf{a} \odot \mathbf{z} + \mathbf{b}$ (Instance Normalization), $f_{\text{LT}}(\mathbf{z}) = W\mathbf{z} + \mathbf{b}$ (Linear Transformation) and $f_{\text{AC}} = [\mathbf{z}_{1:k}, \mathbf{z}_{k+1:d} + \mathbf{t}\left(\mathbf{z}_{1:d}, \mathbf{c}\right)]$ (Additive Coupling). In addition, we combined four building blocks as above to obtain our flow model.

Meanwhile, the flow model allows not only for fast computation of probability distributions, but also for fast sampling from the distributions to obtain multip-hypotheses. In order not to lose generality, we consider the case where no other additional information is available, so instead of taking a direct mode computation from the output probability distribution with $\theta_I^* = \text{argmax}_\theta p_{\Theta|f_I}(\theta \mid f_{\mathbf{I}})$, we sample the distribution to select the larger probability N hypotheses. Therefore, the samples $\theta_i, i \in [1, 2, ..., N]$ drawn from the output distribution are:

$$\theta_i \sim p_{\Theta|\mathbf{I}}(\theta \mid f_{\mathbf{I}}). \tag{4}$$

Then, we use MLP to estimate the SMPL shape β_i and camera parameters π_i using image features f_I and pose θ_i as input:

$$[\beta_i, \pi_i] = \text{MLP}\left(f_I, \theta_i\right). \tag{5}$$

To summarize, we use probabilistic models to obtain a conditional probability distribution of poses, as well as sampling and estimation to obtain the initial human mesh hypotheses $M_i(\theta_i, \beta_i, \pi_i)$. However, these hypotheses are discrepant and insufficient for feature representation and need further enhancement.

3.3 Intra-hypothesis Refinement

After obtaining multiple human mesh recovery hypotheses $M_i(\theta_i, \beta_i, \pi_i)$, we first maintain its mesh information via a learnable positional embedding and encode its features $X_i, i \in [1, 2, ..., N]$ as subsequent inputs, for each hypothesis. To refine single-hypothesis features and enhance those coarse representations independently, the *Intra-hypothesis refinement* module feeds the encoded hypothesis features X_i into several parallel MHSA blocks, which can be represented as:

$$\widetilde{X}_i^l = X_i^{l-1} + \text{MHSA}\left(\text{LN}\left(X_i^{l-1}\right)\right), \qquad (6)$$

where $l \in [1, 2, ..., L_1]$ is the index of *Intra-hypothesis refinement* module.

However it is not enough to process each hypothesis independently, the respective feature enhancements need to be shared. Thus, the hypothesis features are concatenated and fed into the MLP to mix themselves and forming refined hypothesis representations. The procedure can be represented as:

$$
\begin{aligned}
\widetilde{X}_{concat}^l &= \text{Concat}\left(\widetilde{X}_1^l, \widetilde{X}_2^l, \ldots, \widetilde{X}_N^l\right), \\
\text{Concat}\left(\widetilde{X}_1^l, \widetilde{X}_2^l, \ldots, \widetilde{X}_N^l\right) &= \widetilde{X}_{concat}^l + \text{MLP}\left(\text{LN}\left(\widetilde{X}_{concat}^l\right)\right),
\end{aligned} \qquad (7)
$$

where $\text{Concat}(\cdot)$ is the concatenation operation.

3.4 Inter-hypothesis Communication

To capture multi-hypothesis relationships mutually, we inherit the cross-attention mechanism from [38–40] and apply the Multi-Head Cross-Attention (MHCA) to model inter-hypothesis relationships.

Specifically, the multiple hypotheses feature X_i^l are alternately regarded as queries and keys, and fed into the MHCA:

$$X_i^l = X_i^{l-1} + \text{MHCA}\left(\text{LN}\left(X_1^{l-1}\right), \ldots, \text{LN}\left(X_i^{l-1}\right), \ldots\right), \qquad (8)$$

where $l \in [1, 2, ..., L_2]$ is the index of *Inter-hypothesis communication* module, $X_i^0 = \widetilde{X}_i^{L_1}$. As a result, MHCA passes information crosswise among hypotheses to significantly enhance feature representation and modelling capabilities.

Similarly, here we proceed to mix the hypothesis features obtained, as well as forming hypothesis representations after communication:

$$
\begin{aligned}
X_{concat}^l &= \text{Concat}\left(X_1^l, X_2^l, \ldots, X_N^l\right), \\
\text{Concat}\left(X_1^l, X_2^l, \ldots, X_N^l\right) &= X_{concat}^l + \text{MLP}\left(\text{LN}\left(X_{concat}^l\right)\right),
\end{aligned} \qquad (9)
$$

where $\text{Concat}(\cdot)$ is the concatenation operation. Considering that the final single estimation result is obtained, the hypothesis features can be optionally not divided in the last MLP. Note that you can likewise choose to divide and thus obtain multiple reasonable results.

Finally, a regressor is applied to the output feature X^{L_2} to produce the 3D human mesh $M(\theta_i, \beta_i, \pi_i)$.

3.5 Loss Function

We introduce multiple losses as supervision for the probability distribution and mesh recovery hypotheses, respectively.

NLL Loss. As with typical probabilistic models, we use NLL loss to minimize the negative log-likelihood: $\mathcal{L}_{nll} = -\ln p_{\Theta|\mathbf{I}}\left(\boldsymbol{\theta}_{gt} \mid f_{\mathbf{I}}\right)$.

2D Joint Loss. A squared error reprojection loss is applied between the ground truth J_{2D} and estimated 2D joints $\hat{J}_{2D}$: $\mathcal{L}_{2D}(\theta, \beta, \pi) = \|J_{2D} - \hat{J}_{2D}\|_2$.

3D Loss. When 3D annotations (3D joints and/or SMPL parameters) are available, 3D loss is applied to reduce the errors between the ground truth and estimated values: $\mathcal{L}_{3D}(\theta, \beta) = \|J_{3D} - \hat{J}_{3D}\|_2 + \|\beta - \hat{\beta}\|_2 + \|\theta - \hat{\theta}\|_2$.

Orth Loss. The 6D representation proposed in [37] is used in our model to estimate the rotations. Since the absence of any constraint on the 6D representation leads to large differences between examples with partial 3D and or 2D annotations, we use L_{orth} to force the 6D representation of the samples drawn from the distribution to be close to the orthogonal 6D representation.

Overall: In total, the objective function of our model is:

$$\mathcal{L} = \lambda_{nll}\mathcal{L}_{nll} + \lambda_{2D}\mathcal{L}_{2D} + \lambda_{3D}\mathcal{L}_{3D} + \lambda_{orth}\mathcal{L}_{orth}, \tag{10}$$

where λ_{nll}, λ_{2D}, λ_{3D} and λ_{orth} represent the weights of the corresponding losses.

4 Experimental Results

4.1 Datasets

Following the settings of previous work [11,13], our method is trained on a mixture of data from several datasets with 3D and 2D annotations, including Human3.6M [41], MPI-INF-3DHP [42], 3DPW [43], COCO [44], and MPII [45]. In addition, we report experimental results on the evaluation sets of Human3.6M and 3DPW datasets, and apply widely used evaluation metrics, including Mean Per Joint Position Error (MPJPE) and Procrustes-Aligned Mean Per Joint Position Error (PA-MPJPE).

4.2 Comparison

We compare our method with the previous state-of-the-art temporal and frame-based methods on Human3.6M and 3DPW datasets. As shown in Table 1, our method achieves state-of-the-art performance in terms of accuracy in both the indoor dataset Human3.6M and the challenging field dataset 3DPW. It is worth noting that, our method outperforms the state-of-the-art temporal method MAED [20], whereas our method is a frame-based approach.

Figure 3 shows the qualitative results of our method on LSP dataset [46]. We observe that our method can better extract and represent the image features, and achieve more accurate mesh recovery. Moreover, we show the recovery results of our model for challenging monocular image inputs including depth ambiguity, joint occlusion and truncation, in Fig. 4. It can be seen that our model is able to handle them well by refining and communicating multi-hypotheses. We refer to the project website for more qualitative results.

Table 1. Quantitative evaluation of state-of-the-art temporal and frame-based methods on Human3.6M and 3DPW datasets. The best results are highlighted in bold and "-" shows the results that are not available.

Method	Human3.6M		3DPW	
	MPJPE↓	PA-MPJPE↓	MPJPE↓	PA-MPJPE↓
Temporal				
VIBE [16]	65.9	41.5	93.5	56.5
Lee *et al.* [18]	58.4	38.4	92.8	52.2
MAED [20]	56.3	38.7	88.8	50.7
Frame-based				
SPIN [13]	62.5	41.1	96.9	59.2
I2L-MeshNet [15]	55.7	41.1	93.2	57.7
ProHMR [27]	-	41.2	-	59.8
PyMAF [19]	57.7	40.5	92.8	58.9
PARE [21]	-	-	84.3	51.2
Ours	**54.8**	**38.1**	**83.7**	**50.5**

4.3   Ablation Study

We further conduct extensive ablation experiments on the effect of each key component and design in the proposed model. In the top part of Table 2, we report the results with different numbers of initial human mesh hypotheses. Experiments show that generating more hypotheses from the probabilistic model improves performance with a small increase in parameters, but becomes worse instead when $N > 8$. In the middle and bottom parts of Table 2, we report how the different parameters L_1 and L_2 impact the performance of our model, respectively. The validity and importance of our proposed modules for the experiment can be known from the results when $L_1 = 0$ or $L_2 = 0$, and the best performance of the model at $L_1 = 2$ and $L_2 = 2$.

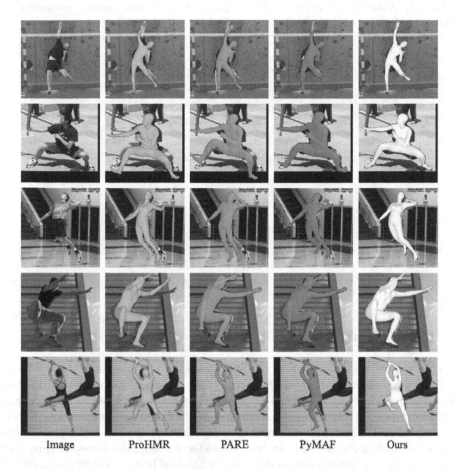

| Image | ProHMR | PARE | PyMAF | Ours |

Fig. 3. Qualitative results on LSP dataset. From left to right: Input images, ProHMR [27] results, PyMAF [19] results, PARE [21] results, Our results.

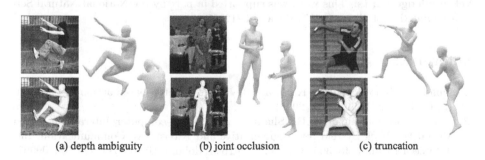

(a) depth ambiguity   (b) joint occlusion   (c) truncation

Fig. 4. Plausible human mesh recovery results generated by our method, especially for ambiguous parts with depth ambiguity, joint occlusion and truncation.

Table 2. Ablation study on different parameters of our model, evaluated on Human3.6M. N is the hypothesis number, L_1 is the number of *Intra-hypothesis refinement* module and L_2 is the number of *Inter-hypothesis communication* module.

N	L_1	L_2	MPJPE↓	PA-MPJPE↓
6	2	2	60.1	44.3
8	2	2	**54.8**	**38.1**
12	2	2	58.7	40.2
20	2	2	61.6	42.1
8	2	0	70.2	50.8
8	2	1	65.9	46.4
8	2	2	**54.8**	**38.1**
8	2	3	59.5	43.7
8	0	2	65.3	47.1
8	1	2	58.3	40.2
8	2	2	**54.8**	**38.1**
8	3	2	60.7	42.5

5   Conclusion

In this paper, we present a multi-hypothesis and probabilistic model-based method, MHPro, for human mesh recovery from monocular images. Unlike most probabilistic modeling and multi-hypothesis methods, we propose to refine and communicate multi-hypothesis for a better image feature representation. Extensive experiments show that our method achieves state-of-the-art performance on two benchmark datasets and can better handle challenging images. Future work could consider continually extending our method to better exploit the ability of multi-hypotheses and promote recovery accuracy considering various ambiguities.

Acknowledgements. This work was supported in part by the National Natural Science Foundation of China (62171317 and 62122058).

References

1. Duan, H., Zhao, Y., Chen, K., et al.: Revisiting skeleton-based action recognition. In: CVPR, pp. 2969–2978 (2022)
2. Liu, Y., Sivaparthipan, C.B., Shankar, A.: Human-computer Interaction Based Visual Feedback System for Augmentative and Alternative Communication. Int. J. Speech Technol. **25**, 305–314 (2022). https://doi.org/10.1007/s10772-021-09901-4
3. Weng, C.Y., Curless, B., Kemelmacher-Shlizerman, I.: Photo wake-up: 3D character animation from a single photo. In: CVPR, pp. 5908–5917 (2019)

4. Khirodkar, R., Tripathi, S., Kitani, K.: Occluded human mesh recovery. In: CVPR, pp. 1715–1725 (2022)
5. Zheng, C., Wu, W., Yang, T., et al.: Deep learning-based human pose estimation: a survey. ArXiv:2012.13392 (2020)
6. Tian, Y., Zhang, H., Liu, Y., et al.: Recovering 3D human mesh from monocular images: a survey. ArXiv:2203.01923 (2022)
7. Loper, M., Mahmood, N., Romero, J., et al.: SMPL: a skinned multi-person linear model. TOG **34**(6), 1–16 (2015)
8. Bogo, F., Kanazawa, A., Lassner, C., Gehler, P., Romero, J., Black, M.J.: Keep it SMPL: automatic estimation of 3D human pose and shape from a single image. In: Leibe, B., Matas, J., Sebe, N., Welling, M. (eds.) ECCV 2016. LNCS, vol. 9909, pp. 561–578. Springer, Cham (2016). https://doi.org/10.1007/978-3-319-46454-1_34
9. Lassner, C., Romero, J., Kiefel, M., et al.: Unite the people: closing the loop between 3D and 2D human representations. In: CVPR, pp. 6050–6059 (2017)
10. Song, J., Chen, X., Hilliges, O.: Human body model fitting by learned gradient descent. In: Vedaldi, A., Bischof, H., Brox, T., Frahm, J.-M. (eds.) ECCV 2020. LNCS, vol. 12365, pp. 744–760. Springer, Cham (2020). https://doi.org/10.1007/978-3-030-58565-5_44
11. Kanazawa, A., Black, M.J., Jacobs, D.W., et al.: End-to-end recovery of human shape and pose. In: CVPR, pp. 7122–7131 (2018)
12. Pavlakos, G., Zhu, L., Zhou, X., et al.: Learning to estimate 3D human pose and shape from a single color image. In: CVPR, pp. 459–468 (2018)
13. Kolotouros, N., Pavlakos, G., Black, M.J., et al.: Learning to reconstruct 3D human pose and shape via model-fitting in the loop. In: ICCV, pp. 2252–2261 (2019)
14. Kolotouros, N., Pavlakos, G., Daniilidis, K.: Convolutional mesh regression for single-image human shape reconstruction. In: CVPR, pp. 4501–4510 (2019)
15. Moon, G., Lee, K.M.: I2L-MeshNet: image-to-lixel prediction network for accurate 3D human pose and mesh estimation from a single RGB image. In: Vedaldi, A., Bischof, H., Brox, T., Frahm, J.-M. (eds.) ECCV 2020. LNCS, vol. 12352, pp. 752–768. Springer, Cham (2020). https://doi.org/10.1007/978-3-030-58571-6_44
16. Kocabas, M., Athanasiou, N., Black, M.J.: VIBE: video inference for human body pose and shape estimation. In: CVPR, pp. 5253–5263 (2020)
17. Jiang, W., Kolotouros, N., Pavlakos, G., et al.: Coherent reconstruction of multiple humans from a single image. In: CVPR, pp. 5579–5588 (2020)
18. Lee, G.H., Lee, S.W.: Uncertainty-aware human mesh recovery from video by learning part-based 3D dynamics. In: ICCV, pp. 12375–12384 (2021)
19. Zhang, H., Tian, Y., Zhou, X., et al.: PyMAF: 3D human pose and shape regression with pyramidal mesh alignment feedback loop. In: ICCV, pp. 11446–11456 (2021)
20. Wan, Z., Li, Z., Tian, M., et al.: Encoder-decoder with multi-level attention for 3D human shape and pose estimation. In: ICCV, pp. 13033–13042 (2021)
21. Kocabas, M., Huang, C.H.P., Hilliges, O., et al.: PARE: part attention regressor for 3D human body estimation. In: ICCV, pp. 11127–11137 (2021)
22. Li, C., Lee, G.H.: Generating multiple hypotheses for 3D human pose estimation with mixture density network. In: CVPR, pp. 9887–9895 (2019)
23. Li, C., Lee, G.H.: Weakly supervised generative network for multiple 3D human pose hypotheses. ArXiv:2008.05770 (2020)
24. Biggs, B., Novotny, D., Ehrhardt, S., et al.: 3D multi-bodies: fitting sets of plausible 3D human models to ambiguous image data. In: NIPS, vol. 33, pp. 20496–20507 (2020)
25. Oikarinen, T., Hannah, D., Kazerounian, S.: GraphMDN: leveraging graph structure and deep learning to solve inverse problems. In: IJCNN, pp. 1–9 (2021)

26. Wehrbein, T., Rudolph, M., Rosenhahn, B., et al.: Probabilistic monocular 3D human pose estimation with normalizing flows. In: ICCV, pp. 11199–11208 (2021)
27. Kolotouros, N., Pavlakos, G., Jayaraman, D., et al.: Probabilistic modeling for human mesh recovery. In: ICCV, pp. 11605–11614 (2021)
28. Sengupta, A., Budvytis, I., Cipolla, R.: Hierarchical kinematic probability distributions for 3D human shape and pose estimation from images in the wild. In: ICCV, pp. 11219–11229 (2021)
29. Li, W., Liu, H., Tang, H., et al.: MHFormer: multi-hypothesis transformer for 3D human pose estimation. ArXiv:2111.12707 (2021)
30. Vaswani, A., Shazeer, N., Parmar, N., et al.: Attention is all you need. In: NIPS, vol. 30 (2017)
31. Dosovitskiy, A., Beyer, L., Kolesnikov, A., et al.: An image is worth 16×16 words: transformers for image recognition at scale. ArXiv:2010.11929 (2020)
32. Lin, K., Wang, L., Liu, Z.: End-to-end human pose and mesh reconstruction with transformers. In: CVPR, pp. 1954–1963 (2021)
33. Jiang, Y., Chang, S., Wang, Z.: TransGAN: two pure transformers can make one strong GAN, and that can scale up. In: NIPS, vol. 34 (2021)
34. Chen, H., Wang, Y., Guo, T., et al.: Pre-trained image processing transformer. In: CVPR, pp. 12299–12310 (2021)
35. Dai, Z., Cai, B., Lin, Y., et al.: UP-DETR: unsupervised pre-training for object detection with transformers. In: CVPR, pp. 1601–1610 (2021)
36. Zeng, Y., Fu, J., Chao, H.: Learning joint spatial-temporal transformations for video inpainting. In: Vedaldi, A., Bischof, H., Brox, T., Frahm, J.-M. (eds.) ECCV 2020. LNCS, vol. 12361, pp. 528–543. Springer, Cham (2020). https://doi.org/10.1007/978-3-030-58517-4_31
37. Zhou, Y., Barnes, C., Lu, J., et al.: On the continuity of rotation representations in neural networks. In: CVPR, pp. 5745–5753 (2019)
38. Chen, C.F.R., Fan, Q., Panda, R.: CrossViT: cross-attention multi-scale vision transformer for image classification. In: ICCV, pp. 357–366 (2021)
39. Wei, X., Zhang, T., Li, Y., et al.: Multi-modality cross attention network for image and sentence matching. In: CVPR, pp. 10941–10950 (2020)
40. Hou, R., Chang, H., Ma, B., et al.: Cross attention network for few-shot classification. In: NIPS, vol. 32 (2019)
41. Ionescu, C., Papava, D., Olaru, V., et al.: Human3.6M: large scale datasets and predictive methods for 3D human sensing in natural environments. TPAMI **36**(7), 1325–1339 (2013)
42. Mehta, D., Rhodin, H., Casas, D., et al.: Monocular 3D human pose estimation in the wild using improved CNN supervision. In: 3DV, pp. 506–516 (2017)
43. von Marcard, T., Henschel, R., Black, M.J., Rosenhahn, B., Pons-Moll, G.: Recovering accurate 3D human pose in the wild using IMUs and a moving camera. In: Ferrari, V., Hebert, M., Sminchisescu, C., Weiss, Y. (eds.) ECCV 2018. LNCS, vol. 11214, pp. 614–631. Springer, Cham (2018). https://doi.org/10.1007/978-3-030-01249-6_37
44. Lin, T.-Y., et al.: Microsoft COCO: common objects in context. In: Fleet, D., Pajdla, T., Schiele, B., Tuytelaars, T. (eds.) ECCV 2014. LNCS, vol. 8693, pp. 740–755. Springer, Cham (2014). https://doi.org/10.1007/978-3-319-10602-1_48
45. Andriluka, M., Pishchulin, L., Gehler, P., et al.: 2D human pose estimation: new benchmark and state of the art analysis. In: CVPR, pp. 3686–3693 (2014)
46. Johnson, S., Everingham, M.: Clustered pose and nonlinear appearance models for human pose estimation. In: BMVC, vol. 2, no. 4, p. 5 (2010)

Image Sampling for Machine Vision

Jiashuai Cui[1], Fan Li[1(✉)], and Liejun Wang[2]

[1] Xi'an Jiaotong University, Xi'an 710049, China
morganc@stu.xjtu.edu.cn, lifan@mail.xjtu.edu.cn
[2] Xinjiang University, Urumqi 830046, China
wljxju@xju.edu.cn

Abstract. Image sampling is one of the basic methods for image compression, which is efficient for image store, transmission, and applications. Existing sampling methods are designed for human-eye perception, which discard unconcerned information to decrease the amount of data considering the visual preference of human. However, these methods cannot adapt to the increasing machine vision tasks since there is a lot of redundant information for machine analysis to ensure the comfort of human eyes. In this paper, we propose an image sampling method for machine vision. We adopt a gray image to retain the main structural information of the image, and construct a concise color feature map based on the dominant channel of pixels to provide color information. Experiments on public datasets including COCO and ImageNet show that our sampling method can adapt to the characteristics of machine vision and greatly reduce the amount of data with little impact on the performance of mainstream computer vision algorithms.

Keywords: Image sampling · Machine vision · Color feature

1 Introduction

With the enrichment of application scenarios and the advancement of hardware devices, it is inefficient to directly store, transmit and process massive high-resolution images. Image sampling is of great significance by preprocessing original images to retain effective information for tasks, which can reduce the amount of data from the source and ensure the efficient processing.

Existing sampling methods are targeted at human eyes perception. Uniform sampling following the Nyquist-Shannon sampling theorem [1] ensure that original images can be restored perfectly without any loss of information, but it contains a lot of redundant information. Since human eyes prefer the foreground and ignore the background, non-uniform sampling methods [2–19] focus on sampling points on the foreground to achieve both great compression and the maintenance of perception. In the industry, considering the sensitivity of human eyes for luminance, the JPEG [20] coding standard converts the image into the YUV space for sampling, keeping the luminance completely and downsampling the color component to obtain a balance between the reduction of data and the good vision effect.

L. Fang et al. (Eds.): CICAI 2022, LNAI 13604, pp. 229–241, 2022.
https://doi.org/10.1007/978-3-031-20497-5_19

However, these sampling methods designed for human eyes can not adapt to the increasing machine vision tasks today. RGB images are the basis of most machine vision tasks. However, because machine vision is only targeted at analysis tasks and does not require fine-grained color distinction, the RGB format is actually redundant for machine vision. In addition, the separation of image acquisition and image analysis is a common scenario in machine vision. In order to avoid the large distortion of compression for transmission, it's necessary to reduce the mount of data from the source. Therefore, the sampling method expected for machine vision tasks is non-RGB, which can retain a little color information for analysis and significantly compress data.

In this paper, we propose an image sampling method for machine vision, which can greatly reduce the amount of data while retaining information effective for downstream vision tasks. In this sampling method, we use the gray feature map with original resolution to retain the main structural information of the image to distinguish objects boundaries. At the same time, we construct a concise color feature map based on the dominant color components of pixels, and downsample its spatial resolution to obtain a very small amount of data to effectively represent the color feature and complement the gray feature. The advantages of the proposed method are showed as:

Compact. It is completed by only simple operations of non-deep learning methods.

Efficient. The amount of data can be greatly compressed, and the performance loss for visual tasks is small.

General. It adapts to various machine vision tasks such as image classification and object detection without modification.

2 Related Work

Nyquist pointed out that for a band-limited signal, as long as the sampling frequency is more than twice the highest frequency, it can be recovered without information loss. For image sampling, the sampling interval of the whole image is determined by the most drastic region, and the sampling theorem must be satisfied in three channels at the same time, so uniform sampling is of serious redundancy.

Non-uniform sampling is proposed, which focuses on assigning more sampling points to the foreground regions of interest. Adaptive mesh sampling is proposed in [2], modeling the distance between pixels as the elastic system to sample points. Elder [3] introduces the farthest point strategy into the field of image sampling, and derives the best sampling points through the error function. The distortion of image luminance is taken into account for sampling in [4]. In addition, researchers [5, 6, 10, 14] propose methods for allocating sampling points from different views. Wavelet is introduced into the field of image sampling [7, 8, 16]. From a perspective of manifold, researchers [9, 11–13] try to model and solve the problem of image sampling. A lot of research focus on the sparsity and low sampling rate [15, 17, 18]. With the development of deep learning, there are some related methods to obtain good performance [19].

In the industry, the JPEG coding standard converts the image into the YUV color space for sampling. The luminance component Y is retained completely, and the color component U and V can be downsampled with different factors taking into account the reduction of the amount of data and the feel of the human eyes.

The above traditional sampling methods are all designed for human eyes, and cannot retain the information interested by machine specially, so the amount of data is redundant. In the coding field, existing work [21, 22] has focused on the necessity of coding for machine vision and we are inspired by them.

3 Method

3.1 Motivation

The sampling method needs to reduce the amount of data on the premise of preserving the main structural information of the image. Gray image sampling is suitable because it contains edge information to distinguish the foreground and the background so that objects are clear in shape. Meanwhile, the data volume of gray images is significantly reduced by two-thirds compared to RGB images.

However, gray images can only distinguish changes in luminance, and lack color information compared to original RGB images, while the basic color information is critical for machine vision.

On the one hand, color information is a key property of objects. The following figures are taken from ImageNet [23]. The broccoli and cauliflower in Figure 1(a) and (b) are unrecognizable in shape and can not be distinguished by gray images. The key difference of attribute is that broccoli is green, while cauliflower is yellow.

(a)Broccoli   (b)Cauliflower

Fig. 1. Color information is a key property of objects.

On the other hand, color information can help objects stand out from the background. The image below is taken from the COCO [24] dataset. The traffic sign in gray image (a) is close to the background and is difficult to identify. If the color information is considered, its red attribute can make it conspicuous in the background. It can be seen from the saliency [25] maps that the color information produces high response at the location of the sign in the saliency, while gray image can not provide this information (Fig. 2).

Color information is important, but in order to represent color features with the smallest amount of data, it is necessary to clarify what the most critical factor in color information is. To this end, we assume that: the important information is not the value of color channels, but the ordinal relationship of the color channels, that is, which channel among R, G and B has the largest value to be the dominant component.

To this end, we conducted the following experiments. For a well-trained ResNet50 [26] classification network, we change the input format of test images respectively: (1)

(a) Gray image and its saliency.   (b) RGB image and its saliency.

Fig. 2. Color information can help objects stand out from the background.

The pixel values of the input image change as a whole. (2) The ordinal relationship of channels change, which means exchanging the values of the maximum and minimum channels. It can be seen from Table 1 that the change of the ordinal relationship of color has a greater impact on the network recognition ability.

Table 1. What is the most critical factor in color information?

	Precision/%	Decrease compared to RGB/%
Numerical change	58.58	−14.18
Ordinal change	51.81	−20.94

The ideal image sampling needs both preserving structural information and concisely supplementing color information. Further, the inter-channel ordinal relationship is critical in color information. Inspired by this, we propose an image sampling method that combines gray information and dominant color channel index information.

3.2 Implementation

The image sampled by the proposed method is stored in two parts. The first part is a gray image to retain main information, and it's the same as the original image in length and width, and the depth is 8 bits. The second part is a color feature map to provide concise color information. Its spatial dimension is half in length and width, and the depth is 2 bits. The specific sampling method is as showed in Fig. 3.

Gray Image. The gray image contains main information of the original image, and the amount of data per pixel is reduced from 24 bits to 8 bits, which can significantly compress the data volume. The lack of color information caused by grayscale operation will be compensated as shown next.

Color Feature. Inspired by our exploration, we adopt the dominant components of the RGB channels to represent the ordinal relationship of the colors.

Concise Representation of Color Feature. At each pixel position of the image, the channel with the largest value among the RGB channels represents the most important color

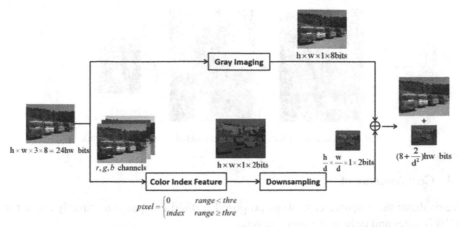

Fig. 3. The proposed image sampling method combining gray image and color index feature. The original image will be sampled as a gray image to decrease the volume of data and a color feature map to save key information for machine vision. The detailed method is as shown: (a) gray imaging is conducted to save main structural information of original images. (b) the index number of channels at pixels with the largest value can be used to construct a color feature. (c) when the RGB channels have little difference and the pixel is nearly gray as a whole, the forth code is adopted but not the index number of channels to represent there is no dominant color component. (d) the color feature map will be downsampled to further reduce the data volume.

component, so the index number of the channel with the largest value can be used to construct a color feature. The index numbers of the three RGB channels have a range of $\{0,1,2\}$, so each pixel of the color feature map only needs space of 2 bits.

Full Use of Feature Space. The 2 bits can represent 4 cases, and the range of index numbers has only 3 cases, so the fourth feature case can be encoded to make full use of the feature space. For a pixel, when the RGB channels have little difference, the pixel is nearly gray as a whole, and there is no dominant component. Therefore, considering this case separately, for pixels whose range of three channels is less than a specific threshold, the color feature will be encoded as the fourth case.

Further Compression of Color Feature. The color information doesn't require a clear and accurate boundary and it only needs to represent the dominant color of the large areas. Therefore, the color feature map will be downsampled to further reduce the data volume without affecting the performance of vision tasks.

3.3 Visualization

Following the above description, the proposed sampling method can obtain gray images and concise color feature maps. The visualization results are shown below. As shown in the Fig. 4, the red sign in the color feature is distinct from the background to supplement the gray image, and the sampling effect is as expected.

Fig. 4. Visualization of sampling results (Color figure online).

3.4 Cost Assessment

We evaluate the resource cost of the proposed method compared to directly using raw RGB images and only using gray images.

Table 2. Source assessment of the proposed sampling method.

Input	Bit/pixel	FLOPs/pixel	Time/ms
RGB	24	0	5.24
Gray	8	5	5.60
Ours	8.5	10	6.55

In terms of space, our method is efficient, saving nearly 2/3 of data compared to the RGB form. With concise color feature, our method has a negligible increase in the amount of data compared to gray images, but can significantly improve the performance of machine vision as discussed in detail next.

In terms of time cost, we discuss the amount of computation and the actual processing time. When the raw RGB image is used, no additional processing is required. And for grayscale processing, average to each pixel, following the grayscale formula as

$$Gray = R \times 0.299 + G \times 0.587 + B \times 0.114 \tag{1}$$

there are 3 multiplications and 2 additions. The color feature sampling will bring extra 5 float operations including 3 comparison and 1 subtraction to calculate the range of channels, 1 comparison to check whether over-threshold, and no calculation in downsampling because of directly adopting the corner value as result in every cell.

The above comparison doesn't take into account actual factors such as data access efficiency. Therefore, we test the actual time to read and process 5000 images of 224*224 size from the COCO validation set on the Intel i5–8400 CPU. The actual time cost of the proposed method is also small.

In summary, the proposed method can greatly reduce the amount of data in space and spend little extra time, so it can serve machine vision tasks at low cost.

4 Experiments

In order to verify the proposed method can retain the effective information of machine vision tasks, we conduct sufficient experiments on multiple datasets and models. It shows our method has a little performance loss while greatly reducing the amount of data. Compared with gray inputs, the proposed method can stably improve the performance of machine vision tasks. The following experiments are carried out on the hardware of NVIDIA GTX 2080TI and the deep learning environment of Pytorch1.7 and CUDA10.2.

4.1 Object Detection

In the following experiments, we adopt mAP as metric. In object detection, Precision is the proportion of correct results in all bounding boxes predicted under the premise of a certain confidence. Recall is the proportion of the bounding boxes predicted by the algorithm in all ground truth in images. Drawing a curve with Precision as the vertical axis and Recall as the horizontal axis, AP is mathematically the area under the curve to balance the accuracy and omission. In multi-class task, mAP is the mean value of APs of each class. In practice, we will follow the COCO [24] standard to calculate the mAP metric where mAP@0.5 means the confidence threshold is 0.5 and mAP@0.5–0.95 is the mean value of each threshold of 0.5 to 0.95.

Different Datasets. We compare the metrics that can be achieved on the YOLOv5-s model [27–30] using raw RGB images, gray images, and sampled images by our method as input. During training, only the HSV augment setting differs since the color feature of sampled images change greatly, and others are kept the same to ensure fairness.

Table 3. YOLOv5-s on different datasets.

Dataset	Input	mAP@0.5/%	mAP@0.5–0.95/%
VOC	RGB	86.6	62.6
	Gray	85.6	60.8
	Ours	85.8	61.4
COCO	RGB	55.4	36.7
	Gray	53.6	35.0
	Ours	54.5	35.7

Compared with gray inputs, the proposed sampling method can provide color information and significantly improve the object detection performance. And on the more challenging dataset COCO, our method brings greater improvement, indicating it can adapt to complex scenarios.

Different Scales of Models. We compare the performance of YOLOv5 networks of different scales on COCO. It can be seen from Table 4 that the proposed sampling method

Table 4. YOLOv5 models of different scale on COCO.

Scale	Params/M	Input	mAP@0.5/%	mAP@0.5–0.95/%
Small	7.3	RGB	55.4	36.7
		Gray	53.6	35.0
		Ours	54.5	35.7
Middle	21.4	RGB	62.8	44.2
		Gray	60.3	42.0
		Ours	61.0	42.8
Large	47.0	RGB	65.4	47.4
		Gray	63.1	44.9
		Ours	64.0	45.8

can be applied to detection networks of different sizes, and has consistent improvement of large, medium and small scale models.

Different Algorithms. On the Pascal VOC dataset, we compare the impact of three inputs on the performance of mainstream object detection algorithms. Table 5 shows that our method can be applied to different paradigms including one-stage, two-stage and anchor-free algorithms. It has a consistent improvement to detection algorithms.

Table 5. Different algorithms on Pascal VOC. (mAP@0.5/%)

	YOLOv5-m	Faster RCNN [31]	CenterNet [32]
RGB	90.1	70.1	74.9
Gray	89.2	65.4	72.4
Ours	89.5	66.0	72.8
Increase	+0.3	+0.6	+0.4

4.2 Image Classification

In the following experiments, we adopt top-1 accuracy as metric. If the class with the highest confidence predicted by the algorithm is the same as the true label of an image, it's correct. Top-1 accuracy is the correct rate on the whole dataset. It reflects the classification ability of the algorithm.

Different Datasets. We compare the achieved accuracy on the classical network ResNet50 with 3 kinds of inputs. It can be seen from Table 6 that the proposed method can achieve better results than gray image.

Table 6. Classification precision of ResNet50 on different datasets. (%)

	Cifar100	ImageNet
RGB	78.65	72.76
Gray	71.44	70.95
Ours	73.92	71.34
Increase	+2.48	+0.39

Different Scales of Models. On the Cifar100 dataset, we compare the performance of ResNet networks of different scales on three input forms. Table 7 shows that the proposed method can be applied to classification networks of different sizes, and it has a consistent improvement on models of different sizes.

Table 7. Classification precision of ResNet models in different sizes on Cifar100. (%)

	Res18 (11.7M)	Res50 (25.6M)	Res101 (44.6M)	Res152 (60.2M)
RGB	76.24	78.65	78.30	78.75
Gray	69.11	71.44	72.01	72.46
Ours	72.28	73.92	74.48	75.83
Increase	+3.17	+2.48	+2.47	+3.37

Different Algorithms. On the Cifar100 dataset, we compare the impact of three input forms to mainstream backbone networks. It can be seen from Table 8 that the proposed sampling method can be applied to image classification networks of different paradigms, and it has a consistent improvement to the mainstream networks.

Table 8. Classification precision of different networks on Cifar100. (%)

	MobileNet-v2 [33]	Vgg16 [34]	DenseNet121 [35]
RGB	68.61	72.38	79.24
Gray	60.45	63.92	72.04
Ours	64.76	67.81	75.62
Increase	+4.31	+3.89	+3.58

4.3 Ablation Experiments

Threshold. The proposed method will judge the three-channel range value of each pixel during color feature sampling to decide whether to encode the pixel as the forth case to represent there is no dominant color. Based on COCO and the YOLOv5 network, we verify the necessity of a threshold and explore the optimal value.

Table 9. Exploring range threshold.

Threshold	mAP@0.5/%	mAP@0.5–0.95/%
No Threshold	53.9	35.4
16	54.3	35.6
24	54.3	35.5
32	**54.5**	**35.7**
40	54.0	35.5
48	53.9	35.4
56	53.9	35.3
64	54.1	35.5

As shown in the Table 9, the performance of networks is significantly lower with sampled images without threshold as input, indicating the necessity to encode the case of no dominant color individually. Further, through the comparison of multiple settings, we choose 32 as the best threshold to divide whether there is a dominant color in the pixel, so as to achieve the best effect.

Downsampling Factor. The proposed method performs downsampling on the color feature map to compress the amount of data. Based on the COCO dataset and the YOLOv5 object detection network, we verify the necessity of downsampling the color feature map and explore the optimal downsampling factor.

Table 10. Exploring downsampling factor.

Factor	Bit/pixel	mAP@0.5/%	mAP@0.5–0.95/%
No Downsampling	2.000	54.2	35.6
1/2	**0.500**	**54.5**	**35.7**
1/4	0.125	53.9	35.3
1/8	0.031	53.8	35.3
1/16	0.008	53.9	35.4
1/32	0.002	53.7	35.1

As shown in the Table 10, appropriate downsampling by 1/2 can actually improve the performance of machine vision tasks. We argue it is because color feature is not as fine as edge information, and may generate error at the boundary of regions. Downsampling can eliminate such tiny distortion, so that the networks can focus on the color information.

In addition, although other factors of downsampling can further reduce the amount of data, the marginal utility is small, and the benefits are not enough to make up for the performance drop. Therefore, downsampling is necessary, and we choose 1/2 as the optimal factor.

4.4 Effect Visualization

In order to illustrate the proposed method can help machine vision focus on key areas by highlighting color information, we visualize the feature map of the sampled image. It can be seen that after sampling, strong response is generated in the shallow, middle, and deep layers of the deep networks at the position of the red traffic sign, indicating the machine can make full use of the color features provided by the sampling method to improve the performance of visual analysis tasks (Fig. 5).

Fig. 5. Responses in shallow, middle and deep feature maps with the sampled image as input.

5 Conclusion

We propose a simple but effective image sampling method. Through constructing the gray image and the concise color feature, it can greatly reduce the performance loss of visual tasks while greatly compressing the amount of data. Our method has been tested on public datasets including COCO, VOC, ImageNet and Cifar, as well as mainstream deep models, which fully proves its effectiveness and generality. In the future, our sampling method will collaborate with encoders and be applied to machine vision task scenarios where image acquisition and image processing are separated.

References

1. Nyquist, H.: Certain topics in telegraph transmission theory. Proc. IEEE **90**(2), 280–305 (1928)
2. Terzopoulos D., Vasilescu M.: Sampling and reconstruction with adaptive meshes. In Computer Vision and Pattern Recognition, pp. 70–75 (1991)
3. Eldar, Y., Lindenbaum, M., et al.: The farthest point strategy for progressive image sampling. IEEE Trans. Image Process. **6**(9), 1305–1315 (1997)
4. Ramoni, G., Carrato, S.: An adaptive irregular sampling algorithm and its application to image coding. Image Vision Comput. **19**(7), 451–460 (2001)

5. Wei, L., Wang, R.: Differential domain analysis for non-uniform sampling. ACM Trans. Graph. **30**(4), 1–10 (2011)
6. Marvasti, F., Liu, C., Adams, G.: Analysis and recovery of multidimensional signals from irregular samples using nonlinear and iterative techniques. Sig. Process **36**, 13–30 (1994)
7. Chen, W., Itoh, S., Shiki, J.: Irregular sampling theorems for wavelet subspace. IEEE Trans. Inf. Theory **44**(3), 1131–1142 (1998)
8. Liu, Y.: Irregular sampling for spline wavelet. IEEE Trans. Inf. Theory **42**(2), 623–627 (1996)
9. Oztireli, A., Alexa, M., Gross, M.: Spectral sampling of manifolds. AMC Trans. Grap. **29**(6), 1–8 (2010)
10. Devir, Z., Lindenbaum, M.: Blind adaptive sampling of images. IEEE Trans. Image Process. **21**(4), 1478–1487 (2012)
11. Sochen, N., Kimmel, R., Malladi, R.: A general framework for low level vision. IEEE Trans. Image Process. **7**(3), 310–318 (1998)
12. Cheng, S., Dey, T., Ramos, E.: A manifold reconstruction from point samples. In: Proceedings of the Sixteenth Annual ACM-SIAM Symposium on Discrete Algorithms, pp. 1018–1027 (2005)
13. Saucan, E., Appleboime, E., Zeevi, Y.: Geometric approach to sampling and communication. Sampl. Theory Sig. Image Process. **11**, 1 (2010)
14. Vipula, S., Navin, R.: Data Compression using non-uniform sampling. In: International Conference on Signal Processing, pp. 603–607 (2007)
15. Ji, S., Xue, Y., Lawrence, C.: Bayesian compressive sensing. IEEE Trans. Sig. Process. **56**(6), 2346–2356 (2008)
16. Bahzad, S., Nazanin, R.: Model-based nonuniform compressive sampling and recovery of natural images utilizing a wavelet-domain universal hidden Markov model. IEEE Trans. Sig. Process. **65**(1), 95–104 (2017)
17. Matthew, M., Robert, N.: Near-optimal adaptive compressed sensing. IEEE Trans. Inf. Theory **60**(7), 4001–4012 (2014)
18. Ali, T., Farokh, M.: Adaptive sparse image sampling and recovery. IEEE Trans. Comput. Imaging **4**(3), 311–325 (2018)
19. Dai, Q., Henry, C., et al.: Adaptive image sampling using deep learning and its application on X-ray fluorescence image reconstruction. IEEE Trans. Multim. **22**(10), 2564–2578 (2020)
20. William, P., Joan, M.: JPEG: Still image data compression standard. ISBN: 978-0442012724
21. Wang, Z., Li, F., Xu, J., Pamela, C.: Human-machine interaction oriented image coding for resource-constrained visual monitoring in IoT. IEEE Intern. Things J. (2022)
22. Mei, Y., Li, L., Li, Z., Li, F.: Learning-based scalable image compression with latent-feature reuse and prediction. IEEE Trans. Multim. **24**, 4143–4157 (2022)
23. Jia, D., Wei, D., Li, F., et al.: ImageNet: a large-scale hierarchical image database. In: IEEE Conference on Computer Vision and Pattern Recognition, pp. 248–255 (2009)
24. Lin, T., Marie, M., et al.: Microsoft COCO: common objects in context. In: European Conference on Computer Vision, pp. 740–755 (2014)
25. Itti, L., Koch, C., Niebur, E.: A model of saliency-based visual attention for rapid scene analysis. IEEE Trans. Pattern Anal. Mach. Intell. **20**(11), 1254–1259 (1998)
26. He, K., Zhang, X., Ren, S., Sun, J.: Deep residual learning for image recognition. In: IEEE Conference on Computer Vision and Pattern Recognition, pp. 770–778 (2016)
27. Joseph, R., Santosh, D., Ross, G., Ali, F.: You only look once: unified, real-time object detection. In: IEEE Conference on Computer Vision and Pattern Recognition, pp. 779–788 (2016)
28. Joseph, R., Ali, F.: YOLO9000: better, faster, stronger. In: IEEE Conference on Computer Vision and Pattern Recognition, pp. 6517–6525 (2017)
29. Joseph, R., Ali, F.: YOLOv3: An incremental improvement. https://arxiv.org/pdf/1804.02767.pdf

30. Glenn J., et al.: YOLOv5 homepage. https://github.com/ultralytics/yolov5
31. Ren, S., He, K., Ross, G., Sun, J.: Faster R-CNN: towards real-time object detection with region proposal networks. IEEE Trans. Pattern Analysis Mach. Intell. **39**(6), 1137–1149 (2017)
32. Zhou, X., Wang, D., Philipp, K.: Objects as points. https://arxiv.org/pdf/1904.07850.pdf
33. Mark, S., Andrew, H., et al.: MobileNetV2: inverted residuals and linear bottlenecks. https://arxiv.org/pdf/1801.04381.pdf
34. Simonyan, K., Zisserman, A.: Very deep convolutional networks for large-scale image recognition. In: International Conference on Learning Representation, pp. 1–14 (2015)
35. Huang, G., Liu, Z., et al.: Densely connected convolutional networks. IEEE Conference on Computer Vision and Pattern Recognition, pp. 2261–2269 (2017)

SMOF: Squeezing More Out of Filters Yields Hardware-Friendly CNN Pruning

Yanli Liu[1], Bochen Guan[1(✉)], Weiyi Li[1], Qinwen Xu[2], and Shuxue Quan[1]

[1] OPPO US Research Center, Innopeak Technology Inc, Palo Alto, CA 94303, USA
bochen.guan@gmail.com
[2] Google LLC, Mountain View, CA 94043, USA

Abstract. Researchers have proposed various structured Convolutional Neural Networks (CNNs) pruning strategies to make them work efficiently on edge devices. However, most of them focus on reducing the number of filter channels per layer without considering the redundancy within individual filter channels. In this work, we explore pruning from another dimension, the kernel size. We develop a CNN pruning framework called SMOF, which Squeezes More Out of Filters by reducing both kernel size and the number of filter channels. Notably, SMOF is friendly to standard hardware devices without any customized low-level implementations, and the pruning effort by kernel size reduction does not suffer from the fixed-size width constraint in SIMD units of general-purpose processors. The pruned networks can be deployed effortlessly with significant running time reduction. We also support these claims via extensive experiments on various CNN structures and general-purpose processors for mobile devices.

Keywords: CNN · Kernel size · Pruning

1 Introduction

Deep convolutional neural networks (CNNs) have made remarkable breakthroughs on various tasks such as computer vision [4,10], image processing [17], natural language processing [29], and medical imaging applications [25]. Recently, the rapid development of communication technologies such as Internet-of-Things and 5G [30] provides a vision of the future where edge devices have a crucial role in providing uninterrupted communications and computations every day. Therefore, there will be an explosive increase in applying deep learning on edge devices to address the new challenges and enable more advisable services. However, successful deep CNN architectures such as ResNet [12] typically contain hundreds of layers and tons of parameters, which require a large memory footprint and increased computational power. Therefore, there has been a high demand for reducing the size and FLOPs of CNNs with acceptable compromise on their performance.

© The Author(s), under exclusive license to Springer Nature Switzerland AG 2022
L. Fang et al. (Eds.): CICAI 2022, LNAI 13604, pp. 242–254, 2022.
https://doi.org/10.1007/978-3-031-20497-5_20

In view of this challenge, various neural network pruning strategies have been developed. It has been shown that the redundancy in CNNs mostly lies in their convolution filters [21,33]. In what follows, we classify pruning methods into two main categories: filter channel pruning and filter weight pruning. Overall, their key idea is to obtain high pruning ratios with acceptable loss in performance [8].

Filter channel pruning approaches are developed by removing the filter channels of a CNN according to certain metrics [18,22]. These methods will change the network structure in a systematic way and only keep basic network blocks to decrease redundancy. Filter channel pruning can achieve high pruning ratios. However, due to the fixed-size width of the SIMD (single instruction, multiple data) unit in general-purpose processors [14], filter channel pruning may not fully utilize the SIMD unit and may not achieve as much of a latency reduction as its FLOPs reduction.

Filter weight pruning approaches such as [5,32] focus on optimizing individual filter weights and achieve a sparse network with acceptable performance degradation. In contrast to channel pruning, weight pruning approaches keep the network structure. Since the sparse weights are often randomly distributed in filters, weight pruning approaches usually need an extra record to locate the sparse weights. However, unstructured sparse convolution does not have an efficient implementation on popular hardware architectures (e.g., ARM and x86) and frameworks (e.g., Tensorflow Lite and TensorRT) [14].

In summary, filter channel and weight pruning methods are mostly developed on an algorithmic level without considering the structural constraints of current edge devices. Therefore, we ask if it is possible to develop a deep CNN pruning method that yields high pruning ratios and runtime reduction ratios under hardware limitations. In this work, we propose SMOF to achieve this goal. We summarize our contributions as follows:

1. We develop a hybrid pruning method called Squeezing More Out of Filters (SMOF), which considers both filter weight pruning and channel pruning by reducing the kernel size and the number of output channels.
2. SMOF is hardware-friendly. The pruned network can be deployed effortlessly on common hardware devices without any customized low-level implementations and also enjoy significant runtime reduction.
3. We demonstrate the efficiency of SMOF for various vision tasks on general-purpose processors of mobile devices.

2   Related Work

2.1   Filter Channel Pruning

Filter channel pruning approaches are proposed to remove filter channels within each layer based on different measuring metrics or importance scores. Channel pruning keeps the predefined network structure and decreases redundancy at the layer level.

Some previous strategies focus on finding better criteria to prune unimportant filter channels. [16] shows the feasibility of using the ℓ_2-norm of filter weights as a measuring metric. [18] find that the variance of the feature maps could be another choice for this metric. Recently, there has been a trend of applying automated machine learning (AutoML) for automatic network compression [3,6]. The key idea of these methods is to explore the total space of network filter configurations for the best candidate. On the other hand, LeGR [6] defines a pair of learnable parameters to adjust the important scores across layers, which leads to a global ranking of filters.

However, these methods only develop ranking and removal mechanisms for filter channels without considering the redundancy within the filters. Moreover, arbitrarily pruned filter channels can not be efficiently implemented on edge devices, where the numbers of output channels should align to the fixed-size width of SIMD units.

2.2   Filter Weight Pruning

Filter weight pruning focuses on removing individual filter weights and producing a sparse network. Some methods such as OBProx-SG [5] embeds the pruning demand into the network training loss and employs a joint strategy of fine-tuning and optimization to learn a sparse CNN. Another recent work [15] enhances the sparsity of weights by adding thresholds to each filter. On the other hand, some other methods focus on converting the network to the spectral domain [11,20], and utilize sparsity of both filters and feature maps to reduce computational cost. However, for the popular edge device hardware architectures such as ARM and x86, these unstructured sparse convolution computations cannot be implemented efficiently. They require an additional record to locate the sparse weights, which takes extra memory and computational resources.

2.3   Hybrid Filter Pruning

In view of the filter redundancy in both channels and weights, several pruning methods are proposed to account for both dimensions. Some of them attempt to use AutoML to search for a compact network structure.

[3] propose to search for a compact structure by shrinking a large network from different dimensions. However, the training is very heavy in both machine time and human labor. Some other approaches add extra components or blocks to help the network learn a sparse structure. For example, SWP [22] assigns a learnable matrix to each filter weight to learn its desired kernel shape by stripe-wise pruning and removes a filter channel when all of its stripes are pruned. In PatDNN [23], the kernel shapes can be chosen from a predefined set, and the number of remaining filter channels at each layer should be smaller than some predefined threshold. However, allowing various kernel shapes requires customized implementation on the hardware. In summary, both regularization methods and kernel shaping methods require a further customized ASIC design [14] or special low-level implementation to fully utilize the hardware

computational capacity. Otherwise, significant runtime reduction ratios cannot be achieved.

3   Proposed Method

In this paper, we propose SMOF for CNN pruning, which Squeezes More Out of Filters by reducing both the kernel size and the number of filter channels at each layer. We assign each convolutional layer a learnable matrix called *Filter Skeleton (FS)* to learn the *kernel shape* of filter channels, and another learnable vector called *Filter Mask (FM)* to learn the importance of individual filter channels. Specifically, let the weight of a convolutional layer be $W \in \mathbb{R}^{N \times C \times K \times K}$, where K is the *kernel size*, and N, C are the number of output and input channels, respectively. We say that each filter channel consists of K^2 *stripes* of the form $\mathbb{R}^{C \times 1}$. We propose SMOF with a focus on reducing K and N in a learnable and coordinated way. See Algorithm 1 for details.

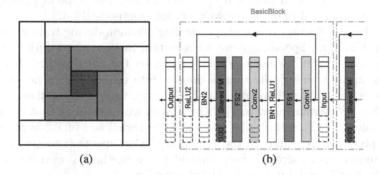

(a)   (b)

Fig. 1. (a) **Kernel size reduction by FS Pruning.** This FS of size 5×5 has 2 slices. During training, if the sum of the absolute values of its FS elements is smaller than $\rho_{\mathrm{FS}} \cdot 4(K^l + 1 - 2i)$, these elements will be pruned to 0, and the kernel size is further reduced from 3 to 1. The central element (in dark blue) will never be pruned in SMOF. (b) **Filter channel reduction by FM pruning.** We show the case of the shortcut connection in BasicBlock. The orange blocks denote BasicBlocks with the same structure, where the shared FM is applied after the FS2 block. The dashed part in shared FM has been pruned to 0, leading the corresponding output channels in Conv2 are also pruned to 0. Since the same shared FM is also applied in the previous BasicBlock, the shortcut connection can be applied safely.

3.1   Filter Skeleton (FS) for Kernel Size Reduction

Let $W^l \in \mathbb{R}^{N^l \times C^l \times K^l \times K^l}$ be the weight of lth convolution layer. Inspired by [22], we assign a learnable parameter called Filter Skeleton $\mathrm{FS}^l \in \mathbb{R}^{K^l \times K^l}$ to W^l to reduce the kernel size K^l. Each element in FS reflects the importance the corresponding stripe in all of the N^l filter channels of W^l, and is initialized as 1. Mathematically, the training loss with FS can be written as:

$$\sum_{(x,y)\in D} \text{loss}(f(x, W \odot FS), y) + \sum_l \sum_{i=1}^{K^l//2} \alpha_i^l \|\text{FS}_i^l\|_g, \tag{1}$$

where K^l is the kernel size of the lth convolutional layer, and FS_i^l denotes the ith *slice* of FS^l (see Fig. 1 (a)), and $\odot$ denotes the dot product. The penalty term in (1) promotes kernel size reduction. Specifically, the $\| \cdot \|_g$-norm induces group sparsity on the 4 edges FS_i^l ($i = 1, 2, 3, 4$).

$$\|\text{FS}_i^l\|_g = \sum_{j=1}^{4} \|\text{FS}_{i,j}^l\|_2. \tag{2}$$

the $\|\text{FS}_i^l\|_g$ term induces structured sparsity on the 4 edges $\text{FS}_{i,j}^l$ ($j = 1, 2, 3, 4$) of FS_i^l, which is inspired from Group Lasso [26,28], This type of penalty term has also been applied in other network pruning methods [19,32].

Kernel size reduction is done in a "peeling" fashion during training, as illustrated in Fig. 1 (a). Specifically, we set a certain ratio $\rho_{\text{FS}} > 0$ during training. Starting from $i = 1$, we consider the 4 edges on the ith slice FS_i^l. If at some iteration during training, the sum of the absolute values of elements on FS^l on these edges are smaller than[1] $\rho_{\text{FS}} \cdot 4(K^l + 1 - 2i)$, we will prune these elements to 0. After FS^l is multiplied to W^l, the stripes with positions that correspond to zero values in FS^l will also be zero, and the kernel size of W^l is reduced by 2, This process is repeated to the remaining FS^l elements (i.e., $i \leftarrow i + 1$) to further reduce kernel size. To keep current progress, the FS^l elements that are pruned to 0 will not be updated at later iterations.

In (1), the coefficients α_i^l are of the form:

$$\alpha_i^l = (K^l//2 + 1 - i)\alpha \quad \text{for some } \alpha > 0. \tag{3}$$

This gives a stronger penalty to the outer slices of FS^l, and encourages pruning to start from outer slices.

3.2   Filter Mask (FM) for Filter Number Reduction

To further improve pruning ratios, we also reduce the number of filter channels at each layer alongside kernel size reduction. For that purpose, we assign a learnable vector called Filter Mask $\text{FM}^l \in \mathbb{R}^{N^l \times 1}$ to the weight $W^l \in \mathbb{R}^{N^l \times C^l \times K^l \times K^l}$. FM^l is multiplied to $W^l \odot \text{FS}^l$ during training, which learns the importance of the N^l output channels. The elements of FM^l are initialized as 1.

---

[1] $4(K^l + 1 - 2i)$ is the initial sum of the FS elements on 4 edges.

Together with FS, we now have the full training loss:

$$\sum_{(x,y)\in D} \mathrm{loss}(f(x, W \odot FS \odot FM), y) + \sum_l \sum_{i=1}^{K^l//2} \alpha_i^l \|FS_i^l\|_g + \sum_l \beta \|FM^l\|_1,$$

(4)

where α_i^l is given by (3), and the last term applies ℓ_1-norm penalty to induce sparsity on FM^l. During training, we set a threshold $\delta_{FM} > 0$, and prune the FM^l elements with absolute values smaller than δ_{FM} to 0. After multiplying FM^l to $W^l \odot FS^l$, any filter channel with a 0 in FM^l is also 0.

For CNNs with special structures such as ResNet [12], arbitrarily pruning channels at different layers may destroy the structures and lead to significant performance degradation. Thus, we apply a shared FM to all the layers that are connected by shortcuts and prune their output channels at the same time (see Fig. 1 (b)). In other words, the shared FM reflects the importance of their output channels altogether.

Algorithm 1 SMOF: Squeezing More Out of Filters yields hardware-friendly CNN pruning

---

1: **Input**: CNN with initial convolution weights W, penalty parameters α, β for Filter Skeleton (FS) and Filter Mask (FM), pruning parameters ρ_{FS}, δ_{FM} for FS and FM. Total Number of iterations K;
2: **Output**: pruned & trained CNN;
3: Initialize the elements of FS and FM as 1;
4: **for** $k = 1, 2, ..., K$ **do**
5:    Update FS of each layer with ratio ρ_{FS};
6:    Update FM of each layer by the procedures in Fig. 1 (b), with threshold δ_{FM};
7:    Apply one iteration of SGD to W and non-zero elements of FM, with the full training loss in (4);
8:    Apply one iteration of proximal gradient descent given by (5) to nonzero elements of FS;
9: **end for**
10: $W \leftarrow W \odot FS \odot FM$;
11: Reduce kernel sizes and number of filter channels at each layer by procedures described in Figs. 1;
12: Adjust zero-padding at each layer based on its kernel size reduction;

3.3   Training and Inference

In order to perform training with the loss function (4), we apply stochastic gradient descent (SGD) on $\{W^l\}$ and $\{FM^l\}$. To deal with the non-differentiable penalty term on $\{FS^l\}$, we apply proximal gradient descent [2]. More specifically, the update on FS^l is given by

$$FS_{i,j}^{l,+} = \mathrm{Prox}_{\eta \alpha_i \|\cdot\|_2}(FS_{i,j}^l - \eta \alpha_i \tilde{g}_{i,j}^l),$$

(5)

where η is the learning rate, $i = 1, 2, ..., K^l//2$, and $j = 1, 2, 3, 4$. $\tilde{g}_{i,j}^l$ is a stochastic gradient of the first term in (4) w.r.t. $\text{FS}_{i,j}^l$. The proximal operator $\text{Prox}_{\eta\alpha_i\|\cdot\|_2}$ has a closed form expression, which is cheap and easy to implement:

$$\text{Prox}_{\eta\alpha_i\|\cdot\|_2}(x) = \frac{x}{\|x\|_2}\max\{0, \|x\|_2 - \eta\alpha_i\}. \tag{6}$$

To prepare the pruned model for inference, we multiply FS^l and FM^l to W^l, and prune the outer stripes of W^l with zero value in FS^l, as well as output channels with zero value in FM^l (see Figs. 1). If the kernel size of W^l is reduced by $2n$, its zero-padding should be decreased by n.

4   Experiments

To validate our proposed approach, we conduct extensive experiments on ResNet [12] for image classification, and UNet [25] for image denoising. We use SNPE (Snapdragon Neural Processing Engine SDK) on Qualcomm Snapdragon SM8250 as our mobile platform and test on two different general-purpose processors: GPU and digital signal processor (DSP).

4.1   ResNet56 on CIFAR-10

Table 1. ResNet56 pruning with CIFAR-10. The baseline ResNet56 model has a GPU runtime of 5.7(ms), and a DSP runtime of 0.845(ms). All DSP runtime are averaged over 20 runs. SMOF achieves the most runtime reduction with an accuracy gain of 0.39%.

Method	Params % ↓	FLOPs % ↓	GPU % ↓	DSP % ↓	Accuracy %
SMOF	48.28	60.50	45.61	21.30	93.18 → 93.57
SWP [22]	77.7	75.6	–	–	93.10 → 92.98
HRank [18]	42.4	50.0	26.32	12.43	93.26 → 93.17
Global Ranking [6]	-	53	29.82	13.01	93.9 → 93.7

Dataset. SMOF is evaluated by ResNet56 [12]) on CIFAR-10 dataset. For the training set, we apply standard data augmentation procedures, including random crop and random horizontal flip.

Implementation Details. We start pruning from pre-trained models and train the model for 180 epochs, where the initial learning rate is 0.1 and divided by 10 at the 90th and 135th epoch. The training algorithm is SGD with a momentum of 0.9, a batch size of 128, and a weight decay of $1e - 4$. We set $\alpha = 1e - 4$, $\rho_{\text{FS}} = 0.425$, $\beta = 1e - 3$, $\delta_{\text{FM}} = 0.2$, and $r = 1/2$. To stop the pruning process and fixes the obtained network structure, we set $\alpha = \beta = \rho_{FS} = \delta_{FM} = 0$ for last 90 epochs. We also set a certain percentage (denoted by r) of FM values to be learnable at each convolution layer, while the rest are always 1. This avoids pruning of all of the channels in one layer and therefore makes training easier[2].

Discussion. In Table 1, we present a pruning ratio and runtime comparison between our SMOF and other pruning strategies. SMOF achieves a higher pruning ratio than HRank [18] and Global Ranking [6], while enjoying a 0.39% accuracy gain. SMOF also saves much more GPU and DSP runtime than HRank [18] and Global Ranking [6]. We speculate that this is because these two strategies only focus on filter channel pruning, while for processors with longer SIMD (e.g., 1024 bit for the DSP processor), the aligning processing explained at the beginning of Sec. 4 cancels some of their pruning efforts. Moreover, the data padding/cropping itself costs extra latency.

Compared with SMOF, SWP [22] has higher pruning ratios as it achieves finer granularity by allowing pruning of individual stripes at each layer. However, the pruned channels typically have irregular kernel shapes, which also vary a lot among channels at the same layer. As a result, customized low-level implementations are required to achieve runtime reduction.

4.2   ResNet18 on ImageNet

Dataset. We evaluate SMOF to ResNet18 [12] on ImageNet dataset [7], which contains 1.28 million training images and 50K test images for 1000 classes.

Table 2. ResNet18 pruning with ImageNet. The pruned models SMOF-1 and SMOF-2 are obtained with parameters and procedures described in Sec. 4.2. The baseline ResNet18 model has a GPU runtime of 24.3(ms), and a DSP runtime of 4.96(ms). * denotes our independent test. All DSP runtime are averaged over 20 runs.

Method	Params % ↓	FLOPs % ↓	GPU % ↓	DSP % ↓	Accuracy %
SMOF-1	24.96	31.02	28.81	29.44	69.76 → 69.21
SMOF-2	25.21	36.60	32.92	33.47	69.76 → 68.55
SWP [22]	-	54.48	–	–	69.76 → 69.59
DMCP [27]	–	43.54	34.57	11.29	70.1 → 69.2
ResRep* [9]	–	40.61	33.33	19.35	69.76 → 69.12
FPGM [13]	-	36.48	36.63	15.32	69.76 → 68.54

---

[2] If we set $r = 1$, then for certain layers of ResNet56, the elements of FM are very similar during training, and all the channels are pruned nearly at the same time. By fixing some FM elements to be 1, we keep the corresponding channels and allow channel pruning for the rest.

Implementation Details. Our training settings are similar to the official PyTorch implementation[3]. Specifically, we apply SGD with momentum $= 0.9$, an initial learning rate of 0.1, a batchsize of 256, and a weight decay factor of $1e-4$.

Throughout this test, we keep all the elements in FilterMasks to be 1 (i.e., $r = 0$). First, we set $\alpha = 1e-6$ and $\rho_{FS} = 0$ for 10 epochs. Then, we either 1) set $\alpha = 2e-4$ and $\rho_{FS} = 0.45$ for 20 epochs, or 2) set $\alpha = 1e-6$ and $\rho_{FS} = 0.625$ for 20 epochs. We call the obtained models SMOF-1 and SMOF-2, respectively. Next, we stop pruning and fix their network structures by setting $\alpha = \rho_{FS} = \beta = \delta_{FM} = 0$, and apply learning rates $1e-1, 1e-2, 1e-3, 1e-4$ for 20 epochs, respectively.

Discussion. In Tables 2, we present a pruning ratio and runtime comparison between SMOF and other strategies. The SMOF-1 model has smaller pruning ratios and a higher accuracy than SMOF-2. Similar to the ResNet56 test, SWP [22] achieves the best pruning ratios but not desired runtime reduction. DMCP [27], ResRep [9], and [13] are channel pruning methods, they have a similar accuracy compared to SMOF-1 or SMOF-2. Though they have higher FLOPs reduction ratios, their GPU runtime are similar to SMOF, and their DSP runtime are even worse. This is caused by the aligned processing mentioned at the beginning of Sec. 4 that their channel pruning is inefficiently implemented especially on the DSP processor with a longer SIMD unit of 1024 bits. Moreover, the data padding/cropping itself costs extra latency.

4.3   U-Net for Image Denoising

Table 3. Comparison of several model pruning methods for image denoising. The noise level of training and testing images is 70. All the methods are tested on BSD68 dataset and FLOPs is reported for a 128×128 image. SMOF achieves more runtime reduction on different general-purpose processors, especially on DSP. $*$ denotes our implementation.

Method	Params % ↓	FLOPs % ↓	PSNR ↓	GPU (ms)	DSP (ms)
DHP [17]	58.25	58.06	0.12	9.85	0.71
Factor-SIC2 [31]	67.65	64.22	0.23	–	31.80
Group [24]	73.45	56.30	0.11	–	19.80
LeGR* [6]	53.09	58.65	0.13	29.20	1.44
Hrank* [18]	56.96	57.77	0.15	–	0.85
SMOF-1	74.74	52.79	0.11	4.60	0.54
SMOF-2	58.89	44.28	0.05	8.47	0.56

---

[3] https://github.com/pytorch/examples/tree/master/imagenet.

Dataset. In this section, we evaluate SMOF on U-Net for image denoising, and compare with five state-of-the-art pruning approaches (DHP [17], Factor-SIC2 [31], Group [24], LeGR [6], and HRank [18]). We train on the DIV2K [1] dataset and evaluate on the BSD68 dataset.

Implementation Details. To ensure a fair comparison, we apply the same network hyperparameters as in the original training strategy [25]. We use SGD with momentum$=$ 0.9, fixed learning rate of $1e-4$, a batch size of 256, and a weight decay factor of $5e-5$. We also apply the same procedures for data preprocessing, weights initialization, and the same image noise level (70). To compare these model compression methods, we measure their performance in six metrics, including the number of parameters, FLOPs, Peak Signal-to-Noise Ratio (PSNR), and runtime on GPU and DSP.

Discussion. We evaluate two models pruned by SMOF for different purposes: one for computational efficiency (SMOF-1) and the other one for high PSNR (SMOF-2). We summarize the test results in Table 3. The procedures for obtaining these pruned models can be found in the appendix.

Compared with LeGR [6] and HRank [18], SMOF-1 saves more runtime with similar performance. Besides, we notice that SMOF-1 achieves a similar PSNR and complexity reduction as Group [24], but with less run-time on CPU and DSP. This might be caused by the inefficient implementations of group convolution on mobile device accelerators [17]. We also notice that, although DHP [17] and Factor-SIC [31] achieve a greater reduction of FLOPs, SMOF-1 performs more efficiently on the processors.

SMOF-2 obtains an excellent PSNR of 25.19, which is very close to 25.24 of the baseline model. Notably, due to the fixed-size width constraint in the

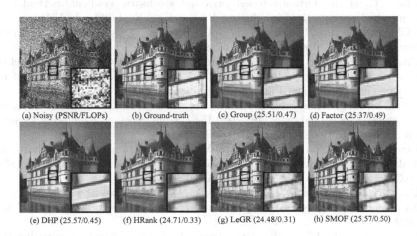

(a) Noisy (PSNR/FLOPs)   (b) Ground-truth   (c) Group (25.51/0.47)   (d) Factor (25.37/0.49)

(e) DHP (25.57/0.45)   (f) HRank (24.71/0.33)   (g) LeGR (24.48/0.31)   (h) SMOF (25.57/0.50)

Fig. 2. Denoising on an image from BSD68 (noise level 50). We report PSNR and FLOPs measured on this image.

processors, SMOF-2 performs more efficiently though it has similar pruning ratios compared with other approaches.

Figure 2 presents the output of SMOF and other algorithms. In terms of the visual quality, the output of SMOF-1 is close to the ground truth. Besides, SMOF remains detailed patterns, which demonstrates the capacity of SMOF to handle Gaussian noise with large noise levels.

5   Conclusions

In this work, we propose a hardware-friendly CNN pruning framework called SMOF, which learns the importance of stripes and channels. It prunes the unimportant stripes and channels in a coordinated way, so that the kernel size and number of channels can be reduced while preserving the network structure. The efficiency of SMOF is demonstrated by several CNNs on different general-purpose processors without any customized low-level implementations.

References

1. Agustsson, E., Timofte, R.: Ntire 2017 challenge on single image super-resolution: dataset and study. In: The IEEE Conference on Computer Vision and Pattern Recognition (CVPR) Workshops (2017)
2. Bauschke, H.H., et al.: Convex analysis and monotone operator theory in Hilbert spaces, vol. 408. Springer (2011). https://doi.org/10.1007/978-1-4419-9467-7
3. Cai, H., Gan, C., Wang, T., Zhang, Z., Han, S.: Once-for-all: train one network and specialize it for efficient deployment. In: International Conference on Learning Representations (2019)
4. Chang, F.J., Tuan Tran, A., Hassner, T., Masi, I., Nevatia, R., Medioni, G.: Faceposenet: making a case for landmark-free face alignment. In: Proceedings of the IEEE International Conference on Computer Vision (ICCV) Workshops (2017)
5. Chen, T., et al.: Orthant based proximal stochastic gradient method for ℓ_1-regularized optimization. In: Hutter, F., Kersting, K., Lijffijt, J., Valera, I. (eds.) ECML PKDD 2020. LNCS (LNAI), vol. 12459, pp. 57–73. Springer, Cham (2021). https://doi.org/10.1007/978-3-030-67664-3_4
6. Chin, T.W., Ding, R., Zhang, C., Marculescu, D.: Towards efficient model compression via learned global ranking. In: Proceedings of the IEEE/CVF Conference on Computer Vision and Pattern Recognition, pp. 1518–1528 (2020)
7. Deng, J., Dong, W., Socher, R., Li, L.J., Li, K., Fei-Fei, L.: Imagenet: a large-scale hierarchical image database. In: 2009 IEEE Conference on Computer Vision and Pattern Recognition, pp. 248–255. IEEE (2009)
8. Deng, L., Li, G., Han, S., Shi, L., Xie, Y.: Model compression and hardware acceleration for neural networks: a comprehensive survey. Proc. IEEE **108**(4), 485–532 (2020). https://doi.org/10.1109/JPROC.2020.2976475
9. Ding, X., Hao, T., Liu, J., Han, J., Guo, Y., Ding, G.: Lossless CNN channel pruning via decoupling remembering and forgetting. arXiv preprint arXiv:2007.03260 (2020)
10. Gorji, S., Clark, J.J.: Going from image to video saliency: augmenting image salience with dynamic attentional push. In: Proceedings of the IEEE Conference on Computer Vision and Pattern Recognition (CVPR) (2018)

11. Guan, B., Zhang, J., Sethares, W.A., Kijowski, R., Liu, F.: Spectral domain convolutional neural network. In: ICASSP 2021–2021 IEEE International Conference on Acoustics, Speech and Signal Processing (ICASSP), pp. 2795–2799. IEEE (2021)
12. He, K., Zhang, X., Ren, S., Sun, J.: Deep residual learning for image recognition. In: Proceedings of the IEEE Conference on Computer Vision and Pattern Recognition, pp. 770–778 (2016)
13. He, Y., Liu, P., Wang, Z., Hu, Z., Yang, Y.: Filter pruning via geometric median for deep convolutional neural networks acceleration. In: Proceedings of the IEEE/CVF Conference on Computer Vision and Pattern Recognition, pp. 4340–4349 (2019)
14. Ignatov, A., et al.: Ai benchmark: All about deep learning on smartphones in 2019. In: 2019 IEEE/CVF International Conference on Computer Vision Workshop (ICCVW), pp. 3617–3635 (2019). https://doi.org/10.1109/ICCVW.2019.00447
15. Kusupati, A., et al.: Soft threshold weight reparameterization for learnable sparsity. In: International Conference on Machine Learning, pp. 5544–5555. PMLR (2020)
16. Li, H., Kadav, A., Durdanovic, I., Samet, H., Graf, H.P.: Pruning filters for efficient convnets. International Conference on Learning Representations (2017)
17. Li, Y., Gu, S., Zhang, K., Van Gool, L., Timofte, R.: DHP: differentiable meta pruning via hypernetworks. In: Vedaldi, A., Bischof, H., Brox, T., Frahm, J.-M. (eds.) ECCV 2020. LNCS, vol. 12353, pp. 608–624. Springer, Cham (2020). https://doi.org/10.1007/978-3-030-58598-3_36
18. Lin, M., et al.: Hrank: filter pruning using high-rank feature map. In: Proceedings of the IEEE/CVF Conference on Computer Vision and Pattern Recognition, pp. 1529–1538 (2020)
19. Liu, B., Wang, M., Foroosh, H., Tappen, M., Pensky, M.: Sparse convolutional neural networks. In: Proceedings of the IEEE Conference on Computer Vision and Pattern Recognition, pp. 806–814 (2015)
20. Liu, Z., Xu, J., Peng, X., Xiong, R.: Frequency-domain dynamic pruning for convolutional neural networks. In: Proceedings of the 32nd International Conference on Neural Information Processing Systems, pp. 1051–1061 (2018)
21. Liu, Z., Sun, M., Zhou, T., Huang, G., Darrell, T.: Rethinking the value of network pruning. In: International Conference on Learning Representations (2018)
22. Meng, F., et al.: Pruning filter in filter. In: Advances in Neural Information Processing Systems, vol. 33, pp. 17629–17640 (2020)
23. Niu, W., et al.: Patdnn: achieving real-time dnn execution on mobile devices with pattern-based weight pruning. In: Proceedings of the Twenty-Fifth International Conference on Architectural Support for Programming Languages and Operating Systems, pp. 907–922 (2020)
24. Peng, B., Tan, W., Li, Z., Zhang, S., Xie, D., Pu, S.: Extreme network compression via filter group approximation. In: Proceedings of the European Conference on Computer Vision (ECCV), pp. 300–316 (2018)
25. Ronneberger, O., Fischer, P., Brox, T.: U-Net: convolutional networks for biomedical image segmentation. In: Navab, N., Hornegger, J., Wells, W.M., Frangi, A.F. (eds.) MICCAI 2015. LNCS, vol. 9351, pp. 234–241. Springer, Cham (2015). https://doi.org/10.1007/978-3-319-24574-4_28
26. Roth, V., Fischer, B.: The group-lasso for generalized linear models: uniqueness of solutions and efficient algorithms. In: Proceedings of the 25th international conference on Machine learning, pp. 848–855 (2008)
27. Shaopeng, G., Yujie, W., Quanquan, L., Yan, J.: Dmcp: differentiable markov channel pruning for neural networks. In: IEEE Conference on Computer Vision and Pattern Recognition (CVPR) (2020)

28. Simon, N., Friedman, J., Hastie, T., Tibshirani, R.: A sparse-group lasso. J. Comput. Graph. Stat. **22**(2), 231–245 (2013)
29. Sun, Z., Sarma, P., Sethares, W., Liang, Y.: Learning relationships between text, audio, and video via deep canonical correlation for multimodal language analysis. In: Proceedings of the AAAI Conference on Artificial Intelligence, vol. 34, pp. 8992–8999 (2020)
30. Wang, F., Zhang, M., Wang, X., Ma, X., Liu, J.: Deep learning for edge computing applications: a state-of-the-art survey. IEEE Access **8**, 58322–58336 (2020)
31. Wang, M., Liu, B., Foroosh, H.: Factorized convolutional neural networks. In: Proceedings of the IEEE International Conference on Computer Vision Workshops, pp. 545–553 (2017)
32. Wen, W., Wu, C., Wang, Y., Chen, Y., Li, H.: Learning structured sparsity in deep neural networks. arXiv preprint arXiv:1608.03665 (2016)
33. Zhu, M., Gupta, S.: To prune, or not to prune: exploring the efficacy of pruning for model compression. arXiv preprint arXiv:1710.01878 (2017)

H-ViT: Hybrid Vision Transformer for Multi-modal Vehicle Re-identification

Wenjie Pan[1], Hanxiao Wu[2], Jianqing Zhu[1(✉)], Huanqiang Zeng[1], and Xiaobin Zhu[3]

[1] College of Engineering, Huaqiao University, Quanzhou 362021, China
jqzhu@hqu.edu.cn
[2] College of Information Science and Engineering, Huaqiao University, Xiamen 361021, China
[3] School of Computer and Communication Engineering, University of Science and Technology Beijing, Beijing 100083, China

Abstract. Vehicle re-identification (ReID) is a critical technology in smart city and has drawn much attention. Many studies focus on single-modal (i.e., visible) vehicle re-identification, which are prone to be deteriorated under bad illumination conditions. Therefore, visible, near-infrared, and thermal-infrared multi-modal vehicle re-identification is worthy to study. This paper proposes a hybrid vision transformer (H-ViT) based multi-modal vehicle re-identification. The proposed H-ViT has two new modules: (1) modal-specific controller (MC) and (2) modal information embedding (MIE) structure. In the feature extraction process, the MC flexibly specifies modal-specific layers for different modal data and controls the sharing attribute of the position embedding to alleviate the difficulty brought by heterogeneous multi-modalities. The MIE structure learns inter- and intra-modal information to reduce feature deviations toward modal variations. Experimental results show that our H-ViT method achieves good performance on multi-modal vehicle re-identification datasets (i.e., RGBNT100 and RGBN300) by integrating MC and MIE modules, which are superior to existing algorithms.

Keywords: Vision transformer · Multi-modality · Vehicle re-identification

1 Introduction

Vehicle re-identification (ReID) aims to retrieve a specific vehicle image from the vehicle gallery set captured by non-overlapping cameras, which has drawn much attention due to its significant role in smart city, intelligent transportation, and social security. Most existing methods [2] often focus on single-modal vehicle ReID based on visible vehicle images, which have limited ability in unsatisfactory light environment. To this end, multi-modal vehicle re-identification is worthy to study.

Same as traditional single-modal vehicle ReID, multi-modal vehicle ReID encounters many challenges, such as viewpoint variations and similar appearances [2,10,13,21–24]. What's worse, there is a huge gap between different modalities, as shown in Fig. 1, which brings a new challenge to multi-modal vehicle ReID.

Fig. 1. Vehicle images were caught by different modal cameras. Here, RGB, NIR and TIR are visible, near-infrared and thermal-infrared, respectively.

Existing multi-modal vehile ReID studies [7,19] apply convolution neural network (CNN) structures [2,7,9], which are weak in capturing global feature due to that CNN uses finite sized kernels. Considering excellent ability of transformer [3,4,6,11] in modeling long-range dependencies at the spatial dimension has been demonstrated by the great results in many computer vision tasks, building a transformer-based model is a promising way to multi-modal vehicle ReID.

Inspired by vision transformer (ViT) [3] and TransReID [6], we propose a transformer-based model, namely, hybrid vision transformer (H-ViT) for multi-modal vehicle ReID. First, in order to solve the difficulty brought by multi-modalities, we propose a modal-specific controller (MC) to assign modal-specific layers for different modal data and specify the sharing type of position embedding. Secondly, a modal information embedding (MIE) method is proposed to alleviate feature deviations towards modal variations by learning intra- and inter-modal information. Using MC and MIE, our H-ViT can learn modal-specific and modal-common information to extract good features for multi-modal vehicle ReID.

The contributions of the paper are summarized as follows. We propose a hybrid vision transformer (H-ViT) for multi-modal vehicle ReID, which contains two novel modules, namely, modal-specific controller (MC) and modal information embedding (MIE). Experimental results on RGBNT100 and RGBN300 demonstrate that our H-ViT outperforms the state-of-the-art methods.

2   Related Work

2.1   Single-Modal Re-identification

Most Vehicle re-identification methods are usually based on visible images [2,5], which suffers from grand challenges, such as similar appearances, viewpoint changes, and insufficient illumination. To solve similar appearances in vehicle re-identification task, Zhu et al. [24] used orientation and camera similarity as penalty to get the final similarity. Wang et al. [13] proposed an orientation-based region proposal module and feature extraction module to capture vehicles' region appearance information. Zhu et al. [22] applied a siamese deep network to extract deep learning features for an input vehicle image pair simultaneously. To handle the viewpoint changes problem, Meng et al. [10] proposed a part perspective transformation module to map the different parts of a vehicle into a unified perspective respectively. Zhou et al. [21] proposed a viewpoint-aware attentive multi-view inference model that only requires visual information to solve the multi-view vehicle ReID problem. Zhu et al. [23] designed a quadruple directional deep learning networks to extract quadruple directional deep learning features of vehicle images. Regarding insufficient illumination problem, due to the superior imaging ability of infrared technology in low illumination environment, the visible-infrared re-identification task has gained widespread interest for improving the ReID performance in light-less environment.

2.2 Multi-modal Re-identification

To overcome the shortcoming of single-modal bringing to ReID task in light-less environment, cross-modal object ReID has drawn much attention [2,15]. Since the convolutional neural network (CNN) was proposed, it has extensively promoted multi-modal re-identification development. Many existing methods are proposed based on CNN-based method to handle the vast modality gap between the cross-modal images. For example, Liu et al. [8] proposed a hetero-center triplet loss to constrain the distance of different class centers from both the same modality and cross modalities . Wang et al. [12] trained an image-level sub-network to translate an infrared image to its visible counterpart and a visible image to its infrared version. Wang et al. [14] proposed a cross-modal interacting module and a multi-modal margin loss to enhance multi-modal learning.

In order to further improve the performance in object ReID, some studies pay attention to identifying objects in multi-modal images. Zheng et al. [19] provided a multi-modal person ReID dataset RGBNT201 and designed a network to learn effective multi-modal features from single to multiple modalities and from local to global views. Li et al. [7] provided two multi-modal vehicle ReID datasets RGBNT100 and RGBN300, and proposed a Heterogeneity-collaboration Aware Multi-stream convolutional Network towards automatically fusing different spectrum features in an end-to-end learning framework.

The great success of CNN-based is demonstrated by these studies' state-of-the-art performance in vehicle ReID tasks. Considering the comparable performance of transformer-based method in computer vision tasks with CNN-based methods [3,4,11], it is also a promising way to build a transformer-based model for vehicle ReID tasks.

2.3   Transformer in Re-identification Task

Transformer, which is a self-attention-based neural network, has draw in attention in ReID task due to the excellent performance in modeling long-range dependencies for spatial and sequential data [3,4,11,16]. He et al. [6] first proposed a pure transformer-based object ReID framework, which achieves state-of-the-arts performance on both person and vehicle ReID benchmarks. Chen et al. [1] proposed a structure-aware positional transformer network to utilize the structural and positional information and learn semantic-aware sharable modality features. Zhang et al. [17] introduced a transformer-based feature calibration to integrate low-level detail information as the global prior for high-level semantic information.

To utilize transformer to model long-range dependencies for modal data, we structure a transformer-based baseline hybrid vision transformer (H-ViT) and design modal-specific controller (MC) to assign the different modal data to their modal-specific layers for multi-modal vehicle ReID. To reduce feature deviations towards modal variations, we propose modal information embedding (MIE) to enhance the ability of transformer in utilizing modal information.

3   Method

The structure of our hybrid vision transformer is shown in Fig. 2, including (1) the normal modules: vision transformer branches (e.g. patch embedding layer and transformer encoders) and loss function (e.g. ID loss and Triplet loss), and (2) the proposed modules: modal-specific controller (MC) and modal information embedding (MIE).

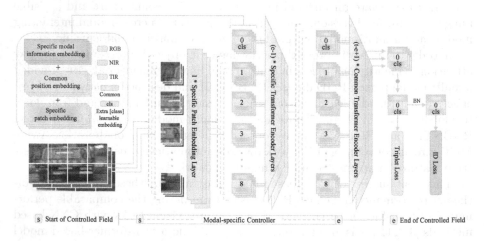

Fig. 2. The structure of hybrid vision transformer (H-ViT).

3.1   Vision Transformer Branches and Loss Function

Inspired by [3,6], each vision transformer branch in H-ViT has two stages: one patch embedding layer and multiple transformer encoders. For an image $x \in \mathbb{R}^{H \times W \times C}$, where H, W, C denote height, width, and the number of channels, respectively, the vision transformer branch treating process is as follows.

Firstly, in the patch embedding layer, images are split into N fixed-sized patches $x_p \in \mathbb{R}^{H_p \times W_p \times C}$, where H_p, W_p denote patch height and weight, respectively. As a result, an image $x \in \mathbb{R}^{H \times W \times C}$ is split into N patches $x_p^1, x_p^2, ..., x_p^N; N = \frac{H}{H_p} \times \frac{W}{W_p}$. Then, each patch is flatten and mapped to D dimensional embedding with trainable linear projections. Besides, an extra D dimension learnable embedding token (denoted as x_{cls}) is collaborated to these patch embeddings and serves as feature representations. Thus, a total of $N+1$ D dimensional embedding will be formed. A D dimension learnable position embedding P is added to these $N+1$ D dimension embeddings for attaching positional information into embedding. In summary, the process of patch embedding layer as shown in Eq. (1).

$$Z_0 = [x_{cls}; E(x_p^1); E(x_p^2); ...; E(x_p^N)] + P \tag{1}$$

where E represents the calculation of transforming a patch into one feature embedding; P is a position embedding.

Secondly, in each transformer encoder, input embeddings are handled with layer normalization (LN), multi-head self-attention (MSA), and residual connections, as formulated in Eq. (2). Then, results of residual connections are further processed with layer normalization (LN), multi-layer perception (MLP), residual connections, as formulated in Eq. (3). Following [3,6], we stack transformer encoders to deepen a model for improving feature extracting.

$$F_0 = MSA(LN(Z_0)) + Z_0 \tag{2}$$

$$T_0 = MLP(LN(F_0)) + F_0 \tag{3}$$

Finally, feature representations from different vision transformer branches are fused (e.g. average fusion and concatenating fusion) and fed into a loss module. Following TransReID [6], the loss module applies identification (ID) loss (Eq. 4) and triplet (T) loss (Eq. (5)).

$$L_{ID} = -\frac{1}{n} \sum_{i=1}^{n} \delta(y_i == c_i) log(p(y_i|f_i)) \tag{4}$$

where n represents the number of samples; δ is a indicator function; y_i and c_i are prediction class and truth class for i-th sample, respectively; f_i is the feature vector for the i-th sample.

$$L_T = log[1 + exp(\|f_a - f_p\|^2 - \|f_a - f_n\|^2)] \tag{5}$$

Table 1. Five types of MC configurations.

Type	ν		k		Patch embedding layer	Transformer encoder layers
	s	e				
FC	0	0	0		Common	Common: all layers
FS	0	$t+1$	$t+1$		Specific	Specific: all layers
SS	0	k	$1 \le k \le t, k \in \mathbb{N}$	Specific	Specific: the first $k-1$ layers
MS	1	$k+1$	$1 \le k \le t, k \in \mathbb{N}$	Common	Specific: the first k layers
DS	$t-k+1$	$t+1$	$1 \le k \le t, k \in \mathbb{N}$	Common	Specific: the last k layers

where f_a is the feature vector for the anchor sample; f_p is the feature vector for a sample holding the same class to the anchor sample, and f_n is the feature vector for a another sample having a different class from the anchor sample.

Figure 2 is an example for three-modal vehicle ReID. For two-modal vehicle ReID, two vision transformer branches are assigned. In what follows, we propose (1) the modal-specific controller (MC) module for assigning the distribution of modal-specific layers to improve multi-modal feature learning; (2) the modal information embedding (MIE) module for reduce the feature deviations toward modal variations by learning intra- and inter-modal information. The details of two modules as shown in Sect. 3.2 and Sect. 3.3.

3.2 Modal-specific Controller

modal-specific controller (MC) can assign the sharing type of structures as follows: (1) the position embedding, (2) the patch embedding layer, and (3) the transformer encoders.

MC specifies the sharing type of position embedding as modal-common and modal-specific. The modal-common type means different modal patch embedding added the same position embedding. The modal-specific type means different modal patch embedding added its modal-specific position embedding.

MC assigns modal-specific layers (i.e., patch embedding layer and transformer encoders) with two parameters. The modal-specific controlling field ν and the number of modal-specific layers k. ν is a left closed and right open interval, and there are two parameters in ν: the start of controlling field s and the end of controlling field e. Therefore, for t transformer layers, ν can be described as following in Eq. (6). k is computed as $k = e - s$.

$$\nu = [s, e) | 0 \le s \le e \le t + 1, s \in \mathbb{N}, e \in \mathbb{N}, t \in \mathbb{N} \tag{6}$$

where $\mathbb{N}$ represents the number of transformer encoders.

We can flexibly assign the modal-specific layers by MC to raise 5 types of configurations as follows. (1) fully modal-common (FC), (2) fully modal-specific (FS), (3) shallow modal-specific (SS), (4) medium modal-specific (MS), and (5) deep modal-specific (DS). The parameters of these configurations are shown in Table 1. In simple terms, MC configures the model as following: the first s layers

Table 2. Statistics of RGBNT100 and RGBN300.

Datasets	Modalities	Subjects	Images	Train	Query	Gallery
RGBNT100 [7]	RGB, NIR, and TIR	100	51750	8675	1715	8575
RGBN300 [7]	RGB and NIR	300	100250	25200	4985	24925

are modal-common, the next k layers are modal-specific, and the last $t + 1 - k$ layers are modal-common. For example, when H-ViT configure $t = 12, k = 9, v = [1, 10)$ in MS, the first layer (patch embedding layer) is modal-common, the first 9 transformer encoder layers are modal-specific, and the last 3 transformer encoder layers are modal-common. Figure 2 shows a H-ViT structure when s is set to 0.

3.3 Modal Information Embedding

Inspired by side information embedding proposed by TransReID [6], we propose modal information embedding (MIE) module to encode non-visual modal information, which can alleviate the feature deviations towards modal variations. Our MIE is a D dimension embedding, which is added to patch embedding and position embedding as following.

$$Z_0 = [x_{cls}; E(x_p^1); E(x_p^2); ...; E(x_p^N)] + P + M \tag{7}$$

where M is a learnable modal information embedding. In H-ViT, due to MIE aiming to alleviate the feature deviations towards modal variations, different from position embedding which is modal-common, it is always modal-specific and it does not change along with changing the sharing type of patch embedding layer.

4 Experiments and Analysis

4.1 Datasets

Table 2 shows statistics of RGBNT100 and RGBN300. RGBNT100 and RGBN300 are released by a research group [7] from Anhui University. RGBNT100 is a three-modal vehicle dataset, in where each vehicle is captured by visible (RGB), near-infrared (NIR), and thermal-infrared (TIR) cameras simultaneously. Also, RGBN300 is a double-modal, which contains vehicle images captured by RGB and NIR cameras.

4.2 Implementation

We conduct experiments by PyTorch with one RTX3090 GPU. All single-modal images are resized to 192 × 192. Training images are augmented with random horizontal flipping, padding, random cropping, and random erasing [20], as done TransReID [6].The batch size is set to have 16 subjects and each subject has

4 images. The momentum and weight decay of the stochastic gradient descent (SGD) optimizer are set to 0.9 and 0.0001, respectively. The learning rate is initialized as 0.008 with cosine learning rate decay. The patch size and stride size are both set to 16 × 16. Following [6], ImageNet pre-trained vision transformer (ViT), which consists of 1 patch embedding layer and 12 transformer encoder layers. Consequently, field of modal-specific controller (MC) is limited to $\nu = [s, e] | 0 \leq s \leq e \leq 13$. Due to RGBNT100 and RGBN300 are three-modal and double-modal datasets, respectively, H-ViT are corresponding modified to triple-modal transformer and dual-modal transformer. That is, on RGBNT100, H-ViT's backbone has three branches, while on RGBN300, H-ViT's backbone has two branches. As last, for performance metrics, commonly-used cumulative matching characteristic (CMC) curves and the mean average precision (mAP) are applied. R1, R5, and R10 denotes rank-1, rank-5, and rank-10 identification rates on a CMC curve, respectively.

Table 3. The performance comparison between the proposed H-ViT and other state-of-the-arts methods on both RGBNT100 and RGBN300.

Methods	RGBNT100				RGBN300			
	mAP(%)	R1(%)	R5(%)	R10(%)	mAP(%)	R1(%)	R5(%)	R10(%)
HAMNet [7]	65.4	85.5	87.9	88.8	61.9	84.0	86.0	87.0
TransReID [6]	60.1	82.2	83.7	84.7	67.1	86.5	88.0	88.7
H-ViT (Ours)	**79.0**	**93.4**	**94.4**	**95.3**	**79.0**	**93.7**	**94.7**	**95.1**

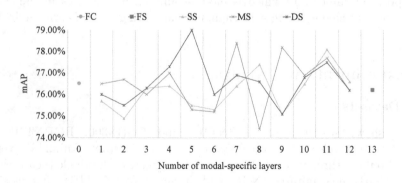

Fig. 3. The comparison of modal-specific controller configurations on RGBNT100.

4.3 Comparison with State-of-the-Art

As shown in Table 3, our H-ViT method acquires best results on both RGBNT100 and RGBN300. Specifically, H-ViT obtains 79.0% mAP, 93.4% R1, 94.4% R5 and 95.3% R10 on RGBNT100, while achieves 79.0% mAP, 93.7% R1,

94.7% R5 and 95.1% R10 on RGBN300. Compared with the CNN-based method HAMNet [7], H-ViT method wins 13.6% mAP on RGBNT100 and 17.1% mAP on RGBN300, respectively. Compared with the transformer-based method TransReID [6], H-ViT outperforms it on RGBNT100 by a 18.9% larger mAP and on RGBN300 by a 11.9% larger mAP. These results demonstrate that our H-ViT method has superior performance both on RGBNT100 and RGBN300.

4.4   Analysis

Impact of Modal-specific Controller. For fully demonstrating the impact of different MC configurations in multi-modal vehicle re-identification (ReID), we conduct 5 types of MC's configurations in Table 1 on RGBNT100, and position embedding is set to modal-common, as shown in Fig. 3.

Firstly, partial modal-specific (i.e. shallow modal-specific, medium modal-specific and deep modal-specific) outperforms fully modal-specific and fully modal-common, and H-ViT achieves the best performance when $k = 5$ is configured in deep modal-specific. Deep modal-specific outperforms shallow modal-specific and medium modal-specific, which due to attention mechanism in transformer encoder is is more sensitive to global features and learn global features such as appearance. Therefore, shallow layers should be configured as modal-common to enhance H-ViT in learning global feature between modalities.

Secondly, H-ViT performs better when the gap between the number of modal-specific layers and the number of modal-common layers is smaller, which is because modal-specific MIE needs enough modal-specific layers and modal-common layers to fully learn intra- and inter-modal information. For example, H-ViT in deep modal-specific reaches 79.0% mAP with a gap of 3 layers ($k = 5, v = [8, 13)$), and 75.5% mAP with a larger gap of 9 layers ($k = 2, v = [11, 13)$). That is, MC should be configured enough modal-specific and modal-common layers to enhance MIE learning feature deviations toward modal variations. From what has been discussed above, to make H-ViT extract global feature and learn intra- and inter-modal information, MC should be configured to deep field, and specified about half of the layers as modal-specific layers.

Furthermore, to investigate the impact of position embedding, we conduct experiments to compare performance resulted from modal-specific and modal-common position embedding on best configurations in 5 types of MC's configurations in Table 1 (e.g. $k = 11$ in shallow modal-specific ($v = [0, 11)$), $k = 9$ in medium modal-specific ($v = [1, 10)$), $k = 5$ in deep modal-specific ($v = [8, 13)$), $k = 0$ in fully modal-common ($v = [0, 0)$), and $k = 13$ in fully modal-specific ($v = [0, 13)$). The experimental results on RGBNT100 and RGBN300 as shown in Table 4, one can see that the fluctuation on RGBNT100 is larger than that on RGBN300. For example, experiments with different types of position embedding have a difference of 1.4% mAP on RGBNT100 and only 0.1% difference mAP on RGBN300 when $v = [8, 13)$. The reason for this situation is the thermal camera's view-point is different from visible and near-infrared cameras which have almost identical view-points. Stable performance of modal-common position embedding shows that modal-common position embedding is more robust than modal-specific position embedding.

Table 4. The comparison of different position embedding (i.e.,modal-specific and modal-common) on RGBNT100 and RGBN300.

ν	Type	RGBNT100				RGBN300			
		mAP(%)	R1(%)	R5(%)	R10(%)	mAP(%)	R1(%)	R5(%)	R10(%)
[0, 0)	Common	76.5	91.5	93.1	93.6	77.2	91.2	92.5	93.1
	Specific	76.1	91.5	92.9	93.4	77.8	92.8	93.6	93.8
[0, 11)	Common	78.1	91.9	92.7	93.2	78.8	93.5	94.5	**95.2**
	Specific	77.7	92.1	92.9	93.7	**79.0**	**93.7**	**94.7**	95.1
[1, 10)	Common	78.2	93.4	94.2	94.8	78.4	93.4	94.4	94.8
	Specific	76.7	91.7	93.1	93.9	78.4	93.2	94.2	94.8
[8, 13)	Common	**79.0**	**93.4**	**94.4**	**95.3**	78.5	92.3	93.1	93.7
	Specific	77.6	90.6	91.6	92.1	78.4	92.8	93.7	94.2
[0, 13)	Common	76.2	92.7	93.6	94.3	77.5	92.4	93.3	94.0
	Specific	76.9	92.8	94.2	94.6	77.2	92.5	93.2	93.7

Role of MIE. Considering the action scope of MIE contain all stages in features extracting, which means the performance of MIE is greatly affected by the configurations of MC. Therefore, we conduct experiments on the best configurations in 5 types of configurations: $k = 11$ in shallow modal-specific ($\nu = [0, 11)$), $k = 9$ in medium modal-specific ($\nu = [1, 10)$), $k = 5$ in deep modal-specific ($\nu = [8, 13)$), $k = 0$ in fully modal-common ($\nu = [0, 0)$), and $k = 13$ in fully modal-specific ($\nu = [0, 13)$). Figure 4 shows the experimental results on RGBNT100 and RGBN300, one can see that MIE provides +1.9% mAP to the best configuration ($\nu = [8, 13)$) on RGBNT100 , and +0.5% mAP to the best configuration ($\nu = [0, 11)$) on RGBN300, which demonstrate that MIE is useful for alleviating feature deviations caused by modal variations. Noticing that MIE has negative impact on RGBNT100 and RGBN300 when MC is configured as $\nu = [0, 13)$ (fully modal-specific), which is caused by its invalid role in all stages of features extracting and lacking information exchanging between different modalities. In short, MIE can alleviate feature deviations towards modal variations, but is greatly impacted by MC's configurations and should not be used in fully modal-specific configuration

Influence of Multi-modal Fusions. Different modal data are fused at the end of feature extracting which is not affected by MC and MIE, so we select the best configuration in Fig. 3 (i.e. $k = 5, \nu = [8, 13)$ in deep modal-specific) with

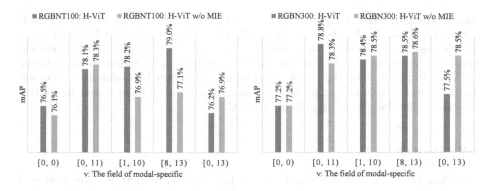

Fig. 4. The ablation study of modal information embedding (MIE). H-ViT w/o MIE means H-ViT without MIE. ν denotes the field of modal-specific layers.

modal-common position embedding to conduct experiments on RGBNT100 and RGBN300 for different multi-modal fusion methods. Table 5 shows the results fusing by average, Hadamard product [18], and concatenating. One can see that the average fusion way acquires best performance, which suggests that the low-pass effect of average fusion could filter out multi-modal heterogeneity, which is beneficial to improve performance.

Table 5. Results of different fusion methods on RGBNT100 and RGBN300, where A, HP, and C denotes average, Hadamard product, and concatenating, respectively.

Fusion	RGBNT100				RGBN300			
	mAP(%)	R1(%)	R5(%)	R10(%)	mAP(%)	R1(%)	R5(%)	R10(%)
A	**79.0**	93.4	94.4	95.3	**78.5**	92.3	93.1	93.7
HP	45.2	63.0	65.9	67.6	72.0	89.1	90.5	91.2
C	74.9	92.4	93.5	94.1	75.6	91.2	92.3	92.9

5 Conclusion

In this paper, we propose a transformer-based baseline, namely, hybrid vision transformer (H-ViT), for multi-modal vehicle ReID tasks. H-ViT has two new modules, (1) the modal-specific controller (MC) and (2) the modal information embedding (MIE). MC can well deal with heterogeneous multi-modal images via flexibly allocating the distribution of modal-specific layers and specify the sharing type of position embedding. MIE is able to reduce feature deviations towards modal variations by learning intra- and inter-modal information. Experiments show that our H-ViT acquires state-of-the-art results.

Acknowledgements. This work was supported in part by the National Key R&D Program of China under the Grant 2019YFB1405900, in part by the National Natural Science Foundation of China under the Grants 61976098, 61871434, 61876178, and 61901183, in part by the Natural Science Foundation for Outstanding Young Scholars of Fujian Province under the Grant 2022J06023, and in part by Collaborative Innovation Platform Project of Fuzhou-Xiamen-Quanzhou National Independent Innovation Demonstration Zone under the Grant 2021FX03.

References

1. Chen, C., Ye, M., Qi, M., Wu, J., Jiang, J., Lin, C.W.: Structure-aware positional transformer for visible-infrared person re-identification. IEEE Trans. Image Process. **31**, 2352–2364 (2022)
2. Deng, J., et al.: Trends in vehicle re-identification past, present, and future: a comprehensive review. Mathematics **9**(24), 3162 (2021)
3. Dosovitskiy, A., et al.: An image is worth 16x16 words: transformers for image recognition at scale (2020). https://arxiv.org/abs/2010.11929
4. Han, K., et al.: A survey on visual transformer (2020). https://arxiv.org/abs/2012.12556
5. Han, X., et al.: Rethinking sampling strategies for unsupervised person re-identification (2021). https://arxiv.org/abs/2107.03024
6. He, S., Luo, H., Wang, P., Wang, F., Li, H., Jiang, W.: Transreid: transformer-based object re-identification (2021). https://arxiv.org/abs/2102.04378
7. Li, H., Li, C., Zhu, X., Zheng, A., Luo, B.: Multi-spectral vehicle re-identification: a challenge. In: Proceedings of the AAAI Conference on Artificial Intelligence, vol. 34, pp. 11345–11353. New York, USA (2020)
8. Liu, H., Tan, X., Zhou, X.: Parameter sharing exploration and hetero-center triplet loss for visible-thermal person re-identification. IEEE Trans. Multimedia **23**, 4414–4425 (2020)
9. Lu, Y., et al.: Cross-modality person re-identification with shared-specific feature transfer. In: Proceedings of the IEEE/CVF Conference on Computer Vision and Pattern Recognition, pp. 13379–13389. Washington, USA (2020)
10. Meng, D., Li, L., Wang, S., Gao, X., Zha, Z.J., Huang, Q.: Fine-grained feature alignment with part perspective transformation for vehicle reid. In: Proceedings of the ACM International Conference on Multimedia, pp. 619–627. Washington, USA (2020)
11. Vaswani, A., et al.: Attention is all you need (2017). https://arxiv.org/abs/1706.03762
12. Wang, Z., Wang, Z., Zheng, Y., Chuang, Y.Y., Satoh, S.: Learning to reduce dual-level discrepancy for infrared-visible person re-identification. In: Proceedings of the IEEE/CVF Conference on Computer Vision and Pattern Recognition, pp. 618–626. California, USA (2019)
13. Wang, Z., et al.: Orientation invariant feature embedding and spatial temporal regularization for vehicle re-identification. In: Proceedings of the IEEE International Conference on Computer Vision, pp. 379–387. Venice, Italy (2017)
14. Wang, Z., Li, C., Zheng, A., He, R., Tang, J.: Interact, embed, and enlarge: boosting modality-specific representations for multi-modal person re-identification. In: Proceedings of the AAAI Conference on Artificial Intelligence, vol. 36, no. 3, pp. 2633–2641 (2022)

15. Ye, M., Shen, J., Lin, G., Xiang, T., Shao, L., Hoi, S.C.: Deep learning for person re-identification: a survey and outlook (2020). https://arxiv.org/abs/2001.04193
16. Yu, Z., Pei, J., Zhu, M., Zhang, J., Li, J.: Multi-attribute adaptive aggregation transformer for vehicle re-identification. Inf. Process. Manage. **59**(2), 102868 (2022)
17. Zhang, G., Zhang, P., Qi, J., Lu, H.: Hat: hierarchical aggregation transformers for person re-identification. In: Proceedings of the ACM International Conference on Multimedia, pp. 516–525. Chengdu, China (2021)
18. Zhao, H., Jia, J., Koltun, V.: Exploring self-attention for image recognition. In: Proceedings of the IEEE/CVF Conference on Computer Vision and Pattern Recognition, pp. 10076–10085. Washington, USA (2020)
19. Zheng, A., Wang, Z., Chen, Z., Li, C., Tang, J.: Robust multi-modality person re-identification. In: Proceedings of the AAAI Conference on Artificial Intelligence, vol. 35, pp. 3529–3537. Vancouver, Canada (2021)
20. Zhong, Z., Zheng, L., Kang, G., Li, S., Yang, Y.: Random erasing data augmentation. In: Proceedings of the AAAI Conference on Artificial Intelligence, vol. 34, pp. 13001–13008. New York, USA (2020)
21. Zhou, Y., Shao, L.: Aware attentive multi-view inference for vehicle re-identification. In: Proceedings of the IEEE Conference on Computer Vision and Pattern Recognition, pp. 6489–6498. Utah, USA (2018)
22. Zhu, J., Zeng, H., Du, Y., Lei, Z., Zheng, L., Cai, C.: Joint feature and similarity deep learning for vehicle re-identification. IEEE Access **6**, 43724–43731 (2018)
23. Zhu, J., et al.: Vehicle re-identification using quadruple directional deep learning features. IEEE Trans. Intell. Transp. Syst. **21**(1), 410–420 (2019)
24. Zhu, X., Luo, Z., Fu, P., Ji, X.: Voc-reid: vehicle re-identification based on vehicle-orientation-camera. In: Proceedings of the IEEE/CVF Conference on Computer Vision and Pattern Recognition Workshops, pp. 602–603. Washington, USA (2020)

A Coarse-to-Fine Convolutional Neural Network for Light Field Angular Super-Resolution

Gaosheng Liu🆔, Huanjing Yue🆔, and Jingyu Yang$^{(\boxtimes)}$🆔

School of Electrical and Information Engineering, Tianjin University, Tianjin, China
{gaoshengliu,huanjing.yue,yjy}@tju.edu.cn

Abstract. Densely-sampled light field (LF) images are drawing increasing attention for their wide applications, such as 3D reconstruction, virtual reality, and depth estimation. However, due to the hardware restriction, it is usually challenging and costly to capture them. In this paper, we propose a coarse-to-fine convolutional neural network (CNN) for LF angular super-resolution (SR), which aims at generating densely-sampled LF images from sparse observations. Our method contains two stages, *i.e.*, coarse-grained novel views synthesis and fine-grained view refinement. Specifically, our method first extracts the multi-scale correspondence in the sparse views and generates coarse novel views. Then we propose a structural consistency enhancement module to regularize them for LF parallax structure preservation. Experimental results on both real-world and synthetic datasets demonstrate that our method achieves state-of-the-art performance. Furthermore, we show the promising application of the reconstructed LF images by our method on the depth estimation task.

Keywords: Light field · Angular super-resolution · View synthesis

1 Introduction

Different from 2D imaging, light field (LF) imaging can record light rays on not only spatial but also angular dimensions, where the geometric information of the real-world scenes is encoded. Benefited from the rich angular clues, the densely-sampled LF images are highly desirable for various applications, such as 3D reconstruction [10,24], post-refocusing [4], and virtual reality [28]. However, it is challenging and costly to acquire densely-sampled LF images. For example, the conventional LF imaging devices, including camera array [19] and computer-control gantry [16], are usually bulky and expensive. The recent hand-held commercial LF cameras [1,2] suffer from the intrinsic tradeoff between spatial and angular resolutions since the sensor is shared for spatial-angular recording. To tackle the tradeoff, developing computational methods to enhance the angular resolutions of LF images is an attractive topic in recent years.

© The Author(s), under exclusive license to Springer Nature Switzerland AG 2022
L. Fang et al. (Eds.): CICAI 2022, LNAI 13604, pp. 268–279, 2022.
https://doi.org/10.1007/978-3-031-20497-5_22

As shown in Fig. 1, the LF image can be represented by an array of sub-aperture images (SAIs). The horizontally or vertically stacked SAIs build up an epipolar-plane image (EPI) volume, and the EPIs are the 2D slices of the EPI volume. In the literature, various approaches have been proposed from different perspectives, $e.g.$ reconstructing novel SAIs, or high-resolution EPI volume (EPIs). And they can be roughly classified into two categories, $i.e.$, non-learning-based methods [12–15,18,29,31] and learning-based methods [8,9,17,20–23,25,27].

The non-learning-based methods usually either predict the scene depth from the sparse views as auxiliary information [12,18] or require handcrafted image priors, such as sparsity in continuous Fourier domain [14] or shearlet transform domain [15]. Recently, following the board application of deep learning technology, the learning-based methods have shown remarkable performance in LF angular SR. Among them, both depth-dependent methods [8,9,20] and depth-independent methods [11,17,21–23,25,27] are widely studied. Specifically, Yoon et $al.$ [27] proposed to jointly reconstruct the high-spatial and -angular resolution LF images. However, their performance is limited by the under-used spatial-angular correlations in surrounding SAIs. Kalantari et $al.$ [9] proposed an end-to-end network, which estimates the scene depth that is utilized to synthesize novel SAIs via a physically-based warping operation. They also proposed a color network to refine the warped views. Yeung et $al.$ [25] proposed to utilize spatial-angular alternating convolutions [26] to explore the spatial-angular clues in the input SAIs, and the final novel SAIs are generated via 4D convolutions. Wang et $al.$ [17] proposed a pseudo-4D CNN framework to reconstruct high-resolution EPI volumes. Wu et $al.$ [21,23] introduced a $blur$-$restoration$-$deblur$ scheme that works on 2D EPIs. Later, they proposed to fuse the pre-upsampled sheared EPIs [20] to generate the final high-resolution EPIs. By taking advantage of the geometry information, Jin et $al.$ [8] proposed a depth-based network for LF images with large baselines. Recently, Wu et $al.$ [22] incorporated the non-local attention mechanism to explore the spatial-angular correlations in the EPI volumes.

Though the previous methods have achieved remarkable performance, the depth-dependent methods rely heavily on the photo-consistency assumption and fail to handle the non-Lambertian effect. The multi-scale correlations in the input SAIs are under-exploited in the depth-independent methods. In addition, there is still room to improve the reconstruction quality of parallax structure in reconstructed LF images. Based on the above observation, in this paper, we develop a depth-independent coarse-to-fine method for LF angular SR. Specifically, our method first models the multi-scale correlations in the sparse views and synthesizes coarse novel views. Then, we propose a structural consistency enhancement module to regularize the intermediate results. We conduct experiments on both real-world and synthetic LF datasets, and the results demonstrate that our method achieves state-of-the-art performance in quantitative results and visual quality.

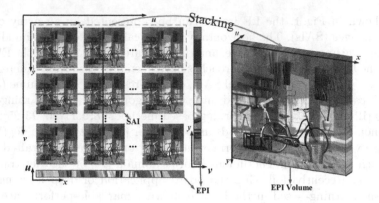

Fig. 1. Illustrations of LF images. The x, y are spatial coordinates and u, v are the angular coordinates. The LF image can be represented as an array of sub-aperture images (SAIs). The epipolar-plane image (EPI) volume is constructed by stacking one-direction SAIs. The EPIs are the 2D slices of the EPI volume.

2   Proposed Method

The two-plane model [5] is widely utilized to parameterize the 4D LF as $L(x, y, u, v) \in \mathbb{R}^{U \times V \times H \times W}$. Given a sparsely-sampled 4D LF image $L_{\mathrm{LR}} \in \mathbb{R}^{U \times V \times H \times W}$ with angular resolution of $U \times V$ and spatial resolution of $H \times W$. This paper aims to reconstruct the corresponding densely-sampled LF image $L_{\mathrm{HR}} \in \mathbb{R}^{\alpha U \times \alpha V \times H \times W}$. We follow previous work [11, 17, 21–23, 25] to perform the proposed method on the Y channel of the input LF images, and the Cb and Cr channels are up-sampled using bicubic algorithm on the angular domain. The overall architecture of our method is depicted in Fig. 2 (a), which consists of a coarse-grained view synthesis sub-network (CVSNet) and a fine-grained view refinement sub-network (FVRNet). Specifically, the CVSNet takes the sparsely-sampled LF image as inputs and generates novel views. Then the input views and the synthesized views are concatenated to generate the intermediate results. Finally, the intermediate results are fed into FVRNet to generate the final densely-sampled LF image. In the following, we give the details of CVSNet and FVRNet.

2.1   Coarse-grained View Synthesis Sub-network

Previous methods [11, 25] utilize spatial-angular alternating convolution or 3D convolution to extract the correlations in the sparsely-sampled LF image. However, the multi-scale correlations are under-exploited. To this end, we introduce CVSNet which is a modified UNet architecture to model the multi-scale correlations in the sparse views. The architecture of CVSNet is depicted in Fig. 2 (b).

As shown in Fig. 2 (b), the backbone of the proposed CVSNet follows the encoder-decoder structure with skip connections of the UNet. The filter num-

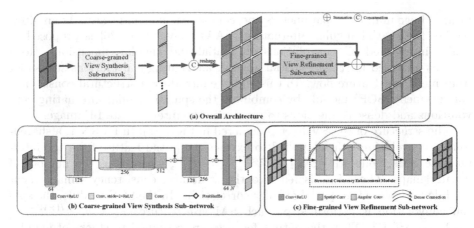

Fig. 2. The Framework of the proposed method. It contains two sub-networks, *i.e.*, coarse-grained views synthesis network (CSVNet), and fine-grained view refinement network (FVRNet). The CSVNet is utilized to synthesize novel views and FVRNet is utilized to refine them.

ber of each convolutional layer is shown at the bottom of each block. The filter number of the last convolutional layer N is the number of novel views to be synthesized (*e.g.*, $N = 60$ for $2 \times 2 \to 8 \times 8$ angular SR). The CVSNet consists of two down-sampling and up-sampling operations. The down-sampling operation is achieved by applying a convolutional layer with stride 2, and the up-sampling operation is achieved by the PixelShuffle layer. Specifically, the input SAIs are stacked along the channel dimension before being fed into CVSNet. Then CVS-Net generates a set of novel SAIs by incorporating the multi-scale correlations in the SAIs of the input sparsely-sampled LF image, which can be represented as

$$L_{\text{Coarse}} = H_{\text{CVSNet}}(L_{\text{LR}}), \tag{1}$$

where the H_{CVSNet} denotes the CVSNet and L_{Coarse} denotes the synthesized views. The generated novel views and the input views are concatenated, which are fed into the FVRNet.

2.2   Fine-grained View Refinement Sub-network

An important property of the LF image is the valuable 4D structure, which is also known as the parallax structure. To produce high-quality high-angular-resolution LF images, the parallax structure should be well preserved. In our coarse views synthesis, the novel views are synthesized without considering the structural consistency among the intermediate views. Therefore, further refinement on the intermediate LF image to enhance the structural consistency is required.

To preserve the LF parallax structure, an intuitive way is to apply high-dimensional (*e.g.*, 4D and 3D) CNNs. However, high-dimensional CNNs will bring a huge number of parameters and computational complexity. As an alternative, the spatial-angular alternating (SAA) convolution [26] is proposed to utilize interleaved 2D convolutions on spatial and angular dimensions. However, as analyzed in [7], the spatial angular alternating convolutions still suffer from inefficient feature flow. To this end, we introduce a structural consistency enhancement (SCE) module by combining the spatial angular alternating convolutions and dense connections to regularize the intermediate LF image.

The structure of the FVRNet is depicted in Fig. 2 (c). In FVRNet, a shared-weight convolution is first applied to extract the initial feature from the intermediate SAIs, generating $\mathcal{F}_{\text{init}} \in \mathbb{R}^{\alpha^2 UV \times C \times H \times W}$, where C is the number of feature maps. Then $\mathcal{F}_{\text{init}}$ is fed into the structural consistency enhancement module to explore the spatial-angular correlations. In the SCE module, the spatial convolution is performed on each SAI-wise feature, $\mathcal{F}_s^i \in \mathbb{R}^{C \times H \times W}$, $i \in \{1, 2, \cdots, \alpha^2 UV\}$. Then the output features are reshaped to stacks of angular patches, i.e., $\mathcal{F}_a \in \mathbb{R}^{HW \times C \times \alpha U \times \alpha V}$. The angular convolution is performed on each angular feature, $\mathcal{F}_a^j \in \mathbb{R}^{C \times \alpha U \times \alpha V}$, $j \in \{1, 2, \cdots, HW\}$.

We apply dense connection in the SCE module to enhance the information flow. Specifically, The output of the k-th $(2 \leq k \leq 4)$ SAA convolution can be formulated by

$$\mathcal{F}_{\text{SAA}}^{(k)} = H_{\text{SAA}}^k([\mathcal{F}_{\text{SAA}}^{(1)}, \cdots, \mathcal{F}_{\text{SAA}}^{(k-1)}]), \tag{2}$$

where $[\cdot]$ denote the concatenation operation, $\mathcal{F}_{\text{SAA}}^{(k)}$ denotes the output feature of the k-th SAA convolution, H_{SAA}^k denotes the k-th SAA convolution.

Specifically, we utilize four SAA convolutions in the SCE module. The output feature of the SCE module is processed by two convolutional layers to output the final results. Finally, a global residual connection in FVRNet is also performed.

2.3 Training Details

We utilize the L_1 loss to minimize the distance between the ground truth and the output of our method

$$\mathcal{L} = \|L_{\text{SR}} - L_{\text{GT}}\|_1, \tag{3}$$

where L_{SR} is the angularly super-resolved LF image. The number of filters of the convolutional layers in FVRNet is set to $C = 32$ (the last convolution has one filter). We cropped the SAIs into patches of 64×64 for training. The batch size was set to one, and the learning rate was initially set to 2e-4 which is reduced by half after every 15 epochs. The training was stopped after 70 epochs. During training, the data is augmented via random flipping and 90-degree rotation. We implemented the network in PyTorch and utilized an NVIDIA RTX 2080 TI GPU to train it. The ADAM algorithm is applied to optimize the network.

Table 1. Quantitative comparisons (PSNR/SSIM) with the state-of-the-arts on real-world datasets for $2 \times 2 \rightarrow 8 \times 8$ angular SR. The best results are highlighted in red.

Test sets	Kalantari et al. [9]	Wu et al. [21]	Wu et al. [20]	Yeung et al. [25]	SAA-Net [22]	Ours
30scenes	39.88/0.979	35.25/0.928	36.74/0.950	40.67/0.979	39.90/0.977	41.83 / 0.993
Occlusions	35.34/0.962	33.02/0.922	32.98/0.943	36.24/0.977	35.04/0.962	37.19 / 0.986
Reflective	34.99/0.940	33.64/0.927	34.38/0.941	35.72/0.945	35.36/0.945	36.27 / 0.970
Average	36.74/0.960	33.97/0.926	34.70/0.945	37.54/0.967	36.77 / 0.961	38.43 / 0.983

3 Experiments

The experiments are conducted on both real-world and synthetic LF scenes. Specifically, we select 100 real-world scenes from Stanford Lytro Archive [3] and Kalantari et al. [9] to train the model. We extract the central 8×8 SAIs from the original 14×14 SAIs for training and testing. For synthetic scenes, we select 20 scenes from *HCInew* dataset [6] to train the model. We compare our methods with five state-of-the-art methods, *i.e.*, Kalantari et al. [9], Yeung et al. [25], Wu et al. [21], Wu et al. [20], and SAA-Net [22]. The Kalantari et al. [9], Yeung et al. [25], and Wu et al. [20] are trained using the same training datasets as ours. Since the training codes of Wu et al. [21] and SAA-Net [22] are not available, we test their methods using their released models. The comparisons are conducted on $2 \times 2 \rightarrow 8 \times 8$ task. Specifically, we sample the input sparse 2×2 views from the four corners of the ground-truth 8×8 views. To compute the PSNR and SSIM scores of the angular SR results, only the Y channel of synthesised views (*e.g.*, 60 novel views for $2 \times 2 \rightarrow 8 \times 8$ angular SR) are utilized for quantitative evaluation.

3.1 Comparison on Real-world Scenes

We used three test sets which contains 70 real-world LF scenes are utilized for performance comparison, namely *30scenes* [9], *Occlusions* [3], and *Reflective* [3].

Table 1 lists the PSNR and SSIM scores for each test set and the average results for the three test sets. From Table 1, it can be observed that our method consistently outperforms other state-of-the-art methods. Compared with Kalantari et al. [9], our method achieves an average gain of 1.69 dB. This is because their method incorporates estimated disparities to warp novel views from input views. However, the warping operation is difficult to handle challenging cases, such as occluded regions and non-Lambertian surfaces. The results of Wu et al. [21] and Wu et al. [20] are inferior to others. The reason is that their methods work on one-direction EPIs, which can not fully exploit the spatial correlations in the SAIs. Our method outperforms Yeung et al. [25] by 1.16 dB on *30scenes* test set. Compared with SAA-Net [22], our method achieves 1.66 dB and 0.022 gain in terms of average PSNR and SSIM.

Figure 3 presents the visual comparison results of two scenes. It can be observed that our method produces fine-grained details in the synthesized views.

Table 2. Quantitative comparisons (PSNR/SSIM) with the state-of-the-arts on synthetic datasets for $2 \times 2 \rightarrow 8 \times 8$ angular SR. The best results are highlighted in red.

Test sets	Kalantari et al. [9]	Wu et al. [21]	Wu et al. [20]	Yeung et al. [25]	SAA-Net [22]	Ours
HCInew	32.37/0.905	28.82/0.773	27.85/0.793	32.07/0.895	30.54/0.862	32.87/0.951
HCIold	38.22/0.944	34.79/0.874	36.03/0.902	37.44/0.927	38.40/0.918	39.89/0.964
Average	35.30 / 0.925	31.81 / 0.824	31.94 / 0.848	34.76/0.911	34.47/0.890	36.38/0.957

The EPI-based method, Wu et al. [21], Wu et al. [20], SAA-Net [22] are prone to producing ghosting artifacts. Kalantari et al. [9] struggles to recover the boundary of the rock in scene *Rock*. The results of Yeung et al. [25] suffer from ringing artifacts. We also provide the EPIs recovered by each method for comparison. We can observe that Wu et al. [21] and Wu et al. [20] can not recover the linear patterns in EPIs. The EPIs reconstructed by Yeung et al. [25] and SAA-Net [22] also have artifacts. By contrast, our method recovers fewer artifacts and more linear structures. This demonstrates that our method is a strong baseline for high-quality LF angular SR.

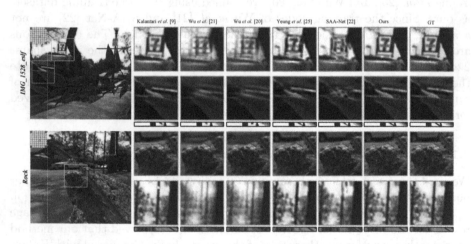

Fig. 3. Visual comparison on real-world scenes for $2 \times 2 \rightarrow 8 \times 8$ angular SR. We selected patches (highlighted using green and red boxes) in SAI that locates at the angular position of $(5, 5)$. The EPIs are cut along the blue line. (Color figure online)

3.2   Comparison on Synthetic Scenes

For synthetic scenes, we select four scenes from *HCInew* and five scenes from *HCIold* dataset for comparison. Table 2 lists the quantitative comparison results with the state-of-the-art methods in terms of PSNR and SSIM. From Table 2, we can observe that our method achieves the best performance. Specifically, our method outperforms Yeung *et al.* [25] by 2.45 dB on *HCIold* dataset. Compared with Kalantari *et al.* [9], our method achieves an average gain of 1.08 dB. Compared with Wu *et al.* [21] and Wu *et al.* [20], Ours achieves more than 4 dB on average. Compared with SAA-Net [22], Ours also achieves an average gain of 1.91 dB.

Figure 4 presents the visual comparisons. It can also be observed that our method produces the most fine-grained details. For scene *Herbs*, the bowls (highlighted in green box) reconstructed by other methods are over smooth. For scene *StillLife*, the tablecloth recovered by Kalantari *et al.* [9], Yeung *et al.* [25], and SAA-Net [22] have severe artifacts. The results of Wu *et al.* [21] and Wu *et al.* [20] are also blurry. By contrast, our method recovers more fine-granular textures.

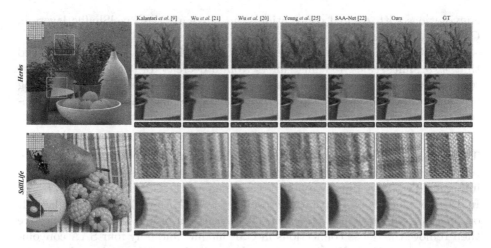

Fig. 4. Visual comparison on synthetic scenes for $2 \times 2 \rightarrow 8 \times 8$ angular SR. We selected patches (highlighted using green and red boxes) in SAI that locates at the angular position of (5, 5). The EPIs are cut along the blue line. (Color figure online)

3.3 Ablation Study

In this subsection, We perform ablation studies to demonstrate the effectiveness of the proposed methods. Specifically, we take advantage of the multi-scale correlations in the sparsely-sampled input, and we propose the SCE module to refine the coarse-grained synthesized views. To this end, we design several variants to verify the effectiveness of the introduced strategy or module. The experiments are conducted on $2 \times 2 \rightarrow 8 \times 8$ task. The models are trained using the real-world 100 scenes, and tested on the *30scenes*, *Occlusions*, and *Reflective* test sets.

The Effectiveness of Multi-scale Modeling. To verify the effectiveness of multi-scale modeling, we design a variant by replacing the down-sampling

Table 3. Ablation results on real-world datasets. The best results are highlighted in red.

Variants	30Scenes	Occlusions	Reflective
w/o_Multi-scale Modeling	41.54/0.9921	36.72/0.9842	36.20/0.9713
w/o_CSE	41.54/0.9917	36.85/0.9845	36.07/0.9714
w/o_Dense Connection	41.67/0.9922	37.04/0.9852	36.16/0.9699
w_2SAAConv	41.68/0.9922	36.92/0.9848	36.14/0.9713
w_3SAAConv	41.72/0.9923	37.02/0.9852	36.18/0.9704
Ours	41.83/0.9925	37.19/0.9857	36.27/0.9704

convolutions with normal convolutions and removing the PixelShuffle layers in CVSNet.

Table 3 lists the quantitative results of the ablation study. It can be observed that w/o_Multi-scale Modeling suffers from a decrease of 0.29 dB on 30scenes test set, and 0.47 dB on Occlusion test set. This is because the down-sampling operations in CVSNet can help enlarge the receptive field and explore the multi-scale correlations in the SAIs, which are beneficial for the view synthesis.

The Effectiveness of CSE. In the FVRNet, we introduced CSE module to refine the intermediate results. We then conduct several experiments to show the influence of CSE module. We first directly remove the CSE module in FVRNet. In Table 3, we can observe that the results of w/o_CSE are decreased by 0.29 dB on 30scenes, which demonstrates the effectiveness of proposed CSE module. We then remove the dense connections in CSE module and only four SAA convolutions are maintained. We can observe that w/o_Dense Connection, the results suffer from a decrease of 0.16 dB on 30scenes. This is because the dense connections can help enhance the feature flow. We also conduct the experiments by utilizing a different number of SAA convolutions in CSE module. From Table. 3, we can observe that the results of w_2SAAConv and w_3SAAConv are inferior to Ours (w_4SAAConv) by 0.15 dB and 0.11 dB on 30scenes test set, respectively.

3.4 Depth Estimation

Since one of the most valuable information of the reconstructed LF image is the geometry information of the real-world scene, we further apply our method to depth estimation task to verify the ability to reveal the geometric structures. We utilize SPO [30] to predict the scene depth estimation from the reconstructed densely-sampled LF image. We also compare the visual quality of estimated depth maps with Wu et al. [20] and SAA-Net [22]. The ground-truth depth map is estimated from the ground-truth densely-sampled LF image. Figure 5 presents the visual results. We can observe that our method achieves promising depth prediction, such as the boundary of leaves in scene *occlusion_2_eslf* and the rock in scene *Rock*.

Fig. 5. Visual comparison of depth estimation.

4 Conclusion

In this paper, we propose a coarse-to-fine network for LF angular SR, which aims to reconstruct densely-sampled LF images from sparsely-sampled ones. We introduce two sub-networks, *i.e.*, a CVSNet to synthesize novel views, and an FVRNet to refine the coarse views. Specifically, CVSNet contains a UNet architecture to extract the multi-scale correspondence in the sparse views and generate coarse novel views. In FVRNet, we propose a structural consistency enhancement module to refine the coarse views and help preserve the parallax structure of LF image. The experiments are conducted on both real-world and synthetic datasets, and the experimental results demonstrate that our method achieves state-of-the-art performance. We further apply our method to the depth estimation task, and the visual results show our promising ability to predict the geometric information from scenes. Our method also has limitations, *e.g.*, the visual reconstruction quality still has obvious distance from the ground-truth images in some challenging regions, such as the tablecloth in scene *StillLife* (Fig. 4). In future work, we will explore more effective strategies to improve the visual quality.

Acknowledgments. This work was supported in part by the National Natural Science Foundation of China under Grant 62072331.

References

1. Lytro illum. https://www.lytro.com/
2. Raytrix. https://www.raytrix.de/
3. The stanford lytro light field archive. http://lightfields.stanford.edu/LF2016.html. Accessed 16 Oct 2021

4. Fiss, J., Curless, B., Szeliski, R.: Refocusing plenoptic images using depth-adaptive splatting. In: 2014 IEEE International Conference on Computational Photography (ICCP), pp. 1–9 IEEE (2014)
5. Gortler, S.J., Grzeszczuk, R., Szeliski, R., Cohen, M.F.: The lumigraph. In: Proceedings of the 23rd Annual Conference on Computer Graphics and Interactive Techniques, pp. 43–54 (1996)
6. Honauer, K., Johannsen, O., Kondermann, D., Goldluecke, B.: A dataset and evaluation methodology for depth estimation on 4D light fields. In: Lai, S.-H., Lepetit, V., Nishino, K., Sato, Y. (eds.) ACCV 2016. LNCS, vol. 10113, pp. 19–34. Springer, Cham (2017). https://doi.org/10.1007/978-3-319-54187-7_2
7. Hu, Z., Yeung, H.W.F., Chen, X., Chung, Y.Y., Li, H.: Efficient light field reconstruction via spatio-angular dense network. IEEE Trans. Instrum. Meas. **70**, 1–14 (2021)
8. Jin, J., Hou, J., Yuan, H., Kwong, S.: Learning light field angular super-resolution via a geometry-aware network. **34**(07), pp. 11141–11148 (2020)
9. Kalantari, N.K., Wang, T.C., Ramamoorthi, R.: Learning-based view synthesis for light field cameras. ACM Trans. Graphics (TOG) **35**(6), 1–10 (2016)
10. Kim, C., Zimmer, H., Pritch, Y., Sorkine-Hornung, A., Gross, M.H.: Scene reconstruction from high spatio-angular resolution light fields. ACM Trans. Graph. **32**(4), 73 (2013)
11. Liu, D., Huang, Y., Wu, Q., Ma, R., An, P.: Multi-angular epipolar geometry based light field angular reconstruction network. IEEE Trans. Comput. Imaging **6**, 1507–1522 (2020)
12. Mitra, K., Veeraraghavan, A.: Light field denoising, light field superresolution and stereo camera based refocussing using a GMM light field patch prior. In: 2012 IEEE Computer Society Conference on Computer Vision and Pattern Recognition Workshops, pp. 22–28 IEEE (2012)
13. Pujades, S., Devernay, F., Goldluecke, B.: Bayesian view synthesis and image-based rendering principles. In: Proceedings of the IEEE Conference on Computer Vision and Pattern Recognition, pp. 3906–3913 (2014)
14. Shi, L., Hassanieh, H., Davis, A., Katabi, D., Durand, F.: Light field reconstruction using sparsity in the continuous fourier domain. ACM Trans. Graphics (TOG) **34**(1), 1–13 (2014)
15. Vagharshakyan, S., Bregovic, R., Gotchev, A.: Light field reconstruction using shearlet transform. IEEE Trans. Pattern Anal Mach. Intell. **40**(1), 133–147 (2017)
16. Vaish, V., Adams, A.: The (new) stanford light field archive (2008). http://lightfield.stanford.edu/
17. Wang, Y., Liu, F., Wang, Z., Hou, G., Sun, Z., Tan, T.: End-to-end view synthesis for light field imaging with pseudo 4DCNN. In: Ferrari, V., Hebert, M., Sminchisescu, C., Weiss, Y. (eds.) ECCV 2018. LNCS, vol. 11206, pp. 340–355. Springer, Cham (2018). https://doi.org/10.1007/978-3-030-01216-8_21
18. Wanner, S., Goldluecke, B.: Variational light field analysis for disparity estimation and super-resolution. IEEE Trans. Pattern Anal. Mach. Intell. **36**(3), 606–619 (2013)
19. Wilburn, B., et al.: High performance imaging using large camera arrays. In: ACM SIGGRAPH 2005 Papers, pp. 765–776 (2005)
20. Wu, G., Liu, Y., Dai, Q., Chai, T.: Learning sheared epi structure for light field reconstruction. IEEE Trans. Image Process. **28**(7), 3261–3273 (2019)
21. Wu, G., Liu, Y., Fang, L., Dai, Q., Chai, T.: Light field reconstruction using convolutional network on epi and extended applications. IEEE Trans. Pattern Anal. Mach. Intell. **41**(7), 1681–1694 (2018)

22. Wu, G., Wang, Y., Liu, Y., Fang, L., Chai, T.: Spatial-angular attention network for light field reconstruction. IEEE Trans. Image Process. **30**, 8999–9013 (2021)
23. Wu, G., Zhao, M., Wang, L., Dai, Q., Chai, T., Liu, Y.: Light field reconstruction using deep convolutional network on epi. In: Proceedings of the IEEE Conference on Computer Vision and Pattern Recognition, pp. 6319–6327 (2017)
24. Wu, J., et al.: Iterative tomography with digital adaptive optics permits hour-long intravital observation of 3d subcellular dynamics at millisecond scale. Cell **184**, 3318–3332.e17 (2021)
25. Yeung, H.W.F., Hou, J., Chen, J., Chung, Y.Y., Chen, X.: Fast light field reconstruction with deep coarse-to-fine modeling of spatial-angular clues. In: Ferrari, V., Hebert, M., Sminchisescu, C., Weiss, Y. (eds.) ECCV 2018. LNCS, vol. 11210, pp. 138–154. Springer, Cham (2018). https://doi.org/10.1007/978-3-030-01231-1_9
26. Yeung, H.W.F., Hou, J., Chen, X., Chen, J., Chen, Z., Chung, Y.Y.: Light field spatial super-resolution using deep efficient spatial-angular separable convolution. IEEE Trans. Image Process. **28**(5), 2319–2330 (2018)
27. Yoon, Y., Jeon, H.G., Yoo, D., Lee, J.Y., So Kweon, I.: Learning a deep convolutional network for light-field image super-resolution. In: Proceedings of the IEEE International Conference on Computer Vision Workshops, pp. 24–32 (2015)
28. Yu, J.: A light-field journey to virtual reality. IEEE MultiMedia **24**, 104–112 (2017)
29. Zhang, F.L., Wang, J., Shechtman, E., Zhou, Z.Y., Shi, J.X., Hu, S.M.: Plenopatch: patch-based plenoptic image manipulation. IEEE Trans. Visual. Comput. Graphics **23**(5), 1561–1573 (2016)
30. Zhang, S., Sheng, H., Li, C., Zhang, J., Xiong, Z.: Robust depth estimation for light field via spinning parallelogram operator. Comput. Vis. Image Underst. **145**, 148–159 (2016)
31. Zhang, Z., Liu, Y., Dai, Q.: Light field from micro-baseline image pair. In: Proceedings of the IEEE Conference on Computer Vision and Pattern Recognition, pp. 3800–3809 (2015)

VSA: Adaptive Visual and Semantic Guided Attention on Few-Shot Learning

Jin Chai[1], Yisheng Chen[2], Weinan Shen[2], Tong Zhang[1],
and C. L. Philip Chen[1(✉)]

[1] School of Computer Science and Engineering,
South China University of Technology, Guangzhou, China
philip.chen@ieee.org
[2] School of Electrical and Computer Engineering, Guangzhou Nanfang College,
Guangzhou, China

Abstract. Training models with only a few samples often bring overfitting and generalization problems. Moreover, it has always been challenging to identify new classes based on small samples. However, studies have shown that humans can use prior knowledge such as vision and semantics to learn new categories from a small number of samples. We propose a bimodal attention mechanism (VSA) based on vision and semantics to better use this prior knowledge like humans. VSA can adaptively combine information from both visual and semantic modalities to guide visual feature extraction, that is, which features should be paid more attention to during feature extraction. Therefore, the new category is more discriminative even if only one sample exists. Meanwhile, our extensive experiments on miniImageNet, CIFAR-FS, and CUB demonstrate that our bimodal attention mechanism is effective and achieves state-of-the-art results on the CUB dataset.

Keywords: Adaptive · Attention · Few-shot learning

1 Introduction

In recent years, with the exponential growth of data size and the improvement of computing power, object classification based on deep learning has made significant progress. However, most deep learning models rely on vast amounts of data. The annotation of large-scale data is a tedious and expensive task. In some tasks, obtaining large-scale data for the training and learning deep learning models is difficult. Training the model using only a small amount of labeled data in most deep learning methods will undoubtedly bring overfitting and generalization problems. Therefore, when faced with only a small amount of data, most deep learning models are not competent. However, studies have shown that humans can learn new classes in very few samples by exploiting prior knowledge and contextual connections [1]. Therefore, few-shot learning is proposed for imitating this generalization ability of humans.

In the task of few-shot learning, the main problem is that when there are only a small number of labeled samples, the features of the new class are not diverse enough, so the machine cannot obtain a comprehensive understanding of the new class. For the machine to better recognize new classes, prior knowledge is essential. In the past decade, most few-shot learning efforts have focused on how to transfer prior knowledge into base classes [2,3]. In recent years, with the development and inspiration of zero-shot learning [4,5], prior knowledge of other modalities has also been applied to few-shot learning [6–8]. In ZSL, the introduction of semantic knowledge is widespread [9,10] because it is challenging to complete ZSL tasks without semantic knowledge or other modal knowledge. In the FSL task, there have also been some FSL works introducing semantic knowledge in recent years [6,8]. Semantic knowledge is gradually introduced for FSL tasks because visual and semantic space is very related, and the alignment between them can be transferred to new classes through class-based computation.

In the task of few-shot learning, especially when the number of samples is only one, the visual features are often noisy or only local [11], making the visual features unobvious. In some cases, semantic knowledge can be more discriminative than visual features. For example, as shown in Fig. 1a, the Siberian husky and the Siberian wolf have no noticeable difference in vision; but in semantic knowledge, one is a canine, and the other is a wolf, and there is a clear difference. Therefore, when faced with this situation, these works [6–8,11,12] all use semantic knowledge to make up for the situation in Fig. 1a, making the visual features more discriminative. However, as shown in Fig. 1b, the two cats in the picture are very different visually, but semantically, they are both cats and are indistinguishable. Therefore, works such as [13,14] use guidance based on the samples to make visual features more discriminative. It is essential to use semantic knowledge to guide visual feature extraction, but it is equally important to use the samples themselves to guide visual feature extraction. Therefore, we propose a bimodal attention mechanism (VSA), which adaptively combines information from visuals and semantics and then pays attention to the visual prototype to make it more discriminative.

siberian husky   siberian wolf   cat   cat

a   b

Fig. 1. Some classes may have similar visual features and different semantic features, and some classes the opposite. Siberian husky and Siberian wolf are visually similar but have different semantic features; cat in b has similar semantic but distinct visual features.

2   Related Works

Small Sample Learning Setting: The setting of small sample learning usually has three sets of data, namely training set, support set, and query set. The support set, query set and training set are disjoint. The support set and query set correspond to the training set and test set in the general classification. On training and evaluation, images of each class are divided into a smaller support set and a larger query set. The number of classes per episode is called the mode, and the number of supporting images per episode is the shot so that a set with five classes and one labeled image forms a "5-way 1-shot"classification problem. Few-shot classifiers are trained on a large, disjoint set of classes, typically using the same scenario scheme for each batch iteration of SGD. Optimizing a few-shot classifier on a task distribution teaches it to generalize from similar distributions to new tasks.

Metric Learning in Few-Shot Learning: The main idea of metric learning methods in few-shot learning [15–17] are to learn a metric space with strong generalization through auxiliary tasks without updating parameters. It can be applied to new tasks. Since this method does not need to update the model parameters, it can avoid the over-fitting phenomenon of the target task to a certain extent. Furthermore, this kind of method can achieve relatively good performance in small sample classification. The classic few-shot learning baseline, the prototype network [6], is based on metric learning. The prototype network uses a neural network to learn a non-linear mapping of the input to the embedding space and takes the prototype of a class as the average of its support set in the embedding space. Then the problem is changed from the original classification problem to the nearest neighbor problem in the embedding space. When testing one sample, its category can be obtained by calculating the Euclidean distance between the sample and the prototype of each category.

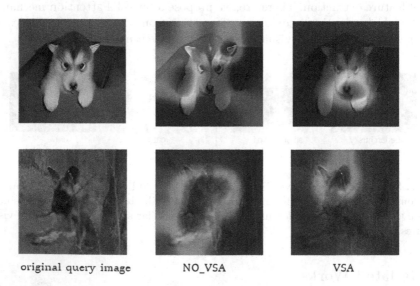

original query image   NO_VSA   VSA

Fig. 2. Our Grad-CAM visualization test on miniImageNet unseen classes in the 1-shot scenario. The first column is query images, and the second and third are Grad-CAM visualizations without and with VSA, respectively; the warmer the color, the higher the value.

Attention in Few-Shot Learning: In the few-shot learning field, sample-guided attention [13,14] and semantic-guided attention [6–8] are two main categories. The classic baseline network matching network for sample-guided attention uses the attention based on the softmax function to guide the prediction of the meta-learning classifier. Similar to the matching network, the cross attention network (cross attention) [14]. It uses the semantic dependencies between the support samples and the query samples to model and adaptively locates the relevant regions so that identifying the embedded features is beneficial to the simulation. Combined to form cross attention and manipulate feature maps. For semantic guided attention, the usual practice is to generate attention maps on visual features through word embeddings to capture the representative feature. The multi-attention network [18] uses word embeddings to generate attention feature maps on the visual features of examples. Like multi-attention networks, [12] developed an attention generator to localize relevant features in example images via word embeddings. Our work is similar to but different from the above work, and we propose an attention mechanism based on the above two categories- a sample-guided and semantic-guided bimodal attention mechanism (VSA). The main contributions of our work are two-fold:

1. We propose an attention mechanism based on two modalities, which adaptively fuses the information of the two modalities to generate a more accurate attention map, which can better capture more representative features.
2. In the case of few samples or fine-grained data, our mechanism can better guide the extraction of visual features. We furthermore achieved state-of-the-art results in experiments on the CUB dataset.

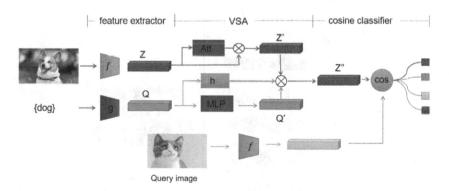

Fig. 3. This is the framework of our proposed VSA method, which consists of three parts: feature extractor, VSA, and cosine classifier. Where $\otimes$ is the Hadamard product, Z is the visual feature vector extracted by f, and Q is the word vector extracted by g.

3 Approach

In 3.1, we established a symbolic definition of the related problem. Then, in 3.2, we will focus on VSA.

3.1 Symbol Definition

Before training, we divide the dataset into a training set (D_{base}) and a support set(D_{novel}). The training set(D_{base}) contains M base classes, and each base class has m (m value is larger) labeled samples, the support set (D_{novel}) has only K (generally K is 1 or 5) labeled samples, and N new class. And $D_{base} \cap D_{novel} = \emptyset$, in other words, $M \cap N = \emptyset$. $\chi \in R^{ds}$ denotes visual space. We provide semantic information for each class $c \in M \cup N$ in terms of semantic information acquisition.

3.2 Framework

Fig. 3 Shows our entire network framework, which mainly consists of three parts: feature extraction, VSA, and cosine classifier.

Feature Extraction: Humans cannot learn a new class without prior knowledge, and the same goes for FSL methods, which cannot learn a new class (D_{novel}) without the help of a base class (D_{base}). We use the base class (D_{base}) to train the feature extractor f in the graph. After training with the base class (D_{base}), we fix the feature extractor as in many works and get the visual space χ and the feature vector Z. For semantic information extraction, we use the GloVe word embedding model [19] as our semantic information extractor g. GloVe is a word embedding model trained on the Wikipedia dataset, and its embeddings have dimension 300. In this way, we get a 300-dimensional word vector.

VSA: As shown in Fig. 3, our VSA module consists of three sub-modules, namely Att, MLP, and h.

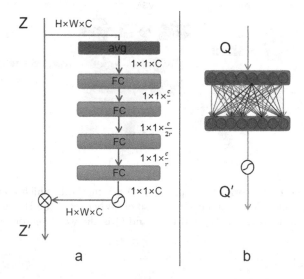

Fig. 4. This is the structure of Att and MLP, two essential components of VSA, , where $\otimes$ is the Hadamard product.

Att: The Att module structure is shown in Fig. 4a, which consists of three fully connected layers and one 2D convolutional layer. Inserting a ReLU between each fully connected layer and finally concatenating a non-linear function is the same as most works [20–22]. We first map the input $Z \in R^{H \times W \times C}$ to $V \in R^{H \times W \times C}$, and then denote the learned filter kernel set by $F = [f1, f2, ..., fc]$, where fc denotes the parameter of the c filter, and then set $V = [v1, v2, ..., vc]$ means output.

$$V_c = F_c * Z = \sum_{s=1}^{c} F_c^s * Z^s \tag{1}$$

Among them, $*$ represents convolution, $F_c = [F_c^1, F_c^2, F_c^3, ..., F_c^{c'}]$, $Z^s = [Z^1, Z^2, Z^3, ..., Z^{c'}]$, $V_c \in R^{H \times W}$, F_c^s a two-dimensional spatial kernel. Then, channel-level statistics are generated by global average pooling; in other words, the statistics $Z \in R^c$ is generated by shrinking V through its spatial dimension $H \times W$, namely:

$$Z_c = \frac{1}{H \times W} \sum_{i=1}^{H} \sum_{j=1}^{W} V_c(i, j) \tag{2}$$

After that, after three full connections and a non-linear function, we get Z_{map}:

$$Z_{map} = \partial(\frac{1}{1 + exp(Z_c)}) = \partial(\frac{1}{1 + exp(\frac{1}{H \times W} \sum_{i=1}^{H} \sum_{j=1}^{W} V_c(i, j))}) \tag{3}$$

Finally, after a 2D convolutional layer, we get the sample-based attention map Z'.

$$Z' = \sigma(conv(Z_{map} \otimes Z)) \tag{4}$$

where σ is the sigmoid activation function, $\otimes$ is the Hadamard product.

MLP: The MLP module is very similar in structure to the Att model. It consists of 2 fully connected layers with a dropout layer, followed by a sigmoid nonlinearity. His role is to map the resulting embedded word vector Q into the visual space. After going through the MLP model, we get the semantic attention map Q' with semantic information.

Weight generator (h): Although the visual space and the semantic spaceare very related, they have different structures. When faced with the situation as shown in Fig. 1, in order to better utilize the two modal information in different scenarios, we introduce an adaptive coefficient ε, to adaptively balance the guidance of the two modal information. For example, it is not easy to distinguish from the visual modalities in Fig. 1a scenario, and the network can use more semantic knowledge to guide visual attention. In Fig. 1b scenario, the information of the visual modalities is relatively apparent, while the semantic information is difficult to distinguish, so the network can use more visual attention to guide feature extraction. Therefore, the network generates the adaptive coefficient ε, which is calculated as follows:

$$\varepsilon = \frac{1}{1 + exp(-h(Q_m))} \tag{5}$$

where Q_m is the label embedding of class m; the h is an adaptive hybrid network with a parameter of θ_h.

Cosine Classifier: In addition to feature extractors, deep learning frameworks generally have a classifier. On multi-classification problems, the simplest classifier is to use softmax to calculate the classification score for classification. However, softmax is not reasonable in a small sample classification because the weights it generates are not controllable. So, in our work, we use the cosine classifier proposed by [23]. The cosine classifier calculates the classification score based on the cosine similarity $score(x) = \cos < x, x_k >$ to obtain the classification result. When using a cosine classifier, the weights of the classifiers are equivalent to the class prototypes in metric learning [23], so we generate the classification weights based on the support set D_{novel}. Based on the prototype network [2] we get the visual prototype of class c:

$$P_{avg}^c = \frac{1}{|D_c^n|} \sum_{(x_i, y_i) \in D_c^n} x_i \tag{6}$$

Due to the lack of samples, the visual prototype at this time is not accurate. Therefore, it is recommended to use our VSA to combine the attention of the two modalities. The final classification weight of class c is

$$W_c = P^c \otimes Z_map \otimes (\varepsilon \cdot Q') \tag{7}$$

Finally, the final classification score of the cosine classifier is:

$$score_c(x) = t \cdot \cos < x, W_c > \tag{8}$$

Among them, t is the cosine similarity coefficient, and $\cos < \cdot >$ is the cosine similarity calculation.

4   Experiments

In this section, we implement our VSA method on three benchmark datasets and compare it with two metric-based methods: Metric learning methods based on visual attention and metric learning methods based on semantic attention. Our experiments show that our VSA is effective. Furthermore, to further demonstrate that our VSA is adequate, we do related ablation experiments and visualizations in this section.

4.1   Comparison with State-of-the-Arts

This section will compare several FSL baseline models and popular methods. Table 1 and Table 2 show the results of the CIFAR-FS and CUB datasets, where KTN [24], TriNet [7], AM3 [8], SEGA [6], and our VSA all use semantic knowledge. In the 5-way 1-shot setting, our VSAs all achieve good performance and outperform methods like [6,8] that also use semantic knowledge. In the 5-way 5-shot setting, our results are not all optimal, but they are also competitive, and on the CUB dataset, our results are all optimal. In the face of this phenomenon, in Fig. 5, we show the reason: Our VSA performance improvement decreases as the number of shots increases. This phenomenon is because fewer samples per new class make the resulting visual prototype poorer and more affected by background and noise. Therefore, when the number of samples is small, the attention of the two modalities from the VSA can effectively avoid these effects and better present the visual prototype. However, as the number of shots increases, the visual information becomes more and more abundant, and the visual prototype tends to be stable and accurate, so our method is less and less helpful for the visual prototype.

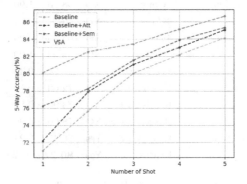

Fig. 5. 5-Way accuracy on CIFAR-FS from 1 to 5 Shot. Among them, baseline+att represents the baseline network plus visual attention, and baseline+Sem represents the baseline network plus semantic-guided attention.

Nevertheless, for the experimental results on the CUB dataset, our method is still beneficial for similar reasons as above. The CUB dataset is fine-grained, and the inter-class distances in the fine-grained dataset are very similar, and our method uses bimodal attention information to make the distinction between classes more obvious. Indirectly expands the distance between classes. Therefore, our method is more efficient on fine-grained data. The results in Table 3 show that our method also achieves good results on the miniImageNet.

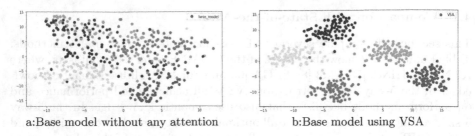

a:Base model without any attention   b:Base model using VSA

Fig. 6. Prototype visualization in visual space under 5-way 1-shot scene based on t-SNE. (a) is the visualization of the base model, and (b) is the visualization using VSA. All prototypes are generated during 500 rounds of testing on CIFAR-FS for five new unseen classes, and the color of the dots represents its class.

Table 1. Compare with other FSL methods on average classification (%). We report the average classification accuracy (%) on the test set of 5000 new classes (with 95% confidence intervals). "Sem" indicates whether to utilize semantic knowledge.

Model	Backbone	Sem	CIFAR-FS	
			5-way 1-shot	5-way 5-shot
MAML (ICML'17) [25]	4Conv	NO	58.90 ± 1.90	71.50 ± 1.00
ProtoNet (NIPS'17) [2]	4Conv	NO	55.50 ± 0.70	72.00 ± 0.60
R2-D2 [26]	4Conv	NO	65.30 ± 0.20	78.30 ± 0.20
RelationNet [17]	4Conv	NO	55.00 ± 1.00	69.30 ± 0.80
MTUNet+WRN [27]	WRN-28–10	NO	68.34 ± 0.49	82.93 ± 0.37
MetaOptNet (CVPR'19) [28]	ResNet-12	NO	72.00 ± 0.70	84.20 ± 0.50
RFS (ECCV'20) [29]	ResNet-12	NO	73.90 ± 0.80	86.90 ± 0.50
DSN-MR [30]	ResNet-12	NO	78.00 ± 0.90	$\mathbf{87.30 \pm 0.60}$
SGEA(WACV2022) [6]	ResNet-12	Yes	78.45 ± 0.24	86.00 ± 0.20
VSA	ResNet-12	Yes	$\mathbf{80.24 \pm 0.24}$	86.54 ± 0.19

Table 2. Results of the study on the CUB dataset. The test setup is the same as above.

Model	Backbone	Sem	CUB	
			5-way 1-shot	5-way 5-shot
MultiSem (CoRR'19) [31]	DenseNet-121	NO	$76.10 \pm n/a$	$82.90 \pm n/a$
FEAT (CVPR'20) [32]	ResNet-18	NO	68.87 ± 0.22	82.90 ± 0.15
Neg-Cosine (ECCV'20) [33]	ResNet-12	NO	69.17 ± 0.85	85.60 ± 0.56
DeepEMD (CVPR'20) [34]	ResNet-12	NO	75.65 ± 0.83	88.69 ± 0.50
AM3 (NIPS'19) [8]	ResNet-12	Yes	73.6	79.9
TriNet (TIP'19) [7]	ResNet-18	Yes	69.16 ± 0.46	84.10 ± 0.35
AGAM(AAAI-2021)	ResNet-12	Yes	79.58 ± 0.23	87.17 ± 0.23
MAP-Net(2022) [35]	ResNet-12	Yes	82.45 ± 0.23	88.30 ± 0.17
SGEA(WACV2022) [6]	ResNet-12	Yes	84.57 ± 0.22	90.85 ± 0.16
VSA	ResNet-12	Yes	$\mathbf{87.71 \pm 0.21}$	$\mathbf{92.66 \pm 0.15}$

4.2 Visualization

In this section, to better understand what our VSA does, we use Grad-CAM [36] to visualize the testing of our backbone model on miniImageNet unseen classes. As shown in Fig. 2, when our backbone network does not use VSA, the backbone network is easily disturbed by background noise so that the background may play a role as an essential feature of this class during recognition. However, when our backbone network adds our VSA, it can be seen that it now pays more attention to the object and does not pay too much attention to the background to obtain more essential features. Furthermore, to demonstrate that our VSA can expand the inter-class distance and shrink the intra-class distance. We used t-SNE for visualization. Figure 6 shows the changes in prototypes before and after applying VSA in the CIFAIR-FS dataset 5-Way 1-Shot scenario. As shown in the figure, before not using VSA, the generated visual prototype is very unstable; after using VSA, the generated visual prototype becomes more stable, the distance between classes becomes large, and the intra-class distance becomes small.

Table 3. Results of the study on the miniImageNet. The test setup is the same as above.

Model	Backbone	Sem	miniImageNet	
			5-way 1-shot	5-way 5-shot
MAML (ICML'17) [25]	4Conv	NO	58.9 ± 1.9	71.5 ± 1.0
Matching Networks (NIPS'16) [3]	4Conv	NO	45.56 ± 0.84	55.31 ± 0.73
ProtoNet (NIPS'17) [2]	4Conv	NO	49.42 ± 0.78	68.20 ± 0.66
KTN (ICCV'19) [24]	4Conv	Yes	64.42 ± 0.72	74.16 ± 0.56
MetaOptNet (CVPR'19) [28]	ResNet-12	NO	62.64 ± 0.61	78.63 ± 0.46
RFS (ECCV'20) [29]	ResNet-12	NO	64.82 ± 0.60	$\mathbf{82.14 \pm 0.43}$
Neg-Cosine (ECCV'20) [33]	ResNet-12	NO	63.85 ± 0.81	81.57 ± 0.56
TriNet (TIP'19) [7]	ResNet-18	Yes	58.12 ± 1.37	76.92 ± 0.69
SGEA(WACV2022) [6]	ResNet-12	Yes	69.04 ± 0.26	79.03 ± 0.18
AM3 (NIPS'19) [8]	ResNet-12	Yes	65.30 ± 0.49	78.10 ± 0.36
VSA	ResNet-12	Yes	$\mathbf{70.32 \pm 0.23}$	80.27 ± 0.17

4.3 Ablation Study

In this subsection, we will conduct ablation experiments on our method to verify further that our method is effective. As shown in Table 4, we compare the use of no attention (first row), only visual attention (second row), only semantic attention (third row), and both (fourth row) performance to infer that our method can significantly improve performance. As shown in Table 4, the performance of our VSA in the CIFAR-FS dataset 5-way 1-shot scenario is 9% higher than that without any attention; 8%, and 4% higher than that with single attention, respectively; In the 10-way 1-shot scenario, it is 8% higher than when no attention using; 6% and 4% higher than when using single attention.

Table 4. Ablation experiments of our proposed method on CIFAR-FS. We report the average classification accuracy (%) (95% confidence interval) on a test set of 5000 novel classes, with *Att* for visual attention, *Sem* for semantic knowledge, and $\sqrt{}$ for usage.

Model	Module	Module	CIFAR-FS	CIFAR-FS
	Att	*Sem*	5-way 1-shot	10-way 1-shot
model1			71.05 ± 0.29	56.47 ± 0.20
model2	$\sqrt{}$		72.19 ± 0.29	58.55 ± 0.20
model3		$\sqrt{}$	76.24 ± 0.25	61.77 ± 0.17
VSA	$\sqrt{}$	$\sqrt{}$	$\mathbf{80.09 \pm 0.24}$	$\mathbf{65.11 \pm 0.17}$

5   Conclusions

In this work, we propose an efficient few-shot learning method, Bimodal Attention (VSA). VSA fuses information from both visual and semantic modalities to provide top-down guidance on which features the network should focus on to capture more representative features better. Our method validates its effectiveness on three benchmarks, especially on fine-grained image datasets and when the new class has only one labeled sample. In addition, we also perform ablation experiments on this to further verify that our VSA is reasonable and practical.

References

1. Markman, E.M.: Categorization and naming in children: problems of induction. MIT Press (1989)
2. Snell, J., Swersky, K., Zemel, R.: Prototypical networks for few-shot learning. Advances in neural information processing systems, vol. 30 (2017)
3. Vinyals, O., et al.: Matching networks for one shot learning. Advances in Neural Information Processing Systems, vol. 29 (2016)
4. Palatucci, M., Pomerleau, D., Hinton, G.E., Mitchell, T.M.: Zero-shot learning with semantic output codes. In: Advances in Neural Information Processing Systems, vol. 22 (2009)
5. Wang, W., Zheng, V.W., Yu, H., Miao, C.: A survey of zero-shot learning: settings, methods, and applications. ACM Trans. Intell. Syst. Technol. (TIST) **10**(2), 1–37 (2019)
6. Yang, F., Wang, R., Chen, X.: Sega: semantic guided attention on visual prototype for few-shot learning. In: Proceedings of the IEEE/CVF Winter Conference on Applications of Computer Vision, pp. 1056–1066 (2022)
7. Chen, Z., Fu, Y., Zhang, Y., Jiang, Y.-G., Xue, X., Sigal, L.: Multi-level semantic feature augmentation for one-shot learning. IEEE Trans. Image Process. **28**(9), 4594–4605 (2019)
8. Xing, C., Rostamzadeh, N., Oreshkin, B., Pinheiro, P.O.O.: Adaptive cross-modal few-shot learning. In: Advances in Neural Information Processing Systems, vol. 32 (2019)

9. Socher, R., Ganjoo, M., Manning, C.D. Ng, A.: Zero-shot learning through cross-modal transfer. In: Advances in Neural Information Processing Systems, vol. 26 (2013)
10. Kodirov, E., Xiang, T., Gong, S.: Semantic autoencoder for zero-shot learning. In: Proceedings of the IEEE Conference on Computer Vision and Pattern Recognition, pp. 3174–3183 (2017)
11. He, K., Fan, H., Wu, Y., Xie, S., Girshick, R.: Momentum contrast for unsupervised visual representation learning, in: Proceedings of the IEEE/CVF Conference on Computer Vision and Pattern Recognition, pp. 9729–9738 (2020)
12. Chu, W.-H., Wang, Y.-C. F.: Learning semantics-guided visual attention for few-shot image classification. In: 2018 25th IEEE International Conference on Image Processing (ICIP), pp. 2979–2983. IEEE (2018)
13. Ren, M., Liao, R., Fetaya, E., Zemel, R.: Incremental few-shot learning with attention attractor networks. In: Advances in Neural Information Processing Systems, vol. 32 (2019)
14. Hou, R., Chang, H., Ma, B., Shan, S., Chen, X.: Cross attention network for few-shot classification. In: Advances in Neural Information Processing Systems, vol. 32 (2019)
15. Koch, G., et al.: Siamese neural networks for one-shot image recognition. In: ICML Deep Learning Workshop, Vol. 2, p. 0. Lille (2015)
16. Nickel, M., Kiela, D.: Poincaré embeddings for learning hierarchical representations. In: Advances in Neural Information Processing Systems, vol. 30 (2017)
17. Sung, F., Yang, Y., Zhang, L., Xiang, T., Torr, P.H., Hospedales, T.M.: Learning to compare: relation network for few-shot learning. In: Proceedings of the IEEE Conference on Computer Vision and Pattern Recognition, pp. 1199–1208 (2018)
18. Wang, P., Liu, L., Shen, C., Huang, Z., Van Den Hengel, A., Tao Shen, H.: Multi-attention network for one shot learning. In: proceedings of the IEEE Conference on Computer Vision and Pattern Recognition, pp. 2721–2729 (2017)
19. Pennington, J., Socher, R., Manning, C.D.: Glove: global vectors for word representation. In: Proceedings of the 2014 Conference on Empirical Methods in Natural Language Processing (EMNLP), pp. 1532–1543 (2014)
20. Hu, J., Shen, L., Sun, G.: Squeeze-and-excitation networks In: Proceedings of the IEEE Conference on Computer Vision and Pattern Recognition, pp. 7132–7141 (2018)
21. Woo, S., Park, J., Lee, J.-Y., Kweon, I.S.: Cbam: convolutional block attention module. In: Proceedings of the European Conference on Computer Vision (ECCV), pp. 3–19 (2018)
22. Park, J., Woo, S., Lee, J.-Y., Kweon, I.S.: Bam: bottleneck attention module, arXiv preprint arXiv:1807.06514 (2018)
23. Qi, H., Brown, M., Lowe, D.G.: Low-shot learning with imprinted weights. In: Proceedings of the IEEE Conference on Computer Vision and Pattern Recognition, pp. 5822–5830 (2018)
24. Peng, Z., Li, Z., Zhang, J., Li, Y., Qi, G.-J., Tang, J.: Few-shot image recognition with knowledge transfer. In: Proceedings of the IEEE/CVF International Conference on Computer Vision, pp. 441–449 (2019)
25. Finn, C., Abbeel, P., Levine, S.: Model-agnostic meta-learning for fast adaptation of deep networks. In: International Conference on Machine Learning, pp. 1126–1135. PMLR (2017)
26. Bertinetto, L., Henriques, J.F., Torr, P.H., Vedaldi, A.: Meta-learning with differentiable closed-form solvers, arXiv preprint arXiv:1805.08136 (2018)

27. Wang, B., Li, L., Verma, M., Nakashima, Y., Kawasaki, R., Nagahara, H.: Match them up: visually explainable few-shot image classification, arXiv preprint arXiv:2011.12527 (2020)
28. Lee, K., Maji, S., Ravichandran, A., Soatto, S.: Meta-learning with differentiable convex optimization. In: Proceedings of the IEEE/CVF Conference on Computer Vision and Pattern Recognition, pp. 10657–10665 (2019)
29. Tian, Y., Wang, Y., Krishnan, D., Tenenbaum, J.B., Isola, P.: Rethinking few-shot image classification: a good embedding is all you need? In: Vedaldi, A., Bischof, H., Brox, T., Frahm, J.-M. (eds.) ECCV 2020. LNCS, vol. 12359, pp. 266–282. Springer, Cham (2020). https://doi.org/10.1007/978-3-030-58568-6_16
30. Simon, C., Koniusz, P., Nock, R., Harandi, M.: Adaptive subspaces for few-shot learning. In: Proceedings of the IEEE/CVF Conference on Computer Vision and Pattern Recognition, pp. 4136–4145 (2020)
31. Schwartz, E., Karlinsky, L., Feris, R., Giryes, R., Bronstein, A.M.: Baby steps towards few-shot learning with multiple semantics, arXiv preprint arXiv:1906.01905 (2019)
32. Ye, H.-J., Hu, H., Zhan, D.-C., Sha, F.: Few-shot learning via embedding adaptation with set-to-set functions. In: Proceedings of the IEEE/CVF Conference on Computer Vision and Pattern Recognition, pp. 8808–8817 (2020)
33. Liu, B., et al.: Negative margin matters: understanding margin in few-shot classification. In: Vedaldi, A., Bischof, H., Brox, T., Frahm, J.-M. (eds.) ECCV 2020. LNCS, vol. 12349, pp. 438–455. Springer, Cham (2020). https://doi.org/10.1007/978-3-030-58548-8_26
34. Zhang, C., Cai, Y., Lin, G., Shen, C.: Deepemd: few-shot image classification with differentiable earth mover's distance and structured classifiers. In: Proceedings of the IEEE/CVF Conference on Computer Vision and Pattern Recognition, pp. 12203–12213 (2020)
35. Ji, Z., Hou, Z., Liu, X., Pang, Y., Han, J.: Information symmetry matters: a modal-alternating propagation network for few-shot learning. IEEE Trans. Image Process. **31**, 1520–1531 (2022)
36. Selvaraju, R.R., Cogswell, M., Das, A., Vedantam, R., Parikh, D., Batra, D.: Grad-cam: visual explanations from deep networks via gradient-based localization. In: Proceedings of the IEEE International Conference on Computer Vision, pp. 618–626 (2017)

Evolutionary Multitasking for Coarse-to-Fine Point Cloud Registration with Chaotic Opposition Search Strategy

Yue Wu[1], Hangqi Ding[1], Maoguo Gong[2(✉)], Hao Li[2], Qiguang Miao[1], and Wenping Ma[3]

[1] School of Computer Science and Technology, Xidian University, Xi'an, China
ywu@xidian.edu.cn, hqding@stu.xidian.edu.cn
[2] School of Electronic and Engineering, Xidian University, Xi'an, China
gong@ieee.org
[3] School of Artificial Intelligence, Xidian University, Xi'an, China
wpma@mail.xidian.edu.cn

Abstract. Point cloud registration is a challenging task in both computer vision and pattern recognition. In general, the success of well-known registration algorithms depends heavily on the assumption of an initial near-optimal transformation. To address this problem, we propose a coarse-to-fine point cloud registration algorithm based on evolutionary multitasking. Specifically, the point cloud registration problem is solved by knowledge sharing before the coarse alignment task and the fine alignment task. In addition, an effective knowledge transfer mechanism and chaotic opposition search strategy are also developed to improve the effective knowledge transfer between tasks and enhance the exploration of more unknown areas in the population, respectively. The performance of the new approach is examined on 14 models from two datasets and compared with 6 competitive methods. Experimental results show that the new approach has the best robustness and accuracy. The new approach improved the registration success rate by 68% through evolutionary multitasking without providing initial transformation information.

Keywords: Evolutionary multitasking · Point cloud registration · Knowledge transfer · Chaotic opposition search

1 Introduction

Point cloud registration is a fundamental task in computer vision, where the goal is to find the optimal transformation between the source point cloud set and the

Supported by the Key-Area Research and Development Program of Guangdong Province (2020B090921001), the National Natural Science Foundation of China (62036006), the Natural Science Basic Research Plan in Shaanxi Province of China (2022JM-327) and the CAAI-Huawei MINDSPORE Academic Open Fund.

target point cloud set. Point cloud registration is widely used in pattern recognition [1], autonomous driving [2], medical images [3], etc. Over the past few decades, numerous registration algorithms have been proposed to obtain accurate alignment results, but they always face some challenges [4–6]. For example, a large number of outliers or noise lead to poor registration robustness, poor initial misalignment leads to trapping in local optima. Therefore, designing a registration approach that is robust and does not require prior alignment information has always been a very important and difficult problem.

Iterative Closest Point (ICP) is a well-known standard to point cloud registration problems, which is often used in the fine registration stage [7]. The ICP method is less robust to partially overlapping cases. Trimmed ICP (TrICP) was proposed to improve the robustness [8]. However, the optimal nature of such methods requires some further assumptions. For example, they assumed that initially provided a near-optimal pose estimate (with small transformations). Otherwise, the alignment process may get stuck in local minima. More critically, there is no reliable way to judge if it is trapped in a local minimum.

One of the main advantages of evolutionary algorithm-based registration methods is that they do not need to provide an accurate estimate of the initial pose [9,11]. Although various evolutionary algorithms have been successfully applied to solve the registration problem, then fine registration methods are used to obtain higher alignment results [12–15]. Existing algorithms are based on an important assumption, i.e., the alignment results should be within the convergence region of fine methods. It is impossible to predict in advance. If the opposite happens, the solution may be far from the optimal solution. Thus, the challenge of coarse-to-fine point cloud registration is the low success rate.

Evolutionary multitasking is an emerging research in evolutionary computation. The goal of evolutionary multitasking is to simultaneously optimize multiple related tasks. The knowledge contained in one task can be leveraged by other tasks to improve the performance of all tasks at hand. Evolutionary multitasking has been widely used in many practical optimization problems, e.g., sparse reconstruction problems [16], job shop scheduling problems [17], and feature selection problems [18]. Inspired by solving complex problems through information sharing in multitasking, this paper develops an efficient coarse-to-fine point cloud registration method based on evolutionary multitasking. This method is designed to address the low success rate of registration.

The two registration tasks in this study consist of the same pair of point cloud data, but the purpose of the tasks and the accuracy of the results are different. Specifically, one registration task is to align the sampled point cloud data. Another task is to align the unsampled point cloud data. Since the two data sets have the target of aligning the same model, a multi-task optimization problem can be formulated. In this multitasking system, the task of aligning the sampled point cloud is used to provide an initial transformation for the task with the original point cloud data, helping it to find a better transformation solution.

The main contributions of this paper are as follows:

1. We proposed a new method for coarse-to-fine point cloud registration via evolutionary multitasking. Knowledge transfer between two related alignment tasks significantly enhances registration success rate.
2. We develop efficient knowledge transfer mechanisms that reduce ineffective the fine registration task. Reasonable application of fine registration operations to improve the quality of task solutions.
3. We design a chaos opposition search strategy, which can effectively enhance the exploration of more unexplored regions in populations during evolution.

This paper is organized as follows. Section 2 gives related works on point cloud registration and multitask optimization. In Sect. 3, we describe the proposed method in detail. Section 4 presents experiments on real datasets, and gives the experimental analysis. Finally, Sect. 5 draws the conclusions.

2 Related Works

2.1 Point Cloud Registration

Coarse Registration. Coarse registration is the initial step when the relative pose of the point cloud is completely unknown, which provides a good initial position for fine registration. Evolutionary algorithms have been successfully applied to coarse registration stage. They are considered a promising approach due to the fact that global search for optimal solutions can be achieved without prior registration knowledge. Various evolutionary algorithms are used, i.e., Particle Swarm Optimization Algorithm [9–11], Differential Evolution Algorithm [12,13], Genetic Algorithm [14,15], Ant Colony Algorithm [19]. All their alignment results need to be further solved by the fine methods. There is no guarantee that their coarse registration results can be accepted by the fine methods.

Fine Registration. Fine registration minimizes spatial position differences between two point clouds. Fine registration methods mainly include ICP-family and probability-based methods [20]. ICP can be regarded as a milestone in point cloud registration. There are many variants of ICP [21–23]. Probabilistic-based methods use Gaussian mixture models to represent point clouds, and the registration problem is reformulated as an alignment problem of two Gaussian mixtures [24,25]. Probability-based methods are less sensitive to initialization than ICP-family. However, the results are not as predictable as ICP.

2.2 Evolutionary Multitask Optimization

Evolutionary Multitask Optimization aims to reveal the multitasking potential of evolutionary algorithms. Evolutionary multitasking builds on the implicit parallelism of swarm-based algorithms, while accelerating the convergence of multiple optimization tasks by exploiting their potential complementarity. In particular, a unified random key scheme is used to combine the design spaces of different tasks into a unified pool of genetic material. Each individual in the population can be decoded as a solution to a specific task. Evolutionary multitasking has been successfully used to solve different optimization problems in practice [16–18, 26].

3   Method

In this section, we propose a novel approach to point cloud registration via evolutionary multitasking. The description of the problem and the definition of the task are given first. The details of the two design mechanisms are then described. Finally, it presents the evaluation function of tasks.

3.1   Problem Statement

Take two point clouds X, Y as an example, the relationship between X and Y can be defined as:

$$y_i = Rx_i + t \tag{1}$$

where $x_i \in X$, $y_i \in Y$. $R \in SO(3)$ is an orthogonal rotation matrix, t is a 3×1 translation vector.

The point cloud registration problems can be formulated as a robust estimation problem:

$$\underset{R,t}{\text{minimize}} \sum_{i=1}^{N} \rho \left(\|y_i - (Rx_i + t)\| \right) \tag{2}$$

where $\{(x_i, y_i)\}_1^N$ is a set of correspondences with noise and outliers, $\rho(\cdot)$ is a robust cost function, and $\| \cdot \|$ is the l_2-norm.

3.2   Task Definition

The alignment process is divided into two stages, namely the coarse registration stage and the fine registration stage. Coarse-to-fine point cloud registration can be considered as a multi-task optimization problem since related tasks have similar functional landscapes. In this study, we develop two different point cloud sets (a sampled subset and the whole original set) based on the same set of point cloud pairs. They have different alignment difficulty and accuracy. ST1 is the coarse alignment of the sampled subset, ST2 is the fine alignment of the entire original point set.

Sampling often degrades the resolution of point clouds, resulting in a loss of registration accuracy. For ST1, the sampled subset has a smaller number of point clouds. It can quickly converge to a rough solution via a robust fitness function. The rough solution is used as the prior knowledge to the fine registration stage. The unsampled original point cloud has a higher resolution and can obtain more accurate alignment results. Evolutionary multitasking is employed to leverage the knowledge of the designed sampled simple task and the original task to improve alignment accuracy, and greatly improve the alignment success rate.

3.3   Knowledge Transfer

Fine alignment requires prior information from coarse alignment. Therefore, it is very important to judge when to pass the information from the coarse alignment task ST1 to the fine alignment task ST2. If the search convergence speed of a task is accelerated, it should appropriately reduce the knowledge exchange with other tasks, and the offspring are mainly produced by the self-evolution of the current task. Conversely, if the search for the current task converges slowly, knowledge from other tasks needs to be used to help it converge. Therefore, we estimate the convergence trend of ST1 by comparing the fitness value of the current individual with that of the previous two generations. let g denote the current generation, i is the i-th individual. The fitness values on task ST1 in the current generation and the two previous generations are recorded as F_g^{ST1}, F_{g-1}^{ST1}, and F_{g-2}^{ST1}. We can get the differences of the fitness value among three generations,

$$D_{1,g}^i = |F_g^i - F_{g-1}^i| \tag{3}$$

$$D_{2,g}^i = |F_{g-1}^i - F_{g-2}^i| \tag{4}$$

where $|\cdot|$ calculates the absolute value.

If $D_{1,g}^i > D_{2,g}^i$, it indicates that the convergence rate of the individual is accelerating. The self-evolution within the task tends to obtain better convergence. If $D_{1,g}^i \leq D_{2,g}^i$, the individual did not gain a better solution by communicating with individuals within the task. Therefore, passing knowledge from another task is more likely to improve the convergence of the task.

We calculate the value of $|D_{1,g}^i - D_{2,g}^i|$ and sort. Then select the individual with the smallest difference and perform knowledge transfer with the fine alignment task ST2.

3.4   Chaos Opposition Search

The limitation of the coarse alignment task ST1 is that its solutions are continuously further optimized by the fine alignment task, which means that the efficiency of ST1 landscape navigation continues to decline. The core of opposite learning is to consider a candidate solution and its corresponding opposite candidate solution simultaneously [27]. Opposite candidate solutions are more likely to be close to the global optimum than randomly generated solutions. Chaotic motion can traverse all states within a certain range according to unique laws [28]. We generalize the concept of opposite learning to the multitasking point cloud registration problem, exploiting the upper and lower bounding to generate opposing solutions. And the chaotic space search strategy is introduced to perturb the opposite solution space to make it have different search ranges.

We take the upper bound U and lower bound L of the unified express space as the search boundaries. The opposite solution of offspring o_1 is

$$o_2 = sr \times (U + L) - o_1 \tag{5}$$

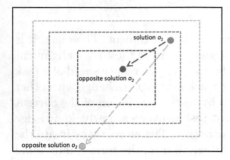
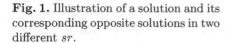
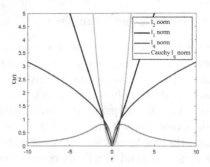

Fig. 1. Illustration of a solution and its corresponding opposite solutions in two different sr.

Fig. 2. The cost function curves, where r represents residual and $C(r)$ represents cost.

where o_2 is opposite solution. sr is a scaling rate, which is determined by dynamic chaos value. Different sr can expand or narrow the spatial search range.

Figure 1 shows an example of a solution o_1 and its opposite solution o_2, where the red rectangle represents the shrinkable search subspace and the blue rectangle represents the extended search subspace. A suitable range of sr can speed up the convergence speed, while increasing diversity. Specifically, a smaller range of sr focuses on searching the local subspace, while a larger range of sr allows to expand exploration in more potential regions. Through the chaos opposition search strategy, the coarse alignment task ST1 can comprehensively search for feasible solutions in different ranges of potential regions.

3.5   Fitness Function

In previous studies, the l_2 distance was used to measure the alignment error. As shown in Fig. 2, the l_2-norm cost curve increases quadratically with residuals, which leads to large deviation caused by outliers and partial overlaps. The l_1-norm distance gives equal emphasis to all residuals, but outliers still largely interfere to the total cost. The curve of l_q-norm is much flatter, which can greatly reduce the influence of outliers. In this paper, we adopt a robust Cauchy weighted l_q-norm error metric. Specifically, we formulate the coarse alignment problem as:

$$\underset{R,t}{\arg\min} \sum_{i=1}^{N} \|w_i(\boldsymbol{y}_i - (\boldsymbol{R}\boldsymbol{x}_i + \boldsymbol{t}))\|_q^q + \tau log(1 + (1 - \frac{I}{N})^2) \qquad (6)$$

where w_i is the weights of residuals, τ is a balance factor, N is the number of pairwise correspondences, and I is the number that is considered to be the true correspondence. We use the Cauchy function to calculate weights:

$$w_i = \frac{1}{1 + (e_i/k)^2} \qquad (7)$$

where k is a scale factor and $e_i = \|\boldsymbol{y}_i - (\boldsymbol{R}\boldsymbol{x}_i + \boldsymbol{t})\|$ is an residual.

For the fine alignment task, the TrICP algorithm is the best alignment for dealing with partially overlapping point clouds. Assume that the overlapping percentage is denoted as r and the corresponding overlapping part of X can be denoted as $X_r \in X$. Then the fine alignment problem can be defined as:

$$\min_{R,t,r} \frac{1}{N'} \sum_{x_i \in X_r} \|y_i - (Rx_i + t)\|^2 \tag{8}$$

where $N' = |X_r|$ is the number of points in X_r.

4   Experiments

4.1   Datasets and Settings

Datasets. We comprehensively evaluate the proposed method on two public and popular real-world point cloud datasets, i.e. the Stanford 3D Scanning Repository and the Statue Model Repository. The Stanford Repository contains partially overlapping and large transformed scan data, and their ground-truth transformations are available. The Statue Model Repository are the datasets containing various types of statues.

Compared Methods. We provide five comparison algorithms, including ICP [7], TrICP [8], GHS [29], AKT [30], and MKT [31]. Among them, ICP and TrICP are classic point cloud registration algorithms. GHS, AKT, and MKT are different evolutionary multitask optimization algorithms proposed for efficient transfer of useful knowledge.

Evaluating Metrics. We adapt two widely used metrics for quantitative evaluation: rotation error E_R and translation error E_t.

$$\begin{cases} E_R = \arccos \dfrac{\operatorname{tr}(R^t (R^e)^T) - 1}{2} \\ E_t = \|t^t - t^e\| \end{cases} \tag{9}$$

where R^t and R^e are the true rotation matrix and the estimated one, respectively. t^t and t^e are the true translation vector and the estimated one, respectively. $\operatorname{tr}(\cdot)$ stands for the trace of a matrix.

In addition, we adopt the root mean square error ($RMSE$) to uniformly evaluate the R^e and t^e of the Statue Model Repository dataset.

$$RMSE = \sqrt{\frac{1}{N} \sum_{i=1}^{N} \|\mathbf{R}^t x_i + t^t - \mathbf{R}^e x_i - t^e\|^2} \tag{10}$$

Experimental Setup. Regarding the hyperparameters, the maximum number of generations is 100 and the population size is 60. For ICP, convergence threshold is set to $1e - 5$ and the maximum number of inner iterations is 100. The overlap rate estimation parameter of TrICP is set to 2. For fair comparisons, the three multitasking optimization methods (GHS, AKT and MKT) use the same parameter settings as ours. Each scan is uniformly downsampled to nearly 3000 points. For each case, we performed the optimizations for 30 different sets of initial solutions. In ablation experiments, we independently optimized the two tasks with the same settings.

4.2   Results and Analysis

Stanford Repository. We first demonstrate the robustness and accuracy of our approach to scan pairs with limited overlap and large transformations on the Stanford Repository. We show alignment results and errors for four sets of point pairs. We then aligned all sets of scan pairs for each model, including 14 pairs of Buddha scans, 14 pairs of Dragon scans, 9 pairs of Bunny scans, 11 pairs of Armadillo scans. We report the mean of rotation errors and translation errors.

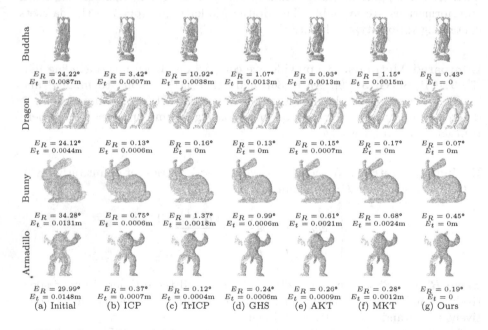

Fig. 3. Comparison of different methods on point clouds with partial overlaps.

Figure 3 compares alignment results on point cloud pairs with partial overlaps. In this registration, no initialization information is provided. ICP and TrICP get trapped in local minima and do not get satisfactory results. In particular, TrICP fail to align Buddha scan pairs ($E_R > 10°$). The three improved multitasking algorithms achieve similar alignment results. But they are not designed for the point cloud registration problems, so they can not take advantage of the coarse alignment task to provide prior knowledge for the fine alignment task. Our approach achieves the best results, which are very close to the ground truth.

Table 1 reports the quantitative evaluations of the average E_R and E_t on the whole 48 scan pairs. We added noise and outliers to each pair of scans to test the robustness of all methods. Without providing any initial pose, ICP and TrCIP mostly fail to align scan pairs. A single poor alignment greatly reduced their average performance. Our method ranks first among all models, while the average performance of GHS, AKT and MKT is comparable. Our method not only retains the advantage that the evolutionary algorithm does not require any initial pose, but also makes the registration results satisfactory through evolutionary multitask optimization.

Table 1. Results on the Stanford 3D Scanning Repository.

Method	Buddha(14 pairs)		Dragon(14 pairs)		Bunny(9 pairs)		Armadillo(11 pairs)	
	$E_R(°)$	$E_t(m)$	$E_R(°)$	$E_t(m)$	$E_R(°)$	$E_t(m)$	$E_R(°)$	$E_t(m)$
Initial	24.00	9.50E-03	24.00	1.75E-02	45.00	1.31E-02	30.01	1.31E-02
ICP	5.72	9.59E-04	3.28	8.15E-04	2.08	9.44E-04	1.86	9.20E-04
TrICP	13.05	4.90E-03	2.05	7.30E-04	2.52	5.80E-03	1.55	4.45E-04
GHS	3.29	7.23E-03	1.83	5.37E-04	1.88	6.89E-04	2.02	6.58E-04
AKT	2.11	3.93E-03	2.55	9.81E-04	1.67	3.60E-03	1.59	9.73E-04
MKT	1.99	4.60E-03	2.91	7.10E-04	2.04	4.50E-03	1.81	2.00E-03
Ours	**0.83**	**1.00E-03**	**0.94**	**2.84E-04**	**1.05**	**6.18E-04**	**0.77**	**4.08E-04**

Statue Model Repository. Then, we evaluate our approach on 10 different models from the Statue Model Repository. In a full model, we use the first 60% of points to create the source set, and the last 60% with a random rigid transformations to construct the target set. Table 2 show the average $RMSE$ for each method over the 10 instances. With a total of 8 instances, our method achieves the lowest $RMSE$ value.

Table 2. Results on the Statue Model Repository.

Method	Bear	Archer	Meduse	Monkeys	Bears	Eagle	Owl	Taichi	Horse	Naiade
ICP	59.4	23.4	8.5	17.2	29.4	17.2	**2**	12.4	12.6	20.7
TrICP	35.2	12.5	4.6	12.5	21.3	6.8	3.4	6.9	**4.3**	25.1
GHS	45.7	17	8.3	5.8	17.8	4.2	4.7	6.6	10.3	22.5
AKT	23.8	34.5	4.9	4.2	26.4	5.3	4	5.2	10.5	14.2
MKT	49.6	11.7	5.7	4.4	13.5	2.7	3.2	5.7	11.7	15.7
Ours	**5.9**	**5.3**	**2.6**	**3.8**	**6.1**	**1.2**	2.6	**2.1**	9.5	**8.3**

Ablation Study. Figure 4 shows the success rate of our method in the ablation experiment, where [0°, 20°), [20°, 40°), [40°, 60°), [60°, 80°) are represented as points 20°, 40°, 60°, 80° in the figure. If $E_R < 2°$ and $E_t < 0.005$ m, the alignment is considered successful. For problems with small rotation angles, all tasks achieve good performance. However, ST2 become very unreliable as the rotation increases, i.e. its success rate drops drastically. In the case of large rotation and translation, the success rate of our method is about 68% higher than that of ST2. Our method is less sensitive to initial translation and rotation than others.

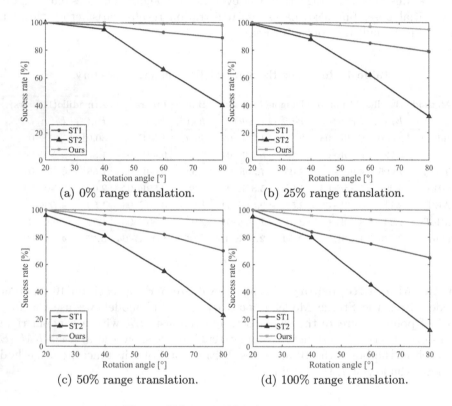

(a) 0% range translation.   (b) 25% range translation.

(c) 50% range translation.   (d) 100% range translation.

Fig. 4. Ablation study of our method.

5   Conclusions

In this paper, the coarse-to-fine point cloud registration problems is transformed into a multi-task optimization problem. We create two tasks, a coarse alignment task that aligns the sampled subsets, and a fine alignment task that aligns the original set of registration points. The division of labor and precision of these two tasks are different. The coarse alignment task requires extensive search of regions where optimal values may exist to provide initial positions for the fine alignment task. The fine alignment task obtains more accurate alignment results. In particular, we propose a new knowledge transfer strategy to achieve robust and efficient multi-task optimization performance. In addition, we propose a novel chaotic opposition search strategy. The search ability of the approach is enhanced by adding chaotic weights to the opposite feasible solutions. Experiments show that our proposed approach outperforms other methods on both real datasets.

References

1. Huang, X., Mei, G., Zhang, J.: Feature-metric registration: a fast semi-supervised approach for robust point cloud registration without correspondences. In: Proceedings of the IEEE Conference on Computer Vision and Pattern Recognition (CVPR), pp. 11366–11374 (2020)
2. Chen, S., Liu, B., Feng, C., Vallespi-Gonzalez, C., Wellington, C.: 3d point cloud processing and learning for autonomous driving: impacting map creation, localization, and perception. IEEE Signal Process. Mag. **38**(1), 68–86 (2020)
3. Wu, Y., Mu, G., Qin, C., Miao, Q., Ma, W., Zhang, X.: Semi-supervised hyperspectral image classification via spatial-regulated self-training. Remote Sens. **12**(1), 159 (2020)
4. Li, J., Zhao, P., Hu, Q., Ai, M.: Robust point cloud registration based on topological graph and Cauchy weighted lq-norm. ISPRS J. Photogramm. Remote. Sens. **160**, 244–259 (2020)
5. Fu, K., Liu, S., Luo, X., Wang, M.: Robust point cloud registration framework based on deep graph matching. In: Proceedings of the IEEE Conference on Computer Vision and Pattern Recognition (CVPR), pp. 8893–8902 (2021)
6. Wu, Y., Ma, W., Miao, Q., Wang, S.: Multimodal continuous ant colony optimization for multisensor remote sensing image registration with local search. Swarm Evol. Comput. **47**, 89–95 (2019)
7. Besl, P.J., McKay, N.D.: Method for registration of 3-D shapes. IEEE Trans. Pattern Anal. Mach. Intell. **14**(2), 239–256 (1992)
8. Chetverikov, D., Svirko, D., Stepanov, D., Krsek, P.: The trimmed iterative closest point algorithm. Object Recogn. Support. Interact. Serv. Robots **3**, 545–548 (2002)
9. Li, H., Shen, T., Huang, X.: Approximately global optimization for robust alignment of generalized shapes. IEEE Trans. Pattern Anal. Mach. Intell. **33**(6), 1116–1131 (2010)
10. Wu, Y., Miao, Q., Ma, W., Gong, M., Wang, S.: PSOSAC: particle swarm optimization sample consensus algorithm for remote sensing image registration. IEEE Geosci. Remote Sens. Lett. **15**(2), 242–246 (2017)
11. Zhan, X., Cai, Y., He, P.: A three-dimensional point cloud registration based on entropy and particle swarm optimization. Adv. Mech. Eng. **10**(12), 1–13 (2018)
12. Li, C.L., Dian, S.Y.: Dynamic differential evolution algorithm applied in point cloud registration. In: IOP Conference Series Materials Science and Engineering, vol. 428, pp. 012032 (2018)
13. Zhang, X., Yang, B., Li, Y., Zuo, C., Wang, X., Zhang, W.: A method of partially overlapping point clouds registration based on differential evolution algorithm. PLoS One **13**(12), 1–12 (2018)
14. Lomonosov, E., Chetverikov, D., Ekárt, A.: Pre-registration of arbitrarily oriented 3D surfaces using a genetic algorithm. Pattern Recognit. Lett. **27**(11), 1201–1208 (2006)

15. Ji, S., Ren, Y., Ji, Z., Liu, X., Hong, G.: An improved method for registration of point cloud. Optik Int. J. Light Electron Opt. **140**, 451–458 (2017)
16. Li, H., Ong, Y.S., Gong, M., Wang, Z.: Evolutionary multitasking sparse reconstruction: framework and case study. IEEE Trans. Evol. Comput. **23**(5), 733–747 (2018)
17. Zhang, F., Mei, Y., Nguyen, S., Zhang, M., Tan, K.C.: Surrogate-assisted evolutionary multitask genetic programming for dynamic flexible job shop scheduling. IEEE Trans. Evol. Comput. **25**(4), 651–665 (2021)
18. Chen, K., Xue, B., Zhang, M., Zhou, F.: An Evolutionary Multitasking-Based Feature Selection Method for High-Dimensional Classification. IEEE Trans, Cybern (2020)
19. Wu, Y., Gong, M., Ma, W., Wang, S.: High-order graph matching based on ant colony optimization. Neurocomputing **328**, 97–104 (2019)
20. Gojcic, Z., Zhou, C., Wegner, J.D., Guibas, L.J., Birdal, T.: Learning multiview 3D point cloud registration. In: Proceedings of the IEEE Conference on Computer Vision and Pattern Recognition (CVPR), pp. 1759–1769 (2020)
21. Deng, Z., Yao, Y., Deng, B., Zhang, J.: A robust loss for point cloud registration. In: Proceedings of the IEEE International Conference on Computer Vision (ICCV), pp. 6138–6147 (2021)
22. Babin, P., Giguere, P., Pomerleau, F.: Analysis of robust functions for registration algorithms. In: International Conference on Robotics and Automation (ICRA), pp. 1451–1457 (2019)
23. Rusinkiewicz, S.: A symmetric objective function for ICP. ACM Trans. Graphics. **38**(4), 1–7 (2019)
24. Eckart, B., Kim, K., Kautz, J.: HGMR: hierarchical gaussian mixtures for adaptive 3D registration. In: Ferrari, V., Hebert, M., Sminchisescu, C., Weiss, Y. (eds.) ECCV 2018. LNCS, vol. 11219, pp. 730–746. Springer, Cham (2018). https://doi.org/10.1007/978-3-030-01267-0_43
25. Hertz, A., Hanocka, R., Giryes, R., Cohen-Or, D.: PointGMM: a neural gmm network for point clouds. In: Proceedings of the IEEE Conference on Computer Vision and Pattern Recognition (CVPR), pp. 12054–12063 (2020)
26. Bi, Y., Xue, B., Zhang, M.: Learning and Sharing: A Multitask Genetic Programming Approach to Image Feature Learning. IEEE Trans. Evol, Comput (2021)
27. Simon, D.: Biogeography-based optimization. IEEE Trans. Evol. Comput. **12**(6), 702–713 (2008)
28. Mozaffari, A., Emami, M., Fathi, A.: A comprehensive investigation into the performance, robustness, scalability and convergence of chaos-enhanced evolutionary algorithms with boundary constraints. Artif. Intell. Rev. **52**(4), 2319–2380 (2019)
29. Liang, Z., Zhang, J., Feng, L., Zhu, Z.: A hybrid of genetic transform and hyperrectangle search strategies for evolutionary multi-tasking. Expert Syst. Appl. **138**, 1–18 (2019)
30. Zhou, L., et al.: Toward adaptive knowledge transfer in multifactorial evolutionary computation. IEEE Trans. Cybern. **51**(5), 2563–2576 (2020)
31. Liang, Z., Xu, X., Liu, L., Tu, Y., Zhu, Z.: Evolutionary Many-task Optimization Based on Multi-source Knowledge Transfer. IEEE Trans. Evol. Comput. **26**(2), 319–333 (2021)

Matching and Localizing: A Simple yet Effective Framework for Human-Centric Spatio-Temporal Video Grounding

Chaolei Tan, Jian-Fang Hu, and Wei-Shi Zheng[✉]

School of Computer Science and Engineering, Sun Yat-sen University,
Guangzhou 510006, China
tanchlei@mail2.sysu.edu.cn, hujf5@mail.sysu.edu.cn, wszheng@ieee.org

Abstract. Human-Centric Spatio-Temporal Video Grounding (HC-STVG) is a recently emerging task that aims to localize the spatio-temporal locations of the target person depicted in a natural language query. To tackle this task, we propose a simple yet effective two-stage framework, which is based on a *Matching and Localizing* paradigm. Under our framework, we decompose HC-STVG into two stages. In the first stage, we conduct cross-modal matching between the query and candidate moments to determine the temporal boundaries. Specifically, we develop an Augmented 2D Temporal Adjacent Network (Aug-2D-TAN) as our temporal matching module. In this module, we improve 2D-TAN [7] from two aspects: 1), A Temporal-Aware Context Aggregation module (TACA) to jointly aggregate the past contexts in forward direction and the future contexts in backward direction, which helps to learn more discriminative moment representations for cross-modal matching. 2), A Random Concatenation Augmentation (RCA) mechanism to combat overfitting and reduce the risk of unreasonably learning query-independent saliency prior, which is mistakenly provided by the training videos that only contain a single salient event. In the second stage, we utilize the pretrained MDETR [4] model to associate the language query with meaningful bounding boxes. Then, we conduct a query-based denoising procedure on the language-aware bounding boxes to obtain the frame-wise prediction for spatial localization. Experiments show that our simple yet effective framework can achieve a promising performance for the challenging HC-STVG task.

Keywords: Human-centric spatio-temporal video grounding ·
Matching and localizing · Temporal-aware context aggregation ·
Random concatenation augmentation

ⓒ The Author(s), under exclusive license to Springer Nature Switzerland AG 2022
L. Fang et al. (Eds.): CICAI 2022, LNAI 13604, pp. 305–316, 2022.
https://doi.org/10.1007/978-3-031-20497-5_25

1   Introduction

In recent years, the community has witnessed a surge of deep learning in the field of artificial intelligence. Once equipped with the powerful computation capacity of modern hardware devices, these data-driven technologies have shown great potential in a wide range of realistic applications, such as computer vision, natural language processing, etc. Nowadays, the multimedia data that people are exposed to in their daily life is incredibly exploding. Therefore, how to achieve intelligent human-computer interaction based on multimedia data has been a long-standing problem in the research community. In this work, we focus on the problem of Human-Centric Spatio-Temporal Video Grounding (HC-STVG) [6], which aims to bridge the two most important types of multimedia data, i.e., video and text, by the question-and-answer interactions between human and machines. Concretely, HC-STVG requires to localize the spatio-temporal locations in an untrimmed video corresponding to the person indicated by a language query. Compared to existing tasks such as temporal video grounding [7,9,10,13] and referring expression comprehension [4,12,15], HC-STVG task is more fascinating and more challenging since it aims to empower the machine with a strong ability to understand the complicated spatio-temporal cross-modal dependencies.

In this work, we propose a simple yet effective framework to tackle the task of HC-STVG in a two-stage manner, which is based on a *Matching and Localizing* paradigm. Under this framework, we first determine the best matching moment boundary from the temporal candidates and then predict the frame-wise spatial locations of the referred person. In the first stage, we mainly rely on the action-linguistic dependencies to conduct cross-modal matching between the query and temporal moments. Specifically, we develop a temporal matching module named Augmented 2D-TAN to determine the moment boundary. In the second stage, we mainly rely on the object-linguistic dependencies to conduct cross-modal localization in each frame that falls within the predicted moment. Specifically, we utilize the pretrained MDETR [4] model to associate the language query with meaningful box proposals, then a denoising procedure is conducted to obtain the frame-wise prediction for spatial localization. We show that by simply combining the two stages, the model can already achieve a promising performance in the challenging HC-STVG task, which demonstrates the effectiveness of our *Matching and Localizaing* paradigm.

In summary, our contributions are three-fold: (1) We propose a simple yet effective two-stage framework to tackle the problem of Human-Centric Spatio-Temporal Video Grounding (HC-STVG), which provides a basic paradigm and a strong baseline for future research progress. (2) We devise a Temporal-Aware Context Aggregation module (TACA) to jointly aggregate the past contexts in forward direction and the future contexts in backward direction, which helps to learn more discriminative moment features for better temporal matching. (3) We introduce the Random Concatenation Augmentation (RCA) into the training phase, which helps to combat overfitting and reduce the risk of mistakenly learning query-independent saliency prior.

2   Related Work

2.1   Referring Expression Comprehension

Referring Expression Comprehension (REC) aims to spatially localize the target object in an image according to a language query. REC is more challenging than the object detection task in computer vision, since it's not limited to a closed set of class labels and is only permitted to train with open queries while test with unseen queries. A large number of approaches [12, 15–18] have been explored and studied over the past few years. Mao et al. [15] introduced the first deep-learning method to jointly tackle referring expression generation and comprehension, they trained a CNN-LSTM network via maximizing the mutual likelihood of training pairs. Hu et al. [16] proposed a modular architecture called Compositional Modular Networks (CMNs) to model the pairwise interactions between image regions and the parsed compositional linguistic structures. Qiu et al. [18] proposed a language-aware deformable convolution model to adaptively extract a key-point object representation instead of the traditional rectangular representation for fine-grained cross-modal interaction.

2.2   Temporal Video Grounding

Temporal Video Grounding (TVG) is a task to localize the corresponding temporal boundaries based on a given language query that describes a specific event. To solve this problem, a variety of methods [7, 9–11, 13, 22–26] are proposed over these years. Gao et al. [10] designed a Cross-modal Temporal Regression Localizer (CTRL) to jointly model text query and video clips, outputting alignment scores and action boundary regression results for candidate clips. Ge et al. [11] proposed an actionness score enhanced Activity Concepts based Localizer (ACL) to mine the activity concepts from both the visual and linguistic modalities for activity localization via language query. Zhang et al. [7] proposed to model the temporal relations between video moments by a two-dimensional map, where moment localization is conducted by mathcing the moment-level features with referring expressions.

2.3   Spatio-Temporal Video Grounding

Human-Centric Spatio-Temporal Video Grounding (HC-STVG) is a challenging task that was recently proposed [6]. Unlike the existing saptial or temporal localization tasks based on referring expressions, HC-STVG requires the capability to conduct simultaneous spatial and temporal localization via referring expressions, i.e. localizaing a spatio-temporal tube in an untrimmed video that is indicated by the linguistic description. To tackle this task, Tang et al. [6] proposed a baseline method called Spatio-Temporal Grounding with Visual Transformers (STGVT), which utilizes Visual Transformers to extract cross-modal representations for video-sentence matching and temporal localization.

3   Methodology

3.1   Overview

Given an untrimmed video V and a language query Q, human-centric spatio-temporal video grounding aims to simultaneously localize the temporal moment of interest and the spatial boxes of referred person in each frame within the moment. Formally, the task could be formulated into the prediction of a spatio-temporal tube $\{o_i\}_{i=t_s}^{t_e}$, where t_s, t_e are the starting frame and ending frame of the target moment, respectively. And o_i indicates the spatial bounding box in the $i - th$ frame that falls within the localized moment (t_s, t_e).

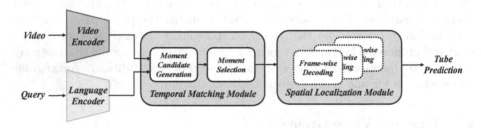

Fig. 1. Framework of our simple yet effective matching and localizing framework.

As presented in Fig. 1, we propose a simple yet effective framework to tackle HC-STVG in a two-stage manner, which mainly consists of a temporal matching module and a spatial localization module. In the first stage, the input video V is first passed into our temporal matching module named Augmented 2D-TAN to obtain a moment prediction $(\hat{t}_s, \hat{t}_e)$, which determines the temporal boundary of the final prediction. Then in the second stage, we feed the frames within the localized moment to the spatial localization module to acquire frame-wise bounding boxes referring to the person specified by the query. More will be discussed in further details below.

3.2   Temporal Matching Module

In this section, we will give a detailed illustration on the temporal matching module in our two-stage framework. Concretely, we devise an Aug-2D-TAN (as illustrated in Fig. 2) for accurate and robust moment matching. Our Aug-2D-TAN is developed based on 2D-TAN (2D Temporal Adjacent Networks) [7], while we mainly improve it from two aspects: 1), we design a Temporal-Aware Context Aggregation module (TACA) to learn more discriminative moment features by capturing the temporal dynamics; 2), we propose a Random Concatenation Augmentation (RCA) mechanism to combat the overfitting issue that most previous methods are prone to suffer from.

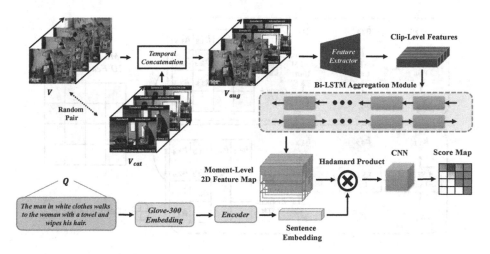

Fig. 2. Architecture of our temporal matching module Aug-2D-TAN.

3.3 2D Temporal Adjacent Network

In this part, we will give a brief recap of 2D-TAN to clarify some necessary preliminaries. Concretely, the input video is first split into N fixed-length clips and clip-wise visual features are extracted by a pretrained 3D-CNN. Then, 2D-TAN generates dense moment candidates in the form of a 2D map. In such a map, each map grid represents a temporal segment spanning across multiple clips, whose starting time and ending time are indicated by the 2D coordinate of the grid. Formally, the dense moment candidates $\mathcal{C}$ could be formulated as:

$$\mathcal{C} = \{C_{ij} = [S_i, S_{i+1}, ..., S_j] \,|\, 1 \leq i \leq j \leq N\} \tag{1}$$

where candidate C_{ij} spans from the i-th clip segment S_i to the j-th clip segment S_j. To obtain a compact representation of each moment candidate, a moment feature aggregation module $MFA(\cdot)$ is adopted to integrate clip-level features into moment-level features. Therefore, a moment-level 2D feature map $\mathcal{M} \in \mathbb{R}^{N \times N \times c}$ is constructed as follows:

$$\mathcal{M}_{ij} = \begin{cases} \text{MFA}\left([F_i, F_{i+1}, ..., F_j]\right) & i \leq j \\ \mathbf{0} & i > j \end{cases} \tag{2}$$

where F_i is the feature representation of clip segment S_i. After the construction of $\mathcal{M}$, we combine $\mathcal{M}$ with the sentence embedding extracted from the query and employ a stack of 2D convolutional layers to model the inter-moment contexts. Finally, an MLP network is used to predict the moment-wise matching scores between M and the language query. The moment with the highest matching score is selected as the temporal boundary of the spatio-temporal tube.

3.4 Temporal-Aware Context Aggregation

In 2D-TAN [7], $MFA(\cdot)$ is instantiated as a max-pooling operation. The max-pooling operation only preserves some globally salient information within the

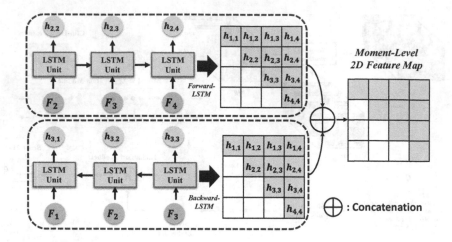

Fig. 3. The proposed Temporal-Aware Context Aggregation (TACA) module.

moment and is neither capable of capturing the intra-moment temporal dynamics nor the rich action details. This will become a significant defect that prevents the network from learning discriminative moment features for cross-modal matching. To improve the representation learning, we devise a Temporal-Aware Context Aggregation (TACA) module to dynamically aggregate the temporal contexts and action details, which is helpful to learn more discriminative and expressive moment representations for better cross-modal matching.

As shown in Fig. 3, the Temporal-Aware Context Aggregation module consists of a Forward-LSTM and a Backward-LSTM to separately encode the past temporal contexts and the future temporal contexts as follows:

$$\overrightarrow{H}_{ij} = \text{Forward-LSTM}([F_i, F_{i+1}, ..., F_j]) \tag{3}$$

$$\overleftarrow{H}_{ij} = \text{Backward-LSTM}([F_j, F_{j-1}, ..., F_i]) \tag{4}$$

$$\mathcal{M}_{ij} = concat\left(\overrightarrow{H}_{ij}, \overleftarrow{H}_{ij}\right) \tag{5}$$

Intuitively, the Forward-LSTM interacts a video clip with the past contexts that has happened before, i.e., learning the temporal dynamics in the forward direction. And the Backward-LSTM interacts a video clip with the future contexts that will happen afterwards, i.e., learning the temporal dynamics in the backward direction. Combining these two complementary components is an effective way to capture the bi-directional temporal dynamics and fine-grained action details within the moment. Consequently, compared to the original 2D-TAN, the moment features learned by our temporal matching module are more suitable for calculating the cross-modal matching score with the language query, leading to more precise temporal boundaries of the predictions. Note that the parameters of the Forward-LSTM and Backward-LSTM are shared across all moments, so we can implement the TACA module in parallel to improve computation efficiency.

3.5   Random Concatenation Augmentation

In the training process of 2D-TAN, we observe severe overfitting issue, which will significantly hurt the generalization ability of the model. Although there have been a large number of works that focus on the task of Temporal Video Grounding (TVG), none of the existing methods have discussed about the impact of data augmentation, which is necessarily needed to avoid unstable and unreasonable model training. In this work, for the first time, we introduce a Random Concatenation Augmentation (RCA) mechanism into the training phase of temporal grounding networks, which randomly selects training samples in pair and concatenates them to augment the training data. Specifically, we randomly select two videos (with similar frame rate) V, V' and their corresponding language queries Q, Q'. We augment the video training data as follows:

$$V_{aug} = \{V(t)\}_{t=\tau_s-\delta_1}^{\tau_e+\delta_2} \oplus \{V'(t)\}_{t=\tau_s'-\delta_1'}^{\tau_e'+\delta_2'}$$

$$s.t. \begin{cases} -\Delta \leq |V_{aug}| - |V| \leq \Delta \\ -\Delta \leq |V| - |V'| \leq \Delta \end{cases} \tag{6}$$

where τ_s (τ_s'), τ_e (τ_e') indicate the start frame index and end frame index of the ground truth moment, respectively. δ_1, δ_2, δ_1', δ_2' are temporal offsets that are randomly generated under the augmentation constraint. Operation $|\cdot|$ indicates getting the duration of a video, and Δ denotes the tolerance threshold for the difference of video duration in our augmentation constraint. We restrict the number of frames in V_{aug} to be similar to that of V, and the number of frames in V to be similar to that of V', as shown in the Eq. (6). $\oplus$ represents concatenation operation along the temporal dimension. We randomly assign Q or Q' as the query of V_{aug}. During training, we perform this augmentation with a probability of 0.5 for each training sample.

The proposed augmentation operation greatly enriches the diversity of training data, thus it helps a lot to alleviate the severe overfitting that previous methods are likely to suffer from. Furthermore, RCA reduces the risk of learning query-independent saliency prior. Empirically, we found that the model may unreasonably learn the query-independent saliency prior, i.e. a wrong prior that any moment containing a salient event would be identified as the output regardless of the language query, which is mistakenly provided by the training videos that contain a single salient event. To address this issue, RCA forces the ground-truth moments from different videos to simultaneously occur in one video. In this way, we guarantee there are at least two salient moments in the same video, hence the model have to learn a query-based cross-modal matching capability to distinguish the correct prediction.

4   Spatial Localization Module

In the second stage, we develop a spatial localization module to predict the frame-wise spatial locations of the target object. For each frame within the predicted moment, we adopt the pretrained MDETR [4] model to associate a set of meaningful bounding boxes with their matching descriptions (i.e., several words extracted from the language query) as language-aware proposals. To find the best matching proposal, we further design a denoising procedure to filter out the redundant bounding boxes in each frame. In more details, we first introduce an external language parser [8] to detect the subject words in the language query. Then, we discard the bounding boxes whose matching descriptions do not contain any one of the subject words or contain more than one subject word. Finally, we select the one with the longest matching description among the remaining bounding boxes in each frame as our output.

5   Experiments

5.1   Experimental Settings

Dataset. We evaluate our proposed framework on the HCSTVG dataset which was specially proposed in [6] for the task of Spatio-Temporal Video Grounding. HCSTVG dataset is human-centric and all the videos are captured in multi-person scenes. The query sentences contain rich and diverse referring expressions towards human activities. It consists of 4,500 and 1,160 moment-sentence pairs for training and testing, respectively.

Evaluation Metrics. We follow the previous work [6] to adopt m_vIoU and vIoU@R as our evaluation metrics. The vIoU metric is calculated as vIoU $= \frac{1}{|T_U|} \sum_{t \in T_I} \text{sIoU}_t$, where sIoU$_t$ indicates the spatial Intersection over Union between the predicted bounding box and the ground-truth bounding box in the i-th frame. T_U and T_I indicate the temporal intersection and temporal union between the predicted moment and the ground-truth moment. The m_vIoU is defined as the average vIoU across all the samples, and vIoU@R indicates the percentage of predictions that have a vIoU higher than R.

5.2   Implementation Details

We use SlowFast Network [2] pretrained on Kinetics-600 [1] and AVA [3] to extract visual features for each video clip, where each clip consists of a fixed number of 32 frames. In the random concatenation augmentation, the counterpart of certain video is randomly selected from those with similar fps, and the length of augmented video is guaranteed not to be too different from that of the original video. The hidden size of LSTM is 512 for the textual encoder module, and 256 for each unidirectional component in TACA module. The CNN is set to be 8-layer with identical kernel size 5. In the training procedure, we adopt Adam to optimize the proposed Aug-2D-TAN. The initial learning rate is set as 0.0001 and the batch size is set as 64.

5.3   Experimental Results

Quantitative Analysis. To quantitatively verify the effectiveness of our proposed framework, we evaluate our model performance on HCSTVG dataset and compare it with the existing methods. As shown in Table 1., we outperforms the previous methods in terms of viou@0.3, and m_viou on the HCSTVG validation set. We further compare our model performance with other methods on the HCSTVG test set, as shown in Table 2. It could be seen that our method also outperforms the others in terms of viou@0.3 and m_viou.

Table 1. Performance comparison on HCSTVG validation set.

Method	viou@0.3	m_viou
Random	0.03	0.00
TALL [10]+WSSTG [19]	19.95	13.37
2D-TAN [7]+WSSTG [19]	19.83	15.43
STGVT [6]	26.81	18.15
STVGBert [20]	29.37	20.42
Stage-1 [21]+2D-TAN [7]	36.07	22.83
Stage-1 [21]+MMN [21]	49.02	30.32
Ours	**50.40**	**30.40**

Table 2. Performance comparison on HCSTVG test set. [†]: quoted from the competition methods in the 3rd Person in Context (PIC) Challenge at HCVG track.

Method	viou@0.3	m_viou
easy_baseline2.5[†]	48.6	30.9
try10[†]	47.9	31.3
2stage[†]	50.2	31.4
Ours	**52.70**	**31.9**

Ablation Study. We conduct ablation experiments to verify the effectiveness of our proposed components, i.e., the Random Concatenation Augmentation (RCA) mechanism and Temporal-Aware Context Aggregation (TACA) module, as shown in Table 3. The RCA mechanism brings an improvement of 0.5% in the m_viou performance. And we actually observe a more stable training process when the RCA is introduced. The TACA module brings consistent gains to all of the performance metrics, which demonstrates the superiority to learn more discriminative moment features via temporal dynamics modeling. Finally, we further ablate our overall contribution by replacing our temporal matching

Table 3. Ablation study on HC-STVG dataset [6].

Method	viou@0.3	m_tiou	m_viou	Split
Baseline	47.2	53.4	29.5	val
+RCA	48.8	54.1	30.0	val
+RCA+TACA	**50.4**	**55.2**	**30.4**	val
Baseline	47.7	53.3	29.4	test
Ours	**52.7**	**56.5**	**31.9**	test

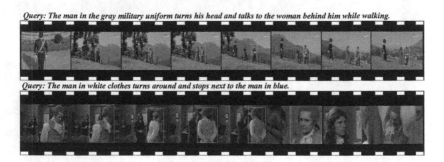

Query: The man in the gray military uniform turns his head and talks to the woman behind him while walking.

Query: The man in white clothes turns around and stops next to the man in blue.

Fig. 4. Qualitative visualization of our proposed method

module with 2D-TAN. It is shown that our model outperforms the baseline by 2.5% of m_viou, which confirms the effectiveness of our contribution. **Qualitative Analysis.** We give some visualization results of typical cases to conduct qualitative analysis on our proposed method, as shown in Fig. 4. In the first row, our model successfully localizes the trajectory of the man which is far away from the camera. And in the second row, we give a typical case in which the referred person is close to the camera, and our model also performs well to tackle such type of cases.

6 Conclusion

In this work, we propose a simple yet effective framework to tackle the problem of Human-Centric Spatio-Temporal Video Grounding (HC-STVG). Through our ablation experiments, we verify the effectiveness of the proposed Temporal-Aware Context Aggregation (TACA) module and Random Concatenation Augmentation (RCA) mechanism, which can facilitate to learn more discriminative moment features and help to combat overfitting. Experiments show that our simple yet effective framework our work can actually provide a basic paradigm and a strong baseline for future research progress in this area.

Acknowledgements. This work was supported partially by the NSFC (U1911401, U1811461, 62076260, 61772570), Guangdong Natural Science Funds Project (2020B151 5120085), Guangdong NSF for Distinguished Young Scholar (2022B1515020009), and the Key-Area Research and Development Program of Guangzhou (202007030004).

References

1. Carreira, J., Noland, E., Banki-Horvath, A., Hillier, C., Zisserman, A.: A short note about kinetics-600. arXiv preprint arXiv:1808.01340 (2018)
2. Feichtenhofer, C., Fan, H., Malik, J., He, K.: Slowfast networks for video recognition. In: IEEE Conference on Computer Vision and Pattern Recognition, pp. 6202–6211 (2019)
3. Gu, C., et al.: Ava: A video dataset of spatio-temporally localized atomic visual actions. In: IEEE Conference on Computer Vision and Pattern Recognition, pp. 6047–6056 (2018)
4. Kamath, A., Singh, M., LeCun, Y., Misra, I., Synnaeve, G., Carion, N.: Mdetr-modulated detection for end-to-end multi-modal understanding. arXiv preprint arXiv:2104.12763 (2021)
5. Kingma, D.P., Ba, J.: Adam: A method for stochastic optimization. arXiv preprint arXiv:1412.6980 (2014)
6. Tang, Z., et al.: Human-centric spatio-temporal video grounding with visual transformers. IEEE Trans. Circuits Syst. Video Technol. (2021)
7. Zhang, S., Peng, H., Fu, J., Luo, J.: Learning 2d temporal adjacent networks for moment localization with natural language. In: Proceedings of the AAAI Conference on Artificial Intelligence, vol. 34, pp. 12870–12877 (2020)
8. Zhang, Y., Li, Z., Min, Z.: Efficient second-order TreeCRF for neural dependency parsing. In: Proceedings of ACL, pp. 3295–3305 (2020). https://www.aclweb.org/anthology/2020.acl-main.302
9. Anne Hendricks, L., Wang, O., Shechtman, E., Sivic, J., Darrell, T., Russell, B.: Localizing moments in video with natural language. In: Proceedings of the IEEE International Conference On Computer Vision. pp. 5803–5812 (2017)
10. Gao, J., Sun, C., Yang, Z., Nevatia, R.: Tall: Temporal activity localization via language query. In: Proceedings of the IEEE International Conference On Computer Vision, pp. 5267–5275 (2017)
11. Ge, R., Gao, J., Chen, K., Nevatia, R.: Mac: Mining activity concepts for language-based temporal localization. In: 2019 IEEE Winter Conference on Applications of Computer Vision (WACV), pp. 245–253. IEEE (2019)
12. Nagaraja, V.K., Morariu, V.I., Davis, L.S.: Modeling context between objects for referring expression understanding. In: Leibe, B., Matas, J., Sebe, N., Welling, M. (eds.) ECCV 2016. LNCS, vol. 9908, pp. 792–807. Springer, Cham (2016). https://doi.org/10.1007/978-3-319-46493-0_48
13. Wu, J., Li, G., Liu, S., Lin, L.: Tree-structured policy based progressive reinforcement learning for temporally language grounding in video. In: Proceedings of the AAAI Conference on Artificial Intelligence, vol. 34, pp. 12386–12393 (2020)
14. Yu, L., Poirson, P., Yang, S., Berg, A.C., Berg, T.L.: Modeling context in referring expressions. In: European Conference on Computer Vision. pp. 69–85. Springer (2016)
15. Mao, J., Huang, J., Toshev, A., Camburu, O., Yuille, A.L., Murphy, K.: Generation and comprehension of unambiguous object descriptions. In: Proceedings of the IEEE Conference On Computer Vision And Pattern Recognition, pp. 11–20 (2016)

16. Hu, R., Rohrbach, M., Andreas, J., Darrell, T., Saenko, K.: Modeling relationships in referential expressions with compositional modular networks. In: Proceedings of the IEEE Conference On Computer Vision And Pattern Recognition, pp. 1115–1124 (2017)
17. Yang, S., Li, G., Yu, Y.: Dynamic graph attention for referring expression comprehension. In: Proceedings of the IEEE/CVF International Conference on Computer Vision, pp. 4644–4653 (2019)
18. Qiu, H., et al.: Language-aware fine-grained object representation for referring expression comprehension. In: Proceedings of the 28th ACM International Conference on Multimedia, pp. 4171–4180 (2020)
19. Chen, Z., Ma, L., Luo, W., Wong, K.Y.K.: Weakly-supervised spatio-temporally grounding natural sentence in video. arXiv preprint arXiv:1906.02549 (2019)
20. Su, R., Yu, Q., Xu, D.: Stvgbert: A visual-linguistic transformer based framework for spatio-temporal video grounding. In: Proceedings of the IEEE/CVF International Conference on Computer Vision, pp. 1533–1542 (2021)
21. Wang, Z., Wang, L., Wu, T., Li, T., Wu, G.: Negative sample matters: A renaissance of metric learning for temporal grounding. arXiv preprint arXiv:2109.04872 (2021)
22. Li, K., Guo, D., Wang, M.: Proposal-free video grounding with contextual pyramid network. In: Proceedings of the AAAI Conference on Artificial Intelligence, vol. 35, pp. 1902–1910 (2021)
23. Mun, J., Cho, M., Han, B.: Local-global video-text interactions for temporal grounding. In: Proceedings of the IEEE/CVF Conference on Computer Vision and Pattern Recognition, pp. 10810–10819 (2020)
24. Wang, H., Zha, Z.J., Chen, X., Xiong, Z., Luo, J.: Dual path interaction network for video moment localization. In: Proceedings of the 28th ACM International Conference on Multimedia, pp. 4116–4124 (2020)
25. Xiao, S., Chen, L., Zhang, S., Ji, W., Shao, J., Ye, L., Xiao, J.: Boundary proposal network for two-stage natural language video localization. In: Proceedings of the AAAI Conference on Artificial Intelligence, vol. 35, pp. 2986–2994 (2021)
26. Zhang, H., Sun, A., Jing, W., Zhen, L., Zhou, J.T., Goh, R.S.M.: Natural language video localization: A revisit in span-based question answering framework. Ieee Trans. Pattern Anal. Mach. Intell. (2021)

Part-Wise Topology Graph Convolutional Network for Skeleton-Based Action Recognition

Xiaowei Zhu[1,2], Qian Huang[1,2(✉)], Chang Li[1,2], Lulu Wang[3], and Zhuang Miao[4(✉)]

[1] Key Laboratory of Water Big Data Technology of Ministry of Water Resources, Hohai University, Nanjing, China
huangqian@hhu.edu.cn
[2] School of Computer and Information, Hohai University, Nanjing, China
[3] Water Conservancy Service Station, Banjing Town, Rugao, Jiangsu, China
[4] Command and Control Engineering College, Army Engineering University of PLA, Nanjing, China
emiao_beyond@163.com

Abstract. Action recognition based on skeleton data has attracted extensive attention in computer vision. Graph convolutional network (GCN) has achieved remarkable performance by modeling the human skeleton as a spatial-temporal graph. The graph topology that dominates feature aggregation is the key for GCN to extract representative features. However, the previous models based on GCN mostly build skeleton topology that are naturally connected or adaptively shared, and lack the exploration of fine-grained relations of multi-level features. In this paper, we propose a novel Part-wise Topology Graph Convolution (PT-GC) for the task of skeleton action recognition. PT-GC first builds part-level topology with two modeling strategies, and then effectively aggregates multi-level joint features by combining global topology and part-level topology, which can accurately construct human topology. Finally, we adopt the two-stream architecture and combine PT-GC with a spatial-temporal modeling module to propose a powerful graph convolutional network named PT-GCN. On the two large-scale datasets, NTU RGB+D and NTU RGB+D 120, PT-GCN exhibits significant performance advantages, proving the effectiveness of our proposed method.

Keywords: Skeleton action recognition · Graph convolutional network · Part-level topology

1 Introduction

With the continuous development of artificial intelligence technology, human action recognition plays an important role in applications such as video surveillance, human-computer interaction, and abnormal behavior monitoring

© The Author(s), under exclusive license to Springer Nature Switzerland AG 2022
L. Fang et al. (Eds.): CICAI 2022, LNAI 13604, pp. 317–329, 2022.
https://doi.org/10.1007/978-3-031-20497-5_26

[1,3,6,23]. In recent years, skeleton-based human action recognition has attracted extensive attention. Skeleton is a compact and expressive modality that is insensitive to complex backgrounds and dynamic camera perspectives, and skeleton data contains higher-level semantic information while having only a small amount of data [19–21].

Early deep learning-based methods regard human skeleton as a set of independent features, which are manually constructed into a sequence of coordinate vectors or a pseudo-image, using a recurrent neural network (RNN) or a convolutional neural network (CNN) to analyze skeleton data and generate predictions [8,27]. However, representing skeleton data as vector sequences or mesh images cannot express the complete spatial-temporal dependencies between correlated joints. Graph Convolutional Network (GCN) can efficiently handle non-Euclidean data such as graphs, and it can generalize convolutions from images to graphs of arbitrary size and shape. In recent years, more and more skeleton action recognition models use GCN-based methods to extract spatial-temporal features [5,10,15,20,22,25].

Yan et al. proposed a spatial-temporal graph convolutional network (ST-GCN), which was the first to use GCN to model skeleton data. They build a spatial topology map based on the natural connections of the human body, and add temporal associations between the same joints in consecutive frames to construct a complete spatial-temporal graph [25]. However, the skeleton topology map in ST-GCN only represents the physical structure of the human body. In actions such as "touching the head" or "clapping hands", there is also a strong dependence between the hands and the head or between the hands. Therefore, the fixed spatial articulation is not optimal. Shi et al. proposed an Adaptive Graph Convolutional Network (AGCN), which uses a self-attention mechanism to change the topology of human skeletons and adaptively learn the connections between previously disconnected bones [20,22]. In fact, adaptively learning the skeleton spatial relationship directly through the attention mechanism will generate a lot of redundant information, and the generated spatial topology graph shared by each channel is not optimal. Liu et al. introduced a multi-scale graph topology to achieve multi-scale joint relationship modeling [14]. Ye et al. proposed Shift-GCN [5], replacing the traditional convolution operator with the Shift convolution operator, using shifted graph convolution. In addition, Song et al. used part attention to obtain the importance of each part, but it did not fully consider the correlation between parts and the differences within parts [24].

In this paper, we fully consider the contribution of human body part information to action occurrence, and propose a novel dynamic modeling spatial topology module, which is guided by human body part information to construct a more complete skeleton topology graph. Specifically, Part-wise Topology Graph Convolution (PT-GC) combines global topology and part-level topology, taking into account both global and local information, to capture the relationship between different channels and joints in more detail. Our proposed refinement method simultaneously models between and within human body parts, effectively eliminating the unreasonable sharing of relational weights between different joints and channels. In addition, we refer to the two-stream network architecture of 2s-AGCN [20] and obtain the final prediction by integrating the prediction scores of Joint-stream and Bone-stream. This method can effectively improve the model performance.

Combining these efforts mentioned above, we finally propose a novel network for skeleton-based action recognition, named Part-wise Topology Graph Convolutional Networks (PT-GCN). Our major contributions are summarized as follows:

(1) We adopt a reasonable human body parts segmentation method and propose two modeling strategies for part-level topology, which can effectively model the importance and correlation of parts.
(2) Our proposed part-wise topology graph convolution, which refines the skeleton topology through the fusion of global graph and part-level graph, can better adapt to the hierarchical structure of GCN and action recognition tasks.
(3) We propose a new skeleton-based action recognition model named PT-GCN. It can accurately capture the relationship between and within parts, and effectively extract the spatial and temporal information of skeleton data.
(4) We conduct experiments on two widely-used datasets: NTU RGB+D [18] and NTU RGB+D 120 [12], on which our proposed method outperforms state-of-the-art approaches.

2   Methods

In this section, we introduce the construction of a spatial-temporal graph of the human skeleton. We elaborate our part-level topology modeling strategies and Part-wise Topology Graph Convolution (PT-GC). Finally, we present the full structure of the proposed model named PT-GCN.

2.1   Graph Construction

Different action samples contain different spatial-temporal information. We construct spatial-temporal skeleton graphs to describe the structured information between these nodes along the spatial and temporal dimensions. The complete spatial-temporal skeleton graph is built according to the natural connection of human body structure and the connection of consecutive frames, so it contains the connection edges between joints and the connection edges between frames. The graph is defined as $\mathcal{G} = (\mathcal{X}, \mathcal{V}, \mathcal{E})$, where $\mathcal{X}$ represents the feature set of vertices, there are V vertices, T frames and C channels, which is represented as a matrix $X \in R^{C \times V \times T}$. $\mathcal{V} = \{v_1, v_2, ..., v_V\}$ represents the vertex set. $\mathcal{E}$ is the set of edges, reflecting the connection strength between vertices. We use the weighted summation of joints in the input feature map through the features of their corresponding neighbor joints to obtain the output feature map. The graph convolution implementation of the feature map is formulated as:

$$f_{out} = \sum_s^S W_s \cdot f_{in} \cdot A_s \tag{1}$$

where f_{in} and f_{out} denote the input and output feature maps. S denotes the sampling area of the spatial dimension. A_s and W_s denote the adjacency matrix and weight function under the sampling area s.

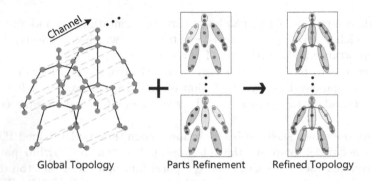

Global Topology   Parts Refinement   Refined Topology

Fig. 1. Refined topology based on parts. The human body is divided into 8 parts, including two palms, two arms, two legs, head and torso. Different colored ellipses indicate importance and relevance of the parts. Nodes with different colors inside the part represent the difference in the weights of the joints for the part.

2.2   Part-Level Topology Modeling Strategy

By aggregating and classifying actions from multiple datasets, we found that almost all actions can be decomposed into single part actions or a combination of part actions. For example, shaking the head can be regarded as the action of the head, pointing with finger can be decomposed into the action of the arm and the palm and clapping can be regarded as the action of the two palms and the arm. Thus, in theory, more accurate dependencies between joints can be obtained by optimizing topology based on human body part information.

Previous part-based models usually aim to extract features from body parts individually or only focus on discovering the importance of different body parts [24, 26]. However, we fully consider the correlation between parts and the differences within parts, and construct a refined part-level topology for the features of each channel, as shown in Fig. 1.

Before performing GCN, body part correlations need to be modeled. Specifically, we first divide the human skeleton into 8 parts, the input feature $X \in R^{N \times C \times T}$ of each joint is aggregated according to the part division strategy, which is formulated as:

$$X_i^{part} = Concat(\{X_j \mid j \in L(i)\})   i = 1, 2, ..., V \tag{2}$$

where V denotes the number of parts, $Concat(\cdot)$ denotes the splicing function, $L(i)$ denotes the set of joint numbers corresponding to the i_{th} part, and X_i^{part} represents the feature of the i_{th} part after aggregation.

Two Modeling Strategy. In order to obtain the best dependencies between parts, we propose two modeling strategies $\mathcal{M}_1(\cdot)$ and $\mathcal{M}_2(\cdot)$ to model the part dependencies. Since each joint contributes to the corresponding part, we perform an average pooling operation on the joints inside the part. In addition, in order to reduce the computation cost, we utilize linear transformations $\psi(\cdot)$ and $\varphi(\cdot)$ to reduce the feature dimension before the part-level topology modeling. The first modeling strategy $\mathcal{M}_1(.)$ calculates the correlation between parts in the temporal dimension in the way of Einstein summation, which can be formulated as:

$$\mathcal{M}_1(i,j) = \sigma(\sum_t^T(\psi(AvgPool_V(X_{it}^{part})) \cdot \varphi(AvgPool_V(X_{jt}^{part})))) \qquad (3)$$

where $AvgPool_V(\cdot)$ denotes the average pooling in the spatial dimension, T denotes the number of frames, and $\sigma(.)$ is activation function. The second modeling strategy $\mathcal{M}_2(.)$ needs to calculate the distance of the channel dimension between different parts, and utilizes the nonlinear transformation of the distance to represent the correlation between parts, which is formulated as:

$$\mathcal{M}_2(i,j) = \sigma(\psi(AvgPool_{VT}(X_i^{part})) - \varphi(AvgPool_{VT}(X_j^{part}))) \qquad (4)$$

where $AvgPool_{VT}(\cdot)$ denotes the average pooling in both spatial and temporal dimensions. By modeling functions $\mathcal{M}_1(.)$ or $\mathcal{M}_2(.)$, the correlation between two parts can be obtained to build the part level topology graph.

Part-Level Topology Modeling. The size of the parts relationship graph is $C_r \times P \times P$, where C_r denotes the number of channel after dimensionality reduction, and P denotes the number of divided parts. It cannot be directly applied to the human skeleton graph, so it needs to be mapped to a graph of size $V \times V$ through a mapping function. According to the relationship between the various parts obtained in the previous section, the part correlation features are first connected into a whole vertex matrix, which is formulated as:

$$G_{part} = Concat(\{Concat(\{\mathcal{M}(i,j) \mid j = 1,2,...,P\}) \mid i = 1,2,...,P\}) \qquad (5)$$

where $\mathcal{M}(i,j)$ is the optimal modeling strategy, and its value denotes the correlation between parts i and j. G_{part} denotes the spliced part relationship graph. It should be noted that the part-level graph expresses different part correlations on each channel, but the joints within a part do not share weights, so the topology needs to be refined while mapping. We optimize the topology through learnable bias and linear transformation, which is formulated as:

$$P_s^{part} = \phi(\mathcal{R}(G_{part}) + B_0) \quad s = 1, 2, ..., S \tag{6}$$

where $\mathcal{R}(\cdot)$ denotes the mapping function of the graph. $\phi(\cdot)$ denotes the linear transformation function. B_0 denotes the positional bias of the channel and joint, which is a learnable parameter. P_s^{part} is the complete part-level graph, which is actually a tensor of (C_{out}, V, V).

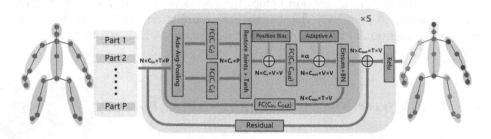

Fig. 2. The proposed PT-GC. C_{in}, C_r, C_{out}, T, P, and V represent the input channel, compressed channel, output channel, number of frames, number of parts, and number of joints, respectively. FC represents the convolution layer with kernel size of 1×1. BN denotes Batch Normalization. Relu is the activation function.

2.3   Part-Wise Topology Graph Convolution

Neighborhood determination is extremely important in graph convolution. [20] captured the relevance of nodes through a self-attention mechanism. [4] focused on the modeling of channel topology as a way to change the neighborhood of nodes. Whereas our part-level modeling strategy captures both part correlations and intra-part differences, expanding the neighborhood of nodes more accurately.

Our proposed PT-GC is more flexible, and the skeleton topology is completely determined by the network adaptive learning. It combines global graph and part-level graph to obtain the correlations of human joints more accurately. The global graph is driven by data and relies on adaptive learning to represent the common features of various actions. The part-level graph is guided by part information, and is synthesized in different channels of the feature map to represent the difference between different actions. A gating mechanism α is introduced in the process of fusing the global graph and the individual refined graph to control the difference in the contribution of required parts and joints in different sampling regions. Finally, the graph convolution can be completed by performing Einstein summation of the part-wise topology and the input features in the spatial dimension.

GCN will dynamically update the global and part-level topology during the inference process to capture the features of the previously disconnected skeleton nodes. Therefore, Eq. 1 is modified into the following form:

$$f_{out} = \sum_s^S W_s \cdot f_{in} \cdot (P_s^{global} + \alpha P_s^{part}) \qquad (7)$$

where P_s^{global} is the global topology, and P_s^{part} is the part-level topology. The global topology is initialized with the natural connection of the human skeleton, and changed by adaptively learning the correlation of actions.

The complete PT-GC module is shown in Fig. 2, and we take the modeling strategy $\mathcal{M}_2$ as an example. The aggregated input features $X_{part} \in R^{N \times C_{in} \times T \times P}$ are subjected to adaptive average pooling, and then input to two fully connected layers for dimensionality reduction operation. After part-level modeling, the associated topology map of parts is obtained. Then it needs to be mapped to the joint topology and fused with the global topology. In addition, multiple sampling regions S are set to learn semantic information at different levels.

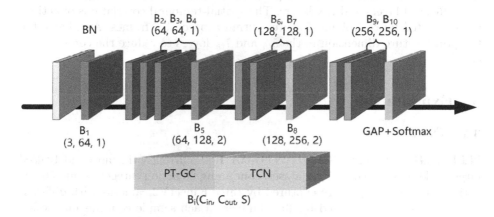

Fig. 3. The overview of the proposed PT-GCN model. The entire part-wise topology graph convolutional block is represented as $B_i(C_{in}, C_{out}, S)$. The three numbers of each block represent the number of input channels, the number of output channels and the stride, respectively. There are a total of 10 blocks. BN represents the batch normalization. GAP represents the global average pooling.

2.4 Model Architecture

As shown in Fig. 3, the overall architecture of PT-GCN is mainly composed of a batch normalization layer, 10 basic blocks and a classification layer. The input data is first normalized by the BN layer. The numbers of output channels for each block are 64, 64, 64, 64, 128, 128, 128, 256, 256, and 256. The residual network is connected between blocks [7], and finally perform global average pooling and softmax classification to obtain behavior prediction results. Each block mainly consists of a part-wise spatial modeling module, a spatial-temporal modeling module and residual connections.

Part-Wise Spatial Modeling. In the spatial modeling module, we use our proposed part-wise graph convolution module. We set up three mapping strategies and use three PT-GCs in parallel to extract semantic information at different levels between parts and joints, as shown in Fig. 2. For a single PT-GC, first utilizes ψ and φ with reduction rate r to extract compact representations, taking the modeling strategy $\mathcal{M}_2(\cdot)$ as an example, using temporal and intra-part spatial pooling to aggregate features. After that, PT-GC conducts pair-wise subtraction and activation, then fused with the global map. Finally, the graph convolution is completed to obtain the output feature map, as shown in Eq. 7.

Spatial-Temporal Modeling. We use a temporal convolutional network TCN [2] as a spatial-temporal modeling module, which is mainly composed of 2D convolutional layers and BN layers. The spatial-temporal correlations of actions are extracted by convolving features within consecutive frames. And halve the temporal feature dimension in the 5_{th} and 7_{th} layers to reduce the computation cost.

3   Experiments

3.1   Datasets

NTU RGB+D. NTU RGB+D (NTU-60) [18] is currently the most widely used large-scale action recognition dataset, containing 60 action categories and 56,000 action clips. The clips were captured by three KinectV2 cameras with different perspectives and performed by 40 volunteers. Each sample contains one action and is guaranteed to have at most 2 subjects. The skeleton information consists of the 3D coordinates of 25 body joints and the corresponding action category labels. NTU-60 recommends two benchmarks [18]: Cross-View Evaluation (X-View) split according to different camera views and Cross-Subject Evaluation (X-Sub) split according to different subjects.

NTU RGB+D 120. NTU RGB+D 120 (NTU-120) [12] extends NTU-60 with a larger scale. It contains 120 action categories and 114,480 action clips. The clips were performed by 106 volunteers in 32 camera setups. NTU-120 also recommends two benchmarks [12]: the first is Cross-Subject Evaluation(X-Sub), which is the same cross-subject evaluation as NTU-60. The other is Cross-Setup Evaluation (X-Set), which splits training and test samples based on the parity of camera setup IDs.

3.2 Implement Details

For the NTU RGB+D dataset, there are at most two peoples in each sample of the dataset. If the number of bodies in the sample is less than 2, we pad the second body with 0. The max number of frames in each sample is 300. For samples with less than 300 frames, we repeat the samples until it reaches 300 frames.

All experiments are conducted on one RTX 3070 TI GPU with the PyTorch deep learning framework. We use the stochastic gradient descent(SGD) with Nesterov momentum(0.9) as the optimizer and the cross-entropy as the loss function. Weight decay is 0.0001. The initial learning rate is set to 0.1 and a warmup strategy [7] is used in the first 5 epochs to make the training procedure more stable. The batch size is 8. The learning rate is divided by 10 at the 30_{th} epoch and 40_{th} epoch. The training process is ended at the 50_{th} epoch.

3.3 Ablation Studies

In this section, we use the X-Sub and X-View benchmarks of the NTU-60 to verify the effectiveness of proposed modules in PT-GCN.

As introduced in Sect. 2.2 and 2.3, our proposed PT-GC module contains two topological graphs, namely the global adaptive graph P^{global} and the part-level graph P^{part}, where the modeling of the P^{part} includes two modeling strategies. We manually delete one of the graphs within PT-GC and use $\mathcal{M}_1$ and $\mathcal{M}_2$ modeling methods for part-level topology, respectively, to test the performance of different configurations of PT-GC. In terms of data stream, we preprocessed the original skeleton data to obtain the Joint-stream and Bone-stream, and compared the model performance of the single-stream network and the dual-stream network in the experiment. Additionally, we adopt ST-GCN [25] as the baseline method, which used a topology fixed in GCN that is not trainable.

Table 1. Comparisons of the validation accuracy of PT-GC with different settings. w/o X means deleting the X.

Methods	Data	$\mathcal{M}$	X-Sub (%)	X-View (%)
Baseline	Joint	−	84.3	92.7
PT-GCN w/o P^{part}	Joint	−	86.4	93.6
PT-GCN w/o P^{global}	Joint	$\mathcal{M}_1$	87.1	93.5
PT-GCN w/o P^{global}	Joint	$\mathcal{M}_2$	87.3	93.7
PT-GCN	Joint	$\mathcal{M}_1$	88.0	94.3
PT-GCN	Joint	$\mathcal{M}_2$	88.2	94.6
PT-GCN	Bone	$\mathcal{M}_2$	88.9	94.3
PT-GCN	Joint+Bone	$\mathcal{M}_2$	**90.7**	**96.0**

The specific ablation experiment configuration and results are shown in Table 1. The experimental results show that our part-level graph is able to obtain the correlation between joints well. The method of combining global graph and part-level graph has better effect than the method of single graph. The part-level topology modeling strategy $\mathcal{M}_2$ has better performance than $\mathcal{M}_1$. The combination of the global graph and the part-level graph, the part-level modeling strategy $\mathcal{M}_2$ and the two-streams network structure are the optimal configuration of this model. Under this configuration, PT-GCN brings improvements of +6.4% and +3.3% over the baseline method on X-Sub and X-View benchmarks, respectively. Experiments fully demonstrate the effectiveness and superiority of this module.

3.4 Comparisons with the State of the Art

We compare the final model with state-of-the-art skeleton-based action recognition methods on the NTU-60 and NTU-120 datasets. The results are shown in Table 2 and Table 3. These methods for comparison include RNN-based methods [11,13,18], CNN-based methods [2,9,28] and GCN-based methods [5,10,15,16,20,25]. Our model achieves significant improvements of +1.0% and +0.7% over 2s Shift-GCN on the X-Sub benchmark of NTU-60 and the X-Set benchmark of NTU-120, respectively. Overall, PT-GCN achieves better performance than other methods on both datasets, which demonstrates the superiority of our model.

Table 2. Comparisons of the validation accuracy with the state-of-the-art methods on the NTU RGB+D dataset.

Methods	X-Sub (%)	X-View (%)
Deep LSTM [18]	60.7	67.3
Ind-RNN [11]	81.8	88.0
TCN [2]	74.3	83.1
HCN [9]	86.5	91.1
SGN [28]	89.0	94.5
ST-GCN [25]	81.5	88.3
AS-GCN [10]	86.8	94.2
2s-AGCN [20]	88.5	95.1
NAS-GCN [15]	89.4	95.7
2s Shift-GCN [5]	89.7	**96.0**
PT-GCN (ours)	**90.7**	**96.0**

Table 3. Comparisons of the validation accuracy with the state-of-the-art methods on the NTU RGB+D 120 dataset.

Methods	X-Sub (%)	X-Set (%)
ST-LSTM [13]	55.7	57.9
SGN [28]	79.2	81.5
ST-GCN [25]	70.7	73.2
AS-GCN [10]	77.9	78.5
Mix-Dimension [16]	80.5	83.2
ST-Transformer [17]	82.7	84.7
2s-AGCN [20]	82.9	84.9
2s Shift-GCN [5]	**85.3**	86.6
PT-GCN (ours)	85.0	**87.3**

4   Conclusion

In this work, we present a novel part-wise topology graph convolutional network (PT-GCN) for skeleton-based action recognition. PT-GC accurately learns the joint correlation of actions in a way that combines global topology and part-level topology, showing powerful correlation modeling capability. We evaluate the proposed model on two large-scale datasets, and the experimental results demonstrate that PT-GC has stronger representation than other graph convolutions, and PT-GCN has excellent performance and generalization ability.

Acknowledgement. This work was supported in part by the National Key Research and Development Program of China under Grant No. 2018YFC0407905, the Key Research and Development Program of Jiangsu Province under Grant No. BE2016904, the Fundamental Research Funds of China for the Central Universities under Grant No. B200202188, and the Jiangsu Water Conservancy Science and Technology Project under Grant No. 2018057.

References

1. Aggarwal, J.K., Ryoo, M.S.: Human activity analysis: A review. Acm Comput. Surv. (Csur) **43**(3), 1–43 (2011)
2. Bai, S., Kolter, J.Z., Koltun, V.: An empirical evaluation of generic convolutional and recurrent networks for sequence modeling. arXiv preprint arXiv:1803.01271 (2018)
3. Carreira, J., Zisserman, A.: Quo vadis, action recognition? a new model and the kinetics dataset. In: proceedings of the IEEE Conference on Computer Vision and Pattern Recognition, pp. 6299–6308 (2017)
4. Chen, Y., Zhang, Z., Yuan, C., Li, B., Deng, Y., Hu, W.: Channel-wise topology refinement graph convolution for skeleton-based action recognition. In: Proceedings of the IEEE/CVF International Conference on Computer Vision, pp. 13359–13368 (2021)

5. Cheng, K., Zhang, Y., He, X., Chen, W., Cheng, J., Lu, H.: Skeleton-based action recognition with shift graph convolutional network. In: 2020 IEEE/CVF Conference on Computer Vision and Pattern Recognition (CVPR), pp. 180–189 (2020)
6. Feichtenhofer, C., Fan, H., Malik, J., He, K.: Slowfast networks for video recognition. In: Proceedings of the IEEE/CVF International Conference On Computer Vision, pp. 6202–6211 (2019)
7. He, K., Zhang, X., Ren, S., Sun, J.: Deep residual learning for image recognition. In: Proceedings of the IEEE Conference On Computer Vision And Pattern Recognition, pp. 770–778 (2016)
8. Ke, Q., Bennamoun, M., An, S., Sohel, F., Boussaid, F.: A new representation of skeleton sequences for 3d action recognition. In: Proceedings of the IEEE Conference On Computer Vision And Pattern Recognition, pp. 3288–3297 (2017)
9. Li, C., Zhong, Q., Xie, D., Pu, S.: Co-occurrence feature learning from skeleton data for action recognition and detection with hierarchical aggregation. arXiv preprint arXiv:1804.06055 (2018)
10. Li, M., Chen, S., Chen, X., Zhang, Y., Wang, Y., Tian, Q.: Actional-structural graph convolutional networks for skeleton-based action recognition. In: Proceedings of the IEEE/CVF Conference On Computer Vision And Pattern Recognition, pp. 3595–3603 (2019)
11. Li, S., Li, W., Cook, C., Zhu, C., Gao, Y.: Independently recurrent neural network (indrnn): Building a longer and deeper rnn. In: Proceedings of the IEEE Conference On Computer Vision And Pattern Recognition, pp. 5457–5466 (2018)
12. Liu, J., Shahroudy, A., Perez, M., Wang, G., Duan, L.Y., Kot, A.C.: Ntu rgb+ d 120: A large-scale benchmark for 3d human activity understanding. IEEE Trans. Pattern Anal. Mach. Intell. **42**(10), 2684–2701 (2019)
13. Liu, J., Shahroudy, A., Xu, D., Wang, G.: Spatio-temporal lstm with trust gates for 3d human action recognition. In: Leibe, B., Matas, J., Sebe, N., Welling, M. (eds.) ECCV 2016. LNCS, vol. 9907, pp. 816–833. Springer, Cham (2016). https://doi.org/10.1007/978-3-319-46487-9_50
14. Liu, Z., Zhang, H., Chen, Z., Wang, Z., Ouyang, W.: Disentangling and unifying graph convolutions for skeleton-based action recognition. In: Proceedings of the IEEE/CVF Conference On Computer Vision And Pattern Recognition, pp. 143–152 (2020)
15. Peng, W., Hong, X., Chen, H., Zhao, G.: Learning graph convolutional network for skeleton-based human action recognition by neural searching. In: Proceedings of the AAAI Conference on Artificial Intelligence, vol. 34, pp. 2669–2676 (2020)
16. Peng, W., Shi, J., Xia, Z., Zhao, G.: Mix dimension in poincaré geometry for 3d skeleton-based action recognition. In: Proceedings of the 28th ACM International Conference on Multimedia, pp. 1432–1440 (2020)
17. Plizzari, C., Cannici, M., Matteucci, M.: Spatial temporal transformer network for skeleton-based action recognition. In: Del Bimbo, A., et al. (eds.) ICPR 2021. LNCS, vol. 12663, pp. 694–701. Springer, Cham (2021). https://doi.org/10.1007/978-3-030-68796-0_50
18. Shahroudy, A., Liu, J., Ng, T.T., Wang, G.: Ntu rgb+ d: A large scale dataset for 3d human activity analysis. In: Proceedings of the IEEE Conference On Computer Vision And Pattern Recognition, pp. 1010–1019 (2016)
19. Shi, L., Zhang, Y., Cheng, J., Lu, H.: Skeleton-based action recognition with directed graph neural networks. In: Proceedings of the IEEE/CVF Conference on Computer Vision and Pattern Recognition, pp. 7912–7921 (2019)

20. Shi, L., Zhang, Y., Cheng, J., Lu, H.: Two-stream adaptive graph convolutional networks for skeleton-based action recognition. In: Proceedings of the IEEE/CVF Conference On Computer Vision And Pattern Recognition, pp. 12026–12035 (2019)
21. Shi, L., Zhang, Y., Cheng, J., Lu, H.: Decoupled spatial-temporal attention network for skeleton-based action-gesture recognition. In: Proceedings of the Asian Conference on Computer Vision (2020)
22. Shi, L., Zhang, Y., Cheng, J., Lu, H.: Skeleton-based action recognition with multi-stream adaptive graph convolutional networks. IEEE Trans. Image Process. **29**, 9532–9545 (2020)
23. Shi, L., Zhang, Y., Cheng, J., Lu, H.: Action recognition via pose-based graph convolutional networks with intermediate dense supervision. Pattern Recogn. **121**, 108170 (2022)
24. Song, Y.F., Zhang, Z., Shan, C., Wang, L.: Stronger, faster and more explainable: A graph convolutional baseline for skeleton-based action recognition. In: Proceedings Of The 28th Acm International Conference On Multimedia, pp. 1625–1633 (2020)
25. Yan, S., Xiong, Y., Lin, D.: Spatial temporal graph convolutional networks for skeleton-based action recognition. In: Thirty-Second AAAI Conference On Artificial Intelligence (2018)
26. Zhang, H., et al.: Resnest: Split-attention networks. arXiv preprint arXiv:2004.08955 (2020)
27. Zhang, P., Lan, C., Xing, J., Zeng, W., Xue, J., Zheng, N.: View adaptive recurrent neural networks for high performance human action recognition from skeleton data. In: Proceedings of the Ieee International Conference On Computer Vision, pp. 2117–2126 (2017)
28. Zhang, P., Lan, C., Zeng, W., Xing, J., Xue, J., Zheng, N.: Semantics-guided neural networks for efficient skeleton-based human action recognition. In: proceedings of the IEEE/Cvf Conference On Computer Vision And Pattern Recognition, pp. 1112–1121 (2020)

A Lightweight Detection Method of Smartphone Assembly Parts

Bo Zhang[1], Wenbai Chen[1(✉)], Xiaohao Wang[1], and Chunjiang Zhao[2]

[1] School of Automation, Beijing Information Science and Technology University, Beijing 100192, China
chenwb03@126.com
[2] Beijing Academy of Agriculture and Forestry Sciences, Beijing 100097, China

Abstract. The object detection algorithm for smartphone assembly parts in the 3C (Computer, Communication, Consumer Electronics) scene occupies many system computing resources, and the flexible targets and small-scale heterogeneous components in the background lead to problems such as low detection accuracy. Based on the YOLOv5n network, we propose a lightweight and high-precision network-YOLOv5n-GTA. First, we replace the ordinary convolution module with the Ghost convolution module in the backbone network and neck, thereby significantly reducing the parameter scale in the network. Second, we add a Transformer module at the end of the backbone network to enhance the feature expression ability of the network and further improve the modeling and representation ability of the backbone network. Then, We use the meta-ACON (Activate or not) activation function to dynamically learn the activation function's linearity and solve the neuron necrosis problem by controlling the nonlinearity of each layer of the network. Experimental results show that our method outperforms other excellent detection algorithms in inference speed and model size evaluation indicators. We compress model parameters to 63% of YOLOv5n and model size to 75% of YOLOv5n at a speed of 24.5 ms per image on GPU.

Keywords: Object detection · Lightweight network · 3C industry

1 Introduction

China is a large manufacturing country globally, but it is not yet a manufacturing power [2]. In particular, there are still many manual operations in the 3C industry. In recent years, with the further aggravation of China's aging population, upgrading the 3C manufacturing industry has important practical significance. Currently, in the 3C scene, the mobile phone parts detection algorithm model is relatively large [14] and takes up more computing resources in actual production. There are many flexible printed circuits and small-scale heterogeneous parts in

Supported by National Natural Science Foundation of China(6227072907).

the mobile phone assembly. Therefore, we hope to combine the rapid development of machine vision and deep learning technology in recent years to propose a lightweight and efficient object detection method for mobile phone assembly parts in the 3C scene.

With the large-scale development of deep learning technology, object detection has benefited from the super feature extraction and learning capabilities of the convolutional neural network [17] (convolutional neural network, CNN), which has made significant progress in the field of object detection. At present, object detection algorithms based on deep learning and widely used can be divided into two categories: Two-stage target detection algorithms, such as Fast R-CNN [6], Faster R-CNN [30], Mask R-CNN [10], etc. This kind of algorithm divides target detection into two stages; first, it generates a pre-selection anchor box, then performs fine-grained object detection, which has high detection accuracy but low detection speed; Single-stage target detection algorithms, such as SSD (Single Shot Multibox Detector) [22], RetinaNet [20], YOLO series (You Only Look Once) [27–29]. They directly generate target location and classification information through the network model, an end-to-end target detection method. Yolov5 detection algorithm is an object detection network framework proposed by Ultralytics in May 2020. This algorithm inherits the advantages of previous generations of the Yolo algorithm. It is one of the most excellent target detection architectures and is also suitable for application in industrial scenarios.

In the mobile phone parts assembly under the 3C scene, there are more flexible printed circuit objects and small-sized heterogeneous parts. Considering the limited computing resources in the actual industrial scene, it has practical production significance to learn more object characteristics, improve the detection performance and reduce the model's weight. We propose a lightweight inspection network structure for mobile phone parts assembly inspection in the 3C scene, which introduces a lightweight convolution module, a transformation module to enhance data feature extraction, and an adaptive activation function. The main contributions of this work are:

1) We propose an improved lightweight network named YOLOv5n-GTA, which consists of a backbone, a neck and a head.
2) A novel, lightweight and high-performance module combination combines the ghost module, the Transformer encoder module and the Meta-ACON adaptive activation function.

2 Related Works

Lightweight Neural Network. In recent years, a new branch of research has been formed to design small and efficient networks for resource-constrained environments commonly found in industrial settings. Although many object detectors achieve excellent accuracy and inference in real-time, most of these models require too many computing resources to deploy on production equipment. The core idea of lightweight neural network design is to optimize the number of parameters and computation [36], trying to reduce the amount of computation and parameters while still making the network model have a strong expressive ability. The lightweight design of the network is mainly to design a more efficient "network computing method". The calculation method here is mainly for the convolution method, which significantly reduces the number of network parameters while considering the excellent network characterization performance. There are dilated convolution [33], deformable convolution [3], depthwise separable convolution [13], etc. Many scholars and institutions have conducted in-depth and extensive research on lightweight networks recently. They have achieved a series of encouraging results, such as SqueezeNet [15], MobileNet series [12,13,31], ShuffleNet series [24,34].

Small Object Detection. Small object detection has always been a challenging problem in computer vision, but the demand for small target detection exists widely in actual production. Many small objects in mobile phone assembly parts in the 3C industry, such as mobile phone front camera, SIM card slot, etc. Because small objects occupy fewer pixel values in the image, in the existing object detection models, the bottom features of the backbone network are generally used to detect small objects. However, the lack of semantic information on the bottom features makes small object detection difficult, so the performance of small object detection still needs improvement. Given this, many improvement strategies for improving small object detection are proposed as follows: 1)Multi-scale Prediction: Multi-scale prediction predicts the classification and coordinates of objects on a feature map of different scales. The SSD [22] algorithm adopts the multi-scale prediction method for the first time. At present, the small object detection method of multi-scale prediction has become the basic operation to improve the performance of small target detection, such as DSSD [5], PANe t[21], TridentNet [19], etc. 2)Improving Feature Resolution: The main idea of this method is to improve the detection accuracy of small objects by increasing the resolution of high-level feature maps and converting the feature expression of small objects into the same or similar feature expression of large and medium objects. The representative algorithms are STDN [35], PGAN [18]. 3)Data Enhancement Technology: Generally, for the small number of samples of small objects is relatively small, we can increase the number of samples of small objects via data enhancement, which will help improve the detection performance. Reference [16] describes copy-pasting small objects (without overlapping other objects in other images) to increase the number of small objects in a single image.

Activation Function. The activation function is a non-linear mapping layer in a convolution neural network designed to enhance the non-linear representation of the network. In the early development of deep learning, the representative activation functions sigmoid and tanh were widely used. However, with the deepening of the model depth, the S-type activation functions appeared to have a gradient diffusion problem. The ReLU(rectified linear units) [25] activation function solves the gradient diffusion problem of the S-type activation function, but its negative semiaxis gradient is always 0, which leads to neuron necrosis [1]. In order to solve the problem of neuron necrosis, the ReLU series activation function [8,11] was proposed to alleviate this problem effectively. The Swish [26] activation function has no upper and lower bounds and is micro-and non-monotonic. The Maxout activation function [7] fits the approximation target convex function through a linear piecewise function. The Maxout activation function has a ReLU slightly linear unsaturation and solves the neuron necrosis problem at the same time.

3 Method

3.1 Overview of Network Architecture

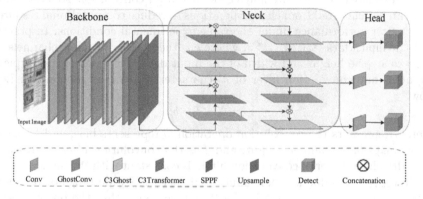

Fig. 1. The Architecture of our proposed the lightweight detection network: YOLOv5n-GTA

YOLOv5n-GTA is a lightweight detection method for Smartphone assembly parts in the 3C scene based on the YOLOv5 nano version. It continues the overall YOLOv5n framework, composed of an Input, a Backbone, a Neck, and an Output Head, as shown in Fig. 1. The input side performs the calculation operations such as Mosaic data enhancement, adaptive picture scaling, and adaptive anchor. The backbone network is mainly used to extract image features. The neck comprises a Feature Pyramid Network and a Path Aggregation Network, which fuse each other. It is mainly used to fuse the features extracted from the backbone network and send the fused results to the prediction layer. After neck fusion, the output side predicts the feature maps by 1×1 convolution and outputs classification information, location information, and object information. The lightweight detection method proposed in this paper mainly replaces the ordinary convolution module with the Ghost convolution module. It adds the C3Transformer module at the end of the backbone network to enhance feature data extraction. At the same time, the adaptive activation function is introduced as the activation function of the whole network to overcome the inherent drawbacks of the activation function.

3.2   Ghost Model

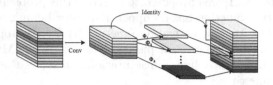

Fig. 2. Ghost model

The Ghost convolution [9] network was proposed in 2020, and there is extensive redundancy in the feature maps generated after convolution, so more feature maps can be generated from cheap operations to reduce computational resources, it has better performance under the same experimental conditions. In practice, given the input data $X \in R^{c \times h \times w}$, where c is the number of input channels and h, and w are the height and width of the input data. The operation of typically generating any convolution layer of N characteristic graphs is shown in Eq. 1. below.

$$Y = X * f + b, \tag{1}$$

Where $*$ represents the convolution operation, b represents bias, and Y has the feature maps of n channel output, and f is the convolution filter of this layer. Generally, the number of convolution filters is consistent with the number of output channels, the value is tremendous, and there is a wide range of redundant feature information. As shown in Fig. 2, it is assumed that the output feature map is the "Ghost" of some intrinsic feature maps with some cheap transformations. These intrinsic feature maps are usually smaller and produced by standard convolution filters.

$$Y^{'} = X * f^{'}, \tag{2}$$

$$y_{ij} = \Phi_{i,j}(y_{i}^{'}), \quad \forall i = 1, ..., m, j = 1, ..., s, \tag{3}$$

Specifically, as shown in Equation 2, m intrinsic feature maps $Y^{'}$ generated using a primary convolution, $f^{'}$ is the utilized filter, and the bias term is omitted for simplicity. The hyper-parameters such as filter size, stride, and padding, are the same as those in the ordinary convolution (Eq. 1) to keep the spatial size of the output feature maps consistent. To further obtain the desired n feature maps, we propose to apply a series of cheap linear operations on each intrinsic feature in $Y^{'}$ to generate s ghost features as shown in Equation 3. where $y_{i}^{'}$ is the i-th intrinsic feature map in $Y^{'}$, $\Phi_{i,j}$ in the above function is the j-th (except the last one) linear operation for generating the j-th ghost feature map y_{ij}. By utilizing Eq. 3, we can obtain $n = m \cdot s$ feature maps as the output data of a Ghost module, as shown in Fig. 2. The linear operations Φ operate on each channel whose computational cost is much less than the ordinary convolution. In practice, we use 5×5 linear kernels in a Ghost module.

The Ghostbottleneck module, as shown in Fig. 3 (a), is composed of a ghost convolution module. It mainly consists of two ghost modules. The first ghost module is used to increase the expansion layer of the number of channels, and the second ghost module is used to reduce the number of channels. The residual shortcut is connected between the input and output of the two ghost modules. The YOLOv5 network uses the CSPNet [32] network to reduce computation and improve inference speed and accuracy. Figure 3 (b) shows that the framework is the CSP network. It is called the C3Ghost module because it is composed of three convolution blocks and the Ghostbottleneck module. This modular design can enhance CNN's learning ability, eliminate bottleneck computing and reduce memory cost.

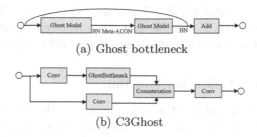

(a) Ghost bottleneck

(b) C3Ghost

Fig. 3. The modules composed of Ghost bottleneck and C3Ghost are called Ghost Modules.

3.3   Vision Transformer Module

In recent years, the transformer architecture has performed well in the NLP field. In 2020, Google applied the transformer architecture to the computer vision field and proposed ViT(Vision Transformer) [4]. The design follows the original transformer architecture as much as possible and achieves excellent results. The Transformer structure breaks the limited receptive field limitation of CNN. It captures the long-distance dependencies of the entire feature map by the self-attention mechanism, which has stronger modeling capabilities. Two layers mainly implement each Transformer module: a multi-head attention layer and a multi-layer perceptron, and residual shortcuts are used between each layer. First, the input data is divided into Patches, the learnable linear projection embeds the position information of the divided Patches, and the input sequence X is generated.

$$Q = XW^Q$$
$$K = XW^K \tag{4}$$
$$V = XW^V$$

As shown in Eq. 4, X is the input sample sequence feature, W^Q, W^K, and W^V are the spatial projection weight matrix, and the input sequence X is multiplied by the weight matrix to generate the Q(query), K(key), V(value).

$$\text{Attention}(Q, K, V) = \text{softmax}(\frac{QK^T}{\sqrt{d_k}})V \qquad (5)$$

Scaled Dot Product Attention is the core calculation formula of the Transformer architecture, as shown in Eq. 5. The input consists of queries and keys of dimension d_k and values of dimension d_v. We compute the dot products of the query with all keys, divide each by $\sqrt{d_k}$, and apply a softmax function to obtain the weights on the values. Similar to the Ghost convolution module shown in Fig. 3(b), the Transformer module also uses the CSPNet architecture, consisting of three convolution modules and a Transformer Block. The Transformer module is followed by the SPPF module, which is a fast version of Spatial Pyramid Pooling and is mainly used to fuse features under different receptive fields.

3.4   Meta-ACON Activation Function

In order to solve the problem of neuron necrosis in the ReLU activation function in the neural network, the detection framework proposed in this paper uses the Meta-ACON activation function [23]; the activation function can optimize the adaptive activation parameters through learning. The Maxout [7] series activation function is approximated to the ACON series activation function by the Smooth maximum principle, as shown in Eq. 6, the Meta-ACON activation function, where X represents the input; p_1 and p_2 are two learnable parameters, which control the upper and lower limits of the first derivative of Meta-ACON, and can obtain an activation function with better performance; The β parameter is learned through a small convolutional network and a sigmoid function, which dynamically controls the linearity and nonlinearity of the activation function, helping to improve generalization and transfer performance.

$$f_{\text{Meta−ACON}}(x) = S_\beta(p_1x, p_2x) = (p_1x - p_2x) \cdot \sigma[\beta(p_1 - p_2)x] + p_2x \qquad (6)$$

4   Experimental Results

4.1   Datasets

The sensor used in data set production is Microsoft Azure Kinect. The sensor is connected to the manipulator's end in the form of the eye in hand. In order to increase the diversity of the data set and enhance the generalization of the model, the selection is carried out in different periods and under different illumination, and the end camera is used to simulate various possible scenes. Aiming at the semi-flexible and small-scale characteristics of smartphone assembly parts in a 3C scenario, the small object enhancement strategy is specially carried out in the construction of datasets, that is, as many small targets and high-resolution images as possible appear in the scene so that the network model can learn enough small target data features. The data set has five objects: flexible cable(FPC), coaxial line(COAX), SIM card slot, mobile phone front camera(CAM), and mobile phone(MP) model. There are 1200 images in the datasets, and the resolution of each image is 2048 × 1536.

4.2   Evaluation Metrics

This paper's evaluation indicators are average precision (AP), mean average precision (mAP), the time required for detection per image, model parameters, and model size.

$$AP_i = \int_0^1 PdR \qquad (7)$$

$$mAP = \frac{\sum_i^N AP_i}{N} \qquad (8)$$

where P is precision; R is recall; i refers to the i-th class. The geometric meaning of average precision is the area enclosed by the curve and horizontal axis formed by Precision and Recall. The mAP is the mean of the average precision of all categories in the dataset, where n represents the number of target classes in the dataset. The number of model parameters and the model size measures the memory space occupied by the model in the system, usually in MB.

4.3   Implementation and Experimental Setup

We use the self-made dataset described earlier to train our model. The training set, validation set, and test set in the experiment are divided according to 8 : 1 : 1. Before network training, the K-Means algorithm is used to calculate the prior anchors' size. During training, the input image size of the network is 640 × 640, and the data augmentation strategies are left-right flipping, horizontal and vertical translation, random scaling, and mosaic. We utilize the SGD optimizer to train our network, and its hyper parameters are set to the default values, where the learning rate is 0.01, the cosine annealing parameter is 0.01, the learning rate momentum is 0.937, and the weight decay coefficient is 0.005. We use automatic batch size, and network iterations are set to 300. The environment for our experiment is the Ubuntu16.04 operating system, Intel (R) Xeon (R) CPU e5-4650 V3 @ 2.10GHz CPU (with 32GB RAM), two NVIDIA Titan XP GPUs (with 12GB memory). The model is built, trained, and tested in python-3.8, PyTorch-1.10.0, and CUDA11.1.

4.4   Ablation Study

In this section, we validate the effectiveness of each critical component used in our model. The ablation experiment mainly controls the Ghost module, Transformer module, and Meta-ACON activation function to analyze their impact on network performance. We use YOLOv5n as the baseline. First, we use the Ghost module to replace the ordinary convolution module in YOLOv5n, marked as YOLOv5n-G in Fig. 4; then, we use the Ghost module and the Transformer module at the same time, which is marked as YOLOv5n-GT in Fig. 4. Finally, under the premise of YOLOv5n-GT, the activation function is replaced with Meta-ACON, marked as YOLOv5n-GTA, as shown in Fig. 4.

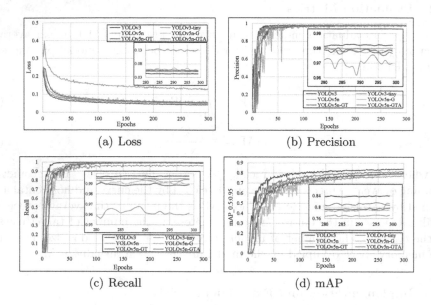

(a) Loss   (b) Precision

(c) Recall   (d) mAP

Fig. 4. Illustration of Loss curve, Precision curve, Recall curve, and mAP curve of ablation experiment and comparison experiment

As we can see, YOLOv5n-GTA has a specific improvement compared to YOLOv5n-G and YOLOv5n-GT in terms of Loss, Precision, and Recall curves. At the same time, for the baseline, yolov5n-GTA can still maintain the same performance as yolov5n after a large-scale reduction of network models.

4.5   Comparison with Other Methods

We compare our method with five state-of-the-art detection methods YOLOv-5n, YOLOv3 and YOLOv3-tiny, NanoDet-Plus, EfficientDet, among them, large-scale YOLOv3, medium-scale EfficientNet, baseline network YOLOv5n and light-weight networks YOLOv3-tiny and NanoDet-Plus are chosen. The specific comparisons are shown in Table 1, and it can be seen that our YOLOv5n-GTA is much smaller than the large-scale network YOLOv3 and the baseline network YOLOv5n in inference speed, parameters, and model size, and it is far superior to the lightweight network YOLOv3-tiny and NanoDet-Plus in accuracy.

In order to further compare the detection results of the algorithms perceptually, Fig. 5 shows the detection results for four algorithms selected, and the

Table 1. comparison of parameters detected by different algorithms on datasets

Method	AP					mAP_0.5:0.95	Speed img/ms		Parameter/million	Model/MB
	CAM	FPC	SIM	COAX	MP		GPU	CPU		
YOLOv3	0.74	0.87	0.80	0.81	0.96	0.84	43.7	426.9	63	127.8
YOLOv3-tiny	0.65	0.82	0.76	0.70	0.91	0.77	10.3	73.2	8.9	18.1
YOLOv5n	0.71	0.85	0.79	0.77	0.94	0.81	36.2	58.7	1.9	4.3
NanoDet-Plus	0.66	0.82	0.77	0.68	0.90	0.77	12.5	55.9	2.5	4.7
EfficientDet	0.68	0.81	0.77	0.72	0.92	0.78	28.0	60.2	12.0	64.3
Ours	0.69	0.84	0.78	0.74	0.93	0.80	24.5	48.2	**1.2**	**2.9**

remaining detection results are similar. The above qualitative and quantitative results show that our method has advantages in inference speed, parameters and model size, and it is lightweight compared with different detection algorithms on our mobile phone parts dataset.

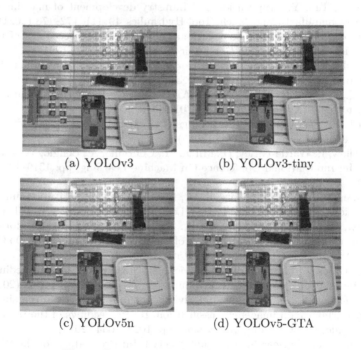

(a) YOLOv3   (b) YOLOv3-tiny

(c) YOLOv5n   (d) YOLOv5-GTA

Fig. 5. Detection results of four algorithms

5 Conclusion

This paper proposes a lightweight object detection algorithm for mobile phone assembly parts in the 3C scene. The proposed YOLOv5n-GTA is a light-weight detection architecture based on YOLOv5n, consisting of three parts: the Backbone, Neck, and Head. We use the Ghost module and Transformer module to reduce the weight of the network while considering the ability of network feature extraction, such as small objects such as the front camera of the mobile phone and the SIM card slot. Our purpose in using the Meta-ACON adaptive activation function is to improve the performance of the network further. By constructing the data set by ourselves, we adopt the strategy of appearing as many small targets in the image as possible to enhance the ability of the network to extract the features of small objects. Finally, many experiments show that our algorithm achieves lightweight and high detection performance in 3C scenarios.

References

1. Clevert, D.A., Unterthiner, T., Hochreiter, S.: Fast and accurate deep network learning by exponential linear units (elus). arXiv preprint arXiv:1511.07289 (2015)
2. Cuicui, L., Tao, Y.: Application and industry development of machine vision in intelligent manufacturing. Mach. Tool Hydraulics **49**(11), 172–178 (2021)
3. Dai, J., et al.: Deformable convolutional networks. In: Proceedings of the IEEE International Conference On Computer Vision, pp. 764–773 (2017)
4. Dosovitskiy, A., et al.: An image is worth 16×16 words: Transformers for image recognition at scale. arXiv preprint arXiv:2010.11929 (2020)
5. Fu, C.Y., Liu, W., Ranga, A., Tyagi, A., Berg, A.C.: Dssd: Deconvolutional single shot detector. arXiv preprint arXiv:1701.06659 (2017)
6. Girshick, R.: Fast r-cnn. In: Proceedings of the IEEE International Conference On Computer Vision, pp. 1440–1448 (2015)
7. Goodfellow, I., Warde-Farley, D., Mirza, M., Courville, A., Bengio, Y.: Maxout networks. In: International Conference On Machine Learning, pp. 1319–1327. PMLR (2013)
8. Gulcehre, C., Moczulski, M., Denil, M., Bengio, Y.: Noisy activation functions. In: International Conference On Machine Learning, pp. 3059–3068. PMLR (2016)
9. Han, K., Wang, Y., Tian, Q., Guo, J., Xu, C., Xu, C.: Ghostnet: More features from cheap operations. In: Proceedings of the IEEE/CVF Conference On Computer Vision And Pattern Recognition, pp. 1580–1589 (2020)
10. He, K., Gkioxari, G., Dollár, P., Girshick, R.: Mask r-cnn. In: Proceedings of the IEEE International Conference On Computer Vision, pp. 2961–2969 (2017)
11. He, K., Zhang, X., Ren, S., Sun, J.: Delving deep into rectifiers: Surpassing human-level performance on imagenet classification. In: Proceedings of the IEEE international Conference On Computer Vision, pp. 1026–1034 (2015)
12. Howard, A., et al.: Searching for mobilenetv3. In: Proceedings of the IEEE/CVF international Conference On Computer Vision, pp. 1314–1324 (2019)
13. Howard, A.G., et al.: Mobilenets: Efficient convolutional neural networks for mobile vision applications. arXiv preprint arXiv:1704.04861 (2017)
14. Huang, Z., Yin, Z., Ma, Y., Fan, C., Chai, A.: Mobile phone component object detection algorithm based on improved ssd. Proc. Comput. Sci. **183**, 107–114 (2021)
15. Iandola, F.N., Han, S., Moskewicz, M.W., Ashraf, K., Dally, W.J., Keutzer, K.: Squeezenet: Alexnet-level accuracy with 50x fewer parameters and< 0.5 mb model size. arXiv preprint arXiv:1602.07360 (2016)

16. Kisantal, M., Wojna, Z., Murawski, J., Naruniec, J., Cho, K.: Augmentation for small object detection. arXiv preprint arXiv:1902.07296 (2019)
17. LeCun, Y., Bottou, L., Bengio, Y., Haffner, P.: Gradient-based learning applied to document recognition. Proceedings of the IEEE **86**(11), 2278–2324 (1998)
18. Li, J., Liang, X., Wei, Y., Xu, T., Feng, J., Yan, S.: Perceptual generative adversarial networks for small object detection. In: Proceedings of the IEEE Conference On Computer Vision And Pattern Recognition, pp. 1222–1230 (2017)
19. Li, Y., Chen, Y., Wang, N., Zhang, Z.: Scale-aware trident networks for object detection. In: Proceedings of the IEEE/CVF International Conference on Computer Vision, pp. 6054–6063 (2019)
20. Lin, T.Y., Goyal, P., Girshick, R., He, K., Dollár, P.: Focal loss for dense object detection. In: Proceedings of the IEEE International Conference On Computer Vision, pp. 2980–2988 (2017)
21. Liu, S., Qi, L., Qin, H., Shi, J., Jia, J.: Path aggregation network for instance segmentation. In: Proceedings of the IEEE Conference On Computer Vision And Pattern Recognition, pp. 8759–8768 (2018)
22. Liu, W., et al.: SSD: single shot multibox detector. In: Leibe, B., Matas, J., Sebe, N., Welling, M. (eds.) ECCV 2016. LNCS, vol. 9905, pp. 21–37. Springer, Cham (2016). https://doi.org/10.1007/978-3-319-46448-0_2
23. Ma, N., Zhang, X., Liu, M., Sun, J.: Activate or not: Learning customized activation. In: Proceedings of the IEEE/CVF Conference on Computer Vision and Pattern Recognition, pp. 8032–8042 (2021)
24. Ma, N., Zhang, X., Zheng, H.-T., Sun, J.: ShuffleNet V2: practical guidelines for efficient cnn architecture design. In: Ferrari, V., Hebert, M., Sminchisescu, C., Weiss, Y. (eds.) Computer Vision – ECCV 2018. LNCS, vol. 11218, pp. 122–138. Springer, Cham (2018). https://doi.org/10.1007/978-3-030-01264-9_8
25. Nair, V., Hinton, G.E.: Rectified linear units improve restricted boltzmann machines. In: Icml (2010)
26. Ramachandran, P., Zoph, B., Le, Q.V.: Searching for activation functions. arXiv preprint arXiv:1710.05941 (2017)
27. Redmon, J., Divvala, S., Girshick, R., Farhadi, A.: You only look once: Unified, real-time object detection. In: Proceedings of the IEEE Conference On Computer Vision And Pattern Recognition, pp. 779–788 (2016)
28. Redmon, J., Farhadi, A.: Yolo9000: better, faster, stronger. In: Proceedings of the IEEE Conference On Computer Vision And Pattern Recognition, pp. 7263–7271 (2017)
29. Redmon, J., Farhadi, A.: Yolov3: An incremental improvement. arXiv preprint arXiv:1804.02767 (2018)
30. Ren, S., He, K., Girshick, R., Sun, J.: Faster r-cnn: Towards real-time object detection with region proposal networks. In: Advances in Neural Information Processing Systems 28 (2015)
31. Sandler, M., Howard, A., Zhu, M., Zhmoginov, A., Chen, L.C.: Mobilenetv 2: Inverted residuals and linear bottlenecks. In: Proceedings of the IEEE Conference On Computer Vision And Pattern Recognition, pp. 4510–4520 (2018)
32. Wang, C.Y., Liao, H.Y.M., Wu, Y.H., Chen, P.Y., Hsieh, J.W., Yeh, I.H.: Cspnet: A new backbone that can enhance learning capability of cnn. In: Proceedings of the IEEE/CVF Conference On Computer Vision And Pattern Recognition Workshops, pp. 390–391 (2020)
33. Yu, F., Koltun, V.: Multi-scale context aggregation by dilated convolutions. arXiv preprint arXiv:1511.07122 (2015)

34. Zhang, X., Zhou, X., Lin, M., Sun, J.: Shufflenet: An extremely efficient convolutional neural network for mobile devices. In: Proceedings of the IEEE Conference On Computer Vision And Pattern Recognition, pp. 6848–6856 (2018)
35. Zhou, P., Ni, B., Geng, C., Hu, J., Xu, Y.: Scale-transferrable object detection. In: proceedings of the IEEE Conference On Computer Vision And Pattern Recognition, pp. 528–537 (2018)
36. Zhou, Y., Chen, S., Wang, Y., Huan, W.: Review of research on lightweight convolutional neural networks. In: 2020 IEEE 5th Information Technology and Mechatronics Engineering Conference (ITOEC), pp. 1713–1720. IEEE (2020)

Illumination-Guided Transformer-Based Network for Multispectral Pedestrian Detection

Fuchen Chu[1], Jiale Cao[1], Zhuang Shao[2], and Yanwei Pang[1(✉)]

[1] School of Electrical and Information Engineering,
Tianjin University, Tianjin, China
{fuchenchu,connor,pyw}@tju.edu.cn
[2] Warwick Manufacturing Group, University of Warwick, Coventry CV47AL, UK
Zhuang.Shao@warwick.ac.uk

Abstract. Multi-modal information (e.g., visible and thermal) can generate reliable and robust pedestrian detection results in various computer vision applications. Despite its broad applications, it remains a crucial problem that how to fuse the two modalities effectively. The self-attention operator of transformer can obtain long-range dependencies and integrate information across the entire input, which has been widely used for cross-modal fusion. However, there is still a lack of further analysis and design for transformer to use in multispectral pedestrian detection task. To benefit from both RGB and thermal modalities, we propose a novel illumination-guided transformer-based network (ITNet) for multispectral pedestrian detection in this paper. Firstly, different from the previous methods that apply the original transformer structure directly, we designed two different transformer-based fusion modules to make the RGB and thermal modalities complement each other. Secondly, an illumination-guided module is used to adaptively re-weight and fuse the multi-modal features according to the illumination conditions. Extensive evaluations on two benchmarks demonstrate the effectiveness of our proposed approach for multispectral pedestrian detection.

Keywords: Multispectral object detection · Cross-modal feature fusion · Transformer · Illumination-guided module

1 Introduction

Pedestrian detection is one of the key tasks in the field of computer vision. It is a fundamental step in various practical applications, such as autonomous driving [19] and intelligent robotics [29]. Although significant improvements have been accomplished over the past few years, pedestrian detection is still a challenging problem in complex and changing real-world environment, such as illumination variation, shadows, and limited external light. In such conditions, it is difficult for a detector that uses only visible spectrum data to achieve a satisfactory result. Hence, multi-modal information have been adopted to improve the reliability and robustness of pedestrian detection. The visible cameras provide visual details (e.g., color and texture), while thermal cameras are sensitive to temperature changes, which is extremely useful for low light detection. Because of these advantages, detectors exploiting the multispectral modalities have been adopted to improve the detection performances in multispectral pedestrian detection.

Driven by the advances in convolutional neural networks (CNN), a growing number of CNN-based detectors [17,21,31] have been proposed. CNNs are useful for extracting local information, but they lack the ability to extract long-range information from global features. By contrast, the self-attention in transformer can obtain relationships between long-range elements. Recently, Fang et al. [25] proposed a simple cross-modality fusion transformer (CFT) module for multispectral object detection. However, this article used the original transformer module for feature fusion directly, without further analysis and modification based on the characteristics of multispectral pedestrian detection task. During the day time, pedestrians in RGB images have clearer texture features than thermal images. On the contrary, under bad illumination conditions, thermal images can provide more accurate pedestrian information than RGB [14]. We argue that the illumination information is a clue to guide us to fuse and extract the features of two modalities. Inspired by this observation, we designed two novel different transformer-based feature fusion module and proposed an illumination-guided module to make our ITNet adapt to different illumination conditions.

In this paper, we propose a novel illumination-guided transformer-based network (ITNet) for multispectral pedestrian detection. We proposed two novel transformer-based feature fusion (TFF) module to make the color and thermal modalities complement each other. The self-attention mechanism of transformer can capture the global context of the scene, which is powerful for multi-modal information fusion. Then, an illumination-guided module (IGM) is used to optimize the output feature of two TFF module adaptively according to illumination conditions. We demonstrate in experiments that our proposed multispectral pedestrian approach achieves comparable performance with an efficient inference speed. The main contributions of this paper are summarized as follows:

- We introduce a novel ITNet for multispectral pedestrian detection.
- We propose a novel TFF module to fuse cross-modal features. Two novel transformer-based multi-modal feature fusion modules are designed and we provide a deep analysis in experiments.
- In our ITNet, an IGM is proposed to make our model adapt to different illumination conditions by re-weighting the multi-modal features adaptively.
- The extensive experiments are evaluated on KAIST [13] and CVC-14 [9] dataset. Comprehensive experimental results prove the effectiveness of our proposed approach.

2   Related Work

2.1   Multispectral Pedestrian Detection

As an essential step in various computer vision tasks, pedestrian detection has been an active field of research for many years [1,2,22]. However, using only color images as the input may have poor detection results under the limitations of the insufficient illumination (*e.g.,* night). Recently, multispectral data have shown great advantages, which additionally utilize thermal modality to compensate for the shortcoming of the color modality. The first large-scale multispectral pedestrian detection benchmark was introduced in [13] and then various methods have been proposed to solve this problem. Hwang et al. [13] proposed an extended aggregated channel features (ACF) method to aggregate color-thermal image pairs for pedestrian detection. With the rapid development of deep learning, the CNN-based solutions [3] significantly improve the multispectral pedestrian detection performances.

How to fuse and extract the information of two modalities is the common concerned problem in multispectral pedestrian detection. Liu et al. [21] designed four different network fusion approaches for multispectral pedestrian detection and reveal the halfway fusion model provides the best performance. Inspired by this article, MSDS-RCNN [17] adopted a two-stream halfway fusion architecture and learned by jointly optimizing pedestrian detection and semantic segmentation tasks to further improve the detection accuracy. Reference [31] introduced a confidence-aware fusion method. The disagreements of predictions between two different modalities are used to select the more informative features while suppressing less useful ones. Zhou et al. [32] proposed MBNet to alleviate the inconsistency between visible and thermal features. A differential modality aware fusion (DMAF) is proposed to facilitate the optimization process of a dual-modality network. Zhang et al. [28] proposed a novel knowledge distillation framework named Modality Distillation (MD) to tackle the hardware and software limitations in multispectral scene analysis.

2.2   The Transformer Architecture

The transformer architecture was initially proposed in natural language processing (NLP) as a substitute to the recurrent scheme to boost its scalability. Dosovitskiy et al. [7] borrowed the transformer architecture for the first time. They proposed Vision Transformers (ViT) to shows the great potentials of generalizing transformers for computer vision by reshaping an image into flattened patches. After that, transformer-based models [4,6,12] have achieved promising performance in various vision tasks. The follow-up work, DeiT [27] further provides an effective ViT training strategy tuned several training strategies to allow ViT to work well on ImageNet-1K image classification. Carion et al. [4] combined the CNN and the transformer to propose a complete end-to-end DETR object detection framework. It is the first approach to successfully utilize transformers for the object detection task. The Swin Transformer [23] decreases the time complexity of self-attention computation by limiting the areas for self-attention computation and achieves SOTA performance in vision tasks such as object detection and semantic segmentation. Unlike most previous transformer-based models, Swin Transformer is a hierarchical architecture which makes it applicable in downstream tasks as a general-purpose backbone network. Inspired by the success of transformer in computer vision, we employ the transformer to perform intra-modal and cross-modal fusion for multispectral pedestrian detection.

3 Our Method

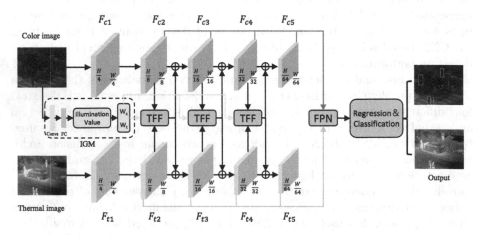

Fig. 1. The overall architecture of our proposed illumination-guided transformer-based network(ITNet). The ITNet adopts ResNet-50 [11] or VGG-16 [26] as the backbone network and embeds TFF module to capture cross-modality information. The IGM is proposed to estimate the illumination value from the given color image and assign weights to two modalities for adapting the model to different illumination conditions. (Color figure online)

3.1 Overall Architecture

An overview of our proposed illumination-guided transformer-based network (ITNet) is illustrated in Fig. 1. The ITNet extends the framework of RetinaNet [11] and the backbone network is transformed into a two-stream convolutional neural network by adding an additional branch. Specifically, our multispectral pedestrian detection architecture takes a color image and a corresponding thermal image as inputs. The two-stream backbone networks have the same structure (e.g. VGG-16 [26] or ResNet-50 [11]), which is used to extract features of two modalities respectively. Then, the thermal features and RGB features are input to the transformer-based feature fusion (TFF) module at different scales in the network for facilitating modal fusion and modal interaction. For the purpose of accurate and robust detection, two different cross-modal feature fusion module is proposed in TFF. Besides, a tiny illumination guided module (IGM) is designed to capture illumination values of the given image. The result of IGM is a key weight to fuse the RGB and thermal features adaptively according to different illumination conditions. With the help of TFF and IGM module, the contribution of each feature map from two modalities will be efficiently integrated and optimized. Finally, the features are input to the regression head and the classification head for detecting objects separately.

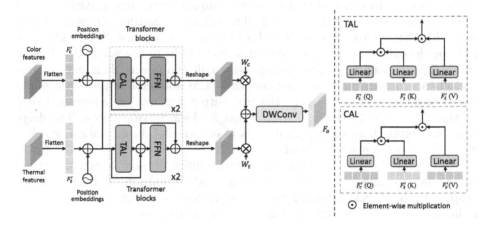

Fig. 2. Details of our transformer-based feature fusion (TFF) module. It takes the color feature map F_c and thermal feature map F_t as inputs. We first generate the flattened and embedded feature F_c' and F_t'. Then, we employ two transformer blocks with our proposed attention module (TAL or CAL) to generate the feature map for each branch with deep intra-modal and cross-modal fusions. Besides, we assign the weights W_c' and W_t' by multiplying with illumination value respectively. Finally, the output features of two branch are added together and go through a 3×3 deep-wise convolution (DWConv) for local fusion to generate the output feature map F_o.

3.2 Transformer-Based Feature Fusion (TFF) Module

It has been widely verified that the RGB modality and the thermal modality are complementary, the combination of them can help to improve pedestrian detection performance [13]. The existing CNN-based methods usually modulate RGB features with the thermal features by concatenation [10], plain fusion [21], or modality-aware fusion [32]. CNNs are efficient in extracting local information, but they lack the ability to learn long-range dependencies from global information. In contrast, transformer [7] can obtain long-range dependencies and integrate information across the entire input. Recently, transformer has been used to overcome the limitations of CNNs in multispectral pedestrian detection

[25]. However, the transformer module has never been analyzed and adjusted to make it more appropriate for multispectral pedestrian detection tasks. Based on the above considerations, we propose a novel transformer-based feature fusion (TFF) module to fuse cross-modal features.

The detail structure of our proposed TFF module is illustrated in Fig. 2. Specifically, we denote the input sequence of TFF as $F_c \in \mathrm{R}^{C \times H \times W}$ and $F_t \in \mathrm{R}^{C \times H \times W}$, where F_c is color feature maps and F_t is thermal feature maps. Next, F_c and F_t are flattened along the height and width dimensions and the flattened feature map is represented as $F'_c \in R^{HW \times C}$ and $F'_t \in R^{HW \times C}$. Then we encode the position information into F'_c and F'_t, and fed them to the transformer module. In order to capture more complementary information between RGB and thermal modality, we designed two different transformer blocks, where each block has an attention layer and a feed-forward network (FFN). Then, we reshape the output features of two transformer blocks to the size of $C \times H \times W$ and assign different weights by element-wise multiplying with illumination value (details are in Sect. 3.3). For each branch, a transformer block has two duplicate transformer blocks. Finally, the two output features are added and then go through a 3×3 deep-wise convolution for local feature fusion. The deep-wise convolution have strong capabilities to enhance local information, which is effective for dense prediction tasks.

To capture the latent interactions between different modalities, our method is proposed to enhance one modality from another modality. The detail of our proposed two different attention module of transformer blocks are shown in the right part of Fig. 2. The attention layer can be written as

$$F_{out} = Softmax(\frac{QK^T}{\sqrt{d_k}})V, \tag{1}$$

where Q, K, V are the query, key, and value inputs of the attention layer, d_k represents feature dimension. In thermal-based attention layer (TAL), we generate Q by F'_c and K, V by F'_t with a convolutional layer respectively and in color-based attention layer (CAL), we generate K by F'_t and Q, V by F'_c with a convolutional layer respectively. In our proposed attention layer, V retains the original features and Q, K performs inter-modality information fusion. For example, the output of TAL has the information of thermal features and compensates according to color features. The key idea of our proposed CAL and TAL is to deeply fuse intra-modal and cross-modal information. By explicitly modeling of RGB and thermal features, the complementary features learning can be enhanced. Then, the feed-forward network (FFN) contains two fully-connected layers with a GELU non-linearity. Besides, there is a residual connection and a normalization operation after attention layer and FFN. The W'_c and W'_t then control the weight of the output of TAL and CAL based on different illumination conditions. The fully-connected layer and deep-wise convolution provide a local cross-modal feature fusion, and our attention layer provides cross-modal fusion by building long-range dependencies. In order to make sufficient use of cross-modality complements, our TFF module is densely inserted in each ResNet block. The ablation study in Sect. 4.4 proves the effectiveness of our module.

3.3 Illumination-Guided Module

Normally, color and thermal modalities are complementary with each other since they provide different information. However, the confidence of the two modalities is different under different lighting conditions. The thermal images can provide more accurate pedestrian information at nighttime [18]. This indicates that taking illumination conditions into account can improve the performance of detection. Motivated by the above idea, we develop an illumination-guided module (IGM) as shown in the left of Fig. 1. Inspired by [18], only RGB images are used as input because thermal images are less sensitive to illumination changes, and the input image is resized to 56×56 pixels to facilitate training and testing efficiency. Then, the resized image is input to two 3×3 convolutional layers and two subsequent fully-connected layers for extracting features. The network is trained by minimizing the softmax loss between the predicted illumination values and the label, and the softmax score of day category is used as the output illumination value W_c. The value of W_t is obtained by W_c because the sum of them is 1. W_c and W_t represent the predicted illumination values of the day and night respectively. Then W_c and W_t are embedded into the transformer-based feature fusion module for adaptive optimizing the weights of refined color and thermal modalities under different illumination conditions. For example, in the case of poor illumination, the value of W_t is larger than W_c, so the weight of thermal features will be larger during fusion. By element-wise multiplying with the illumination weight W_c and W_t, the features of two modalities have different proportion for fusion. With the help of IGM, the illumination condition is token into account and the contribution of each modality will be efficiently integrated and optimized for accurate and robust detection.

4 Experiments

4.1 Datasets and Metrics

The KAIST dataset [13] contains 95,328 well-aligned color and thermal image pairs. The images on KAIST dataset were captured in various traffic environments with a resolution of 640×480. As is common practice, we adopts the log-averaged miss rate metric for performance evaluation, where the miss rate is log-averaged over false positives per image (FPPI) of $[10^{-2}:10^0]$. We use the training annotations improved by Zhang et al. [31]. The test set contains 2,252 image pairs sampled every 20 frames and we use the test annotations from [21].

CVC-14 [9] is a dataset of visible (grayscale) and thermal video sequences, which is captured at day and night. The training dataset consists of 7085 aligned visible and thermal infrared sequential image pairs with 8105 dense pedestrian annotations. CVC-14 testing dataset contains 1433 image pairs in which 706 pairs were captured during daytime and others in nighttime. The images on CVC-14 dataset were captured in city traffic environments with a resolution of 640×480. In CVC-14 dataset, all annotations are individually provided in each modality since the cameras are not well calibrated. The CVC-14 dataset also adopts the log-averaged miss rate for performance evaluation.

4.2 Implementation Details

Our detector uses the deep model ResNet-50 [11] or VGG-16 [26] as the backbone network, which is pre-trained on the ImageNet dataset [16]. The input image is resized during training and testing and the shorter edge is 512 pixels. All the images are horizontally flipped and randomly color distorted for data augmentation. Our proposed method is optimized by Adam and trained on NVIDIA TitanX GPU. The initial learning rate of 0.0001 for the first 8 epochs and $1e^{-5}$ for the last 2 epochs. Focal loss [20] and Balanced L1 loss [8] are adopted as the classification loss and the bounding box regression loss to optimize the object detection task. We plan to support it with MindSpore in future work.

Table 1. State-of-the-art comparison in terms of miss rate and inference time on KAIST dataset [13]. Miss rate is used as the evaluation metric. The results on all, day, and night test sets are shown. Our ITNet achieves a favorable performance on KAIST test set. Note that NVIDIA 1080Ti GPU is faster than NVIDIA TitanX GPU.

Method	Backbone	All ↓	Day ↓	Night ↓	Inference time (s)	Platform
Halfway Fusion [21]	VGG-16	25.75	24.88	26.59	0.43	TITAN X
Fusion RPN [15]	VGG-16	20.67	19.55	22.12	0.80	MATLAB
IAF R-CNN [18]	VGG-16	15.73	14.55	18.26	0.21	TITAN X
IATDNN+IASS [10]	VGG-16	14.95	14.67	15.72	0.25	TITAN X
CIAN [30]	VGG-16	14.12	14.77	11.13	0.07	1080 Ti
MSDS-RCNN [17]	VGG-16	11.34	10.53	12.94	0.22	TITAN X
AR-CNN [31]	VGG-16	9.34	9.94	**8.38**	0.12	1080 Ti
ITNet(Ours)	VGG-16	**8.37**	**8.38**	8.76	0.08	TITAN X
MBNet [32]	ResNet-50	8.13	8.28	7.86	0.07	1080 Ti
ITNet(Ours)	ResNet-50	**7.88**	**8.15**	**7.33**	0.10	TITAN X

Table 2. State-of-the-art comparison in terms of miss rate on CVC-14 test set [9]. The results on all, day, and night test sets are shown. Our ITNet achieves a favorable performance on CVC-14 test set.

Method	Backbone	All ↓	Day ↓	Night ↓
Halfway Fusion [24]	VGG-16	31.99	36.29	26.29
Choi et al. [5]	VGG-16	47.30	49.30	43.80
Park et al. [24]	VGG-16	31.40	31.80	30.80
AR-CNN [31]	VGG-16	22.10	24.70	18.10
ITNet(Ours)	VGG-16	**21.30**	**24.40**	**14.30**
MBNet [32]	ResNet-50	21.10	24.70	13.50
ITNet(Ours)	ResNet-50	**20.60**	**23.90**	**12.90**

Table 3. The impact of progressively integrating different modules of our ITNet, including TFF in Sect. 3.2 and IGM in Sect. 3.3. The baseline only use concat for fusion. Miss rate is used for evaluation. The detector is evaluated on KAIST [13] dataset.

Baseline	TFF	IGM	KAIST		
			All	Day	Night
✓			14.53	15.79	13.16
✓	✓		9.26	10.41	8.77
✓	✓	✓	7.88	8.15	7.33

4.3 Comparison with State-of-the-Art Methods

In this subsection, we provide some results of our proposed ITNet and other state-of-the-art methods to show the effectiveness of our method. We first provide the comparisons on the KAIST dataset in Table 1. Our proposed ITNet achieves 8.15 MR, 7.33 MR, and 7.88 MR on the day, night and all-day subset, respectively. It can be observed that our method achieves state-of-the-art performance on this dataset. For example, our ITNet outperforms AR-CNN and MBNet by 0.97% and 0.25% on all test set with the same backbone. Besides, we also compare the running time of our method with other state-of-the-art methods. ITNet has a comparable performance on computational efficiency. Namely, our ITNet achieves a favorable performance on the KAIST test set.

Table 4. Effectiveness of the TFF in Sect. 3.2. The detector is evaluated on KAIST [13] dataset. For fair comparisons, all experiments are implemented without IGM. Miss rate is used for evaluation.

Method	All	Day	Night
Baseline	14.53	15.79	13.16
Only CAL	12.05	12.88	10.34
Only TAL	11.37	12.06	9.91
CAL & TAL	9.26	10.41	8.77

Table 2 shows the experimental results of existing methods and our method on the CVC-14 dataset. We fine-tune from the KAIST pretrained model in the training of CVC-14 dataset. We follow the protocol in [24] to conduct the evaluation experiments and adopt the strategy in [31]. The pedestrians in the RGB modality are used as the training target and pedestrians in the thermal modality are acted as a reference. The result in Table 2 shows that our ITNet can also have good performance, which demonstrates the robustness of our method to different multispectral pedestrian detection domain.

4.4   Ablation Study

We first show the impact of progressively integrating different modules of our ITNet in Table 3. We train our detector on KAIST dataset for all ablation experiments. When we directly perform the baseline pedestrian detection, which use simple concatenation without illumination-guided module (IGM) to fuse two modalities, it achieves a miss rate of 14.53% on the test set. When we integrate transformer-based feature fusion (TFF) module, it achieves a miss rate of 9.26%, which is much better than baseline. It demonstrates that our TFF module can efficiently capture the complementary modality information and generates more accurate detection results. When we further add IGM, it has a improvement and the miss rate is 7.88%. By introducing the adaptive weights to the RGB and thermal features, our method has a favorable performance under different illumination conditions.

Fig. 3. Qualitative comparison of MBNet [32] and our ITNet on the KAIST dataset. The first two columns show the results of visible images, while the last two columns show the results of thermal images.

We further compare the effectiveness of different feature fusion designs in Table 4, including only concatenation design, only color-based attention layer (CAL) or thermal-based attention layer (TAL) for all transformer block, and CAL and TAL for each branch respectively as our ITNet. The experimental results demonstrate that our two different transformer-based fusion modules are effective for improving the detection performance. CAL and TAL can capture the complementary modality information in a more explicit way.

4.5   Visualized Results

We show the qualitative comparison of MBNet [32] and our ITNet in Fig. 3. Compared to MBNet, our ITNet successfully detects small persons and persons at night scene. The visualized results demonstrate that our depth-based method can significantly improve the performance of object detection.

5   Conclusion

In this work, we propose a novel illumination-guided transformer-based network (ITNet) for multispectral pedestrian detection. Our ITNet consists of a transformer-based feature fusion (TFF) module and an illumination-guided module (IGM). The TFF module first integrate and fuse cross-modality features and the illumination values of IGM adaptively optimize the weight of features. Experiments are performed on two multispectral pedestrian datasets to show the effectiveness of our proposed method. How to fuse the information of cross-modality efficiently is the common concerned problem in various multi-modal computer vision task. We hope that our design can inspire the future research on cross-modality multispectral pedestrian detection.

Acknowledgment. This work was supported in part by the National Key R&D Program of China (Grant No. 2018AAA0102802), Tianjin Research Program of Science and Technology (Grant No. 19ZXZNGX00050) and CAAI-Huawei MindSpore Open Fund.

References

1. Cao, J., Pang, Y., Li, X.: Pedestrian detection inspired by appearance constancy and shape symmetry. In: Proceedings of the IEEE Conference on Computer Vision and Pattern Recognition, pp. 1316–1324 (2016)
2. Cao, J., Pang, Y., Li, X.: Learning multilayer channel features for pedestrian detection. IEEE Trans. Image Process. **26**(7), 3210–3220 (2017)
3. Cao, Y., Guan, D., Wu, Y., Yang, J., Cao, Y., Yang, M.Y.: Box-level segmentation supervised deep neural networks for accurate and real-time multispectral pedestrian detection. ISPRS J. Photogram. Remote Sens. **150**, 70–79 (2019)
4. Carion, N., Massa, F., Synnaeve, G., Usunier, N., Kirillov, A., Zagoruyko, S.: End-to-end object detection with transformers. In: Vedaldi, A., Bischof, H., Brox, T., Frahm, J.-M. (eds.) ECCV 2020. LNCS, vol. 12346, pp. 213–229. Springer, Cham (2020). https://doi.org/10.1007/978-3-030-58452-8_13
5. Choi, H., Kim, S., Park, K., Sohn, K.: Multi-spectral pedestrian detection based on accumulated object proposal with fully convolutional networks. In: 2016 23rd International Conference on Pattern Recognition (ICPR), pp. 621–626. IEEE (2016)
6. Dong, J., Hu, Z., Zhou, Y.: Revisiting knowledge distillation for image captioning. In: Fang, L., Chen, Y., Zhai, G., Wang, J., Wang, R., Dong, W. (eds.) CICAI 2021. LNCS, vol. 13069, pp. 613–625. Springer, Cham (2021). https://doi.org/10.1007/978-3-030-93046-2_52
7. Dosovitskiy, A., et al.: An image is worth 16×16 words: transformers for image recognition at scale. arXiv preprint arXiv:2010.11929 (2020)
8. Girshick, R.: Fast R-CNN. In: Proceedings of the IEEE International Conference on Computer Vision, pp. 1440–1448 (2015)
9. Gonzalez, A., et al.: Pedestrian detection at day/night time with visible and FIR cameras: a comparison. Pattern Recogn. **16**(6), 820 (2016)
10. Guan, D., Cao, Y., Yang, J., Cao, Y., Yang, M.Y.: Fusion of multispectral data through illumination-aware deep neural networks for pedestrian detection. Inf. Fusion **50**, 148–157 (2019)

11. He, K., Zhang, X., Ren, S., Sun, J.: Deep residual learning for image recognition. In: Proceedings of the IEEE International Conference on Computer Vision (2016)
12. Huang, B., Xue, J., Lu, K., Tan, Y., Zhao, Y.: MPNet: multi-scale parallel codec net for medical image segmentation. In: Fang, L., Chen, Y., Zhai, G., Wang, J., Wang, R., Dong, W. (eds.) CICAI 2021. LNCS, vol. 13069, pp. 492–503. Springer, Cham (2021). https://doi.org/10.1007/978-3-030-93046-2_42
13. Hwang, S., Park, J., Kim, N., Choi, Y., So Kweon, I.: Multispectral pedestrian detection: benchmark dataset and baseline. In: Proceedings of the IEEE Conference on Computer Vision and Pattern Recognition, pp. 1037–1045 (2015)
14. Kieu, M., Bagdanov, A.D., Bertini, M., del Bimbo, A.: Task-conditioned domain adaptation for pedestrian detection in thermal imagery. In: Vedaldi, A., Bischof, H., Brox, T., Frahm, J.-M. (eds.) ECCV 2020. LNCS, vol. 12367, pp. 546–562. Springer, Cham (2020). https://doi.org/10.1007/978-3-030-58542-6_33
15. Konig, D., Adam, M., Jarvers, C., Layher, G., Neumann, H., Teutsch, M.: Fully convolutional region proposal networks for multispectral person detection. In: Proceedings of the IEEE Conference on Computer Vision and Pattern Recognition (2017)
16. Krizhevsky, A., Sutskever, I., Hinton, G.E.: ImageNet classification with deep convolutional neural networks. In: Proceedings of the Advances in Neural Information Processing Systems (2012)
17. Li, C., Song, D., Tong, R., Tang, M.: Multispectral pedestrian detection via simultaneous detection and segmentation. In: Proceedings of the British Machine Vision Conference (2018)
18. Li, C., Song, D., Tong, R., Tang, M.: Illumination-aware faster R-CNN for robust multispectral pedestrian detection. Pattern Recogn. **85**, 161–171 (2019)
19. Li, C., Chen, D., Chen, J., Dai, H.: A cross-layer fusion multi-target detection and recognition method based on improved FPN model in complex traffic environment. In: Fang, L., Chen, Y., Zhai, G., Wang, J., Wang, R., Dong, W. (eds.) CICAI 2021. LNCS, vol. 13069, pp. 323–334. Springer, Cham (2021). https://doi.org/10.1007/978-3-030-93046-2_28
20. Lin, T.Y., Goyal, P., Girshick, R., He, K., Dollár, P.: Focal loss for dense object detection. In: Proceedings of the IEEE International Conference on Computer Vision, pp. 2980–2988 (2017)
21. Liu, J., Zhang, S., Wang, S., Metaxas, D.N.: Multispectral deep neural networks for pedestrian detection. In: Proceedings of the British Machine Vision Conference (2016)
22. Liu, W., Liao, S., Ren, W., Hu, W., Yu, Y.: High-level semantic feature detection: a new perspective for pedestrian detection. In: Proceedings of the IEEE Conference on Computer Vision and Pattern Recognition (2019)
23. Liu, Z., et al.: Swin transformer: hierarchical vision transformer using shifted windows. In: Proceedings of the IEEE International Conference on Computer Vision (2021)
24. Park, K., Kim, S., Sohn, K.: Unified multi-spectral pedestrian detection based on probabilistic fusion networks. Pattern Recogn. **80**, 143–155 (2018)
25. Qingyun, F., Dapeng, H., Zhaokui, W.: Cross-modality fusion transformer for multispectral object detection. arXiv preprint arXiv:2111.00273 (2021)
26. Simonyan, K., Zisserman, A.: Very deep convolutional networks for large-scale image recognition. arXiv:1409.1556 (2014)
27. Touvron, H., Cord, M., Douze, M., Massa, F., Sablayrolles, A., Jégou, H.: Training data-efficient image transformers & distillation through attention. In: Proceedings of the International Conference on Machine Learning (2021)

28. Zhang, H., Fromont, E., Lefèvre, S., Avignon, B.: Low-cost multispectral scene analysis with modality distillation. In: Proceedings of the IEEE Winter Conference on Applications of Computer Vision (2022)
29. Zhang, H., Huang, R., Yuan, L.: Robust indoor visual-inertial SLAM with pedestrian detection. In: 2021 IEEE International Conference on Robotics and Biomimetics (ROBIO), pp. 802–807. IEEE (2021)
30. Zhang, L., et al.: Cross-modality interactive attention network for multispectral pedestrian detection. Inf. Fusion 50, 20–29 (2019)
31. Zhang, L., Zhu, X., Chen, X., Yang, X., Lei, Z., Liu, Z.: Weakly aligned cross-modal learning for multispectral pedestrian detection. In: Proceedings of the IEEE International Conference on Computer Vision (2019)
32. Zhou, K., Chen, L., Cao, X.: Improving multispectral pedestrian detection by addressing modality imbalance problems. In: Vedaldi, A., Bischof, H., Brox, T., Frahm, J.-M. (eds.) ECCV 2020. LNCS, vol. 12363, pp. 787–803. Springer, Cham (2020). https://doi.org/10.1007/978-3-030-58523-5_46

3D Face Cartoonizer: Generating Personalized 3D Cartoon Faces from 2D Real Photos with a Hybrid Dataset

Ming Guo[1], Shunfei Wang[2], Zhibo Wang[1], Ming Lu[3], Xiufen Cui[2], Xiao Ling[2], and Feng Xu[1(✉)]

[1] School of Software and BNRist, Tsinghua University, Beijing, China
xufeng2003@gmail.com
[2] Guangdong OPPO Mobile Telecommunications Corp., Ltd., Dongguan, China
[3] Intel Labs, Beijing, China

Abstract. Cartoon face is a prevalent kind of stylized face, which is widely used in movies, TVs and advertisements. Although plenty of methods have been proposed to generate 2D cartoon faces, it is still challenging to learn personalized 3D cartoon faces directly from 2D real photos. To solve this problem, we contribute the first 3D cartoon face hybrid dataset with both large amounts of low-quality and a small number of high-quality face triplets. Each triplet contains a 2D real face, as well as its corresponding 2D and 3D cartoon faces. To leverage the hybrid dataset, we propose *Recon2AGen* which first pretrains our network with low-quality triplets in a reconstruction-then-generation manner and then finetunes it with high-quality triplets in an adversarial manner. In this way, we solve the 2D-to-3D ambiguity and the real-to-cartoon transformation by disentangling the task into three progressively learned subtasks. And the hybrid dataset is fully explored to achieve generalizable and high accuracy results. Extensive experiments show that our generated 3D cartoon faces are of high quality and can be easily edited and animated, enabling extensive practical applications. Code and dataset will be available at https://github.com/mingsjtu/3DCartoonGenerator.

Keywords: 3D face generation · Cartoon face · Dataset

1 Introduction

As a popular kind of stylized face, cartoon faces have rich application scenarios. Generating cartoon faces directly and automatically from real faces can largely extend the ability of digital content creation, and is widely demanded in applications such as movies, advertisements, games and virtual reality.

Although many previous works can generate high-quality 2D cartoon faces [5,9,12,18,21,22], the generation of 3D cartoon faces still mainly relies on tedious manual works by artists with professional 3D modeling software. Therefore, high-quality 3D cartoon faces are usually only used in high-end fields such as game

© The Author(s), under exclusive license to Springer Nature Switzerland AG 2022
L. Fang et al. (Eds.): CICAI 2022, LNAI 13604, pp. 356–367, 2022.
https://doi.org/10.1007/978-3-031-20497-5_29

2D Real   2D Cartoon   [25]   [3]   Ours   Ours w/ Tex

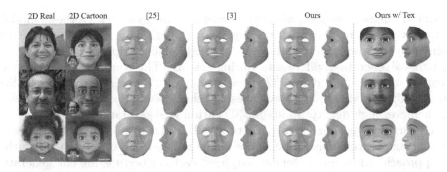

Fig. 1. We propose 3D Face Cartoonizer to generate personalized 3D cartoon faces directly from 2D real face photos. From left to right: input real faces, 2D cartoon faces, 3D cartoon face results of [25] and [3], and our results without and with texture. Notice that neither [25] nor [3] can directly obtain the results from real photo inputs as we do. They rely on the 2D cartoon faces.

and film production. As for ordinary users, it is challenging to customize 3D cartoon faces. Although there are some 3D stylized face generation methods, most of them focus on caricatures, which are quite different from cartoon faces. Besides, they usually require sketches as additional input [10, 11] or need to know the 3D model of the input real face [24].

In this paper, we introduce a learning-based method to generate both the shape and texture of 3D cartoon faces directly from 2D real face images, as shown in Fig. 1. To achieve this, we built a hybrid dataset, consisting of 6,842 low-quality and 130 high-quality face triplets. Each triplet contains a 2D real face image, its corresponding 2D cartoon face and textured 3D cartoon face. The 2D cartoon face is generated using a popular web application called ToonMe[1]. For the low-quality triplets, the 3D cartoon faces are generated by a landmark-guided deformation method inspired by [25], which only fits "coarse shapes". We get a large number of low-quality triplets as the fitting is automatic given the landmark annotations. The high-quality triplets contain 3D cartoon faces of much higher quality, but obtaining them is expensive and time-consuming as the creation heavily relys on professional artists. So, we just collect a relatively small number of high-quality triplets in the hybrid dataset. In general, our hybrid dataset strikes a balance between high quality, large quantity, and low costs.

Given the hybrid dataset, generating 3D cartoon faces from 2D face images is still challenging. For geometry generation, learning the relationship between 3D cartoon faces and 2D real faces suffers not only the 2D-to-3D ambiguity but also the real-to-cartoon transformation. We address this by a novel training strategy, called *Recon2Gen*, that learns reconstruction before generation by just using the low-quality dataset. This strategy is effective as it utilizes an easier task (reconstruction) to pretrain the network, making the final task (generation) can be achieved even with low-quality training data. Next, to make our

---

[1] https://toonme.com.

results of "higher quality", we further finetune our geometry synthesis module in an adversarial manner with the high-quality data. Given the model already trained by the low-quality data, only 90 high-quality triplets for training are enough to generate vivid results during testing. This three-stage progressive learning strategy, named *Recon2AGen* (adding an "*A*" to *Recon2Gen* standing for the adversarial training), leverages the characteristic of our hybrid dataset and achieves high-quality results for 3D carton face generation.

To further synthesize a fully textured 3D cartoon face, we integrate style transfer and texture generation into a single geometry-aware UV-space synthesis approach, which gives personal-stylized cartoon texture for our generated cartoon meshes. In summary, the contributions can be concluded as follows:

(i) To the best of our knowledge, 3D Face Cartoonizer is the first method that generates 3D cartoon faces directly from 2D facial images with high-quality geometry and texture.
(ii) We contribute the first hybrid dataset for 3D cartoon face generation, which contains 2D facial images and their corresponding 2D and 3D cartoon faces (with different qualities for the 3D cartoon faces), and will be released for future research.
(iii) We propose a novel *Recon2AGen* method which fully explores our hybrid dataset and solves both the 2D-to-3D ambiguity and the real-to-cartoon transformation.

2 Related Work

3D Stylized Face Reconstruction. Thanks to the rapid development of 3D human face reconstruction, several stylized face reconstruction works have emerged recently. However, almost all of them are focused on caricatures. Due to the considerable geometrical difference between caricatures and real faces, previous work [25] has demonstrated that directly using normal face models such as 3DMM [27], FaceWareHouse [4], FaceScape [26] and FLAME [16] cannot fit them correctly. Approaches that aim to address this limitation can be divided into two categories. In the first category, the problem is solved by manually making 3D meshes for caricatures and using the results to build a specific parametric model, such as [19]. However, it is time-consuming and costly for artists to make a great number of 3D caricatures. In the second category, the problem is solved by designing parametric models beyond the scope of normal face models, such as [25] and [3]. However, they both only consider sparse constraints of landmarks, so the results are not so satisfying and lack details. While plenty of methods are proposed for 3D caricature faces, as one popular style type, 3D cartoon faces are never studied by existing methods to the best of our knowledge.

3D Stylized Face Generation. Similar to 3D stylized face reconstruction, existing works on 3D stylized face generation primarily focus on caricature face generation. Some of them are based on the 3D models of real faces and generate caricatures by exaggerating the difference between the input face and the mean face [15, 24]. Other methods require additional input like sketches drawn by users [10, 11]. Although they can obtain 3D caricatures, the above methods are highly dependent on the quality of the input sketch and are not totally automatic. [17] uses 2D real faces as input, while the generated results are limited in a predefined PCA space.

Face Texture Generation. The texture is essential for 3D faces generation. However, as the texture of cartoon faces is quite different from real faces, existing statistical texture models [2, 16] built on real faces cannot be applied to 3D cartoon faces. To extend the space of the predefined linear model, GAN is used to generate real face texture in high fidelity [6, 8]. [5] designs a GAN-based cycle-consistency network to transfer the color style from real faces to caricatures for 2D caricatures generation. Other methods [1, 20, 23] try to solve face style translation tasks by designing an encoder for StyleGAN [14]. These style transfer methods focus only on 2D cartoon portrait generation but not complete UV texture.

3   Hybrid Cartoon Dataset

To facilitate the learning of 3D cartoon face generation, we construct a hybrid cartoon dataset with both low and high-quality data. It connects real and cartoon face domains, providing both 2D and 3D information with different quality as Fig. 2a. Specifically, our dataset contains 6,972 data triplets, each of which includes a real facial image I_r, its corresponding 2D cartoon image I_c generated by ToonMe, and its 3D cartoon face mesh M_c with texture T_c. For the 6,842 low-quality data triplets, the 3D cartoon face meshes M_c^l are generated by a denser-landmark guided face fitting algorithm. To provide more explicit 3D cartoon guidance, our dataset also contains 130 high-quality 3D cartoon faces M_c^h created by expert artists based on M_c^l, forming the high-quality triplets. Details are described as follows.

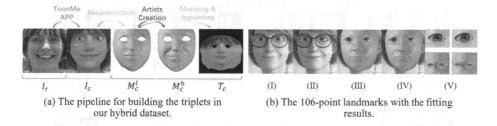

| I_r | I_c | M_c^l | M_c^h | T_c | (I) | (II) | (III) | (IV) | (V) |

(a) The pipeline for building the triplets in our hybrid dataset.

(b) The 106-point landmarks with the fitting results.

Fig. 2. Preparation process of our hybrid cartoon dataset.

The real face photos I_r are selected from FFHQ dataset [14] and we manually filter out samples whose generated 2D cartoon faces have obvious artifacts. From the 2D cartoon images I_c, we construct the 3D cartoon faces of two quality levels $(M_c^l$ and $M_c^h)$ with cartoon textures T_c.

Low-Quality Data. To get a large amount of low-quality faces M_c^l from given 2D cartoon images automatically, we refine the landmark-guided fitting-based stylized face reconstruction method [25] with extra style-related landmarks. Notice that the standard 68-point landmark-setting (blue points in Fig. 2b(II)) used in [25] fails to reconstruct accurate eyelid and nose shapes of a cartoon face as shown in Fig. 2b(III). Therefore, we introduce extra landmarks around the eyelids and nostrils, annotated as red and green points in Fig. 2b(II) respectively to get the final 106-point landmarks setting. These extra landmarks can be automatically located by extracting the eyelid and nostril edges via Sobel operator [7] with the help of the pre-mentioned 68-point landmarks. As shown in Fig. 2b(IV–V), this helps the fitting algorithm reconstruct better 3D cartoon faces with smoother and more natural eyelid contours and the characteristic chubby nose shapes in this cartoon style.

High-Quality Data. The cartoon face reconstruction method above only relies on landmarks and fails to capture the detailed stylized shapes of the cartoon faces, *e.g.*, deep nasolabial folds. Therefore, to enhance the quality of the 3D cartoon faces, we select 130 representative faces from the low-quality 3D cartoon data and ask three expert artists to refine these 3D models according to the corresponding 2D cartoon images with the 2D real photos as extra identity reference. These are referred to as high-quality data in our dataset.

Texture. As textures are one of the key components in reflecting cartoon style, we reconstruct cartoon textures based on the 2D cartoon images and the 3D cartoon faces. We first obtain a coarse cartoon texture map by mapping the 2D cartoon face image onto the 3D cartoon mesh. Then, for the invisible facial regions, we set their texture color as their symmetrical counterparts on the visible areas and finally apply Poisson inpainting to achieve complete cartoon texture maps as T_c in Fig. 2a.

4   Method

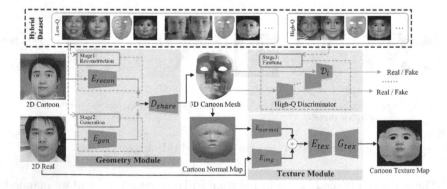

Fig. 3. Overview of our 3D Face Cartoonizer framework. Our framework contains two modules for geometry generation and texture generation. Notice that we only need 2D cartoon faces for training, which are not required for real usage.

The architecture of the proposed 3D Face Cartoonizer is shown in Fig. 3. Our method consists of a geometry module and a texture module which are trained on our hybrid cartoon dataset. We will introduce the two modules separately below.

4.1 Geometry Module

The geometry module is the most critical component of our method. It is trained to output a 3D cartoon facial geometry from a single real facial image. In order to generate high-quality outputs, we carefully design its network structures and train it using a novel training strategy *Recon2AGen*.

Network Structure. We use a special encoder-decoder architecture for the geometry module. It contains two encoders E_{recon} and E_{gen} which can regress the feature vectors from 2D cartoon images and 2D real images respectively. The feature vectors can be divided into a geometry feature vector which only encodes the 3D cartoon facial geometry, and a 3D pose $P \in se(3)$. The geometry feature, either output by E_{recon} or E_{gen}, will then be fed into a shared decoder D_{share}, which has the same network architecture as [3]. The decoder D_{share} predicts deformation representation in [25] instead of directly outputting the vertex positions of the 3D cartoon face. By applying the estimated deformation gradient to the mean 3D cartoon face, the geometry module can generate the final shape of the 3D cartoon face.

Recon2AGen Training Strategy. Generating a high-quality 3D cartoon face from a single real facial image is not easy as there are three major difficulties in learning this task: *1)* Recovering a 3D face from one 2D image is an ill-posed problem. *2)* Converting real faces to cartoon style needs to preserve the user-specific identity information. *3)* Learning to generate high-quality 3D cartoon faces is not easy when most of the training data is low-quality. Training the geometry module to solve the three problems in one stage will make the task even harder as all these difficulties will be coupled together. Therefore, we propose *Recon2AGen*, a progressive training strategy, in which the geometry module learns to solve these three problems respectively in three different stages. In *Stage 1*, the geometry module learns reconstruction using E_{recon} and D_{share}. It is trained to reconstruct the 3D cartoon face from a given 2D cartoon image, supervised by a large quantity of low-quality training data to overcome the ill-posed problem. In *Stage 2*, we fix the decoder D_{share} and train a new encoder E_{gen} from scratch to transfer the input 2D real image to 3D cartoon domain. In *Stage 3*, to enhance the quality of the 3D cartoon face generation, we finetune the geometry module on the artist-made high-quality data in a region-based adversarial manner. Specifically, we train 8 independent discriminators $\mathcal{D}_i$, $i \in \{1, \cdots, 8\}$, to distinguish the generated 3D face shapes in different local regions from the artist-made data while the geometry module is finetuned to fool these discriminators.

Training Losses. To cooperate with *Recon2AGen* training strategy, we implement well-designed training losses L to train the geometry module:

$$L = w_{geo}L_{geo} + w_{lmk}L_{lmk} + w_{sm}L_{sm} + w_{adv}L_{adv}, \tag{1}$$

where L_{geo} is a geometry loss, L_{lmk} is a landmark loss, L_{sm} is a smoothing loss, and L_{adv} is an adversarial loss. w_{geo}, w_{lmk}, w_{sm} and w_{adv} are the corresponding weights for different loss functions.

The geometry loss L_{geo} measures the difference between the generated 3D cartoon face $\hat{M}_c$ and the ground truth M_c:

$$L_{geo} = \|\hat{M}_c - M_c\|_2^2. \tag{2}$$

The landmark loss is used to maintain the consistence between the ground truth 2D landmarks and the corresponding 3D vertices:

$$L_{lmk} = \sum_{i \in \mathcal{K}_{lmk}} \|\boldsymbol{\Pi}\boldsymbol{P}\hat{\boldsymbol{v}}_i - \boldsymbol{k}_i\|_2^2, \tag{3}$$

where $\boldsymbol{k}_i$ is the detected 2D landmark and $\hat{\boldsymbol{v}}_i$ is its corresponding vertex on the estimated 3D cartoon face. $\mathcal{K}_{lmk}$ is the set of the 3D landmark indices on the mesh. $\boldsymbol{\Pi}$ is the camera projection matrix.

Inspired by the Laplacian smoothing algorithm, we use a smoothing loss L_{sm} to alleviate artifacts such as folding surfaces and self-intersections by constraining the Laplacian coordinates of the estimated cartoon faces to be similar to those of the ground truth. The L_{sm} is expressed as:

$$L_{sm} = \|\mathcal{L}\hat{M}_c - \mathcal{L}M_c\|_2^2, \tag{4}$$

where $\mathcal{L}$ denotes the Laplacian operator,

To extract the characteristics of the artist-made high-quality data, we use an adversarial loss which is formulated with the 8 discriminators. The discriminators are trained to distinguish the generated cartoon faces from the ground truth. The geometry module tries to fool the discriminators while keeping fitting the ground truth meshes. The L_{adv} is written as:

$$L_{adv} = \sum_{i=1}^{8} \mathbb{E}[\log \mathcal{D}_i(M_c)] + \mathbb{E}[\log(1 - \mathcal{D}_i(\hat{M}_c))]. \tag{5}$$

The geometry module is trained progressively in three stages. In the first two training stages, we set the loss weight w_{geo} to 10, w_{lmk} to 1×10^{-4}, w_{sm} to 1×10^3 and w_{adv} to 0. In *Stage 3*, we set w_{adv} to 5×10^{-4} while keeping the other loss weights unchanged. In this stage, the geometry module and the discriminators are trained in an adversarial manner, formulated as:

$$(E_{gen}, D_{share})* = \underset{E_{gen}, D_{share}}{\operatorname{argmin}} \ \underset{\mathcal{D}_i}{\max} L. \tag{6}$$

4.2   Geometry-Aware Texture Synthesis

Based on the proposed hybrid dataset, we train a geometry-aware GAN-structured network to synthesize complete cartoon texture from an input real facial image. As textures are strongly correlated to facial geometry, the texture module is guided by the geometric information of the 3D cartoon face predicted by the geometry module, as shown in Fig. 3. Our geometry-aware GAN does not directly concatenate the input image with the geometry guidance. Instead, we first use two shallow encoders, noted as E_{img} and E_{normal}, to transfer the input image and the normal map in UV-space predicted by the geometry module into two feature maps to combine these two pieces of information in feature space. They will be added and then injected into pSp [20] which is the state-of-the-art encoder for StyleGAN (noted as E_{tex}). Finally, the pretrained StyleGAN using our texture dataset will generate texture maps in the UV-space with the input feature map output by E_{tex}.

5   Experiments

In this section, we evaluate the proposed hybrid dataset and 3D Face Cartoonizer with thorough qualitative and quantitative experiments.

Experimental Settings. We train and evaluate both the geometry module and the texture generation module on our hybrid cartoon dataset. For the geometry module, we randomly choose 6140 triplets for training and the rest 702 triplets for testing from the low-quality data. In the high-quality data, there are 90 triplets for training and 40 triplets for testing. When training the texture generation module, we remove all triplets with eyeglasses to achieve clean facial textures. Finally, 4889 triplets are used for training leaving 556 triplets for testing. Both the real and cartoon images are aligned and resized to 224×224 before being fed into our network. The total training process costs about 6 days on a single GTX 2080 GPU. The average time to process an image in the inference stage is 0.02 ms for the geometry module and 0.08 s for the texture module.

5.1   Comparisons

To the best of our knowledge, there is no previous method that can directly convert a real portrait to a 3D cartoon face. Therefore, prior to our work, a naive way to automatically generate a 3D cartoon face from a real image is to concatenate 2D real-to-cartoon translation and 2D stylized face reconstruction techniques. We combine ToonMe App with two state-of-the-art stylized face reconstruction methods separately, including a fitting-based method proposed by [25] and a learning-based method proposed by [3]. Note that [3] is retrained on our proposed dataset. We compare our methods with these two naive methods both qualitatively and quantitatively.

Qualitative Comparisons. The qualitative comparisons among our 3D Face Cartoonizer and these two indirect solutions are shown in Fig. 4. Compared

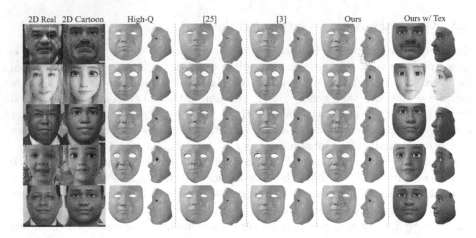

Fig. 4. Qualitative comparisons of our 3D cartoon face generation with other 3D cartoon face reconstruction methods ([25] and [3]).

with the two baselines, our geometry generation performs better in the following aspects. (1) On the "identity similarity", our results have more personalized overall face shapes (the 1st and 3rd row). (2) On the "style similarity", our results better represent the cartoon style, such as the chubby noses (the 1st row), the sharp curvatures of lips (the 2nd row), and plump shapes around cheekbones (the 1st and 3th row). (3) Our results also have richer "details" such as nasolabial folds shown in all rows. Besides, [3] suffers from unpleasant wrinkled surfaces(the 2nd row). Again, it should be noted that these naive solutions require ToonMe App to convert the real facial image to cartoon style and this will lead to more computation time. [25] also requires extra landmark annotations. On the contrary, our geometry module can synthesize high-quality 3D cartoon faces directly from an input real facial image and greatly enhance the convenience of 3D cartoon face generation.

We also demonstrate the effect of our texture generation module in the last column in Fig. 4 by rendering the 3D cartoon face results with the generated textures. To make our results more vivid, we add 3D eye models by calculating the size and the location of the eyeballs according to the eyelids of the generated 3D cartoon face and selecting a suitable iris color based on the estimated race of the input photo using [13]. The generated textures dramatically enhance aesthetics and the identity similarity with the input face image.

Quantitatively Comparisons. We also quantitatively compare our method with [25] and [3]. As there is no "accurate" ground truth for 3D cartoon face generation, we conduct a perceptual study to demonstrate the visual quality of these methods. We invite 30 volunteers and each volunteer scores the results of the same input achieved by all approaches simultaneously. To get a thorough and quantitative evaluation of each method, we design 3 scoring dimensions (artistry, identity similarity and style similarity) according to previous works on similar

Table 1. Perceptual study of different 3D cartoon face generation methods.

Metrics	[25]	[3]	Ours	High-Q
Artistry	2.67	2.88	**4.39**	4.27
Identity similarity	2.56	2.75	3.72	**4.01**
Style similarity	2.84	3.31	4.23	**4.28**

tasks [17,24]. Table 1 presents the average scores from the 30 volunteers. Our method achieves the most favorite results in all the aspects among all automatic methods and even outperforms the high-quality data in the artistry dimension.

5.2   Ablation Study

In this subsection, we evaluate the effect of the proposed *Recon2AGen* training strategy and *AGen* finetuning in 3D Face Cartoonizer.

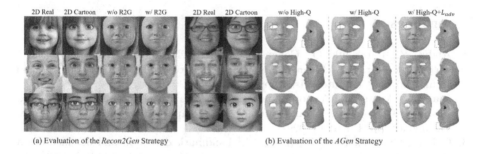

(a) Evaluation of the *Recon2Gen* Strategy   (b) Evaluation of the *AGen* Strategy

Fig. 5. Qualitative evaluations of the key components in our technique.

***Recon2Gen* Training.** We measure the effectiveness of our *Recon2Gen* training strategy in improving the quality of cartoon face generation in Fig. 5a. Without the *Recon2Gen* training strategy (noted as "w/o R2G", the geometry module fails to generate accurate face contours and sometimes leads to inaccurate face orientations. By pre-training on the task of cartoon face reconstruction (noted as "w/ R2G"), the geometry module generates better facial poses (the 1st row), expressions (the 2nd row), and more accurate facial contours (the last row).

***AGen* Finetuning.** To demonstrate the effect of *AGen* finetuning, We compare our method with two extra ablations, including one geometry module only trained with the low-quality data and another finetuned with the high-quality data without using the adversarial loss. As shown in Fig. 5b, directly introducing high-quality data in the training brings minor improvement to the generated cartoon faces. By using an adversarial training loss, the geometry module is able to learn the style of the artist-made cartoon faces, such as shaper eye corner

contours (the 1st row), a more vivid smile (side view of the 1st row), more pro-
nounced nasolabial folds (the 2nd row), and a chubby and protruding chin (the
3rd row).

6 Conclusion

We proposed 3D Face Cartoonizer, the first automatic solution that directly generate a high-quality 3D cartoon face from a single facial image. In our solution,
the method *Recon2AGen* solves the 2D-to-3D ambiguity and the real-to-cartoon
transformation in a progressive manner with limited high-quality data, avoiding
the huge cost of building a large scale artists-made 3D cartoon face dataset.

Acknowledgements. This work was supported by Beijing Natural Science Foundation (JQ19015), the NSFC (No. 62021002, 61727808), the National Key R&D Program
of China (2018YFA0704000), and the Key Research and Development Project of Tibet
Autonomous Region (XZ202101ZY0019G). This work was also supported by THUIBCS,
Tsinghua University, and BLBCI, Beijing Municipal Education Commission.

References

1. Alaluf, Y., Patashnik, O., Cohen-Or, D.: ReStyle: a residual-based StyleGAN
   encoder via iterative refinement. In: Proceedings of the IEEE/CVF International
   Conference on Computer Vision, pp. 6711–6720 (2021)
2. Blanz, V., Vetter, T.: A morphable model for the synthesis of 3D faces. In: Proceedings of the 26th Annual Conference on Computer Graphics and Interactive
   Techniques, pp. 187–194 (1999)
3. Cai, H., Guo, Y., Peng, Z., Zhang, J.: Landmark detection and 3D face reconstruction for caricature using a nonlinear parametric model. Graph. Models **115**,
   101103 (2021)
4. Cao, C., Weng, Y., Zhou, S., Tong, Y., Zhou, K.: FaceWarehouse: a 3D facial
   expression database for visual computing. IEEE Trans. Visual. Comput. Graph.
   20(3), 413–425 (2013)
5. Cao, K., Liao, J., Yuan, L.: CariGANs: unpaired photo-to-caricature translation.
   arXiv preprint arXiv:1811.00222 (2018)
6. Deng, J., Cheng, S., Xue, N., Zhou, Y., Zafeiriou, S.: UV-GAN: adversarial facial
   UV map completion for pose-invariant face recognition. In: Proceedings of the
   IEEE Conference on Computer Vision and Pattern Recognition, pp. 7093–7102
   (2018)
7. Duda, R.O., Hart, P.E., et al.: Pattern Classification and Scene Analysis, vol. 3.
   Wiley, New York (1973)
8. Gecer, B., Ploumpis, S., Kotsia, I., Zafeiriou, S.: GANFIT: generative adversarial
   network fitting for high fidelity 3D face reconstruction. In: Proceedings of the
   IEEE/CVF Conference on Computer Vision and Pattern Recognition (CVPR),
   June 2019
9. Gong, J., Hold-Geoffroy, Y., Lu, J.: AutoToon: automatic geometric warping for
   face cartoon generation. In: Proceedings of the IEEE/CVF Winter Conference on
   Applications of Computer Vision, pp. 360–369 (2020)

10. Han, X., Gao, C., Yu, Y.: DeepSketch2Face: a deep learning based sketching system for 3D face and caricature modeling. ACM Trans. Graph. (TOG) **36**(4), 1–12 (2017)
11. Han, X., et al.: CaricatureShop: personalized and photorealistic caricature sketching. IEEE Trans. Visual. Comput. Graph. **26**(7), 2349–2361 (2018)
12. Jang, W., Ju, G., Jung, Y., Yang, J., Tong, X., Lee, S.: StyleCariGAN: caricature generation via StyleGAN feature map modulation. ACM Trans. Graph. (TOG) **40**(4), 1–16 (2021)
13. Karkkainen, K., Joo, J.: FairFace: face attribute dataset for balanced race, gender, and age for bias measurement and mitigation. In: Proceedings of the IEEE/CVF Winter Conference on Applications of Computer Vision, pp. 1548–1558 (2021)
14. Karras, T., Laine, S., Aila, T.: A style-based generator architecture for generative adversarial networks. In: Proceedings of the IEEE/CVF Conference on Computer Vision and Pattern Recognition, pp. 4401–4410 (2019)
15. Lewiner, T., Vieira, T., Martínez, D., Peixoto, A., Mello, V., Velho, L.: Interactive 3D caricature from harmonic exaggeration. Comput. Graph. **35**(3), 586–595 (2011)
16. Li, T., Bolkart, T., Black, M.J., Li, H., Romero, J.: Learning a model of facial shape and expression from 4D scans. ACM Trans. Graph. **36**(6), 194–1 (2017)
17. Liu, J., et al.: Semi-supervised learning in reconstructed manifold space for 3D caricature generation. In: Computer Graphics Forum, vol. 28, pp. 2104–2116. Wiley Online Library (2009)
18. Pinkney, J.N., Adler, D.: Resolution dependent GAN interpolation for controllable image synthesis between domains. arXiv preprint arXiv:2010.05334 (2020)
19. Qiu, Y., et al.: 3DCaricShop: a dataset and a baseline method for single-view 3D caricature face reconstruction. In: Proceedings of the IEEE/CVF Conference on Computer Vision and Pattern Recognition, pp. 10236–10245 (2021)
20. Richardson, E., et al.: Encoding in style: a StyleGAN encoder for image-to-image translation. In: Proceedings of the IEEE/CVF Conference on Computer Vision and Pattern Recognition, pp. 2287–2296 (2021)
21. Shi, Y., Deb, D., Jain, A.K.: WarpGAN: automatic caricature generation. In: Proceedings of the IEEE/CVF Conference on Computer Vision and Pattern Recognition, pp. 10762–10771 (2019)
22. Song, G., et al.: AgileGAN: stylizing portraits by inversion-consistent transfer learning. ACM Trans. Graph. (TOG) **40**(4), 1–13 (2021)
23. Tov, O., Alaluf, Y., Nitzan, Y., Patashnik, O., Cohen-Or, D.: Designing an encoder for StyleGAN image manipulation. arXiv preprint arXiv:2102.02766 (2021)
24. Vieira, R.C.C., Vidal, C.A., Cavalcante-Neto, J.B.: Three-dimensional face caricaturing by anthropometric distortions. In: 2013 XXVI Conference on Graphics, Patterns and Images, pp. 163–170. IEEE (2013)
25. Wu, Q., Zhang, J., Lai, Y.K., Zheng, J., Cai, J.: Alive caricature from 2D to 3D. In: Proceedings of the IEEE Conference on Computer Vision and Pattern Recognition, pp. 7336–7345 (2018)
26. Yang, H., et al.: FaceScape: a large-scale high quality 3D face dataset and detailed riggable 3D face prediction. In: Proceedings of the IEEE/CVF Conference on Computer Vision and Pattern Recognition, pp. 601–610 (2020)
27. Zhu, X., Lei, Z., Yan, J., Yi, D., Li, S.Z.: High-fidelity pose and expression normalization for face recognition in the wild. In: Proceedings of the IEEE Conference on Computer Vision and Pattern Recognition, pp. 787–796 (2015)

Low Light Video Enhancement Based on Temporal-Spatial Complementary Feature

Gengchen Zhang, Yuhang Zeng, and Ying Fu$^{(\boxtimes)}$

School of Computer Science and Technology, Beijing Institute of Technology,
Beijing, China
{3120220991,zengyuhang,fuying}@bit.edu.cn

Abstract. Under low light conditions, the quality of video data is heavily affected by noise, artifacts, and weak contrast, leading to low signal-to-noise ratio. Therefore, enhancing low light video to obtain high-quality information expression is a challenging problem. Deep learning based methods have achieved good performance on low light enhancement tasks and a majority of them are based on Unet. However, the widely used Unet architecture may generate pseudo-detail textures, as the simple skip connections of Unet introduce feature inconsistency between encoding and decoding stages. To overcome these shortcomings, we propose a novel network 3D Swin Skip Unet (3DS^{2}Unet) in this paper. Specifically, we design a novel feature extraction and reconstruction module based on Swin Transformer and a temporal-channel attention module. Temporal-spatial complementary feature is generated by two modules and then fed into the decoder. The experimental results show that our model can well restore the texture of objects in the video, and performs better in removing noise and maintaining object boundaries between frames under low light conditions.

Keywords: Low light video enhancement · Swin-Transformer · Attention mechanism

1 Introduction

When taking photos in a dark scene or at a backlight angle, the captured images are often with low brightness, low contrast, low color perception, which affect the visual effects. In addition, darkness and noise hide the details in the image and cause low signal-to-noise ratio. These problems have negative effects on a range of downstream computer vision tasks such as object detection [1] and semantic segmentation [4]. To solve this, in this paper, we focus on low light video enhancement to produce visual pleasing videos, which have the potential to be used in automated driving and surveillance systems under low light conditions.

Deep learning has been widely used in low light enhancement tasks, and promising performances have been achieved in the past decades. Among these methods, many of them [3,6] are based on Unet architecture [19]. We notice

L. Fang et al. (Eds.): CICAI 2022, LNAI 13604, pp. 368–379, 2022.
https://doi.org/10.1007/978-3-031-20497-5_30

that simple skip connection between encoders and decoders plays an important role in Unet. However, feature fused by simple skip connection may impair the enhance performance of the model due to the large differences in features between encoders and decoders. As a result, in low light video enhancement tasks, it may cause pseudo-detail texture or information loss without fully utilizing the space domain information and time domain information.

To solve these problems, we consider extracting temporal-spatial complementary feature during skip connection and make it consistent with decoded feature. So we propose 3D Swin Skip Unet (3DS^{2}Unet) with two novel modules added to skip connection. In order to capture global temporal-spatial context in encoded feature and establish long range dependency on the moving object in low light video, we design a feature extraction and reconstruction module based on 3D Swin-Transformer [13] which has strong ability to extract information across the spatial and temporal dimensions. To increase consistency between features, we propose temporal-channel attention module that fuses reconstructed feature output by first module and the decoded feature. Temporal-spatial complementary feature with stronger capability for video expression is output by this module and fed into next decoder. Our model is evaluated on SMOID [6] dataset and outperforms state-of-the-art methods on quantitative metrics. Visualization results also validate our advantages in clear textures and few artifacts.

2   Related Work

2.1   Low Light Image Enhancement

The existing traditional low light image enhancement methods can be divided into three categories, including histogram equalization (HE) based method, Retinex [9] based method and dehazing based method. Based on histogram equalization, CVC [2] uses inter-pixel context information to enhance the contrast of the input image. LDR [10] uses layered difference representation of 2D histograms and enhances image contrast by amplifying the gray-level differences between adjacent pixels. Another series of dark light image enhancement methods are derived from Retinex theory. SSR [7] uses Gaussian convolution function to estimate brightness and then calculates the reflection of the image for dark enhancement. Li et al. [11] propose a Robuse-Retinex model which considers the influence of strong noise on enhancement performance. After the low light image is inverted, the inverted image is similar to the hazy image in visualization and in intensity distribution. Dong et al. [5] apply the dehazing algorithm to inverted low light images to achieve low light enhancement. In general, traditional modeling approaches require task-specific adjustments to improve the validity of model assumptions and are limited by certain prerequisites.

More and more deep learning based method has been developed to do low light [22,23]. Lore et al. [14] first introduce deep learning to low light image enhancement tasks. They propose a sparse denoising autoencoder LLNet to adaptively enhance and denoise image. The dataset used by LLNet is obtained by adding gamma correction and Gaussian noise, which cannot reflect the real dark light environment. Chen *et al.* [3] make paired low light dataset SID which contains more than five 5000 paires of low light raw images and normal light RGB images. They use the dataset to train Unet [19] and attain good performance on low light image enhancement. Ren *et al.* [18] propose a hybrid network with two distinct streams to simultaneously learn the global content and structure of enhanced images. Some researchers combine Retinex theory with CNN and propose low light enhancement networks based on Retinex. Msr-net [20] transforms the multiscale Retinex architecture into a deep convolutional network. RetinexNet [24] expresses the image decomposition, adjustment and reconstruction process in Retinex with the CNN models respectively.

2.2   Low Light Video Enhancement

Since videos consist of a series of images, image enhancement methods can be applied to video in the frame-by-frame way. However, frames in a video are continuous and correlated, directly performing image enhancement method frame by frame may lead to flickering effect, object shape inconsistency between frames, unnecessary artifacts and so on.

Researchers have developed a series of methods on low light video enhancement tasks. In recent years, more and more deep learning based methods are developed for low light video enhancement. MBLLVEN [15] uses 3D convolution to extract and enhance image features. Jiang *et al.* [6] replace 2D convolution layers in the Unet with 3D convolution layers to improve performance on low light videos. RViDeNet [25] adopts temporal fusion and spatial fusion to make use of correlation between adjacent frames in the video. EMVD [16] processes the video in three stages, including fusion stage, denoising stage and refinement stage. These stages operate on a transform-domain that simultaneously increases accuracy and decreases complexity. $3D^2$Unet [26] uses 3D deformable convolution in Unet to adaptively extract information from the video within and between frames. It attains better video recovery accuracy and visual effect. Zhang *et al.* [27] infers optical flow from image to sythesize low light video which is hard to collect.

Unet has been widely used in low light image and video enhancement [6,26]. In the Unet architecture, features concatenated between skip connection are inconsistent which may cause degradation in accuracy. To solve this problem, we propose feature extraction and reconstruction module based on Swin-Transformer to extract context from temporal and spatial domain. We also propose temporal-channel attention module to make it consistent with decoded feature. We add these two modules to 3DUnet and forms 3D Swin Skip Unet ($3DS^2$Unet) that outperforms state-of-the-art low light video enhancement methods.

3   Method

In this section, we present our novel low light video enhancement method. Our method takes low light raw video with F frames in Bayer pattern as input. We pack $F \times H \times W$ raw video into four color channels and the size becomes half of the original. The $4 \times F \times \frac{H}{2} \times \frac{W}{2}$ packed video is then processed with our model 3DS^{2}Unet that outputs RGB enhanced video.

3.1 Overall Architecture

Our low light video enhancement model 3DS^{2}Unet is shown in Fig. 1. Its overall architecture is based on 3DUnet and it uses 3D convolution block as encoder and decoder to extract and reconstruct multi-scale video features. In order to better fuse the image features between encoding and decoding stages, we introduce a feature extraction and reconstruction module based on Swin-Transformer and a temporal-channel attention module. These two modules connect the encoder and decoder of the same layer to replace the skip connection part of the original Unet structure. The Swin Skip connection can be represented by

$$F_{TSC} = M_{TCA}(M_{FER}(F_E), F_D) \tag{1}$$

where F_E is the encoded feature and F_D is the decoded feature in the same layer. F_{TSC} is the temporal-spatial complementary feature generated by Swin Skip. M_{FER} is the feature extraction and reconstruction module, M_{TCA} is the temporal-channel attention module. We will present more information about these two modules and describe our optimization target in the following.

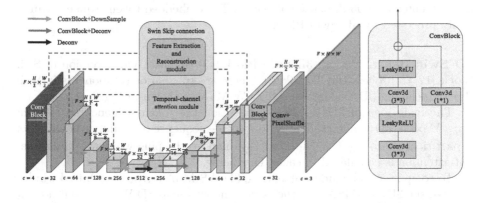

Fig. 1. Overall architecture of our 3DS^{2}Unet. Our model takes packed raw video as input. The encoded feature maps (blue blocks) with different scale are obtained by ConvBlock and downsampling. The decoder generate decoded feature maps (orange blocks) symmetrical with encoded feature maps. The Swin Skip connection fuses encoded feature and decoded feature and outputs temporal-spatial complementary feature (yellow block) which extract context in both temporal and spatial dimension of low light video. (Color figure online)

3.2 Feature Extraction and Reconstruction Module

We design feature extraction and reconstruction module based on 3D Swin-Transformer. It generates reconstructed feature with global receptive field in spatial and temporal domain. It can be further divided into three parts, including feature embedding module, 3D Swin Blocks and feature reconstruction module. The input feature from the encoder is stretched into token sequence of a specific length by the feature embedding module. Then the token sequence is fed into four consecutive 3D-Swin Blocks for further feature extraction and processing, and obtain output tokens sequence. Finally, feature reconstruction module convert the output token sequence to reconstructed features with the same size as encoded feature. This process can be expressed by

$$F_R = M_{FER}(F_E) = Recon(3DSwin^4(Embed(F_E))) \qquad (2)$$

where F_R is the reconstructed feature. $Embed$, $3DSwin$ and $Recon$ represents feature embedding, 3D Swin Block and feature reconstruction respectively. These three parts are elaborated in the following.

Feature Embedding Module. The function of the feature embedding module is to transform the feature map into a token sequence, as shown in Fig. 2(a). We first split the $C \times F \times H \times W$ encoded feature map into several feature patches with size $C \times 2 \times 4 \times 4$. Then we use 3D convolution with kernel size and stride equals to $2 \times 4 \times 4$ to generate a $96 \times \frac{F}{2} \times \frac{H}{4} \times \frac{W}{4}$ token sequence. Each token is represented as a 96-dimensional vector. The embedded token sequence can be easily processed by 3D Swin Block.

3D Swin Block. We use 3D Swin Block [13] that is a video version of Swin Block [12] to process the 3D tokens. There are two major components in Swin Block, including 3D W-MSA and 3D SW-MSA as shown in Fig. 2(c).

The main idea of 3D W-MSA is partition the token sequence into several $P \times M \times M$ 3D windows. The $\frac{F}{2} \times \frac{H}{4} \times \frac{W}{4}$ sequence of 96-dimensional token is partitioned into $\lceil \frac{F}{2P} \rceil \times \lceil \frac{H}{4M} \rceil \times \lceil \frac{W}{4M} \rceil$ non-overlapping windows. Multi-head self-attention is calculated in each 3D window.

To compute cross-window attention, 3D WS-MSA introduces shifted window mechanism. 3D WS-MSA uses the same window size as 3D W-MSA, but its windows shift $(\frac{P}{2}, \frac{M}{2}, \frac{M}{2})$ along temporal and spatial axes. Multi-head self-attention is also calculated in each shifted 3D window that makes each token percept other tokens in adjacent windows. Using several stacked 3D Swin blocks, each token can get global context directly or indirectly.

Feature Reconstruction Module. Feature extraction module based on 3D Swin Blocks does not change the shape of token sequence. However, these compressed tokens cannot concatenate and fuse with features generated by decoders. We use feature reconstruction module to convert token sequence to a feature map (see Fig. 2(b)). We first upsample the token sequence with scale equals to $2 \times 4 \times 4$ and generate a $96 \times F \times H \times W$ feature map. Then we perform 3D convolution to reconstruct feature dimension and use Batch Normal (BN) layer and ReLU activation function to introduce nonlinearity. The feature reconstruction module finally outputs $C \times F \times H \times W$ feature map F_R.

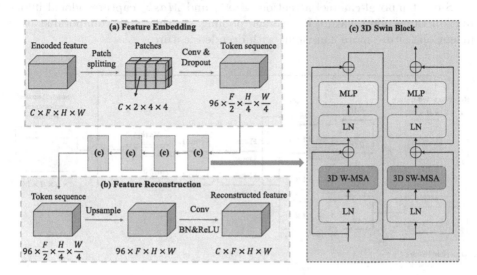

Fig. 2. Feature extraction and reconstruction module based on 3D Swin-Transformer. (a) Feature embedding module. (b) Feature reconstruction module. (c) 3D Swin Block. Encoded feature is embedded into token sequence then processed by four consecutive 3D Swin Blocks and finally converted into reconstructed feature.

3.3 Temporal-Channel Attention Module

$3DS^2$Unet uses the temporal-channel attention module to fine-tune and fuse the reconstructed and decoded features, as shown in Fig. 3. With this, we can obtain temporal-channel attention and temporal-spatial complementary feature.

We first perform global average pooling on the reconstructed feature F_R and decoded feature F_D in channel dimension to produce $C \times 1 \times 1 \times 1$ vector $GAP_1(F_R)$ and vector $GAP_1(F_D)$. The channel attention $Mask_1$ is obtained by averaging the sum of the two vectors, then performing a linear mapping and a nonlinear ReLU operation, constructing attention with Sigmoid at last. Similarly, we also perform global average pooling in temporal dimension to produce $F \times 1 \times 1 \times 1$ vectors $GAP_2(F_R)$ and $GAP_2(F_D)$. The temporal attention $Mask_2$ is calculated from these two vectors in the same way as $Mask_1$. Temporal-channel attention can be represented by

$$Mask_i = Sigmoid(ReLU(Linear_i(\frac{GAP_i(F_R) + GAP_i(F_D)}{2}))), i = 1, 2 \quad (3)$$

where GAP is global average pooling in temporal or channel dimension.

The temporal-spatial complementary feature F_{TSC} is calculated by Eq. 4 that fuses reconstructed feature and temporal-channel attention. It is then concatenated with decoded feature to serve as input of next decoder.

$$F_{TSC} = F_R \times Mask_1 \times Mask_2 \tag{4}$$

Since temporal-channel attention $Mask_1$ and $Mask_2$ captures global information in decoded feature by average pooling. So they make temporal-spatial attention feature more consistent with decoded feature.

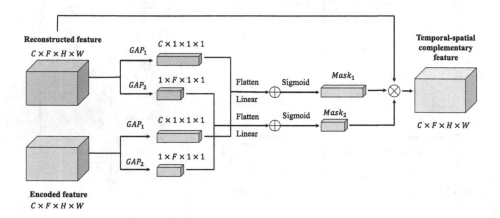

Fig. 3. Temporal-channel attention module.

3.4   Learning Detail

Our method uses an asymptotic optimization approach to update the model parameters. The training process of the complete model can be divided into two steps. In the first step, we pre-train the 3DUnet model and update the parameters of encoder and decoder. In the second step, we add feature extraction reconstruction module and temporal-channel attention module to obtain the complete model. We load the pre-trained parameters of the encoder and decoder to the complete model and optimize jointly optimize all parameters.

The optimization objection in pre-train stage is

$$\Theta_1 = \arg\min_{\Theta_1} \|V_{RGB}^{NL} - N_{\Theta_1}(V_{RAW}^{LL})\|_1 \tag{5}$$

where V_{RGB}^{NL} and V_{RAW}^{LL} represent ground-truth video in RGB data format under normal light condition and the video to be processed in RAW data format under low light condition, $N_{\Theta_1}(\cdot)$ is 3DUnet model and Θ_1 is trainable parameters of encoders and decoders.

The optimization objection in refining stage is

$$(\Theta_1, \Theta_2) = \underset{(\Theta_1, \Theta_2)}{\arg\min} ||V_{RGB}^{NL} - N_{(\Theta_1, \Theta_2)}(V_{RAW}^{LL})||_1 \qquad (6)$$

where Θ_1 is initialized with pre-trained result, $N_{(\Theta_1, \Theta_2)}(\cdot)$ is the complete model and Θ_2 represents parameters of feature extraction reconstruction module and temporal-channel attention module.

4 Experiment

4.1 Setup

We use the dataset in SMOID [6] that consists of low light RAW format video and corresponding RGB format ground-truth video in normal light. The SMOID dataset has 179 pairs of real street view videos under different gain levels (0, 5, 10, 15, 20). The Gain level affects the quality of the captured images. Generally, higher Gain level makes video brighter. Raw images are obtained by cameras with Bayer filter, so we decompose and pack the raw images into 4 channels in "GBRG" order.

For the SMOID dataset, we select 125 video sequences as the training set, 27 sequences for validation, and the remaining 27 sequences for testing. In training phase, we extract all the sub-videos of 16 consecutive frames from the original video of 200 frames. Then the sub-videos are randomly cropped with a 512×512 window. To further augment the data size, they are flipped randomly up, down, left and right. Considering that the images of the SMOID dataset have some blurry artifacts at the edges, we do not test on the full images. Instead, we evaluate image blocks of size 512×512 cropped from original raw image. Finally, since the SMOID dataset collects data at 5 different Gain levels and the amount of data in each set is sufficient, our model training and testing processes are performed separately at each Gain level.

All the methods are trained with ADAM optimizer [8] with parameters set as $\beta_1 = 0.9, \beta_2 = 0.999, \epsilon = 10^{-8}$ and batch size is set to 1. Learning rate is set to 1e−4 at pre-train stage and change to 5e−5 at refining stage. Our model is built on Pytorch [17] and trained with one RTX 3090 GPU. In the test phase, we use PSNR and SSIM to measure the performance of the models.

4.2 Results

To evaluate the performance of our method, we compare 3DS^{2}Unet with state-of-the-art low light video enhancement methods such as MBLLVEN [15] and SMOID [6]. Besides, we train and test low light image enhancement methods on the SMOID dataset frame by frame to compare with our model. These methods includes PMRID [21] and SID [3]. We also compare our model with some state-of-the-art video denoising models such as EMVD [16] and RViDeNet [25]. For MBLLVEN and PMRID that takes RGB format images as the input, we change

MBLLVEN   SMOID   PMRID   SID   EMVD   RViDeNet   3DS²Unet

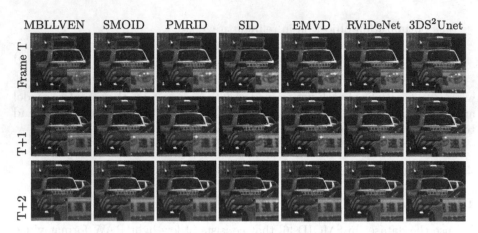

Fig. 4. Virtual comparison on SMOID dataset at Gain = 0.

the input channel of their first layer to fit our packed 4-channel raw video. These methods are assessed with quantitative metrics and visual effect on the SMOID dataset at all Gain levels.

Table 1. Quantitative results of different methods on SMOID dataset at all Gain levels. The experimental results are measured by two metrics PSNR and SSIM. The results are the average values on the test set.

Method	Gain0		Gain5		Gain10		Gain15		Gain20	
	PSNR	SSIM	PSNR	SSIM	PSNR	SSIM	PSNR	SSIM	PSNR	SSIM
MBLLVEN [15]	29.10	0.9291	26.13	0.9002	28.66	0.9330	28.81	0.9067	26.32	0.9165
SMOID [6]	29.64	0.9255	28.99	0.9085	31.00	0.9396	29.07	0.8992	30.55	0.9421
PMRID [21]	27.86	0.9020	27.83	0.8996	31.05	0.9319	29.52	0.8897	30.79	0.9328
SID [3]	27.99	0.9147	26.82	0.9054	27.81	0.9103	28.04	0.8879	28.93	0.9181
EMVD [16]	30.14	0.9262	29.39	0.9141	32.22	0.9428	30.04	0.8970	32.77	0.9475
RViDeNet [25]	32.98	0.9535	29.54	**0.9188**	33.90	0.9590	30.10	0.8977	34.76	**0.9627**
3DS²Unet	**33.42**	**0.9567**	**29.69**	0.9178	**34.25**	**0.9614**	**30.14**	**0.9080**	**34.81**	0.9626

The experimental results on SMOID dataset at different Gain levels are shown in Table 1. By analyzing the quantitative results, our 3DS²Unet outperforms the compared methods at all Gain levels. Compared with methods based on Unet such as SMOID and SID, 3D²Unet achieves 1.1 dB to 6.44 dB increment on PSNR at different Gain levels. Our method outperforms MBLLVEN by 8.49 dB on PSNR because it is more suitable for RAW2RGB low light enhancement tasks. 3DS²Unet is slightly lower than RViDeNet when measured with SSIM at Gain = 5 and Gain = 20, but surpasses it on PSNR at all Gain levels.

Figure 4 shows the visualization results of obtained by different image enhancement methods when Gain level equals 0. Our method is superior to other methods in many aspects including the ability of removing low light video noise, recovering object boundaries as well as maintaining texture and other image details. MBLLVEN and PMRID fails to accurately recover the color when enhancing low light raw video. SMOID has a lack of ability to remove noise from the video. Due to the lack of temporal information, there are flickering artifacts in the videos enhanced with SID.

4.3   Ablation Study

To validate the two modules proposed in our work, we conduct a series of ablation study. We use SMOID dataset at Gain = 0 as training and test sets. We remove the feature extraction and reconstruction module based on Swin-Transformer and the encoded feature map is fed directly into temporal-channel attention module. We also test the model without temporal-channel attention module that directly feeds reconstructed feature map into next decoder. Table 2 shows the comparison of these two models with the original $3DS^2Unet$ model. We find that PNSR drops 0.33 dB and 0.52 dB after removing feature extraction and reconstruction module and temporal-channel attention module. We also find that removing any of the modules may cause severe artifacts in the enhanced image. So we can conclude that both modules improve the feature's ability to describe information from temporal, spatial and channel dimensions.

Table 2. Ablation study on the SMOID dataset at Gain=0.

Feature extraction and reconstruction	Temporal-channel attention	PSNR	SSIM
×	√	33.09	0.9554
√	×	32.90	0.9541
√	√	**33.42**	**0.9567**

5   Conclusion

In this paper, we propose a novel model for low light video enhancement based on 3DUnet. Our model uses temporal-spatial complementary feature instead of encoded feature in the skip connection. To generate the temporal-spatial complementary feature, we propose feature extraction and reconstruction module based on 3D Swin Transformer and temporal-channel attention module. In the future, we will focus on improving its efficiency and develop realtime video enhancement method.

Acknowledgments. This work was supported by the National Natural Science Foundation of China under Grants No. 62171038, No. 61827901, and No. 62088101.

References

1. Bochkovskiy, A., Wang, C.Y., Liao, H.Y.M.: YOLOv4: optimal speed and accuracy of object detection. arXiv preprint arXiv:2004.10934 (2020)
2. Celik, T., Tjahjadi, T.: Contextual and variational contrast enhancement. IEEE Trans. Image Process. **20**(12), 3431–3441 (2011)
3. Chen, C., Chen, Q., Xu, J., Koltun, V.: Learning to see in the dark. In: Proceedings of Conference on Computer Vision and Pattern Recognition (CVPR), pp. 3291–3300 (2018)
4. Chen, L.-C., Zhu, Y., Papandreou, G., Schroff, F., Adam, H.: Encoder-decoder with atrous separable convolution for semantic image segmentation. In: Ferrari, V., Hebert, M., Sminchisescu, C., Weiss, Y. (eds.) ECCV 2018. LNCS, vol. 11211, pp. 833–851. Springer, Cham (2018). https://doi.org/10.1007/978-3-030-01234-2_49
5. Dong, X., et al.: Fast efficient algorithm for enhancement of low lighting video. In: Proceedings of International Conference on Multimedia and Expo (ICME), pp. 1–6 (2011)
6. Jiang, H., Zheng, Y.: Learning to see moving objects in the dark. In: Proceedings of International Conference on Computer Vision (ICCV), pp. 7324–7333 (2019)
7. Jobson, D.J., Rahman, Z.U., Woodell, G.A.: Properties and performance of a center/surround Retinex. IEEE Trans. Image Process. **6**(3), 451–462 (1997)
8. Kingma, D.P., Ba, J.: Adam: a method for stochastic optimization. arXiv preprint arXiv:1412.6980 (2014)
9. Land, E.H.: The Retinex theory of color vision. Sci. Am. **237**(6), 108–129 (1977)
10. Lee, C., Lee, C., Kim, C.: Contrast enhancement based on layered difference representation of 2D histograms. IEEE Trans. Image Process. 5372–5384 (2013)
11. Li, M., Liu, J., Yang, W., Sun, X., Guo, Z.: Structure-revealing low-light image enhancement via robust Retinex model. IEEE Trans. Image Process. **27**(6), 2828–2841 (2018)
12. Liu, Z., et al.: Swin transformer: hierarchical vision transformer using shifted windows. In: Proceedings of International Conference on Computer Vision (ICCV), pp. 10012–10022, October 2021
13. Liu, Z., et al.: Video Swin Transformer. arXiv preprint arXiv:2106.13230 (2021)
14. Lore, K.G., Akintayo, A., Sarkar, S.: LLNet: a deep autoencoder approach to natural low-light image enhancement. Pattern Recogn. **61**, 650–662 (2017)
15. Lv, F., Lu, F., Wu, J., Lim, C.: MBLLEN: low-light image/video enhancement using CNNs. In: Proceedings of British Machine Vision Conference (BMVC), vol. 220, p. 4 (2018)
16. Maggioni, M., Huang, Y., Li, C., Xiao, S., Fu, Z., Song, F.: Efficient multi-stage video denoising with recurrent spatio-temporal fusion. In: Proceedings of Conference on Computer Vision and Pattern Recognition (CVPR), pp. 3466–3475 (2021)
17. Paszke, A., et al.: PyTorch: an imperative style, high-performance deep learning library (2019)
18. Ren, W., et al.: Low-light image enhancement via a deep hybrid network. IEEE Trans. Image Process. **28**(9), 4364–4375 (2019)
19. Ronneberger, O., Fischer, P., Brox, T.: U-Net: convolutional networks for biomedical image segmentation. In: Navab, N., Hornegger, J., Wells, W.M., Frangi, A.F. (eds.) MICCAI 2015. LNCS, vol. 9351, pp. 234–241. Springer, Cham (2015). https://doi.org/10.1007/978-3-319-24574-4_28
20. Shen, L., Yue, Z., Feng, F., Chen, Q., Liu, S., Ma, J.: MSR-net: low-light image enhancement using deep convolutional network. arXiv preprint arXiv:1711.02488 (2017)

21. Wang, Y., Huang, H., Xu, Q., Liu, J., Liu, Y., Wang, J.: Practical deep raw image denoising on mobile devices. In: Vedaldi, A., Bischof, H., Brox, T., Frahm, J.-M. (eds.) ECCV 2020. LNCS, vol. 12351, pp. 1–16. Springer, Cham (2020). https://doi.org/10.1007/978-3-030-58539-6_1

22. Wei, K., Fu, Y., Yang, J., Huang, H.: A physics-based noise formation model for extreme low-light raw denoising. In: Proceedings of Conference on Computer Vision and Pattern Recognition (CVPR), pp. 2758–2767 (2020)

23. Xiang, Y., Fu, Y., Zhang, L., Huang, H.: An effective network with ConvLSTM for low-light image enhancement, pp. 221–233 (2019)

24. Yang, W., Wang, W., Huang, H., Wang, S., Liu, J.: Sparse gradient regularized deep Retinex network for robust low-light image enhancement. IEEE Trans. Image Process. **30**, 2072–2086 (2021)

25. Yue, H., Cao, C., Liao, L., Chu, R., Yang, J.: Supervised raw video denoising with a benchmark dataset on dynamic scenes. In: Proceedings of Conference on Computer Vision and Pattern Recognition (CVPR), pp. 2301–2310 (2020)

26. Zeng, Y., Zou, Y., Fu, Y.: 3D^{2}Unet: 3D deformable Unet for low-light video enhancement. In: Ma, H., et al. (eds.) PRCV 2021. LNCS, vol. 13021, pp. 66–77. Springer, Cham (2021). https://doi.org/10.1007/978-3-030-88010-1_6

27. Zhang, F., Li, Y., You, S., Fu, Y.: Learning temporal consistency for low light video enhancement from single images. In: Proceedings of Conference on Computer Vision and Pattern Recognition (CVPR), pp. 4967–4976 (2021)

Compound Label Learning for Affective Image Content Analysis

Qingzhu Zhang and Tongtong Yuan[✉]

Beijing University of Technology, Chaoyang, China
yuantt@bjut.edu.cn

Abstract. The single label of an affective image cannot well reflect the emotions underneath, thus converting the single label into compound affective labels better reveals the complex emotions of the image. However, building new datasets on human annotation has high labor costs, and the results are quite subjective. To address this issue, our paper proposes a model for constructing compound affective labels from single-label datasets with a CNN-based model. First, we enhance the ability of image sentiment classification by applying a new classifier loss. Second, we adopt the knowledge distillation model for retaining more sentiment information in image labels. Third, we integrate the attention mechanism within the knowledge distillation to transfer the attention map to the student network for improving its performance. Finally, we attain the compound affective labels from the label probability distribution of the distilled model. The generated image datasets with compound labels can be applied in various fields. They can serve for psychological analysis and evaluation, and provide richer affective references in art design, interactive media, advertising products, etc.

Keywords: Affective Image Content Analysis · Knowledge distillation · Image classification

1 Introduction

With the rapid development of today's mobile network, more and more people tend to express their emotions by posting affective images on social media platforms such as Weibo, Instagram, and Twitter. Although the related research on image semantic recognition has made great progress at present, the research on Affective Image Content Analysis (AICA) is not deep enough. One of the main difficulties in sentiment analysis is the lack of large-scale sentiment datasets with emotional labels. First of all, the collection of large-scale datasets with manual-tagged labels is usually labor-intensive. Moreover, emotions are quite subjective [1]. The emotions one feels from images are intimately related to one's experience, personality, and cultural background [2]. Therefore, the construction of the emotion datasets is affected by a variety of interference factors, resulting in very limited large-scale emotion datasets at present. It is a common approach to avoid subjectivity by majority voting [3, 4], in which case the same image will be tagged by multiple annotators and choosing a dominant emotion category as the ground

© The Author(s), under exclusive license to Springer Nature Switzerland AG 2022
L. Fang et al. (Eds.): CICAI 2022, LNAI 13604, pp. 380–391, 2022.
https://doi.org/10.1007/978-3-031-20497-5_31

truth label, but the human cost associated with such an approach is rather high. In addition, and most importantly, the emotional information in an image is extremely rich [5], while the description of image emotion by a single label lacks complexity and depth, which is particularly one-sided and fragile, failing to portray the emotions of the images adequately. Therefore, it is of great significance to build datasets with compound affective labels in an automatic way.

The construction of affective image datasets with multi-labels also has considerable potential practical value. First of all, they can be applied to the field of psychology. With the diverse emotional information in the datasets, researchers can evaluate the psychological status of the individual by observing the individual's emotional reactions to different affective images or the emotional contents they uploaded on the internet, then conduct research on psychological analysis and therapy. Secondly, the multi-dimensional emotional information of images provides references in art design [6] and advertising, bringing more diverse creative inspirations. As well in the realms of interactive media and entertainment, images with compound affective labels contribute various ways for sentiment semantics understanding, offering users abundant matching methods for image semantic retrieval [7], which has broad application prospects.

Focusing on addressing the problem of the singleness of current labels of affective image datasets and the difficulty of manual annotation, we propose a model to generate compound affective labels from the original affective dataset.

The main contributions of this paper are as follows:

(1) According to the idea of Label Distribution Learning (LDL), we access the emotion probability distribution through the output of emotion classification and build compound affective labels grounding the distribution.
(2) By adopting the method of knowledge distillation learning, we train the student model with Soft Targets, the probabilities of each category in the Softmax function of the teacher model, instead of the one-hot labels, so as to retain more valuable sentimental information about the images and facilitate the student model to construct more reasonable multi-label dataset on the basis of the original single label.
(3) We optimize the traditional classifier loss with the introduction of AM-Softmax loss to increase the aggregation within the categories, refining the classification performance of the teacher model.
(4) Jointed with the Attention-Transfer mechanism, the student model learns the attention map of the teacher model through Attention Loss during knowledge distillation, thus improving the performance in image emotion recognition.

2 Related Works

Domestic and foreign research on the construction of datasets with compound affective labels originated from sentiment analysis of images, and currently focuses on the optimization of image sentiment classification and prediction of sentiment distribution, and generates image multi-label datasets based on label distribution learning.

In [8], two algorithms based on conditional probability neural network, BCPNN and ACPNN, were proposed by employing the method of Label Distribution Learning

(LDL). BCPNN encodes the image label into binary representation and the ACPNN model expands the emotion distribution by adding noise to the labels. Then they built two new datasets based on the original datasets. [9] built the new labels in light of the theories related to Gaussian distribution. The Gaussian distribution loss was constructed from two aspects: giving distribution to all emotion categories and to the emotions with the same valence as the dominant label. The total loss is the weighted sum of loss functions of two different distributions.

In this paper, we deconstruct the task of generating the compound emotion-labeled dataset into image sentiment classification and distribution prediction, and relevant research results at home and abroad are explored according to these directions.

2.1   Affective Representation Model Emotional Representation Model

Nowadays, there are two commonly employed types of visual emotion representation models [10], namely, Categorical Emotion States (CES) based on category classification and Dimensional Emotion Space (DES) [11] based on dimensional space. The most favored CES model is Mikel's eight emotions model [12], including "Amusement", "Contentment", "Awe", "Excitement", "Fear", "Sadness", "Disgust" and "Anger". Among the DES models, the VAD model [13] is a widely used one. Valence, Arousal, and Dominance in VAD represent the three-dimensional characteristics of emotions. Compared with DES model, the CES model is easier for understanding [10] and labeling, thus widely used in visual sentiment research. Therefore, we also adopt Mikel's emotion 8-categories model based on CES for emotion representation of the images.

2.2   Image Sentiment Classification Based on Deep Learning

In recent years, with the wide application of CNN), image sentiment analysis technology has been further developed. On this basis, new models for sentiment analysis have also been gradually built via CNN techniques [14, 15]. Based on SentiBank, [15] presented a new deep learning algorithm for image sentiment analysis --Deep SentiBank. They adopted the concept of adjective-noun pairs (ANP) for image processing and selected 1 million online photos on Flickr, trained them with ANP, and classified them via the Deep Convolution Neural Network. [16] presented a Deep Neural Network model which filters out the error information in the training set through a feedback mechanism, thus making the emotion classification more effective. From the psychological point of view, [17] used the semantic quantization method to construct emotional feature space and the feature expressions of object words, respectively, and combines the two to classify image emotions. [18] put forward a multi-level region-based convolutional neural network, which can automatically extract multi-level depth features from images. [19] introduced a model of transferring emotional information from one high-marked area to another low-marked area by Transfer Learning.

2.3   Label Distribution Learning

In traditional image classification tasks, each image instance is associated with only one label. However, this method of processing labels separately ignores the relationship between other labels. Therefore, [20] put forward a scheme of Multi-Label Learning (MLL), in which each example in the training set is presented by a single feature vector and is associated with compound labels. However, the Multi-Label Learning approach has difficulty in accurately describing the exact features of each label [21].

Different from the traditional Single-Label Learning (SLL) and MLL, in Label Distribution Learning (LDL) [22], the original ground-truth label is represented by a discrete distribution. The label distribution is a probability distribution in which each feature reflects the significance of the corresponding label for the image. Compared with one-hot labels, this label probability distribution can better represent the overall state of a sample comprehensively.

In our paper, we generate the labels in light of the concept of label distribution learning, that is, converting the single label into the form of the probability distribution. Using convolutional neural network and knowledge distillation mechanism, the label probability distribution is generated by the output of Softmax function.

3 The Proposed Model

To generate compound affective labels from the original single-labeled datasets, the model requires a certain capability of affective recognition. Therefore, we divide our work into two parts: the classification of emotions in images, and the prediction of label distribution. The sentiment classification performance of the model is enhanced in three directions: adjusting the Softmax loss, employing knowledge distillation methods, and introducing the spacial attention maps. Grounded on the theory of Label Distribution Learning (LDL), the top-ranked best results of the Softmax probability distribution from this model are used as predictive compound affective labels.

In this paper, we use ResNet-50 [23] as the backbone network and adopt the knowledge distillation learning method for model training (Fig. 1).

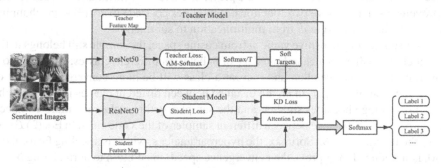

Fig. 1. Illustration of our model. As shown in this figure, the teacher's feature map is passed on to the student model as knowledge by the Attention Loss. AM-Softmax loss is introduced as the Teacher Loss instead of the traditional cross-entropy loss, which increases the aggregation within the category and improves the classification ability of the model. The Student Loss function of the model includes knowledge distillation loss (KD Loss) and Attention Loss based on the Attention-Transfer mechanism.

Based on the idea of Label Distribution Learning (LDL), we take the probability distribution in the output of the Softmax function in the final model as the basis of label construction and take the distribution of category probability as the judgment basis to generate compound emotional labels. In the experiment, we find that when the corresponding probability in Softmax of the current category is less than 0.12, this category of emotion makes little contribution to the image. Therefore, this paper selects the categories with the corresponding Softmax value greater than 0.12 as the generated compound labels. Among them, the category to which the maximum value in the probability distribution is taken as the main label to compare with the ground truth for evaluation.

3.1 Classifier Loss

At present, Softmax loss (Eq. 1) is the most widely used loss function for classification as it is useful for distinguishing classes, yet it does not condense features within the same class. Although there are some methods to improve the discriminability of features by combining Softmax loss with contrastive loss [24] and center loss [25]. However, those loss functions require careful selection of image pairs and triples, which is not only time-consuming but also greatly affects the recognition performance [26]. To tackle this issue, we adopt AM-Softmax to optimize the model classifier, which is proposed by [26] and was first used for face recognition. Its distinguishing feature is that it can widen the gap between classes while narrowing the gap within the same class.

$$\mathcal{L}_S = -\frac{1}{n}\sum_{i=1}^{n}\log\frac{e^{W_{y_i}^T f_i}}{\sum_{j=1}^{c}e^{W_j^T f_i}} = -\frac{1}{n}\sum_{i=1}^{n}\log\frac{e^{|W_{y_i}||f_i|\cos(\theta_{y_i})}}{\sum_{j=1}^{c}e^{|W_j||f_i|\cos(\theta_j)}} \tag{1}$$

L-Softmax [27]and A-Softmax [28] have been proposed in previous studies as an improvement to Softmax by introducing a parameter m, and thus the cosine distance of W and F in Softmax (Eq. 1) is transformed from $\cos(\theta)$ to $\cos(m\theta)$, adjusting the space between different classes. As in the previous cases, AM-Softmax has made further improvements in the above two functions. It modifies $\cos(m\theta)$ to $\cos(\theta) - m$, changing the hyperparameter margin m from multiplication to subtraction.

After subtracting a positive value m from cosine space, the sample still belongs to the current class, so there is a clear boundary of m between different classes. When the loss converges, θ becomes smaller, and that intra-class will be more converged. In light of the introduction of the margin m, the distance between different classes is widened, the inter-classes range becomes smaller, and the samples within a class are more compact, thus narrowing the distance between different samples of the same class. In Eq. (2) $\mathcal{L}_{AMS}$ shows the function of AM-Softmax, the hyperparameter s, which is a scaling factor fixed at 30, is introduced to improve the convergence speed. In addition to normalizing $b = 0$ and weight, the feature vector x is also normalized, so that $\|W\|=1$, $\|x\|=1$, simplifing the format and operation of L-Softmax and A-Softmax (Fig. 2).

$$\mathcal{L}_{AMS} = -\frac{1}{n}\sum_{i=1}^{n}\log\frac{e^{s\cdot(\cos\theta_{y_i}-m)}}{e^{s\cdot(\cos\theta_{y_i}-m)}+\sum_{j=1,j\neq y_i}^{c}e^{s\cdot\cos\theta_j}}) \tag{2}$$

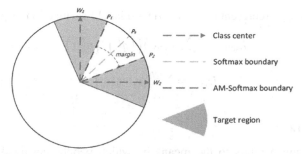

Fig. 2. Comparison of constraints between AMSoftmax and Softmax function on inter-class boundaries. For the traditional Softmax, the decision boundary is Po, where $W_1^T P_0 = W_2^T P_0$. For AM-Softmax, the decision boundary P1 of the first kind, in which $W_1^T P_1 - m = W_2^T P_1 = W_1^T P_2$, as the value of margin m also controls the size of the classification boundaries [27].

3.2 Knowledge Distillation

Generating compound affective labels from a single-label dataset relies on more abundant visual sentiment information in the original dataset labels, so the model is required to preserve more sentiment information in the output probability distribution. CNN is usually used to classify affective images with single-category labels, namely, the Hard Target. Since traditional models only consider the correct category and ignore the information on the probability of other categories, it leads us to fail to make good use of the information embedded in the label distribution [29].

On this basis, a model based on knowledge distillation [29] can solve this problem as well as achieve better classification results. Its core idea is to distill the knowledge contained in the trained model into another model. In this method, the teacher-student model is introduced. The results of the teacher model's Softmax function represent the distribution of the prediction probability corresponding to each category and carry more valuable information, which is also known as Soft Target and is applied as part of Total loss to induce the training of the student network in order to realize knowledge transfer. In addition, the learning method of knowledge distillation also introduces the temperature parameter T into the Softmax function. As temperature parameter T increases, the distribution of soft labels in the network model becomes more even and more information of other categories can be retained.

In Eqs. (3) and (4), q_i^T and p_j^T respectively represent the output Softmax value of class i of the Student and the Teacher network when the temperature value is T.

$$q_i^T = \frac{\exp(z_i/T)}{\sum_{i=1}^N \exp(z_k/T)} \tag{3}$$

$$p_j^T = \frac{\exp(v_i/T)}{\sum_{k=1}^N \exp(v_k/T)} \tag{4}$$

The total loss function of knowledge distillation L_{KD} is the combination of the Soft Loss L_{soft} and Hard Loss L_{hard} and the weight coefficient α is introduced to adjust their respective proportions. In this experiment, we take $T = 20$, $\alpha = 0.3$:

$$L_{KD} = \alpha L_{soft} + (1 - \alpha)L_{hard} \tag{5}$$

where: L_{soft} and L_{hard} represent the soft and hard label loss function respectively.

$$L_{\text{soft}} = \sum_{j=1}^{N} p_j^T \log\left(\left(q_j^T\right)/\left(p_j^T\right)\right) \tag{6}$$

$$L_{\text{hard}} = \sum_{j=1}^{N} c_j \log(q_j) \tag{7}$$

3.3 Attention Loss

Attention mechanism refers to the means by which people can quickly filter valuable information from the vast amount of information with limited attention resources. Researchers have found that the combination of the attention mechanism and CNN can be used to rapidly analyze data, identify important features, and focus attention on meaningful information or targets, ignoring irrelevant information and insignificant regions, in order to achieve a more effective acquisition of image feature information [30].

In the process of knowledge distillation, the attentional map from the teacher network can also be regarded as a kind of knowledge [31]. Therefore, the attentional transfer mechanism allows the student network to learn the attentional map by shortening the distance between the student's and teacher's attention map, enhancing its performance. [31] introduced the Attention-Transfer mechanism and presented three activation-based methods of generating the attention map. They supposed that if the absolute value of the activation function of a hidden neuron is larger, the more important and attention-worthy the neuron is, so the attention map is an accumulation of the tensor of the activation function output in the channel dimension.

In this paper, the attention map is obtained by multiplying and then accumulating the feature maps. First, we divide the student and teacher networks into equal-sized units to ensure that the final attentional feature map of the student model is equal in size to that of the teacher model and then calculate the square of the absolute value of each point in the feature map, where the multiplication serves to focus the important regions of the image noticed by the model on the later convolutional layers. Then the feature maps of multiple channels are added together to form a single channel and flattened so that the feature map of size $(C \times W \times H)$ of the last convolution layer is transformed into a two-dimensional tensor of size $(1 \times W \times H)$.

As shown in Eq. (8), where A is the feature map of the size $(C \times W \times H)$ of a layer's output. Define the mapping function F and take the absolute value of the tensor of each channel of the feature map, calculate its power, and then sum them up. The size of the feature map is converted from $(C \times H \times W)$ to $(1 \times H \times W)$:

$$F_{\text{sum}}^p (A) = \sum_{i=1}^{C} |A_i|^p \tag{8}$$

$$\mathcal{L}_{\text{AT}} = \frac{\beta}{2} \sum_{i=1}^{N} |\frac{F(A_i^s)}{|F(A_i^s)|_2} - \frac{F(A_i^t)}{|F(A_i^t)|_2}|_p \tag{9}$$

In Eq. (9), $\mathcal{L}_{AT}$ is the total Attention Loss, where s represents the student network and t represents the teacher network. $F(A_i^s)$ and $F(A_i^t)$ are respectively the j-th attentional map of the student and the teacher in vectorized form, and p refers to the norm type, in the experiment, $p = 2$.

4 Experiment and Analysis

In the experiment, we adopt the FI (Flicker and Instagram) [3] dataset. It is a large-scale affective image dataset collected from two social networks, Flicker and Instagram, with affective labels based on Mikel's eight emotions models [12] including "Amusement", "Contentment", "Anger", "Excitement", "Fear", "Sadness" and "Awe", for a total of 22700 images. Among them, there are 18,156 training sets, accounting for 80%; 3,408 test sets, accounting for 15%, and 1,136 verification sets, accounting for 5%.

4.1 Model Evaluations

Compared with the baseline network. We take the label that has the maximum value in the probability distribution as the main label to compare with the ground truth label for model evaluation. As shown in Table 1, the accuracy of our model outperforms many baseline networks. The ablation analysis is revealed in Table 2. After pre-training a large number of image data, combined with the optimized loss and knowledge distillation mode, our model has achieved better performance among the six commonly used image sentiment classification models.

Table 1. The comparison to the baseline networks. Among them, ResNet-50, ResNet-101 [24], VGGNet-19 [32] and AlexNet [33] are pre-trained based on ImageNet [35], and the FI dataset is used for emotion classification.

Model name	Accuracy
Deep Senti Bank	61.54%
AlexNet	58.61%
VGGNet-19	59.32%
ResNet-101	60.82%
ResNet-50 (Backbone)	64.67%
Our Model	68.83%

Table 2. Shows the ablation analysis results of the proposed model.

Model name	Accuracy
ResNet-50	64.67%
ResNet-50 + AMSoft Loss	67.80%
ResNet-50 + Knowledge Distillation	65.49%
ResNet-50 + KD + Attention Loss	66.98%
Our Model	68.83%

Compared with previous models. The results in Table 3 show that our model has certain advantages in terms of the model depth and the architecture of the loss functions. The pre-trained ResNet network has already achieved a good level of performance in image classification, and the introduction of AM-Softmax loss and the knowledge distillation loss with attention features further improve the performance of the network.

Table 3. The comparison to the model proposed in previous researches.

Model name	Accuracy
Rao, 2016	67.24%
Yang, 2017	67.48%
Yang, 2018	67.64%
Our Model	68.83%

Among them, [Rao, 2016] [19], a deep network named MldrNet, which can learn the multi-level depth representation of image emotion classification combine different levels of features, to classify the emotion types of different types of images. [Yang, 2017] [9], a multi-task deep learning framework based on VGGNet is proposed to predict visual emotion by using the ambiguity and relationship between emotion categories, and predict the probability distribution of image emotion by Gaussian distribution functions. [Yang, 2018] [34], a model based on GoogleNet Inception with Deep Metrics Learning for emotional understanding, a multi-task depth framework is proposed to explore the relationship between emotional labels with emotional loss, so as to optimize the retrieval and classification goals.

4.2   The Construction of Multi-labels

In this paper, we use the probability distribution of the Softmax function of the final model as the basis for the construction of the multi-labels. The category with the maximum value in the probability distribution is regarded as "label 1" (the primary label), the category with the second-highest probability distribution is regarded as "label 2", and so on. The "ground-truth" is the original single label of the image in the test dataset (Fig. 3).

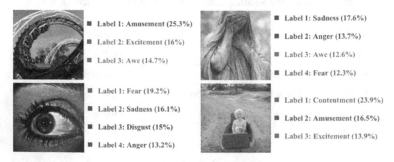

Fig. 3. The generated multi-label images

Through analysis, it can be found that there is some connection among the predicted multi-labels. Usually, these labels belong to the same polarity (Valence). According to the theory of affective psychology, Amusement, Contentment, Awe, and Excitement are positive emotions, while Fear, Sadness, Disgust, and Anger are negative. Even though the model had not trained in valence with polarity classification, the results suggest that the model still shows some regularity in terms of emotion polarity. It can be concluded that the model has the ability to discriminate between positive and negative emotions.

Some of the ground-truth labels of image data are not consistent with the emotions generated by human affections, and for some images, the predicted labels are closer to the feelings generated by humans than the original labels. From this, it shows that the generated emotion dataset not only enriches emotion information but also optimizes the original dataset to some extent.

5 Conclusion

In this work, we develop a model for generating compound affective labels from a single label, improve the image classification performance by optimizing the classification loss function, using knowledge distillation as well as combining attention mechanisms, and generate compound affective labels using the label distribution of the model. The accuracy of the model in our paper surpasses some baseline models and models in the previous works. The generated compound affective labels not only enrich the original single-label dataset but also to some extent update and optimize the undesirable labels in the original dataset.

References

1. Siersdorfer, S., Minack, E., Deng, F., Hare, J.: Analyzing and predicting sentiment of images on the social web. In: Proceedings of the 18th ACM international conference on Multimedia, pp. 715–718 (2010)
2. Joshi, D., et al.: Aesthetics and emotions in images. IEEE Sig. Process. Mag. 28(5), 94–115 (2011)
3. You, Q., Luo, J., Jin, H., Yang, J.: Building a large-scale dataset for image emotion recognition: The fine print and the benchmark. In: Proceedings of the AAAI Conference on Artificial Intelligence, vol. 30 (2016)
4. Machajdik, J., Hanbury, A.: Affective image classification using features inspired by psychology and art theory. In: Proceedings of the 18th ACM international conference on Multimedia, pp. 83–92 (2010)
5. Plutchik, R.: A general psycho evolutionary theory of emotion. In: Theories of Emotion, pp. 3–33. Elsevier, Amsterdam (1980)
6. Jia, J., Wu, S., Wang, X., Hu, P., Cai, L., Tang, J.: Can we understand van gogh's mood? learning to infer affects from images in social networks. In: Proceedings of the 20th ACM International Conference on Multimedia, pp. 857–860 (2012)
7. Wei-Ning, W., Ying-Lin, Y., Sheng-Ming, J.: Image retrieval by emotional semantics: A study of emotional space and feature extraction. In: 2006 IEEE International Conference on Systems. Man and Cybernetics, vol. 4, pp. 3534–3539. IEEE, New York (2006)
8. Yang, J., Sun, M., Sun, X.: Learning visual sentiment distributions via augmented conditional probability neural network. In: Thirty-First AAAI Conference on Artificial Intelligence (2017)

9. Yang, J., She, D., Sun, M.: Joint image emotion classification and distribution learning via deep convolutional neural network. In: IJCAI, pp. 3266–3272 (2017)

10. Zhao, S., Yao, X., Yang, J., Jia, G., Ding, G., Chua, T.S., Schuller, B.W., Keutzer, K.: Affective image content analysis: Two decades review and new perspectives. In: IEEE Transactions on Pattern Analysis and Machine Intelligence (2021)

11. Gunes, H., Schuller, B.: Categorical and dimensional affect analysis in continuous input: Current trends and future directions. Image Vision Comput. **31**(2), 120–136 (2013)

12. Mikels, J.A., Fredrickson, B.L., Larkin, G.R., Lindberg, C.M., Maglio, S.J., Reuter Lorenz, P.A.: Emotional category data on images from the international affective picture system. Behav. Res. Methods **37**(4), 626–630 (2005)

13. Schlosberg, H.: Three dimensions of emotion. Psychol. Rev. **61**(2), 81 (1954) Campos, V., Salvador, A., Giro-i Nieto, X., Jou, B.: Diving deep into sentiment: Understanding fine-tuned CNNs for visual sentiment prediction. In: Proceedings of the 1st International Workshop on Affect and Sentiment in Multimedia, pp. 57–62 (2015)

14. Peng, K.C., Chen, T., Sadovnik, A., Gallagher, A.C.: A mixed bag of emotions: Model, predict, and transfer emotion distributions. In: Proceedings of the IEEE Conference on Computer Vision and Pattern Recognition, pp. 860–868 (2015)

15. Chen, T., Borth, D., Darrell, T., Chang, S.F.: DeepSentiBank: Visual sentiment concept classfication with deep convolutional neural networks. arXiv preprint arXiv:1410.8586 (2014)

16. You, Q., Luo, J., Jin, H., Yang, J.: Robust image sentiment analysis using progressively trained and domain transferred deep networks. In: Twenty-Ninth AAAI Conference on Artificial Intelligence (2015)

17. Wang, J., Fu, J., Xu, Y., Mei, T.: Beyond object recognition: Visual sentiment analysis with deep coupled adjective and noun neural networks. In: IJCAI, pp. 3484–3490 (2016)

18. Rao, T., Li, X., Zhang, H., Xu, M.: Multi-level region-based convolutional neural network for image emotion classification. Neurocomputing **333**, 429–439 (2019)

19. He, Y., Ding, G.: Deep transfer learning for image emotion analysis: Reducing marginal and joint distribution discrepancies together. Neural Process. Lett. **51**(3), 2077–2086 (2020)

20. Zhang, M.L., Wu, L.: Lift: Multi-label learning with label-specific features. IEEE Trans. Pattern Anal. Mach. Intell. **37**(1), 107–120 (2014)

21. Geng, X.: Label distribution learning. IEEE Trans. Knowl. Data Eng. **28**(7), 1734–1748 (2016)

22. Geng, X., Yin, C., Zhou, Z.H.: Facial age estimation by learning from label distributions. IEEE Trans. Pattern Anal. Mach. Intell. **35**(10), 2401–2412 (2013)

23. He, K., Zhang, X., Ren, S., Sun, J.: Deep residual learning for image recognition. In: Proceedings of the IEEE conference on computer vision and pattern recognition. pp. 770–778 (2016)

24. Sun, Y., Chen, Y., Wang, X., Tang, X.: Deep learning face representation by joint identification-verification. Adv. Neural Inf. Process. Syst. **27** (2014)

25. Wen, Y., Zhang, K., Li, Z., Qiao, Y.: A discriminative feature learning approach for deep face recognition. In: European Conference on Computer Vision, pp. 499–515. Springer, New York (2016)

26. Wang, F., Cheng, J., Liu, W., Liu, H.: Additive margin softmax for face verification. IEEE Sig. Process. Lett. **25**(7), 926–930 (2018)

27. Liu, W., Wen, Y., Yu, Z., Yang, M.: Large-margin softmax loss for convolutional neural networks. arXiv preprint arXiv:1612.02295 (2016)

28. Liu, W., Wen, Y., Yu, Z., Li, M., Raj, B., Song, L.: Sphereface: Deep hypersphere embedding for face recognition. In: Proceedings of the IEEE Conference on Computer Vision and Pattern Recognition, pp. 212–220 (2017)

29. Hinton, G., Vinyals, O., Dean, J., et al.: Distilling the knowledge in a neural network. arXiv preprint arXiv:1503.02531 **2**(7) (2015)

30. Vaswani, A, Shazeer, N, Parmar, N.: Attention is all you need. Adv. Neural Info. Proces. Syst. **30** (2017)

31. Zagoruyko, S., Komodakis, N.: Paying more attention to attention: Improving the performance of convolutional neural networks via attention transfer. arXiv preprint arXiv:1612.03928 (2016)

32. Simonyan, K., Zisserman, A.: Very deep convolutional networks for large-scale image recognition. arXiv preprint arXiv:1409.1556 (2014)

33. Krizhevsky, A., Sutskever, I., Hinton, G.E.: ImageNet classification with deep convolutional neural networks. Adv. Neural Inf. Process. Syst. **25** (2012)

34. Yang, J., She, D., Lai, Y.K., Yang, M.H.: Retrieving and classifying affective images via deep metric learning. In: Proceedings of the AAAI Conference on Artificial Intelligence, vol. 32 (2018)

35. Xu, C., Cetintas, S., Lee, K., Li, L.: Visual sentiment prediction with deep convolutional neural networks (2014). arXiv preprint arXiv:1411.5731

Weakly Supervised Learning of Instance Segmentation with Confidence Feedback

Yu Yang[1](ID), Fang Wan[2](ID), Qixiang Ye[2](ID), and Xiangyang Ji[1(✉)](ID)

[1] Tsinghua University, BNRist, Beijing, China
yang-yu16@mails.tsinghua.edu.cn
[2] UCAS, Cheltenham, UK

Abstract. Only provided with image category supervision, weakly supervised instance segmentation is a challenging yet significant task when required to simultaneously learn object locations and instance segmentation. In this paper, we propose a region-based multibranch network with feed-forward and feedback procedures to estimate image classifiers, object detectors, and mask predictors in an end-to-end manner. In the feed-forward procedure, the instance confidences estimated by the image classification branch are transferred to train object detectors and mask predictors. In the feedback procedure, the instance confidences retrieved from detection outputs and mask confidences obtained from segmentation outputs are employed for classifier enhancement. With iterative feed-forward and feedback procedures, our approach produces a closed-loop multitask learning mechanism that can efficiently correct object localization while generating high-quality instance segmentation. On PASCAL VOC benchmark datasets, our methods greatly improve the performance of weakly supervised object detection (WSOD) and weakly supervised instance segmentation (WSIS).

Keywords: Object detection · Instance segmentation · Weakly supervised learning

1 Introduction

Prevalent deep learning based instance segmentation algorithms [11,15], despite their striking performance, require extensive human efforts on pixel-level dense annotations, which limit their practical application in many situations. This inspires weakly supervised instance segmentation (WSIS) [25], which learns to segment objects of interest given solely the image-level annotations indicating the presence or absence of some class of objects in images.

To tackle the above challenging WSIS problem, the peak response map (PRM) method [25] first leverages class activation maps (CAMs) [24] to highlight

Supplementary Information The online version contains supplementary material available at https://doi.org/10.1007/978-3-031-20497-5_32.

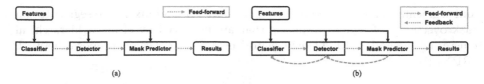

Fig. 1. With confidence feed-forward and feedback, the closed-loop learning mechanism incorporates image classification, object detection, and instance segmentation tasks. (a) WS-MRCNN. (b) WS-MRCNN with confidence feedback.

the object locations and then retrieves segmentation proposals to learn instance segmentation models. However, this method faces two main drawbacks. First, the CAMs produced from a classification network are insufficient to accurately indicate the full extent of a given object. Second, the segmentation proposals are generated by a separated algorithm and are not learnable.

Inspired by the prevalent Mask R-CNN [11] in fully-supervised instance segmentation, we design a region-based multibranch deep network, referred to as the weakly-supervised Mask R-CNN (WS-MRCNN), to tackle the challenging WSIS problem. The WS-MRCNN includes three branches that perform image classification, object detection, and mask prediction. Given image and region proposals as inputs, the classification branch performs both image classification and estimates instance confidences (object locations) in a multiple instance learning way [3]. These estimated instance confidences are then transferred to the detector and mask prediction branches for their optimization.

Learning from the transferred instance confidences, the detector and mask prediction branch attain a higher object localization capability [17,21] than that of the classification branch. We thus design a feedback procedure, which leverages the detection and segmentation results to correct object localization. With feed-forward and feedback procedures, a closed-loop multitask learning system is constructed (Fig. 1). With multiple learning iterations, the accuracy of object localization is enhanced, and the image classification, object detection, and mask prediction branches are collaboratively improved.

The contributions of this paper can be summarized as:

(1) A region-based multibranch deep network can simultaneously perform weakly supervised object detection (WSOD), weakly supervised instance segmentation (WSIS), and image classification in an integrated manner.

(2) A closed-loop learning method with feed-forward and feedback mechanisms explicitly utilizes the relationship between multiple tasks to collaboratively enhance the performance of each task.

2   Related Work

Supervised Instance Segmentation. Instance segmentation requires segmentation of every object of interested classes [6]. The dominant approaches to this problem are region-based two-stage approaches [11,15] where detection and segmentation are formulated as a classification and pixel-wise segmentation task over a set of region proposals that are produced by either a hierarchical clustering method [2,19,26] or a neural network, *i.e.* region proposal network (RPN) [16].

Weakly Supervised Object Detection (WSOD). WSOD learns to localize every object of interested classes from images with only category labels. WSOD is usually formualted as a multiple instance learning (MIL) problem [5,23], where image is treated as a bag, and object proposals are regarded as instances in a bag. With the rise of deep learning, MIL networks [3,17,21] emerge as a promising solution to WSOD. The first MIL network, weakly supervised deep detection network (WSDDN) [3], proposes two-streams structure, one stream to classify each instance MIL networks infer image classification with a soft selection of object proposal classification [3], improve the selection (*i.e.* object localization) correctness with context information [12], and refine the implicitly learned object proposal classification with online instance classifier [17]. Our work is also based on MIL framework. Unlike the above methods that only concern WSOD, our MIL network also learns WSIS.

Weakly Supervised Semantic Segmentation (WSSS). WSSS learns to segment images into regions of different semantic classes with only image class labels provided. Prevalent methods usually inspects the class activation map [4] inside a classification network by apply the classification head to the feature maps of the input images. These activation maps roughly highlight the small regions of interested classes but do not maintain enough quality for segmentation. Therefore, these maps are further refined with confidence propagation [20] or semantic affinity [1] to yield quality semantic segmentation. In our work, we use WSSS method to precompute the semantic decomposition of the whole image for the generation of pseudo labels of instance segmentation.

Weakly Supervised Instance Segmentation (WSIS). WSIS aims at learning instance segmentation from less costly annotation such as bounding box annotation [13] of objects or class annotation of images. In this paper, we mainly focus on the latter one, which is still lack of exploration. Previous method, PRM [25], attempts to resolve this problem by activating object parts and retrieving instance masks from a set of precomputed segment proposals. Our work instead construct an end-to-end network to fulfill WSIS which yields segmentation with more semantic consistency.

3 Method

3.1 Overview

Figure 2 presents the architecture of the proposed WS-MRCNN. It comprises a backbone network plus three heads for classification, detection and instance

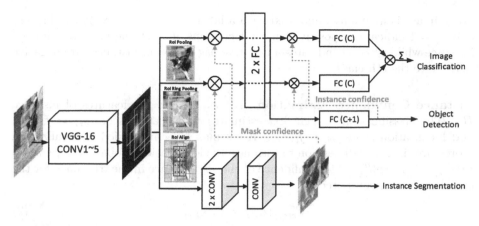

Fig. 2. Network architecture. Our WS-MRCNN comprises a backbone CNN, a classification branch, a detection branch and an instance segmentation branch. The green dashed line indicates the confidence feedback. (Color figure online)

segmentation respectively. Given an image region proposals as inputs, the backbone network produces feature maps for each image region. Taking these region features as input, the classification branch estimates image classification score with soft selection of instance confidences via MIL [3], the detection branch performs an instance classification to achieve object detection, and the instance segmentation branch performs pixel-wise classification to produce segmentation masks. Among these head branches, only the classification branch is supervised by manual annotation of image classes while the learning of the rest branches are supervised by pseudo labels generated by processing the instance confidence produced by the classification branch. Based on the observation that the learned detection and instance segmentation branch acquire a higher object localization capability than the classification branch [17,21], we further introduce a feedback procedure to leverage the prediction of detection and instance segmentation branches to correct object localization in the classification branch. The joint loss function is defined as:

$$\mathcal{L} = \lambda_c \mathcal{L}_{cls} + \lambda_d \mathcal{L}_{det} + \lambda_m \mathcal{L}_{msk}. \tag{1}$$

In the following sections, we will first describe how pseudo is generated, also known as confidence feed-forward procedure in Sect. 3.2 and then present our feedback mechanism in Sect. 3.3

3.2 Confidence Feed-Forward Procedure

Following MIL [3] framework, we regard images as bags and image regions as instances in bags. Formally, given an image $B_i \in \mathcal{B} \subset \mathbb{R}^{3 \times H \times W}$ which contains instances $\{B_{i1}, B_{i2}, \ldots, B_{ij}, \ldots, B_{iN_i}\}$, where N_i denotes the number of instances and N is the number of images in the training set. In WSIS setting, every image is manually annotated with a label $y_i^c \in \mathcal{Y}_{cls}$, where $\mathcal{Y}_{cls} = \{1, -1\}$ and $y_i^c = 1$ indicates a positive bag that contains at least one positive cth-class instance while $y_i^c = -1$ indicates a negative bag where all instances are negative relative to the cth class.

Instance Confidence Estimation. Let ϕ_{ij} denote the features of instance B_{ij}. The classification branch first estimates classification score $s_{ij} = f_c(\phi_{ij})$ and localization score $l_{ij} = f_l(\phi_{ij})$. A softmax layer is applied to localization scores over instance dimension to estimate the localization probability, $i.e.$ $p_{ij}^c = exp(l_{ij}^c)/\sum_k exp(l_{ik}^c)$. The confidence of the jth instance in the ith image for the cth class is then computed as

$$S_{cls\_f}^c(i, j) = s_{ij}^c * p_{ij}^c. \tag{2}$$

For image classification, the score of the ith image for the cth class is predicted as the sum of instance confidences:

$$o_i^c = \sum_j S_{cls\_f}^c(i, j). \tag{3}$$

By Eq. 3, the relationship between the image and instance confidences is established. When training the classification branch with manual labels, the network selects the discriminative instances to contribute to image classification. Then it progressively learns the instance confidences which are later used to produce pseudo labels for training the object detector and instance segmentation.

From Classification to Detection. Given the instance confidence S_{cls_f} estimated by the classification branch, the instance of the highest confidence, B_{ij*}^c, is selected as the pseudo ground-truth to train the detector, where j^* is defined as:

$$j^* = \arg\max_j S_{cls\_f}^c(i, j). \tag{4}$$

Accordingly, when there are only cth-class instances present in the image, the label y_{ij}, for instance B_{ij}, is assigned as:

$$y_{ij} = \begin{cases} c, & if \, y_i^c = 1 \; \& \; IoU(B_{ij}, B_{ij*}^c) > 0.6 \\ 0, & if \; 0.1 < IoU(B_{ij}, B_{ij*}^c) < 0.4 \\ -1, & otherwise \end{cases}, \tag{5}$$

where $y_{ij} = c$ denotes that B_{ij} is a positive instance of the cth class, and $y_{ij} = 0$ indicates that B_{ij} is the background. For $y_i^c = -1$, instance B_{ij} is ignored by the detection loss. When there are multiple classes present, Eq. 5 is applied for each class and the maximum intersection over union (IoU) is considered instead.

Given instances $\{B_{ij}\}$ and estimated labels $\{y_{ij}\}$, a detector $f_d(\phi_{ij}; \theta_d)$ with parameters θ_d can be learned. Similar to the image classification task, the learned detector can predict the instance confidence, as:

$$S_{det\_f}(i, j) = f_d(\phi_{ij}; \theta_d). \tag{6}$$

From Detection to Mask Prediction. In the mask prediction branch, we again select the instance of the highest confidence as the pseudo ground-truth B_{ij*}^c, as expressed in Eq. 4 and label other instances based on Eq. 5, considering the feed-forward confidence S_{det_f}. However, learning instance segmentation requires pixel-level annotations. To solve this problem, we introduce the segmentation mask of the WSSS method [1] to annotate pixels. The generation process of the segmentation mask comprises two steps. First, CAMs [24] are applied to generate the most discriminative area and most confident background area, which are regarded as seed areas. Second, we train an AffinityNet [1] to learn the similarity between pixels and then employ its results to expand the seed areas. The expanded areas, further refined with a dense conditional random field (CRF) [14], are adopted as the pseudo ground truth mask. We denote the foreground pixel set in the pseudo ground-truth mask as M^c for the cth class. For each foreground instance ($y_{ij} \neq 0$), the label of pixel B_{ijk} is determined as:

$$y_{ijk}^c = \begin{cases} 1, \ y_{ij} = c \ \& \ B_{ijk} \in B_{ij*}^c \cap M^c \\ 0, \ y_{ij} = c \ \& \ B_{ijk} \notin B_{ij*}^c \cap M^c \ , \\ -1, \ otherwise \end{cases} \quad (7)$$

where $y_{ijk}^c = 1$ denotes that pixel B_{ijk} is a foreground pixel for the cth class, 0 indicates the background class and -1 indicates ignorance. This suggests that for each pseudo ground truth box B_{ij*}^c, the inside semantic mask $B_{ij*}^c \cap M^c$ is set as the pseudo ground truth foreground mask, and the foreground mask is leaned in a class-aware manner [11]. With these pixel-level pseudo labels, a mask predictor is trained.

3.3 Confidence Feedback Procedure

From Mask Prediction to Detection. Given the prediction of instance segmentation branch, the instance confidence is calculated by averaging the confidences of foreground pixels for the cth class as:

$$S_{msk\_b}(i, j, k) = \max_c f_m(\phi_{ijk}; \theta_m^c). \quad (8)$$

Based on the instance confidence feedback S_{msk_b} originating from the mask prediction task, $i.e.$ Eq. 8, and the instance confidence S_{cls_f} transferred from the image classification task, $i.e.$ Eq. 2, the loss function for object detection is defined as:

$$\mathcal{L}_{det}(\theta_d, S_{cls\_f}, S_{msk\_b}) = -\frac{1}{N} \sum_i \mathbb{E}_j \left[\delta(y_{ij}, -1) \log f_d\left(\hat{\phi}_{ij}; \theta_d^{y_{ij}}\right) \right], \quad (9)$$

where $\hat{\phi}_{ij} = g(\hat{\phi}_{ijk})$, $\hat{\phi}_{ijk}$ is defined as:

$$\hat{\phi}_{ijk} = [(1 - w(\gamma_m)) + w(\gamma_m) \cdot S_{msk\_b}(i, j, k)] \cdot \phi_{ijk}, \quad (10)$$

In the above, $g(\cdot)$ comprises two FC layers, f_d is an object detector with an FC layer and a softmax layer, $w(\gamma_m)$ is the feedback rate which is controlled by parameter γ_m, and $w(\gamma_m)$ linearly increases from 0 to γ_m during training.

Table 1. Ablation study on the feedback mechanism.

Methods	Feedback		Ins. Segmentation		Obj. Detection			
	Det.	Seg.	$mAP^r_{0.25}$	$mAP^r_{0.5}$	$mAP^{cls}_{0.5}$	$mAP^{cls}_{0.7}$	$mAP^{det}_{0.5}$	$mAP^{det}_{0.7}$
WS-MRCNN			50.56	32.55	32.31	14.95	39.41	18.68
WS-MRCNN	✓		52.26	33.88	35.52	17.87	41.44	19.59
+Feedback	✓	✓	51.53	35.41	35.71	17.41	42.07	20.67

According to Eq. 5, instances spatially close to the pseudo ground-truth are labeled as positives. This step can be regarded as an expansion of valuable instances based on the spatial prior [16]. This step also ensures that the model is robust to biased locations. Furthermore, the detector acquires a higher capability to discriminate positive instances from negative instances than does the classifier [17,21]. We therefore apply the feedback instance confidence from detection S_{det_b}, which is defined as:

$$S_{det\_b}(i, j) = \max_{c=1,...,C} f^c_d \left(\hat{\phi}_{ij}; \theta_d \right). \tag{11}$$

The above equation refines the instance confidence in the image classification task, where f^c_d denotes the detector for the cth class.

From Detection to Classification. In image classification, the feature of B_{ij} is updated based on feedback instance confidence $S^c_{det\_b}(i, j)$ originating from object detection as:

$$\tilde{\phi}_{ij} = [(1 - w(\gamma_d)) + w(\gamma_d) \cdot S^c_{det\_b}(i, j)] \cdot \hat{\phi}_{ij}, \tag{12}$$

where $w(\gamma_d)$ is the feedback rate similar to $w(\gamma_m)$ in Eq. 10. Accordingly, p^c_{ij} and s^c_{ij} are updated as $\tilde{p}^c_{ij}$ and $\tilde{s}^c_{ij}$, respectively, considering their definitions in Sect. 3.2. The image classification score is further updated as $\tilde{o}^c_i = \mathbb{E}_{j \sim \tilde{p}^c_{ij}} \tilde{s}^c_{ij}$ The image classifier is updated by minimizing the hinge loss between the classification score and ground truth label as

$$\mathcal{L}_{cls}(\theta_c, S_{det\_b}) = \mathbb{E}_{i \in \{1,...,N\}} \left[\frac{1}{C} \sum_c^C \max(0, 1 - y^c_i \tilde{o}^c_i) \right], \tag{13}$$

where C denotes the number of image classes.

4 Experiments

The proposed WS-MRCNN is evaluated on the PASCAL VOC 2007 and PASCAL VOC 2012 datasets [9]. The mean average precision (mAP) [10] is computed to evaluate the performance of the instance segmentation task. The object detection and image classification performance level are evaluated with both mAP [9] and correct localization (CorLoc) metrics [7]. Details about experiment setup are available in the appendix.

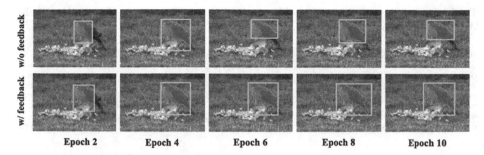

Fig. 3. Evolution of the object detection and mask prediction tasks during training the training process. By introducing the feedback mechanism, localization is corrected for both object detection and mask prediction (best viewed in color).

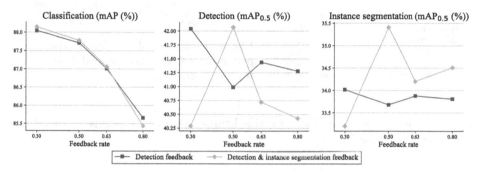

Fig. 4. Performance (%) of image classification (left), object detection (middle), and instance segmentation (right) with respect to feedback rate.

4.1 Ablation Study

Effect of the Feedback Mechanism. Table 1 presents the effect of the feedback procedure. For the instance segmentation task, the introduction of different feedback mechanisms (Fig. 2) improves the performance by 1.3%–2.86% for $mAP_{0.5}^r$ and 0.97%–1.7% for $mAP_{0.25}^r$. Specifically, with solely the feedback originating from detection to classification, the instance segmentation performance is improved by 1.47% for $mAP_{0.5}^r$ and 1.7% for $mAP_{0.25}^r$. When further introducing the feedback from segmentation into detection, the instance segmentation performance is improved by 2.86% for $mAP_{0.5}^r$, which explicitly demonstrates the effectiveness of the proposed closed-loop learning mechanism with feedback.

We further evaluate the effect of feedback on object detection (Table 1). $mAP_{0.5}^{cls}$ and $mAP_{0.7}^{cls}$ denote the detection performance of the classifier, and $mAP_{0.5}^{det}$ and $mAP_{0.7}^{det}$ denote that of the object detector. With confidence feedback, the performance levels of both object detection and image classification are improved, which indicates that the confidence feedback originating from detection enforces the localization effect of the image classification branch and enhances the classification performance (by 0.91%–3.4%). Confidence feedback also improves the object detection performance by adopting more accurate for-

Table 2. Detection performance (%) on the VOC 2007 test set. Comparison of the WS-MRCNN to other approaches.

Method	Aero	Bike	Bird	boat	bottle	bus	car	cat	chair	cow	table	dog	horse	mbike	person	plant	sheep	sofa	train	tv	mAP
WSDDN [3]	39.4	50.1	31.5	16.3	12.6	64.5	42.8	42.6	10.1	35.7	24.9	38.2	34.4	55.6	9.4	14.7	30.2	40.7	54.7	46.9	34.8
OICR [17]	58.0	62.4	31.1	19.4	13.0	65.1	62.2	28.4	24.8	44.7	30.6	25.3	37.8	65.5	15.7	24.1	41.7	46.9	**64.3**	**62.6**	41.2
WCCN [8]	49.5	60.6	38.6	29.2	16.2	**70.8**	56.9	42.5	10.9	44.1	29.9	42.2	47.9	64.1	13.8	23.5	45.9	54.1	60.8	54.5	42.8
TS²C [22]	59.3	57.5	43.7	27.3	13.5	63.9	61.7	59.9	24.1	46.9	36.7	45.6	39.9	62.6	10.3	23.6	41.7	52.4	58.7	56.6	44.3
WeakRPN [18]	57.9	**70.5**	37.8	5.7	**21.0**	66.1	**69.2**	59.4	3.4	57.1	**57.3**	35.2	**64.2**	**68.6**	**32.8**	**28.6**	50.8	49.5	41.1	30.0	45.3
MELM [21]	55.6	66.9	34.2	29.1	16.4	68.8	68.1	43.0	**25.0**	**65.6**	45.3	53.2	49.6	**68.6**	2.0	25.4	**52.5**	56.8	62.1	57.1	47.3
Ours	**61.5**	66.0	**48.4**	**35.2**	19.1	65.8	67.1	**63.9**	17.7	48.4	45.2	**59.2**	52.1	66.3	16.2	23.4	47.6	**58.0**	60.2	62.4	**49.2**

Table 3. Weakly supervised instance segmentation performance (%) on the VOC 2012 segmentation validation set.

Backbone	Methods	$mAP^r_{0.25}$	$mAP^r_{0.5}$
ResNet50	PRM [25]	44.3	26.8
VGG16	PRM [25]	–	22.0
	MELM+MCG [25]	36.9	22.9
	WS-MRCNN (ours)	50.56	32.55
	WS-MRCNN+FB (ours)	**51.53**	**35.41**

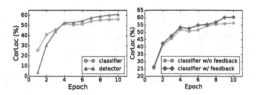

Fig. 5. Evolution of the localization performance of the classifier and detector during training.

ward confidences as input. This is verified through pseudo supervision visualization during training (Fig. 3).

Effect of the Feedback Rate. The effect of the feedback rate, as defined in Eqs. 10 and 12, is shown in Fig. 4. We compare the performance of all the tasks under different feedback rates. The results indicate that a very low or high feedback rate leads to little performance improvement. When the rate is very low, the feedback information can hardly correct the instance confidence. When the rate is very high, the feedback confidence can produce major discrepancies with the initial confidence and thereby disturb the optimization process. A proper feedback rate is crucial to comprehensively improve the performance of all tasks.

4.2   Comparison to Previous Approaches

Weakly Supervised Instance Segmentation. Table 3 summarizes our instance segmentation performance in terms of mAP with thresholds of 0.25, 0.5. "MELM+MCG" indicates that the min-entropy latent model (MELM) [21] is used to generate the detection boxes utilized to retrieve the most matching instance from the set of mask proposals produced via multiscale combinatorial grouping (MCG). It is observed that with VGG16, our proposed WS-MRCNN outperforms the state-of-art "MELM+MCG" approach by a large margin, i.e. 13.66% for $mAP^r_{0.25}$ and 9.65% for $mAP^r_{0.5}$. It should be noted that the WS-MRCNN with VGG16 even significantly outperforms the PRM method [25] with ResNet50 by 6.26% and 5.75% for $mAP^r_{0.25}$ and $mAP^r_{0.5}$, respectively, which verifies that the WS-MRCNN is a new and more effective framework for

Fig. 6. Instance segmentation examples of the proposed WS-MRCNN on the PASCAL VOC 2012 dataset. The first two rows show successful cases while the last row shows failure cases (best viewed in color).

the WSIS task. By introducing confidence feedback, the performance is further increased to 51.53% and 35.41% for $mAP_{0.25}^r$ and $mAP_{0.5}^r$ respectively. Figure 6 shows instance segmentation examples for our methods, where the first two rows show successful cases and the last row shows failure cases.

Weakly Supervised Object Detection. Since the WS-MRCNN can learn object detectors, it is compared to other WSOD approaches on the popular PASCAL VOC 2007 dataset. Table 2 indicates that WS-MRCNN outperforms previous methods "TS^{2}C", "WeakRPN", and "MELM" by 5.3%, 4.3%, and 2.3%, respectively. The improvements are significant for the challenging WSOD task. Figure 5 shows the CorLoc performance during training. The performance of the learned detector gradually exceeds that of the classifier. With the feedback mechanism, the localization ability of the image classifier is improved, which further benefits the object detection and mask prediction.

5 Conclusions

WSIS is a challenging task when provided with image category supervision but required to simultaneously learn object locations, instance masks, and instance segmentation models. In this paper, we proposed an effective network architecture, referred to as the WS-MRCNN, to estimate image classifier, object detector, and mask predictor in an integrated manner. With the designed confidence feedforward and feedback procedures, the WS-MRCNN achieves good performance of WSIS and WSOD compared to previous approaches.

Acknowledgement. This work was supported by the National Key R&D Program of China under Grant 2018AAA0102801, National Natural Science Foundation of China under Grant 61620106005, and partially supported by 62006216.

References

1. Ahn, J., Kwak, S.: Learning pixel-level semantic affinity with image-level supervision for weakly supervised semantic segmentation. In: CVPR (2018)
2. Arbelaez, P., Ponttuset, J., Barron, J., Marques, F., Malik, J.: Multiscale combinatorial grouping. In: CVPR (2014)
3. Bilen, H., Vedaldi, A.: Weakly supervised deep detection networks. In: CVPR (2016)
4. Chen, L.C., Papandreou, G., Kokkinos, I., Murphy, K., Yuille, A.L.: DeepLab: semantic image segmentation with deep convolutional nets, atrous convolution, and fully connected CRFs. TPAMI **40**(4), 834–848 (2017)
5. Cinbis, R.G., Verbeek, J.J., Schmid, C.: Weakly supervised object localization with multi-fold multiple instance learning. TPAMI **39**(1), 189–203 (2017)
6. Dai, J., He, K., Sun, J.: Instance-aware semantic segmentation via multi-task network cascades. In: CVPR (2016)
7. Deselaers, T., Alexe, B., Ferrari, V.: Weakly supervised localization and learning with generic knowledge. IJCV **100**, 275–293 (2012). https://doi.org/10.1007/s11263-012-0538-3
8. Diba, A., Sharma, V., Pazandeh, A., Pirsiavash, H., Van Gool, L.: Weakly supervised cascaded convolutional networks. In: Proceedings of the IEEE Conference on Computer Vision and Pattern Recognition, pp. 914–922 (2017)
9. Everingham, M., Eslami, S.M.A., Van Gool, L., Williams, C.K.I., Winn, J., Zisserman, A.: The PASCAL visual object classes challenge: a retrospective. Int. J. Comput. Vis. **111**(1), 98–136 (2014). https://doi.org/10.1007/s11263-014-0733-5
10. Hariharan, B., Arbeláez, P., Girshick, R., Malik, J.: Simultaneous detection and segmentation. In: Fleet, D., Pajdla, T., Schiele, B., Tuytelaars, T. (eds.) ECCV 2014. LNCS, vol. 8695, pp. 297–312. Springer, Cham (2014). https://doi.org/10.1007/978-3-319-10584-0_20
11. He, K., Gkioxari, G., Dollár, P., Girshick, R.: Mask R-CNN. In: ICCV (2017)
12. Kantorov, V., Oquab, M., Cho, M., Laptev, I.: ContextLocNet: context-aware deep network models for weakly supervised localization. In: Leibe, B., Matas, J., Sebe, N., Welling, M. (eds.) ECCV 2016. LNCS, vol. 9909, pp. 350–365. Springer, Cham (2016). https://doi.org/10.1007/978-3-319-46454-1_22
13. Khoreva, A., Benenson, R., Hosang, J.H., Hein, M., Schiele, B.: Simple does it: weakly supervised instance and semantic segmentation. In: CVPR (2017)
14. Krahenbuhl, P., Koltun, V.: Efficient inference in fully connected CRFs with gaussian edge potentials. In: NIPS (2011)
15. Li, Y., Qi, H., Dai, J., Ji, X., Wei, Y.: Fully convolutional instance-aware semantic segmentation. In: CVPR (2017)
16. Ren, S., He, K., Girshick, R., Sun, J.: Faster R-CNN: towards real-time object detection with region proposal networks. In: NeurIPS (2015)
17. Tang, P., Wang, X., Bai, X., Liu, W.: Multiple instance detection network with online instance classifier refinement. In: CVPR (2017)

18. Tang, P., et al.: Weakly supervised region proposal network and object detection. In: Ferrari, V., Hebert, M., Sminchisescu, C., Weiss, Y. (eds.) ECCV 2018. LNCS, vol. 11215, pp. 370–386. Springer, Cham (2018). https://doi.org/10.1007/978-3-030-01252-6_22

19. Uijlings, J.R.R., van de Sande, K.E.A., Gevers, T., Smeulders, A.W.M.: Selective search for object recognition. IJCV **104**(2), 154-171 (2013)

20. Vernaza, P., Chandraker, M.: Learning random-walk label propagation for weakly-supervised semantic segmentation. In: CVPR (2017)

21. Wan, F., Wei, P., Jiao, J., Han, Z., Ye, Q.: Min-entropy latent model for weakly supervised object detection. In: CVPR (2018)

22. Wei, Y., et al.: TS^{2}C: tight box mining with surrounding segmentation context for weakly supervised object detection. In: Ferrari, V., Hebert, M., Sminchisescu, C., Weiss, Y. (eds.) ECCV 2018. LNCS, vol. 11215, pp. 454–470. Springer, Cham (2018). https://doi.org/10.1007/978-3-030-01252-6_27

23. Ye, Q., Zhang, T., Qiu, Q., Zhang, B., Chen, J., Sapiro, G.: Self-learning scene-specific pedestrian detectors using a progressive latent model. In: CVPR (2017)

24. Zhou, B., Khosla, A., Lapedriza, A., Oliva, A., Torralba, A.: Learning deep features for discriminative localization. In: CVPR (2016)

25. Zhou, Y., Zhu, Y., Ye, Q., Qiu, Q., Jiao, J.: Weakly supervised instance segmentation using class peak response. In: CVPR (2018)

26. Zitnick, C.L., Dollár, P.: Edge boxes: locating object proposals from edges. In: Fleet, D., Pajdla, T., Schiele, B., Tuytelaars, T. (eds.) ECCV 2014. LNCS, vol. 8693, pp. 391–405. Springer, Cham (2014). https://doi.org/10.1007/978-3-319-10602-1_26

Robust Face-Swap Detection Based on 3D Facial Shape Information

Weinan Guan[1,2], Wei Wang[2(✉)], Jing Dong[2], Bo Peng[2], and Tieniu Tan[2]

[1] School of Artificial Intelligence, University of Chinese Academy of Sciences, Beijing, China
[2] Center for Research on Intelligent Perception and Computing, CASIA, Beijing, China
`weinan.guan@cripac.ia.ac.cn`, {`wwang,jdong,bo.peng,tnt`}`@nlpr.ia.ac.cn`

Abstract. Maliciously-manipulated images or videos - so-called deep fakes - especially face-swap images and videos have attracted more and more malicious attackers to discredit some key figures. Previous pixel-level artifacts based detection techniques always focus on some unclear patterns but ignore some available semantic clues. Therefore, these approaches show weak interpretability and robustness. In this paper, we propose a biometric information based method to fully exploit the appearance and shape feature for face-swap detection of key figures. The key aspect of our method is obtaining the inconsistency of 3D facial shape and facial appearance, and the inconsistency based clue offers natural interpretability for the proposed face-swap detection method. Experimental results show the superiority of our method in robustness on various laundering and cross-domain data, which validates the effectiveness of the proposed method.

Keywords: Deep-fake detection · 3D facial shape

1 Introduction

Recently, with the developing of deep learning, especially Generative Adversarial Networks (GAN) [8], some studies of facial manipulation have shown rapid progress. The manipulated images or videos, so-called deep fakes, are always maliciously used to deceive the public. Face swapping, as one of deep fakes, is generated by replacing the target face with the source face but reserving the expressions of the target face. It attracts increasing attention of malicious people to slander some key figures. Therefore, deep-fake detection has arisen significant concerns.

In the past years, deep-fake detection studies has seen a remarkable advance [13,20,21]. Researchers exploit multiple clues to authenticate face-swap images and videos, such as details in the eye and teeth areas [11], the combination of local and global features [23] and 3D head poses [22]. For detecting deep-fake videos, the sequential information is also an important cue [9,18]. Deep-fake detection is

L. Fang et al. (Eds.): CICAI 2022, LNAI 13604, pp. 404–415, 2022.
https://doi.org/10.1007/978-3-031-20497-5_33

actually a statistical classification problem. Some classification neural networks can be applied to detect deep fakes and achieve satisfied performance. Previous work in deep-fake detection mostly captures the flaws of appearance as the detection clues in face-swap images and videos.

In this paper, we propose to leverage the inconsistency between 3D facial shape and facial appearance information for protecting key figures from face-swap images and videos. The facial appearance in a face-swap image or video is of the source individual, while 3D facial shape remains the target individual. The inherent flaw is employed to robustly detect face-swap images or videos, that 3D facial shape does not belong to the claimed person. Unlike previous work on modelling human behavior [3,4], which requires the sequential information to follow head movements or trace facial expression, the biometric shape information can be extracted from a single image. Our proposed method shows the superior robustness against laundering counter-measures and on cross-domain data, compared to some previous pixel-level artifacts based approaches. And it can be generalized well in the wild. We summarize our main contributions as:

- We propose a novel clue and framework to detect the inconsistency between facial appearance and 3D facial shape information, and the inconsistency based clue provides the interpretability for the proposed face-swap detection method.
- We model the distance measurement of intra-class and inter-class data in order to fully exploit the data distribution for improving the detection performance.
- Extensive experiments against most laundering counter-measures and on cross-domain data demonstrate the superiority of our method in robustness and generalization.

2   Related Work

In this section, some previous work related to face swapping is introduced, and then some detection methods are discussed.

2.1   Face-Swap Manipulation

Face swapping has attracted extensive attention of researchers. Several manipulation methods are proposed to generate compelling fake images and videos, including *FaceSwap* [2], *Deepfakes* [1], and *FSGAN* [14].

FaceSwap is a graphics-based approach to transfer the face region from a source video to a target video [17]. This method performs face swapping by fitting the 3D model to landmarks in the source face and aligning it to the target face. The rendering and color correction are then applied to improve the visualization of fake images and videos.

Unlike traditional approaches that are based on computer-graphics, some methods rely on deep-learning algorithms, especially GANs, to generate face-swap images and videos. For two specific individuals, *Deepfakes* trains two autoencoders with a shared encoder to reconstruct the source and the target faces, respectively [17]. The face-swap image is produced from the source face by the trained encoder and target decoder. The fake face is then blended with the target image using Poisson image editing [16,17]. However, this technique is needed to train a model for every pair of faces. *FSGAN* is subject agnostic, which can be applied to pairs of faces without training on those faces [14].

2.2 Face-Swap Detection

By the continuous development of technology for detecting face-swap images and videos, numerous novel methods are emerged to capture various flaws of face-swap deep fakes [20]. Here, we concentrate on some current methods based on different clues, including pixel-level artifacts based low-level approaches and semantic clues based high-level approaches [3].

Pixel-level artifacts based low-level approaches detect deep fakes relying on the marks of generation process. Researchers utilize some classification networks to capture the pixel-level artifacts, such as *XceptionNet* [6], and *EfficientNet* [19]. The former shows good performance on *FaceForensics++* Dataset [17], and is also proposed as a baseline method in the *Deepfake Detection Challenge (DFDC)* [7]. And the latter has similar or better detection performance. However, these methods always suffer from simple laundering counter-measures which can easily destroy the measured artifacts (e.g., additive noise, recompression, smoothing) [4]. This results the performance of the models is decreased dramatically on laundering data, and the models are even non-effective on cross-domain data.

Semantic clues based high-level approaches utilize some semantically meaningful features for detecting manipulations [3], like the color clues [12], 3D head poses [22], and blending boundaries [10]. In [12], the authors prove the difference of color between the images from a real camera and a network. Researchers in [22] observe the inconsistency between 3D head poses estimated from the facial landmarks and the central face region. In another attempt [10], the blending boundaries are detected in deep fakes, which is generated by blending the altered face into an existing background image.

Different from them, in our method, we describe a robust clue for protecting key figures from face-swap deep fakes. The inconsistency between appearance and 3D facial shape is leveraged by our method for defending most laundering counter-measures and cross-domain data. And our method also shows good performance in the wild.

3   The Proposed Method

Figure 1 shows the proposed detection framework. In order to capture the inconsistency of 3D facial shape and facial appearance in face-swap images and videos, we first utilize 3DMM (3D morphable model) [5] to extract 3D facial shape features of face-swap images and template videos (Subsect. 3.2). Then, we calculate *Mahalanobis Distance* between the shape features of suspected images and corresponding templates, and the distance is further utilized to authenticate the suspected images by comparing with the fixed threshold (Subsect. 3.3).

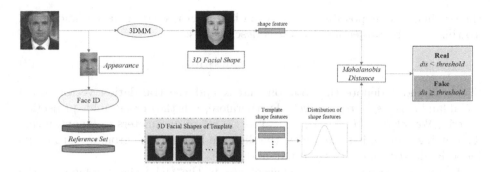

Fig. 1. An overview of our authentication pipeline.

3.1 Face-Swap Artifacts

In the process of confrontation between generation and detection methods, the facial appearance in face-swap images and videos has been constantly enhanced. For this reason, it is difficult for face-swap detection only relying on the facial flaws. However, face swapping only performs manipulation on the facial region. It focuses on changing the facial appearance in the target faces. Therefore, it ignores to transfer other biometric information from source faces to target faces. We concentrate on the inherent flaw in face-swap deep fakes, and build our framework for face-swap detection based on a cross-modal clue.

Specifically, we utilize the inconsistency between facial appearance and 3D facial shape in face-swap deep fakes for detection. For a specific individual, his/her facial shape should not change significantly in diverse images and video footage. In face-swap deep fakes, current methods only replace the target faces with the source faces but retain facial shapes of target images. Hence, the flaw of the cross-modal inconsistency provides us a novel clue for face-swap detection.

3.2 3D Facial Shape

3D morphable model is proposed to estimate 3D facial model from a single face [5]. In this work, we utilize the 3DMM fitting model [15,24] to reconstruct the 3D face with facial shape and texture information. It only fits the 3D facial shape based on the correspondences of 3D and 2D facial landmarks.

Based on [15] and [24], the facial shape with expression can be estimated:

$$S = \bar{S} + A_{id}\alpha_{id} + A_{exp}\alpha_{exp} \tag{1}$$

where $\bar{S}$ denotes the mean vector of 3D facial shape, A_{id} and A_{exp} are the matrices comprised by the principal components of 3D facial shape variances representing identification and expression respectively, and α_{id} and α_{exp} denote the weighted coefficients for A_{id} and A_{exp}. Thus, α_{id} and α_{exp} are the determinants of various facial shape and expression, respectively. The method further projects 3D facial landmarks into 2D plane. Moreover, the correspondences in the original face as possible are achieved by the projected 2D facial landmarks. To this end, the projection process is described as:

$$s_{2D}(P, R, t, \alpha_{id}, \alpha_{exp}) = PR(s_{3D}(\alpha_{id}, \alpha_{exp}) + t) \tag{2}$$

where R and t denote the rotation matrix and the translation vector of 3D facial landmarks s_{3D}, respectively. Furthermore, P is the orthographic projection matrix. We set $\theta = \{P, R, t, \alpha_{id}, \alpha_{exp}\}$ as the set of parameters to be optimized. The fitting process is to minimize the distance between the ground truth of 2D facial landmarks and the projected landmarks.

In our framework, we only concentrate on the facial shape related to the identity irrespective of expression. Therefore, α_{id} is the only required parameter. For simplicity, we also perform feature selection on α_{id} to obtain facial shape features. The details of feature selection are shown in Subsect. 4.3.

3.3   Inconsistency Measure

Here, we introduce a measurement method to calculate the distance between the shape features of a manipulated image and the corresponding template. Then, the distance is compared with a given threshold for detecting deep fakes. In our method, due to the inaccuracy of estimation, the template is enrolled with a set of 3D facial shape features and a particular distribution is modeled for the features. Therefore, for the comprehensive utilization of the template information, we use *Mahalanobis Distance* for measurement. Compared to other common measurements, *Mahalanobis Distance* is scale-invariant and uses the relations of various features. Moreover, it can compute the distance between a point and a distribution. Consequently, in our approach, we utilize *Mahalanobis Distance* to calculate the distance between 3D facial shape features in a manipulated image and the distribution modeled by the corresponding template. The formula of *Mahalanobis Distance* is described as follows:

$$D(\vec{x}) = \sqrt{(\vec{x} - \vec{\mu})^T \Sigma^{-1} (\vec{x} - \vec{\mu})} \tag{3}$$

where, $\vec{x}$ denotes the 3D facial shape feature vector of the manipulated image, and $\vec{\mu}$ and Σ are the mean vector and the covariance matrix of the corresponding template, respectively. The formula shows that *Mahalanobis Distance* utilizes the covariance matrix to integrate the relations of various features and distribution information of a template. It is noticed that regarding the inverse covariance matrix, the number of images in the template must not be less than the feature dimensions.

After measuring the distance, a threshold needs to be determined in the training phase for detecting deep fakes. It is obvious that the 3D facial shape features of a genuine image should be close to the corresponding template. Thus, an image is classified as fake if the computed distance between it and its template is above the given threshold. We tune and fix our threshold with the criterion of approximate accuracy between genuine and manipulated images.

4   Experiments

4.1   Dataset

Since we mainly concentrate on face-swap detection in this paper, deep fakes created by *FaceSwap*[1] and *Deepfakes*[2] from FaceForensics++ Dateset [17] are used as our experimental dataset. In the following, more details about the dataset are provided.

FaceForensics++ Dataset [17]. FaceForensics++ Dataset is a large-scale facial forgery dataset, which has $1,000$ pristine videos collected from the Internet. The face-swap videos in the dataset are generated by *FaceSwap* and *Deepfakes*, respectively. *FaceSwap* is a graphics-based method to swap the faces of a source video to a target video, while *Deepfakes* is a deep learning based method of face swapping. In the generation process of face-swap videos, the $1,000$ pristine videos are randomly split into 500 pairs for face swapping. In every pair, face swapping is conducted by *FaceSwap* and *Deepfakes*, respectively. Thus, both *FaceSwap* and *Deepfakes* generate $1,000$ fake videos respectively.

Facial Shape Registration. Since we try to utilize facial shape information to authenticate the subject featured by his/her facial appearance, the shape features of each protected person should be registered as a template. We first calculate the shape coefficients α_{id}s (Eq. 2) of each individual from the first five seconds of the corresponding video (the first seven seconds for a video with fps less than 20). We further perform feature selection on α_{id}s to obtain our facial shape features and then we determine the mean vector and the covariance matrix of the features for each person as his/her facial shape template.

Dataset Splitting. For impartial comparison with previous methods mentioned in FaceForensics++ Dataset, we arrange our training, testing, and validation data with the official procedure. In the training phase, only genuine videos and face-swap videos manipulated by *FaceSwap* are used for training and validating. Furthermore, they all undergo *FFmpeg*[3] *CRF23* compression for saving disk space. Moreover, we further utilize *Deepfakes* as cross-domain data for assessment in the testing phase.

Laundering Attacks. *CRF40* compressed videos are also provided by Face-Forensics++ Dataset with lower quality compared to *CRF23*. To assess the robustness of our method, we also attempt more laundering attacks, such as additive noise and smoothing. Gaussian smoothing (*GS*) are used to *CRF23*

---

[1] https://github.com/MarekKowalski/FaceSwap/.
[2] https://github.com/deepfakes/faceswap.
[3] FFmpeg. http://ffmpeg.org/.

videos by *OpenCV*[4] package. The sizes of the the gaussian kernels are 7 and 13 corresponding to standard deviations 1.4 and 2.3, respectively. Furthermore, gaussian noise (*GN*) with zero means are added in each channel of RGB frames. We take into account two various noise levels with the variance of 0.001, and 0.01, respectively.

4.2   Experiment Setup

Our proposed method conducts face-swap detection through the inconsistency between 3D facial shape and appearance. Specifically, a face-swap image always retains the facial shape of the target face but preserves the appearance of the source face. Hence, this clue is capable of face-swap detection as a result of the different facial shapes in different individuals. And we conduct the first experiment to validate the differences of facial shape in different individuals. As shown in the red part of Fig. 3(b), we calculate *Mahalanobis Distance* between the mean vector of 3D facial shape features in a template and other templates. And the green part shows the discrepancy between an individual and his/her template. It is noticed that *Mahalanobis Distance* over 100 are reduced to 100 for simplicity. The figure separates the two part strongly supporting our hypothesis.

Furthermore, we try to examine the resilience of our method to laundering attacks and cross-domain data and compare the results with some previous pixel-level artifacts based methods. In particular, we further set *XceptionNet* and *EfficientNet* as comparison methods, where *XceptionNet* shows the best performance in the FaceForensics++ Dataset. Specifically, we replace the output layer of *XceptionNet* and *EfficientNet* with a fully connected layer of single output and a *Sigmoid* activation is appended. In our approach, the direction of training is to obtain a threshold with approximate accuracy between genuine and manipulated images, which is used in the testing phase.

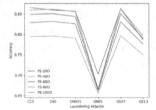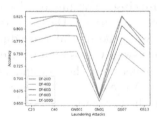

Fig. 2. The performance of five feature selection strategies on laundering (top) and cross-domain (bottom) testing data.

---

[4] OpenCV. https://opencv.org/.

4.3   Ablation Study

Shape Feature Selection. For simplicity, we perform feature selection based on 3D facial shape features. We set 100 frames as the minimum duration of each registered video. Then, due to the employment of *Mahalanobis Distance*, the maximum dimension of the shape features is limited to 100.

We design five feature selection strategies, selecting the top 20, 40, 60, 80, 100 dimensions of the α_{id}s as facial shape features, respectively. They are assessed on the validation dataset and the strategy with best performance is employed in our method. The accuracy of different feature selection (from 20 to 100) on validation data is 0.873, 0.866, 0.854, 0.834 and 0.805, respectively. Therefore, the feature selection strategy of taking the top 20 dimensions has the best performance for face-swap detection on validation data. Furthermore, we also assess the five strategies on all testing data. In Fig. 2, our strategy is still superior for authenticating laundering and cross-domain data. It verifies the effectiveness of our feature selection strategy.

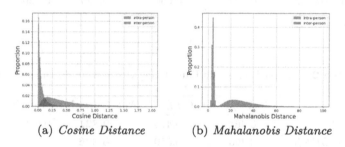

(a) *Cosine Distance*   (b) *Mahalanobis Distance*

Fig. 3. *Cosine Distance* (a) and *Mahalanobis Distance* (b) between 3D facial shape features in templates are shown here. The red/green part corresponds to the distance between mean vectors/3D facial features of a template/a frame and corresponding/other templates. (Color figure online)

Distance Metrics. We also report the results of another measurement method *Cosine Distance*. According to Fig. 3, we use various inconsistency measurement methods to examine the distinguishability between various characters under the same experimental setting.

Specifically, in Fig. 3(a), for the green part, we determine *Cosine Distance* between facial shape features of all frames in the registered videos and the mean vectors of the corresponding templates. The red part is *Cosine Distance* from the mean vectors of other templates. In Fig. 3(b), the measurement method is substituted with *Mahalanobis Distance*.

In Fig. 3(a), the red and green parts have a large overlapping area indicating that in our task, the facial shape features of different individuals cannot be distinguished by *Consine Distance* and the given threshold. This problem is significantly weakened with *Mahalanobis Distance*.

We further conduct comparison experiments on testing data, including laundering data and cross-domain data. The experimental results are shown in Tables 1 and 2. Compared to our method with *Consine Distance* (Ours(C)), our method with *Mahalanobis Distance* (Ours(M)) outperforms on most testing data. The results of the two experiments demonstrate that *Mahalanobis Distance* is more appropriate for our task than other measurement methods.

Table 1. Comparison of the Laundering Data. *ACC*

	XceptionNet	EfficientNet	Ours (M)	Ours (C)
*CRF23	0.974	**0.980**	0.866	0.750
CRF40	0.855	0.816	**0.860**	0.754
GN(var=0.001)	0.790	0.842	**0.857**	0.746
GN(var=0.01)	0.600	0.596	**0.703**	**0.706**
GS(std=1.4)	0.770	0.720	**0.863**	0.751
GS(std=2.3)	0.694	0.666	**0.787**	0.720

Table 2. Comparison of the Laundering Cross-Domain Data. *ACC*

	XceptionNet	EfficientNet	Ours (M)	Ours (C)
CRF23	0.464	0.470	**0.821**	0.679
cre CRF40	0.493	0.510	**0.826**	0.688
GN(var=0.001)	0.572	0.548	**0.827**	0.682
GN(var=0.01)	0.533	0.510	**0.698**	0.649
GS(std=1.4)	0.515	0.507	**0.826**	0.683
GS(std=2.3)	0.514	0.507	**0.768**	0.666

4.4 Face-Swap Detection in the Wild

Here, we further examine the effectiveness of our method in the wild. We gather four video clips of Donald Trump in various surroundings, including a template video. Moreover, two face-swap video clips replacing the faces of others with Trump are downloaded from the Internet. Figure 4 shows the faces from collected videos. We further extract 3D facial shape features of all frames in each video, and determine *Mahalanobis Distance* with the template.

We utilize a scatter plot to show the experimental results of face-swap detection in the wild. According to Fig. 4, these points calculated from genuine faces are mainly distributed below the red line of the threshold. And they are effectively distinguished from those computed by the manipulated faces. Therefore, it demonstrates the effectiveness of our method in the wild. Moreover, note that the distribution of the points calculated from genuine faces does not alter with changes in the surroundings significantly. Consequently, the robustness of the feature expression of the facial shape is also demonstrated by the experiments.

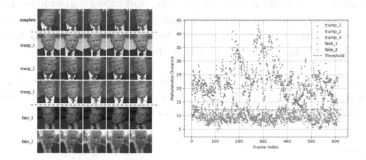

Fig. 4. Shown above are faces from genuine and face-swap videos of Donald Trump in the wild. Shown below is distribution of mahalanobis distances between the template and all faces in five videos.

4.5 Experiment Results and Analysis

The experimental results on laundering data and laundering cross-domain data are presented in Tables 1 and 2. According to Table 1, our proposed approach shows strong robustness against laundering attacks. We train our model, *XceptionNet* and *EfficientNet* on *CRF23* data, and test them against various laundering counter-measures. Table 1 summarizes the performance of all methods. Our proposed approach maintains similar performance when detecting different laundering data, while the effect of the pixel-level artifacts based methods are weakened. Moreover, our approach outperforms them on all laundering data and the accuracy of face-swap detection only has light fluctuation.

We further validate our method on cross-domain data generated by a previously unseen manipulation, *Deepfakes*. In Table 2, our proposed method significantly outperforms the pixel-level artifacts based methods. *XceptionNet* and *EfficientNet* lose effects on the cross-domain data, while our proposed method shows comparable performance with the previous experiments, even on laundering cross-domain data. The performance of our method against different laundering counter-measures is similar. It further demonstrates the feature expression of 3D facial shape is robust on laundering and cross-domain data.

5 Conclusions

We tackle the task of face-swap detection with good robustness on laundering and cross-domain data. Our proposed method leverages the inconsistency between 3D facial shape information and facial appearance information to detect face-swap images. We further propose to utilize *Mahalanobis Distance* for measuring the inconsistency and present its superiority in our task. Moreover, we demonstrate that our approach is less vulnerable to laundering counter-measures and has good robustness against unseen face-swap methods. Finally, our proposed method also shows remarkable performance on the genuine and face-swap videos in the wild. In our method, 3D facial shape information plays a crucial role to detect face-swap images. In the future work, we will focus on more advanced facial shape estimation methods for better detection performance.

Acknowledgement. This work is supported by the National Key Research and Development Program of China under Grant No. 2020AAA0140003 and the National Natural Science Foundation of China (NSFC) under Grants 61972395, U19B2038.

References

1. Deepfakes. https://github.com/deepfakes/faceswap. Accessed 07 Nov 2020
2. Faceswap. https://github.com/MarekKowalski/FaceSwap/. Accessed 07 Nov 2020
3. Agarwal, S., El-Gaaly, T., Farid, H., Lim, S.N.: Detecting deep-fake videos from appearance and behavior (2020)
4. Agarwal, S., Farid, H., Gu, Y., He, M., Nagano, K., Li, H.: Protecting world leaders against deep fakes. In: Proceedings of the IEEE/CVF Conference on Computer Vision and Pattern Recognition (CVPR) Workshops (2019)
5. Blanz, V., Vetter, T.: A morphable model for the synthesis of 3D faces. In: Proceedings of the 26th Annual Conference on Computer Graphics and Interactive Techniques (1999)
6. Chollet, F.: Xception: deep learning with depthwise separable convolutions. In: The IEEE Conference on Computer Vision and Pattern Recognition (CVPR), pp. 1800–1807 (2017)
7. Dolhansky, B., Howes, R., Pflaum, B., Baram, N., Ferrer, C.C.: The deepfake detection challenge (DFDC) preview dataset (2019)
8. Goodfellow, I., et al.: Generative adversarial nets. In: Advances in Neural Information Processing Systems 27, pp. 2672–2680 (2014). http://papers.nips.cc/paper/5423-generative-adversarial-nets.pdf
9. Güera, D., Delp, E.J.: Deepfake video detection using recurrent neural networks. In: 2018 15th IEEE International Conference on Advanced Video and Signal Based Surveillance (AVSS) (2018)
10. Li, L., et al.: Face x-ray for more general face forgery detection. In: Proceedings of the IEEE/CVF Conference on Computer Vision and Pattern Recognition (2020)
11. Matern, F., Riess, C., Stamminger, M.: Exploiting visual artifacts to expose deepfakes and face manipulations. In: 2019 IEEE Winter Applications of Computer Vision Workshops (WACVW) (2019)
12. McCloskey, S., Albright, M.: Detecting GaN-generated imagery using color cues (2018)
13. Mirsky, Y., Lee, W.: The creation and detection of deepfakes: a survey. arXiv: 2004.11138 (2020)
14. Nirkin, Y., Keller, Y., Hassner, T.: FSGAN: subject agnostic face swapping and reenactment. In: Proceedings of the IEEE/CVF International Conference on Computer Vision (ICCV) (2019)

15. Peng, B., Wang, W., Dong, J., Tan, T.: Automatic detection of 3D lighting inconsistencies via a facial landmark based morphable model. In: 2016 IEEE International Conference on Image Processing (ICIP), pp. 3932–3936 (2016)
16. Pérez, P., Gangnet, M., Blake, A.: Poisson image editing. In: ACM SIGGRAPH 2003 Papers (2003)
17. Rossler, A., Cozzolino, D., Verdoliva, L., Riess, C., Thies, J., Niessner, M.: FaceForensics++: learning to detect manipulated facial images. In: The IEEE International Conference on Computer Vision (ICCV) (2019)
18. Sabir, E., Cheng, J., Jaiswal, A., AbdAlmageed, W., Masi, I., Natarajan, P.: Recurrent convolutional strategies for face manipulation detection in videos. In: Proceedings of the IEEE/CVF Conference on Computer Vision and Pattern Recognition (CVPR) Workshops (2019)
19. Tan, M., Le, Q.V.: EfficientNet: rethinking model scaling for convolutional neural networks. In: International Conference on Machine Learning(ICML), pp. 6105–6114 (2019)
20. Tolosana, R., Vera-Rodríguez, R., Fiérrez, J., Morales, A., Ortega-Garcia, J.: DeepFakes and beyond: a survey of face manipulation and fake detection. arXiv: 2001.00179 (2020)
21. Yadav, D., Salmani, S.: DeepFake: a survey on facial forgery technique using generative adversarial network. In: 2019 International Conference on Intelligent Computing and Control Systems (ICCS), pp. 852–857 (2019)
22. Yang, X., Li, Y., Lyu, S.: Exposing deep fakes using inconsistent head poses. In: ICASSP 2019–2019 IEEE International Conference on Acoustics, Speech and Signal Processing (ICASSP), pp. 8261–8265 (2019)
23. Zhou, P., Han, X., Morariu, V.I., Davis, L.S.: Two-stream neural networks for tampered face detection. In: 2017 IEEE Conference on Computer Vision and Pattern Recognition Workshops (CVPRW), pp. 1831–1839 (2017)
24. Zhu, X., Lei, Z., Yan, J., Yi, D., Li, S.Z.: High-fidelity pose and expression normalization for face recognition in the wild. In: The IEEE Conference on Computer Vision and Pattern Recognition (CVPR), pp. 787–796 (2015)

Prompt Learning with Cross-Modal Feature Alignment for Visual Domain Adaptation

Jinxing Liu, Junjin Xiao, Haokai Ma, Xiangxian Li, Zhuang Qi,
Xiangxu Meng, and Lei Meng$^{(\boxtimes)}$

Shandong University, Jinan, Shandong, China
{liujinxing,mahaokai,xiangxian_lee}@mail.sdu.edu.cn, mxx@sdu.edu.cn,
lmeng@sdu.edu.cns

Abstract. Exploring the capacity of pre-trained large-scale models to learn common features of multimodal data and the effect of knowledge transfer on downstream tasks are two major trends in the multimedia field. However, existing studies usually use pre-trained models as feature extractors, or as the teacher model to achieve knowledge distillation of downstream tasks. Therefore, the cross-modal knowledge transfer mechanism and the knowledge forgetting problem of pre-trained large models have not been fully investigated.To address the above issues, this paper explores the fine-tuning strategy, feature selection strategy and semantic guidance approach in the migration process of pre-trained large models.Aiming at the problem of knowledge forgetting during "fine-tuning", an image classification algorithm (PMHANet) integrating a pre-trained large-scale model and heterogeneous feature alignment is proposed.More importantly, this provides a cross-modal knowledge transfer paradigm for multimodal pre-training of large models.We conducted experiments on VireoFood-172 and NUS-WIDE and found that large models trained on datasets such as COCO performed better on the similar domain dataset NUS-WIDE than the small domain dataset VireoFood-172; PMHANet effectively implements multimodal representation enhancement in downstream tasks based on a partially fine-tuned pre-trained large model to achieve SOTA performance on both datasets.

Keywords: Pre-trained multimodal models · Cross-modal knowledge transfer · Heterogeneous feature alignment · Image classification

1 Introduction

In recent years, knowledge transfer based on multimodal pre-trained large models has received wide attention due to its excellent performance [10,15], which can bridge the semantic gap between different modal data and improve the performance of downstream tasks. However, current large models rely on large-scale multimodal data, while the data distribution and data modality are often limited in downstream tasks, leading to unsatisfactory performance after knowledge

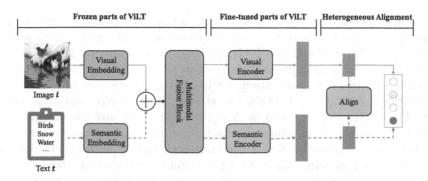

Fig. 1. Illustration of the PMHANet. Combining cross-modal transfer and heterogeneous feature alignment mechanisms with existing pre-trained large models, image representation enhancement is achieved by maximising the consistency between multimodal representations.

transfer. Therefore, how to combine the knowledge of multimodal pre-trained large models with small domain data to improve the performance of downstream tasks and explain their mechanisms is an urgent problem.

There are two main approaches to knowledge transfer for multimodal pre-trained models, one is to use the model as a feature extractor and fine-tune [7, 21], and the other is to use the model as a teacher to achieve knowledge distillation [20]. However, existing methods may lead to knowledge forgetting when transfering, limiting the performance of knowledge transfer. To address this issue, we use heterogeneous feature alignment to supplement the interaction information in the transfer phase. Heterogeneous feature alignment is an important technique for feature enhancement with multimodal data [3, 11, 14, 16], but the effectiveness of alignment is currently limited due to the different distribution and value range between heterogeneous features.

To address the above issues, this paper explores how to use multimodal pre-trained large models for cross-modal knowledge transfer and proposes a model transfer method based on partial heterogeneous modal feature alignment (PMHANet). Specifically, this paper explores the transfer method for pre-trained large models by comparing the feature capabilities of different stages and types. Based on the above exploration, we use semantic information to enhance image representation and propose an image classification algorithm (PMHANet) that incorporates a pre-trained large model and partially heterogeneous modal feature alignment. As shown in Fig. 1, this paper divides the pre-trained large model into four modules, which Shallow Feature Extraction(SFE), Feature Fusion Network(FFN), Fine-tune Network(FTN), and Heterogeneous Feature Alignment(HFA). Specifically, in the SFE Module, PMHANet forms shallow features for multimodal interactions by mapping visual modality and semantic modality information, respectively. To achieve heterogeneous modal feature interactions, PMHANet fuses the underlying features of images and text and implements self-focused implicit feature alignment in the FFN; to achieve fine-grained feature extraction, PMHANet retrains the transfer network module on a segmented domain task dataset to enhance the image representation capability of the model in the FTN. Finally, to mitigate the loss of interaction information during multimodal large-scale model transfer, PMHANet learns text-enhanced visual representations for image classification by maximizing the distributional consistency between visual and semantic representations in the HFA. The PMHANet proposed in this paper solves the problem of interaction information loss during multimodal large-scale model transfer, achieves the effective transfer of multimodal pre-trained large-scale models in image classification tasks, and culminates in a fine-tuning paradigm for pre-trained models.

We conducted performance comparisons, an ablation study of the alignment method, and several in-depth analyses of the transfer paradigm of the pre-trained large model on two real-world datasets, VireoFood-172 and NUS-WIDE. The results show that PMHANet can further improve the image classification performance by partial fine-tuning and heterogeneous feature alignment. To summarize, this paper includes two main contributions:

(1) Based on ViLT, we explore the knowledge transfer capability of features at different stages and types of features, and propose a knowledge transfer paradigm for multimodal pre-trained large models.
(2) An image classification method (PMHANet) is proposed based on heterogeneous feature alignment, which can achieve semantic-guided image feature enhancement and effectively improve image classification performance.

2   Related Works

2.1   Multi-modal Pre-trained Large-Scale Models

Multimodal pre-trained large-scale models are capable of automatically learning different modal features without supervision and quickly migrating to different down- stream tasks. Most of the current multimodal pre-trained large models are based on BERT [4] which can be structurally classified into single-stream and dual-stream models. Single-stream models such as VisualBERT [10], UNI-CODER [6], VL-BERT [12], and ImageBERT [15] use the collocation of visual and semantic features of image-text pairs as input to the interaction network, and multimodal information is fused without constraints at an early stage. In contrast, in dual-stream models such as ViLBERT [12], LXMERT [17], and ERNIE-ViL [22], different modal data are encoded respectively and the resulting embeddings interact through a co-attentive-based encoding layer. However, less research has been done to explore the transfer mechanism of pre-trained large models, and how to combine the knowledge of pre-trained large models to achieve feature enhancement for downstream tasks is still a problem waiting to be solved.

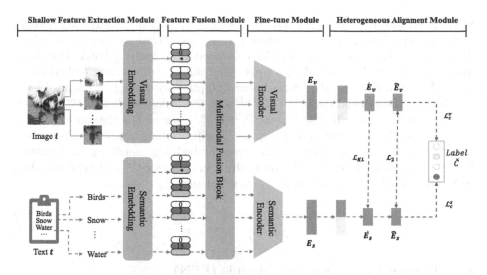

Fig. 2. Illustration of the PMHANet. PMHANet combines heterogeneous feature alignment mechanisms with existing pre-trained large-scale models to enhance image characterization and enable cross-modal knowledge transfer.

2.2   Heterogeneous Feature Alignment

Heterogeneous feature alignment techniques are able to learn linear or nonlinear mappings to align features from different domains in the latent space.Current research typically uses shared neural networks to learn high-level features of heterogeneous data and constrain their similarity, such as the KL-divergence [14], the loss of generative adversarial networks [3] and the covariance matrix of feature distributions [16].However, the existing methods do not address the inherent heterogeneity of data in different domains and cannot resolve the differences between text features and image features heterogeneous modalities in terms of feature distribution and value domain range, resulting in limited mapping effect of heterogeneous feature alignment techniques between modalities.

3   Technique

3.1   Framework Overview

In view of the powerful characterization ability of pre-trained large models and the feature enhancement ability of heterogeneous feature alignment, this paper proposes an image classification algorithm PMHANet.As shown in the Fig. 2, PMHANet contains four main submodules.

3.2   Shallow Feature Extraction Module (SFE)

PMHANet generates low-level and shallow features for information interaction in Feature Fusion Module by linearly mapping image and text in the

Shallow Feature Extraction Module respectively.Specifically, PMHANet accepts multi-modal original image text pairs $\{(I_j, T_j) \mid j = 1, \ldots, N\}$ as input, where N represents the number of samples contained in a training batch.The input image $I \in \mathbb{R}^{C \times H \times W}$ is sliced into equal-sized image patches, and embedded to $v \in \mathbb{R}^{L \times D}$ through visual feature linear mapping layer $\mathcal{M}_v(\cdot)$. Then add the absolute position encoding $E_v^{pos} \in \mathbb{R}^{L \times D}$ and the type encoding $E_v^{type} \in \mathbb{R}^{L \times D}$ to generate the visual shallow feature $F_v \in \mathbb{R}^{L \times D}$, where L is the content tokens and D is the hidden dimension of features. The processing of text data is similar. After the text data t is mapped into a word embedding matrix by the semantic feature embedding layer $\mathcal{M}_s(\cdot)$, the position encoding E_s^{pos} and type encoding E_s^{type} are added to form semantic shallow features F_s.

$$F_v = \mathcal{M}_v(I) + E_v^{pos} + E_v^{type} \tag{1}$$

$$F_s = \mathcal{M}_s(T) + E_s^{pos} + E_s^{pos} \tag{2}$$

3.3   Feature Fusion Network Module (FFN)

In order to leverage the generic knowledge in the multimodal pre-trained model and to enhance the representational power of the model when migrating to downstream tasks of image classification, we extract interaction features based on the multimodal feature fusion layer of the pre-trained large model.In the Feature Fusion module, PMHANet fuses heterogeneous modal features F_v and F_s and facilitates multimodal information interaction based on pre-trained knowledge to reduce the variability of distribution of heterogeneous features in the feature space and generate multimodal interaction features:

$$F_{sv} = (\theta\,(LN\,(MSA\,(LN\,[F_s : F_v]))) \cdots) \tag{3}$$

where $MSA(\cdot)$ denotes multi-headed self-attention, $LN(\cdot)$ denotes LayerNorm normalization method, $\theta(\cdot)$ denotes two-layer fully connected network.

3.4   Fine-Tune Network Module (FTN)

The Transfer Network Module fine-tunes the layers to generate fine-grained features in the segment and alleviates data limitations between the pre-training and downstream datasets such as data distribution.In detail, the fine-grained heterogeneous feature extraction was achieved by mapping interaction features to different feature spaces via visual mapping $\mathcal{T}_v(\cdot)$ and semantic mapping $\mathcal{T}_s(\cdot)$.After the multimodal interaction features are subjected to multi-headed attention operations, the content representation information is aggregated and the visual representation feature E_v is generated through the visual perceptual mapping module.Multimodal interaction features aggregate content representation information through semantic information mapping and generate semantic representation features E_s. The specific formulas are as follows:

$$E_v = \mathcal{T}_v\,(LN\,(MSA\,(LN\,(F_{sv})))) \tag{4}$$

$$E_s = \mathcal{T}_s\,(F_{sv}) \tag{5}$$

Table 1. Datasets used in the experiment.Tags means the number of text words

Dataset	Class	Tags	Train Split	Test Split
Vireo-Food172	172	353	68,175	25,250
NUS-WIDE	81	1,000	121,962	81,636

3.5   Heterogeneous Feature Alignment Module (HFA)

Visual and semantic encoders are able to learn visual and semantic features E_v and E_s independently, and given that semantic embeddings have better discriminative power on classification tasks, aligning visual and semantic features directly allows their distribution to converge and enables semantically guided visual feature enhancement.However, the inherent variability of heterogeneous modal characteristics leads to limited effects in alignment.

To solve this problem, we align the shared information of visual and semantic features in the HFA module, i.e. the partial heterogeneous alignment method. Based on the assumption that the embedding E_k consists of E_k^1, which represents label information, and E_k^2, which represents stylistic information.Therefore separating E_v^1 and E_s^1 from E_v and E_s and aligning them can alleviate the heterogeneity between heterogeneous modes, and endow visual features with semantic information, ultimately enhancing visual representation.To preserve the semantic modal feature distribution, we used a one-way KL-divergence loss function for cross-modal feature alignment to compensate for heterogeneous modal distribution differences. In addition, we use the ℓ_2 norm alignment method to align the heterogeneous modal features in the potential space.

$$\mathcal{L}_{KL} = KL\left(\dot{\mathbf{E}}^s \| \dot{\mathbf{E}}^v\right) \qquad (6)$$

$$\mathcal{L}_{\text{align}} = \left\| \hat{\mathbf{E}}^v - \hat{\mathbf{E}}^s \right\|_2 \qquad (7)$$

The representations output the category prediction information through a nonlinear mapping and use cross-entropy (CE) loss and binary cross-entropy (BCE) loss to calculate the classification loss in single-label classification and multi-label classification tasks, respectively.

$$\mathcal{L}_c^v = CE\left(\text{softmax}\left(\phi\left(\hat{\mathbf{E}}^v\right)\right), y\right) \qquad (8)$$

$$\mathcal{L}_c^s = CE\left(\text{softmax}\left(\phi\left(\hat{\mathbf{E}}^s\right)\right), y\right) \qquad (9)$$

4   Experiments

4.1   Datasets

We conducted experiments on two datasets, Vireo-Food172 and NUS- WIDE, and the statistical information corresponding to the datasets is given in Table 1:

Table 2. Compare the experimental results, where the VireoFood-172 dataset uses the accuracy (Acc) of top1 and top5 as a measure of single classification task, and the NUS-WIDE dataset uses the precision (Prec) and recall (Recall) of top1 and top5 as the performance performance of multi-classification task

	Algorithm	Vireo-Food172		NUS-WIDE			
		Acc@1	Acc@5	Prec@1	Prec@5	Recall@1	Recall@5
Visual Classification	ResNet50	81.6	95.0	73.2	36.1	39.8	86.4
	WRN	82.3	95.5	73.4	36.5	39.8	78.7
	WISeR	82.8	96.5	73.7	36.7	40.1	79.0
	ViLT	69.4	90.2	80.7	40.5	45.8	88.0
Heterogeneous Feature Alignment	IG-CMAN	82.9	96.4	73.3	37.0	42.0	80.0
	ATNet	82.9	93.1	75.7	35.8	41.3	77.1
	MSMVFA	83.1	96.6	78.2	39.3	43.7	85.6
	PMHANet	**83.7**	**96.7**	**81.6**	**41.1**	**46.3**	**88.8**

- **VireoFood-172** [1]: A single-label classification dataset containing a total of 110,241 images of dishes, corresponding to 172 categories and 353 semantic elements with an average of three semantic elements annotated per image.We sliced all images according to the design in paper [1].
- **NUS-WIDE** [2]: A multi-label classification dataset containing a total of 269,648 image samples corresponding to 81 categories and 1000 semantic elements.We refer to the related paper [2,18,19], preprocessed the original dataset and divided the remaining 203,598 samples.

4.2   Model Details

In our experiments, we followed the feature dimension setting of the pre-trained model VILT [9], and the input image resolution was resized to 384. Model was optimised using the Adam optimiser during training, with the learning rate picked from 5e-5 to 5e-3 and with every four periods completed, the optimiser's learning rate decayed to a factor of 0.1 of the original.For NUS-WIDE, the positive sample weights for setting BCE losses were selected from 20 to 150.

4.3   Performance Comparison

In this section, we show the effect of PMHANet on two datasets, comparing the performance of the base vision models ResNet50 [5] and the improved models WRN [23] and WISeR [13] based on ResNet50, and we also compare ViLT [9] transferred directly to the classification task. To compare with multimodal inference methods, we experimented with ATNet [14] and MSMVFA [8] methods based on feature alignment, and ARCH-D [1] methods based on multimodal information constraints based on ResNet50. As shown in Table 2.

- **For pre-trained basic vision models**: models with deeper layers such as ResNet50 and VGG19 achieved better results than ResNet-18 in both

Table 3. Performance of the PMHANet with different semantic guidance approaches on the Vireo172 and NUS-WIDE datasets.FT: partial fine-tuned ViLT.

Algorithm	VIreo172		NUS-WIDE			
	Acc@1	Acc@5	Prec@1	Prec@5	Recall@1	Recall@5
Baseline	69.4	90.2	80.5	40.5	45.4	87.6
+FT	82.9	96.3	80.7	40.6	45.8	88.0
+FT+l2norm	82.9	96.5	80.7	40.6	45.8	88.0
+FT+KL	83.5	96.6	81.2	40.8	46.1	88.4
+FT+l2norm+KL	**83.7**	**96.7**	**81.6**	**41.1**	**46.3**	**88.8**

datasets.Improvements in model structure by the WRN and WISeR models yielded better predictive performance than ResNet50. This shows that structural improvements and parametric enhancement enhance the task migration capability of the model

- **For the large pre-trained model ViLT**: it produced inconsistent results when migrating to the classification task on both datasets. Compared to ResNet50, ViLT showed a 14.9% decrease in Top-1 on the VireoFood172 dataset, but a 10.2% increase on the NUS-WIDE dataset, indicating that the pre-trained large model is susceptible to data distribution in downstream task migration, which leads to inconsistent quality of its learned representations.
- **For multimodal inference methods**, the visual representation is enhanced by feature alignment-based or multimodal information constraint methods, thus improving the classification performance, where the MSMVFA method fuses multi-scale information and the CMRR method adds constraints on the local information thus further enhancing the inference capability.
- **PMHANet achieves the best results on both datasets**, and obtains a 20.6% Top-1 accuracy improvement relative to the original ViLT on the Vireo-Food172 dataset. This demonstrates the effectiveness of the design of partial fine-tuning and heterogeneous feature alignment, allowing the model to learn a better visual representation , which also demonstrates the potential of PMHANet to facilitate model learning for out-of-distribution data.

4.4 Ablation Study

In addition to the overall performance comparison, we conducted ablation experiments in order to explore the effectiveness of the heterogeneous feature alignment method in PMHANet. The results are shown in Table 3, and we have the following findings:

- **Partial fine-tuning facilitates cross-modal knowledge transfer:** Due to the significant heterogeneity between the task targeted by the pre-trained large model and the downstream task, it is difficult to directly migrate it to the image classification task, so only 69.4% top1 accuracy is obtained on vireo172. In contrast, fine-tuning the model according to the downstream task

Table 4. Classification performance of ViLT combined with different fine-tuning strategies and token features.Ft-3 fine-tunes the last three layers of the ViLT

Token Type	Accuracy	Frozen	FT-3	FT-6	FT-9	FT-all
Class token	Acc@1	35.3	74.7	79.5	82.7	83.1
	Acc@5	66.5	93.4	95.1	96.5	96.5
Content token	Acc@1	69.4	78.6	82.3	82.7	82.9
	Acc@5	90.3	95.1	96.1	96.3	96.3
Fusion token	Acc@1	68.9	78.6	82.3	82.7	83.2
	Acc@5	90.1	95.0	96.0	96.4	96.5

to achieve cross-modal knowledge transfer for segmented datasets can achieve a performance improvement of 19.4%. Meanwhile, the performance improvement of "baseline+FT" on the NUS-WIDE dataset is not obvious, which may be due to the similar data distribution between the training dataset of the pre-trained large model and NUS-WIDE.

– **Heterogeneous feature alignment facilitates image feature enhancement:** L2norm can achieve similarity of heterogeneous features by aligning heterogeneous modal features in a uniform feature space, but bi-directional similarity cannot achieve specific feature enhancement.KL Divergence can asymmetrically achieve one-way similarity from image features to text features, which eventually yields 83.5% top1 accuracy on vireo172 and a simultaneous boost on nuswide. Combining l2norm and KL-divergence, the model can mitigate the semantic "gap" when migrating from the pre-trained large model to the downstream task by fine-grained heterogeneous alignment of visual and semantic modal representations through partial feature alignment methods, and compensate for the information loss during migration, thus achieving the best classification improvement on both datasets.

4.5   In-depth Analysis of PMHANet

In this section, we investigate the impact of using different fine-tuning strategies, feature selection approaches, and semantic guidance approaches when pre-trained large models are used in the knowledge migration process, thus providing insight into the design of PMHANet on model migration.

Comparison of Feature Selection Methods. We explore the impact of fine-tuning strategy and the choice of token feature type on migration performance on the VireoFood-172 dataset, and the results are shown in Table 4.

– **At the level of the fine-tuning strategy:** We compare the effects of tuning different fine-tuning layers on the model. The fine-tuned network layers (from frozen to FT-3, FT-6) enable fine-grained extraction of features, which leads to a significant improvement in its classification performance. As the

Table 5. Comparison of transfer ability of pre-trained models with features at different stages in classification tasks. Shallow: features generated by Embedding; Frozen: features generated by frozen ViLT; Fine-tune: features generated by fine-tuned ViLT

Feature		Vireo172		NUS-WIDE			
		Acc@1	Acc@5	Prec@1	Prec@5	Recall@1	Recall@5
Image	Shallow	5.2	17.0	42.3	25.6	19.5	57.0
	Frozen	69.4	90.2	80.5	40.5	45.4	87.6
	Fine-tune	82.9	96.3	80.7	40.6	45.8	88.0
Text	Shallow	97.1	99.6	71.9	36.7	39.7	80.3
	Frozen	76.9	93.8	42.5	26.1	20.0	57.0
	Fine-tune	97.9	99.9	75.0	37.7	41.7	82.2
Multi-modal	Shallow	82.4	95.7	67.3	34.9	37.2	77.6
	Frozen	90.9	98.3	80.9	40.5	46.0	88.0
	Fine-tune	98.6	99.9	84.3	41.8	48.1	90.5

number of fine-tuned layers rises (FT-9 and FT-all), the generalization ability of shallow networks may be weakened, limiting their performance improvement. More importantly, the fine-tuning of more layers brings an increase in computational overhead. Therefore, FT-6 is chosen for our algorithm to balance the model performance and computational efficiency.

– **At the level of the feature selection strategy:** In the case of partial fine-tuning, the information obtained by class token in the shallow pre-trained knowledge deviates more from the information in the downstream task, while content token and fusion token are able to better combine the pre-trained knowledge with the multimodal information in the downstream task and therefore obtain better classification results. Since the content token already has sufficient representational power, it is used in this model.

Analysis of Cross-Modal Migration Ability. In this section, we analyze the experimental results of image, text and multimodal data for the features extracted from different layers to analyze the cross-modal knowledge transfer capability of ViLT, as shown in Table 5. Due to the diversity of image data the shallow features lack category-related information and thus have poor performance. The interaction space information provided by the pre-trained interaction network and further extraction of image features can improve the prediction of the model. However, due to the problem of data distribution differences in knowledge migration, the model still needs to be fine-tuned to achieve better classification performance. Compared to images, text features mapped by semantic embedding can obtain sufficient classification information. However, the hybrid knowledge of the pre-trained interaction network makes the representation of text features less capable due to the different value range and distributions of heterogeneous modal features. The use of multimodal fusion features consistent

Table 6. Experimental comparison of semantic guidance modalities on the ability to represent visual features.

Approaches	Vireo172		NUS-WIDE			
	Acc@1	Acc@5	Prec@1	Prec@5	Recall@1	Recall@5
Deep PI	81.4	96.1	80.7	40.5	45.6	88.0
Shallow PI	81.5	96.2	80.7	40.5	45.7	88.0
Concat	83.7	96.8	81.6	41.1	46.3	88.8

with pre-training can fully utilize the pre-training just to achieve the best performance.

Comparison of Semantic Guidance Approaches. In this section, we conduct experiments to compare the effects of different semantic guidance approaches on image features, as shown in Table 6. The Deep PI method passes different modal data asynchronously through the feature extraction network to map to the same feature space, FTN Module is affected by the optimization of text classification and degrades the image classification performance. The Shallow PI method achieves semantic enhancement of visual features by directly aligning shallow text features with deep image features and avoids the influence of text on FTN Module. The best results can be achieved by stitching image and text features together according to the ViLT settings, making full use of pre-training knowledge, and achieving feature fusion and interaction through self-attention in a shallow network.

5   Conclusion

In this paper, we propose an image classification algorithm PMHANet that combines multimodal pre-trained large model and heterogeneous feature alignment, and propose a "fine-tuning" paradigm for the pre-trained large model. The experimental results show that partial heterogeneous feature alignment can further improve the image representation capability of the model. Future work in this research is focused on two directions.First, the learning capability of the model for multimodal interaction representations is improved by introducing higher-order graph structure information between image and text information. Second, causal inference techniques can help the model learn the relationship between context and target, combined with the mapping alignment of heterogeneous modalities to further alleviate the semantic gap problem between modalities.

Acknowledgments. This work is supported in part by the Excellent Youth Scholars Program of Shandong Province (Grant no. 2022HWYQ-048) and the Oversea Innovation Team Project of the "20 Regulations for New Universities" funding program of Jinan (Grant no. 2021GXRC073).

References

1. Chen, J., Ngo, C.W.: Deep-based ingredient recognition for cooking recipe retrieval. In: Proceedings of the 24th ACM International Conference on Multimedia, pp. 32–41 (2016)
2. Chua, T.S., Tang, J., Hong, R., Li, H., Luo, Z., Zheng, Y.: Nus-wide: a real-world web image database from national university of Singapore. In: Proceedings of the ACM International Conference on Image and Video Retrieval, pp. 1–9 (2009)
3. Chung, Y.A., Weng, W.H., Tong, S., Glass, J.: Unsupervised cross-modal alignment of speech and text embedding spaces. In: Advances in Neural Information Processing Systems 31 (2018)
4. Devlin, J., Chang, M.W., Lee, K., Toutanova, K.: BERT: pre-training of deep bidirectional transformers for language understanding. arXiv preprint arXiv:1810.04805 (2018)
5. He, K., Zhang, X., Ren, S., Sun, J.: Deep residual learning for image recognition. In: Proceedings of the IEEE Conference on Computer Vision and Pattern Recognition, pp. 770–778 (2016)
6. Huang, H., et al.: Unicoder: a universal language encoder by pre-training with multiple cross-lingual tasks. arXiv preprint arXiv:1909.00964 (2019)
7. Iki, T., Aizawa, A.: Effect of visual extensions on natural language understanding in vision-and-language models. arXiv preprint arXiv:2104.08066 (2021)
8. Jiang, S., Min, W., Liu, L., Luo, Z.: Multi-scale multi-view deep feature aggregation for food recognition. IEEE Trans. Image Process. **29**, 265–276 (2019)
9. Kim, W., Son, B., Kim, I.: ViLT: vision-and-language transformer without convolution or region supervision. In: International Conference on Machine Learning, pp. 5583–5594. PMLR (2021)
10. Li, L.H., Yatskar, M., Yin, D., Hsieh, C.J., Chang, K.W.: VisualBert: a simple and performant baseline for vision and language. arXiv preprint arXiv:1908.03557 (2019)
11. Lin, T.Y., Goyal, P., Girshick, R., He, K., Dollár, P.: Focal loss for dense object detection. In: Proceedings of the IEEE International Conference on Computer Vision, pp. 2980–2988 (2017)
12. Lu, J., Batra, D., Parikh, D., Lee, S.: VilBert: pretraining task-agnostic visiolinguistic representations for vision-and-language tasks. In: Advances in Neural Information Processing Systems 32 (2019)
13. Martinel, N., Foresti, G.L., Micheloni, C.: Wide-slice residual networks for food recognition. In: 2018 IEEE Winter Conference on Applications of Computer Vision (WACV), pp. 567–576. IEEE (2018)
14. Meng, L., et al.: Learning using privileged information for food recognition. In: Proceedings of the 27th ACM International Conference on Multimedia, pp. 557–565 (2019)
15. Qi, D., Su, L., Song, J., Cui, E., Bharti, T., Sacheti, A.: ImageBert: cross-modal pre-training with large-scale weak-supervised image-text data. arXiv preprint arXiv:2001.07966 (2020)
16. Sun, B., Saenko, K.: Deep coral: correlation alignment for deep domain adaptation. In: Hua, G., Jégou, H. (eds.) ECCV 2016. LNCS, vol. 9915, pp. 443–450. Springer, Cham (2016). https://doi.org/10.1007/978-3-319-49409-8_35
17. Tan, H., Bansal, M.: Lxmert: learning cross-modality encoder representations from transformers. arXiv preprint arXiv:1908.07490 (2019)

18. Tang, J., Shu, X., Li, Z., Qi, G.J., Wang, J.: Generalized deep transfer networks for knowledge propagation in heterogeneous domains (2016)
19. Tang, J., et al.: Tri-clustered tensor completion for social-aware image tag refinement. IEEE Trans. Pattern Anal. Mach. Intell. **39**(8), 1662–1674 (2016)
20. Tang, Z., Cho, J., Tan, H., Bansal, M.: VidLanKD: improving language understanding via video-distilled knowledge transfer. In: Advances in Neural Information Processing Systems 34 (2021)
21. Wang, J., Wang, H., Deng, J., Wu, W., Zhang, D.: EfficientcCLIP: efficient cross-modal pre-training by ensemble confident learning and language modeling. arXiv preprint arXiv:2109.04699 (2021)
22. Yu, F., et al.: ERNIE-ViL: knowledge enhanced vision-language representations through scene graphs. In: Proceedings of the AAAI Conference on Artificial Intelligence, vol. 35, pp. 3208–3216 (2021)
23. Zagoruyko, S., Komodakis, N.: Wide residual networks. arXiv preprint arXiv:1605.07146 (2016)

Tile Defect Detection Based on the Improved S2C-YOLOv5

Limei Song[✉], Jiatong Xiao, Zhichao Wu, Mengya Liu, and Zhonghao Xiang

Tianjin Key Laboratory of Intelligent Control of Electrical Equipment, Tiangong University, Tianjin 300387, China
songlimei@tiangong.edu.cn, xiaojt0214@yeah.net

Abstract. For the problem of complex tile surface pattern background, different defect features, low efficiency, and high leakage rate of manual and traditional recognition, this paper proposes a deep learning-based tile surface defect detection method. First, the YOLOv5 backbone network is replaced with a lightweight network ShuffleNetV2, and then, the convolutional block attention module (CBAM) is added. Finally, a lightweight tile detection system is constructed by using CrossEntropyLoss instead of the loss function in the original network. The comparison experiments with six networks such as YOLOv4, Faster RCNN, and SSD show that the algorithm detects tile defects with 95.10% Precision and 92.91% mAP, which is 3.02 percentage points better than the defect recognition accuracy of the network before improvement. It solves the industry-wide problem of long-term reliance on manual visual recognition for tile surface defect detection, realizes automatic and high-precision detection of tile defects, and the resulting tile defect detection technology can be put into stable and reliable operation in the ceramic industry.

Keywords: Tile · Surface defect detection · Deep learning · Recognition

1 Introduction

Ceramic tiles are now widely used in the construction field, and the surface quality of ceramic tiles directly affects the appearance and service life. At present, the domestic mass production process of ceramic wall and floor tiles still uses the manual inspection method for quality assessment, which is not only slow and error-prone but also difficult to meet the modern industrial inspection requirements of high-speed, high-precision, automatic online inspection. Complex tile surface texture is intricate and complex, and the background information can interfere with defect detection, so it is difficult to detect.

With the rapid development of target detection technology, traditional methods of machine vision are applied to defect detection in the industry. To solve these problems of low efficiency and low accuracy of traditional vision inspection, more and more scholars are using different techniques for tile surface defect detection. Machine vision inspection relies on image processing techniques to detect external defects and is now able to be put to use in modern industry. L. Guangya et al. [1] proposed a visual inspection method

© The Author(s), under exclusive license to Springer Nature Switzerland AG 2022
L. Fang et al. (Eds.): CICAI 2022, LNAI 13604, pp. 429–440, 2022.
https://doi.org/10.1007/978-3-031-20497-5_35

for tile surface defects based on Gabor transform and region growing for the detection of cracks, holes, pockmarks, and color difference defects in tiles. Zhang et al. [2] used the method of color space distribution difference of tile surface defects to detect tiles and the types of defects detected were cracks, scratches, spots, and breakage. Junhua Li et al. [3] used the improved SIFT and color moment fusion features as regions of tile images, and then classified the tiles for defects by SVM classifier. Maria et al. [4] used RGB color conversion based on the gray matrix, segmentation, and feature extraction, and fed the extracted features into an artificial neural network to build a tile surface defect detection model.

Most of the current traditional machine learning methods require specific preprocessing methods to extract features, which is a tedious process and incomplete in terms of extracted features, resulting in low accuracy and efficiency of defect detection. These methods are often only for a specific texture background of tiles, which is not applicable enough.

To address the limitations of the currently existing methods, this paper takes tiles with three different texture backgrounds as the research object and uses YOLOv5s6 as the base deep learning training model. For the problems of small defect sizes and complex textures in the dataset, we improve the models in turn.

The main contributions of this study are summarized as follows:

- A tile defect detection system was constructed based on the YOLOv5s6 model with high accuracy and speed.
- Replaced the CSPDarknet backbone network with ShuffleNetV2 and added the CBAM attention module to make the network model more lightweight while reducing the interference of complex texture background on the results.
- Using CrossEntroyLoss instead of BCEWithLogitsLoss function in Yolov5 to evaluate the class loss and confidence loss of the target and prediction frames. The S2C-YOLOv5 model proposed in this paper is finally obtained.

2 Related Work

With its powerful feature extraction capability and excellent generalization performance, deep learning techniques have emerged as a mature research result in many industrial inspection tasks. There are also many scholars studying the application of deep learning to defect detection. L. Zehui et al. [5] introduced a convolutional self-encoder in YOLOv3 for weak defect reconstruction to enhance the input of the network, which can effectively identify holes, pinholes, and scratch-like defects on the surface of polished tiles, but it is only limited to the detection of polished tiles, and the generalization is not strong. Taochuan Zhang et al. [6] designed a two-stream convolutional neural network model using a maximal fusion strategy, taking the original image of the tile and its corresponding binary image of the defect region as input, extracting features to achieve feature fusion separately and then inputting them to an SVM classifier to achieve defect classification and recognition. Masch et al. [7] used a five-layer convolutional neural network for image classification of steel defect types, demonstrating that the deep learning approach outperforms classical machine vision algorithms that combine hand-engineered features with support vector machines, however, their work is limited to shallow networks without batch normalization. Lin et al. [8] used inter-frame deep convolutional networks to simulate the differential operations of biological vision to characterize suspicious defective regions.

Currently, the YOLO family of target detection algorithms [9–12], which are widely used in industry, reduces the complexity of network computation and increases the speed of target detection. Compared with other networks, the performance is stronger for the same size data set and has been steadily improving. Therefore, in this paper, we adopt the YOLOv5 model as the baseline, and use ShuffleNetV2 to replace the original backbone network to build a lighter network with higher detection accuracy and faster speed for the small tile defect target and complex background texture information and incomplete feature extraction, and add the attention module to remove the interference of complex texture information on the detection results and improve the Loss function to further improve the accuracy of defect detection.

3   S2C-YOLOv5 Model

The YOLOv5 model is a common target detection algorithm. This detection model has high detection accuracy and fast inference speed, with a maximum inference speed of 140 FPS. The FLOPS of YOLOv5s6 model is only 0.4 worse than YOLOv5s, but the mAP value is 6.6 higher than YOLOv5s. Considering various factors, YOLOv5s6 is chosen as the base model for this study.

The three parts of backbone network selection, model training, and classification recognition are the three major tasks of image classification and recognition [16]. In this paper, the improvement of the YOLOv5 network is mainly from three aspects to improve, which are the replacement and enhancement of the backbone and the improvement of the loss function, and then improve the detection accuracy of the tile defect detection model.

3.1   Backbone Network Improvements

The backbone network of YOLOv5 is CSPDarknet [17], which is considerable in speed but has low accuracy due to complex tile texture information and small defect detection targets. Then, four-slice operations are used in the upper structure of feature extraction to form the Focus layer, but multiple slice operations lead to significant growth in computation and the number of parameters. It is proved that the frequent use of the C3 Layer will occupy more cache space and slow down the operation speed, and the parallel operation of SPP structure and C3 structure will affect the speed. Therefore, in this paper, we propose to improve the network structure of YOLOv5 by using the lightweight idea in ShuffleNetV2 [18] to further improve the network in terms of speed and accuracy.

ShuffleNetV2 achieves the optimal trade-off between speed and accuracy because it follows four lightweight network design guidelines after a detailed analysis of the impact of input and output channels, the number of grouped convolutional groups, the degree of network fragmentation, and element-by-element operations on speed and memory access cost (MAC) on different hardware, as shown in Table 1.

Table 1. ShuffleNetV2 lightweight network design criterions.

Serial number	Criterions
1	The smallest memory access MAC when the number of input and output channels is the same
2	Group convolution with too many groups increases the MAC
3	Fragmented operations (multiple paths, making the network very wide) are not friendly to parallel acceleration
4	Element-wise operations (e.g. ReLU, Shortcut-add, etc.) bring non-negligible memory and time consumption

ShuffleNetV2 introduces a new operation Channel Split, which starts by splitting the input feature map into two branches in the channel dimension: the number of channels is c' and $c - c'$. $c' = c/2$ For the actual implementation. The input and output channels are the same, which is following criterion 1. The two 1×1 convolutions are no longer group convolutions, which is consistent with criterion 2. The other two branches form two groups to avoid multiple channels, which is consistent with criterion 3. The channel shuffle is performed on the two branch concat results to ensure the information exchange between the two branches. One of the concat and channel shuffles can be combined with the Channel Split of the next module unit to form an element-level operation, which is following criterion 4.

The incorporation of ShuffleNetV2 in YOLOv5 makes the network lighter and deeper. Deeper network layers mean better nonlinear representation and a higher ability to learn more complex transformations. As a result, more complex feature inputs can be fitted, thus greatly improving model performance.

3.2   Integration of CBAM Attention Mechanisms

For tiles with complex background texture information, the texture information can obscure some of the defective features and affect the detection accuracy during feature extraction. The introduction of the CBAM convolutional block attention mode can eliminate the influence of confusing information on the detection results and focus on useful target information [19].

CBAM is a feed-forward convolutional neural network, which contains two independent sub-modules, Channel Attention Module, and Spatial Attention Module. Channel Attention Module uses the channel relationship between features to generate a channel attention graph, and its specific structure is shown in Fig. 1.

The channel's attention is focused on the information of a given input image whose calculation formula is shown as Eq. 1:

$$M_C(F) = \sigma\left(W_1\left(W_0\left(F_{avg}^c\right)\right) + W_1\left(W_0\left(F_{max}^c\right)\right)\right) \tag{1}$$

where σ is the sigmoid function, $W_0 \in R^{C/r \times C}$, $W_1 \in R^{C \times C/r}$, The weights W_0 and W_1 of MLP are shared and are ReLU activation functions before W_0.

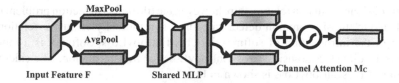

Fig. 1. Channel Attention Module structure schematic.

The spatial Attention Module is used to generate spatial attention graphs by using the spatial relationship between features. Its specific structure is shown in Fig. 2. The Spatial Attention Module is concerned with the location information of the input image as a complement to the Channel Attention Module.

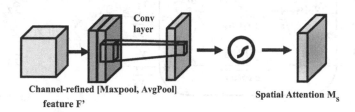

Fig. 2. Spatial Attention Module structure schematic.

To calculate the spatial attention, firstly, apply the average pooling and maximum pooling operations along the channel axis to aggregate the channel information of a feature map to generate two 2D maps, and then perform the join and convolution operations using a standard convolution layer to obtain a 2D spatial attention map, as shown in Eq. 2:

$$M_C(F) = \sigma\left(f^{7\times7}\left(\left[F_{avg}^s; F_{max}^s\right]\right)\right) \tag{2}$$

where σ is the sigmoid function, $f^{7\times7}$ is the convolution kernel of size 7×7, Fsavg $\in R^{1\times H\times W}$ denotes the average pooling characteristic of the channel and Fsmax $\in R^{1\times H\times W}$ denotes the maximum pooling characteristic of the channel.

Integrating the CBAM attention mechanism into the lightweight network ShuffleNetV2 adds a layer of CBAM modules, and another layer is added to the backbone network.

3.3 Improvement of the Loss Function

BCEWithLogitsLoss is used in YOLOv5 to evaluate the class loss and confidence loss of target frames and prediction frames, which is usually used for multi-label classification, i.e., a target can belong to one or more classes. The internal calculation process of BCEWithLogitsLoss is shown in Eq. 3:

$$BCEWithLogitsLoss = Sigmoid + BCELoss \tag{3}$$

Sigmoid is an inclusion relationship, however, the tile defect detection problem in this paper listed in the six common defect categories is a mutually exclusive relationship, because of the introduction of softmax in CrossEntropyLoss, Softmax is a mutually exclusive relationship, so using CrossEntropyLoss for transformation. The calculation diagram of CrossEntropyLoss is shown in Fig. 3.

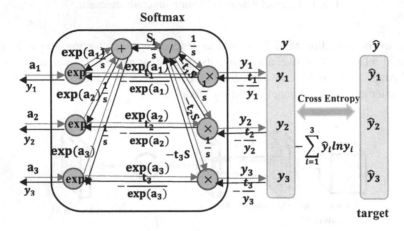

Fig. 3. CrossEntropyLoss calculation chart.

Cross-Entropy loss is usually defined as shown in Eq. (4):

$$Loss = - \sum_{i=1}^{N} \hat{y}_i * \log(y_i) \tag{4}$$

where $\hat{y}_i$ is Ground truth values.

The calculation process inside CrossEntropyLoss is shown in Eq. 5:

$$CrossEntropyLoss = LogSoftmax + NLLLoss \tag{5}$$

$$softmax(z_j) = \frac{e^{z_j}}{\sum_{k=1}^{K} e^{z_k}} for\, j = 1, \ldots, K \tag{6}$$

Softmax is calculated as shown in Eq. 6 and then log(softmax) is calculated.

Because the values after the Softmax formula are between 0 and 1, the value domain after the log is negative infinity to 0. Therefore, NLLLoss processing is required, as shown in Eq. 7. OneHot vector is encoded in log(softmax(input)), and the prediction result of the subscript position corresponding to the target value of each sample is taken for the negative summation operation.

$$NLL(log(softmax(input)), target)$$
$$= - \sum_{i=1}^{n} OneHot(target)_i \times log(softmax(input)_i) \tag{7}$$

Finally, the values of sigmoid and NLLLoss are added together as shown in Eq. 5 to obtain CrossEntropyLoss.

The backbone network and loss function are jointly improved YOLOv5 named S2C-YOLOv5. The structure diagram of the improved network S2C-YOLOv5 is shown in Fig. 4.

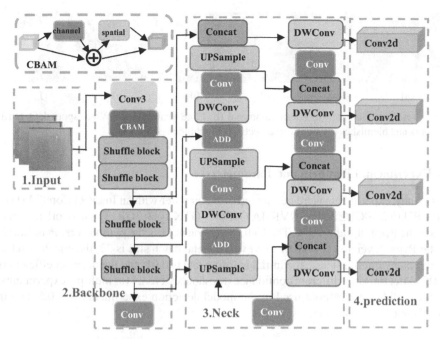

Fig. 4. S2C-YOLOv5 network structure diagram.

4 Experiment

In this section, we first introduce the data set used in this paper, and then, we present a detailed analysis of the improved model and experimental results.

4.1 Dataset Processing

The defective tiles dataset used in this paper was obtained from a tile manufacturing plant in Tianjin. A total of 400 different types of defective tiles were collected, and the resolution of the images was 3456*3456. To demonstrate the generalizability of the method in this paper, we selected tiles with different textures for testing. The types of tile defects produced by the production line of this tile factory mainly include six categories of tiles: Angle abnormal, Edge abnormal, White spots defects, Dark spots and blemishes, Aperture defects, Light block defects, and the defective tiles are shown in Fig. 5.

Firstly, the original images were sliding sliced with an overlap rate of 0.2 to obtain an image size of 800*800, and the defects of the sliced images were obvious. Then the data set was expanded by taking the methods of image rotation, mirroring, cropping, and brightness/contrast transformation, and finally, 7410 sample images were obtained. In the experiment, the data set was divided into the training set, test set, and validation set according to the ratio of 8:1:1. The final training set, test set, and validation set contain 5928, 741, and 741 images.

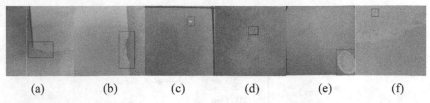

$$\begin{array}{cccccc} \text{(a)} & \text{(b)} & \text{(c)} & \text{(d)} & \text{(e)} & \text{(f)} \end{array}$$

Fig. 5. Defective tile type. (a) Angle abnormal (b) Edge abnormal (c) White spots defects (d) dark spots and blemishes (e) Aperture defects (f) Light block defects.

4.2 Experimental Platform and Parameters

In this study, experiments were conducted on a computer with an Intel(R) Core(TM) i7–7700 CPU @ 3.60GHz and an NVIDIA GeForce GTX 1060 3GB. The network model is built on the Pytorch framework. The CUDA version is 11.6, the python version is 3.8.12, and the Pytorch version is 1.10.0. The experimental batch size is 32, the epoch is set to 500, the momentum is 0.937, the initial learning rate is 0.01, and the decay coefficient is 0.0005. After training, different confidence thresholds were set for multiple experiments, and the confidence threshold used in the model detection experiments was 0.5, taking into account various factors.

4.3 Model Evaluation Metrics

To evaluate the performance of the model and verify whether the model can detect tile defects well, we use the metrics Precision, Recall, Accuracy, F1, AP, mAP, Loss, FPS, and model size to evaluate the model. The specific formulas for these metrics are shown in Eqs. 8–11:

$$Precision = \frac{TP}{TP+FP} \times 100\% \tag{8}$$

$$F1 = \frac{2TP}{2TP+FP+FN} \times 100\% \tag{9}$$

where TP is the number of positive samples predicted by positive samples; FP is the number of positive samples predicted by negative samples; FN is the number of negative samples predicted by positive samples.

$$AP = \sum_{I=1}^{n-1}(r_{i+1} - r_i)P_{inter}(r_i + 1) \tag{10}$$

where $r_1, r_2 \ldots r_n$ are the Recall values corresponding to the first interpolation of the Precision interpolation segment in ascending order. The AP of all categories is mAP.

$$mAP = \frac{\sum_{i=1}^{k} AP_i}{k} \tag{11}$$

where k is the number of APs.

4.4 Comparison with Other Object Detection Models

To further illustrate the effectiveness of the improved model in this paper for tile defect detection, our model was compared with other target detection models, and the models for comparison experiments were YOLOv4 [20], YOLOv5s6, Faster RCNN [21], YOLOv5s, SSD [22], and EfficientDet [23]. The data sets and software conditions in the experiments are the same, and the experimental results are shown in Table 2.

Table 2. Experimental results of different models.

Model	Precision (%)	mAP (%)	F1 (%)	FPS	Modelsize (MB)
YOLOv4	82.95	81.36	80.01	45.2	246.7
YOLOv5s6	92.08	91.34	89.44	90.6	16.3
SSD-VGG16	80.62	78.50	79.32	41.8	41.8
YOLOv5s	90.85	90.01	89.23	111.1	14.2
Faster RCNN	81.51	79.27	78.59	42.3	108.3
EfficientDet	87.43	86.44	85.33	44.1	52
S2C-YOLOV5	95.10	92.91	91.06	85.2	15.8

By comparing the seven sets of experimental results in the table, we find that the improved S2C-YOLOv5 model proposed in this paper outperforms other models in all metrics, and has very obvious advantages over SSD-VGG16, Faster RCNN, YOLOv4, and EfficientDet. Compared with the original network YOLOv5s6, Precision and mAP have 3.02 and 1.57 percentage points advantages, and the model size is reduced by 1.8 MB. Compared with YOLOv5s, although the FPS difference is 25.9, it meets the industrial requirements, and Precision, mAP, and F1 aspects are improved. Therefore, the improved S2C-YOLOv5 model in this paper improves detection accuracy with guaranteed speed, and the model is smaller than the network model before improvement, which is truly lightweight and easier to deploy to hardware devices.

4.5 Ablation Experiments

To verify the necessity of each module improved in this paper, we set up four sets of experiments for comparison. The first set of experiments is a blank control experiment, and the backbone is YOLOv5s6. The second set of experiments, S-YOLOv5, is a replacement of the backbone network ShuffleNetV2, naming this improvement SNV2. The third set of experiments, SC-YOLOv5, is a CBAM attention module added to S-YOLOv5, and the fourth set of experiments, S2C- YOLOv5 is to improve the loss function in the SC-YOLOv5 network, naming this improvement as loss+. The data set and parameters such as hardware and software conditions, threshold, and initial learning rate are the same for the four sets of experiments. The experimental results of the model before and after the improvement are shown in Table 3. The experimental results of the model before and after improvement for different tile defects are shown in Table 4.

Table 3. Experimental results before and after improvement.

Models	SNV2	CB AM	Loss+	Base line	Precision	mAP	F1	FPS
YOLOv5s6				√	92.08	91.34	89.44	90.6
S-YOLOv5	√			√	93.15	92.45	90.56	73.2
SC-YOLOv5	√	√		√	94.23	93.81	90.31	76.9
S2C-YOLOv5	√	√	√	√	95.10	92.91	92.06	85.2

Table 4. Detection accuracy of each defect before and after improvement.

Type of defects	YOLOv5s6		S-YOLOv5		SC-YOLOv5		S2C-YOLOv5	
	Precision	F1	Precision	F1	Precision	F1	Precision	F1
Edge	87.2	86.3	90.4	89.5	91.5	90.0	92.7	90.0
Angle	92.6	91.7	90.4	91.6	95.1	94.9	97.1	96.9
White spot	85.9	80.3	86.9	84.3	88.4	87.5	90.6	91.5
Light block	80.5	81.6	83.3	85.1	87.6	88.1	88.3	87.6
Dark spots	88.6	85.9	90.6	89.0	92.1	94.3	93.7	94.8
Aperture	91.4	92.6	92.7	93.2	94.6	93.4	97.2	96.2

The comparison of the trends of Loss and precision during the training of S2C-YOLOv5 and YOLOv5s6 models is shown in Fig. 6. The Loss of S2C-YOLOv5 can converge to 0.02 after training 500 epochs, which is 0.004 lower than that of YOLOv5s6.

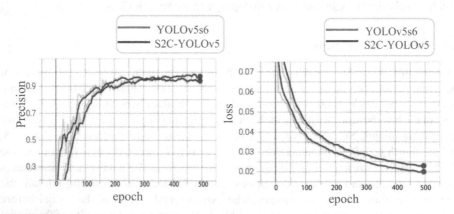

Fig. 6. Comparison of S2C-YOLOv5 and YOLOv5s6 training precision and Loss curves.

4.6 Results and Analysis

According to the analysis of the experimental results, firstly, for S-YOLOv5, Precision, mAP and F1 increased by 1.07, 1.11, and 1.12 percentage points, compared with the original network, and after using ShuffleNetV2 as the backbone network, the feature information characterization of defects was stronger and the extracted feature information was more comprehensive. Although the FPS has decreased, it still meets the industrial requirements.

Then, for SC-YOLOv5, after adding the CBAM module, the Precision and mAP are improved by 1.08 and 1.36 percentage points, and for Light block defects and White spots defects, two types of defects with very low precision, there is 7.1 and 2.5 percentage points improvement. The reason is that Light block defects and White spots defects are similar to the background texture information of tiles, and the CBAM module enhances the characteristics of the defect information and reduces the interference of the background information, which also improves the overall experimental results.

Finally, for S2C-YOLOv5, Precision and F1 are improved by 0.87 and 1.75 percentage points based on the original one, and Precision for different defects is improved substantially because the softmax in CrossEntropyLoss is mutually exclusive, which is more applicable to the category information of mutually exclusive relationship and clears the obstacle of ambiguity in the classification of different defects. The effectiveness of the improved method in this paper is fully verified by the comparison of four sets of ablation experiments.

5 Conclusion

In this paper, deep learning techniques are applied to tile defect detection, and an improved S2C-YOLOv5 model is proposed. First, to address the problems of large cache space occupation, low operation efficiency, and low detection accuracy due to the module operation of the network itself, ShuffleNetV2 replaces the backbone network to construct a more lightweight network with guaranteed accuracy. Then, the CBAM module is added to reduce the interference of tile texture information. Finally, CrossEntroyLoss is used to be more applicable to the defect class of mutually exclusive relations. After extensive experiments, the improved model in this paper can effectively achieve accurate recognition of tile defect detection. The final experimental results show that Precision is 95.10%, mAP is 92.91%, F1 is 92.06%, and FPS is 85.2. There are obvious advantages compared with other deep learning network models. Compared with the model of YOLOv5s6 before improvement, Precision, mAP, and F1 improved by 3.02, 1.57, and 2.62 percentage points. It provides the basis that it can be put into operation stably and reliably in the ceramic industry.

References

1. Guangya, L., et al.: Research on visual detection method of tile surface defects based on gabor transformation and region growing. Modern Comput. **24**, 37–42 (2019)
2. Huialiang, Z., et al.: Detection of surface defects in ceramic tiles with complex texture. IEEE Access **9**, 92788–92797 (2021)

3. Junhua, L., et al.: Research on defect detection algorithm of ceramic tile surface with multi-feature fusion. Comput. Eng. Appl. **56**(15), 191–198 (2020)
4. Mariyadi, B., et al.: 2D detection model of defect on the surface of ceramic tile by an artificial neural network. J. Phys. Conf. Ser. **1764**(1), 012176 (2021)
5. Zehui, L.: Research on Visual Detection System and Algorithm of Polished Tile Surface Defects. The Guangdong University of Technology, Guangdong (2021)
6. Taochuan, Z. et al.: Development of an online fast non-destructive testing system for ceramic tiles based on deep learning. Mech. Eng. Autom. **6**, 129–130+133 (2020)
7. Masci, J., Meier, U., Ciresan, D., Schmidhuber, J., Fricout, G.: Steel defect classification with Max-Pooling convolutional neural networks. In: The 2012 International Joint Conference on Neural Networks, IJCNN, pp. 1–6 (2012)
8. Lin, J., Yao, Y., Ma, L., Wang, Y.: Detection of a casting defect tracked by deep convolution neural network. The International Journal of Advanced Manufacturing Technology **97**(1–4), 573–581 (2018). https://doi.org/10.1007/s00170-018-1894-0
9. Redmon, J., et al.: You only look once: Unified, real-time object detection. In: Proceedings of the IEEE Conference on Computer Vision and Pattern Recognition, pp. 779–788 (2016)
10. Redmon, J., et al.: Better, faster, stronger. In: IEEE Conference on Computer Vision and Pattern Recognition, p. 6517—652. IEEE, New York (2017)
11. Redmon, J., et al.: Yolov3: An Incremental Improvement. In: IEEE Conference on Computer Vision and Pattern Recognition (2018)
12. Bochkovskiy, A., et al.: YOLOv4: Optimal speed and accuracy of object detection. In: IEEE Conference on Computer Vision and Pattern Recognition (2020)
13. Li, W., et al.: Garbage classification and detection based on YOLOv5s network. Pack. Eng. **42**(8), 50–56 (2021)
14. Fangbo, Z., et al.: Safety helmet detection based on YOLOv5. In: 2021 IEEE International Conference on Power Electronics. Computer Applications (ICPECA), pp. 6–11. IEEE, New York (2021)
15. Misra, D.: Mish: A self regularized non-monotonic neural activation function (2019)
16. Yanan, S.: et al.: Rail surface defect detection method based on YOLOv3 deep learning networks. In: 2018 Chinese Automation Congress (CAC), pp. 1563–1568 (2018)
17. Bo, G.: et al.: Fabric defect detection algorithm based on improved YOLOv5 model. J. Zhejiang Sci-Tech Univ. Nat. Scie. Ed. (2020)
18. Wenbin, X.: et al.: Real-time static gesture recognition method based on ShuffleNetv2-YOLOv3 model. J. Zhejiang Univ. Eng. Sci. **55**(10), 1815–1824+ 1846 (2021)
19. Yang, Y., et al.: An improved CNN fault diagnosis model fusion depth separable small convolution kernel and CBAM. Electron. Meas. Technol. **45**(6), 171–178 (2022)
20. Yuchun, C., et al.: Research on knowledge distillation algorithm for target detection based on YOLOv4. Comput. Sci. **49**(S1), 337–344 (2022)
21. Bin, Z., Cong, Z.: Dense crowd detection algorithm based on Faster-RCNN. Comput. Appl. 1–7 (2022)
22. Muqin, L., et al.: Vehicle detection based on SSD-mobilenet V3 model. Sens. Microsyst. **41**(6), 142–145 (2022)
23. Liye, S., et al.: Power grid components and defect identification method based on improved EfficientDet. J. Electrotech. Technol. **37**(9), 2241–2251 (2022)

Human-Object Interaction Detection: A Survey of Deep Learning-Based Methods

Fang Li[1,2], Shunli Wang[1,2], Shuaiping Wang[1,2], and Lihua Zhang[1,2,3,4(✉)]

[1] Academy for Engineering and Technology, Fudan University, Shanghai, China
lihuazhang@fudan.edu.cn
[2] Engineering Research Center of AI and Robotics, Ministry of Education,
Beijing, China
[3] Jilin Provincial Key Laboratory of Intelligence Science and Engineering,
Changchun, China
[4] Artifical Intelligence and Unmanned Systems Engineering Research Center
of Jilin Province, Changchun, China

Abstract. In recent years, rapid progress has been made in detecting and identifying single object instances. In order to understand the situation in the scene, computers need to recognize how humans interact with surrounding objects. Human-object interaction (HOI) detection aims to identify a set of interactions in images or videos. It involves the positioning of interactive subjects and objects and the classification of interactive types. It is crucial to realize high-level semantic understanding of people-centered scenarios. The study of HOI detection is also conducive to promoting the research of other advanced visual tasks. In this paper, we introduce the previous works on HOI detection based on deep learning, which are raised from the two primary development trends of sequential and parallel methods. Secondly, we summarize the main challenges faced by the HOI detection task. Further, we introduce the most popular HOI detection datasets, including image and video datasets, and main metrics. Finally, we summarize the future research directions for the HOI detection task.

Keywords: Human-object interaction (HOI) Detection · Computer vision · Deep learning

1 Introduction

Due to the vigorous development of deep learning, the performance of machines in multi-domain tasks has exceeded or approached the human level. Many researchers have also begun to make machine learning understand higher semantic level visual tasks such as visual relationship detection tasks [5, 23] and visual language tasks such as Image Caption [29] and Visual Question Answer (VQA) [1]. Machines not only need to recognize objects but also need to understand the relationships between objects in vision.

This work is supported by Shanghai Municipal Science and Technology Major Project (2021SHZDZX0103) and National Key R&D Program of China (2021ZD0113503).

L. Fang et al. (Eds.): CICAI 2022, LNAI 13604, pp. 441–452, 2022.
https://doi.org/10.1007/978-3-031-20497-5_36

HOI detection is an important and relatively new visual relationship detection task necessary for deeper scene understanding. It needs to locate people and objects and identify their complex interactions. The specific task can be described as: given an image or a video, the purpose of HOI detection is to detect triples $<people, interaction, object>$. Unlike the general visual relationship detection, the subject of the triplet is fixed as a human, and the interaction is an action. HOI detection is vital to realizing high-level semantic understanding of human-centered scenes. It has many applications such as activity analysis, human-computer interaction and intelligent monitoring.

In this paper, we summarize the previous research works on HOI detection, dividing HOI detection methods into two major streams: sequential and parallel. In addition, we also present the challenges faced by the current HOI detection task. Then, we also summarize datasets and metrics used for HOI detection. Finally, we prospect the future development directions of HOI detection.

2   Methods

HOI detection was first proposed in [10]. Gupta *et al.* introduce visual semantic role annotation. We can divide the HOI detection task into two modules: object detection and interaction prediction. We use the way in [14] to classify the past works according to the model's execution order of object detection and interaction prediction, which is divided into sequential and parallel methods as is shown in Fig. 1. At the same time, we also summarize some typical HOI detection works, as shown in Table 1.

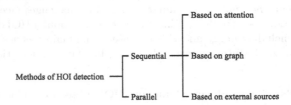

Fig. 1. Methods classification of HOI detection.

2.1   Sequential HOI Detectors

The main idea of the sequential HOI detection method is to use an external object detector to detect the target, and each pair of detected objects uses a separate neural network to predict the interaction. Consequently, the sequential HOI method is also called a two-stage strategy. The model of the sequential method can be summarized in Fig. 2. These approaches first use the detected bounding boxes from a pre-trained detector to extract Region-of Interest (RoI) features from the backbone. Then a multi-stream architecture is employed to

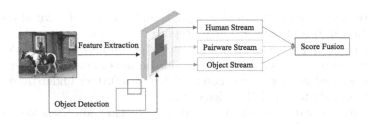

Fig. 2. Sequential method model of HOI detection.

fuse the three parallel streams, getting the final interaction results of all human object pairs.

Gkioxari *et al.* [8] proposed InteractNet. This work assumes that people's appearance, posture, clothing, and movement characteristics are powerful clues to locate the objects they interact with. It extends the existing object detectors and introduces an action-specific density graph to locate the object based on the human-centered appearance and predict the interaction based on the character-istics of each box. However, the lack of context information often troubles the interactive detection of visual cues based on a single box.

Inspired by [8], Gao *et al.* proposed iCAN [7] by using the appearance char-acteristics of people and objects. The module learns to dynamically generate an attention map for each detected person or object to highlight the areas related to the task. Suppose that the appearance of an instance provides hints about where we should pay attention in the image.

The graph-based methods have also proposed frameworks that can explicitly represent the HOI structure with graphs [6, 22, 25, 27, 30]. Liu *et al.* [22] proposed ConsNet,which is a knowledge perception framework. It explicitly encodes the relationships among objects, actions and interactions into an undirected graph that becomes a consistency graph. GATs [28] uses a graph attention network to spread knowledge between knowledge classification and its components. This model takes the visual features of candidate object pairs and the word embedding of HOI tags as inputs and maps them to the visual semantic joint embedding space. The detection results are obtained by measuring their similarity.

DRG [6] uses an abstract spatial-semantic representation to describe each HOIs and aggregates the context information of the scene through a dual relation graph, effectively capturing the discrimination clues in the scene and solves the ambiguity problem in local prediction.

Qi *et al.* [25] introduced GPNN. For a given scene, GPNN infers an analytic graph of HOI structure, represented by the adjacency matrix and the node label. Using the structural representation of the HOI graph, GPNN can explicitly use rich relationships to integrate information from various elements and propagate it structurally effectively.

VSGNet [27] takes the relative spatial reasoning and structural connection between objects as the basic clue for analyzing interaction as the starting point. It extracts visual features from human object pairs, refines the features using the spatial configuration of human object pairs, and uses the structural connection between human object pairs through graph convolution.

Wang *et al.* [30] proposed a heterogeneous graph network. It models people and objects as different types of nodes and contains in-class messages between homogeneous and heterogeneous nodes, giving us a further understanding of the graph network structure of HOI detection.

Deep context attention [31] proposed an HOI detection framework based on context attention. The proposed attention module adaptively selects relevant context information centered on examples to highlight image areas that may contain human-object interaction.

Subsequently, various external sources such as linguistic priors [6] or human posture information [11] are used to further improve the performance of HOI detection. Although sequential HOI detection has a fairly intuitive pipeline and reliable performance, it is time-consuming and expensive because of the additional neural network reasoning after the stage of object detection. In addition, the multi-stage model mainly focuses on performance like average accuracy, which is far from meeting the needs of high performance and real-time detection.

2.2   Parallel HOI Detectors

To overcome the redundant reasoning structure of sequential HOI detectors, some research works [13, 20, 32] proposed parallel HOI detectors, whose main idea is to perform object detection and interactive prediction in parallel, and associate them with simple heuristic methods such as distance or the IoU.The model of most parallel methods is summarized as shown in Fig. 3. We can see object detection and interaction prediction are executed in parallel, which is the most fundamental difference between parallel and sequential methods.

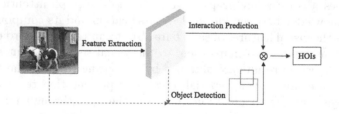

Fig. 3. Parallel method model of HOI detection.

Wang *et al.* [32] proposed a novel full convolution method directly detecting the interaction between human and object pairs. This network predicted the interaction points, pairing with the interaction vector of dense prediction. These points are associated with detecting people and objects to obtain the final prediction. This work firstly proposes HOI detection as a key point detection and grouping problem.

PPDM [20] is the first method to realize real-time detection of HOI, which is significantly ahead of the synchronous way in detection speed and accuracy. It proposes that the center of the detection frame is the person and object point, and the interaction point is the midpoint of the person and object point. In the new parallel architecture of PPDM, the interaction point implicitly provides context and regularization for human and object detection, suppresses the isolated detection box that cannot form a meaningful HOI triad, and improves the accuracy of HOI detection.

Kim et al. proposed UnionDet [13] driven by a novel joint level detector. This network captures the joint region of human-object interaction. It directly detects the interacting human object pairs instead of associating the object detection results by inputting each object pair into a separate neural network, eliminating the need for a lot of neural network reasoning after object detection. Joint level detection seems intuitive. Detecting joint areas is more challenging than instance-level detection.

These parallel HOI detection works clearly locate the interaction localization with the interaction point [20,32] or the union box [13]. Because interaction prediction can be parallelized with existing object detectors, these ways all have the characteristics of fast reasoning time. However, there still are some shortcomings. To correlate local interaction and object detection results, these parallel HOI require a manual post-processing stage to manually search the threshold and pair each object with local interaction points, creating additional time complexity. In addition, their result prediction accuracy is not as high as that of sequential methods.

3   Challenges

There are also significant challenges in the research of HOI detection, which can be summarized into three aspects.

Complex Scenes. Because of the subtle differences between human-centered fine-grained actions, it is challenging to detect HOI: 1) an image may contain multiple people interacting the same; 2) Interact with multiple objects, multiple people share the same interaction and objects; 3) The fine-grained interactions.

Long-Tail Distribution of Interaction Behaviors. The common problem is that the categories of interaction behavior in HOI detection are seriously unbalanced. Some varieties appear with high frequency, and some emerge with low frequency. It brings a severe long-tail distribution effect, and the lack of positive labels will directly lead to the low classification accuracy of these categories.

Polysemy of Verbs. Existing researches usually assume that the same verb has similar visual characteristics in different HOI categories but ignores the different semantic meanings of verbs. This semantic difference may be huge, resulting in a sharp change in the importance of the same type of visual features with the change in the object of interest.

Table 1. Summary of existing HOI detection methods.

Class	Work	Published	Feature backbone	Dataset	Metrics	Website
Sequential	InteractNet [8]	CVPR 2018	ResNet-50-FPN	V-COCO HICO-DET	mAP	–
	iCAN [7]	BMVC 2018	ResNet-50	V-COCO HICO-DET	mAP	https://github.com/vt-vl-lab/iCAN
	ConsNet [22]	ACM-MM2020	ResNet-50-FPN	V-COCO HICO-DET	mAP	–
	DRG [6]	ECCV 2020	ResNet-50-FPN	V-COCO HICO-DET	mAP	https://github.com/vt-vl-lab/DRG
	GPNN [25]	ECCV 2018	ResNet-101	V-COCO HICO-DET	mAP	https://github.com/SiyuanQi/gpnn
				CAD-120	F1-score	
	VSGNet [27]	CVPR 2020	ResNet-152	V-COCO HICO-DET	mAP	https://github.com/ASMIftekhar/VSGNet
	Wang et al. [30]	ECCV 2020	ResNet-50	V-COCO HICO-DET	mAP	–
	Wang et al. [31]	ICCV 2019	ResNet-50	V-COCO HICO-DET HCVRD	mAP_{role}	–
	Gupta et al. [11]	ICCV 2019	–	HICO-DET	mAP	https://github.com/BigRedT/no_frills_hoi_det
Parallel	Wang et al. [32]	CVPR 2020	Hourglass-104	V-COCO HICO-DET	mAP_{role}	https://github.com/vaesl/IP-Net
	PPDM [20]	CVPR 2020	Hourglass-104 DLA-34	HICO-DET HOI-A	mAP	https://github.com/YueLiao/PPDM
	UnionDet [13]	ECCV 2020	ResNet50-FPN	V-COCO	AP_{role}	–
				HICO-DET	mAP	

4 Datasets

4.1 Image Datasets

Here, we briefly introduce the most commonly used image datasets. See Table 2 for more details.

Visual Genome. Krishna *et al.* proposed the Visual Genome dataset [16], one of the earliest datasets to provide object interaction and attribute detailed labels. Unlike previous datasets such as MS-COCO [21], Visual Genome contains annotations of many objects but also a general representation of the visible world, which is not biased towards specific tasks.

HICO. Chao *et al.* [3] proposed HICO to identify the interaction between human and objects. HICO, a large image data set with 47774 pictures, provides different interactions for each object category and is the first benchmark for image-level HOI classification to classify whether there are HOI classes in the image.

V-COCO. Gupta et al. [10] proposed a V-COCO dataset, annotated and refined a part of the subset of the COCO dataset. V-COCO contains 10346 images in total, including 16199 personnel instances. V-COCO allows multiple people in an image but restricts one person to only one type of operation on one object.

HCVRD. Zhang *et al.* [33] built HCVRD dataset based on Visual Genome dataset [16]. It provides 1,824 object categories and more than 900 predicate categories. Such a large label space also leads to the long tail distribution of data. Some categories may have thousands of training instances, while others have only a few.

HICO-DET. Chao *et al.* [2] introduced HICO-DET dataset, which adds instance annotation based on HICO [3] and further annotates the HOI instances presented in each image. Since the instance annotation is based on the HOI class annotation of HICO, HICO-DET also has a long tail distribution in the number of instances of each HOI class as in HICO.

Ambiguous-HOI. Considering the existing HOI benchmark mainly focuses on the evaluation of universal HOI and has no unique ability to check and process 2D pose and appearance fuzziness, Li *et al.* proposed ambiguous-HOI dataset [18] based on HICO-DET dataset [2]. They selected the HOI category from HICO-DET and marked the HOI of the image according to the HICO-DET settings.

HAKE. Li *et al.* [19] built a HAKE dataset based on human part status. According to the existing activity dataset, the part states of all people in all images are marked to establish the relationship between instance activity and body part states. Using HAKE, we can alleviate the learning difficulties caused by the long-tail data distribution and bring interpretability.

H^2O. Orcesi *et al.* proposed H^2O dataset [24], which is composed of 10,301 images in the V-COCO dataset [10] and 3666 images in the field selected from the COCO dataset [21]. Unlike the existing data sets, H^2O presents the interaction between people and objects and between people.

4.2 Video Datasets

Unlike still images, videos contain much information about the physical world and are very detailed. The following are typical video datasets that can be used for HOI detection. See Table 3 for more details.

CAD-120. Koppla *et al.* proposed CAD-120 dataset [15], which consists of 61,585 RGB-D video frames in total, including 120 activity sequences of 10 different high-level activities performed by 4 different subjects, and each high-level activity is performed three times.

Action Genome. Ji *et al.* proposed Action Genome [12] composed of spatiotemporal scene graph, which is regarded as a time-varying version of scene graph for Visual Genome [16]. The goal of Visual Genome is to use objects and visual relationships to intensify and represent scenes, while Action Genome aims to decompose actions.

Table 2. Image datasets for HOI detection.

Datasets	Images	Object categories	Verbs	HOI categories	Interactions/ Relationships
Visual genome [16]	108077	33877	68111	–	–
HICO [3]	47774	80	Over 117	600	–
V-COCO [10]	10346	80	26	–	26539
HCVRD [33]	52855	1824	927	9852	–
HICO-DET [2]	47774	80	117	–	Over 150 K
Ambiguous-HOI [18]	8996	40	48	87	25188
HAKE [19]	Over 118 K	–	–	–	724 K
H^2O [24]	13967	–	51	214	128969

AVA. Gu *et al.* proposed AVA dataset [9], annotated 80 atomic visual actions in 15 to 30 min video clips of 437 different movies. The bounding box is used to locate each person, and the attached label corresponds to one or more actions the person performs.

VidHOI. Chiou *et al.* proposed VidHOI [4] based on Vidor [26], using a keyframe-centered evaluation strategy to bypass the challenge of how to obtain accurate tracks with correct start and end timestamps.

V-HICO. Since the relationship between Vidor datasets [26] and VidHOI datasets [4] is not necessarily people-centered and cannot be directly used to evaluate video-based human-object interaction detection, Li *et al.* collected V-HICO dataset [17],which is a large and different HOI video dataset. Each video contains human-object interaction and also has a richer outdoor scene.

Table 3. Video datasets for HOI detection.

Dateset	Videos	Video hours	Annotated images/frames	Object categories	Predicate categories	HOI categories	HOI instances
CAD-120 [15]	0.5 K	0.57	61 K	13	6	10	32 K
Action Genome [12]	10 K	82	234 K	35	25	157	1.7 M
AVA [9]	437	108	3.7 M	–	49	80	1.6 M
VidHOI [4]	7122	70	7.3 M	78	50	557	755 K
V-HICO [17]	6594	–	–	244	99	756	–

5 Metrics

5.1 mAP

Average Precision(AP) is often used in object detection tasks, which comes from the Accuracy and Recall. AP is usually evaluated in a specific category, calculated separately for each object type. For the HOI detection task, it is considered that only the following three conditions are met at the same time: 1) the IoU ratio between the predicted human frame and the real human frame is greater than or equal to 0.5; 2) the IoU between the predicted object frame and the real object frame is greater than or equal to 0.5; 3) the predicted interaction between people and objects is consistent with the real interaction marked on the label, which is recognized as True Positive (TP).

Table 4. Confusion matrix.

Confusion matrix		Real	
		True	False
Predict	Positive	TP	FP
	Negative	FN	TN

The confusion matrix calculates the AP value, as shown in the following Table 4. Precision is defined as the proportion of true positive samples to all positive samples predicted by the human-object interaction detection model, as shown in Eq. (1):

$$Precision = \frac{TP}{TP + FP} \tag{1}$$

Recall refers to the proportion of positive samples predicted to be correct by the human-object interaction detection model in all real positive examples, as shown in Eq. (2):

$$Recall = \frac{TP}{TP + FN} \tag{2}$$

AP refers to accuracy rates and proportion in the number of images in this category, which is defined as:

$$AP = \int_0^1 p(r)dr \tag{3}$$

Here, p stands for Precision, r stands for Recall, and $p(r)$ is a function with r as the independent variable. The integral of the function is expressed as the average accuracy AP, which can be used to measure the quality of the model judgment results in a single category.

The mean average precision (mAP) is often used to evaluate HOI detection. It is the average value of AP and all categories' average precision. It can measure the prediction results of the HOI detection model in all categories and is defined as:

$$mAP = \frac{AP}{C} \tag{4}$$

where C represents the total number of HOI categories.

5.2   mPD

Considering that mAP may not be enough to simulate synthesis generalization well, Liu *et al.* [26] proposed a new metric mPD (mean Performance Degradation). It can directly measure generalization in HOI learning to evaluate the performance gap between different objects and the same verb composition. In detail, we calculate the relative performance gap between the best and other verb object combinations (the lower, the better) for a given verb and its corresponding object. For verb $v \epsilon V$, we denote the object categories available for v as O_v, $AP_{(v,o)}$ as the average precision for HOI composition$<v, o>$. Then mPD is formulated as:

$$mPD = \frac{1}{|V|} \sum_{v \in V} \frac{AP_{<v,o_{max}>} - \overline{AP_v}}{AP_{<v,o_{max}>}} \tag{5}$$

where $O_{max} = \text{argmax}_o AP_{<v,o>}$, $\overline{AP_v} = \frac{1}{|O_v|} \sum_{o_v} AP_{<v,o>}$ is the mean AP for compositions $<v, o>$ with o_v. The mPD measures the performance gap between the best detection and other combinations. The higher the mPD, the greater the performance gap of the model on different objects, and the worse the generalization.

6   Conclusion and Future Research Directions

In this paper, we summarize the previous deep learning-based research addressing the human-object interaction detection problem from images or video and organize approaches into two categories: sequential and parallel HOI methods. Further, we introduce the challenges faced in HOI, main HOI datasets, and metrics.

The parallel HOI detection methods have a high detection speed, but their detection accuracy is not high. More works can concentrate on improving the parallel method's performance in the future.

In VQA, SGG and other vision tasks, Causal Inference is used to eliminate the influence that plays a significant role in the retention of side effects of functions to remove the deviation caused by training. Therefore, Causal Inference may be applied to HOI detection tasks to alleviate the long-tail distribution problem. The polysemy in HOI detection is also a research direction in the future. Most currently available datasets in HOI detection are public scene datasets, and there is no dataset in a specific scene. Future research can focus on building more special datasets in scenarios such as intelligent medical treatment, intelligent transportation or intelligent sports for HOI detection.

References

1. Antol, S., et al.: VQA: visual question answering. In: Proceedings of the IEEE International Conference on Computer Vision (ICCV) (2015)

2. Chao, Y., Liu, Y., Liu, X., Zeng, H., Deng, J.: Learning to detect human-object interactions. In: Winter Conference on Applications of Computer Vision (WACV) (2018)

3. Chao, Y., Wang, Z., He, Y., Wang, J., Deng, J.: HICO: a benchmark for recognizing human-object interactions in images. In: Proceedings of the IEEE International Conference on Computer Vision (ICCV) (2015)

4. Chiou, M.J., Liao, C.Y., Wang, L.W., Zimmermann, R., Feng, J.: ST-HOI: a spatial-temporal baseline for human-object interaction detection in videos. In: Proceedings of the 2021 Workshop on Intelligent Cross-Data Analysis and Retrieval (ICDAR) (2021)

5. Chiou, M.J., Zimmermann, R., Feng, J.: Visual relationship detection with visual-linguistic knowledge from multimodal representations. IEEE Access **9**, 50441–50451 (2021)

6. Gao, C., Xu, J., Zou, Y., Huang, J.-B.: DRG: dual relation graph for human-object interaction detection. In: Vedaldi, A., Bischof, H., Brox, T., Frahm, J.-M. (eds.) ECCV 2020. LNCS, vol. 12357, pp. 696–712. Springer, Cham (2020). https://doi.org/10.1007/978-3-030-58610-2_41

7. Gao, C., Zou, Y., Huang, J.: iCAN: instance-centric attention network for human-object interaction detection. CoRR (2018)

8. Gkioxari, G., Girshick, R., Dollar, P., He, K.: Detecting and recognizing human-object interactions. In: Proceedings of the IEEE Conference on Computer Vision and Pattern Recognition (CVPR) (2018)

9. Gu, C., et al.: AVA: a video dataset of Spatio-temporally localized atomic visual actions. In: Proceedings of the IEEE Conference on Computer Vision and Pattern Recognition (CVPR) (2018)

10. Gupta, S., Malik, J.: Visual semantic role labeling. CoRR (2015)

11. Gupta, T., Schwing, A., Hoiem, D.: No-frills human-object interaction detection: factorization, layout encodings, and training techniques. In: Proceedings of the IEEE International Conference on Computer Vision (ICCV) (2019)

12. Ji, J., Krishna, R., Fei-Fei, L., Niebles, J.C.: Action genome: actions as compositions of Spatio-temporal scene graphs. In: Proceedings of the IEEE Conference on Computer Vision and Pattern Recognition (CVPR) (2020)

13. Kim, B., Choi, T., Kang, J., Kim, H.J.: UnionDet: union-level detector towards real-time human-object interaction detection. In: Vedaldi, A., Bischof, H., Brox, T., Frahm, J.-M. (eds.) ECCV 2020. LNCS, vol. 12360, pp. 498–514. Springer, Cham (2020). https://doi.org/10.1007/978-3-030-58555-6_30

14. Kim, B., Lee, J., Kang, J., Kim, E.S., Kim, H.J.: HOTR: end-to-end human-object interaction detection with transformers. In: Proceedings of the IEEE Conference on Computer Vision and Pattern Recognition (CVPR) (2021)

15. Koppula, H.S., Gupta, R., Saxena, A.: Learning human activities and object affordances from RGB-D videos. CoRR (2012)

16. Krishna, R., et al.: Visual genome: connecting language and vision using crowd-sourced dense image annotations. Int. J. Comput. Vision **123**, 32–73 (2017)

17. Li, S., Du, Y., Torralba, A., Sivic, J., Russell, B.: Weakly supervised human-object interaction detection in video via contrastive spatiotemporal regions. In: Proceedings of the IEEE International Conference on Computer Vision (ICCV) (2021)

18. Li, Y.L., et al.: Detailed 2D-3D joint representation for human-object interaction. In: Proceedings of the IEEE Conference on Computer Vision and Pattern Recognition (CVPR) (2020)

19. Li, Y., et al.: HAKE: human activity knowledge engine. CoRR (2019)

20. Liao, Y., Liu, S., Wang, F., Chen, Y., Qian, C., Feng, J.: PPDM: parallel point detection and matching for real-time human-object interaction detection. In: Proceedings of the IEEE Conference on Computer Vision and Pattern Recognition (CVPR) (2020)
21. Lin, T.Y., et al.: Microsoft COCO: common objects in context. In: Fleet, D., Pajdla, T., Schiele, B., Tuytelaars, T. (eds.) ECCV 2014. LNCS, vol. 8693, pp. 740–755. Springer, Cham (2014). https://doi.org/10.1007/978-3-319-10602-1_48
22. Liu, Y., Yuan, J., Chen, C.W.: ConsNet: learning consistency graph for zero-shot human-object interaction detection (2020)
23. Lu, C., Krishna, R., Bernstein, M., Fei-Fei, L.: Visual relationship detection with language priors. In: Leibe, B., Matas, J., Sebe, N., Welling, M. (eds.) ECCV 2016. LNCS, vol. 9905, pp. 852–869. Springer, Cham (2016). https://doi.org/10.1007/978-3-319-46448-0_51
24. Orcesi, A., Audigier, R., Toukam, F.P., Luvison, B.: Detecting human-to-human-or-object (H2O) interactions with DIABOLO. In: 2021 16th IEEE International Conference on Automatic Face and Gesture Recognition (FG 2021) (2021)
25. Qi, S., Wang, W., Jia, B., Shen, J., Zhu, S.-C.: Learning human-object interactions by graph parsing neural networks. In: Ferrari, V., Hebert, M., Sminchisescu, C., Weiss, Y. (eds.) ECCV 2018. LNCS, vol. 11213, pp. 407–423. Springer, Cham (2018). https://doi.org/10.1007/978-3-030-01240-3_25
26. Shang, X., Di, D., Xiao, J., Cao, Y., Yang, X., Chua, T.S.: Annotating objects and relations in user-generated videos. In: Proceedings of the 2019 on International Conference on Multimedia Retrieval (2019)
27. Ulutan, O., Iftekhar, A.S.M., Manjunath, B.S.: VSGNet: spatial attention network for detecting human object interactions using graph convolutions. In: Proceedings of the IEEE Conference on Computer Vision and Pattern Recognition (CVPR) (2020)
28. Velickovic, P., Cucurull, G., Casanova, A., Romero, A., Lio, P., Bengio, Y.: Graph attention networks. Stat **1050**, 20 (2017)
29. Vinyals, O., Toshev, A., Bengio, S., Erhan, D.: Show and tell: a neural image caption generator. In: Proceedings of the IEEE Conference on Computer Vision and Pattern Recognition (CVPR) (2015)
30. Wang, H., Zheng, W., Yingbiao, L.: Contextual heterogeneous graph network for human-object interaction detection. In: Vedaldi, A., Bischof, H., Brox, T., Frahm, J.-M. (eds.) ECCV 2020. LNCS, vol. 12362, pp. 248–264. Springer, Cham (2020). https://doi.org/10.1007/978-3-030-58520-4_15
31. Wang, T., et al.: Deep contextual attention for human-object interaction detection. In: Proceedings of the IEEE International Conference on Computer Vision (ICCV) (2019)
32. Wang, T., Yang, T., Danelljan, M., Khan, F.S., Zhang, X., Sun, J.: Learning human-object interaction detection using interaction points. In: Proceedings of the IEEE Conference on Computer Vision and Pattern Recognition (CVPR) (2020)
33. Zhuang, B., Wu, Q., Shen, C., Reid, I.D., van den Hengel, A.: Care about you: towards large-scale human-centric visual relationship detection. CoRR (2017)

Change Detection of Flood Hazard Areas in Multi-Source Heterogeneous Earth Observation Image Time Series Based on Spatiotemporal Enhancement Strategy

Zhihao Wang, Xueqian Wang, and Gang Li[✉]

Department of Electronic Engineering, Tsinghua University, Beijing, China
gangli@tsinghua.edu.cn

Abstract. Change detection (CD) on multiple remote sensing images has been widely used for monitoring flood changes. In this paper, we innovatively propose a spatiotemporal enhanced CD (STECD) algorithm, which exploits the spatial and temporal dependence of multi-source heterogeneous (MSH) Earth Observation image time series (EOITS). Our STECD algorithm mainly contains two steps, i.e., spatial clustering and temporal enhancement. In the spatial clustering step, we propose a sparse Markov random field (SMRF)-based strategy to iteratively optimize the boundaries of flood areas in accordance with contextually spatial features in each image of MSH EOITS. In the temporal enhancement step, the historical incremental information of flood areas is employed as constraints to effectively reduce the effects of terrain shadows (in synthetic aperture radar (SAR) images) and cloud shadows and topography shadows (in optical images) on spatial clustering results in accordance with the temporal dependence among MSH EOITS. Experiments on real MSH EOITS show that the overall detection accuracy of our proposed STECD algorithm is higher than existing commonly used methods for CD of flood hazard areas.

Keywords: Spatiotemporal enhanced change detection · Multi-source remote sensing · Flood

1 Introduction

Rising greenhouse gases emissions are continuing shifting the intensification in the Earth's hydrological cycle, leading to a series of extreme natural disasters typified by floods [1,2]. A considerable amount of literature has underlined that floods are the one of the costliest natural disasters, which significantly threat

Supported by National Key R&D Program of China under Grant 2021YFA0715201, National Natural Science Foundation of China under Grants 61790551, 61925106, and 62101303, and Autonomous Research Project of Department of Electronic Engineering at Tsinghua University.

L. Fang et al. (Eds.): CICAI 2022, LNAI 13604, pp. 453–465, 2022.
https://doi.org/10.1007/978-3-031-20497-5_37

human lives and world economy [3–5]. With the rapid development of remote sensing technology, the remote sensing data derived from Earth Observation (EO) satellites have been widely applied for flood monitoring, which improves the efficiency and stability of flood monitoring systems [6].

Currently, there is a booming development in the context of change detection (CD) of flood areas based on bi-temporal remote sensing images. Optical remote sensing images with good interpretation can be obtained under fine weather conditions especially before flood events. Amarnath [7] proposed a normalized difference surface water index (NDSWI)-based algorithm to produce CD results of flood hazard areas. But the NDSWI algorithm is often affected by the cloud contamination, terrain shadows, and limited spatiotemporal resolution [7]. Synthetic aperture radar (SAR) sensors have all-weather imaging capabilities and have been widely used to detect the flood area in day and night [8]. In [9–11], a number of flood detection methods applied backscatter thresholds on SAR images, due to the very low backscatter of water areas (i.e., the reflected energy by the smooth and open water surface is near-completely not received by the SAR sensors [4]). Note that the quality of flood detection using SAR images may be degraded by high clutter and sidelobe levels therein [12].

There is also a flourish in the literature regarding CD algorithms that combine the superiorities of bi-temporal SAR and optical remote sensing images. Liu et al. [13,14] proposed homogeneous transformation-based CD methods, where heterogeneous remote sensing data are transformed into a homogeneous feature space to perform the CD analysis. Gong et al. [15,16] proposed unsupervised deep neural networks based on bi-temporal heterogeneous images to obtain the CD results in the high-dimensional feature space. These aforementioned algorithms [13–16] may show limited flood detection performance in Earth Observation image time series (EOITS) because these methods [13–16] do not exploit the historical flood information that is crucial to construct the temporal dependence among three or more temporal remote sensing images.

For the problem of CD within multi-source heterogeneous (MSH) EOITS, Li et al. [17] show that the synergistic use of three flood detection algorithms contributing to a significant improvement of flood detection accuracy, in comparison with single-source based methods. But the algorithms used in [17] mainly focus on the design of global thresholds to find flood areas and do not pay attention to enhance the local flood features in MSH EOITS.

In this paper, we propose a novel spatiotemporal enhanced CD (STECD) algorithm based on MSH EOITS to enhance the exploitation of spatial and temporal dependence in flood detection mission in comparison with existing methods [13–17]. Our STECD algorithm mainly includes two steps, i.e., spatial clustering and temporal enhancement. In the spatial clustering step, the hierarchical fuzzy C-means clustering (HFCM) algorithm [18] is introduced to initialize the pixel intensity threshold matrix and then generate the initial flood detection results. Moreover, we propose sparse Markov random field (SMRF)-based operation to iteratively optimize the initial flood detection results and improve the local flood feature extraction capability with larger conceptive fields. In the temporal enhancement step, we exploit the temporal dependence of MSH EOITS to realize the cross-reduction of false alarms derived from terrain shadows in SAR images and cloud shadows and topography shadows in optical images, which further refines the spatial clustering results and increases the detection accuracy of the flood areas. Experimental results derived from four datasets have verified that the proposed STECD algorithm has better CD performance of flood hazard areas than existing commonly used CD methods.

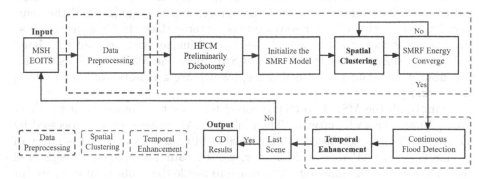

Fig. 1. The framework of our STECD algorithm for CD of flood hazard areas.

2 Method

2.1 Overview of STECD

The framework of our proposed STECD algorithm is shown in Fig. 1, including data preprocessing, spatial clustering, and temporal enhancement. We use $\Psi = \{\Psi_t\}_{1 \leq t \leq S}$ to represent S coregistered MSH EOITS, where $\Psi_t \in R^{M \times N}$ is the image obtained at time t.

Data Preprocessing. In preprocessing stage, image coregistration, SAR images filtering, data truncation, and data mapping are performed to enhance the quality of MSH EOITS and make it convenient to extract flood features.

Spatial Clustering. Firstly, we initial (binary) flood detection results of each image in MSH EOITS based on the HFCM algorithm. Then, we iteratively calculate the SMRF energy function to enhance the boundaries of initial flood detection results in accordance with contextually spatial features in MSH EOITS. The energy-adaptive sparse expansion of the spatial neighborhood system (SNS) in SMRF adaptively increases the receptive fields of flood detection without noticeable increase of computation cost compared with the commonly used second-order SNS in MRF [19].

Temporal Enhancement. Firstly, we initialize the temporal enhancement constraints and the global flood area proportion of Ψ_t based on the spatial clustering results. Then the spatiotemporal enhanced flood detection results are obtained by eliminating the suspected flood areas under the temporal enhancement constraints. This temporal enhancement stage utilizes the historical incremental information of the flood detection results as clustering constraints to realize the global optimization of flood detection results based on temporal dependence characteristics in MSH EOITS.

2.2   Data Preprocessing

The pixel intensities of the water areas are generally low according to the spectral characteristics of water in the near-infrared band image [20] and the near-completely reflection of radar waves on the water surface [4]. Considering these physical properties of water, we only use optical images with near-infrared band and single vision complex (SLC) data of SAR images in MSH EOITS as the initial input of the data preprocessing step, which are generally available in flood monitoring [4,17].

Firstly, all the MSH EOITS are coregistered by the Environment for Visualizing Images (ENVI) software. Then, all the SAR images are preprocessed by the probabilistic patch-based (PPB) weights filter [21] to lighten the effect of speckle noise in SAR images. Moreover, we truncate and map the coregistered MSH EOITS into the same intensity range to tackle the problem of inconsistent data distribution in MSH EOITS [22]. In detail, we truncate the intensities of optical images with near-infrared bands and SLC SAR images:

$$\boldsymbol{\Psi}_t(i,j) = \begin{cases} Min_t, & \boldsymbol{\Psi}_t(i,j) \leq Min_t \\ Max_t, & \boldsymbol{\Psi}_t(i,j) \geq Max_t \\ \boldsymbol{\Psi}_t(i,j), & otherwise \end{cases} \tag{1}$$

for $t = 1, \ldots, S$, where $i = 1, 2, .., M, j = 1, 2, ..., N$, Min_t and Max_t represent the intensity values corresponding with 1% and 99% numbers of the pixels in intensity histogram of $\boldsymbol{\Psi}_t$ (see Fig. 2), respectively. Then, $\boldsymbol{\Psi}_t$ is uniformly mapped to the range of $[0, 255]$, for $t = 1, \ldots, S$.

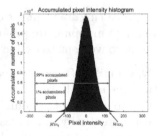

Fig. 2. The accumulated pixel intensity histogram of $\boldsymbol{\Psi}_t$.

2.3   Spatial Clustering

The spatial clustering step is summarized in Algorithm 1. First of all, we initialize the preliminary pixel intensity threshold matrix using HFCM algorithm to get the initial flood detection results. At each iteration, the flood detection results are iteratively updated based on the dynamical threshold matrix of pixels to refine flood detection results by minimizing the SMRF energy function. The iteration is terminated when the decay ratio of the SMRF energy smaller than 0 or the maximum of the iteration index is reached.

Algorithm 1: The spatial clustering step

Input: The MSH EOITS $\Psi = \{\Psi_t\}_{1 \leq t \leq S}$.
Initialization: Let $iter$ represent the iteration index and $iter = 0$. For $t = 1, \ldots, S$, initialized dynamical threshold matrix is $Th_t^{iter} \in \mathcal{R}^{M \times N}$ in accordance with HFCM algorithm [see (2)]. Initialized the spatial clustering results are $D_t^{iter} \in \mathcal{R}^{M \times N}$. If $\Psi_t(i,j) < Th_t^{iter}(i,j)$, $D_t^{iter}(i,j) = 0$, otherwise, $D_t^{iter}(i,j) = 1$, for $t = 1, \ldots, S$, $i = 1, 2, .., M$, and $j = 1, 2, ..., N$.
Iteration:
  1) Calculate the SMRF energy function $U_t\left(N(\Psi_t), D_t^{iter}\right)$ between $N(\Psi_t)$ and D_t^{iter}, where $N(\Psi_t) = \Psi_t/255$ is performed to keep data distribution range consistent between Ψ_t and D_t^{iter} [see (3)].
  2) $iter = iter + 1$ and update the iterative spatial clustering results $D_t^{iter} \in \mathcal{R}^{M \times N}$ [see (4)] based on Th_t^{iter}.
  3) Update Th_t^{iter} [see (5)(6)] to get the spatial constraints Dis_t^{iter}.
  4) Calculate $U_t\left(N(\Psi_t), D_t^{iter}\right)$ between $N(\Psi_t)$ and D_t^{iter}, [see (3)].
  5) Calculate the decay ratio EDR_t between $U_t\left(N(\Psi_t), D_t^{iter}\right)$ and $U_t\left(N(\Psi_t), D_t^{iter-1}\right)$ when all the pixels satisfied with $\{(i,j)|D_t^{iter}(i,j) = 0 \ and \ Dis_t^{iter}(i,j) < \varepsilon_3\}$ are traversed [see (7)] and update the SNS in SMRF [see (8)].
  6) Repeat step 1 to step 5. If $EDR_t < 0$ or $iter = itermax$, stop the iterations.
Output: The final spatial clustering results $D_t = 1 - D_t^{iter-1}$.

Firstly, the initialization step is operated. We separate Ψ_t into several intensity intervals by employing HFCM algorithm, which has been used to distinguish flood and non-flood areas in MSH remote sensing data. $C_t = [C_t^1, C_t^2, ..., C_t^8]$ denotes the eight clustering centers of Ψ_t derived from the HFCM algorithm. We determine the maximum threshold as $T_1 = (C_t^1 + C_t^2)/2$ to avoid aliasing effect of each interval classification. When the pixel intensity of $\Psi_t(i,j) > \varepsilon_1$, the pixel is more likely to be the non-flood area, when the pixel intensity of $\Psi_t(i,j) < \varepsilon_2$, the current pixel is pre-classified as flood pixel, where ε_1 and ε_2 denote the intensity thresholds. Th_t^{iter} is initialized as

$$Th_t^0(i,j) = \begin{cases} C_t^2 - C_t^1, & if \ T_1 \leq \varepsilon_1 \ and \ C_t^2 < \varepsilon_2 \\ T_1, & if \ T_1 \leq \varepsilon_1 \ and \ C_t^2 \geq \varepsilon_2 \\ 0, & otherwise. \end{cases} \tag{2}$$

Without loss of generality, we set $\varepsilon_1 = 255/4$ and $\varepsilon_2 = 255/8$.

The main purpose of spatial clustering step is to iteratively optimize flood detection results based on the SMRF energy function $U_t(\cdot)$ and finally obtain the local minimum of $U_t(\cdot)$. SMRF energy function is defined as

$$U_t\left(N(\boldsymbol{\Psi}_t), \boldsymbol{D}_t^{iter}\right) = U_{data}\left(N(\boldsymbol{\Psi}_t), \boldsymbol{D}_t^{iter}\right) + \varepsilon U_{context}\left(\boldsymbol{D}_t^{iter}\right) \qquad (3)$$

where $U_{data}(\cdot)$ and $U_{context}(\cdot)$ are determined in [19], which represent pixel-level classification dependence and statistics of the dichotomy of the $\boldsymbol{\Psi}_t$, respectively. ε is a hyper-parameter to balance the contributions of $U_{data}(\cdot)$ and $U_{context}(\cdot)$. Note that different from the MRF energy function in $U_{context}(\cdot)$ of [19] (see Fig. 3(a)), our $U_{context}(\cdot)$ uses the energy-adaptive sparse SNS (see Fig. 3(b)) to expand or shrink the receptive fields of flood detection. And $U_t\left(N(\boldsymbol{\Psi}_t), \boldsymbol{D}_t^{iter}\right)$ represents the SMRF energy function between $N(\boldsymbol{\Psi}_t)$ and $\boldsymbol{D}_t^{iter}$.

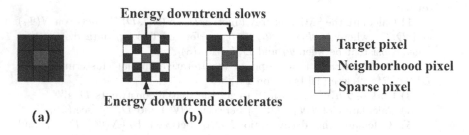

Fig. 3. (a) The SNS in MRF [19]. (b) The SNS in SMRF.

Next, we start the iteration $iter = iter + 1$ and realize the spatial clustering in each iteration by updating the threshold of the pixels in the suspected flood area. Aiming to get the iterative spatial clustering results, when $\boldsymbol{\Psi}_t(i,j) < \boldsymbol{Th}_t^{iter}(i,j)$, we determine that the pixel at (i,j) belongs to the flood areas ($\boldsymbol{D}_t^{iter}(i,j) = 0$). On the contrary, if $\boldsymbol{\Psi}_t(i,j) \geq \boldsymbol{Th}_t^{iter}(i,j)$, the pixel at (i,j) belongs to the non-flood areas ($\boldsymbol{D}_t^{iter}(i,j) = 1$). The binary flood detection results $\boldsymbol{D}_t^{iter}$ of $\boldsymbol{\Psi}_t$ is defined as

$$\boldsymbol{D}_t^{iter}(i,j) = \begin{cases} 0, & \boldsymbol{\Psi}_t(i,j) < \boldsymbol{Th}_t^{iter}(i,j) \\ 1, & otherwise. \end{cases} \qquad (4)$$

We take neighborhood features of a pixel into account to achieve local detection optimization because a pixel is more likely to be affected by its surrounding pixels. Specifically, we extract the edge contour $\boldsymbol{Bd}_t^{iter} \in \mathcal{R}^{M \times N}$ of $\boldsymbol{D}_t^{iter}$, where $\boldsymbol{Bd}_t^{iter}(i,j) = 1$ represents the edge contour and $\boldsymbol{Bd}_t^{iter}(i,j) = 0$ represents the background. Moreover, we employ the global Manhattan distance (MD) matrix $\boldsymbol{Dis}_t^{iter}$ (the minimum of MDs between the pixels with labels 0 and 1 in $\boldsymbol{Bd}_t^{iter}$) as the spatial constraints of $\boldsymbol{Th}_t^{iter}$. According to the river continuum concept (RCC) [23], the flood area is closely connected. Thus, we choose to increase the threshold $\boldsymbol{Th}_t^{iter}(i,j)$ satisfied with $\{(i,j)|\boldsymbol{D}_t^{iter}(i,j) = 0 \text{ and } \boldsymbol{Dis}_t^{iter}(i,j) < \varepsilon_3\}$. In this case, $\boldsymbol{Th}_t^{iter}$ is updated as

$$Th_t^{iter}(i,j) = \begin{cases} (Th_t^{iter-1}(i,j)+1) \cdot V, & if\ D_t^{iter}(i,j) = 0\ and\ Dis_t^{iter}(i,j) < \varepsilon_3 \\ Th_t^{iter-1}(i,j)+1, & otherwise \end{cases} \quad (5)$$

where $V = 1.01$ represents the augmentation factor. We set $\varepsilon_3 = 8$ based on the comprehensive consideration of spatial constraints and computational complexity. Dis_t^{iter} is defined as

$$Dis_t^{iter}(i,j) = M\big((i,j), \{(i_k, j_k)|Bd_t^{iter}(i_k, j_k) = 1\}\big), \quad if Bd_t^{iter}(i,j) = 0 \quad (6)$$

where (i_k, j_k) represents the coordinates of $Bd_t^{iter}(i_k, j_k) = 1$. $M(\cdot)$ represents the minimum of the MDs between the target pixel $Bd_t^{iter}(i,j) = 0$ and all the pixels with label 1 in Bd_t^{iter}. Bd_t^{iter} is updated as soon as D_t^{iter} is updated.

Then, we calculate the SMRF energy decay ratio and update the SNS in SMRF. In order to make the SNS in SMRF dynamically change with the rate of energy downtrend, we define the SMRF energy function decay ratio EDR_t to distinguish increasing and decreasing rate of energy downtrend. When EDR_t decreases, the local consistency between Ψ_t and D_t^{iter} is getting higher and we should select the smaller SNS to speed up the local convergence, otherwise, we should increase the SNS to expand the receptive fields of local flood detection optimization. When all the pixels $\{(i,j)|D_t^{iter}(i,j) = 1 \cap Dis_t^{iter}(i,j) < \varepsilon_3\}$ in Ψ_t are traversed, EDR_t is computed as

$$EDR_t = \frac{U_t\left(N(\Psi_t), D_t^{iter-1}\right) - U_t\left(N(\Psi_t), D_t^{iter}\right)}{U_t\left(N(\Psi_t), D_t^{iter-1}\right)}. \quad (7)$$

We set the SNS in SMRF as $W_t^{iter} \times W_t^{iter}$ and $W_t^0 = 5$. Considering the computation complexity and local optimization capability, when $EDR_t \le \varepsilon_4$, we set $W_t^{iter} = 3$ to narrow the SNS in SMRF, otherwise, we set $W_t^{iter} = 5$ to expand the SNS in SMRF. At the $iter$th iteration, W_t^{iter} is updated as

$$W_t^{iter} = \begin{cases} 3, & EDR_t \le \varepsilon_4 \\ 5, & otherwise \end{cases} \quad (8)$$

where $\varepsilon_4 = 0.01$.

In each iteration, we update formulas (3)–(8). And we set termination condition of the total optimization as $\{if\ EDR_t < 0\ or\ iter = itermax\}$. When the iterations stop, the local flood detection optimum is reached. In order to intuitively represent the flood area, $D_t = 1 - D_t^{iter-1}$ is determined as the final spatial clustering results.

2.4   Temporal Enhancement

The temporal enhancement step is summarized in Algorithm 2. We employ the historical incremental information $Incre_t$ of the spatial clustering results as constraints to realize the cross-reduction of the effect derived from terrain shadows

---

Algorithm 2: The temporal enhancement step

Input: The spatial clustering results $D = \{D_t\}_{1 \leq t \leq S}$ derived from the MSH EOITS.

for $t = 1 : S$ **do**

    Initialization: Let the historical incremental information $Incre_t$ be dynamically initialized in the acquisition interval constraints [see (9)], $Thresh_t$ represents the global flood area proportion of Ψ_t, and num represents the total number of kth four-connected regions in D_t.

    for $k = 1 : num$ **do**

        1) Calculate the overlap ratio $\alpha = \frac{\sum_{i=1}^{M}\sum_{j=1}^{N}(D_t(k) \odot Incre_t)(i,j)}{\sum_{i=1}^{M}\sum_{j=1}^{N}(D_t(k))(i,j)}$ between $D_t(k)$ and $Incre_t$, where $D_t(k)$ represents kth four-connected regions of D_t.

        2) If $\alpha > Thresh_t$, $D_t(k)$ is determined as the reliable flood area of Ψ_t, [see (10)].

    end

end

return $STE = \{STE_t\}_{1 \leq t \leq S}$, where STE_t represents the spatiotemporal enhanced flood detection results of Ψ_t.

Output: The STECD results $CD_{t \to (t-l)}$ between Ψ_t and Ψ_{t-l} for $1 \leq l < t$, [see (11)].

---

in SAR images and cloud shadows and topography shadows in optical images in flood detection results (see Fig. 4). First, we initialize $Incre_t$ and the global flood area proportion of Ψ_t as the temporal enhancement constraints. Under the constraints of $Incre_t$ and Ψ_t, the spatiotemporal enhanced flood detection results STE_t is obtained by eliminating the suspected flood areas. Finally, the STECD results are obtained by comparing the spatiotemporal enhanced flood detection results of the specific two images.

Firstly, if and only if the accumulated MSH EOITS exceed 3 scenes, the historical incremental information $Incre_t$ is initialized as temporal constraints. Considering the rapid change of flood areas, we set ω as the acquisition interval constraints between Ψ_t and Ψ_{t-3} to dynamically adjust $Incre_t$. When $\omega > 6\ days$, the spatial clustering results of the two images from MSH EOITS obtained before the current time are employed as constraints. When $\omega \leq 6\ days$, the spatial clustering results of the three images from MSH EOITS acquired before the current time are used as constraints. $Incre_t$ is calculated by

$$Incre_t(i,j) = \begin{cases} 1, & if\ A_t(i,j) \geq 1\ and\ \omega \leq 6\ days \\ 1, & if\ B_t(i,j) \geq 1\ and\ \omega > 6\ days \\ 0, & otherwise \end{cases} \quad (9)$$

where $A_t = D_t \odot (D_{t-1} + D_{t-2} + D_{t-3})$ and $B_t = D_t \odot (D_{t-1} + D_{t-2})$ represent the temporal constraints and they are constructed based on the complementary characteristics of MSH EOITS (all-weather imaging capability of SAR sensors and different imaging angles of the other sensors).

Secondly, we eliminate the suspected flood area using the constraints $Incre_t$. Changes in the flood zone often occur continuously over a densely continuous observation of the same area in accordance with RCC. Specifically, we compare the four-connected regions between D_t and $Incre_t$. When the overlap ratio α between $D_t(k)$ and $Incre_t$ is larger than $Thresh_t$ (the global flood area proportion of Ψ_t), $D_t(k)$ is determined as the reliable flood area of Ψ_t. The final spatiotemporal enhanced flood detection results of Ψ_t is formulated as

$$STE_t(k) = \begin{cases} D_t(k), & \alpha > Thresh_t \\ 0, & otherwise \end{cases} \tag{10}$$

where $STE_t(k)$ represents the kth four-connected regions of STE_t, $Thresh_t = \frac{\sum_{i=1}^{M}\sum_{j=1}^{N} D_t(i,j)}{M \times N}$ is determined by the ratio of the overall number of pixels onto flood areas to the total number of pixels in Ψ_t, and $\alpha = \frac{\sum_{i=1}^{M}\sum_{j=1}^{N}(D_t(k) \odot Incre_t)(i,j)}{\sum_{i=1}^{M}\sum_{j=1}^{N}(D_t(k))(i,j)}$ is determined as the overlap ratio between $D_t(k)$ and $Incre_t$.

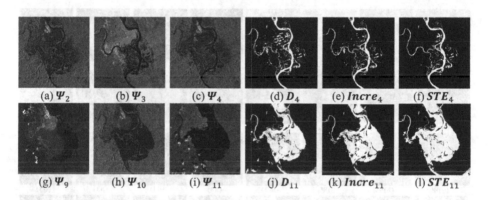

Fig. 4. (a)–(f) $Incre_4$ applied in the reduction of terrain shadows of Ψ_4. (g)–(l) $Incre_{11}$ applied in the reduction of cloud shadows of Ψ_{11}. (White: flood areas. Black: non-flood areas.)

Finally, the CD results of the $\{\Psi_t\}_{1 \leq t \leq S}$ are obtained. Based on the incremental feature constraints of MSH EOITS, the flood features extracted from different data sources can be fused, which can effectively eliminate the effects of terrain shadows in SAR images and cloud shadows and topography shadows in optical images. Aiming to acquire the change map $CD_{t \rightarrow (t-l)}$ between Ψ_t and Ψ_{t-l}, when $(STE_t - STE_{t-l})(i,j) > 0$, we determine the pixel $CD_{t \rightarrow (t-l)}(i,j) = 1$ as changed flood area, otherwise, we set $CD_{t \rightarrow (t-l)}(i,j) = 0$ as non-changed area. The CD results between Ψ_t and Ψ_{t-l} is defined as

$$CD_{t \rightarrow (t-l)}(i,j) = \begin{cases} 1, & (STE_t - STE_{t-l})(i,j) > 0 \\ 0, & otherwise. \end{cases} \tag{11}$$

3   Results and Discussion

We tested the effectiveness of the proposed algorithm on four datasets in Huma Town (HT), China, 2021. The parameters of the STECD algorithm are fixed for all experiments. We set $\varepsilon = 1.6$, $\varepsilon_1 = 255/4$, $\varepsilon_2 = 255/8$, $\varepsilon_3 = 8$, $\varepsilon_4 = 0.01$, and $itermax = 100$ in experiments without loss of generality. All the MSH EOITS in HT were coregistered at the same spatial resolution of 16 m × 16 m (1401 × 1401 pixels). And the ground truth (GT) of each dataset was labeled by ENVI software, which is the difference map between the two specific image.

The evaluation indicators including the overall classification accuracy P_o, the overall error (OE) detection rate OE_r, the Kappa coefficient KC, and the first error measure F_1 are used in this paper. The detailed definitions of these evaluation indicators can be found in [24].

The proposed STECD algorithm is compared with three CD algorithms, which are implemented by the default parameters in PCANet [25], IFBCD [26], and S^3N [14], respectively. The MSH EOITS of HT, GTs of four datasets, and

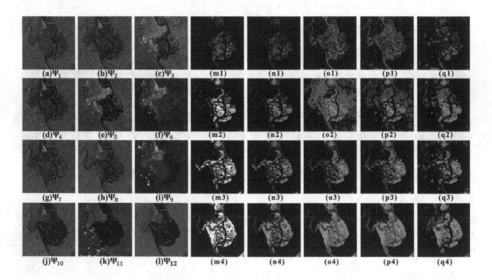

Fig. 5. MSH EOITS of HT, GTs of four datasets, and change detection results produced by 4 algorithms. (a)–(l) Ψ_1–Ψ_{12}. (m1)–(m4) GTs of flood area change based on $\Psi_1 \& \Psi_3, \Psi_4 \& \Psi_6, \Psi_7 \& \Psi_9, and \; \Psi_7 \& \Psi_{12}$, respectively. (n1)–(n4) CD results derived from the proposed STECD algorithm based on Ψ_1–Ψ_3, Ψ_4–Ψ_6, Ψ_7–Ψ_9, and Ψ_7–Ψ_{12}, respectively. (o1)–(o4) CD results derived from the PCANet algorithm based on $\Psi_1 \& \Psi_3, \Psi_4 \& \Psi_6, \Psi_7 \& \Psi_9, and \; \Psi_7 \& \Psi_{12}$, respectively. (p1)–(p4) CD results derived from the IFBCD algorithm based on $\Psi_1 \& \Psi_3, \Psi_4 \& \Psi_6, \Psi_7 \& \Psi_9, and \; \Psi_7 \& \Psi_{12}$, respectively. (q1)–(q4) CD results derived from the S^3N algorithm based on $\Psi_1 \& \Psi_3, \Psi_4 \& \Psi_6, \Psi_7 \& \Psi_9, and \; \Psi_7 \& \Psi_{12}$, respectively. (White: ground truth of incremental flood areas. Green: incremental flood areas are correctly detected. Red: unchanged areas are incorrectly detected as changed flood areas. Blue: incremental flood areas are incorrectly detected as unchanged areas.) (Color figure online)

change detection results produced by 4 algorithms are shown in Fig. 5 where the proposed STECD algorithm produces better change maps than the other three methods. The quantitative experimental results are listed in Table 1. Table 1 shows that PCANet, IFBCD, and S^3N are more suitable to wide-ranging flood hazard area detection, but these three algorithms are sensitive for the local small-scale changed areas. Due to PCANet's and IFBCD's applicability of CD in the SAR data, the KC and F_1 of PCANet and IFBCD algorithms in the fourth dataset (Gaofen-3 and Sentinel-1) are higher than their measures in the other three datasets. S^3N algorithm needs to manually extract a small range of unchanged pixels as online training samples to obtain CD results, which often suffers from the uncertainty of detection accuracy derived from the incorrect selection of training samples. The proposed STECD algorithm obtains higher performance measures of flood areas and non-flood areas than the other three algorithms in the four datasets, benefiting from the utilization of the temporal and spatial dependence of MSH EOITS.

Table 1. CD results analysis on four datasets of MSH EOITS in HT, 2021.

Methods	CD results analysis on Ψ_1–Ψ_3				CD results analysis on Ψ_4–Ψ_6			
	P_o	OE_r	KC	F_1	P_o	OE_r	KC	F_1
PCANet	0.8482	0.3644	0.2429	0.2920	0.5691	0.5541	0.1520	0.2888
IFBCD	0.7993	0.3257	0.2046	0.2587	0.7911	0.3597	0.3469	0.4399
S^3N	0.8755	0.7519	0.1324	0.1835	0.8434	0.4085	0.3956	0.4741
STECD	**0.9704**	**0.1676**	**0.6827**	**0.6977**	**0.9583**	**0.2463**	**0.7578**	**0.7808**
Methods	CD results analysis on Ψ_7–Ψ_9				CD results analysis on Ψ_7–Ψ_{12}			
	P_o	OE_r	KC	F_1	P_o	OE_r	KC	F_1
PCANet	0.9168	0.3704	0.6141	0.6615	0.8826	0.2060	0.6681	0.7403
IFBCD	0.9118	0.2486	0.6418	0.6916	0.8781	0.1968	0.6625	0.7371
S^3N	0.8831	0.4123	0.5137	0.5801	0.8742	0.3380	0.6105	0.6884
STECD	**0.9640**	**0.1873**	**0.8260**	**0.8464**	**0.9562**	**0.1664**	**0.8501**	**0.8767**

4   Conclusions

In this article, we established a two-stage CD algorithm of flood hazard areas based on MSH EOITS. In the spatial clustering step, we firstly perform the HFCM model to initialize the preliminary pixel intensity threshold matrix. Secondly, we propose SMRF-based operation to iteratively optimize the boundaries of initial flood detection results based on the spatial dependence of MSH EOITS. In the temporal enhancement step, we set temporal clustering constraints to lighten the effect derived from terrain shadows in SAR images and cloud shadows and topography shadows in optical images based on the historical increment information of flood detection results. Experimental results based on 4 measured datasets have confirmed the effectiveness of the proposed algorithm for the CD of flood hazard areas. In the future, we will try to collect more MSH EOITS regarding flood hazard areas and establish deep neural networks with sustainable learning capability.

References

1. Mora, C., et al.: Broad threat to humanity from cumulative climate hazards intensified by greenhouse gas emissions. Nat. Clim. Change **8**(12), 1062–1071 (2018)
2. Willner, S., Otto, C., Levermann, A.: Global economic response to river floods. Nat. Clim. Chang. **8**(7), 594–598 (2018)
3. Li, S., et al.: Automatic near real-time flood detection using Suomi-NPP/VIIRS data. Remote Sens. Environ. **204**, 672–689 (2018)
4. DeVries, B., Huang, C., Armston, J., Huang, W., Jones, J., Lang, M.: Rapid and robust monitoring of flood events using Sentinel-1 and Landsat data on the Google Earth Engine. Remote Sens. Environ. **240**, 111664 (2020)
5. Le, T., Froger, J., Ho Tong Minh, D.: Multiscale framework for rapid change analysis from SAR image time series: case study of flood monitoring in the central coast regions of Vietnam. Remote Sens. Environ. **269**, 112837 (2022)
6. Voigt, S., et al.: Global trends in satellite-based emergency mapping. Science **353**(6296), 247–252 (2016)
7. Amarnath, G.: An algorithm for rapid flood inundation mapping from optical data using a reflectance differencing technique. J. Flood Risk Manag. **7**(3), 239–250 (2013)
8. Torres, R., et al.: GMES Sentinel-1 mission. Remote Sens. Environ. **120**, 9–24 (2012)
9. Chini, M., Hostache, R., Giustarini, L., Matgen, P.: A hierarchical split-based approach for parametric thresholding of SAR images: flood inundation as a test case. IEEE Trans. Geosci. Remote Sens. **55**, 6975–6988 (2017)
10. Twele, A., Cao, W., Plank, S., Martinis, S.: Sentinel-1-based flood mapping: a fully automated processing chain. Int. J. Remote Sens. **37**, 2990–3004 (2016)
11. Matgen, P., Hostache, R., Schumann, G., Pfister, L., Hoffmann, L., Savenije, H.H.G.: Towards an automated SAR-based flood monitoring system: lessons learned from two case studies. Phys. Chem. Earth **36**, 241–252 (2011)
12. Wang, X., Li, G., Zhang, X.-P., He, Y.: A fast CFAR algorithm based on density-censoring operation for ship detection in SAR images. IEEE Signal Process. Lett. **28**, 1085–1089 (2021)
13. Liu, Z., Li, G., Mercier, G., He, Y., Pan, Q.: Change detection in heterogenous remote sensing images via homogeneous pixel transformation. IEEE Trans. Image Process. **27**(4), 1822–1834 (2018)
14. Jiang, X., Li, G., Zhang, X., He, Y.: A semisupervised siamese network for efficient change detection in heterogeneous remote sensing images. IEEE Trans. Geosci. Remote Sens. **60**, 1–18 (2022)
15. Gong, M., Zhang, P., Su, L., Liu, J.: Coupled dictionary learning for change detection from multisource data. IEEE Trans. Geosci. Remote Sens. **54**(12), 7077–7091 (2016)
16. Liu, J., Gong, M., Qin, K., Zhang, P.: A deep convolutional coupling network for change detection based on heterogeneous optical and radar images. IEEE Trans. Neural Netw. Learn. Syst. **29**(3), 545–559 (2018)

17. Li, C., et al.: Increased flooded area and exposure in the White Volta river basin in Western Africa, identified from multi-source remote sensing data. Sci. Rep. **12**(1), 1–13 (2018)

18. Wang, Z., Li, G., Jiang, X.: Flooded area detection method based on fusion of optical and SAR remote sensing images. J. Radars **9**(3), 539–553 (2020)

19. Bruzzone, L., Prieto, D.F.: Automatic analysis of the difference image for unsupervised change detection. IEEE Trans. Geosci. Remote Sens. **38**(3), 1171–1182 (2000)

20. Tong, Q.X., Tian, G.L.: Analysis of Spectrum and Characteristics of Typical Land Features in China. Science Press, Beijing (1990)

21. Deledalle, C.A., Denis, L., Tupin, F.: Iterative weighted maximum likelihood denoising with probabilistic patch-based weights. IEEE Trans. Image Process. **18**(12), 2661–2672 (2009)

22. Zhang, J.: Multi-source remote sensing data fusion: status and trends. Int. J. Image Data Fusion **1**(1), 5–24 (2010)

23. Vannote, R.L., Minshall, G.W., Cummins, K.W., et al.: The river continuum concept. Can. J. Fish. Aquat. Sci. **37**(1), 130–137 (1980)

24. Gong, M., Zhan, T., Zhang, P., Miao, Q.: Superpixel-based difference representation learning for change detection in multispectral remote sensing images. IEEE Trans. Geosci. Remote Sens. **55**(5), 2658–2673 (2017)

25. Gao, F., Dong, J., Li, B., Xu, Q.: Automatic change detection in synthetic aperture radar images based on PCANet. IEEE Geosci. Remote Sens. Lett. **13**(12), 1792–1796 (2016)

26. Zhao, M., Ling, Q., Li, F.: An iterative feedback-based change detection algorithm for flood mapping in SAR images. IEEE Geosci. Remote Sens. Lett. **16**(2), 231–235 (2019)

Reinforcement Learning Based Plug-and-Play Method for Hyperspectral Image Reconstruction

Ying Fu[✉] and Yingkai Zhang

Beijing Institute of Technology, Beijing, China
{fuying,3120220996}@bit.edu.cn

Abstract. Hyperspectral images have multi-dimensional information and play an important role in many fields. Recently, based on the compressed sensing (CS), spectral snapshot compressive imaging (SCI) can balance spatial and spectral resolution compared with traditional methods, so it has attached more and more attention. The Plug-and-Play (PnP) framework based on spectral SCI can effectively reconstruct high-quality hyperspectral images, but there exists a serious problem of parameter dependence. In this paper, we propose a PnP hyperspectral reconstruction method based on reinforcement learning (RL), where a suitable policy network through deep reinforcement learning can adaptively tune the parameters in the PnP method to adjust the denoising strength, penalty factor of the deep denoising network, and the terminal time of iterative optimization. Compared with other model-based and learning-based methods and methods with different parameters tuning policies, the reconstruction results obtained by the proposed method have advantages in quantitative indicators and visual effects.

Keywords: Plug-and-Play hyperspectral reconstruction method · Reinforcement learning

1 Introduction

Spectrum is composed of polychromatic light passing through dispersive elements, and represents the light intensity of different wavelength bands. Hyperspectral image (HSI) provides abundant spectral and spatial information compared with red-green-blue (RGB) image, due to small interval and multiple sampling. In view of muti-dimensional information, HSIs can solve the metamerism problem in traditional gray/RGB images, and distinguish observation targets more comprehensively and clearly. Therefore, HSI is widely used in medical diagnosis [16], remote sensing [18], and food safety [9], *etc.*

At present, how to obtain high-quality spectral images is a challenging problem. Traditional imaging systems mainly use the principles of spectroscopy and interference to obtain target information, *e.g.*, push-broom [2], and spectral scanning [31]. However, they require sacrificing temporal dimension for high spatial and spectral resolution information. Thanks to compressive sensing (CS)

L. Fang et al. (Eds.): CICAI 2022, LNAI 13604, pp. 466–477, 2022.
https://doi.org/10.1007/978-3-031-20497-5_38

[8] and decompressive algorithm, computational spectroscopy system can effectively solve the trade-off between temporal and spatial-spectral resolution, which is also called spectral snapshot compressive imaging (SCI). Spectral SCI avoids the limitations of the hardware devices of the traditional imaging systems. In addition to the hardware coupling system, it also mainly depends on the software decoupling part, i.e., spectral recoupling construction method.

Traditional methods, i.e., model-based methods usually require manual embedding of prior knowledge of spectral images. These handcrafted priors are called regularization, such as sparsity [25], total variation [24], low-rank priors [11], and adaptive spatial-spectral dictionary learning [10] etc. Optimization algorithms based on various priors can produce relatively high-quality spectral image results, but their main bottleneck lies in their reconstruction speed. Affected by the development of deep learning, learning-based methods are also gradually used for hyperspectral image reconstruction. Convolutional neural networks (CNN) is used to solve the inverse problem. The most direct one is the end-to-end network [26], and other methods like Autoencoders [6], and patch-based end-to-end network [13]. Through the implicit learning of spectral images, the learning-based methods are often better than the model-based methods, but implicit learning does not utilize known spectral priors, which makes the network poorly interpretable.

Considering the advantages and disadvantages of the model-based and learning-based methods, the joint model and learning methods have also been proposed, i.e., Plug-and-Play (PnP) method. It has attracted great attention due to its effectiveness and flexibility in dealing with various inverse imaging problems. Although the existing PnP method can obtain better spectral reconstruction results, the key problem is that PnP method is very dependent on the selection of parameters, e.g., the terminal time, denoising strength, and penalty factor. There are some existing parameter selection methods or manual setting strategies (manual tweaking [19] and handcrafted principle [20]). However, they cannot adjust parameters adaptively and still rely on human-assisted adjustment.

In this paper, we combine reinforcement learning (RL) and the PnP method (RLPnP) to automatically adjust parameters, which can avoid manual multiple experiments. We use an actor-critic network architecture, and the actor network, i.e., the policy network determines the final parameters. After the comparison with other hyperspectral reconstruction methods and other parameters tuning policies, we demonstrate our method can obtain better performance in hyperspectral image reconstruction. Our contributions are as follows:

1. We introduce RL algorithm into the PnP method for hyperspectral image reconstruction, which can automatically adjust parameters and avoid experimental replication.
2. We propose a RL algorithm that combines the model-free and model-based algorithms to obtain parameters in PnP method through an efficient policy structure.

3. We demonstrate that our method outperforms competing methods, in terms of both quantitative and visual results, which shows the robustness and flexibility of our method.

2   Related Work

In this section, we review the related work from the PnP method.

2.1   PnP

The PnP method is the combination of optimization algorithm and prior denoising. The optimization algorithm currently includes the half-quadratic splitting algorithm (HQS) [32], the primal-dual algorithm [17], and the alternating direction multiplier algorithm (ADMM) [4].

Prior denoising methods include block matching and 3D joint filtering method [5] (BM3D), low-rank Bayesian tensor factorization method [28], deep network-based denoiser [32], and deep plug-and-play prior [14] *etc.* Dabov *et al.* [7] proposed an image denoising policy based on enhanced sparse representation in transform domain, which group similar 2D patches into 3D array to process. Zhang *et al.* [32] proposed a method to solve inverse problems via training a CNN denoiser and integrating it into model-based optimization method as a deep prior. In addition to these aspects, There are some existing manual setting strategies for parameter selection. Manual tweaking [19] can set the correct parameters for the method, but it requires several experiments, which is time-consuming. Handcrafted principle [20] can semi-automatically adjust parameters to reduce labor burden, but it is difficult to choose the initial range, which is crucial to the algorithm. After several experiments and observation, the optimal parameters range for different images may be distinct.

Different from existing parameters selection strategies, our method automatically tune parameters for every single image, which avoids the consumption of handcrafted tuning.

3   Method

This section mainly proposes a reinforcement learning based Plug-and-Play hyperspectral reconstruction method (RLPnP). Spectral SCI is consisted of SD-CASSI system and reconstruction algorithm. The overall architecture is shown in Fig. 1.

3.1   Spectral SCI System

Traditional spectral imaging systems often capture the spectral information in an array detector, sacrificing time in exchange for high-resolution spatial and spectral information. To better balance time and spatial-spectral resolution, systems

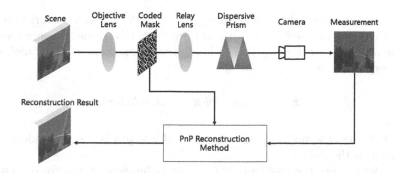

Fig. 1. Spectral SCI system. The upper part is the SD-CASSI system, and the lower part is the reconstruction method.

based on CS are widely used, *e.g.*, SD-CASSI (single disperser coded aperture snapshot spectral imager) [21] system.

In SD-CASSI system, Spectral collection for a scene with λ spectral dimension. Each channel data can be expressed as $\{x_i\,(m,n)\,|_{i=1,2,\cdots,\lambda}\}$, where (m,n) represents the spatial dimension position and i represents the spectral dimension index. Suppose $1 \leq m \leq W, 1 \leq n \leq H, 1 \leq \lambda \leq B$, where H, W represent the height and width of the image, and B represents the spectral dimension size. Then the specific compressed image representation can be expressed as

$$y(m,n) = \sum_{i=1}^{\lambda} c_i(m - \Phi(\lambda), n)x_i(m - \Phi(\lambda), n, \lambda)\phi_i(\lambda), \qquad (1)$$

where $y(m,n)$ denotes the compressed image, $\phi_i(\lambda)$ is the response function of the detector or camera, $c_i(m,n)$ is the coupling of the coded mask, $\Phi(\lambda)$ is expressed as the wavelength-dependent dispersion function of the prism in the system, and its matrix form is

$$\mathbf{Y} = \boldsymbol{\Psi}\mathbf{X} + \epsilon, \qquad (2)$$

where $\mathbf{Y} \in \mathbb{R}^{W \times (H+B-1)}$ is the observation data, $\boldsymbol{\Psi}$ represents the observation matrix of the coded mask, $\mathbf{X} \in \mathbb{R}^{W \times (H+B-1) \times B}$ represents the spectral images to be reconstructed, and ϵ represents the noise.

3.2   PnP Method

The forward process of SCI can be described as the process of generating measurement, and the inverse imaging problem is to reconstruct the original data from the measurement. Suppose $x = vec(\mathbf{X}) \in \mathbb{R}^{W(H+B-1)B}$, $y = vec(\mathbf{Y}) \in \mathbb{R}^{W(H+B-1)}$. According to Eq. (2), the SCI forward model can be expressed as

$$\mathbf{y} = \boldsymbol{\Psi}(\mathbf{x}) + \epsilon, \qquad (3)$$

where ϵ is the sensing noise, and $\boldsymbol{\Psi}$ represents the sensing matrix.

From a statistical inference point of view, the Maximum a posteriori estimation (MAP) can be used for the inverse problem. Given the measured value y and the forward model Eq. (3) to estimate the unknown x in the model, which can be expressed as

$$\hat{x} = \arg\min_{x} \frac{1}{2}\|\Psi x - y\|_2^2 + \lambda R(x), \tag{4}$$

where λ denotes the noise balance factor, $\frac{1}{2}\|\Psi x - y\|_2^2$ is the data fidelity item, and $\lambda R(x)$ is the data prior.

In order to solve the problem, ADMM algorithm is used iteratively to update the three subproblems. The optimization subproblems can be expressed as

$$x^{k+1} = \arg\min_{x} \frac{1}{2}\|y - \Psi x\|_2^2 + \rho\|x - z^k + v^k\|^2, \tag{5}$$

$$z^{k+1} = \arg\min_{z} \frac{\rho}{2}\|z - x^{k+1} - v^k\|_2^2 + \lambda R(z), \tag{6}$$

$$v^{k+1} = v^k + (x^{k+1} - z^{k+1}), \tag{7}$$

where $k \in [0, \tau]$ is the number of iterations, and τ denotes the terminal time.

The x subproblem in Eq. (5) is a least squares estimation problem, so its analytical solution is

$$x^{k+1} = (\Psi\Psi^T + \rho I)^{-1}[\Psi^T y + \rho(z^k - v^k)]. \tag{8}$$

where ρ denotes the penalty factor.

For z subproblem in Eq. (6), suppose $\sigma = \sqrt{\frac{\lambda}{\rho}}$. We can rewrite it as

$$z^{k+1} = \arg\min_{z} R(z) + \frac{1}{2\sigma^2}\|z - x^{k+1} - v^k\|_2^2 = \mathcal{D}_\sigma(x^{k+1} + v^k), \tag{9}$$

where σ is the denoising strength. We use a pre-trained network (Qrnn3D [29]) as the deep prior.

3.3   Reinforcement Learning for Parameters Tuning

For PnP method, the selection of parameters, **penalty factor** ρ, **denoising strength** σ in Eq. (8) and (9), and **terminal time** τ have a great impact on the final reconstruction results. There are some existing parameter selection methods or manual setting strategies. However, these parameter tuning methods all require manual tuning based on experience or repeating a large number of experiments, which consume much resources. Therefore, this work proposes a reinforcement learning method to adjust the parameters, as shown in Fig. 2.

The main idea of the parameter tuning method is to dynamically adjust the parameters in views of the intermediate variables of the current iteration. The process of the proposed method is to select a series of denoising strengths σ and penalty factors ρ to minimize the optimized objective function. It can be

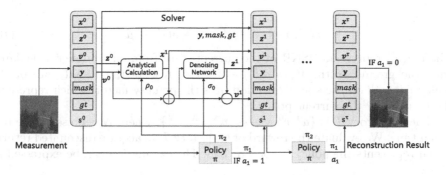

Fig. 2. Parameters tuning method based on reinforcement learning. The calculation process is composed of two parts, solver and policy. First, the intermediate state s^t is stored, which includes variables (x, z, v), measurement y, coding mask $mask$, and ground truth gt. The policy generates two actions, which determine the parameters separately. The solver plays the role of state-transition.

found that this selection (decision-making) process can be regarded as a Markov Decision Process (MDP), so the selection of parameters can be learned through reinforcement learning.

Basic Formula. MDP can be expressed as $(\mathcal{S}, \mathcal{A}, \pi, f, r)$.

$\mathcal{S}$ is represented as the state space, which saves the optimization variables separated by ADMM algorithm in Eq. (8), (9), and (7). In Fig. 2, the intermediate state s includes variables (x, z, v), measurement y, coding mask, and ground truth gt.

$\mathcal{A}$ denotes the action space, which determines the parameters, terminal time τ, denoising strength σ and penalty factor ρ. The goal of the parameter tuning method is to learn a policy π, *i.e.*, to make decisions and perform actions according to the current state. The policy is divided into two parts, π_1 and π_2, which can make two action a_1 and a_2 respectively. a_1 is determined by the stochastic policy π_1, which represents the terminal time τ. If $a_1 = 1$, the iteration goes on, else stops. a_2 is determined by the deterministic policy π_2, which represents the denoising strength σ and penalty factor ρ. We directly update the parameters directly based on the outcome of policy π_2.

f is represented as the state-transition function, *i.e.*, the next state is obtained according to the last state and the executed action, which can be represented as $f(s^{t+1}|s^t, a^t)$. The transition is composed of a single action execution or multiple consecutive action executions. In hyperspectral reconstruction, we create a *solver* to receive the current state (x, z, v) and action (σ, ρ, τ), and generate the next state.

r represents reward function, which can be expressed as $r(s^t, a^t)$, *i.e.*, the evaluation reward given by the environment according to the current state and action. We use peaksignal-to-noise ratio (PSNR) as the indicator for evaluating reconstructed images. We calculate the PSNR based on the image data obtained from the current environment state with the ground truth. The formula is as follows

$$r(s^t, a^t) = \delta(f(s^t, a^t)) - \delta(s^t) + \mu, \tag{10}$$

where $\delta(s^t)$ represents PSNR of the current state from environment calculated with the ground truth, $\delta(f(s^t, a^t)) - \delta(s^t)$ represents the PSNR gain of the policy network on the state transition. μ is the penalty factor, which represents the penalty for the current policy.

The trajectory T is $\{a^0, r^0, s^0, \cdots, a^N, r^N, s^N\}$, where N represents the terminal time. We evaluate the reward of trajectory T to acquire discounted return, which represents the policy is good or bad. The calculation can be expressed as

$$R^t = \sum_{i=0}^{N-t} \eta^i r(s^{t+i}, a^{t+i}), \tag{11}$$

where R^t represents the sum of discounted return after t, and η^i is discount factor. The state and action value functions as

$$V_\pi(s) = \mathbb{E}_{T\sim\pi}[R^t | s^t = s], \tag{12}$$

$$Q_\pi(s, a) = \mathbb{E}_{T\sim\pi}[R^t | s^t = s, a^t = a], \tag{13}$$

where $V_\pi(s)$ represents the state value function and $Q_\pi(s, a)$ represents the action value function. The optimization goal is

$$J(\pi) = \mathbb{E}_{s\sim S, T\sim\pi}[R], \tag{14}$$

where $\mathbb{E}$ represents the expectation, s and S represent the state and its distribution, R represents the discount return from the start to the end, $i.e.$, total PSNR gain between initial state and final state. We hope to maximize the objective function to acquire high-quality reconstructed results.

Policy and Value Learning. The parameter tuning algorithm is mainly based on the DDPG (Deep Deterministic Policy Gradient) algorithm [15], using the Actor-Critic network structure. Actor network is a policy-based network and Critic is a value-based network based on the ResNet-18 [12]. The training of the two networks is performed alternately, and training data come from experience pool D, which stores the historical training intermediate states, such as, optimization variables (x, z, v), mask code and ground truth, $etc.$

The value network training mainly optimizes the network parameters by minimizing the loss function

$$L = \mathbb{E}_{s\sim D, a\sim\pi}[\frac{1}{2}(r(s, a) + \eta V'_\pi(f(s, a)) - V_\pi(s))^2], \tag{15}$$

where V'_π is the critic target network, and V_π is the critic network. In the experiment, we use Mean Square Error (MSE) to calculate the loss. Afterwards, the critic target network is updated by soft update, which can be expressed as

$$\theta' = \beta\theta + (1 - \beta)\theta', \tag{16}$$

where θ' represents the critic target network parameters, θ represents the critic network parameters, and β represents the update factor.

The update of the policy network is divided into two parts of the policy update (stochastic policy π_1 and deterministic policy π_2). Applying the policy gradient theorem, the calculation formula is as follows

$$\nabla_{\theta_1} J(\pi_\theta) = \mathbb{E}_{s \sim D, a \sim \pi}[\nabla_{\theta_1}(Q_\pi(s,a) - V_\pi(s))\pi_1(a_1|s)], \tag{17}$$

$$\nabla_{\theta_2} J(\pi_\theta) = \mathbb{E}_{s \sim D, a \sim \pi}[\nabla_{a_2} Q_\pi(s,a)\nabla_{\theta_2}\pi_2(s)], \tag{18}$$

where θ_1 denotes the critic network parameters, θ_2 denotes the actor network parameters, $Q_\pi(s,a) \approx r(s,a) + \eta V'_\pi(f(s,a))$ represents the action value function can be approximated by state value function and the discount return.

4 Experimental Results

In this section, we first introduce the dataset and metrics for quantitative evaluation in our experiments. Then, our method is compared with several methods. In addition, we compare several different parameters tuning policies with our method.

4.1 Dataset and Metrics

We mainly conduct experiments on natural HSIs, the ICVL dataset [1]. The ICVL dataset currently contains 200 spectral images at a spatial resolution of 1392×1300. The data are normalized and divided into 256×256 according to the center position, and 50 images with low quality are eliminated. 101 randomly selected images are used for training and the remaining 50 are used for testing.

Three quantitative image quality metrics are utilized to evaluate the performance of all methods, including peaksignal-to-noise ratio (PSNR), structural similarity (SSIM) [27], and relative dimensionless global error in synthesis (ERGAS) [22].

4.2 Implementation Details

The experiments in this paper are mainly divided into two parts. The first part is the comparison between the RLPnP and other spectral reconstruction methods, including three model-based methods (*i.e.*, a total variation-based method (TV) [3], a sparse representation-based method (NSR) [23], a low-rank matrix approximation-based method (LRMA) [11]) and two learning-based methods (*i.e.*, HSCNN method [30], Autoencoder-based method (Autoencoder) [6]).

The second part is the ablation study, *i.e.*, the comparison between the RLPnP spectral image reconstruction method and other methods with different parameters tuning policies. 1. Fixed parameters method (fixed, $\sigma = 40$). The denoising strength σ and penalty factor ρ are determined before starting the iteration and fixed during the iteration. 2. Handcrafted tuning parameters method (handcrafted). As the number of iterations increases, the denoising strength σ is reduced from a larger value 50 to a smaller value 40 by log function. From the corresponding equation $\sigma = \sqrt{\frac{\lambda}{\rho}}$ to get penalty factor ρ (fixed parameter λ), which is used in IRCNN [32]. 3. Greedy tuning parameters method (greedy). A value range of the denoising strength σ is divided before the iteration starts. Then each iteration selects the optimal parameters and intermediate states from the results within the preset parameter range, $e.g.$, $\sigma = (50, 45)$. Meanwhile, the number of iterations for all methods is set to 30.

Our method uses the RL algorithm to adjust the parameters in the PnP method (terminal time τ, denoising strength σ and penalty factor ρ), so it is necessary to set the relevant parameters: according to experience and actual running effects, set the number of iterations to 5 and the maximum time step to 6, $i.e.$, a total of 30 iterations at most. The Adam optimizer is used to optimize the network, and the batch size is 10. The learning rates of the policy and value networks are respectively set to 1×10^{-3} and 3×10^{-4}, but after 1000 iterations, reduce to 3×10^{-4} and 1×10^{-4} to improve learning efficiency. The experiment is set up to perform 10 gradient updates of network parameters in each training iteration.

4.3   Results

Table 1 shows the experimental results of the RLPnP and other computational spectral reconstruction methods on the ICVL dataset. From Table 1, we can see that the PSNR index of other methods is lower than 30dB and the SSIM index is lower than 0.95. The proposed method outperforms other methods.

Table 1. Reconstructed results of different methods on ICVL

Methods	PSNR	SSIM	ERGAS
TV [3]	26.1524	0.8921	15.3213
NSR [23]	27.9382	0.8974	12.3244
LRMA [11]	29.9748	0.9265	9.9027
HSCNN [30]	29.4753	0.9281	10.037
Autoencoder [6]	29.3929	0.9185	10.4887
RLPnP	**30.4466**	**0.9543**	**9.1312**

In addition, three groups of comparative visualization results are randomly selected from the 50 test results, and the data is selected from spectral image results of all compared methods, as shown in Fig. 3. It can be seen that RLPnP produces visually pleasing results with fewer artifacts and sharper edges, which is consistent with numerical metrics.

The experimental results of the parameter tuning comparison between the PnP methods are shown in Table 2. In contrast, the performance of RLPnP achieves better in various evaluation indicators.

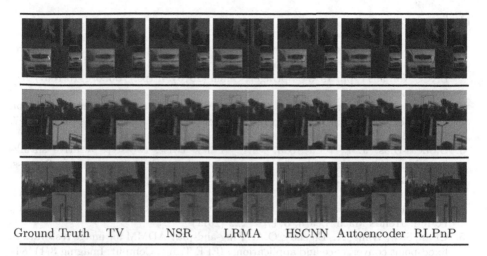

Ground Truth   TV   NSR   LRMA   HSCNN Autoencoder RLPnP

Fig. 3. Visual quality comparison of different methods on ICVL

Table 2. Reconstructed results of different policies on ICVL

Metrics	Greedy	Handcrafted	Fixed	RLPnP
PSNR	29.8509	29.7004	29.611	**30.4466**
SSIM	0.9486	0.9512	0.949	**0.9543**
ERGAS	12.0297	11.6826	12.7645	**9.1312**

5 Conclusion

In this paper, we present RLPnP, a PnP reconstruction method based on reinforcement learning. It can train an appropriate policy network and value network through deep reinforcement learning, and adaptively adjust the parameters for every images in the PnP method. According to the experiments, we demonstrate that the policy network can generate suitable parameters, and can show high-quality hyperspectral reconstruction results in comparison with other methods of the same type and methods with different parameter settings.

In future, it is worth investigating how to improve RL algorithm, especially the policy setting, to conserve computing resources and improve algorithm performance.

Acknowledgments. This work was supported by the National Natural Science Foundation of China under Grants No. 62171038, No. 61827901, and No. 62088101.

References

1. Arad, B., Ben-Shahar, O.: Sparse recovery of hyperspectral signal from natural RGB images. In: Leibe, B., Matas, J., Sebe, N., Welling, M. (eds.) ECCV 2016. LNCS, vol. 9911, pp. 19–34. Springer, Cham (2016). https://doi.org/10.1007/978-3-319-46478-7_2
2. Basedow, R.W., Carmer, D.C., Anderson, M.E.: Hydice system: implementation and performance. In: Proceedings of Imaging Spectrometry, vol. 2480, pp. 258–267. SPIE (1995)
3. Bioucas-Dias, J.M., Figueiredo, M.A.: A new twist: two-step iterative shrinkage/thresholding algorithms for image restoration. IEEE Trans. Image Process. **16**(12), 2992–3004 (2007)
4. Boyd, S., Parikh, N., Chu, E., Peleato, B., Eckstein, J., et al.: Distributed optimization and statistical learning via the alternating direction method of multipliers. Found. Trends Mach. Learn. **3**(1), 1–122 (2011)
5. Chan, S.H., Wang, X., Elgendy, O.A.: Plug-and-play ADMM for image restoration: fixed-point convergence and applications. IEEE Trans. Comput. Imaging **3**(1), 84–98 (2016)
6. Choi, I., Kim, M., Gutierrez, D., Jeon, D., Nam, G.: High-quality hyperspectral reconstruction using a spectral prior. Technical report (2017)
7. Dabov, K., Foi, A., Katkovnik, V., Egiazarian, K.: Image denoising by sparse 3-D transform-domain collaborative filtering. IEEE Trans. Image Process. **16**(8), 2080–2095 (2007)
8. Donoho, D.L.: Compressed sensing. IEEE Trans. Inf. Theory **52**(4), 1289–1306 (2006)
9. Feng, Y.Z., Sun, D.W.: Application of hyperspectral imaging in food safety inspection and control: a review. Crit. Rev. Food Sci. Nutr. **52**(11), 1039–1058 (2012)
10. Fu, Y., Lam, A., Sato, I., Sato, Y.: Adaptive spatial-spectral dictionary learning for hyperspectral image restoration. Int. J. Comput. Vision **122**(2), 228–245 (2017)
11. Fu, Y., Zheng, Y., Sato, I., Sato, Y.: Exploiting spectral-spatial correlation for coded hyperspectral image restoration. In: Proceedings of the IEEE Conference on Computer Vision and Pattern Recognition, pp. 3727–3736 (2016)
12. He, K., Zhang, X., Ren, S., Sun, J.: Deep residual learning for image recognition. In: Proceedings of the IEEE Conference on Computer Vision and Pattern Recognition, pp. 770–778 (2016)
13. Huang, H., Nie, G., Zheng, Y., Fu, Y.: Image restoration from patch-based compressed sensing measurement. Neurocomputing **340**, 145–157 (2019)
14. Lai, Z., Wei, K., Fu, Y.: Deep plug-and-play prior for hyperspectral image restoration. Neurocomputing **481**, 281–293 (2022)
15. Lillicrap, T.P., et al.: Continuous control with deep reinforcement learning. arXiv preprint arXiv:1509.02971 (2015)
16. Hohmann, M., et al.: In-vivo multispectral video endoscopy towards in-vivo hyperspectral video endoscopy. J. Biophotonics **10**(4), 553–564 (2016)
17. Ono, S.: Primal-dual plug-and-play image restoration. IEEE Signal Process. Lett. **24**(8), 1108–1112 (2017)
18. Plaza, A., et al.: Recent advances in techniques for hyperspectral image processing. Remote Sens. Environ. **113**, S110–S122 (2009)
19. Rick Chang, J., Li, C.L., Poczos, B., Vijaya Kumar, B., Sankaranarayanan, A.C.: One network to solve them all-solving linear inverse problems using deep projection models. In: Proceedings of the IEEE International Conference on Computer Vision, pp. 5888–5897 (2017)

20. Tirer, T., Giryes, R.: Image restoration by iterative denoising and backward projections. IEEE Trans. Image Process. **28**(3), 1220–1234 (2018)
21. Wagadarikar, A., John, R., Willett, R., Brady, D.: Single disperser design for coded aperture snapshot spectral imaging. Appl. Opt. **47**(10), B44-51 (2008)
22. Wald, L.: Quality of high resolution synthesised images: is there a simple criterion? In: Proceedings of Third Conference Fusion of Earth Data: Merging Point Measurements, Raster Maps and Remotely Sensed Images, pp. 99–103. SEE/URISCA (2000)
23. Wang, L., Xiong, Z., Shi, G., Wu, F., Zeng, W.: Adaptive nonlocal sparse representation for dual-camera compressive hyperspectral imaging. IEEE Trans. Pattern Anal. Mach. Intell. **39**(10), 2104–2111 (2017)
24. Wang, L., Xiong, Z., Gao, D., Shi, G., Wu, F.: Dual-camera design for coded aperture snapshot spectral imaging. Appl. Opt. **54**(4), 848–858 (2015)
25. Wang, L., Xiong, Z., Gao, D., Shi, G., Zeng, W., Wu, F.: High-speed hyperspectral video acquisition with a dual-camera architecture. In: Proceedings of the IEEE Conference on Computer Vision and Pattern Recognition, pp. 4942–4950 (2015)
26. Wang, L., Zhang, T., Fu, Y., Huang, H.: Hyperreconnet: joint coded aperture optimization and image reconstruction for compressive hyperspectral imaging. IEEE Trans. Image Process. **28**(5), 2257–2270 (2018)
27. Wang, Z., Bovik, A.C., Sheikh, H.R., Simoncelli, E.P.: Image quality assessment: from error visibility to structural similarity. IEEE Trans. Image Process. **13**(4), 600–612 (2004)
28. Wei, K., Fu, Y.: Low-rank Bayesian tensor factorization for hyperspectral image denoising. Neurocomputing **331**, 412–423 (2019)
29. Wei, K., Fu, Y., Huang, H.: 3-D quasi-recurrent neural network for hyperspectral image denoising. IEEE Trans. Neural Netw. Learn. Syst. **32**(1), 363–375 (2020)
30. Xiong, Z., Shi, Z., Li, H., Wang, L., Liu, D., Wu, F.: HSCNN: CNN-based hyperspectral image recovery from spectrally undersampled projections. In: Proceedings of the IEEE International Conference on Computer Vision Workshops, pp. 518–525 (2017)
31. Yamaguchi, M., et al.: High-fidelity video and still-image communication based on spectral information: natural vision system and its applications. In: Proceedings of Spectral Imaging: Eighth International Symposium on Multispectral Color Science, vol. 6062, pp. 129–140. SPIE (2006)
32. Zhang, K., Zuo, W., Gu, S., Zhang, L.: Learning deep CNN denoiser prior for image restoration. In: Proceedings of the IEEE Conference on Computer Vision and Pattern Recognition, pp. 3929–3938 (2017)

AGFNet: Attention Guided Fusion Network for Camouflaged Object Detection

Zeyu Zhao[1], Zhihao Liu[1], and Chenglei Peng[1,2(✉)]

[1] School of Electronic Science and Engineering, Nanjing University, Nanjing, China
pcl@nju.edu.cn
[2] Nanjing Institute of Advanced Artificial Intelligence, Nanjing, China

Abstract. The camouflaged object detection (COD) task is challenging because of the high similarity between target and background. Most of the existing COD methods are based on the transfer learning of salient object detection (SOD) network, which is not efficient for the COD task. It is also difficult to accurately capture the edge information of the object after the coarse-grained localization of the camouflaged object. In this paper, we propose a novel network: Attention Guided Fusion Network (AGFNet), for the task of COD. We use low-level and high-level features to extract edge and semantic information. To solve the problem of discriminating and localizing the camouflaged object, we adopt a dual-attention module, which can selectively determine the more discriminate information of the camouflaged object. In addition, our method applies a module to fuse edge and semantic information for refinement to generate sharp edges. The experiments demonstrate the effectiveness and superiority of the proposed network over state-of-the-art methods.

Keywords: Camouflaged object detection · Attention mechanism · Feature fusion

1 Introduction

Camouflage is the concealment of an animal or object by any combination of material, coloration, or illumination that makes the target object difficult to detect or disguises it as something else [23]. Existing methods used for camouflaged object detection (COD) are categorized into two types, salient object detection (SOD) and generic object detection (GOD). The networks proposed for SOD [17,27,34] and GOD [8,16,35] do not perform as well on the camouflaged object detection dataset, which further illustrates the difficulty and distinctiveness of the COD task. Those models designed explicitly for COD [3,4,12,19] concentrate on how to extract features to discern and locate camouflaged objects. However, ignorance of much edge information makes it difficult to trace the

This work was supported by Natural Science Foundation of Jiangsu Province of China via Grant BK20211149.

L. Fang et al. (Eds.): CICAI 2022, LNAI 13604, pp. 478–489, 2022.
https://doi.org/10.1007/978-3-031-20497-5_39

contour of the camouflaged object accurately. Therefore, this paper focuses on extracting rich edge and semantic information from existing encoder-decoder structures and fusing them to generate the final feature map.

Much of the previous work use side-outputs across a network to extract distinct features [2–4,19]. However, these approaches ignore the implication of network depth and utilize all of the side-outputs to extract semantic information. Low-level and high-level maps can effectively extract edge features and semantic information. Therefore we can extract the corresponding features by processing the deep and shallow side-outputs differently, which increases the efficiency and interpretability of the network. Multi-level aggregation is emphasized in the decoder to incorporate multi-level representations. Some existing studies propose methods that minimize discrepancies in implementing the feature fusion [21,25,31], and others aggregate several layers of side-outputs directly to obtain a decoded feature map [2,3,27]. To further improve the performance of the network, it is essential to adopt methods selectively according to different characteristics over different levels and highlight critical parts of encoded features in the downstream processing phrases.

This study proposes an attention-guided fusion network that fuses edge information and semantic information. We focus on extracting edge information in the shallow encoder and use edge truth maps for deep supervision. Considering the unbalanced data distribution in the edge ground truth, we utilize a class-balancing loss function. We are dedicated to detecting semantic features in the deep encoder to discriminate and localize the object. Then we apply multi-level receptive fields block, inner-layer union, and dual-attention after the shallow and deep encoder. Multi-level receptive field block emphasizes learning rich hierarchical representations. The inner-layer aggregation module incorporates three layers of features to minimize discrepancies between different layers of features. The dual-attention determines the critical part in the channel-wise and spatial-wise features to respectively generate the edge feature map and first object feature map in the shallow and deep phrase. Subsequently, we use two feature maps to guide the fusing edge and semantic information training. We supervise the hidden layers in the fusion process, save them as feature maps, and finally get the prediction map by calculating their average.

2   Related Work

COD. The research on COD has a tremendous impact on advancing our understanding of visual perception, which has a long and rich history in biology and the arts [23]. Existing approaches can be classified into two categories: handcrafted low-level feature-based models and deep learning-based networks. Traditional models rely on handcrafted features (color, texture, motion, etc.) [6,15,18,24] to represent the object. These methods work for a few simple cases but often fail in complex scenes. ANet [12] proposes an end-to-end network to classify and separate camouflaged objects. MGL [30] initially locates the camouflaged object and then leverages information of mutual graph feature to smelt boundaries of the camouflaged object. Fan et al. propose SINet [3], which contains two primary modules: the search module and the identification module. They also constructed a COD dataset COD10K.

Attention Mechanism. Once the attention mechanism was proposed, it was widely used in various tasks to extract informative features and achieved excellent results. SE Block [9] utilizes attention modules, which assign different weights to channels to reinforce those channels that significantly impact the results. CBAM [26] successively uses attention modules in channels and spatial dimensions to extract discriminate features. For the COD task, PFNet [19] employs self-attention modules in the channel and spatial dimension consecutively to locate the camouflaged object. Another proposed method, PRANet [4], utilizes reverse attention to guide model training and refines the feature step by step.

Edge Refinement. It has been proved that enhancing edge features can improve the performance of object detection since the pixels closer to the edges are less predictable. To improve the accuracy of SOD, available studies [5,22,28,33] use various methods to represent edge features and use these features to refine the prediction. However, previous approaches do not use edge refinement modules in the COD task. The use of these modules is fundamental when we need to retain sharp edges.

3   Our Method

In this section, we introduce the AGFNet, which consists of a backbone encoder network and three attention-guided decoder modules (i.e., edge detection, semantic features extraction and fusion refinement), as illustrated in Fig. 1.

3.1   Architecture Overview

The model proposed in this study is a deeply-supervised network, where the final prediction feature is supervised along with some hidden layers, which has been proved to improve the performance and enhance the generalization ability [13]. As shown in Fig. 1, multi-level receptive fields block (MRFB) processes the five sets of features extracted from the backbone network. And the shallow features are used for edge information extraction while the deep features are utilized for semantic representations collection. We combine the information of both to generate the final prediction feature map. Our model utilize a set of training data, denoted as $S = \{(X_n, Y_n, E_n), n = 1, ..., N\}$, where $X_n = \left\{x_j^{(n)}, j = 1, \ldots, |X_n|\right\}$ represents input graph, $Y_n = \left\{y_j^{(n)}, j = 1, \ldots, |X_n|\right\}, y_j^{(n)} \in \{0, 1\}$ denotes ground truth corresponding to the input, $E_n = \left\{e_j^{(n)}, j = 1, \ldots, |X_n|\right\}, e_j^{(n)} \in \{0, 1\}$ denotes the edge truth corresponding to the input. Similar to many existing object detection networks, our algorithm uses backbone network to encode the input graph and then decode features along with specialized modules. We

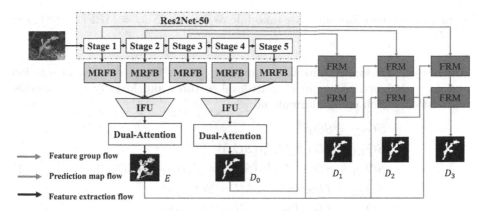

Fig. 1. Architecture overview. The input is processed by the extraction flow (black line) to extract the semantic feature map and edge feature map as the prediction. The orange line indicates the feature group flow, while the green line shows the prediction map flow. The prediction map and feature groups are continuously interacted in the fusion refinement module (FRM) to complement each other and to obtain new prediction maps and feature groups. (Color figure online)

adopt Res2Net-50 [7] as the backbone network, which contains 5 stages with five side-outputs, denoted as $SO = (SO^1, ..., SO^5)$. $\{SO^1, SO^2, SO^3\}$ are used as input for edge detection, described in Subsect. 3.2, $\{SO^3, SO^4, SO^5\}$ are used as input features for discriminating and localizing semantic information mining, described in Subsect. 3.3. Finally, we use Inner-later Features Union (IFU) and Dual-Attention Block to process the above side-outputs group and combine the edge information and semantic information with discrimination and location function to generate the final prediction feature map. We will discuss this in Subsect. 3.4.

3.2 Edge Features Extraction

Multi-level Receptive Field Block. Detecting small objects is critical for COD performance. Motivated by this, we process each output with MRFB to diversify the receptive field, focusing on global and local features with multiple receptive fields. Because the channel size and resolution of the side outputs at different stages are different, we use features of different sizes to represent these side-outputs. For shallow (1, 2, 3) and deep (3, 4, 5) stages, the channel size is separately reduced to 32, 64, and 128 by a 3×3 convolution operation. MRFB includes one residual connection and four independent branches $\{b_i,$ i $=$ 1, 2, 3, 4$\}$ with different kernel size and dilation rate. The four branches use a 1×1 convolution operation at first. Then a $(2i - 1) \times 1$ convolution operation, a $1 \times (2i - 1)$ convolution operation, and a dilated convolution operation with dilation rate $(2i - 1)$ are followed on branches b_2, b_3, b_4. Finally, we concatenate these features and reduce channel size to the initial size with a 1×1 convolution operation. We can formulate this module as follows: $SO_i = \text{MRFB}\left(SO^i\right), i = 1, ..., 5$.

Inner-layer Features Union. Inspired by [27], a inner-layer features union module is designed to combine multi-level features and identify more specific information, which can be formulated as:

$$
\begin{aligned}
SO_{3\_1} &= SO_3 \\
SO_{2\_1} &= SO_2 \otimes f\left(Up\left(SO_3\right)\right) \\
SO_{1\_1} &= SO_1 \otimes f\left(Up\left(SO_2\right)\right) \otimes f\left(Up\left(Up\left(SO_3\right)\right)\right) \\
SO_{2\_2} &= f\left(\text{cat}\left[SO_{2\_1}, f\left(Up\left(SO_{3\_1}\right)\right)\right]\right) \\
SO_{1\_2} &= f\left(\text{cat}\left[SO_{1\_1}, f\left(Up\left(SO_{2\_2}\right)\right)\right]\right)
\end{aligned}
\tag{1}
$$

where $f(\cdot)$ denotes a 3×3 convolutional operation and cat $(\cdot)$ means a channel-wise concatenation operation. The subscripts indicate the intermediate variables for the processing of SO_i, where SO_{i_1} means the features after the first step of processing SO_i and SO_{i_2} denotes the features after further process of SO_{i_1}. Different feature maps have different channels and resolutions, so upsample operation $Up(\cdot)$ is utilized before element-wise multiplication $\otimes$.

Dual-Attention. Inspired by [14], this module is designed to detect the more substantial context in the representations, as shown in Fig. 2. This module has two successive sub-modules: channel attention and spatial attention. In the channel attention module, we first use global average pooling (GAP) to reduce the feature size to 1 for each channel. This is followed by three 3×3 convolution operations to obtain three vectors: Q_s, K_s, and V_s. The channel-wise weight vector, denoted as α, is generated as follows:

$$
\alpha = \text{Softmax}(Q_s K_s^T) V_s \tag{2}
$$

To determine more discriminate parts of the aggregated features SO_{1_2}, we apply channel-wise weight vector as follows: $X = (SO_{1\_2} \otimes \alpha + SO_{1\_2})$. Finally, we regularize and perform a mask operation to X. The mask operation means to exclude the channels with α values in the last 10%. Then in the spatial attention module, the output of the channel attention module is processed by three 3×3 convolution operations to reduce channel size to 1 and generate 3 vectors: Q_c, K_c, and V_c. The decoded edge feature map is retained as follows: $E = \text{Softmax}(Q_c K_c^T) V_c$.

Class-Balancing Loss. For the edge ground truth of a standard image, the distribution of edges and non-edges is considerably biased which results in the malfunction of prediction. We utilize the same loss function as [29], which is tackled as follow:

$$
\ell\left(W\right) = -\beta \sum_{j \in E^+} \log \sigma\left(y_j = 1 \mid X; W\right) - (1 - \beta) \sum_{j \in E^-} \log \sigma\left(y_j = 0 \mid X; W\right)
\tag{3}
$$

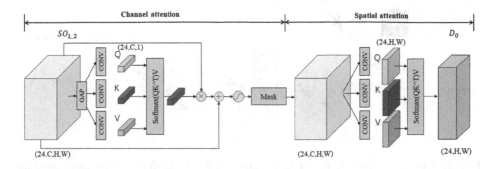

Fig. 2. Dual-attention. It illustrates implementing details of two sub-modules: channel attention module and spatial attention module.

where E^- and E^+ denote non-edge and edge pixels in ground truth. β is calculated as follows: $\beta = \frac{Y^-}{Y^- + Y^+}$. And we assign a weight to the result, as shown in Eq. 4.

$$\mathcal{L}(W) = \alpha \times \ell(W) \tag{4}$$

where α is a hyper-parameter. The detailed reason and value of the setting are described in Sect. 4.1.

3.3 Semantic Features Extraction

For the features encoded in the third, fourth and fifth stages of the backbone network, we adopt a similar approach to decode the features encoded in the first, second and third stages. Firstly, the features are processed with the MRFB in Subsect. 3.2 Multi-level receptive field block, aiming to expand the perception field to consider both local and global information. Secondly, the features after MRFB are aggregated, and the way performs the aggregation of the three features is shown in Subsect. 3.2 Inner-layer features union. Finally, we utilize the Dual Attention Module to extract concealed information from the channel and spatial dimension, so that our network focus only on the detection of the camouflaged objects. With the Dual Attention module used for representations learning, we roughly capture the camouflaged object and generate parameter D_0, which contains the discriminate information of whether it is camouflaged and the localization information of the object.

The traditional cross-entropy loss function is strongly influenced by data distribution. Moreover, we should emphasize pixels that are close to the edges. Considering the outstanding performance of the adaptive pixel intensity loss function [14], we adopt this as our loss function.

3.4 Fusion Refinement

We now have an edge feature map and a decoded feature map of the object. Motivated by [27], we design a fusion refinement module (FRM) to continuously

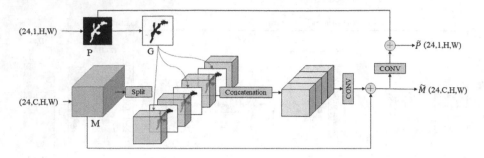

Fig. 3. Fusion refinement. It illustrates the details of the fusion refinement module (FRM), which contains two inputs (P and M) and two outputs ($\tilde{P}$ and $\tilde{M}$).

refine the prediction by utilizing edge feature and decoded feature to complement and correct existing features. As shown in Fig. 3, each module contains two inputs (P and M) and two outputs (refined feature map, denoted as $\tilde{P}$, and a set of refined features, denoted as $\tilde{M}$). The guidance map is obtained as follows: $G = -\operatorname{sigmoid}(P) + 1$. We split the other input features into several groups and put G in the middle of every two groups. Subsequently, we concatenate them and perform a 3×3 convolution operation to reduce the channel size to C. We sum these features with the initial input features, denoted as $\tilde{M}$. Then we use $\tilde{M}$ as one output. Moreover, we perform a 3×3 convolution operation on $\tilde{M}$ to reduce channel size to 1. The other output is represented by the sum of this feature and P, denoted as $\tilde{P}$.

As illustrated in Fig. 1, the network contains six fusion refinement modules. The three modules on the up side input $D_i, (i = 0, 1, 2)$ as P and input SO^1, SO^2, SO^3 as M. Then they output three sets of refined features, denoted as $\tilde{M}$. The three modules on the down side input them as M and input E as P. Finally, they output three decoded camouflaged object feature map: D_i, $(i = 1, 2, 3)$.

4   Experiments

4.1   Implementation Details

Dataset. Since camouflage object detection is a relatively new task with limited relevant datasets, we combine CHAMELEON [20], CAMO [12], and COD10K [3] as datasets in this paper. The CAMO dataset has 2500 images, of which 2000 are used for train and 500 for test. It has two subsets, CAMO and MS-CAMO, having 1250 images each. COD10K is the largest camouflage object detection dataset up to now, containing 10,000 images, of which 6,000 were used for train and 4,000 for test. In this paper, we use the training sets of CAMO and COD10K. The CHAMELEON dataset has 76 images, so it is only used for test.

Data Augmentation. We enhance the dataset by flipping, cropping, rotating, and changing the brightness, contrast, color balance, and sharpness of images. The data might be flipped left and right when loaded with half probability while being clipped within the bounds of 30. For the rotation, the probability of 0.2 is set, and the rotation angle is randomly selected from 15° clockwise to 15° counterclockwise. Finally, the color space of pictures is also enhanced by four aspects: brightness, contrast, color balance, and sharpness. In addition, to further strengthen the diversity of the dataset, we also set random salt and pepper noise to the images to improve the robustness of the network.

Experiments Settings. This paper utilizes the COD benchmark [2], using the CAMO test set, CHAMELEON dataset, and COD10K test set for testing and evaluation. The network is implemented with PyTorch, using Adam optimizer [11]. The batch size is set to 24 and the initial learning rate is set to 0.00005. The network is trained on an NVIDIA RTX3090 GPU with 24G memory. The edge feature map is multiplied by a parameter when calculating the class-balancing loss function, and this parameter is set to 100. The primary purpose of this weight is to keep the loss function value of the edge and the loss function value of the camouflaged object in the same order of magnitude. Therefore, updating the parameters can be kept at the same speed during backpropagation in case one side is over-fitting while the other is under-fitting.

4.2 Comparison with Other Methods

Quantitative Results. As shown in Table 1, this paper achieved the best results on the MAE metric on the CHAMELEON dataset. Although it did not perform the best on the other three evaluated metrics, we also achieved values very close to the best ones. We achieved the best evaluation results in the CAMO test set in all four data. In the COD10K test set, the best results were obtained for MAE and F_β^w while the best results were obtained for the other two indicators. All in all, our network model achieves excellent performance over state-of-the-art algorithms.

Qualitative Results. The comparison with the qualitative analysis of other networks from Fig. 4 shows that the detection of our model is the most accurate one, especially in the second figure, other models are vague for the second object, but the result of our model is clearer. The other models in the fourth picture only detect the human head but not the human body. The detection result in the fifth image shows that our model result is the clearest and has no unnecessary information.

4.3 Ablation Studies

To verify the effectiveness of edge information refinement for camouflaged object detection, we make ablation experiments in this section. In the fusion refinement

Table 1. Results of our model compared with 13 other models. ↑ indicates the higher the score better. The best scores are highlighted in bold.

Model	CHAMELEON				CAMO-Test				COD10K-Test			
	S_α ↑	E_ϕ ↑	F_β^W ↑	M ↓	S_α ↑	E_ϕ ↑	F_β^W ↑	M ↓	S_α ↑	E_ϕ ↑	F_β^W ↑	M ↓
FPN [16]	0.794	0.783	0.590	0.075	0.684	0.677	0.483	0.131	0.697	0.691	0.411	0.075
MaskRCNN [8]	0.643	0.778	0.518	0.099	0.574	0.715	0.430	0.151	0.613	0.748	0.402	0.080
PSPNet [32]	0.773	0.758	0.555	0.085	0.663	0.659	0.455	0.139	0.678	0.680	0.377	0.080
UNet++ [35]	0.695	0.762	0.501	0.094	0.599	0.653	0.392	0.149	0.623	0.672	0.350	0.086
PiCANet [17]	0.769	0.749	0.536	0.085	0.609	0.584	0.356	0.156	0.649	0.643	0.322	0.090
MSRCNN [10]	0.637	0.686	0.443	0.091	0.617	0.669	0.454	0.133	0.641	0.706	0.419	0.073
PFANet [34]	0.679	0.648	0.378	0.144	0.659	0.622	0.391	0.172	0.636	0.618	0.286	0.128
CPD [27]	0.853	0.866	0.706	0.052	0.726	0.729	0.550	0.115	0.747	0.770	0.508	0.059
HTC [1]	0.517	0.489	0.204	0.129	0.476	0.442	0.174	0.172	0.548	0.520	0.221	0.088
ANet-SRM [12]	-	-	-	-	0.682	0.685	0.484	0.126	-	-	-	-
EGNet [33]	0.848	0.870	0.702	0.050	0.732	0.768	0.583	0.104	0.737	0.779	0.509	0.056
PraNet [4]	0.860	**0.907**	**0.763**	0.044	0.769	0.824	0.663	0.094	**0.789**	**0.861**	0.629	0.045
SINet [3]	**0.869**	0.891	0.740	0.044	0.751	0.771	0.606	0.100	0.771	0.806	0.551	0.051
Ours	0.831	0.869	0.751	**0.034**	**0.778**	**0.827**	**0.689**	**0.071**	0.780	0.817	**0.639**	**0.036**

Subsect. 3.4, we remove guiding attention modules about edge features for training. As in Table 2, we kept three decimal places for all evaluation values and the best performance in that evaluation metric is indicated in bold (when some metrics in the figure are equal in value, the specific comparison refers to the case of the value after the thousandth percentile). Comparing the fused edge information with the non-fused edge information, it is obvious that the performance after fusing the edge information is better than that without fusing. In summary, fusing edge information can bring more detailed edges to the final prediction graph of the model and improve the performance in general.

Table 2. Ablation analysis. We do ablation analysis for the selection of prediction map and the presence of FRM with edge feature map. Selection 'LAST' means selecting D_3 as the final map, while 'AVERAGE' means the average of the D_0, D_1, D_2, and D_3.

Modules	Selection		FR with E		CHAMELEON				CAMO-Test				COD10K-Test			
	LAST	AVERAGE	yes	no	S_α ↑	E_ϕ ↑	F_β^W ↑	M ↓	S_α ↑	E_ϕ ↑	F_β^W ↑	M ↓	S_α ↑	E_ϕ ↑	F_β^W ↑	M ↓
1		✓	✓		0.831	0.869	0.751	**0.034**	0.778	0.827	**0.689**	**0.071**	0.780	0.817	**0.639**	0.036
2		✓		✓	**0.836**	**0.887**	**0.761**	0.035	0.763	0.801	0.666	0.079	0.769	0.804	0.621	0.037
3	✓		✓		0.833	0.872	0.747	0.035	**0.780**	**0.827**	0.686	0.072	**0.780**	**0.824**	0.634	0.037
4	✓			✓	0.835	0.887	0.761	0.035	0.763	0.801	0.666	0.079	0.769	0.803	0.620	0.037

In addition, we also test the influence of selecting different output feature maps (D_0, D_1, D_2, D_3) as the final prediction map. The results, shown in Table 2, indicate that the performance of the two selection ways is very similar and each performs better in some metrics. The average of four maps is determined as the final result because we focus more on the performance of the MAE and F_β^W metrics.

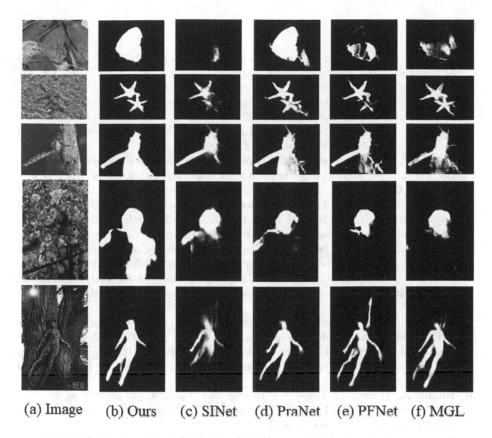

(a) Image   (b) Ours   (c) SINet   (d) PraNet   (e) PFNet   (f) MGL

Fig. 4. Qualitative results of our AGFNet and other typical networks.

5   Conclusion

In this paper, we studied existing COD frameworks and found their shortcomings. Subsequently, we further mined some practical modules from SOD and designed some novel modules according to the specificity of COD. Based on these, we propose a novel network: AGFNet. It both extracts the edge and semantic information with different multi-level receptive fields. Moreover, we apply the dual-attention module to determine more essential parts of the features. We finally obtain both sharp edges and precise object semantics by fusing edge and semantic representations with a fusion refinement module. Extensive experiments demonstrate that our model is competitive compared with other SOTA methods.

References

1. Chen, K., et al.: Hybrid task cascade for instance segmentation. In: Proceedings of the IEEE/CVF Conference on Computer Vision and Pattern Recognition, pp. 4974–4983 (2019)
2. Fan, D.P., Ji, G.P., Cheng, M.M., Shao, L.: Concealed object detection. IEEE Trans. Pattern Anal. Mach. Intell. (2021)
3. Fan, D.P., Ji, G.P., Sun, G., Cheng, M.M., Shen, J., Shao, L.: Camouflaged object detection. In: IEEE CVPR, pp. 2777–2787 (2020)
4. Fan, D.-P., et al.: PraNet: parallel reverse attention network for polyp segmentation. In: Martel, A.L., et al. (eds.) MICCAI 2020. LNCS, vol. 12266, pp. 263–273. Springer, Cham (2020). https://doi.org/10.1007/978-3-030-59725-2_26
5. Feng, M., Lu, H., Ding, E.: Attentive feedback network for boundary-aware salient object detection. In: Proceedings of the IEEE/CVF Conference on Computer Vision and Pattern Recognition, pp. 1623–1632 (2019)
6. Galun, M., Sharon, E., Basri, R., Brandt, A.: Texture segmentation by multiscale aggregation of filter responses and shape elements. In: ICCV, vol. 3, p. 716 (2003)
7. Gao, S.H., Cheng, M.M., Zhao, K., Zhang, X.Y., Yang, M.H., Torr, P.: Res2Net: a new multi-scale backbone architecture. IEEE Trans. Pattern Anal. Mach. Intell. **43**(2), 652–662 (2019)
8. He, K., Gkioxari, G., Dollár, P., Girshick, R.: Mask R-CNN. In: Proceedings of the IEEE International Conference on Computer Vision, pp. 2961–2969 (2017)
9. Hu, J., Shen, L., Sun, G.: Squeeze-and-excitation networks. In: Proceedings of the IEEE Conference on Computer Vision and Pattern Recognition, pp. 7132–7141 (2018)
10. Huang, Z., Huang, L., Gong, Y., Huang, C., Wang, X.: Mask scoring R-CNN. In: Proceedings of the IEEE/CVF Conference on Computer Vision and Pattern Recognition, pp. 6409–6418 (2019)
11. Kingma, D.P., Ba, J.: Adam: a method for stochastic optimization. arXiv preprint arXiv:1412.6980 (2014)
12. Le, T.N., Nguyen, T.V., Nie, Z., Tran, M.T., Sugimoto, A.: Anabranch network for camouflaged object segmentation. Comput. Vis. Image Underst. **184**, 45–56 (2019)
13. Lee, C.Y., Xie, S., Gallagher, P., Zhang, Z., Tu, Z.: Deeply-supervised nets. In: Artificial Intelligence and Statistics, pp. 562–570. PMLR (2015)
14. Lee, M.S., Shin, W., Han, S.W.: Tracer: extreme attention guided salient object tracing network. arXiv preprint arXiv:2112.07380 (2021)
15. Li, S., Florencio, D., Zhao, Y., Cook, C., Li, W.: Foreground detection in camouflaged scenes. In: 2017 IEEE International Conference on Image Processing (ICIP), pp. 4247–4251. IEEE (2017)
16. Lin, T.Y., Dollár, P., Girshick, R., He, K., Hariharan, B., Belongie, S.: Feature pyramid networks for object detection. In: Proceedings of the IEEE Conference on Computer Vision and Pattern Recognition, pp. 2117–2125 (2017)
17. Liu, N., Han, J., Yang, M.H.: Picanet: learning pixel-wise contextual attention for saliency detection. In: Proceedings of the IEEE Conference on Computer Vision and Pattern Recognition, pp. 3089–3098 (2018)
18. Liu, Z., Huang, K., Tan, T.: Foreground object detection using top-down information based on EM framework. IEEE Trans. Image Process. **21**(9), 4204–4217 (2012)

19. Mei, H., Ji, G.P., Wei, Z., Yang, X., Wei, X., Fan, D.P.: Camouflaged object segmentation with distraction mining. In: Proceedings of the IEEE/CVF Conference on Computer Vision and Pattern Recognition, pp. 8772–8781 (2021)
20. Skurowski, P., Abdulameer, H., Baszczyk, J., Depta, T., Kornacki, A., Kozie, P.: Animal camouflage analysis: chameleon database (2018)
21. Pang, Y., Li, Y., Shen, J., Shao, L.: Towards bridging semantic gap to improve semantic segmentation. In: Proceedings of the IEEE/CVF International Conference on Computer Vision, pp. 4230–4239 (2019)
22. Qin, X., Zhang, Z., Huang, C., Gao, C., Dehghan, M., Jagersand, M.: Basnet: boundary-aware salient object detection. In: Proceedings of the IEEE/CVF Conference on Computer Vision and Pattern Recognition, pp. 7479–7489 (2019)
23. Stevens, M., Merilaita, S.: Animal camouflage: current issues and new perspectives. Philos. Trans. R. Soc. B Biol. Sci. **364**(1516), 423–427 (2009)
24. Tankus, A., Yeshurun, Y.: Convexity-based visual camouflage breaking. Comput. Vis. Image Underst. **82**(3), 208–237 (2001)
25. Wei, J., Wang, S., Huang, Q.: F^3net: fusion, feedback and focus for salient object detection. In: Proceedings of the AAAI Conference on Artificial Intelligence, vol. 34, pp. 12321–12328 (2020)
26. Woo, S., Park, J., Lee, J.Y., Kweon, I.S.: CBAM: convolutional block attention module. In: Proceedings of the European Conference on Computer Vision (ECCV), pp. 3–19 (2018)
27. Wu, Z., Su, L., Huang, Q.: Cascaded partial decoder for fast and accurate salient object detection. In: Proceedings of the IEEE/CVF Conference on Computer Vision and Pattern Recognition, pp. 3907–3916 (2019)
28. Wu, Z., Su, L., Huang, Q.: Stacked cross refinement network for edge-aware salient object detection. In: Proceedings of the IEEE/CVF International Conference on Computer Vision, pp. 7264–7273 (2019)
29. Xie, S., Tu, Z.: Holistically-nested edge detection. In: Proceedings of the IEEE International Conference on Computer Vision, pp. 1395–1403 (2015)
30. Zhai, Q., Li, X., Yang, F., Chen, C., Cheng, H., Fan, D.P.: Mutual graph learning for camouflaged object detection. In: Proceedings of the IEEE/CVF Conference on Computer Vision and Pattern Recognition, pp. 12997–13007 (2021)
31. Zhang, Z., Zhang, X., Peng, C., Xue, X., Sun, J.: Exfuse: enhancing feature fusion for semantic segmentation. In: Proceedings of the European Conference on Computer Vision (ECCV), pp. 269–284 (2018)
32. Zhao, H., Shi, J., Qi, X., Wang, X., Jia, J.: Pyramid scene parsing network. In: Proceedings of the IEEE Conference on Computer Vision and Pattern Recognition, pp. 2881–2890 (2017)
33. Zhao, J.X., Liu, J.J., Fan, D.P., Cao, Y., Yang, J., Cheng, M.M.: EGNet: edge guidance network for salient object detection. In: Proceedings of the IEEE/CVF International Conference on Computer Vision, pp. 8779–8788 (2019)
34. Zhao, T., Wu, X.: Pyramid feature attention network for saliency detection. In: Proceedings of the IEEE/CVF Conference on Computer Vision and Pattern Recognition, pp. 3085–3094 (2019)
35. Zhou, Z., Rahman Siddiquee, M.M., Tajbakhsh, N., Liang, J.: UNet++: a nested U-net architecture for medical image segmentation. In: Stoyanov, D., et al. (eds.) DLMIA/ML-CDS -2018. LNCS, vol. 11045, pp. 3–11. Springer, Cham (2018). https://doi.org/10.1007/978-3-030-00889-5_1

Spatial-Temporal Contextual Feature Fusion Network for Movie Description

Yihui Liao, Lu Fan, Huiming Ding, and Zhifeng Xie[✉]

Shanghai University, Shanghai, China
zhifeng_xie@shu.edu.cn

Abstract. The movie description task aims to generate narrative textual descriptions that match the content of the movie. Most of the current methods lack the ability to consider comprehensive visual content analysis and contextual information utilization simultaneously, resulting in inaccurate or incoherent in the generated descriptions. In order to tackle the problem, we propose a new method called spatial-temporal contextual feature fusion network (ST-CFFNet) to capture both spatial-temporal and contextual information in movie by building the stacked visual graph attention encoding unit and the contextual feature fusion module. We also propose a spatial-temporal context loss to constrain the effectiveness of ST-CFFNet in spatial-temporal relation analysis and context modeling. The experimental results on LSMDC dataset show that our method achieves more accurate and coherent movie descriptions.

Keywords: Movie description · Spatial-temporal context · Graph attention network

1 Introduction

Movie description aims to generate accurate and coherent text descriptions for movie content, which can be applied in movie retrieval, movie composing, accessible movie production, etc. The automatic generation of movie description greatly improves the efficiency and reduces the costs in movie editing. However, due to the complexity of movie content, how to understand movie plots and generate accurate descriptions effectively is challenging. To this end, many researchers jointly organized the large-scale movie description challenge (LSMDC) [13] to promote future research on movie description.

Early research in movie description focused on extracting information from external scripts [14] or books [18]. With the release of movie description datasets, some researchers apply the methods [10,23] for video caption to movie description. They adopt an encoder-decoder framework, which encodes the video by convolutional neural networks (CNN), and decodes it with recurrent neural networks (RNN). However, movie is more complex and the results from video caption are too simple to meet the requirement of movie descriptions. Recently, some researchers proposed to divide multiple segments into a group [4,27], using

L. Fang et al. (Eds.): CICAI 2022, LNAI 13604, pp. 490–501, 2022.
https://doi.org/10.1007/978-3-031-20497-5_40

contextual information to generate coherent descriptions. But the previous work neglects the analysis of visual information in movies, so the generated descriptions still have the problems of inaccurate semantics and incomplete content.

To address above problems, we propose a new dual-channel based framework called Spatial-temporal Contextual Feature Fusion Network (ST-CFFNet). As shown in Fig. 1, ST-CFFNet includes three main modules: Spatial-temporal Graph Attention module (ST-GA), Contextual Feature Fusion module (CFF) and the GPT-2 language generator. ST-GA module consists of stacked ST-GA unit, each of them enables to analyze spatial-temporal relations by constructing multiple distinct attention graphs, and the stacked structure can encode deeper semantics. CFF integrates the contextual information to capture spatial-temporal context. GPT-2 can leverage the rich visual representation to generate high quality descriptions. Besides, we propose a new loss named spatial-temporal context loss, including consistency constraint, disparity constraint and coherence constraint. Consistency constraint and disparity constraint can improve the multi-view visual representation capability of the network by enhancing the correlation and independence among different attention graphs. The coherence constraint enforces the text representation of a segment to predict the visual representations within its neighborhood well for better coherence among descriptions. We evaluate our method on the public LSMDC dataset both at sentence level and set level. The results show that our method exhibits competitive performance on all different metrics.

The main contributions of our work can be summarized as follows:

1. We propose a novel dual-channel movie description network called Spatial-temporal Contextual Feature Fusion Network (ST-CFFNet). The network constructs stacked visual graph encoding units on temporal and spatial channels respectively, captures complex spatial-temporal relations from multiple perspectives, and fuses contextual features, which has the ability to generate more accurate and coherent movie descriptions.
2. We propose a spatial-temporal context loss, which can enhance the independence and correlation between stacked graph structures and improve the association among adjacent descriptions by defining the constraint function from consistency, disparity and coherence.

2   Related Work

2.1   Movie Description

Early work of movie description was mainly based on statistical model [14], Dijkstra algorithm [18] analyzing aligned books or scripts to get descriptions. But the collection of the books and scripts is difficult. To cope with these difficulties, Rohrbach et al. [13] released the LSMDC dataset and organized the first large-scale movie description challenge (LSMDC2015). Shetty et al. [16] won the first place whose method was based on image caption [5]. Subsequently, some

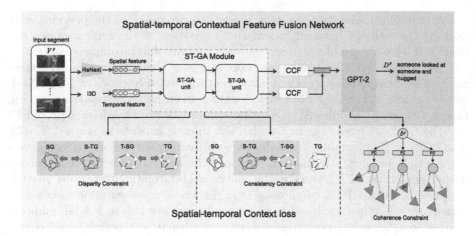

Fig. 1. Overview of our method. The Spatial-temporal Contextual Feature Fusion Network (ST-CFFNet) takes ST-GA and CFF as encoder to analyze spatial and temporal features spatial feature and takes GPT-2 as decoder to generate movie descriptions. The Spatial-temporal Context loss is designed to optimize the encoder.

researchers used video caption-based methods [10,23] to generate single sentence for movie segment. But the movie consists of multiple consecutive segments and similar visual content can be described very differently depending on context. For this reason, LSMDC2019 presented a task of multi-sentence movie description. TAPM [27] performed best, which used an adaptive loss to exploit the context information within 5 segments. Besides, Han et al. [4] split 7 segments into a block, and generate 7 descriptions for each block by computing the mean of the loss in it. Inspired by them, we take 3 movie segments as a group, extract context information for fusion to achieve better movie description.

2.2   Graph Attention Network

Graph attention network (GAT) [21] is a variant of graph neural network (GNN) [15], which updates node representation over its neighbors with self-attention. Since GAT can assign larger weights to more important neighbors and learn with arbitrary graph structure, some methods [9,30] have applied GAT to visual relation reasoning and achieved excellent performance. Recently, Zhong et al. [29] captured the importance of spatial features from adjacent frames via GAT. Wang et al. [24] proposed DualVGR, which captured the relations between problem-related appearance features and motion features by GAT. Inspired by them, our method models the spatial-temporal relations from multiple views via GAT to achieve a deeper understanding of the visual information in movies.

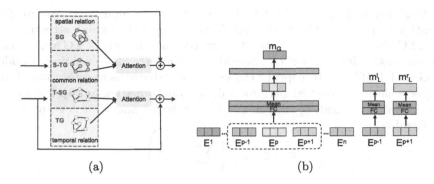

(a)   (b)

Fig. 2. ST-GA unit and Contextual Feature Fusion Module (CFF). (a) is the structure of ST-GA unit, $\oplus$ stands for residual connection. (b) is the structure of CFF.

2.3 Movie Description Datasets

Torabi et al. [19] proposed the first movie description dataset named M-VAD based on audio description (AD), which is a high-quality audio description of movie content. M-VAD transcribed AD to text and aligned it with movies, containing 92 complete movies. Rohrbach et al. [12] proposed the MPII-MD dataset, where they provided both textual descriptions and the matched movie script annotations. Later, Rohrbach et al. [13] proposed a more accurate dataset named LSMDC, which combined the M-VAD and MPII-MD. LSMDC includes more than 118 K sentence-segment pairs and has been updating in recent years to provide more accurate annotations. We choose to demonstrate the performance of our method on the most challenging LSMDC dataset.

3   Method

Figure 1 illustrates the overall architecture of ST-CFFNet, which mainly consists of spatial-temporal graph attention module (ST-GA), contextual feature fusion module (CFF) and GPT-2 language generator. Given m movie segments $V = \{V^1, V^2, \ldots, V^m\}$, the goal of ST-CFFNet is to generate m coherent sentences $D = \{D^1, D^2, \ldots, D^m\}$ that match their visual content.

3.1   Spatial-Temporal Graph Attention Module

Inspired by DualVGR [24], we build the Spatial-temporal Graph Attention module (ST-GA) with stacked ST-GA unit to encode spatial-temporal information in movies. The input temporal features can be represented as $V_t^p = \{v_{t,1}^p, v_{t,2}^p, \ldots, v_{t,c}^p\} \in \mathbb{R}^{d \times c}$ and the input spatial features can be represented as $V_s^p = \{v_{s,1}^p, v_{s,2}^p, \ldots v_{s,c}^p\} \in \mathbb{R}^{d \times c}$, where t stands for temporal feature, s stands for special feature, p is the p-th input segment and c is the number of clips in each segment, obtained by dividing the frame features from feature extractors equally and performing mean pooling operation on it.

As shown in Fig. 2(a), the ST-GA unit decouples input features into four attention graphs: SG, TG, S-TG and T-SG via multi-head graph attention network. SG aims to capture the important spatial information G_s. TG aims to capture the motion information G_t embedding in changing clips over time. Besides, S-TG and T-SG aim to capture the correlation shared across the spatial and temporal channels. We first perform a linear transformation on clip feature and then take it as the node c_i^p in each graph, and the learning of each graph can be described as:

$$\widetilde{c}_i^p = \|_{h=1}^H \sigma \left(\sum_{j \in N_i} a_{ij}^{p,h} c_j^p \right) \tag{1}$$

where $\widetilde{c}_i^p$ is the updated node feature; $\|$ is the concatenation operation; H is the number of attention head; N_i denotes some neighbor nodes of node i in graph; σ is nonlinear transformation; $a_{ij}^{p,h}$ is the attention score of head h between two nodes, which means the importance of node i to node j, can be calculated by:

$$a_{ij}^{p,h} = \frac{exp\left(\delta\left(W_a\left[c_i^p \parallel c_j^p\right]\right)\right)}{\sum\limits_{z \in N_i} exp\left(\delta\left(W_a\left[c_i^p \parallel c_z^{\,p}\right]\right)\right)} \tag{2}$$

where $W_a \in \mathbb{R}^{2d_1 \times 1}$ is learnable parameter; $\delta(\cdot)$ refers to $LeakyReLU$ activation function.

Learning through multi-head GAT, we get the features G_s and G_{st} from spatial channel, G_t and G_{ts} from temporal channel. We consider G_{st} and G_{ts} as supplementary information for G_s and G_t, and we use a simple attention mechanism for feature fusion. In spatial channel, for the n-th node feature $g_{s,n}^p \in \mathbb{R}^{Hd1 \times 1}$ in the input G_s and the n-th node feature $g_{st,n}^p \in \mathbb{R}^{Hd1 \times 1}$ in the G_t, the attention score $\alpha_{s,n}^p$ for $g_{s,n}^p$ can be calculated by:

$$\alpha_{s,n}^p = \frac{exp\left(W_f\varphi\left(g_{s,n}^p\right)\right)}{exp\left(W_f\varphi\left(g_{s,n}^p\right)\right) + exp\left(W_f\varphi\left(g_{st,n}^p\right)\right)} \tag{3}$$

where $\varphi(\cdot)$ refresh to nonlinear transformation; $W_f \in \mathbb{R}^{Hd_1 \times 1}$ is learnable parameter. The attention score for $g_{st,n}^p$ can be calculated in the same way. Finally, we perform a weighted summation of features with its attention scores to obtain the enhanced features $\widetilde{v}_{s,n}^p$.

Then, a residual connection is introduced to alleviate the vanishing gradient problem, and we get the final spatial representation $E_s^p = \{\widetilde{v}_{s,1}^p + v_{s,1}^p, \widetilde{v}_{s,2}^p + v_{s,1}^p, \ldots, \widetilde{v}_{s,c}^p + v_{s,c}^p\}$. Similarly, we perform the same attention mechanism and residual connection in temporal channel, and obtain the final temporal representation $E_t^p = \{\widetilde{v}_{t,1}^p + v_{t,1}^p, \widetilde{v}_{t,2}^p + v_{t,2}^p, \ldots, \widetilde{v}_{t,c}^p + v_{t,c}^p\}$. Finally, the ST-GA unit is stacked as a chain to perform the final ST-GA module:

$$\{E_s^p, E_t^p\} = [STGA(V_s^p, V_t^p)]^K \tag{4}$$

where K is the number of ST-GA unit.

3.2   Contextual Feature Fusion Module

CFF aims to extract contextual information from adjacent segments. As shown in Fig. 2(b), for the m segments features $E = \{E^1, E^2, \ldots, E^m\}$ output by ST-GA, CCF divides E^{p-1}, E^p and E^{p+1} into a group, and extracts contextual feature from them. Specifically, We perform one linear transformation and two mean pooling operations on the three segments to obtain the global contextual feature m_G. Than we perform a linear transformation and a mean pooling on E^{p-1} to get one of the local contextual feature m_L^l, and we perform the same operation on E^{p+1} to get another feature m_L^r. Finally, we concatenate the three features and the segment feature E^p as the final context representation Z^p.

We perform the same CCF module on temporal and spatial channels to obtain Z_s^p and the Z_t^p, respectively. Finally, the tow features are further concatenated into a more compact representation $\bar{V}^p = \{\bar{v}_1^p, \bar{v}_2^p, \ldots, \bar{v}_c^p\}$ to model spatial-temporal context information.

3.3   GPT-2 Language Generator

GPT-2 [11] is pretrained on a corpus dataset of 8 million web pages, containing rich semantic and grammar knowledge, which is important for language generation. Therefore, we take it as the decoder of our network to help better descriptions. For the encoded features $\{\bar{V}^1, \bar{V}^2, \ldots, \bar{V}^m\}$, GPT-2 aims to generate m coherent sentences $D = \{D^1, D^2, \ldots, D^m\}$ auto-regressively. In the decoding step i for $\bar{V}^p$:

$$\hat{s}_i^p = GPT2\left(\hat{s}_{1:i-1}^p, \bar{V}^p\right) \tag{5}$$

where $\hat{s}_i^p$ is the i-th token in D^p. We can get the word probability of $\hat{s}_i^p$, and than chose the next word until the end-of-sentence token [eos] appears, or the output sentence reaches the predefined maximum length.

3.4   Spatial-Temporal Context Loss

The spatial-temporal context loss aims to further improve the multi-view spatial-temporal encoding ability and context modeling ability of the network by defining disparity constraint, consistency constraint, and coherence constraint. In detail, the disparity constraint adopts Hilbert-Schmidt Independence Criterion (HSIC) [17] to increase the difference of graphs within the same channel in ST-GA such as G_t and G_{ts}, to ensure that they capture the specific information. In spatial channel, the disparity constraint between G_s and G_{st} can be given by:

$$HSIC\left(G_s, G_{st}\right) = (n-1)^2 \, tr\left(K_s H K_{st} H\right) \tag{6}$$

where n is the number of nodes in G_s and G_{st}; the K_s and K_{st} are the Gram matrices with $k_{s,ij} = k_s\left(G_s^i, G_s^j\right)$ and $k_{st,ij} = k_{st}\left(G_{st}^i, G_{st}^j\right)$; $R = I - \frac{1}{n}ee^T$; where I is an identity matrix and e is an all-one column vector; Follow DualVGR [24], we use the inner product kernel function for K_s and K_{st}. Similarly, the disparity constraint $HSIC\left(G_t, G_{ts}\right)$ between G_t and G_{ts} in the temporal channel can be defined by the same formula.

Then we set the disparity constraint $\mathcal{L}_d$ for the whole network as:

$$\mathcal{L}_d = \frac{1}{K} \sum_{k=1}^{K} \left(HSIC^{(k)}\left(G_s, G_{st}\right) + HSIC^{(k)}\left(G_t, G_{ts}\right) \right) \tag{7}$$

where $HSIC^{(k)}\left(G_s, G_{st}\right)$ and $HSIC^{(k)}\left(G_t, G_{ts}\right)$ are the disparity constraint of G_s, G_{st} and G_t, G_{ts} in the k-th ST-GA unit respectively.

Consistency constraint aims to enhance the commonality between G_{st} and G_{ts}. Firstly, we use L_2-normalization to normalize the G_{st} and G_{ts} into G_{stnor} and G_{tsnor} respectively. Then, the similarity of the n nodes in each graph can be captured by multiplying the feature vectors with their respective normalized vectors. The consistency implies that the two similarity matrices should be similar, which gives rise to the following constraint:

$$\mathcal{L}_c = \frac{1}{K} \sum_{k=1}^{K} \left(\left\| S_{st}^{(k)} - S_{ts}^{(k)} \right\|^2 \right) \tag{8}$$

where $\mathcal{L}_c$ is the consistency constraint of whole network; $S_{st}^{(k)}$ and $S_{ts}^{(k)}$ are the similarity matrices of n nodes in G_{st} and G_{ts} respectively in k-th ST-GA unit.

The coherence constraint minimize the difference among the textual representation $\hat{D}^p$ generated from GPT-2 and the visual representation $\bar{V}^p$ and its adjacent segments $\bar{V}^{p-1}$ and $\bar{V}^{p+1}$ to improve the correlation among descriptions. First, for the input feature sequence $\bar{V}^p$, we get a single vector representation $\hat{V}^p$ via mean pooling, and then project $\hat{V}^p$ into the past, current and future visual spaces through their respective FC layers, finally the margin ranking losses between the text representation and the candidate video representations are calculated in each visual space to encourage correct match. The coherence constraint $\mathcal{L}_s$ is the sum of the past, current, and future matching losse:

$$\mathcal{L}_s = \sum_{j \neq i-1} l\left(\hat{V}^j, \hat{V}^{p-1}, f(\hat{D}^p)\right) + \sum_{j \neq i} l\left(\hat{V}^j, \hat{V}^p, f(\hat{D}^p)\right) + \sum_{j \neq i+1} l\left(\hat{V}^j, \hat{V}^{p+1}, f(\hat{D}^p)\right) \tag{9}$$

where $l(\cdot)$ denotes the margin ranking losses; $f(\cdot)$ means linear transformation; j indicates the index for wrong matches.

Finally, the spatial-temporal context loss $\mathcal{L}_{st}$ is formed as the weighted summation of the three constraints, which can be described as:

$$\mathcal{L}_{st} = \lambda_d \mathcal{L}_d + \lambda_c \mathcal{L}_c + \lambda_s \mathcal{L}_s \tag{10}$$

where the λ_d, λ_c and λ_s weight the influence of each constraint. We set $\lambda_d = 1e-6$, $\lambda_c = 1$ and $\lambda_s = 0.9$, which can ensure that the content of current segment are captured while the correlation among adjacent segments are also considered.

Follow the TAPM [27], we employ a two-stage training strategy. Before finetuning the pretrained GPT-2, we first fix the weights of it, train with the spatialtemporal context loss for visual encoding, and then with the task of generate descriptions, we calculate the cross-entropy loss between the predicted descriptions and the ground truth to optimize the entire network jointly.

4 Experiment

4.1 Datasets

To evaluate the effectiveness of proposed method, we train and test our framework on the challenging LSMDC dataset [13]. The dataset consists of complete segments from 200 movies, with 128085 high-quality text annotations. For each segment in LSMDC, we use the ResNeXt [25] pretrained on Instagram hashtags [8] and the I3D [2] pretrained on Kinetics [6] to extract frame features.

4.2 Experiment Settings

The ST-GA module is built with $K = 2$ identical unit, $H = 3$ attention heads. The dimension $d = 768$, $d1 = 256$ and the number of clip $c = 3$. We set $\lambda_d = 1e-6$, $\lambda_c = 1$, $\lambda_{sc} = 0.9$ for the proposed loss function and train the model using use Adam optimizer [26] with linear learning rate decay. The learning rate is 5e−5, which is warmed up for the first 4000 steps. In all experiments, we set 5 epochs for the first-stage training and 17 epochs for second stage. Our model is implemented by PyTorch and trained on NVIDIA TITAN Xp GPUs.

4.3 Evaluation Metrics

We evaluate our method both at sentence level and set level. For sentence level, we evaluate the quality of descriptions sentence by sentence with three standard metrics, including METEOR [1], ROUGE-L [7] and CIDEr [20]. For set level, we concatenate all descriptions within a set of 5 segments as proposed by LSMDC2019, and evaluate the coherence in a set with CIDEr and METEOR.

4.4 Quantitative Evaluation

We compare our method against the current state-of-art methods in movie description on LSMDC dataset, including S2VT [22], Base-SAN [28], CT-SAN

Table 1. Comparison with state-of-art methods on the testing set of LSMDC dataset.

Method	Sentence level			Set level	
	CIDEr	METEOR	ROUGE-L	CIDEr	METEOR
S2VT [22]	8.20	7.00	14.90	/	/
Base-SAN [28]	9.00	6.60	15.00	/	/
CT-SAN [28]	10.00	7.10	15.90	/	/
hLSTMat [3]	10.40	5.60	14.90	/	/
LSMDC2019 [13]	11.90	8.25	/	7.00	12.0
TAPM [27]	14.71	8.39	19.72	8.70	**12.1**
Ours	**16.20**	**8.53**	**19.98**	**9.30**	**12.1**

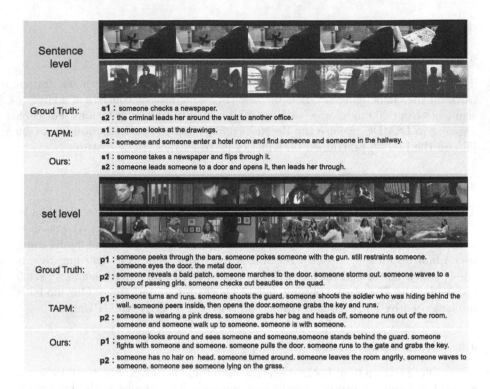

Fig. 3. Qualitative comparison with TAPM [27]. The images in sentence level come form one segment while the set level come from five segments. Examples of each level correspond to descriptions 1 and 2 in order. Green and red fonts indicate correct and erroneous descriptions, respectively. Blue shows the coherence between sentences. (Color figure online)

[28], hLSTMat [3], TAPM [27] and the official baseline in LSMDC2019 [13], which is simply called LSMDC2019. Table 1 shows the results both at the sentence level and set level. We can see that our ST-CFFNet achieves the best performance on all metrics, which verifies the effectiveness of our method. Notably, our method reachs 16.20 score in CIDEr at the sentence and 9.3 score at set level, which is a significant improvement, proving that the descriptions generated by our method are more accurate and coherent in sementics and closer to human descriptions.

4.5   Qualitative Evaluation

We compare our ST-CCFNet to TAPM [27] and the ground truth descriptions on qualitative and the results are shown in Fig. 3. At sentence level, we can get more accurate descriptions, such as "newspapers" and "flips", and for the complex long sentences, we still get the correct semantics. At set level, our method can describe a sequence of actions coherently, while TAPM repeats the description, which is considered to be overly dependent on context leading to a lack of discrimination.

Table 2. Ablation study on the testing set of LSMDC dataset.

Methods	Sentence level			Set level	
	CIDEr	METEOR	ROUGE-L	CIDEr	METEOR
ST-CFFNet	**16.20**	**8.53**	19.98	**9.3**	**12.1**
w/1 ST-GA	15.03	8.51	20.00	8.4	12.0
w/t ST-GA	14.66	8.32	19.94	8.3	11.9
w/o CFF	14.46	8.22	19.70	7.3	11.7
w/o STCl	14.45	8.49	19.79	8.1	12.1
w/o D	15.23	8.50	20.07	8.4	11.9
w/o C	15.19	8.53	**20.11**	8.8	12.1
w/o S	14.59	8.39	19.95	8.3	11.9

4.6 Ablation Study

To analyze our method in depth, we performed ablation studies to evaluate the effect of each component, and we also analyze the effect of each constraint in the spatial-temporal context loss. We test seven variants: (1) (w/1 ST-GA) method with only one ST-GA unit. (2) (w/t ST-GA) method uses a simple encoder with three stacked ResBlock instead of ST-GA. (3) (w/o CFF) method removes the CFF module. (4) (w/o STCl) method removes the Spatial-temporal Context loss. (5) (w/o D) method removes the disparity constraint. (6) (w/o C) method removes the consistency constraint. (7) (w/o S) method removes the coherence constraint.

From Table 2, we can find the full model performs best, showing the effectiveness of our network. When we stack two ST-GA unit, the CIDEr score increased from 14.66 to 16.20, indicating that our ST-GA can capture richer information and the stacked structure is more efficient. Without CFF, we get the lowest CIDEr score at set level, proving that fusing context is beneficial for coherent descriptions. As for STCl, it also improves a lot, demonstrating that constraining both at vision and text can promote higher-quality descriptions. Besides, when removing the consistency constraint or disparity constraint, CIDEr metrics are significantly reduced at both tow level, validating that they are important for achieving accurate content understanding. With the help of coherence constraint, ST-CFFNet shows improvement on all metrics, indicating that it is helpful to consolidate the accuracy and coherence of descriptions.

5   Conclusion

In this paper, we propose a spatial-temporal contextual feature fusion network (ST-CFFNet) to achieve more accurate and coherent movie descriptions by capturing visual information from multiple perspectives and modeling context information. Experiments on LSMDC dataset demonstrated the effectiveness of the proposed method. But our method only generate descriptions with someone as subject, lack the ability to capture the identities of characters in movie. Therefore, our future work is to introduce high-order feature interaction [26] and explore the character grounding movie description.

Acknowledgments. This work was supported by the Shanghai Natural Science Foundation of China No. 19ZR1419100.

References

1. Banerjee, S., Lavie, A.: Meteor: an automatic metric for MT evaluation with improved correlation with human judgments. In: Proceedings of the ACL Workshop on Intrinsic and Extrinsic Evaluation Measures for Machine Translation and/or Summarization, pp. 65–72 (2005)
2. Carreira, J., Zisserman, A.: Quo vadis, action recognition? A new model and the kinetics dataset. In: Proceedings of the IEEE Conference on Computer Vision and Pattern Recognition, pp. 6299–6308 (2017)
3. Gao, L., Li, X., Song, J., Shen, H.T.: Hierarchical LSTMs with adaptive attention for visual captioning. IEEE Trans. Pattern Anal. Mach. Intell. **42**(5), 1112–1131 (2019)
4. Han, S.H., Go, B.W., Choi, H.J.: Multiple videos captioning model for video storytelling. In: 2019 IEEE International Conference on Big Data and Smart Computing (BigComp), pp. 1–4. IEEE (2019)
5. Karpathy, A., Fei-Fei, L.: Deep visual-semantic alignments for generating image descriptions. In: Proceedings of the IEEE conference on computer vision and pattern recognition, pp. 3128–3137 (2015)
6. Kay, W., et al.: The kinetics human action video dataset. arXiv preprint arXiv:1705.06950 (2017)
7. Lin, C.Y.: Rouge: a package for automatic evaluation of summaries. In: Text Summarization Branches Out, pp. 74–81 (2004)
8. Mahajan, Dhruv, Girshick, Ross, Ramanathan, Vignesh, He, Kaiming, Paluri, Manohar, Li, Yixuan, Bharambe, Ashwin, van der Maaten, Laurens: Exploring the limits of weakly supervised pretraining. In: Ferrari, Vittorio, Hebert, Martial, Sminchisescu, Cristian, Weiss, Yair (eds.) ECCV 2018. LNCS, vol. 11206, pp. 185–201. Springer, Cham (2018). https://doi.org/10.1007/978-3-030-01216-8_12
9. Mi, L., Chen, Z.: Hierarchical graph attention network for visual relationship detection. In: Proceedings of the IEEE/CVF Conference on Computer Vision and Pattern Recognition, pp. 13886–13895 (2020)
10. Pan, P., Xu, Z., Yang, Y., Wu, F., Zhuang, Y.: Hierarchical recurrent neural encoder for video representation with application to captioning. In: Proceedings of the IEEE Conference on Computer Vision and Pattern Recognition, pp. 1029–1038 (2016)
11. Radford, A., Wu, J., Child, R., Luan, D., Amodei, D., Sutskever, I., et al.: Language models are unsupervised multitask learners. OpenAI blog **1**(8), 9 (2019)
12. Rohrbach, A., Rohrbach, M., Tandon, N., Schiele, B.: A dataset for movie description. In: Proceedings of the IEEE Conference on Computer Vision and Pattern Recognition, pp. 3202–3212 (2015)
13. Rohrbach, A., et al.: Movie description. Int. J. Comput. Vision **123**(1), 94–120 (2017)

14. Ronfard, R., Thuong, T.: A framework for aligning and indexing movies with their script. In: 2003 Proceedings of International Conference on Multimedia and Expo. ICME 2003 (Cat. No. 03TH8698), vol. 1, pp. 1–21 (2003). https://doi.org/10.1109/ICME.2003.1220844

15. Scarselli, F., Gori, M., Tsoi, A.C., Hagenbuchner, M., Monfardini, G.: The graph neural network model. IEEE Trans. Neural Netw. **20**(1), 61–80 (2008)

16. Shetty, R., Laaksonen, J.: Video captioning with recurrent networks based on frame-and video-level features and visual content classification. arXiv preprint arXiv:1512.02949 (2015)

17. Song, L., Smola, A., Gretton, A., Borgwardt, K.M., Bedo, J.: Supervised feature selection via dependence estimation. In: Proceedings of the 24th International Conference on Machine Learning, pp. 823–830 (2007)

18. Tapaswi, M., Bauml, M., Stiefelhagen, R.: Book2movie: aligning video scenes with book chapters. In: Proceedings of the IEEE Conference on Computer Vision and Pattern Recognition, pp. 1827–1835 (2015)

19. Torabi, A., Pal, C., Larochelle, H., Courville, A.: Using descriptive video services to create a large data source for video annotation research. arXiv preprint arXiv:1503.01070 (2015)

20. Vedantam, R., Lawrence Zitnick, C., Parikh, D.: Cider: Consensus-based image description evaluation. In: Proceedings of the IEEE Conference on Computer Vision and Pattern Recognition, pp. 4566–4575 (2015)

21. Veličković, P., Cucurull, G., Casanova, A., Romero, A., Lio, P., Bengio, Y.: Graph attention networks. arXiv preprint arXiv:1710.10903 (2017)

22. Venugopalan, S., Rohrbach, M., Donahue, J., Mooney, R., Darrell, T., Saenko, K.: Sequence to sequence-video to text. In: Proceedings of the IEEE International Conference on Computer Vision, pp. 4534–4542 (2015)

23. Wang, H., Gao, C., Han, Y.: Sequence in sequence for video captioning. Pattern Recogn. Lett. **130**, 327–334 (2020)

24. Wang, J., Bao, B., Xu, C.: Dualvgr: A dual-visual graph reasoning unit for video question answering. IEEE Trans. Multimed. (2021)

25. Xie, S., Girshick, R., Dollár, P., Tu, Z., He, K.: Aggregated residual transformations for deep neural networks. In: Proceedings of the IEEE Conference on Computer Vision and Pattern Recognition, pp. 1492–1500 (2017)

26. Xie, Z., Zhang, W., Sheng, B., Li, P., Chen, C.L.P.: BagFN: broad attentive graph fusion network for high-order feature interactions. IEEE Trans. Neural Netw. Learn. Syst. 1–15 (2021). https://doi.org/10.1109/TNNLS.2021.3116209

27. Yu, Y., Chung, J., Yun, H., Kim, J., Kim, G.: Transitional adaptation of pretrained models for visual storytelling. In: Proceedings of the IEEE/CVF Conference on Computer Vision and Pattern Recognition, pp. 12658–12668 (2021)

28. Yu, Y., Ko, H., Choi, J., Kim, G.: End-to-end concept word detection for video captioning, retrieval, and question answering. In: Proceedings of the IEEE Conference on Computer Vision and Pattern Recognition, pp. 3165–3173 (2017)

29. Zhong, R., Wang, R., Zou, Y., Hong, Z., Hu, M.: Graph attention networks adjusted Bi-LSTM for video summarization. IEEE Signal Process. Lett. **28**, 663–667 (2021)

30. Zhou, W., Xia, Z., Dou, P., Su, T., Hu, H.: Double attention based on graph attention network for image multi-label classification. ACM Trans. Multimed. Comput. Commun. App. (TOMM) (2022)

A Transformer-Based Network for Deformable Medical Image Registration

Yibo Wang, Wen Qian, Mengqi Li, and Xuming Zhang[✉]

Department of Biomedical Engineering, College of Life Science and Technology,
Huazhong University of Science and Technology, Wuhan, China
zxmboshi@hust.edu.cn

Abstract. Deformable medical image registration plays an important role in clinical diagnosis and treatment. Recently, the deep learning (DL) based image registration methods have been widely investigated and showed excellent performance in computational speed. However, these methods cannot provide enough registration accuracy because of insufficient ability in representing both the global and local features of the moving and fixed images. To address this issue, this paper has proposed the transformer based image registration method. This method uses the distinctive transformer to extract the global and local image features for generating the deformation fields, based on which the registered image is produced in an unsupervised way. Our method can improve the registration accuracy effectively by means of self-attention mechanism and bi-level information flow. Experimental results on such brain MR image datasets as LPBA40 and OASIS-1 demonstrate that compared with several traditional and DL based registration methods, our method provides higher registration accuracy in terms of dice values.

Keywords: Image registration · Deep learning · Transformer · Registration accuracy

1 Introduction

Image registration is one of the fundamental and challenging tasks in medical image processing and analysis. Its goal is to find the correspondence between the moving and fixed images to facilitate such tasks as disease diagnosis and surgical navigation. Up to now, the various image registration methods have been proposed. For the traditional registration methods [1,2,12], the similarity metric is firstly constructed between the fixed and moving images. Then, the objective function based on the constructed metric is optimized to produce the registered image. These methods are time-consuming because of the complicated iterative optimization.

To improve image registration efficiency, the deep learning (DL) based registration methods have been presented. Given numerous moving and fixed images,

L. Fang et al. (Eds.): CICAI 2022, LNAI 13604, pp. 502–513, 2022.
https://doi.org/10.1007/978-3-031-20497-5_41

the deep neural networks can be trained to generate the registered image efficiently. Depending on how the networks are trained, these methods can be categorized into the supervised learning and unsupervised learning ones. In the supervised approaches, the ground-truth deformation fields or anatomical landmarks are needed [5,17,19,21,23,26]. Sokooti et al. [23] have proposed a convolution neuron network (CNN) to directly estimate the displacement vector field (DVF) using the artificially generated DVFs. Cao et al. [5] have developed a deformable inter-modality image registration method which estimates the deformation fields using the deep neural network supervised by intra-modality similarity. The registration performance of these methods greatly depends on the ground-truths which are generally difficult to acquire in clinical scenarios. As for the unsupervised learning based methods [3,11,13,24,27,28], they need no the ground truth of the deformation field. Balakrishnan et al. [3] have proposed a 3D medical image registration model, voxelmorph, which reconstructs the registered result using a CNN with a spatial transform layer. Zhao et al. [28] have designed a volume tweening network (VTN) including the cascaded subnetworks to improve the registration performance recursively. Kim et al. [11] have presented a cycle-consistent deformable image registration method called cyclemorph, which can enhance the registration performance by introducing the cycle consistency into the network loss.

Although the existing DL based registration approaches can provide higher computational efficiency than the traditional ones, they cannot capture the long-range dependence in the moving and the fixed image effectively because of the adoption of such networks as the CNN which has the limited ability of extracting the global image features. Therefore, the registration accuracy of these DL based methods is influenced disadvantageously especially when the large deformation is involved between the fixed and moving images. Recently, the transformer has become an important network in the fields of natural language processing and computer vision because it can explore the long-range dependence based on the self-attention mechanism. Distinctively, the transformer can extract the global image features effectively, thus it has been applied to such tasks as image classification [8,10], image denoising [14,25] and image segmentation [4,6,15]. To overcome the disadvantages of existing CNN based registration methods, we have presented a novel deformable medical image registration network called Transformer-UNet (TUNet). This network introduces the vision transformer (VIT) [8] into the framework of UNet [20] to extract the global and local features from the moving and fixed images, thereby generating the deformation field effectively. Besides, the skip connections are established in the bi-level layers to guarantee the correct information flow between the rough features and the fine features.

Experiments have been done on LPBA40 and OASIS-1 to test the performance of our method. The qualitative and quantitative evaluations demonstrate that the proposed method is provided with higher registration accuracy than the compared traditional and DL based registration methods.

The paper is organized as follows. Section 2 describes our method. Section 3 presents the experimental results of our method on two datasets. Conclusion is given in Sect. 4.

2   Method

The framework of the TUNet is shown in Fig. 1. Here, a moving image M and a fixed image F are input into the TUNet. The deformation field ϕ is computed based on the parameters learned in the different network layers. By means of the spatial transform layer, M is deformed to produce the registered image R. The TUNet is trained using the loss defined by the dissimilarity between F and M and the smoothness constraint of ϕ to produce the registered result in an unsupervised way.

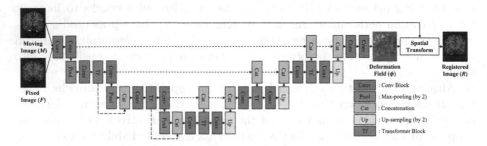

Fig. 1. The overall framework of the proposed method, Transformer-UNet, for deformable medical image registration. Here, the short and long dashed lines denote the skip connection and the bi-level connection, respectively.

2.1   Architecture of the Transformer-UNet

Our Transformer-UNet is built on the encoder-decoder architecture of the UNet [20], but improves the latter by introducing the bi-level connection and an unique Transformer block. As shown in Fig. 1, the proposed Transformer-UNet uses a single input formed by concatenating M and F in the dimension channel. In the encoder, the two Conv layers are used to extract image features, where each block is composed of a convolutional module followed by the Rectified Linear Unit (ReLU). The kernel size and stride in the convolutional module will be set to $3\times3\times3$ and 1, respectively. The Max-pooling layer, Conv layers and Transformer blocks are combined to produce image features at different levels. In some layers in the encoder, the concatenation layer is additionally introduced to concatenate the features produced by the Transformer block at the previous layer and those resulting from the pooling layer. In the decoder, the Conv layers, Transformer blocks and Up-sampling layer are combined to store the spatial resolution of the feature maps at different levels. The features at the same levels produced by the encoder and decoder will be concatenated by the concatenation layers. At the end of decoder, the concatenated features will be processed by the two Conv layers to output the final features. Note that the stride of Max-pooling layer and Up-sampling layer is set to 2, and thus the encoder reduces the spatial resolution of input volumes by a factor of 8 in total and the decoder restores the features to the original size. As the key component of our method, the Transformer block is distributed at different layers in the encoder and decoder. It receives the convolutional features and outputs two different feature maps.

2.2 Transformer Block

Inspired by the VIT [8], we will build the Transfomer block shown in Fig. 2. Compared with the VIT, this block retains the multi-head self-attention mechanism, which is necessary for improving network's awareness for the global information. Meanwhile, we have made some modifications on the VIT to produce the distinctive Transfomer block. Firstly, the redundant position embedding is removed after the patch embedding. Secondly, the convolution module is used to directly compute the weight matrix instead of the original patch embedding and the linear mapping, which will reduce the computational complexity and meet the need of 3D image registration better. Finally, an additional output path has been designed. By using the convolution module with a stride of 2 or the deconvolution module, we have established a bridge for information flow in the bi-level features.

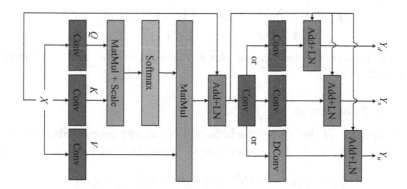

Fig. 2. The structure of the proposed transformer block.

As shown in Fig. 2, the input feature X is processed by the three different convolution modules to generate the query matrix Q, the key matrix K and the value matrix V as:

$$Q = W_Q \cdot X; K = W_K \cdot X; V = W_V \cdot X, \qquad (1)$$

The matrices Q, K and V are reshaped into a sequence of flattened 3D patches: Q, K, and $V \in \mathbb{R}^{B \times N \times (P^3 \cdot C)}$, where B is the mini-batch, C is the number of channels, (P, P, P) is the resolution of each volume patch, and $N = HWD/P^3$ is the resultant number of patches with (H, W, D) denoting the resolution of the input feature. By splitting the heads from the embed channels and swapping the order of axis, we will change them into a 4D vector: Q, $V \in \mathbb{R}^{B \times k \times N \times d_k}$, $K \in \mathbb{R}^{B \times k \times d_k \times N}$, where k is the number of heads and $d_k = (P^3 \cdot C)/k$ is the number of the embedding channels per head. The matrix multiplication, scaling and softmax operations will be implemented for Q, K and V to produce the output Y.

$$Y = softmax(\frac{QK^T}{\sqrt{d_k}})V, \tag{2}$$

The output Y will be added to the input X and then is processed by the layer-norm (LN) operation. To promote the information interaction between two different levels of features, we will add the convolution module with a stride of 2 or the deconvolution (DConv) module at the end of block. Similarly, the LN will be applied again. In this way, our Transformer block will generate two output feature maps. One called Y_s has the same size as the input feature map while another Y_d or Y_u has half or twice the size of the input feature map.

2.3   Spatial Transform

For the spatial transform, we will choose the 3D transformation function with the bilinear interpolation defined as:

$$M \circ \phi = \sum_{q \in G(\phi(p))} M(q) \prod_{d \in \{x,y,z\}} (1 - |\phi_d(p) - q_d|), \tag{3}$$

where p is a voxel, $G(\phi(p))$ means the 8-neighbors of $\phi(p)$ and $\circ$ is the spatial transform function.

2.4   Loss Function

The loss function of the TUNet includes a dissimilarity term related to the local cross correlation (CC) and a smoothness regularization term of ϕ, and it is defined as:

$$\mathcal{L}(M, F, \phi) = -CC(M \circ \phi, F) + \lambda \sum_{p \in \Omega} \|\nabla \phi(p)\|, \tag{4}$$

where λ is a hyper-parameter and Ω denotes the 3D volume and $CC(A, B)$ is computed as:

$$CC(A, B) = \sum_{v \in \Omega} \frac{(\sum_{v_i}(A(v_i) - \bar{A}(v))(B(v_i) - \bar{B}(v)))^2}{\sum_{v_i}(A(v_i) - \bar{A}(v))^2 \sum_{v_i}(B(v_i) - \bar{B}(v))^2}, \tag{5}$$

where v_i is chosen as the $9 \times 9 \times 9$ patch, $\bar{A}(v)$ and $\bar{B}(v)$ mean the local mean of $A(v)$ and $B(v)$, respectively.

3   Experimental Results and Discussion

3.1   Experimental Settings

Datasets. We have chosen LPBA40 [22] and OASIS-1 [16] for experiments. The LPBA40 contains 40 T1-weighted brain MR images, where 56 anatomical areas are segmented from each image. The OASIS-1 contains 414 T1-weighted brain MR images, where each image includes 35 segmented cortical regions. Here, all scans are sampled to a 256×256×256 grid with 1mm isotropic voxel. The affine spatial normalization and brain extraction are carried out using FreeSurfer [9]. The images are further cropped into 192 × 160 × 192. For the LPBA40, we have trained our model on 25 subjects, validated it on 5 subjects and tested it on 5 subjects. For the OASIS-1, we have used 324 subjects for model training, 42 subjects for validation and 40 subjects for testing. What's more, we use random rotation and flipping to form 12× data augmentation.

Implementation Details. We will focus on atlas-based registration, in which a fixed volume is chosen as atlas and each volume in the dataset is registered to it. Here, because of high memory cost in the training stage, we will extract patches of size 128×128×64 from a whole volume, and set the corresponding batch size according to the GPU memory usage. To avoid over-fitting, the random rotation is implemented on each training volume pair to realize data augmentation. We set hyper-parameter λ to 0.1 and adopt Adam optimization with a learning rate of 1e-4. Our model is realized using the MindSpore Lite tool [18] and it trained for 30 epochs on a single NVIDIA RTX 2080Ti GPU.

Compared Methods. In order to verify the superiority of the TUNet, we will compare it with several popular image registration methods including SyN [2] from Advanced Normalization Tools, VoxelMorph (VM) [3], VTN [28], CycleMorph (CM) [11], TransUnet (TF1) [6] and SwinUnet (TF2) [4]. As regards the VoxelMorph, we will choose VoxelMorph-1 [3] as the baseline network with the same parameters to our method for the fair comparison. Since TransUnet [6] and SwinUnet [4] are image segmentation methods using transformer thinking, we rewrite them as registration method while retaining their structure.

Evaluation Metrics. The registration performance is evaluated by Dice [7], which is defined as the overlap rate between the segmented results of registered and fixed images.

$$Dice(R, F) = 2 \cdot \frac{|R \cap F|}{|R| + |F|} \tag{6}$$

Perfectly overlapped regions come with a Dice value of 1. The Dice value explicitly measures the coincidence between two regions and thereby reflects the quality of registration. Considering multiple anatomical structures annotated, we compute the Dice score with respect to each and take an average.

3.2   Ablation Experiment

To investigate different components' individual contribution towards model's overall performance, we progressively integrate our main contributions (Transformer Block and Bi-level Connection) into the model. Corresponding results in Table 1 reveals the importance of introducing Transformer Block together with Bi-level Connection along with the basic UNet architecture. Data in Table 1 are composed of 56 regional Dice averages from all test samples on LPBA40. We can notice that all of these components contribute towards model's performance. We also observe intriguing accuracy improvement created by Transformer Block (2.5%). Compared with Transformer Block, Bi-level Connection's effect is less satisfactory in that it only brings a slight increase in Dice value (0.6%).

Table 1. Ablation experiment on LPBA40.

Methods	Dice
UNet	0.5747
UNet + TransBlock	0.5895
UNet + TransBlock + BiLevelConnection	0.5932

3.3   Computational Efficiency

Considering actual implementation of the model, we compares the computation efficiency of different methods according to Giga Floating-point Operations Per Second (GFLOPs) and inference time on CPU (Intel(R) Core(TM) i7-6950X 3.00 GHz) and GPU (NVIDIA RTX 2080Ti). Our results in Table 2 suggest that the inference time of the SyN is much longer than that of the DL-based methods. On CPU, all DL-based methods can realize image registration in 30 s while the SyN requires more than 1800 s seconds. If GPU is used, the implementation time of DL-based methods can be shortened to less than 1 s. Apart from running time, GFLOPs can also reflect the superiority of our method. Although the TUNet is more computationally expensive than the fully convolutional networks [3,28], it still outperforms other transformer-based methods [4,6].

Table 2. Comparison of running time and FLOPs

Metric	SyN	VM	VTN	CM	TF1	TF2	TUNet
Time (CPU)	1853.16	7.76	23.28	31.04	23.58	24.32	29.24
Time (GPU)	None	0.15	0.44	0.61	0.75	0.86	0.57
GFLOPs	None	97.44	292.32	389.76	418.77	472.31	296.07

3.4   Registration Results

Quantitative Evaluation. Figure 3 visualizes the Dice values for 16 evaluated anatomical structures across all test samples on OASIS-1. For better visualization purpose, we combine the same structures from the left and right hemisphere together. For most of structures, our TUNet model achieves higher scores than VoxelMorph [3] in short-range registration and TransUnet [6] in long-range registration. In particular, on some structures such as Cerebellum cortex, Cerebral white matter, Cerebral cortex, Putamen and Hippocampus, our TUNet performs much better than the compared methods. As can be seen from Fig. 3, the Dice values of our method exceed those of the fully convolutional models, which indicates the proposed Transformer Block's unique contribution. Compared with other methods with transformer, the proposed method has better registration performance, which proves that our designed bi-level skip connection is effective and irreplaceable.

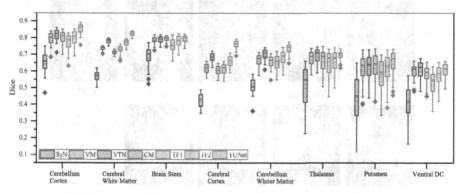

(a) Boxplots of Dice values on the first 8 anatomical structures

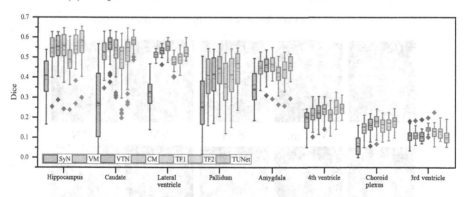

(b) Boxplots of Dice values on the last 8 anatomical structures

Fig. 3. Boxplots of Dice values for the SyN, VTN, VM, CM, TF1, TF2 and TUNet performed on the anatomical structures.

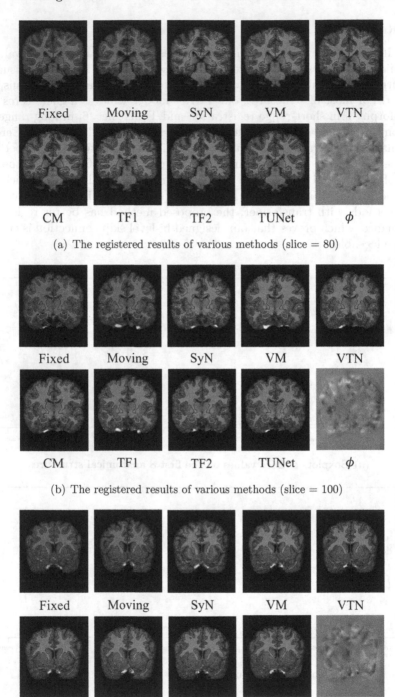

(a) The registered results of various methods (slice = 80)

(b) The registered results of various methods (slice = 100)

(c) The registered results of various methods (slice = 120)

Fig. 4. The registered results of the various methods on OASIS-1. (Color figure online)

Qualitative Evaluation. The results of atlas-based OASIS-1 MR image registration are shown in Fig. 4. The proposed TUNet method can accurately register each pair of moving and fixed images, which can be specifically verified with the segmentation boundaries of several brain structures (blue outlines represent Cerebral White Matter, green outlines represent Hippocampus and red outlines represent Putamen respectively). Besides, the observation from Fig. 4 shows that the other compared methods cannot restore the deformation of some internal brain structures and brain contour effectively. By comparison, the proposed TUNet can provide the most similar registered results to the fixed image in terms of the different brain tissues among all evaluated methods. Especially, the proposed method can preserve some fine image details better than the other methods, which can be verified with the red and green outlines. Indeed, the superiority of the TUNet to other methods lies in its outperforming ability to extract both the global and local features, which can be seen from the blue outlines and the deformation field.

4   Conclusion

In this paper, we have presented a Transformer-UNet based unsupervised deformable medical image registration method. The framework is built on the Transformer model which is introduced into the UNet. By means of the distinctive Transformer-UNet, the global and local features can be extracted from the moving and fixed images effectively, thereby ensuring good registration performance. The experimental results show that our method outperforms several traditional and deep learning based registration methods in terms of visual evaluations and such quantitative metrics as Dice. Future research will be focused on the extension of our method to multi-modal medical image registration.

Acknowledgment. This work was sponsored by the National Natural Science Foundation of China (Grant No. 61871440) and CAAI-Huawei MindSpore Open Fund. We gratefully acknowledge the support of MindSpore.

References

1. Ashburner, J.: A fast diffeomorphic image registration algorithm. Neuroimage **38**(1), 95–113 (2007)
2. Avants, B.B., Epstein, C.L., Grossman, M., Gee, J.C.: Symmetric diffeomorphic image registration with cross-correlation: evaluating automated labeling of elderly and neurodegenerative brain. Med. Image Anal. **12**(1), 26–41 (2008)
3. Balakrishnan, G., Zhao, A., Sabuncu, M.R., Dalca, A.V., Guttag, J.: An unsupervised learning model for deformable medical image registration. In: Proceedings of the IEEE/CVF Conference on Computer Vision and Pattern Recognition, pp. 9252–9260. IEEE (2018)
4. Cao, H., et al.: Swin-Unet: Unet-like pure transformer for medical image segmentation. arXiv preprint arXiv:2105.05537 (2021)

5. Cao, X., Yang, J., Wang, L., Xue, Z., Wang, Q., Shen, D.: Deep learning based inter-modality image registration supervised by intra-modality similarity. In: Shi, Y., Suk, H.-I., Liu, M. (eds.) MLMI 2018. LNCS, vol. 11046, pp. 55–63. Springer, Cham (2018). https://doi.org/10.1007/978-3-030-00919-9_7

6. Chen, J., et al.: TransUNet: Transformers make strong encoders for medical image segmentation. arXiv preprint arXiv:2102.04306 (2021)

7. Dice, L.R.: Measures of the amount of ecologic association between species. Ecology **26**(3), 297–302 (1945)

8. Dosovitskiy, A., et al.: An image is worth 16x16 words: Transformers for image recognition at scale. arXiv preprint arXiv:2010.11929 (2020)

9. Fischl, B.: Freesurfer. Neuroimage **62**(2), 774–781 (2012)

10. He, X., Tan, E.L., Bi, H., Zhang, X., Zhao, S., Lei, B.: Fully transformer network for skin lesion analysis. Med. Image Anal. **77**, 102357 (2022)

11. Kim, B., Kim, D.H., Park, S.H., Kim, J., Lee, J.G., Ye, J.C.: CycleMorph: cycle consistent unsupervised deformable image registration. Med. Image Anal. **71**, 102036 (2021)

12. Klein, S., Staring, M., Murphy, K., Viergever, M.A., Pluim, J.P.: Elastix: a toolbox for intensity-based medical image registration. IEEE Trans. Med. Imaging **29**(1), 196–205 (2009)

13. Lei, Y., et al.: 4d-CT deformable image registration using multiscale unsupervised deep learning. Phys. Med. Biol. **65**(8), 085003 (2020)

14. Luthra, A., Sulakhe, H., Mittal, T., Iyer, A., Yadav, S.: EFormer: Edge enhancement based transformer for medical image denoising. arXiv preprint arXiv:2109.08044 (2021)

15. Ma, M., Xia, H., Tan, Y., Li, H., Song, S.: HT-Net: hierarchical context-attention transformer network for medical CT image segmentation. Appl. Intell. **52**, 1–14 (2022)

16. Marcus, D.S., Wang, T.H., Parker, J., Csernansky, J.G., Morris, J.C., Buckner, R.L.: Open access series of imaging studies (oasis): cross-sectional MRI data in young, middle aged, nondemented, and demented older adults. J. Cogn. Neurosci. **19**(9), 1498–1507 (2007)

17. Miao, S., Wang, Z.J., Zheng, Y., Liao, R.: Real-time 2d/3d registration via CNN regression. In: 2016 IEEE 13th International Symposium on Biomedical Imaging (ISBI), pp. 1430–1434. IEEE (2016)

18. MindSpore: https://www.mindspore.cn/

19. Rohé, M.-M., Datar, M., Heimann, T., Sermesant, M., Pennec, X.: SVF-Net: learning deformable image registration using shape matching. In: Descoteaux, M., Maier-Hein, L., Franz, A., Jannin, P., Collins, D.L., Duchesne, S. (eds.) MICCAI 2017. LNCS, vol. 10433, pp. 266–274. Springer, Cham (2017). https://doi.org/10.1007/978-3-319-66182-7_31

20. Ronneberger, O., Fischer, P., Brox, T.: U-Net: convolutional networks for biomedical image segmentation. In: Navab, N., Hornegger, J., Wells, W.M., Frangi, A.F. (eds.) MICCAI 2015. LNCS, vol. 9351, pp. 234–241. Springer, Cham (2015). https://doi.org/10.1007/978-3-319-24574-4_28

21. Salehi, S.S.M., Khan, S., Erdogmus, D., Gholipour, A.: Real-time deep pose estimation with geodesic loss for image-to-template rigid registration. IEEE Trans. Med. Imaging **38**(2), 470–481 (2018)

22. Shattuck, D.W., et al.: Construction of a 3d probabilistic atlas of human cortical structures. Neuroimage **39**(3), 1064–1080 (2008)

23. Sokooti, H., de Vos, B., Berendsen, F., Lelieveldt, B.P.F., Išgum, I., Staring, M.: Nonrigid image registration using multi-scale 3D convolutional neural networks. In: Descoteaux, M., Maier-Hein, L., Franz, A., Jannin, P., Collins, D.L., Duchesne, S. (eds.) MICCAI 2017. LNCS, vol. 10433, pp. 232–239. Springer, Cham (2017). https://doi.org/10.1007/978-3-319-66182-7_27

24. de Vos, B.D., Berendsen, F.F., Viergever, M.A., Staring, M., Išgum, I.: End-to-end unsupervised deformable image registration with a convolutional neural network. In: Cardoso, M.J., et al. (eds.) DLMIA/ML-CDS -2017. LNCS, vol. 10553, pp. 204–212. Springer, Cham (2017). https://doi.org/10.1007/978-3-319-67558-9_24

25. Wang, Z., Xie, Y., Ji, S.: Global voxel transformer networks for augmented microscopy. Nat. Mach. Intell. **3**(2), 161–171 (2021)

26. Yang, X., Kwitt, R., Styner, M., Niethammer, M.: Quicksilver: fast predictive image registration-a deep learning approach. Neuroimage **158**, 378–396 (2017)

27. Yoo, I., Hildebrand, D.G.C., Tobin, W.F., Lee, W.-C.A., Jeong, W.-K.: ssEMnet: serial-section electron microscopy image registration using a spatial transformer network with learned features. In: Cardoso, M.J., et al. (eds.) DLMIA/ML-CDS -2017. LNCS, vol. 10553, pp. 249–257. Springer, Cham (2017). https://doi.org/10.1007/978-3-319-67558-9_29

28. Zhao, S., Dong, Y., Chang, E.I., Xu, Y., et al.: Recursive cascaded networks for unsupervised medical image registration. In: Proceedings of the IEEE/CVF International Conference on Computer Vision, pp. 10600–10610. IEEE (2019)

Context Alignment Network for Video Moment Retrieval

Chaolei Tan, Jian-Fang Hu, and Wei-Shi Zheng[✉]

School of Computer Science and Engineering, Sun Yat-sen University,
Guangzhou 510006, China
tanchlei@mail2.sysu.edu.cn, hujf5@mail.sysu.edu.cn, wszheng@ieee.org

Abstract. Video Moment Retrieval (VMR) is a challenging cross-modal retrieval task that aims to retrieve the most relevant moment from an untrimmed video via a given language query. In this task, cross-modal semantics should be thoroughly comprehended and supervisory signal of limited annotations should be efficiently mined. Toward this end, we develop a Context Alignment Network (CAN) to tackle VMR by modeling and aligning cross-modal contexts. First, we employ fine-grained fusion to preserve rich low-level information and conduct complementary local-global context modeling to translate low-level information into high-level semantics. Second, we propose a novel context alignment learning to utilize additional context alignment supervision during training. The intuitive motivation is that contextual information around the predicted moment boundaries should be similar to that of the ground truth moment boundaries. Therefore, we define the alignment degree of boundary contexts between video moments as a proxy measure of their temporal overlap. By minimizing the context alignment loss, the model is driven to learn a context-level alignment relationship between moment boundaries. We find context alignment learning is effective to improve the retrieval accuracy by exploiting context alignment as additional supervisory signal. Extensive experiments show that CAN attains competitive performance compared with state-of-the-arts on Charades-STA and TACoS datasets, demonstrating the effectiveness of our proposed method.

Keywords: Cross-modal retrieval · Regression-based moment retrieval · Cross-modal context modeling · Context alignment learning

1 Introduction

With the rapid development of modern society, people are exposed to ever-increasing multimedia information in their daily life. In realistic scenarios, people hunger for the convenience to localize something they are interested in from the raw multimedia data with redundancy. Video Moment Retrieval (VMR) is a task to meet this demand, which requires to localize the moment that best matches the description of a given language query from an untrimmed video.

Although lots of existing methods [1,6,12,28,31] have been studied in the field of VMR, there are still some critical issues to be addressed. First of all,

L. Fang et al. (Eds.): CICAI 2022, LNAI 13604, pp. 514–525, 2022.
https://doi.org/10.1007/978-3-031-20497-5_42

the commonly adopted cross-modal fusion in existing methods is in a coarse-grained manner, i.e., simply combining the visual features with sentence embedding. However, during such fusion process, plenty of low-level information will be blurred or lost at the early stage, which hurts the retrieval performance. Secondly, we find it suboptimal to conduct prediction right on top of the fusion module, since the low-level cross-modal representation is not adaptive to support the high-level query-based retrieval. Furthermore, due to the limited annotations of VMR, it become crucial to efficiently mine the hidden supervisory signal in the training data. Up to now, only coordinate-level supervision is explored, i.e. they train the model by minimizing the coordinate distances. Actually, We find the monotonous adoption of coordinate-level supervision limits the model performance to some extent.

To address the above issues, in this work, we develop a regression-based framework called Context Alignment Network (CAN) for video moment retrieval. In the early stage, We employ fine-grained fusion to integrate the frame-level visual features and word-level textual features by cross-modal co-attention. For thorough cross-modal semantics comprehension, we propose to complementarily model the local and global contexts in the cross-modal space. Afterwards, we aggregate the high-level contexts into a compact representation, from which the moment boundaries are predicted. In order to exploit additional context alignment supervision to boost the retrieval performance, we further propose a novel training paradigm named context alignment learning. The intuitive motivation stems from our observation that contextual information around the predicted boundaries should be similar to that of the ground-truth boundaries. In context alignment learning, we define the alignment degree of boundary contexts between video moments as a proxy measure of their temporal overlap. During training, this proxy measure would be minimized to align the boundary contexts, which will in turn facilitate the alignment of moment boundaries.

In summary, the contributions of our work are as follows: 1) we develop a Context Alignment Network (CAN) to effectively tackle the problem of VMR by modeling and aligning cross-modal contexts; 2) We propose a novel context alignment learning to utilize additional context alignment supervision by aligning the context-level representations of the predicted moment boundaries and ground-truth boundaries, which is effective to improve the retrieval accuracy; 3) we conduct extensive experiments and in-depth analysis on large-scale publicly available video moment retrieval benchmarks, which demonstrates the effectiveness of our proposed method.

2   Related Work

Video-text retrieval. Video-Text Retrieval (VTR) aims to retrieve the best matching video from a video corpus according to a given language query. As a coarse-grained cross-modal retrieval task, VTR is often tackled as a ranking problem in previous works [5,25,32], where similarity scores between all possible video-text pairs are calculated to select the result with the highest score.

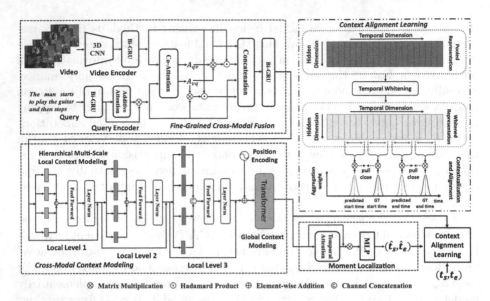

⊗ **Matrix Multiplication** ⊙ **Hadamard Product** ⊕ **Element-wise Addition** © **Channel Concatenation**

Fig. 1. The architecture of Context Alignment Network. We adopt fine-grained fusion and complementary context modeling for better semantics understanding. A novel context alignment learning is proposed to improve the retrieval accuracy.

Video Moment Retrieval. Video Moment Retrieval (VMR) aims to retrieve the temporal boundaries of the video moment corresponding to a given language query. This task is recently proposed in [1,6]. VMR is more challenging than VTR because it's a fine-grained cross-modal retrieval task. To facilitate the development of VMR, a variety of methods have been explored [1,6,20,28,31] over these years. Concretely, a majority of the existing methods [6,31] employ a two-stage proposal-based framework and they focus on generating and ranking proposals. However, these methods are heavily relying on dense proposal generation where the number of proposals is proportional to the square of the duration of the video, which will lead to unacceptable computation cost when the video is very long. In comparison, one-stage methods are promising to provide flexible and fast query-based video moment retrieval. In this work, we propose a novel one-stage approach named Context Alignment Network (CAN) which directly regress the starting/ending time of the target moment.

3   Context Alignment Network

3.1   Problem Formulation

Given an untrimmed video V and a language query Q, the target of video moment retrieval is to retrieve the moment from V which is most relevant to Q. The input video V can be denoted as $\{v_i\}_{i=1}^{T}$, meaning that it consists of T

frames or clip-level segments. The input query Q with N words can be denoted as $\{w_i\}_{i=1}^{N}$. The predicted moment and the moment of interest can be denoted by their temporal boundaries $(\hat{t}_s, \hat{t}_e)$ and (t_s, t_e), where $\hat{t}_s$, t_s are the starting times and $\hat{t}_e$, t_e are the ending times. Details will be discussed later.

3.2 Unimodal Encoders

We first employ two separate unimodal encoders to extract features from raw videos and queries, respectively. Their architectures are described below.

Video encoder. For an untrimmed video, we first divide it into a sequence of fixed-length clips and uniformly sample the sequence to T clips. The clips are then fed to the visual feature extractor, which contains a pretrained 3D Convolutional Neural Network (3D-CNN) [3,9] followed by a 2-layer Bidirectional Gated Recurrent Unit (Bi-GRU) to model temporal variations.

Query encoder. For a text sentence query, we adopt a pretrained Glove [13] word2vec model to encode it into word-level embeddings. Afterwards, a 2-layer Bi-GRU and an additive self-attention [2] module are employed to capture the sequential and global textual information, respectively.

3.3 Fine-Grained Cross-Modal Fusion

One of the key components in our proposed framework is a fine-grained fusion module, which effectively integrates the visual and linguistic unimodal features into an expressive and informative low-level cross-modal representation. Similar to existing methods [17,24] in machine reading comprehension, we design a cross-modal attention module. First, we calculate the Bahdanau attention weight [2] between a pair of video clip and text word as the following:

$$A_{i,j} = \mathbf{W}_s^{\mathrm{T}}(\mathrm{Tanh}(\mathbf{W_v}\mathcal{V}_i + \mathbf{W_w}\mathcal{Q}_j + \mathbf{b})) \tag{1}$$

where $\mathbf{W_v}$, $\mathbf{W_w} \in \mathbb{R}^{D \times D}$, $\mathbf{W_s}$, $\mathbf{b} \in \mathbb{R}^D$ are learnable parameters. $\mathcal{V}_i$ and $\mathcal{Q}_j$ indicate the i-th clip-level feature and j-th word-level feature in a given video-query pair, respectively. Then we normalize $A_{i,j}$ by applying softmax along the column and row axis to obtain the video-to-query attention map $\mathbf{A}_{vq}$ and query-to-video attention map $\mathbf{A}_{qv}$, respectively. $\mathbf{A}_{vq}$ and $\mathbf{A}_{qv}$ associate the vision-language modalities by attending to the important modality-specific information as $\mathcal{Q}' = \mathbf{A}_{vq}\mathcal{Q}, \mathcal{Q}'' = \mathbf{A}_{vq}\mathbf{A}_{qv}^{\mathrm{T}}\mathcal{V}$, where $\mathcal{Q}'$, $\mathcal{Q}'' \in \mathbb{R}^{T \times D}$ are clip-specific query representations aggregated by video-to-query attention and by both of video-to-query and query-to-video attention, respectively. The separate modalities are integrated as follows:

$$\mathcal{M} = \mathrm{Linear}(\mathrm{Bi\text{-}GRU}(\mathrm{Concat}([\mathcal{V}, \mathcal{Q}', \mathcal{V} \odot \mathcal{Q}', \mathcal{V} \odot \mathcal{Q}'']))), \tag{2}$$

where $\odot$ denotes Hadamard product and $\mathcal{M} \in \mathbb{R}^{T \times D}$ is an informative low-level cross-modal representation.

3.4   Cross-Modal Context Modeling

Cross-modal context modeling is a key component to achieve thorough cross-modal semantics understanding. Although the cross-modal representation $\mathcal{M}$ is rich in low-level information, it's not adaptive to achieve high-level query-based retrieval. To mend this gap, we propose to conduct cross-modal context modeling locally and globally as described following.

Local Context Modeling. Local context modeling is significant for fine-grained cross-modal retrieval, since it captures fleeting actions and helps to distinguish between similar local details. We note that the event of interest involved in VMR is usually a combination of several atomic actions at diverse temporal scales. This composite nature raises further demand for the capability of modeling hierarchical multi-scale local contexts. To achieve this goal, we propose a temporal Inception layer to capture multi-scale local context. Given a local size k, we construct multiple local branches (i.e., temporal convolutions and temporal pooling) with different receptive fields based on the local size, and integrate them into a multi-scale representation via inter-branch interactions. Denote the input as $\mathcal{I}$, the branches of a temporal Inception layer with local size k are constructed as:

$$\mathcal{B}_1 = \text{TConv}_1(\mathcal{I}), \mathcal{B}_2 = \text{TConv}_{2,2}(\text{TConv}_{2,1}(\mathcal{I})), \quad (3)$$

$$\mathcal{B}_3 = \text{TConv}_{3,2}(\text{TConv}_{3,1}(\mathcal{I})), \mathcal{B}_4 = \text{TConv}_4(\text{Pooling1D}(\mathcal{I})), \quad (4)$$

where TConv_1, $\text{TConv}_{2,1}$, $\text{TConv}_{3,1}, \text{TConv}_4$ are temporal convolutions with kernel size 1, TConv_{22} and TConv_{32} are temporal convolutions with kernel size k and $2k - 1$. Pooling1D is a temporal max-pooling layer with kernel size k. Then, we concatenate the branch outputs and interact them by a Feed Forward Network (FFN) followed by a Layer Normalization. A residual connection path is also added to maintain the identity information flow. To model different local levels, we further build a local hierarchy by stacking several temporal Inception layers with various local sizes, each of which models a certain local level in the holistic hierarchy. The hierarchical multi-scale local contexts $\mathcal{M}_l$ is obtained by feeding $\mathcal{M}$ to the local hierarchy. As shown in Figure 1, we empirically construct three local levels by stacking three temporal Inception layers, where the local size in each layer is twice of that in its previous layer.

Global Context Modeling. Modeling global contexts is indispensable for thorough cross-modal semantics understanding. Considering the attention layer proposed in Transformer [19] is well-known for its powerful capacity of capturing long-term dependencies, we simply implement our global module as a vanilla transformer encoder. We input local contexts $\mathcal{M}_l$ to the transformer encoder to obtain the high-level global contextual representation $\mathcal{M}_g$. Hierarchical multi-scale local contexts and the high-level global contexts jointly enable the model to capture complicated multi-scale local details and take a global view of the temporal relation cues. These two parts form a cohesive whole and are complementary to each other according to our experiments.

3.5   Context Alignment Learning

In VMR task, it's conventional to train the network by minimizing the coordinate distance. For example, the adoption of Smooth L1 loss is widely explored in a variety of methods [6,8,12,20,22,27,28]. However, existing methods overlook the fact that context alignment between moment boundaries could also be exploited as additional supervisory signal. Our motivation stems from our observation that contextual information around the boundaries of two aligned moments should be similar. Therefore, we can define the alignment degree of boundary contexts between video moments as a proxy measure of their temporal overlap. By minimizing this proxy measure, the model is driven to align the cross-modal contexts, which will in turn facilitate the alignment of moment boundaries. To put it another way, we aim to align the predictions and ground-truth in the context space rather than the coordinate space. We achieve this by first defining a location contextualization operation that maps a boundary location $L \in \{\hat{t}_s, \hat{t}_e, t_s, t_e\}$ to a contextualized representation $\mathcal{C}_L$ which represents the unique contextual information around location L. In such a context space, we align the predicted boundaries and the ground-truth by minimizing the following context alignment loss:

$$\mathcal{L}_{ctx} = \left\| \mathcal{C}_{\hat{t}_s} - \mathcal{C}_{t_s} \right\|_2^2 + \left\| \mathcal{C}_{\hat{t}_e} - \mathcal{C}_{t_e} \right\|_2^2. \tag{5}$$

In the following, we will introduce how we obtain the contextualized representation $\mathcal{C}_L$ corresponding to location L.

Location Contextualization. The proposed location contextualization maps a location to a contextualized representation. Specifically, we use two parameterized gaussian distributions to aggregate the adjacent contexts around a given location L as the following:

$$\mathcal{C}_L = \sum_{t=1}^{T} \delta_L(t) \mathcal{Z}^{\mathrm{w}}(t), \delta_L(t) = \frac{1}{\sum_t exp\left(-\frac{(t-L)^2)}{2\sigma^2}\right)} exp\left(-\frac{(t-L)^2)}{2\sigma^2}\right), \tag{6}$$

where $\mathcal{C}_L$ is the contextualized representation corresponding to location L, $\delta_L(\cdot)$ is the gaussian aggregation weights, σ^2 is the gaussian variance which is manually set as a constant, and the gaussian mean is set as the inputted location L. $\mathcal{Z}^{\mathrm{w}}(t)$ is a whitened representation (will be introduced next) from M_g at timestamp t. The location contextualization operation is differentiable with respect to the network's predictions $(\hat{t}_s, \hat{t}_e)$ and high-level representation M_g, hence it can enforce the network to learn precise boundary retrieval during the process of aligning location contexts.

Temporally Whitened Representation. Intuitively, the contextualized representation should be able to reflect the unique information of locations at a context level, only in this way can we impose a strict alignment constraint on the contextualized representations of different locations for better retrieval learning. We learn a temporally whitened representation $\mathcal{Z}^{\mathrm{w}}$ from $\mathcal{M}_g$ as input to the location contextualization operation. We first feed $\mathcal{M}_g$ to two temporal convolutional layers, and then downsample it by mean pooling (with a pooling stride s) to reduce the temporal resolution and obtain $\mathcal{C}_p \in \mathbb{R}^{T/s \times D}$. Since the representation $\mathcal{C}_p$ of neighboring clips can be very similar, it is not suitable for providing strong alignment supervision in our context alignment loss. We further propose to decorrelate the representation along temporal dimension, which is called temporal whitening. In temporal whitening, we first employ L2 standardization on $\mathcal{C}_p$ to get $\mathcal{Z}$ and then apply whitening on $\mathcal{Z}$ to obtain the whitened representation $\mathcal{Z}^w$ which satisfies the rigorous property for alignment as follows:

$$\mathcal{Z}^w(t_1))^T \mathcal{Z}^w(t_2) = \begin{cases} 1, t_1 = t_2 \\ 0, t_1 \neq t_2 \end{cases} \tag{7}$$

Temporal whitening disentangles the mutual interference between representations of different locations, which is significant for context alignment to be a consistent proxy objective of moment retrieval, i.e. the predicted boundaries aligned with the ground-truth better as the context alignment loss is minimized.

3.6   Prediction Head

We predict moment boundaries from the cross-modal contexts. Firstly, we calculate the temporal weights α from $\mathcal{M}_g$ by a linear layer, then $\mathcal{M}_g$ is aggregated into a compact representation $\mathcal{G} = \sum_{t=1}^{T} \alpha(t)\mathcal{M}_g(t)$. Finally, a two-layer MLP is used to predict the moment boundaries $(\hat{t}_s, \hat{t}_e)$ from $\mathcal{G}$.

3.7   Loss Function

We train our model with 4 loss terms: context alignment loss $\mathcal{L}_{ctx}$, location regression loss $\mathcal{L}_{loc}$, temporal attentive loss $\mathcal{L}_{ta}$ and IoU regression loss $\mathcal{L}_{iou}$. The total training loss is defined as $\mathcal{L} = \lambda_1 \mathcal{L}_{ctx} + \lambda_2 \mathcal{L}_{loc} + \lambda_3 \mathcal{L}_{ta} + \lambda_4 \mathcal{L}_{iou}$, where $\lambda_1, \lambda_2, \lambda_3, \lambda_4$ control the contributions of different loss terms. In the following, we will describe each loss term.

Context Alignment Loss.   The proposed context alignment loss $\mathcal{L}_{ctx}$ is described previously in Eq. 5.

Location Regression Loss. The traditional location regression loss is adopted to regress the L2 distance of the predicted coordinates and the ground-truth coordinates. It is defined as $\mathcal{L}_{loc} = \left\| \hat{t}_s - t_s \right\|_2^2 + \left\| \hat{t}_e - t_e \right\|_2^2$.

Temporal Attentive Loss. Cross-modal semantics within the ground-truth is extraordinarily significant for retrieval, we impose temporal attentive loss following [27] to pay more attention on the query-related video contents, which is given by $\mathcal{L}_{ta} = \frac{-\sum_{t=1}^{T} m_t log\alpha_t}{\sum_{t=1}^{T} m_t}$, where m_t takes 1 if t is within the ground-truth moment, otherwise m_t takes 0. α_t is the attention weight for the t-th video clip.

IoU Regression Loss. Intersection over union (IoU) is also an important metric to measure the overlapping degree of two moments. Specifically, we design an IoU regression loss as $\mathcal{L}_{iou} = \left(1 - \frac{\min(\hat{t}_e, t_e) - \max(\hat{t}_s, t_s)}{\max(\hat{t}_e, t_e) - \min(\hat{t}_s, t_s)}\right)^2$.

Table 1. Performance comparison with state-of-the-art approaches. Bold and underlined numbers represent the best and second best performance, respectively.

Dataset	Charades-STA				TACoS			
Method	R@0.3	R@0.5	R@0.7	mIoU	R@0.1	R@0.3	R@0.5	mIoU
TALL [6]	-	23.63	8.89	-	24.32	18.32	13.30	-
CBP [20]	-	36.80	18.87	35.74	-	-	-	-
DEBUG [11]	54.95	37.39	17.69	36.34	41.15	23.45	11.72	16.03
TripNet [8]	54.64	38.29	16.07	-	-	23.95	19.17	-
GDP [4]	54.54	39.47	18.49	36.34	39.68	24.14	-	16.18
BPNet [22]	65.48	50.75	31.64	46.34	-	25.96	20.96	19.53
SCDM [26]	-	54.44	33.43	-	-	26.11	21.17	-
DRN [28]	-	53.09	31.75	-	-	23.17	-	-
VSLNet [30]	70.46	54.19	35.22	50.02	-	31.86	27.64	26.25
LGI [12]	72.96	59.46	35.48	51.38	-	-	-	-
CAN(ours)	**73.47**	**62.45**	**39.17**	**53.00**	**54.76**	**40.81**	**28.59**	**27.78**

4 Experiments

4.1 Experimental Setting

Datasets. We conduct experiments on Charades-STA [6] and TACoS datasets. Charades-STA dataset [6] is built upon the original Charades dataset [18] for video moment retrieval, containing 6672 untrimmed videos of indoor activities. There are 12408 and 3720 moment-sentence pairs for training and testing, respectively. Each video is about 30 s with 2.4 annotated moments on average, and the average duration of target moments is 8.2 s. TACoS [15] consists of 127 untrimmed videos collected from MPII Cooking Composite Activities dataset [16]. Averagely, each of the videos is 4.79 min long and contains 148 moments of interest. Following the standard split in [6], we obtain 10146, 4589 and 4083 moment-sentence pairs for training, validation and testing, respectively.

Evaluation Metrics. Following the previous works [1,6,12,30], we adopt the "R@m" and "mIoU" metrics to evaluate the retrieval performance. Specifically, "R@m" is simply defined as the top-1 recall at an IoU threshold of m and "mIoU" denotes the averaged temporal Intersection over Union (IoU) of the predictions and ground-truth over the total dataset.

Implementation Details. For visual features, we employ the pretrained I3D [3] network for Charades-STA and C3D [9] network for TACoS. We uniformly sample 64, 128 clips per video for Charades-STA and TACoS, respectively. All the clips have the same length of 16 frames and are overlapped with each other by 50%. RAdam [10] optimizer with a batch size of 64 is adopted to train the network and the learning rate is set to be 0.0001. The loss balance factors λ_1,

Table 2. Ablation results of our proposed CAN on Charades-STA and TACoS datasets.

Dataset	Method	R@0.5	mIoU
Charades-STA	w/o fine-grained fusion	56.13	48.17
	w/o local context modeling	60.67	52.16
	w/o global context modeling	60.35	51.48
	w/o context alignment learning	60.81	52.08
	full model	**62.45**	**53.00**
TACoS	w/o fine-grained fusion	25.62	26.75
	w/o local context modeling	27.22	27.60
	w/o global context modeling	18.45	20.62
	w/o context alignment learning	26.54	26.57
	full model	**28.59**	**27.78**

λ_2, λ_3, λ_4 are set as 1, 10, 1, 1. For the three-level local hierarchy, local size is specified as 3 and 5 for Charades-STA and TACoS, respectively.

4.2 Performance Comparison

In this section, We compare our proposed CAN with state-of-the-arts and results are presented in Table 1. On the Charades-STA dataset, our method surpasses LGI in all metrics and for the strictest metric R@0.7, our approach outperforms LGI by a large margin of 3.69%. On the TACoS dataset, CAN surpasses VSLNet by 8.92%, 0.95% and 1.53% in R@0.1, R@0.3 and R@0.5, respectively. Overall, our approach achieve the best performance on both datasets. The main reason is that CAN thoroughly comprehends the cross-modal semantics by conducting cross-modal context modeling on top of the low-level cross-modal representation, and efficiently exploits additional context-level supervision to improve the retrieval accuracy by context alignment learning.

4.3 Ablation Study

In this section, we give a detailed ablation study on the architecture components and context alignment learning. The results are illustrated in Table 2.

Effect of Fine-Grained Fusion. To verify the importance of integrating modalities by fine-grained fusion, we ablate this component by deliberately replacing it with a coarse-grained fusion module based on hadamard product of the sentence-level embeddings and frame-level features, which is widely adopted in cross-modal retrieval tasks. As shown in Table 2, the model performances drop by a clear margin across all datasets, which confirms that fine-grained fusion is a fundamental step for cross-modal semantics comprehension.

Effect of Cross-Modal Context Modeling. As shown in Table 2, we can see that local and global context modeling are both helpful for better cross-modal representation learning, because removing any one of them will hurt the performance. Further, we find that local and global context modeling are complementary to each other, which is reflected by some suggestive facts in our experiments. On the TACoS dataset, we can see global context modeling dominates the joint effect of local-global cross-modal context modeling, this is because the annotated moments of the same video on TACoS are much more densely distributed compared to Charades-STA dataset. Therefore, given a language query and a reference video of TACoS, we need to make a lot more efforts to figure out the mutual relationships of different events and finally reason out the moment we want. The aforementioned relation reasoning process is primarily dependent on the effect of global context modeling. On the Charades-STA dataset, the annotated moments are more evenly distributed compared to TACoS, thus the impact of local context modeling and global context modeling are relatively similar.

Effect of Context-Level Supervision. As shown in Table 2, adopting context alignment learning in CAN will consistently improve the performance by a considerable margin in terms of all metrics on Charades-STA and TACoS datasets, which shows that context-level supervision works well to improve the retrieval accuracy in VMR. Note that the context-level supervision provided by context alignment learning is able to bring considerable gains over the baseline where coordinate-level supervision is fairly strong. This verifies that the monotonous adoption of coordinate-level supervision limits the model performance to some extent. We demonstrate that jointly exploiting context-level and coordinate-level supervision is an efficient way to train a model for VMR task.

5   Conclusion

In this paper, we develop a novel Context Alignment Network (CAN) that tackles Video Moment Retrieval by modeling and aligning cross-modal contexts. To thoroughly comprehend cross-modal semantics, we conduct complementary local-global cross-modal context modeling on top of fine-grained cross-modal fusion. Besides, we propose context alignment learning aiming to utilize additional context alignment supervision during the training, which is proved to be effective for boosting retrieval accuracy. Extensive experiments on Charades-STA and TACoS datasets verify the effectiveness of our method.

Acknowledgements. This work was supported partially by the NSFC (U1911401, U1811461, 62076260, 61772570), Guangdong Natural Science Funds Project (2020B15 15120085), Guangdong NSF for Distinguished Young Scholar (2022B1515020009), and the Key-Area Research and Development Program of Guangzhou (202007030004).

References

1. Anne Hendricks, L., Wang, O., Shechtman, E., Sivic, J., Darrell, T., Russell, B.: Localizing moments in video with natural language. In: CVPR (2017)

2. Bahdanau, D., Cho, K., Bengio, Y.: Neural machine translation by jointly learning to align and translate. arXiv preprint arXiv:1409.0473 (2014)
3. Carreira, J., Zisserman, A.: Quo vadis, action recognition? A new model and the kinetics dataset. In: CVPR (2017)
4. Chen, L., et al.: Rethinking the bottom-up framework for query-based video localization. In: AAAI (2020)
5. Cheng, X., Lin, H., Wu, X., Yang, F., Shen, D.: Improving video-text retrieval by multi-stream corpus alignment and dual softmax loss. arXiv preprint arXiv:2109.04290 (2021)
6. Gao, J., Sun, C., Yang, Z., Nevatia, R.: Tall: temporal activity localization via language query. In: ICCV (2017)
7. Ghosh, S., Agarwal, A., Parekh, Z., Hauptmann, A.: EXCL: extractive clip localization using natural language descriptions. arXiv preprint arXiv:1904.02755 (2019)
8. Hahn, M., Kadav, A., Rehg, J.M., Graf, H.P.: Tripping through time: efficient localization of activities in videos. arXiv preprint arXiv:1904.09936 (2019)
9. Ji, S., Xu, W., Yang, M., Yu, K.: 3d convolutional neural networks for human action recognition. In: TPAMI (2012)
10. Liu, L., Jiang, H., He, P., Chen, W., Liu, X., Gao, J., Han, J.: On the variance of the adaptive learning rate and beyond. arXiv preprint arXiv:1908.03265 (2019)
11. Lu, C., Chen, L., Tan, C., Li, X., Xiao, J.: Debug: a dense bottom-up grounding approach for natural language video localization. In: EMNLP-IJCNLP (2019)
12. Mun, J., Cho, M., Han, B.: Local-global video-text interactions for temporal grounding. In: CVPR (2020)
13. Pennington, J., Socher, R., Manning, C.D.: Glove: global vectors for word representation. In: EMNLP (2014)
14. Ramachandran, P., Zoph, B., Le, Q.V.: Searching for activation functions. arXiv preprint arXiv:1710.05941 (2017)
15. Regneri, M., Rohrbach, M., Wetzel, D., Thater, S., Schiele, B., Pinkal, M.: Grounding action descriptions in videos. In: Transactions of the Association for Computational Linguistics (2013)
16. Rohrbach, M., Regneri, M., Andriluka, M., Amin, S., Pinkal, M., Schiele, B.: Script data for attribute-based recognition of composite activities. In: Fitzgibbon, A., Lazebnik, S., Perona, P., Sato, Y., Schmid, C. (eds.) ECCV 2012. LNCS, vol. 7572, pp. 144–157. Springer, Heidelberg (2012). https://doi.org/10.1007/978-3-642-33718-5_11
17. Seo, M., Kembhavi, A., Farhadi, A., Hajishirzi, H.: Bidirectional attention flow for machine comprehension. arXiv preprint arXiv:1611.01603 (2016)
18. Sigurdsson, G.A., Varol, G., Wang, X., Farhadi, A., Laptev, I., Gupta, A.: Hollywood in homes: crowdsourcing data collection for activity understanding. In: Leibe, B., Matas, J., Sebe, N., Welling, M. (eds.) ECCV 2016. LNCS, vol. 9905, pp. 510–526. Springer, Cham (2016). https://doi.org/10.1007/978-3-319-46448-0_31
19. Vaswani, A., et al.: Attention is all you need. In: NIPS (2017)
20. Wang, J., Ma, L., Jiang, W.: Temporally grounding language queries in videos by contextual boundary-aware prediction. In: AAAI (2020)
21. Wu, J., Li, G., Liu, S., Lin, L.: Tree-structured policy based progressive reinforcement learning for temporally language grounding in video. In: AAAI (2020)
22. Xiao, S., et al.: Boundary proposal network for two-stage natural language video localization. In: AAAI (2021)
23. Xu, H., He, K., Plummer, B.A., Sigal, L., Sclaroff, S., Saenko, K.: Multilevel language and vision integration for text-to-clip retrieval. In: AAAI (2019)

24. Yu, A.W., Dohan, D., Luong, M.T., Zhao, R., Chen, K., Norouzi, M., Le, Q.V.: QANet: Combining local convolution with global self-attention for reading comprehension. arXiv preprint arXiv:1804.09541 (2018)
25. Yu, Y., Kim, J., Kim, G.: A joint sequence fusion model for video question answering and retrieval. In: Ferrari, V., Hebert, M., Sminchisescu, C., Weiss, Y. (eds.) ECCV 2018. LNCS, vol. 11211, pp. 487–503. Springer, Cham (2018). https://doi.org/10.1007/978-3-030-01234-2_29
26. Yuan, Y., Ma, L., Wang, J., Liu, W., Zhu, W.: Semantic conditioned dynamic modulation for temporal sentence grounding in videos. arXiv preprint arXiv:1910.14303 (2019)
27. Yuan, Y., Mei, T., Zhu, W.: To find where you talk: temporal sentence localization in video with attention based location regression. In: AAAI (2019)
28. Zeng, R., Xu, H., Huang, W., Chen, P., Tan, M., Gan, C.: Dense regression network for video grounding. In: CVPR (2020)
29. Zhang, D., Dai, X., Wang, X., Wang, Y.F., Davis, L.S.: Man: Moment alignment network for natural language moment retrieval via iterative graph adjustment. In: CVPR (2019)
30. Zhang, H., Sun, A., Jing, W., Zhen, L., Zhou, J.T., Goh, R.S.M.: Natural language video localization: A revisit in span-based question answering framework. IEEE Trans. Pattern Anal. Mach. Intell. (2021)
31. Zhang, S., Peng, H., Fu, J., Luo, J.: Learning 2d temporal adjacent networks for moment localization with natural language. In: AAAI (2020)
32. Zhu, L., Yang, Y.: ActBERT: learning global-local video-text representations. In: CVPR (2020)

Underwater Object Detection Using Restructured SSD

Andi Huang, Guoqiang Zhong$^{(\boxtimes)}$, Hao Li, and Daewon Choi

College of Computer Science and Technology, Ocean University of China,
Qingdao 266100, China
gqzhong@ouc.edu.cn

Abstract. Deep learning has been widely used in computer vision tasks such as image classification, semantic segmentation and object detection, which has achieved many breakthrough results in recent years. Compared with conventional object detection tasks, due to objective factors such as uneven illumination, low contrast, and more impurities in the underwater environment, these is no guarantee of high quality for underwater images, which brings challenges to the underwater object detection task. In this paper, we construct an underwater object detection model based on multi-scale feature fusion (called Multi-scale Feature Fusion Network for Underwater Object Detection, MFFNet). MFFNet uses SSD model as the baseline, then makes an improvement by adding three different modules, which are improved FPN, assisting backbone and CBAM attention module. Based on VGG-16 and ResNet-50 as the backbone network, the composite backbone connection is performed; the attention mechanism CBAM module is involved to make the network pay more attention to the objects; the feature pyramid FPN structure is used for multi-scale feature detection. To verify the effectiveness of the network model proposed in this paper, experiments are carried out on three datasets, i.e., VOC 2007, UPRC and Fish4knowledges. The experimental results show that compared with other main object detection models, the network model proposed in this paper has obvious advantages in underwater object detection, and can obtain higher detection accuracy.

Keywords: Underwater object detection · Attention mechanism · Multi-scale detection

1 Introduction

Ocean economy accounts for a significant amount of value creation for the world economy. International organizations such as OECD (Organization for Economic Co-operation and Development) estimate that marine resources are prone to rapid depletion overtime due to unscrupulous and irresponsible fishing activities.

Therefore, it is very important to understand how to protect and use limited marine resources while providing long-term development for sound and sustainable fishery activities. One of the important mechanisms for the protection

© The Author(s), under exclusive license to Springer Nature Switzerland AG 2022
L. Fang et al. (Eds.): CICAI 2022, LNAI 13604, pp. 526–537, 2022.
https://doi.org/10.1007/978-3-031-20497-5_43

of marine resources is to fully understand different species that allow fishery activities, as well as species that are prone to extinction. In this context, how to enable machines to automatically detect different marine species is a very valuable research direction, and also promotes the research and development of underwater object detection technology.

The main task of object detection is to find out the objects of interest in the image, and to determine their categories and positions. It is one of the core problems in the field of computer vision that convolutional neural networks are used to solve, while the accuracy of object detection is constantly improving. However, for underwater objects, due to problems such as image blur, unbalanced illumination, and object occlusion that may be caused by underwater scenes, using existing object detection models directly for underwater object detection cannot bring good results. Based on the above reasons, papers and methods for underwater object detection are constantly being proposed. At the same time, in order to promote the development and progress of underwater robots, underwater robot competitions are held year by year, and visual object detection has also become an important part of the competition project.

Based on the one-stage detector SSD [2] model, our proposed method consists of several parts: (i) Using the structure similar to FPN [4], the features of different layers are fused. In this paper, some improvements have been made by combining the output features of the front layer and the rear layer, then we use the result as the output of this current layer, and complete the prediction with the features obtained through the fusion. (ii) We use different backbone networks for feature extraction to work together, that is, the same corresponding feature extraction layer, in which the output features of one backbone network are transformed and added to the input of the other backbone network. Hence, the backbone network can get stronger feature extraction capability. (iii) We use channel and space attention as the attention mechanism, which is used to allow the object to get more attention, enhancing the detection ability to blurring objects.

2 Related Work

When the conventional object detection model is directly used on images of the underwater complex environment, it cannot achieve good results. Because of the instability of the underwater light source, the image collection is limited to the performance of underwater photography equipment. The pictures obtained are inevitably of low quality, such as blur, low contrast, and darker color occur.

Therefore, in order to conduct underwater object detection, it is usually considered from two angles: underwater images enhancement and improving the original model or proposing new models to make it have better performance. The main purpose of underwater image enhancement technology is to improve the quality of the image. Generally, it includes removing image noise and image super-resolution to achieve the enhanced effect. Dmitry et al. [9] have utilized a mixed dataset of fish, none-fish, above water and underwater images to train models. With this multi-domain combination of images, the trained Xception-based binary (fish/none-fish) classifier has achieved 0.17% false-positives and 0.61% false-negatives on the 20,000 negative and 16,000 positive holdout test images, respectively. It has achieved 99.94% for the area under the ROC curve (AUC). Cui et al. [11] have employed a combined approach to CNN based optimization. A tandem method of data augmentation, network simplification, training acceleration has yielded a higher performance for fish image classification. Olsvik et al. [10] utilize an innovative pre-filtering dataset mechanism. Conventional pre-filtering involves a separation of background images from fish images, or enhancing fish images by removing the background noise. In [17], the authors propose a method for image enhancement. This method is mainly aimed at the existence of mutual obstruction between the objectives in the underwater scene, while the image collected is blurry. Li et al. [18] have compiled 12 current mainstream underwater images to show the practice and achievement of some existing methods in detail. Hitam et al. [19] propose CLAHE-mix, which uses different CLAHE [21] in RGB space and HSV space to enhance image contrast.

In addition to enhancement of images, many people try to improve on the common objective detection model. By increasing the module or modifying the model structure, it can improve the corresponding performance on underwater detection tasks. Ge et al. [1] use CNN based fine-grained image classification with dimensional reduction of internal fully connected layers, in conjunction with layer-restricted retraining to avoid retraining the entire network. Rathi, Jain and Indu [5] use deep CNN with Otsu binarization and thresholding for pyramid mean shifting of fish image data, which has demonstrated an accuracy level of 96.29%. Mandal et al. [6] use an object detector termed as Faster R-CNN, producing a Region Proposal Network (RPN), which has resulted in a very high accuracy.

Sun et al. [8] use FishNet to directly propagate the gradient information from deep layers to shallow layers. On ImageNet-1k, the accuracy of FishNet is higher than that of DenseNet and ResNet using fewer parameters. Rekha et al. [7] use a three stage method of augmentation, detection and classification. The real time images obtained by bost-cameras are first augmented and transmitted to the detection stage. This stage uses CNN to identify regions with higher probability of fish image features. Then, the third stage uses CNN classifier architecture for species classification based on eight categories. Kristian et al. [13] drawing on previous work on fish classification model, introduce a dual method of You Only Look Once (YOLO) fish image detection, with the Squeeze-and-Excitation (SE) architecture for fish classification. Salman et al. [12] employ a Region-Based Convolutional Neural Network (RB-CNN) for fish image processing to diminish noise for fish object detection and localization. Chen et al. [20] propose SWIPENet to deal with underwater small-sample. It adopts the sample heavy weight algorithm IMA and empty convolution to improve the single-stage detector and improve the ability to detect underwater objects.

In our paper, we introduce a novel approach which differs susbstantively from the aforementioned methods. We have combined SSD model with derived convolution block attention module (CBAM) and special attention model, to create a new hybrid model. This approach has not been implemented yet by other papers, thus, constitutes an unique and innovative method which could render higher performance, as explained below.

3 The Proposed Method

In this section, aiming at the problem of poor performance of conventional single-stage detectors in underwater objective detection, we construct the Multi-Scale Feature Fusion Network for Underwater Object Detection (MFFNET).

3.1 SSD Model

In this paper, we adopt the SSD model as our baseline, which is a classic one-stage object detection model. Its detection accuracy is comparable to Faster RCNN while its running speed is comparable to YOLO. We use VGG16 as the backbone of the model, the last two full connection layers of VGG16 are changed into convolutional layers, and 4 convolutional layers are added. Particularly, each detection box generates four coordinate values (x, y, W, H), where (x, y) is the coordinates of the center, W and H are width and height, respectively.

3.2 SSD_FPN

In the idea of FPN, it fuses feature maps with strong low-resolution semantic information and feature maps with high-resolution weak semantic information but rich spatial information on the premise of increasing less computational complexity, thereby obtaining feature maps with both good spatial information and strong semantic information. Based on this idea, we adopt the SSD_FPN method to fuse the intermediate feature maps of multiple scales. As shown in the Fig. 1, the output feature map of conv8_2 undergoes a 1×1 convolution to transform the number of channels. The same principle converts the output feature maps of conv7 and conv9_2 to the same number of channels, and then combines their final results to conv7 as the final output in the FPN structure. Through experiments, we have proved that this method can indeed improve our detection results.

3.3 Assisting Backbone

In our work, we use VGG16 as the lead backbone and ResNet50 as the assisting backbone. The high-level features in ResNet are transformed and added to the low-level features of VGG16 to assist in feature learning. The transformation operation includes using a 1×1 convolution to make them the same number of channels, then using a normalization layer and upsampling to make them the same size, and then adding them.

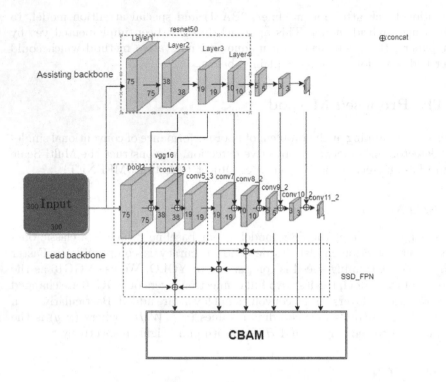

Fig. 1. Architectures of our network. The top is the resnet50 used as the assisting backbone, the middle is the vgg16 as the lead backbone, the below of vgg16 is the SSD_FPN structure, and the bottom is the CBAM module.

Compared with the traditional single backbone, the features extracted at each stage includes some features extracted by the convolution kernel of a certain stage for many times. It can be roughly understood that the convolutional kernel at this stage has repeatedly passed several times. At the same time, in order to prevent the model from being too complicated and causing the expansion of the calculation and parameters, we only use one assisting and one lead backbone. The specific connection method is shown in Fig. 1.

3.4   Attention Mechanism

The attention mechanism CBAM [3] module has also been proposed and proved to be effective, and its specific manifestation is to add attention in the channel and space dimensions. This paper also uses channel and space attention mechanism, which is added to the middle feature layer of the SSD model, namely conv4_3, Conv7, Conv8, Conv9_2, Conv10_2, Conv11_2. After the six convolutional layers, the attention map is calculated from the two different dimensions of channel and space, and then the obtained attention map is multiplied by the input feature map for adaptive feature refinement, as shown in Fig. 2 and Fig. 3.

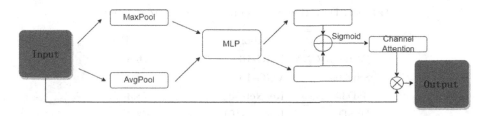

Fig. 2. Channel attention module

The input feature map F (H × W × C) is respectively subjected to global maximum pooling and global average pooling based on the width W and height H of the feature map to obtain two 1 × 1 × C feature maps, and then separate them. The separated ones are then fed into a two-layer neural network, and the two-layer neural network is shared. The features output by this neural network are added element-by-element, and then the sigmoid activation operation is performed to generate the final channel attention feature map. This feature map and the input feature map are multiplied element by element to generate the channel attention module. The output is used as input into the spatial attention module.

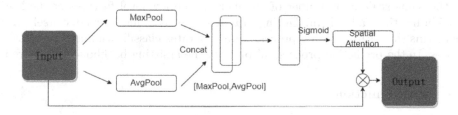

Fig. 3. Spatial attention module

The spatial attention module first performs a channel-based global maximum pooling and global average pooling to obtain two H × W × 1 feature maps, and then splice these two feature maps into channels. Then after a convolutional operation, the dimensionality is reduced to 1 channel, that is, H × W × 1. Then it generates a spatial attention feature map through the sigmoid function, and finally multiply the feature map and the input feature map of the module element by element to obtain the final generated feature.

Table 1. Detection results on the VOC 2007 dataset.

Model	Backbone	mAP
Faster R-CNN	VGG-16	76.5
SSD300	VGG-16	76.3
SSD300	ResNet-50	78.3
DSSD	ResNet-101	78.8
Ours	**VGG-16+ResNet-50**	**80.1**

3.5   MFFNET

In MFFNET, the output of the fused feature maps are fed into the CBAM module, which takes attention to the channel and spatial dimensions. In this way, the feature covers more parts of the object to be identified. And then, the output of the CBAM module is used as the final result of conv5_3 for subsequent operations. Similarly, we perform the same operation on conv7, conv8_2, conv9_2, conv10_2 and conv11_2.

At the same time, the ResNet50 used for assisting also participates in our training process. The high-level features of this assisting backbone are subjected to 1×1 convolution, and the normalization layer and upsampling layer makes it the same scale and number of channels as the low-level features of the lead backbone, then add them. During training, the assisting backbone itself also performs the entire training process, and generates classification and regression losses. In the prediction process, all parts of the assisting backbone are ignored.

3.6   Loss Function

The SSD model adopts two principles in the priori box matching, and we continue to use these two principles:

For each ground truth object in the image, find the a priori box with the largest IOU. The a priori box is a positive sample. If a prior box does not match any ground truth, it is a negative sample.

For the remaining unmatched a priori boxes, if the IOU with a certain ground truth is greater than a certain threshold (usually 0.5), the a priori box also matches the ground truth.

Similarly, we can continue to use the loss function of the SSD model:

$$L(x, c, l, g) = \frac{1}{N}(L_{conf}(x, c) + \alpha L_{loc}(x, l, g)), \tag{1}$$

where N is the number of positive samples of the a priori box, the smooth L1 loss is used for the position error L, and the softmax loss is used for the confidence error L_{loc}.

Table 2. Detection results of individual classes on the UPRC dataset.

Species	Faster R-CNN	SSD	Ours
Holothurian	28.1	25.1	**31.4**
Echiinus	64.1	65.5	**69.4**
Scallop	27.2	25.3	**31.3**
Starfish	45.8	46.4	**50.9**
mAP	41.3	40.6	**45.8**

Table 3. Detection results of average accuracy on the UPRC dataset.

Model	Backbone	mAP
Faster R-CNN	VGG-16	41.3
Cascade R-CNN	ResNet-101	45.7
SSD	VGG-16	40.6
DSSD	ResNet-101	41.4
YOLO	DarkNet-53	40.4
RefineDet	VGG-16	42.4
ours	**VGG-16+ResNet-50**	**45.8**

4 Experiments

4.1 Datasets

There are three data sets that we used in the experiments: Pascal VOC, UPRC and Fish4knowledges.

The Pascal VOC 2007 dataset contains 9963 images, including 5011 training images, 4,952 test images, of 20 types of objects. This dataset is provided in the Pascal VOC Challenge. It is a standardized dataset for computer visual tasks. It mainly provides images of objects in some real scenes.

The URPC dataset contains sea cucumber, sea urchin, scallops and starfish images. It originally includes 5443 training images and 800 test images. All data are provided by Pengcheng Labs in the underwater object detection algorithm competition in the national underwater robot competition. In order to obtain more data sets, we merged different image data provided by the National Underwater Robot Contest in recent years, and expanded the UPRC dataset, and finally got more than 10,000 pictures.

Another dataset is from Fish4Knowledge [16]. This fish data are acquired from a live video dataset, resulting in 27370 verified fish images. The whole dataset is divided into 23 clusters and each cluster is presented by a representative species, which is based on the synapomorphies characteristic from the extent that the taxon is monophyletic. We selected 6 kinds of fish, and the number of images of each fish was greater than 299, and then constructed a new dataset for experimentation.

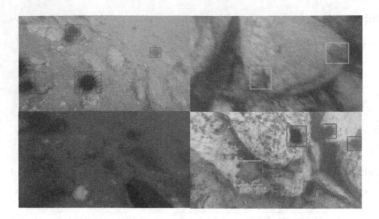

Fig. 4. Results visualization on the UPRC dataset.

4.2 Results

Table 1 shows the comparison results of some mainstream detection algorithms on the VOC 2007 data set. It is easy to see, our method performs the best among others.

For the UPRC dataset, we use the Stochastic Gradient Descent (SGD) method to update the model parameter in the training process, and set the Nesterov momentum (Momentum) to 0.9. At the same time, both VGG16 and ResNet50 use the pre-trained weights. We set the Batch Size to 32. Moreover, the initial learning rate is 0.0001, the weight attenuation coefficient is 0.0005, a total of 24,000 training is conducted, the parameters are saved every 2000 times, and the last-time model is used for test.

After training, the four species contained in the data set are calculated separately for predictive accuracy. The results are shown in Table 2. As we can see, the proposed method outperforms the compared ones.

Due to the characteristics of the UPRC data set, the images have problems, such as blur, low contrast, and object coverage. Our model can obtain better results than existing ones, as shown in Table 3 and Fig. 4.

In addition, we conduct comparison experiment on the Fish4knowledge dataset. It can be seen from Table 4 that the proposed model obtains promising results.

Finally, by gradually removing the assisting backbone model, CBAM and the improved FPN module, we construct ablation study to verify the role of each module and the degree of contribution to the entire model detection accuracy. The results are shown in Table 5.

Table 4. Detection results of individual classes on the Fish4knowledge dataset.

Species	Faster R-CNN	SSD	Ours
Plectroglyphidodon dickii	**90.9**	90.6	89.8
Chromis chrysura	**91.7**	90.8	91.5
Amphiprion clarkii	91.6	90.8	**91.6**
Chaetodon lunulatus	**92.2**	90.9	91.7
Myripristis kuntee	88.4	88.1	**88.4**
Neoniphon sammara	93.3	90.8	**96.9**
mAp(50)	91.4	90.3	**91.6**

Table 5. Ablation experiments on the UPRC dataset.

ASSISTING	CBAM	SSD_FPN	mAp
			40.6
√			41.8
	√		42.5
		√	44.5
√	√		43.8
	√	√	44.8
√		√	45.2
√	√	√	**45.8**

5 Conclusion

This paper introduces three different modules, including improved FPNs, assisting backbone, and CBAM, to the original SSD model, and constructs a new deep architecture called MFFNet for underwater object detection. The improved FPN structure is used for multi-scale feature detection. Based on VGG16 and ResNet50 as the main network, a composite backbone connection is added. The CBAM module is introduced to help the network pay more attention to the detection objects. Experimental results on three used datasets show that the proposed model MFFNET effectively improves the detection results over existing approaches. For the future work, we would like to apply MFFNct to more challenging images, such as those with noise and small objects.

Acknowledgment. This work was partially supported by the National Key Research and Development Program of China under Grant No. 2018AAA0100400, the Natural Science Foundation of Shandong Province under Grants No. ZR2020MF131 and No. ZR2021ZD19, and the Science and Technology Program of Qingdao under Grant No. 21-1-4-ny-19-nsh.

References

1. Ge, Z., McCool, C., Sanderson, C., Corke, P.I.: Modelling local deep convolutional neural network features to improve fine-grained image classification. CoRR, vol. abs/1502.07802 (2015). http://arxiv.org/abs/1502.07802
2. Liu, W., et al.: SSD: single shot multibox detector. CoRR, vol. abs/1512.02325 (2015). http://arxiv.org/abs/1512.02325
3. Woo, S., Park, J., Lee, J., Kweon, I.S.: CBAM: convolutional block attention module. CoRR, vol. abs/1807.06521 (2018). http://arxiv.org/abs/1807.06521
4. Lin, T., et al.: Feature pyramid networks for object detection. CoRR, vol. abs/1612.03144 (2016). http://arxiv.org/abs/1612.03144
5. Rathi, D., Jain, S., Indu, S.: Underwater fish species classification using convolutional neural network and deep learning. CoRR, vol. abs/1805.10106 (2018). http://arxiv.org/abs/1805.10106
6. Mandal, R., Connolly, R.M., Schlacher, T.A., Stantic B.: Assessing fish abundance from underwater video using deep neural networks. CoRR, vol. abs/1807.05838 (2018). http://arxiv.org/abs/1807.05838
7. Rekha, B.S., Srinivasan, G.N., Reddy, S.K., Kakwani, D., Bhattad, N.: Fish detection and classification using convolutional neural networks. In: Smys, S., Tavares, J.M.R.S., Balas, V.E., Iliyasu, A.M. (eds.) ICCVBIC 2019. AISC, vol. 1108, pp. 1221–1231. Springer, Cham (2020). https://doi.org/10.1007/978-3-030-37218-7_128
8. Sun, S., Pang, J., Shi, J., Yi, S., Ouyang, W.: Fishnet: a versatile backbone for image, region, and pixel level prediction. CoRR, vol. abs/1901.03495 (2019). http://arxiv.org/abs/1901.03495
9. Konovalov, D.A., Saleh, A., Bradley, M., Sankupellay, M., Marini, S., Sheaves, M.: Underwater fish detection with weak multi-domain supervision. CoRR, vol. abs/1905.10708 (2019). http://arxiv.org/abs/1905.10708
10. Olsvik, E., et al.: Biometric fish classification of temperate species using convolutional neural network with squeeze-and-excitation. CoRR, vol. abs/1904.02768 (2019). http://arxiv.org/abs/1904.02768
11. Cui, S., Zhou, Y., Wang, Y., Zhai, L.: Fish detection using deep learning. Appl. Comput. Intell. Soft Comput. **2020**(11), 1–13 (2020)
12. Salman, A., Siddiqui, S.A., Shafait, F., Mian, A.S., Schwanecke, U.: Automatic fish detection in underwater videos by a deep neural network-based hybrid motion learning system. ICES J. Mar. Sci. (2019)
13. Knausgård, K.M., et al: Temperate fish detection and classification: a deep learning based approach. CoRR, vol. abs/2005.07518 (2020). http://arxiv.org/abs/2005.07518
14. Iqbal, M.A., Wang, Z., Ali, Z.A., Riaz, S.: Automatic fish species classification using deep convolutional neural networks. Wirel. Personal Commun. **116**(1), 1043–1053 (2021)
15. Liu, Y., et al.: CBNet: a novel composite backbone network architecture for object detection (2019)
16. Boom, B.J., Huang, X., He, J., Fisher, R.B.: Supporting ground-truth annotation of image datasets using clustering (2012)
17. Lin, W.-H., Zhong, J.-X., Liu, S., Li, T., Li, G.: ROIMIX: proposal-fusion among multiple images for underwater object detection. In: ICASSP 2020–2020 IEEE International Conference on Acoustics, Speech and Signal Processing (ICASSP), pp. 2588–2592 (2020)

18. Li, C., et al.: An underwater image enhancement benchmark dataset and beyond. IEEE Trans. Image Process. **29**, 4376–4389 (2020)
19. Hitam, M.S., Awalludin, E.A., Jawahir Hj Wan Yussof, W.N., Bachok, Z.: Mixture contrast limited adaptive histogram equalization for underwater image enhancement. In: 2013 International Conference on Computer Applications Technology (ICCAT), pp. 1–5 (2013)
20. Chen, L., et al.: Underwater object detection using invert multi-class adaboost with deep learning. In: 2020 International Joint Conference on Neural Networks (IJCNN), pp. 1–8 (2020)
21. Reza, A.M.: Realization of the contrast limited adaptive histogram equalization (CLAHE) for real-time image enhancement. J. VLSI Signal Process. Syst. Signal Image Video Technol. **38**(1), 35–44 (2004)

A Multi-branch Cascade Transformer Network (MBCT–Net) for Hand Gesture Segmentation in Cluttered Background

Zhenchao Cui[1], Guoyu Zhou[1], Jing Qi[1(✉)], Huimin Wang[2], and Xilun Ding[3]

[1] School of Cyber Security and Computer, Hebei University, Baoding, China
jingqi@buaa.edu.cn
[2] Beijing University of Technology, Beijing, China
[3] Robotics Institute, Beihang University, Beijing, China
xlding@buaa.edu.cn

Abstract. Hand gesture segmentation is an initial and essential step to classify hand gestures, which provides a simple, intuitive, concise and natural way for human–computer interaction, human–robot interaction. However, hand gestures segmentation with various hand shapes cluttered background is still a challenging problem. To solve the problem, a Multi-Branch Cascade Transformer Network (MBCT–Net) is proposed to segment hand regions from the cluttered background based on encoder-decoder convolutional neural networks, the encoder of the MBCT–Net consists of a deep convolutional neural network (DCNN) module and a multi-branch cascade Transformer (MBCT) module. Furthermore, the MBCT module is designed to represent local details and global semantic information of hand gestures. Moreover, to enhance semantical interaction between different windows and expand the receptive fields of MBCT-Net, we design a multi–window self-attention (MWSA) block in each branch of MBCT module to extract features of hand gestures. The MWSA block not only reduces the amount of calculation, but also enhances semantic interactions between different windows. To verify effectiveness of the proposed MBCT–Net, corresponding experiments have been conducted, and the experimental results prove correctness of the MBCT–Net.

Keywords: Hand gesture segmentation · Deep learning · Transformer

1 Introduction

With rapid developments of robots, human-robot interaction (HRI) has become more and more important. Hand gestures can provide simple, intuitive and concise modality for HRI, and thus vision–based hand gesture recognition has attracted a lot of attention of scholars. Moreover, vision–based hand gesture recognition mainly consists of two steps: hand detection/segmentation and classification. Hand detection is to detect and label hand regions using bounding boxes in an image, if there are hand regions in the image. Hand segmentation is to segment the detected hand region as the region of interest

© The Author(s), under exclusive license to Springer Nature Switzerland AG 2022
L. Fang et al. (Eds.): CICAI 2022, LNAI 13604, pp. 538–550, 2022.
https://doi.org/10.1007/978-3-031-20497-5_44

from the image, to reduce the amount of calculation for subsequent operations. Moreover, the hand detection/segmentation step is an initial and essential step of classification, the accuracy of hand segmentation greatly affects the accuracy of gesture recognition.

Scholars utilize traditional methods to detect/segment hand regions. Some researchers employ skin color [1], shape and texture (such as, histogram of oriented gradient [2], Haar-like [3], scale invariant feature transform [4] features), combination of skin color, shape and texture [5], fusion of motion and skin color [6] information to segment hand regions using a monocular camera.

Many methods of hand gesture segmentation are based on fully convolutional neural networks, which use a series of convolutional and down-sampling layers to expand the receptive fields of the network model and capture the deep features of gestures, and then use up-sampling methods to restore the spatial resolution of the feature maps to achieve the purpose of gesture segmentation. The more typical semantic segmentation neural networks include IASPP-ResNet [7], DeepLabV3 + [8], U-Net [9], and PSPNet [10]. The excellent performance of these convolutional neural network-based methods in various semantic segmentation tasks demonstrates that convolutional neural networks have strong feature learning capability.

However, in convolutional neural networks, the extraction of features often starts from local regions and gradually acquires a global view, and CNN-based methods have difficulty learning global as well as remote semantic information interactions. Limitations still exist when global features are extracted including using methods such as atrous convolution [8, 11, 12] or image pyramids [10]. In the literature [13], the use of transformer is proposed for image recognition, where 2D images are divided into equal-sized blocks as input and trained on each dataset to obtain similar performance to CNN methods. The literature [14] proposes a window-based transformer structure that limits the self-attentive computation to a window of a certain size, and it shows excellent feature learning capability in image classification, target detection, and semantic segmentation tasks. The successful applications of swin transformer shows that transformer has some potential in the field of computer vision.

A hand has many joints, and hand postures have various shape and texture, thus hand gesture segmentation in cluttered background is challenging. To solve the problem, motivated by self-attention strategy, both local details and global information is employed to segment hand regions, and a Multi-Branch Cascade Transformer Network (MBCT–Net) is proposed in this work. Specifically, multiple branches are used to obtain multiple scale information of hand postures, cascaded structure is employed to preserve detailed information, and self-attention strategy is utilized to select representative features. In addition, and the main contributions of the proposed MBCT-Net are shown as follows:

(1) A multi-branch cascade transformer (MBCT) module is proposed in this case. The module can obtain both local details and global features of hand gestures.
(2) The proposed MBCT module utilizes multi-window self-attention block to extract features of hand gestures. Moreover, the multi-window self-attention block not only reduce calculation of the MBCT module, but also enhance semantic interaction between different windows, so as to obtain more local detailed features of hand gestures.

(3) A multi-branches cascade Transformer module is applied to encode-decode structures to learn local details and global semantic information of intermediate feature
maps of hand gestures in this work.

The paper is organized as follows: Sect. 2 describes the methods related to gesture
segmentation. Section 3 details the proposed multi-branch cascade Transformer network.
To demonstrate effectiveness of the proposed MBCT–Net, corresponding experiments
have been conducted, and the experimental results are shown in Sect. 4. In addition,
conclusions are drawn in Sect. 5.

2 Related Works

2.1 Methods Based on Machine Learning

Methods of hand detection based on machine learning can be mainly divided into four
categories: motion, skin color, shape and texture, combination of shape, texture and
color.

2.1.1 Skin Color

Skin differs in color from background objects. Moreover, skin color has rotational and
translational invariance, and methods of skin color detection is simple and fast. Thus, skin
color information is often used in hand detection, but skin color detection is susceptible
to illumination, races and skin color background objects. In addition, modelling of skin
color is essential to detect skin regions, and the first step is to select an appropriate
color space. To adapt changes of illumination in the environment, the color space, which
separates saturation from chrominance, should be selected, such as, YCbCr and HSV
color space.

According to the distance between a user and a camera, hand postures can be mainly
divided into two categories: only containing hands, and containing both faces and hands.
For images only containing hands, scholars mostly utilized skin color models [1] and
adaptive thresholds [15, 16] to detect/segment hand regions. However, some images
contain both faces and hands, if only skin color information is utilized, it is difficult
to distinguish between face and hand regions. To solve the problem, some scholars [4]
detect skin color areas, then remove faces from the detected skin color regions, so hand
regions are obtained.

2.1.2 Shape and Texture

Shape and texture are important characteristics of hand postures, and these features are
utilized by some researchers to detect/segment hand regions. Specifically, they select and
train a specific classifier using a training data set to classify hand postures. It is assumed
that hand postures differentiate themselves on the basis of their shape or texture, and
these methods generally utilize shape or texture features, such as, haar-like wavelet
[3], histogram of oriented gradient (HOG) [2] and scale invariant feature transform
(SIFT) [4] to classify hand postures. In addition, some scholars use multiple features

simultaneously [17], and some of them [18] add context information to improve accuracy of hand detection.

2.1.3   Fusion of Color, Shape and Texture

To improve the accuracy of hand detection, some scholars [5] use both skin color, shape and texture information to detect hand regions.

2.1.4   Motion

To detect motion regions, the frame difference [19, 20] and background subtraction [21] algorithms were mainly used, and some researchers employed both frame difference and background subtraction algorithm [22] to detect motion regions. Whereas some researchers used a method of background subtraction with Gaussian mixture model (GMM) [23]to detect motion regions.

The scholars not only use motion information alone, but also combined skin color and motion information [21] to detect hand areas accurately. Moreover, some researchers deployed motion, skin color and morphology information [22], motion, skin color and edge information [20] to detect hand regions. Furthermore, researchers used thresholds in different color space [21], skin color constraints [20], skin color classifiers [22], histograms [19], skin threshold rules [23] to detect skin color regions.

2.2   CNN-Based Methods

With developments of deep learning methods, CNN-based methods achieve good performance. Some researchers apply convolutional neural networks (CNN)–based methods to detect/segment hand regions. Tang et al. [24] use single shot multibox detector to detect hand regions. Al-Hammadi et al. [25] utilize multiple deep learning architectures to segment hand regions. Dadashzadeh et al. [26] use convolutional residual network and astrous spatial pyramid pooling to segment hand regions. Wei et al. [27], on the other hand, incorporated the target detection model SSD (Single Shot multi box Detector, SSD) into gesture segmentation, but this model leads to the omission of hand detail information when performing thresholding. Cui et al. [7] proposed the IASPP-ResNet model, which is designed to enable the network to extract the multi-scale information of gestures, enrich the feature representation of gestures, and obtain more accurate gesture segmentation results. Many methods of hand gesture segmentation are based on fully convolutional neural networks, they apply a series of convolutional and down-sampling layers to expand the receptive fields of the network and obtain features of hand gestures, then they utilize up-sampling layers to restore the intermediate feature maps to segment hand gestures.

2.3   Transformer–Based Approaches

Transformer initially served the field of natural language processing, where it achieved state-of-the-art performance [28]. Recently Transformer are widely used in the field of computer vision, and researchers in [13] proposed ViT, which is pre-trained on large datasets with position-embedded 2D image patches as inputs. Experiments show that its performance is comparable to that of CNN-based methods. However, ViT requires a large number of datasets for training, and to solve this problem, Deit was proposed in [29], which allows the transformer to be trained on medium-sized datasets. The literature [14] proposed swin transformer, which is used as the backbone network to achieve state-of-the-art performance in image classification, target detection and semantic segmentation. The specific implementation is to restrict the computation of the self-attentive mechanism to a fixed-sized window to reduce the computation, while using the shifted window mechanism to enhance the semantic information interaction between different windows, which expands the receptive fields of the model in the process of continuous down-sampling and finally obtains a more superior performance. Inspired by the methods of window-based self-attention, we design a Multi-Branch Cascade Transformer Network (MBCT–Net) using the self-attention mechanism with different sizes of windows to extract local details and global semantical features of hand gestures.

3 MBCT–Net

3.1 Overview of the Proposed Network

The MBCT-Net is based on encoder-decoder neural network structures, and the encoder structure in the MBCT–Net is composed of two modules: a deep convolutional neural network (DCNN) module and a multi-branch cascade Transformer (MBCT) module.

The structure of the proposed MBCT-Net is shown in Fig. 1. The input of MBCT-Net is a color image, which consists of RGB channels, and the image is processed by the DCNN module to obtain an intermediate feature maps f_d, then they are fed into the MBCT module to extract features of hand gestures with multiple scales f_m. Furthermore, the features extracted by the DCNN and MBCT modules f_d and f_m are concatenated as input of the decoder to segment hand gestures. Specifically, in the decoder, a series of convolution and transposed convolution operations are conducted, then the feature map is concatenated with the original image to obtain more details of hand gestures, and the result is conducted a 1×1 convolution operation to obtain the segmentation result.

3.2 DCNN

The DCNN module is designed to extract features of hand gestures. The DCNN module consists of a 7×7 convolution block, a 1×1 convolution block, and 4 residual groups. Furthermore, to reduce calculation of the DCNN module and fuse local details of hand gestures, a 1×1 convolution layer is added after the first convolution layer and the 1st and 4th residual groups, respectively.

3.3 The Multi-branch Cascade Transformer Module

3.3.1 Overview of the MBCT Module

The multi-branch cascade Transformer (MBCT) module is designed to extract local details and global semantical information of hand gestures. The MBCT module utilizes

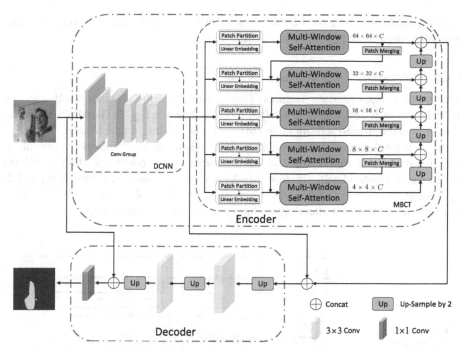

Fig. 1. The diagram of the proposed MBCT–Net.

a cascade of branches to extract features of hand gesture with different scales, and the results of each branch are concatenated step by step after up-sampling to integrate to obtain a total feature map of hand gestures. Furthermore, to enhance semantical interaction between different windows and expand the receptive fields of MBCT-Net, a multi–window self-attention (MWSA) block in each branch of MBCT module is designed to extracts features of hand gestures. The architecture of the MBCT module is shown in Fig. 1, and the process of feature extraction is shown as follows:

The feature maps extracted from the DCNN module f_d are fed into the partition layer, and the patch partition layer splits the pixel matrix of the feature map with a patch containing $i \times i$ pixels to obtain non-overlapping patches. Where i is the size of the patch, and the size of the patch differs for each branch in MBCT. Furthermore, a linear embedding layer is utilized to change the dimension of the feature into a specific dimension, which is denoted as C. After that, the feature map is fed into the MWSA block of each branch of the MBCT module to extract multi-scale features of hand gestures. To expand the receptive fields of MBCT-Net and obtain more local details of hand gestures, the output of each branch is passed to the next branch for feature extraction after patch merging layer of the MBCT module, so the input of the last branch of the MBCT module contains the features extracted from the first four branches of the MBCT module. And the Patch Merging layer is different from the pooling operation, in which the values in the same position in each small window are taken out and put together into a new patch, and then all the patches are concatenated and finally expanded. The channel dimension is then adjusted by a fully connected layer. Moreover, the result of each branch of the

MBCT module is up-sampled layer by layer from bottom to top, and the results are gradually concatenated to obtain a total feature map.

3.3.2 Multi-window Self-attention Blocks

To extract both fine and coarse features of hand gestures, the multi–window self-attention (MWSA) block is designed. The MWSA block is shown in Fig. 2. The MWSA block is a cascade of multi-head self-attention (MHSA) submodules, in which different sizes of windows is employed to represent both fine and coarse features of hand gestures at the same feature level. Furthermore, each MHSA submodule is composed of a LayerNorm (LN) layer, multi-head self-attention (MSA) module, residual connection (LN) and 2-layer MLP with GELU non-linearity. Moreover, $W_1 - MSA$, $W_2 - MSA$ and $W_3 - MSA$ represent multi-head self-attention modules with different sizes of windows.

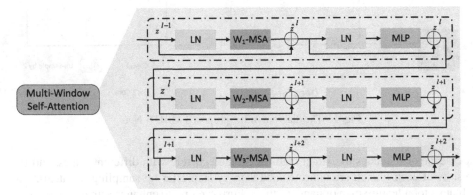

Fig. 2. Architecture of the multi-window self-attention block.

In addition, the self-attention mechanism is applied to focus on a specific window in the MWSA block, which reduces calculation of the MBCT–Net, whereas differences in size between different windows enhances semantic interaction between different windows, which increases receptive field of the MBCT–Net. The MWSA block can be formulated as follow:

$$
\begin{aligned}
\hat{z}^l &= W_1 - MSA(LN(z^{l-1})) + z^{l-1}, \\
z^l &= MLP(LN(\hat{z}^l)) + \hat{z}^l, \\
\hat{z}^{l+1} &= W_2 - MSA(LN(z^l)) + z^l, \\
z^{l+1} &= MLP(LN(\hat{z}^{l+1})) + \hat{z}^{l+1}, \\
\hat{z}^{l+2} &= W_3 - MSA(LN(z^{l+1})) + z^{l+1}, \\
z^{l+2} &= MLP(LN(\hat{z}^{l+2})) + \hat{z}^{l+2}
\end{aligned}
\tag{1}
$$

where $\hat{z}^l$ denotes the output of the lth W_l-MSA module, and z^l represents output of the MLP module of the lth block. Self-attention is calculated as follows [30, 31]:

$$Attention(Q, K, V) = SoftMax(\frac{QK^T}{\sqrt{d}} + B)V, \tag{2}$$

where $Q, K, V \in \mathbb{R}^{M^2 \times d}$ denote the query, key and value matrices, M^2 denotes the number of patches in a window, and d represents the dimension of the *query* or *key*. The values in B are taken from the bias matrix $\hat{B} \in \mathbb{R}^{(2M-1) \times (2M+1)}$.

4 Experimental Results and Analyses

4.1 Datasets and Evaluation Metrics

To demonstrate effectiveness of the proposed MBCT–Net, corresponding experiments are conducted on the public dataset, i.e. OUTHANDS [32]. The OUTHANDS dataset consists of 10 types of hand gestures, which are performed by 23 subjects. Furthermore, in the dataset, 2000 images are selected as the training set, whereas 1000 images are used for testing. The image in the dataset, whose size is 512×512 pixels, is captured in different conditions, such as, different illumination, cluttered background, part occlusions.

To evaluate performance of the MBCT–Net, Mean Intersection over Union ($MIoU$), Pixel Accuracy (PA) [33], Precision (P_r), Recall (Re), and Balanced F-score (F-score) [34] are utilized as evaluation metrics to assess the performance of the MBCT-Net. Moreover, $MIoU$ is used as the main evaluation metric to calculate the average of all category intersection sets, as defined by Eq. (3).

$$MIoU = \frac{1}{n+1} \sum_{i=0}^{n} \frac{p_{ii}}{\sum_{j=0}^{n} p_{ij} + \sum_{j=0}^{n} p_{ji} - p_{ii}}, \tag{3}$$

where the formula $n+1$ denotes the number of categories to be segmented in the dataset, and the 0th category denotes the background. p_{ii} denotes the pixel, which is correctly classified. p_{ij} denotes the pixel, which belongs to the category i, however, it is predicted to belong to the category j, whereas p_{ji} denotes the pixel, which belongs to the category j,however it is predicted to belong to the category i.

PA is a pixel-based evaluation metric in the segmentation task, and it represents the ratio of the number of correctly classified pixels to total pixels, and the PA is defined as follows:

$$PA = \frac{\sum_{i=0}^{n} p_{ii}}{\sum_{i=0}^{n} \sum_{j=0}^{n} p_{ij}} \tag{4}$$

P_r and Re are simple evaluation indicators in the segmentation task, and they are defined by Eq. (5), where N_c denotes the number of pixels which are correctly segmented,

N_r denotes the number of all pixels, and N_g denotes the number of pixels which are in ground–truth.

$$P_r = \frac{N_c}{N_r}, \mathrm{Re} = \frac{N_c}{N_g} \tag{5}$$

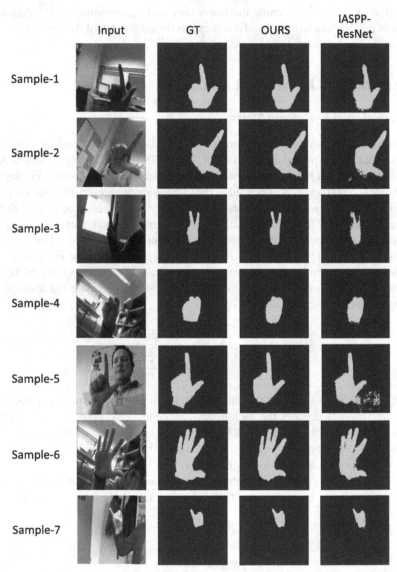

Fig. 3. Some segmentation results using different methods

The F-score is usually calculated by Eq. (6), where β is used to adjust the weight between P_r and Re, when $\beta = 1$, it is called $F_1 - Score$.

$$F_\beta = (1 + \beta^2) \times \frac{P_r \times \text{Re}}{(\beta^2 \times P_r) + \text{Re}} \tag{6}$$

4.2 Experiment Results

To evaluate performances of the MBCT–Net, corresponding experiments have been conducted on the OUTHANDS dataset. Furthermore, the experiments have been implemented on a platform, that is a Nvidia 3060 GPU with 10GB of RAM, and Python and Pytorch are used in the experiments. The experiments are shown in Figs. 3, 4 and Table 1. The experimental results demonstrate effectiveness and robustness of the proposed MBCT–Net on different conditions, such as, different illuminations, skin color background, cluttered background.

In addition, we compare our approach with the state–of–the–art methods, and the performances of different methods are shown in Fig. 5 and Table 1. As the results shown, the proposed MBCT–Net achieves 97.71%, 98.12%, 98.95% and 98.85% on the four evaluation metrics of $MIoU$, PA, Re and F-score, respectively. Furthermore, the proposed MBCT–Net almost always performs better than other methods.

Table 1. Performances of different approaches

Method	MIoU	PA	Pr	Re	F-Score
FCN-8s [27]	0.7830	0.9393	0.9939	0.9367	0.9644
PSPNet [10]	0.8134	0.9506	0.9942	0.9492	0.9712
ICNET [35]	0.7728	0.9351	0.9884	0.9375	0.9623
Deeplabv3 [36]	0.7970	0.9442	**0.9943**	0.9419	0.9674
Deeplabv3 + [8]	0.8872	0.9736	0.9904	0.9795	0.9849
IASPP-ResNet [7]	0.8960	0.9775	0.9907	0.9820	0.9863
MBCT-Net	**0.9771**	**0.9812**	0.9874	**0.9895**	**0.9885**

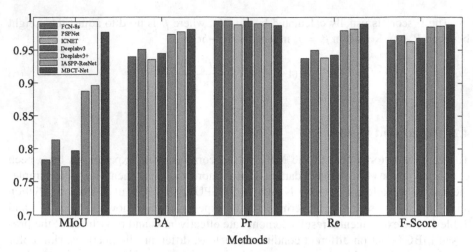

Fig. 4. Experimental results of different methods

5   Conclusions

To segment hand regions from cluttered background, a Multi-Branch Cascade Transformer Network (MBCT–Net) has been developed based on encoder–decoder convolutional neural network in this work. The encoder of the MBCT–Net consists of a deep convolutional neural network (DCNN) module and a multi-branch cascade Transformer (MBCT) module. To extract local details and global semantical of hand gestures with different scales, the MBCT module is designed. The MBCT module utilizes a cascade of multiple branches of Transformer to integrate local detail and global semantical information of hand gestures to expand receptive fields of the MBCT-Net and increase the ability of the MBCT-Net to learn details of hand gestures. Furthermore, the Multi-Window Self-Attention (MWSA) blocks in the MBCT module is designed to reduce calculation of the MBCT-Net, enhance semantical interaction between different windows and expand the receptive fields of MBCT-Net. To verify correctness of the MBCT–Net, corresponding experiments have been conducted, and the experimental results demonstrate robustness and effectiveness of the MBCT–Net.

Acknowledgment. This work was supported by Scientific Research Foundation for Talented Scholars of Hebei University (Grant No. 521100221081), Innovation and Entrepreneurship Training Program for College students of Hebei University (Grant No. 2022156), Scientific Research Foundation of Colleges and Universities in Hebei Province (Grant No. QN2022107) and Science and Technology Program of Hebei Province (Grant No. 22370301D).

References

1. Zheng, Y., Zheng, P.: Hand segmentation based on improved gaussian mixture model. In: 2015 International Conference on Computer Science and Applications (CSA). IEEE, New York (2015)

2. Zhao, Y., Song, Z., Wu, X.: Hand detection using multi-resolution HOG features. In: IEEE International Conference on Robotics and Biomimetics (ROBIO). IEEE, New York (2012)
3. Chen, Q., Georganas, N.D., Petriu, E.M.: Hand gesture recognition using Haar-like features and a stochastic context-free grammar. IEEE Trans. Instrum. Measur. **57**(8), 1562–1571 (2008)
4. Dardas, N.H., Georganas, N.D.: Real-time hand gesture detection and recognition using bag-of-features and support vector machine techniques. IEEE Trans. Instrum. Measur. **60**(11), 3592–3607 (2011)
5. Chuang, Y.L., Chen, L., Chen, G.C.: Saliency-guided improvement for hand posture detection and recognition. Neurocomputing **133**, 404–415 (2014)
6. Mocanu, C., Suciu, G.: Automatic recognition of hand gestures. In 11th International Conference on Electronics, Computers and Artificial Intelligence (ECAI), Pitesti, Romania. IEEE, New York (2019)
7. Cui, Z., et al.: Hand gesture segmentation against complex background based on improved atrous spatial pyramid pooling. J. Amb. Intell. Hum. Comput. (2022)
8. Chen, L.-C., et al.: Encoder-decoder with atrous separable convolution for semantic image segmentation. In: European Conference on Computer Vision (2018)
9. Ronneberger, O., Fischer, P., Brox, T.: U-net: Convolutional networks for biomedical image segmentation. In: International Conference on Medical Image Computing and Computer-Assisted Intervention. Springer, New York (2015)
10. Zhao, H., et al. Pyramid scene parsing network. In: Proceedings of the IEEE Conference on Computer Vision and Pattern Recognition (2017)
11. Yu, F., Koltun, V.: Multi-Scale Context Aggregation by Dilated Convolutions. In: Computer Vision and Pattern Recognition (2015)
12. Zhang, Z.F., et al.: CENet: A Cabinet Environmental Sensing Network. In: Sensors (2010)
13. Dosovitskiy, A., et al.: An image is worth 16x16 words: Transformers for Image recognition at scale. In: Learning (2020)
14. Liu, Z., et al.: Swin transformer. hierarchical vision transformer using shifted windows. In: Computer Vision and Pattern Recognition (2021)
15. Liu, C., et al.: Adaptive threshold gesture segmentation algorithm based on skin color (2016)
16. Wang, W., Pan, J.: Hand segmentation using skin color and background information. In 2012 International Conference on Machine Learning and Cybernetics. IEEE, New York (2012)
17. Sun, J.-H., et al.: Research on the hand gesture recognition based on deep learning. In: 2018 12th International Symposium on Antennas, Propagation and EM Theory (ISAPE). IEEE, New York (2018)
18. Mei, K.Z., et al.: Training more discriminative multi-class classifiers for hand detection. Patt. Recog. **48**(3), 785–797 (2015)
19. Dadgostar, F., Sarrafzadeh, A., Messom, C.: Multi-layered hand and face tracking for real-time gesture recognition. In: International Conference on Neural Information Processing. Springer, New York (2008)
20. Chen, F.-S., Fu, C.-M., Huang, C.-L.: Hand gesture recognition using a real-time tracking method and hidden Markov models. Image Vision Comput. **21**(8), 745–758 (2003)
21. Karishma, S.N., Lathasree, V.: Fusion of skin color detection and background subtraction for hand gesture segmentation. Int. Jo. Eng. Res. Technol. **3**, 2 (2014)
22. Stergiopoulou, E., et al.: Real time hand detection in a complex background. Eng. Appl. Artif. Intell. **35**, 54–70 (2014)
23. Pedro, L.M., et al.: Hand gesture recognition for robot hand teleoperation. In: ABCM Symposium Series in Mechatronics (2012)
24. Tang, J.W., et al.: Position-free hand gesture recognition using single shot multibox detector based neural network. In: 16th IEEE International Conference on Mechatronics and Automation (IEEE ICMA), Tianjin, China (2019)

25. Al-Hammadi, M., et al.: Deep learning-based approach for sign language gesture recognition with efficient hand gesture representation. IEEE Access **8**, 192527–192542 (2020)
26. Dadashzadeh, A., et al.: HGR-Net: a fusion network for hand gesture segmentation and recognition. IET Comput. Vis. **13**(8), 700–707 (2019)
27. Long, J., Shelhamer, E., Darrell, T.: Fully convolutional networks for semantic segmentation. In Proceedings of the IEEE Conference on Computer Vision and Pattern Recognition (2015)
28. Devlin, J., et al.: BERT: Pre-training of deep bidirectional transformers for language understanding. In: North American Chapter of the Association for Computational Linguistics (2018)
29. Touvron, H., et al.: Training data-efficient image transformers and distillation through attention. In: Computer Vision and Pattern Recognition (2020)
30. Hu, H., et al.: Local relation networks for image recognition. In: International Conference on Computer Vision (2019)
31. Hu, H., et al., Relation networks for object detection. In: Computer Vision and Pattern Recognition (2018)
32. Matilainen, M., et al.: OUHANDS database for hand detection and pose recognition. In: International Conference on Image Processing (2016)
33. Garcia-Garcia, A., et al.: A Review on Deep Learning Techniques Applied to Semantic Segmentation. abs/1704.06857
34. Zhang, Q., et al.: Segmentation of Hand Posture against Complex Backgrounds Based on Saliency and Skin Colour Detection
35. Zhao, H., et al., ICNet for real-time semantic segmentation on high-resolution images. In: European Conference on Computer Vision (2017)
36. Chen, L.-C., et al.: Rethinking Atrous Convolution for Semantic Image Segmentation. In: Computer Vision and Pattern Recognition (2017)

Relative Position Relationship Learning Network for Scene Graph Generation

Zhi Chen[1,2] and Yibing Zhan[1,2(✉)]

[1] Hangzhou Dianzi University, Hangzhou, China
zhixiao996@hdu.edu.cn
[2] JD Explore Academy, Beijing, China
zhanyibing@jd.com

Abstract. Scene graph generation (SGG) aims to detect objects along with their relationships in images. It is well believed that the position of objects is a significant consideration when analyzing object relationships. However, current SGG methods generally adopted the absolute positions of objects, which are less effective to describe relationships between two objects when the two objects are placed into different positions of one image. In this paper, we propose a relative position relationship learning network (RPRL-Net) to explicitly represent relationships between different positional objects. Specifically, RPRL-Net develops relative positional self-attention (RPSA) modules to analyze context features from objects by exploring relative positional information between pairwise objects. Afterward, RPRL-Net integrates absolute positional features, relative positional features, and context features of object pairs to predict the final predicates. We conducted comprehensive experiments on the Visual Genome dataset. The experimental results compared with the state-of-the-art demonstrate the superiority of RPRL-Net.

Keywords: Relative position · Self-attention · Scene graph generation

1 Introduction

Scene graph generation (SGG) aims to generate scene graphs of images to model objects and their relationships. In the summary graph, the nodes represent detected objects, and the edges represent the relationships between object pairs. Scene graphs have been adopted in a wide range of high-level visual tasks, such as image captioning [1] and visual question answering [2]. Due to the wide application of scene graphs [3–6], SGG has become a hot topic recently.

In scene graph generation, a scene graph is collection of a visual triplets: subject-predicate-object, such as woman-holding-food and man-eating-food, which as shown in Fig. 1. When predicting relationships, one key is to explore and exploit the rich semantic and spatial information of pairwise objects. However, most current SGG methods only exploited visual information, semantic information and absolute positional information [7] of single objects, which can not explicitly and effectively model their

This work is supported by the Major Science and Technology Innovation 2030 "New Generation Artificial Intelligence" key project (No. 2021ZD0111700) and the National Natural Science Foundation of China (Grant No. 62002090).

L. Fang et al. (Eds.): CICAI 2022, LNAI 13604, pp. 551–559, 2022.
https://doi.org/10.1007/978-3-031-20497-5_45

woman-*holding*-food   boy-*eating*-food

Fig. 1. Examples of different relative positional information represent different relationships

relationships among pairwise objects. It is more significant to model the relative positional information of pairwise objects since different relative positional features may represent different relationships. As shown in Fig. 1 on the left, the food is far away from the woman, so holding is predicted. in Fig. 1 on the right, the food is near to the man, eating better describes their relationship between man and food than holding. Inspired by [8], we model relative positional information between object pairs by using the relative positions, including relative distances, relative scales and relative orientations. Methodologically, most existing approaches model semantic and spatial information by using the CNN framework [9], the RNN framework [10], or the attention framework [11]. Despite the success of these methods, they usually use an iterative modeling strategy to represent the single object context, which may limit the capability of modeling the contextualized representations.

In this paper, we propose a relative position relationship learning network (RPRL-Net) to explore and exploit the relative positional information of pairwise objects for SGG. To overcome the suboptimality of modeling the absolute positional information of single object and the iterative context modeling mechanism, a relative positional self-attention(RPSA) module is proposed to encode the relative positional information into objects and relationship contexts. Besides, in order to facilitate the fusion of semantic and relative positional information, a new technique is developed to encourage increased interaction between query, key and relative position embedding in the RPSA. Finally, we propose positional triplets,i.e., the absolute positional feature of subject and object as well as the relative positional feature between them, respectively. By fusing relationship contexts and positional triplets to predict relationships. The main contributions of this paper lie in two aspects:

- In this paper, we propose a relative position relationship learning network(RPRL-Net) to explicitly represent their relationships between different positional objects for SGG. Besides, a relative positional self-attention(RPSA) module is developed to encode the relative positional information into object and relation contexts.
- We perform extensive experiments on the Visual Genome (VG) dataset [12] and compare RPRL-Net with state-of-the-art scene graph generation methods. Experimental results verify the superior performance of the RPRL-Net compared with the state-of-the-art approaches.

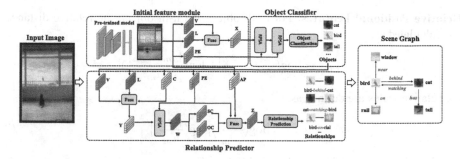

Fig. 2. Flowchart of RPRL-Net consists of three modules: an initial feature module (IFM), an object classifier and a relationship predictor. RPRL-Net first obtains visual features (V), linguistic features (L) and relative positional features (PE) based on the IFM. Then, fusion features (X) and PE are fed to stacked RPSA module to obtain updated context features (C) and predict object label. Afterwards, updated fusion features (Y) and PE are fed to stacked RPSA module to obtain context features (W). The relationship predictor finally predicts the relationships based on updated context features (Z).

The rest of this paper is organized as follows. Section 2 presents the details of our methods. Section 3 presents the experiments, followed by conclusion in Section 4.

2 Approach

In this section, we introduce the architecture of relative position relationship learning network (RPRL-Net) for SGG. Firstly, the feature representations from the input image based on a pre-trained object detector model is described. Then, we explain the details of RPSA module. Finally, the details of object classifier and relationship predictor are explained. An overview flowchart of RPRL-Net is shown in Fig. 2.

2.1 Initial Feature Module

We use Faster R-CNN to detect objects of input images [13]. For one image I, the initial feature module generates four types of features.

Visual Features: Each detected object is represented as a 4096-d vector by extracting fc7 feature after RoI Align and fc6 layer. Finally, the visual features represent $V \in \mathbb{R}^{m \times 4096}$.

Linguistic Features: We use a pretrained 300-d word embedding model [14] to transform the discrete labels into continuous linguistic features, obtaining a linguistic feature matrix of $L \in \mathbb{R}^{m \times 300}$.

Absolute Positional Features: Absolute positional feature $AP \in \mathbb{R}^{m \times 9}$ includes the bounding box $(\frac{x_1}{w}, \frac{y_1}{h}, \frac{x_2}{w}, \frac{y_2}{h})$, center $(\frac{x_1+x_{i2}}{2w}, \frac{y_1+y_2}{2h})$, sizes $(\frac{x_2-x_1}{w}, \frac{y_2-y_1}{h}, \frac{(x_2-x_1)(y_2-y_1)}{wh})$. Here, (x_1, y_1, x_2, y_2) are the bounding box coordinates of object proposals B. w and h are the image width and height.

Relative Positional Features: For m-th object and n-th object, the relative distances are calculated as:

$$d_{mn} = [\log(\frac{|x_m - x_n|}{w_m}), \log(\frac{|y_m - y_n|}{h_m})] \tag{1}$$

the relative scales are defined as:

$$s_{mn} = [\log(\frac{|w_n|}{w_m}), \log(\frac{|h_n|}{h_m})] \tag{2}$$

and the relative orientation is calculated as a cosine function:

$$o_{mn} = \frac{x_m - x_n}{\sqrt{(x_m - x_n)^2 + (y_m - y_n)^2}} \tag{3}$$

Finally, the relative positional features are represented as:

$$pos_{mn} = [d_{mn}, s_{mn}, o_{mn}] \tag{4}$$

This 5-d relative positional features are embedded to a high-dimensional representation by method in [15], which computes cosine and sine functions of different wavelengths.

$$PE_{(i,pos)} = (\sin(pos/1000^{2i/d_{model}}) || \cos(pos/1000^{2i/d_{model}})) \tag{5}$$

where pos is the relative position and i is the dimension. That is, each dimension of the positional encoding corresponds to a sinusoid. d_{model} is the dimension of output feature. Finally, we obtain a feature matrix of $PE \in \mathbb{R}^{m \times n \times 64}$.

Fusion Features: We concatenate V and L are concatenated together and then linearly transform them to a matched dimensionality, resulting in the fused features $X \in \mathbb{R}^{m \times 1024}$. The process is calculated as:

$$X = \text{Linear}(V || L) \tag{6}$$

2.2 Relative Position Self-attention Module

Let $X \in \mathbb{R}^{N \times d_o}$ denote the fusion feature set of objects. d_o is the feature dimension of X. X is first fed into three parallel linear layers to obtain the queries Q, keys K, and values V, respectively. Q, K, V is defined as:

$$Q = \text{Linear}(X), K = \text{Linear}(X), V = \text{Linear}(X) \tag{7}$$

where $Q, K, V \in \mathbb{R}^{m \times d_k}$, d_k is output feature dimension. Original self-attention module uses a scaled dot-product, which represents to compute similarity of fusion features. Inspired by [8], we encode the relative positional features into fusion features. The self-attention mechanism be rewritten as:

$$SA(Q, K, V, RP) = \text{Softmax}(\frac{QK^T}{\sqrt{d_k}} + RP)V \tag{8}$$

where $\sqrt{d_k}$ is a scaling factor following [15]. $RP \in \mathbb{R}^{m \times 64}$ is the updated relative positional feature. RP is defined as:

$$RP = FC(Q + K + FC(PE)) \tag{9}$$

where FC (PE) corresponds to a linear layer applied to the last axis of PE. RP is the sum of query, key and relative position feature, which increases the interaction among them. In this method, RP serves as a gate to filter out the dot product of query and key. This gate would prevent a query from attending to a similar key (content-wise) heavily if the query and key positions are far away from each other.

The multihead variant of the attention module is popularly used which allows the model to jointly attend to information from different representation sub-spaces, and is defined as

$$\text{Multi-Head}(Q, K, V, RP) = \text{Concat}(\text{head}_1, \cdots, \text{head}_H)W^o \tag{10}$$

$$\text{head}_k = \text{SA}(Q, K, V, RP) \tag{11}$$

Finally, we further combine with the FFN layer to generate the relative positional self-attention module, which contains two fully connected layers:

$$\text{FFN}(X) = \text{FC}_{o1}(\sigma(\text{FC}_{o2}(X))) \tag{12}$$

where σ indicates ReLU. The residual connection with layer normalization [15], which is defined as $X = X + \text{LN}(\text{Fun}(X))$, is added to each attention network and each FFN. Here, X is the input feature set, $\text{LN}(\cdot)$ indicates layer normalization, and $\text{Fun}(\cdot)$ represents either an attention network or a FFN.

2.3 Object Classifier

In object classification, with considering the relative positional information and the interaction among the key, query, and relative position embedding, the fusion features and relative positional features are fed into stacked RPSA module to obtain the object context features. Then, the object context features X are projected into c-dimensional vectors $O \in \mathbb{R}^{m \times c}$, where c is the number of object classes. Finally, we predict the refined object labels by using a softmax cross-entropy loss based on the c-dimensional vectors.

2.4 Relationship Predictor

Suppose an object proposal set $\mathcal{B} = \{b\}$ is given. The updated fusion features Y of object proposals $\mathcal{B}$ is initialized by fusing the visual features, linguistic features obtained from the corresponding object proposals $\mathcal{B}$ and the object context features obtained from the last RPSA module layer. Y of $\mathcal{B}$ is calculated as:

$$Y = \sigma(\text{FC}(V\|L\|C)) \tag{13}$$

Then, we feed Y into stacked RPSA module to obtain subject context features of subject proposals SC and object context features OC of object proposals, respectively.

Afterwards, the edge context features Z_{so} between object pairs v_{so} is calculated as:

$$Z_{so} = \sigma(\text{FC}_{v3}(\text{FC}_{v1}(SC)\|\text{FC}_{v2}(OC)\|\text{FC}(PE_{so} + AP_s + AP_o))) \tag{14}$$

Table 1. Performance comparison on SGDet of the VG dataset. We compute the R@20, R@50, R@100 and their mean with and without Graph constrained. "–" indicates the results are unavailable. The best performance is highlighted in boldface.

Method	With graph constraint				Without graph constraint			
	R@20	R@50	R@100	Mean	R@20	R@50	R@100	Mean
IMP [16,17]	18.1	25.9	31.2	25.1	18.4	27.0	33.9	26.4
VtransE [12,17]	23.1	29.9	34.7	29.2	24.4	33.1	39.8	32.4
Motif [17,18]	25.5	32.8	37.2	31.8	27.0	36.6	43.4	35.7
VCTree [17,19]	24.5	31.9	36.2	30.9	26.1	35.7	42.3	34.7
Motif-cKD [20]	25.2	32.5	37.1	31.6	–	36.3	43.2	–
VCTree-cKD [20]	24.8	32.0	36.1	31.0	–	35.9	42.4	–
RPRL-Net	**25.6**	**33.1**	**37.6**	**32.1**	**27.3**	**37.2**	**44.1**	**36.2**

where the AP_s-PE_{so}-AP_o indicates a position triplets, which consists of the absolute positional features of subject and object as well as the relative positional features between subject and object, respectively. Finally, we use the binary cross-entropy loss predict the relationship labels.

3 Experiments

In this section, we conduct experiments to verify the effectiveness of the RPRL-Net on the commonly used benchmark.

3.1 Experimental Settings

Dataset: We use the Visual Genome dataset [12] to conduct all experiments. The VG dataset contains 108,077 images with average annotations of 38 objects and 22 relations per image. Following previous works in [17,18], the most frequent 150 object categories and 50 predicate categories are utilized for evaluation, which split the dataset into 70K/5K/32K as train/validation/test sets.

Evaluation Tasks and Metrics: Following [17], scene graph detection (SGDet) task for SGG is adopted. SGDet generates scene graphs of images to predict the label of objects and relationships without extra-label information. Recall@K (R@K) is calculated by averaging the recall of the top K relationships of all images [21]. We use recall as the evaluation metric and $K = \{20, 50, 100\}$ is reported in our experiments. The performance with and without graph constraint [18] is considered.

3.2 Implementation Details

To ensure a fair comparison of previous SGG, we use the codebase and pre-trained object detection model provided by [17]. The backbone is the Faster R-CNN with

Table 2. Ablation studies

Method	With constraint		Without constraint	
	R@50	R@100	R@50	R@100
Baseline	32.4	36.8	36.4	43.1
B+SA	32.5	37.0	36.6	43.4
B+SA+P	32.8	37.4	36.9	43.8
B+O-RPSA	33.0	37.5	37.1	43.9
RPRL-Net	**33.1**	**37.6**	**37.2**	**44.1**

ResNeXt-101-FPN [22]. The hyperparameters mostly followed [17]. The SGD optimizer with a momentum of 0.9 is adopted. The warm-up strategy [15] is used to increase the learning rate from 0 to 0.001 in the first 5000 iterations. Then, the learning rate is decayed by 0.1 at 18,000 and 24,000 iterations. All training last for 30,000 iterations. The base learning rate is set to 0.001 and the batch size is set to 12. For each image, the top-80 object proposals are provided, and 256 relationship proposals, we set background/foreground ratio for relationship detection as 3/1.

3.3 Performance Comparison

Table 1 presents the results of RPRL-Net and six SGG methods on SGDet of the VG dataset. The results with and without graph constraints are provided. The best performance is highlighted in boldface. From Table 1, we use the same detector and backbone to extract object features. Compared with the second-best methods, RPRL-Net obtains a gain of 0.9% and 1.6% on R@50, and 1.0% and 1.6% on R@100 with and without graph constraint. RPRL-Net consistently outperforms existing state-of-the-art approaches in terms of R@20, R@50 and R@100 metrics on SGDet. These improvements again reveal the ability of RPRL-Net.

3.4 Ablation Studies

A number of experiments are conducted to explore the reasons behind RPRL-Net's success. The results are shown in Table 2 and discussed below. We design four types of variants with different combinations: **Baseline** does not use RPSA module in object classifier and relationship predictor. **B+SA** use self-attention module without relative positional feature and interaction of Q, K and relative positional feature. **B+SA+P** use self-attention module with relative positional feature but does not use interaction of Q, K and relative positional feature. **B+O-PRSA** represent RPSA module is used in object classifier but not used in relationship predictor.

From Table 2, **B+SA** outperforms **Baseline** and **B+SA+P** outperforms **B+SA**. These improvements validate that relative positional information and the interaction of Q, K, relative positional feature have a positive influence on SGG. **RPRL-Net** outperforming **B+O-PRSA** indicate that using RPSA module both in object classifier and relationship predictor is better than only in object classifier.

4   Conclusion

In this paper, we propose a relative position relationship learning network (RPRL-Net) for SGG to explicitly represent their relationships between different positional objects because of the suboptimality of absolute position. The core of RPRL-Net is the relative positional self-attention (RPSA) module to encode the relative positional information into object and relation context. Moreover, the interaction of context feature as well as Q, K and relative positional feature is proposed to facilitate the understanding of object and relation semantics. Comprehensive experiments are conducted on the VG dataset. The experimental results demonstrate that RPRL-Net has high reasoning and integrating abilities.

References

1. Yao, T., Pan, Y., Li, Y., Mei, T.: Exploring visual relationship for image captioning. In: Ferrari, V., Hebert, M., Sminchisescu, C., Weiss, Y. (eds.) Computer Vision – ECCV 2018. LNCS, vol. 11218, pp. 711–727. Springer, Cham (2018). https://doi.org/10.1007/978-3-030-01264-9_42
2. Teney, D., Liu, L., van Den Hengel, A.: Graph-structured representations for visual question answering. In: Proceedings of the IEEE Conference on Computer Vision and Pattern Recognition, pp. 1–9 (2017)
3. Lin, X., Ding, C., Zhan, Y., Li, Z., Tao, D.: HL-Net: heterophily learning network for scene graph generation. In: Proceedings of the IEEE/CVF Conference on Computer Vision and Pattern Recognition, pp. 19476–19485 (2022)
4. Zhan, Y., Jun, Yu., Ting, Yu., Tao, D.: Multi-task compositional network for visual relationship detection. Int. J. Comput. Vis. **128**(8), 2146–2165 (2020)
5. Chen, C., Zhan, Y., Yu, B., Liu, L., Luo, Y., Du, B.: Resistance training using prior bias: toward unbiased scene graph generation. arXiv preprint arXiv:2201.06794 (2022)
6. Lin, X., Ding, C., Zhang, J., Zhan, Y., Tao, D.: RU-Net: regularized unrolling network for scene graph generation. In: Proceedings of the IEEE/CVF Conference on Computer Vision and Pattern Recognition, pp. 19457–19466 (2022)
7. Zellers, R., Yatskar, M., Thomson, S., Choi, Y.: Neural motifs: scene graph parsing with global context (2017)
8. Hu, H., Gu, J., Zhang, Z., Dai, J., Wei, Y.: Relation networks for object detection. In: 2018 IEEE/CVF Conference on Computer Vision and Pattern Recognition (CVPR) (2018)
9. Yang, J., Lu, J., Lee, S., Batra, D., Parikh, D.: Graph R-CNN for scene graph generation (2018)
10. Xu, D., Zhu, Y., Choy, C.B., Fei-Fei, L.: Scene graph generation by iterative message passing (2017)
11. Qi, M., Li, W., Yang, Z., Wang, Y., Luo, J.: Attentive relational networks for mapping images to scene graphs. In: 2019 IEEE/CVF Conference on Computer Vision and Pattern Recognition (CVPR) (2019)
12. Krishna, R., Zhu, Y., Groth, O., Johnson, J., Fei-Fei, L.: Visual genome: connecting language and vision using crowdsourced dense image annotations. Int. J. Comput. Vis. **123**(1), 32–73 (2017)
13. Ren, G., et al.: Scene graph generation with hierarchical context. IEEE Trans. Neural Netw. Learn. Syst. (2020)
14. Pennington, J., Socher, R., Manning, C.: Glove: global vectors for word representation. In: Conference on Empirical Methods in Natural Language Processing (2014)

15. Vaswani, A., et al.: Attention is all you need. In: Advances in Neural Information Processing Systems, pp. 5998–6008 (2017)
16. Li, Y., Ouyang, W., Zhou, B., Wang, K., Wang, X.: Scene graph generation from objects, phrases and region captions. In: Proceedings of the IEEE International Conference on Computer Vision, pp. 1261–1270 (2017)
17. Tang, K., Niu, Y., Huang, J., Shi, J., Zhang, H.: Unbiased scene graph generation from biased training. In: Proceedings of the IEEE/CVF Conference on Computer Vision and Pattern Recognition, pp. 3716–3725 (2020)
18. Zellers, R., Yatskar, M., Thomson, S., Choi, Y.: Neural motifs: scene graph parsing with global context. In: Proceedings of the IEEE Conference on Computer Vision and Pattern Recognition, pp. 5831–5840 (2018)
19. Tang, K., Zhang, H., Wu, B., Luo, W., Liu, W.: Learning to compose dynamic tree structures for visual contexts. In: Proceedings of the IEEE Conference on Computer Vision and Pattern Recognition, pp. 6619–6628 (2019)
20. Wang, T.-J.J., Pehlivan, S., Laaksonen, J.: Tackling the unannotated: scene graph generation with bias-reduced models. arXiv preprint arXiv:2008.07832 (2020)
21. Xu, D., Zhu, Y., Choy, C.B., Fei-Fei, L.: Scene graph generation by iterative message passing. In: Proceedings of the IEEE Conference on Computer Vision and Pattern Recognition, 5410–5419 (2017)
22. Lin, T.-Y., Dollár, P., Girshick, R., He, K., Hariharan, B., Belongie, S.: Feature pyramid networks for object detection. In: Proceedings of the IEEE Conference on Computer Vision and Pattern Recognition, pp. 2117–2125 (2017)

Person Re-identification Based on CNN with Multi-scale Contour Embedding

Hao Chen[1], Yan Zhao[1(✉)], and Lihua Zhang[2,3(✉)]

[1] College of Communication Engineering, Jilin University, Changchun, Jilin, China
chenh20@mails.jlu.edu.cn, zhao_y@jlu.edu.cn
[2] Academy for Engineering and Technology, Fudan University, Shanghai, China
lihuazhang@fudan.edu.cn
[3] United Key Laboratory of Intelligent Science and Engineering of Jilin Province, Changchun, Jilin, China

Abstract. Person Re-identification (Re-ID) plays an important role in the search for missing people and the tracking of suspects. Person Re-identification based on deep learning has made great progress in recent years, and the application of pedestrian contour map has also been concerned. In the study, we found that the pedestrian contour feature is not enough in the shallow expression of CNN. On this basis, in order to improve the recognition performance of Re-ID network, we propose a multi-scale pedestrian contour embedding method. The proposed method uses ResNet50 as the backbone to extract the global features of people. We use the pedestrian contour map as a feature map and reduce its dimension. The pedestrian contour is added to the previous layers of CNN network as a supplement to feature map extraction. In addition, we also apply our method to the local convolution baseline (AlignedReID++). The experimental results show that our method improves the mAP and Rank-1 of the baseline model by 4.5% and 3.6% respectively on Market1501. The mAP and Rank-1 of the local baseline model AlignedReID++ are increased by 0.8% and 1.4%. The final result of our experiment achieves 88.3% mAP and 92.3% Rank-1 accuracy for Market1501, 81.7% mAP and 86.5% Rank-1 accuracy for DukeMTMC-reID.

Keywords: Person Re-identification · Pedestrian contour · Multi-scale architecture

1 Introduction

Person Re-identification (Re-ID), also known as cross camera pedestrian tracking, aims to recognize the same person image under different cameras [1]. Monitoring equipment has become more and more popular in the cities. Re-ID technology plays an important role in the tracking of suspects or the search for lost people [2], which can save a lot of time and labor costs.

In the early research of Person Re-identification, the extraction of person features depends on the prior knowledge, and the obtained features are often limited to manual

L. Fang et al. (Eds.): CICAI 2022, LNAI 13604, pp. 560–571, 2022.
https://doi.org/10.1007/978-3-031-20497-5_46

features, such as color, texture and so on [3]. The research focus is not on feature extraction, but on how to get more powerful similarity metrics [4].

In recent years, deep learning algorithm based on convolutional neural network has emerged in the field of machine vision. CNN network is very excellent for image feature extraction, so it has occupied a major position in the Re-ID task. From the aspect of feature extraction, Re-ID research can be divided into two categories.

First, most methods focus on using CNN to learn the global features of person images. For example, Ahmed et al. [5] proposed Siamese network to extract global features of person images, and used the obtained feature vectors to detect people. Considering the limitations of person images, the global feature vector cannot well express a person's characteristics. Sun et al. [6] used the horizontal segmentation method to divide the person image into six identical blocks to extract local features and calculate the distance between the corresponding local features. In order to solve the problems of occlusion and pedestrian posture dislocation in person images, Zhao et al. [7] estimated the pedestrian body key points by using the pedestrian posture estimation model, extracted local features according to the key points, and also aligned the person image space according to the key points.

Second, in order to learn more recognizable person image features, an attention mechanism is introduced to learn the local features. Liu et al. [8] proposed an attention model into the Re-ID task for the first time to dynamically generate attention features to locate different local areas. Zhao et al. [9] proposed an attention model based on CNN, which uses the similarity information of paired human images to learn the part of the body used for matching. Wang et al. [10] proposed an attention model combining hard attention and soft attention, which can simultaneously learn multi-scale local and pixel level feature maps in an end-to-end manner.

Contour information also plays an important role in the field of image recognition. Some works [11] have deeply understood the expression of CNN in depth visual features. Experiments on Imagenet showed that the CNN based deep learning model prefers texture based features to shape based features. Moreover, the embedded hybrid model based on texture and contour has also been proved to improve the performance of image classification and object detection [12]. Pedestrian contour is also applied to Re-ID tasks. Chen et al. [13] first attempted to utilize contour explicitly in deep Re-ID models, and proposed a contour guidance, which greatly proves the application prospect of pedestrian contour. Yang et al. [14] believed that on the basis that the change of person clothing is not strong (strong refers to the gap between winter clothing and summer clothing), the pedestrian contour also has the ability to distinguish person characteristics. Based on this, the pedestrian contour map is used as the input of feature extraction for Cross- Dressing person Re-ID, and good results are achieved. In the recently released research [15], they proposed a multi-scale appearance and contour deep infomax (MAC-DIM) to maximize mutual information between pedestrian color image features and pedestrian contour features, utilized contour feature learning as regularization to mine more effective shape aware feature representation from color images.

To sum up, the pedestrian contour map (see Fig. 1(b)) has been proved to have certain feature recognition ability and application prospect. In the previous method of using pedestrian contour map in Re-ID task, the general idea is to send the pedestrian contour map to CNN network and use the characteristic map output by the network. In this paper, we propose a person Re-ID method based on multi-scale contour embedding. When extracting shallow features, it can be found that the expression of pedestrian contour is not very obvious (see Fig. 1(c)).So we directly use the pedestrian contour map as a feature map and embed it into the shallow part of CNN network to solve the problem (see Fig. 1(d)). Taking ResNet50 as an example, we embed the contour map in the first convolution layer output position and the first residual block output position of the network. We also apply our method to the local baseline model, AlignedReID++, verifying that the proposed method is compatible in the part-based model with performance bonus.

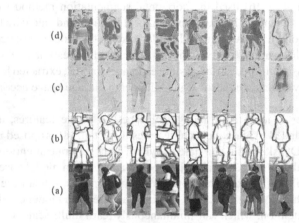

Fig. 1. a) Person images in Market-1501 [16] and DukeMTMC-reID [17]. (b) Corresponding pedestrian contour maps. (c) Shallow features of RGB images in network. (d) Shallow features with embedding pedestrian contour maps.

2 Proposed Method

2.1 Re-iD with Multi-scale Contour Embedding

The overview of our proposed multi-scale contour embedding method is shown in Fig. 2. Many existing Re-ID models take ResNet50 as the backbone, because the residual block of ResNet50 can well prevent the gradient explosion problem and improve the feature extraction ability of the model. In order to verify the method in this paper, we also take ResNet50 as the backbone.

In the embedding method proposed in this paper, we use the pedestrian contour map directly as the feature map instead of the feature map extracted from the contour map through CNN network as in the usual method. We add a pedestrian contour at the output position of the first convolution layer Conv2D of ResNet50 and the output position of the first residual block Layer1. To this end, we need to define the dimensions of the two-level output feature map, set the input image of the network as $I_{RGB} \in \mathbb{R}^{(3 \times 256 \times 128)}$, the output after the first Conv2D layer is $F_{Conv2D}^{RGB} \in \mathbb{R}^{(64 \times 128 \times 64)}$, and the output after the first residual block layer is $F_{Layer1}^{RGB} \in \mathbb{R}^{(256 \times 64 \times 32)}$. If the pedestrian contour is to be embedded in the ResNet50, the corresponding dimension reduction operation is required. In this paper, two different convolution layers are proposed. The first convolution layer is set as Conv2d (7×7), then the contour drawing is output as.

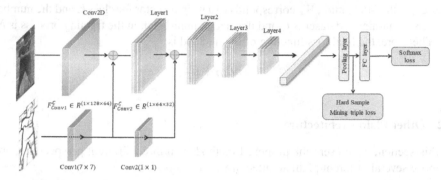

Fig. 2. The overview of our proposed multi-scale contour embedding method.

$F_{Conv1}^{C} \in \mathbb{R}^{(1 \times 128 \times 64)}$; The second convolution layer is set as Conv2d (1×1), and the output of F_{Conv1}^{C} through it is $F_{Conv2}^{C} \in \mathbb{R}^{(1 \times 64 \times 32)}$.

Then the embedding operation of the output position of Conv2D layer is:

$$F_{Layer1}^{In} = F_{Conv2D}^{RGB} \oplus F_{Conv1}^{C} \tag{1}$$

The embedding operation of the output position of the first residual block is:

$$F_{Layer2}^{In} = F_{Layer1}^{RGB} \oplus F_{Conv2}^{C} \tag{2}$$

where, $\oplus$ denotes element-wise addition, $F_{Layer1}^{In} \in \mathbb{R}^{(64 \times 128 \times 64)}$ is the first residual block input, and $F_{Layer2}^{In} \in \mathbb{R}^{(256 \times 64 \times 32)}$ is the second residual block input.

We use the global feature map for the final recognition task, in training stage, and we add Batch Normalization and ReLU layers before the global average pooling layer(GAP). In the loss function, like many person Re-ID methods, we also use softmax loss and hard sample mining (trihard loss) [18]. We denote L_{ID} and L_T^g as the softmax loss and TriHard loss of the global branch respectively.

The L_T^g is calculated after gap of global feature map:

$$L_T^g = \frac{1}{P \times K} \sum_{a \in batch} (\max_{p \in A} d_{a,p} - \min_{n \in B} d_{a,n} + \alpha)_+ \tag{3}$$

where, P represents the number of person ID in a batch, randomly select K pictures for each person ID. a represents the anchor point, p represents the positive sample, and n represents the negative sample. A is the set of positive samples and B is the set of negative samples. $\max d_{a,p}$ Represents the most difficult positive sample, $\max d_{a,n}$ represents the most difficult negative sample. α Means margin and is set to 0.3.

The L_{ID} is calculated after passing through the fully connected layer(FC):

$$L_{ID} = -\sum_{i=1}^{N} \log \frac{e^{W_{y_i}^T f_i}}{\sum_{k=1}^{C} e^{W_k^T f_i}} \qquad (4)$$

where f_i is the i-th feature, W_k corresponds to a weight vector for class k, and the number of classes in training dataset is C and the size of mini-batch in the training process is N.

Therefore, the final loss function of this method is:

$$L = L_{ID} + L_T^g \qquad (5)$$

2.2 Other Plain Architecture

In this section, we present the proposed method from three different perspectives, and propose several different plain architectures.

Architecture with Different Embedding Method. The contour map is used as the feature rather than the weight in this paper, so the method of element-wise multiplication is abandoned and we choose concat and element-wise addition as embedding methods(see Fig. 3). For different embedding methods, we propose two different embedding positions. The first is to embed the contour map in the first convolution layer output position and the first residual block output position of ResNet50, the second is to embed only at the output position of first convolution layer of ResNet50. Therefore, the four architectures in Fig. 3 are named from left to right as A-1, A-2, A-3, A-4. In each architecture, the RGB branch uses the pre-trained ResNet50, the first convolution layer in contour branch is set as Conv2d (7×7), and the second is set as Conv2d (1×1).

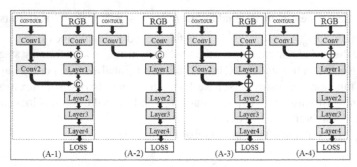

Fig. 3. The plain architecture with different embedding method. In the proposed method where $\oplus$ denotes element-wise addition, © denotes concat operation.

Architecture with Different Embedding Position. In fact, contour features have been used only as shallow features. Moreover, as an end-to-end feature extraction tool, convolutional neural network cannot quantitatively describe the specific results of the feature map after convolution layer calculation. Therefore, we speculate that if we want to add the contour map as a feature to the middle layer of CNN network, it is not that the more layers you add, the better the final result. In order to find the best embedding position of contour feature map, several multi-scale feature embedding methods are used, as shown in Fig. 4. Resnet50 has five layers in structure. Because the output of the last residual block is the final feature map, multi-scale feature embedding is only applied to the output of the first convolution layer and the first three residual blocks.

We embed the contour map by element-wise addition. In each architecture, the RGB branch uses the pre-trained ResNet50, in contour branch, the convolution layers we use are Conv2d (7 × 7) and three Conv2d (1 × 1) from shallow to deep. The first four architectures in the figure are named from left to right as B-1, B-2, B-3, B-4.

In addition, we propose architecture B-5, which adds contour features after layer 2 and layer 3 to verify the correctness of contour features used in the shallow layer of the network.

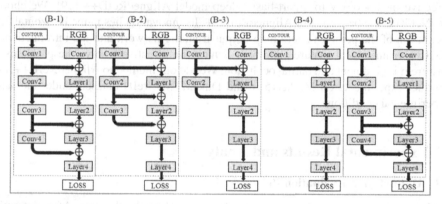

Fig. 4. The plain architecture with different embedding position. In the proposed method where ⊕ denotes element-wise addition.

Architecture with Different Selection of Convolution Layer. The central idea of our method is to use the pedestrian contour map as a feature map, so it is also very important to select the convolution layer that plays the role of dimension reduction. Although convolution layers of different kernel_size can provide the same dimensionality reduction effect, they provide different receptive fields. In this section, three different convolution layers are set(see Fig. 5): the class C convolution layer, which is each network layer of the pre-trained ResNet50 network, the first convolution layer is set as C-conv1, and the first residual block is set as C-layer1. The class D convolution is set as Conv2d (7 × 7), and the class E convolution is set as Conv2d (1 × 1). The reason for setting class C is that the pre-trained ResNet50 performs well in recognition tasks, and the trained parameters have a good comparative value with the convolution layer of random initialization parameters. The D-type convolution layer has a large receptive field. The function of setting class E convolution layer is to reduce the dimension. We embed the pedestrian contour map at the output of the first convolution layer and the first residual block of ResNet50 network.

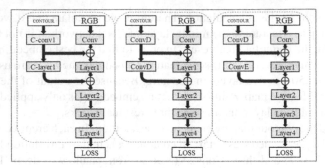

Fig. 5. The plain architecture with different convolution layers. In the proposed method where ⊕ denotes element-wise addition.

AlignedReID++ with Multi-Scale Contour Embedding. We further transfer our effective methodology to a part-based deep model AlignedReID++ [19]. We choose ResNet50 as the backbone of AlignedReID++. Its innovation lies in the horizontal segmentation of the person feature map output from the network and the introduction of DMLI dynamic local feature alignment, which can effectively solve the problems of posture misalignment and partial occlusion. We add our method to AlignedReID++, and conduct experiments on Market1501 and DukeMTMC-reID datasets under the same experimental conditions.

3   Experimental Results and Analysis

3.1   Datasets and Evaluation Protocol

In the confirmatory experiment, we use Market1501 as the datasets. After determining the multi-scale contour embedding method, we conducted experiments on Market1501 and DukeMTMC-reID.For evaluation protocol,we use cumulative maching characteristic(CMC) [20] and mean average precision(mAP) [16] metrics.

3.2   Implementation Details

In the work of extracting pedestrian contour, we use a powerful edge detection model RCF. In the experiments, we use the pytoch framework, and ResNet50, which is pretrained on Imagenet, is used as the backbone of convolutional neural network. The optimizer uses the Adam. In the training phase, a total of 400 epochs are trained, and the learning rate of the first 150 epochs is set to 2×10^{-4}, the remaining learning rate decays to 2×10^{-5}. The weight decay rate is set to 5×10^{-4}, ,and remains unchanged. Each image(including RGB image and pedestrian contour image) is resized into 256×128 pixels. The data augmentation includes random horizontal flipping and cropping. The margins of TriHard loss is set 0.3. Under the above experimental conditions, the average training time of the baseline model is 3 h and 15 min. The training time of any plain architecture proposed in this paper is similar to it, and it will not increase the computation cost.

3.3 Experiment of Contour Embedding Method

We conducted experiments on the public datasets Market1501 to compare the performance of these four methods in Fig. 3. The experimental results are shown in Table 1. The element-wise addition method is used to embed the person image into the network middle layer, which has obvious advantages over the concat method. In terms of data, mAP is about 6% higher and Rank-1 is 3.4% higher. Therefore, the method of element-wise addition is determined.

Table 1. Architecture performance comparison between different embedding methods.

Methods	mAP	Rank-1	Rank-5	Rank-10
A-1 (Conv + Layer(cat))	69.6	86.4	94.8	96.8
A-2 (Conv(cat))	71.9	87.8	95.5	96.9
A-3 (Conv + Layer(+))	**75.4**	**89.8**	**95.6**	97.4
A-4 (Conv(+))	75.1	88.8	95.3	97.4

3.4 Experiment of Contour Embedding Position

We conducted experiments on the public datasets Market1501 to compare the performance of these five methods in Fig. 4. As shown in the experimental results in Table 2, it is credible to add contour features to the shallow layer, and it is not that the more layers are added, the better the effect. In fact, the best person Re-ID results can be obtained by adding the pedestrian contour map at the output of the first convolution layer and the first residual block of ResNet50.

Table 2. Architecture performance comparison between different embedding position.

Methods	mAP	Rank-1	Rank-5	Rank-10
B-1	75.2	89.1	96.0	97.6
B-2	74.9	89.2	**96.0**	**97.7**
B-3 (Ours)	**75.4**	**89.8**	95.6	97.4
B-4	75.1	88.8	95.3	97.4
B-5	74.4	88.7	96.0	97.5

3.5 Experiment on Selection of Contour Branch Convolution Layer

We conducted experiments on the public datasets Market1501 to compare the performance of these three methods in Fig. 5. According to the experimental results in Table 3, in the contour branch, the first convolution layer selects Conv2d (7×7) with large receptive field, and the second convolution layer selects Conv2d (1×1) for dimension reduction operation, so as to build the final multi-scale contour embedding method.

Table 3. Architecture performance comparison between different selection of convolution layer.

Convolution Layers	mAP	Rank-1	Rank-5	Rank-10
Trained (conv + layer1)	68.7	86.0	94.7	96.7
ConvD + ConvD	74.8	89.0	95.4	**97.8**
Ours(ConvD + ConvE)	**75.4**	**89.8**	**95.6**	97.4

3.6   Performance on AlignedReID++

Table 4 shows the performance improvement of our method for the baseline model, on dataset Market1501, mAP is increased by 4.5% and Rank-1 is increased by 3.6%, on dataset DukeMTMC-reID, mAP is increased by 3.6% and Rank-1 is increased by 3%. Our method also improves the performance of AignedReID++, on Market1501, mAP is increased by 0.8% and Rank-1 is increased by 0.5%, on DukeMTMC-reID, Rank-1 is increased by 1.3%.

Table 4. Comparison with the baseline model and the performance of our method on AlignedReID ++.

Methods	Market1501				DukeMTMC-reID			
	Global		Global + DMLI		Global		Global + DMLI	
	mAP	Rank-1	mAP	Rank-1	mAP	Rank-1	mAP	Rank-1
Baseline	70.9	86.4	72.1	87.1	61.0	76.9	63.1	78.5
Ours	75.4	89.8	–	–	64.6	79.9	–	–
AlignedReID + +	75.9	89.2	77.6	91.0	65.6	79.3	68.0	80.7
Ours + AlignedReID++	**76.7**	**90.6**	**78.4**	**91.5**	**65.8**	**81.0**	68.0	**82.0**

3.7   Comparison with Other Methods

Table 5 shows the comparison results between our multi-scale contour embedding method and some other methods in recent years. We compare on two common datasets Market1501 and DukeMTMC-reID. In the experimental results, we not only verify the effectiveness of our method, but also apply our method to AlignedReID++. In the aspect of experimental performance improvement, we use label smooth(LS) [21] and k-reciprocal re-ranking(RK) [22]. By comparing to other methods, we can further verify the effectiveness of the proposed method and the portability in other existing technologies.

Table 5. Comparison between ours and other methods.

Methods	Market1501		DukeMTMC-reID	
	mAP	Rank-1	mAP	Rank-1
PCE&ECN [23]	69.0	87.0	62.0	79.8
AML [24]	74.1	89.5	–	–
AWTL [25]	75.7	89.5	63.4	79.8
AlignedReID++	77.6	91.0	68.0	80.7
Ours + AlignedReID++	**78.4**	**91.5**	68.0	**82.0**
PCB-Contour	76.7	91.2	68.8	82.8
Ours	75.4	89.8	64.6	79.9
CamStyle(RK) [26]	71.5	89.5	57.6	78.3
Ours(RK)	87.2	91.5	78.8	83.4
Ours(LS + RK)	**88.3**	**92.3**	**81.7**	**86.5**

In the comparison of experimental data, we compare the multi-scale contour embedding method based on AlignedReID++ with the PCB-Contour [13] based on local convolution, which also uses pedestrian contour. On dataset Market1501, mAP is increased by 1.7% and Rank-1 is increased by 0.3%. The final result of our our method achieves 88.3% mAP and 92.3% Rank-1 accuracy for Market1501, 81.7% mAP and 86.5% Rank-1 accuracy for DukeMTMC-reID.

4   Conclusion

In this paper, we propose a person Re-ID method based on multi-scale contour embedding, which adds the pedestrian contour map as a feature to the middle layer of convolutional neural network. We get the best multi-scale contour embedding model through a large number of experiments. Experiments not only prove the feasibility of this method, because of the experimental results are better than the baseline model and some other experimental methods, but also proves the importance of adding contour feature map to the shallow features of CNN network. We also apply our method to the local based model AlignedReID++ to verify its feasibility in different methods. The results show that the proposed method is still valuable for person Re-ID based on local features.

References

1. Ye, M., Shen, J., Lin, G., et al.: Deep learning for person re-identification: a survey and outlook. IEEE Trans. Pattern Anal. Mach. Intell. (99), 1–1 (2021)

2. Chen, K.W., Lai, C.C., Lee, P.J., et al.: Adaptive learning for target tracking and true linking discovering across multiple non-overlapping cameras. IEEE Trans. Multimedia **13**(4), 625–638 (2011)

3. Khamis, S., Kuo, C.-H., Singh, V.K., Shet, V.D., Davis, L.S.: Joint learning for attribute-consistent person re-identification. In: Agapito, L., Bronstein, M.M., Rother, C. (eds.) ECCV 2014. LNCS, vol. 8927, pp. 134–146. Springer, Cham (2015). https://doi.org/10.1007/978-3-319-16199-0_10

4. Yang, X., Wang, M., Tao, D.: Person re-identification with metric learning using privileged information. IEEE Trans. Image Process. **2018**, 1 (2018)

5. Ahmed, E., Jones, M., Marks, T.K.: An improved deep learning architecture for person re-identification. In: 2015 IEEE Conference on Computer Vision and Pattern Recognition (CVPR), pp. 3908–3916 (2015)

6. Sun, Y., Zheng, L., Yang, Y., et al.: Beyond part models: person retrieval with refined part pooling. In: European Conference on Computer Vision, pp. 480–496 (2017)

7. Zhao, H., Tian, M., Sun, S., et al.: Spindle net: person re-identification with human body region guided feature decomposition and fusion. In: 2017 IEEE Conference on Computer Vision and Pattern Recognition (CVPR), pp. 1077–1085 (2017)

8. Liu, H., et al.: End-to-end comparative attention networks for person re-identification. IEEE Trans. Image Process. **26**(7), 3492–3506 (2017)

9. Zhao, L., et al.: Deeply-learned part-aligned representations for person re-identification. In: 2017 IEEE International Conference on Computer Vision (ICCV), pp. 3219–3228. IEEE (2017)

10. Wang, C., Zhang, Q., Huang, C., Liu, W., Wang, X.: Mancs: a multi-task attentional network with curriculum sampling for person re-identification. In: Ferrari, V., Hebert, M., Sminchis-escu, C., Weiss, Y. (eds.) ECCV 2018. LNCS, vol. 11208, pp. 384–400. Springer, Cham (2018). https://doi.org/10.1007/978-3-030-01225-0_23

11. Geirhos, R., Rubisch, P., Michaelis, C., et al.: ImageNet-trained CNNs are biased towards texture; increasing shape bias improves accuracy and robustness (2018)

12. Jiang, Z., Yuan, Y., Wang, Q.: Contour-aware network for semantic segmentation via adaptive depth. Neurocomputing, **284**(APR.5), 27–35 (2018)

13. Chen, J., Yang, Q., Meng, J., Zheng, W.-S., Lai, J.-H.: Contour-guided person re-identification. In: Lin, Z., et al. (eds.) PRCV 2019. LNCS, vol. 11859, pp. 296–307. Springer, Cham (2019). https://doi.org/10.1007/978-3-030-31726-3_25

14. Yang, Q., Wu, A., Zheng, W.S.: Person re-identification by contour sketch under moderate clothing change. IEEE Trans. Pattern Anal. Mach. Intell. **43**(6), 2029–2046 (2019)

15. Chen, J., Zheng, W.S., Yang, Q., Meng, J., Hong, R., Tian, Q.: Deep shape-aware person re-identification for overcoming moderate clothing changes. IEEE Trans. Multimedia (2021)

16. Zheng, L., Shen, L., Tian, L., Wang, S., Wang, J., Tian, Q.: Scalable person re-identification: a benchmark. In: Proceedings of the IEEE International Conference on Computer Vision, pp. 1116–1124. IEEE, Santiago (2015)

17. Ristani, E., Solera, F., Zou, R., Cucchiara, R., Tomasi, C.: Performance measures and a data set for multi-target, multi-camera tracking. In: Hua, G., Jégou, H. (eds.) ECCV 2016. LNCS, vol. 9914, pp. 17–35. Springer, Cham (2016). https://doi.org/10.1007/978-3-319-48881-3_2

18. Hermans, A., Beyer, L., Leibe, B.: In Defense of the Triplet Loss for Person Re-Identification (2017)

19. Luo, H., Jiang, W., Zhang, X., et al.: AlignedReID++: dynamically matching local information for person re-identification. Pattern Recogn. **94**, 53–61 (2019)

20. Bolle, R.M., Connell, J.H., Pankanti, S., et al.: The relation between the ROC curve and the CMC. In: IEEE Workshop on Automatic Identification Advanced Technologies, pp. 15–20. IEEE (2005)

21. Szegedy, C., Vanhoucke, V., Ioffe, S., et al.: Rethinking the inception architecture for computer vision. In: 2016 IEEE Conference on Computer Vision and Pattern Recognition (CVPR), pp. 2818–2826. IEEE (2016)
22. Zhong, Z., Zheng, L., Cao, D., et al.: Re-ranking person re-identification with k-reciprocal encoding. In: 2017 IEEE Conference on Computer Vision and Pattern Recognition (CVPR) IEEE Computer Society, pp. 1318–1327 (2017)
23. Sarfraz, M.S., Schumann, A., Eberle, A., et al.: A pose-sensitive embedding for person re-identification with expanded cross neighborhood re-ranking. In: 2018 IEEE/CVF Conference on Computer Vision and Pattern Recognition, pp. 420–429. IEEE (2018)
24. Wang, J., Zhou, S., Wang, J.J., et al.: Deep ranking model by large adaptive margin learning for person re-identification. Pattern Recogn. **74**, 241–252 (2018)
25. Ristani, E., Tomasi, C.: Features for multi-target multi-camera tracking and re-identification. In: 2018 IEEE/CVF Conference on Computer Vision and Pattern Recognition (CVPR), pp. 6036–6046. IEEE (2018)
26. Zhong, Z., Liang, Z., Zheng, Z., et al.: Camera style adaptation for person re-identification. In: 2018 IEEE/CVF Conference on Computer Vision and Pattern Recognition, pp. 5157–5166. IEEE (2018)

Causal Inference with Sample Balancing for Out-of-Distribution Detection in Visual Classification

Yuqing Wang, Xiangxian Li, Haokai Ma, Zhuang Qi, Xiangxu Meng, and Lei Meng[✉]

Shandong University, Jinan, Shandong, China
{wang_yuqing,xiangxian_lee,mahaokai,z_qi}@mail.sdu.edu.cn
{mxx,lmeng}@sdu.edu.cn

Abstract. Image classification algorithms are commonly based on the Independent and Identically Distribution (IID) assumption, but in practice, the Out-Of-Distribution (OOD) problem is widely existing, i.e., the contexts of images in the model predicting are usually unseen during training. In this case, existing models trained under the IID assumption are limiting generalization. Causal inference is an important method to enhance the out-of-distribution generalization of models by partitioning various contexts from data and leading models to learn context-invariant predictions in different situations. However, existing methods mostly have imbalance problems due to the lack of constraints when partitioning data, which weakens the improvement of generalization. Therefore, we propose a Balanced Partition Causal Inference (BP-Causal) method, which automatically generates fine-grained balanced data partitions in an unsupervised manner, thereby enhancing the generalization ability of models in different contexts. Experiments on the OOD datasets NICO and NICO++ demonstrate that BP-Causal achieves stable predictions on OOD data, and we also find that models using BP-Causal focus more accurately on the foreground of images compared with the existing causal inference method, which effectively improves the generalization ability.

Keywords: Out-of-distribution generalization · Causal inference · Invariant learning

1 Introduction

Image classification algorithms based on deep learning have shown good performance under the Independent and Identically Distributed (IID) assumption. However, real-world datasets usually suffer from out-of-distribution (OOD) generalization problems, i.e., contexts of images in the inferring phase are mostly unseen by the modal in the training phase. Existing models trained under IID assumption are hard to generalize well in this case. How to efficiently and accurately extract cross-environment invariant features from the complex data distribution in OOD environments is a problem that remains to be studied.

© The Author(s), under exclusive license to Springer Nature Switzerland AG 2022
L. Fang et al. (Eds.): CICAI 2022, LNAI 13604, pp. 572–583, 2022.
https://doi.org/10.1007/978-3-031-20497-5_47

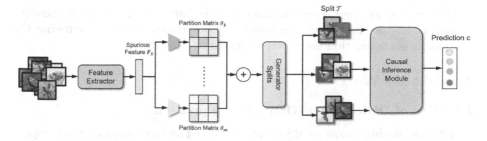

Fig. 1. The causal learning method based on Balanced Partition Causal Inference (BP-Causal) divides the input data set by training multiple partition matrices, and divides it into subsets with different contexts in a fine-grained manner.

Causal inference is effective to alleviate OOD problems, and there are two main approaches. The first is invariant causal prediction (ICP) [10,18,19], which improves the stability of generalization by controlling the covariance of different subsets. But this approach has limited effectiveness in complex scenes. The second is invariant learning, typified by invariant risk minimization [2,3,12,23] that extracts causal features that are invariant across environments by dividing the data and training a classifier that is optimal across all environments. However, these methods are lacking of constraints, which will lead to the imbalance of the divided data and impact the context invariant learning.

To address the aforementioned problems, we propose a Balanced Partition Causal Inference method BP-Causal. By adding balance constraints, the division effect of causal inference on data subsets is improved, the learning of the model in different environments is further enhanced, and the effect of extracting invariant causal features is improved, thereby enhancing the generalization ability in the OOD environment. As shown in Fig. 1, BP-Causal consists of three main modules, Feature Extractor Module, Balance Split Module, and Causal Inference Module. The Feature Extractor Module learns to extract the causal features, confounding features and their mixed features from the input image; the Balance Split Module uses the information in the confounding features to partition the dataset and will be balanced for better learning in different situation; Causal Inference Module use causal features and mix features to incorporate knowledge learned from subsets of data from different contexts to further identify causal features that are invariant across contexts, improving the generalization ability of the model.

We conduct experiments on two OOD image classification datasets, NICO and NICO++, to demonstrate the effect of BP-Causal balanced partitioning, as well as its predictive ability on OOD data, and study the mechanism on generalization performance through ablation studies. Further case analysis shows that BP-Causal can focus on causal features that are invariant across environments. In conclusion, the main contributions of this paper are:

– A balanced partition causal inference method BP-Causal is proposed, which enhances the generalization of models on OOD data by self-learning manner.

– We demonstrate that a more balanced subset partitioning can have a positive impact on the model learning context-free features, thereby improving the model's generalization ability on OOD data.

2   Related Works

2.1   Out-of-Distribution (OOD) Generalization

Traditional machine learning algorithms are based on the assumption of independent and identical distribution, but in reality the i.i.d. assumption is difficult to satisfy, so people correspondingly put forward the problem of out-of-distribution (OOD) generalization [1,11,15]. The OOD problem addresses challenging settings where the test distribution is unknown and different from training, which is a big challenge for machine learning work. Some of the more challenging OOD settings that exist are: debiasing [4,6,14], domain adaption [7,17,22], long-tailed recognition [13,16,21], etc. To better deal with the OOD problem, [9] proposed a real-world OOD dataset NICO. We follow the OOD settings for the NICO dataset, including long-tailed, zero-shot, and orthogonal.

2.2   Causal Inference

Causal inference [26] is an effective means to solve the OOD problem, which usually assumes the existence of heterogeneity and causality within the data. There are two main methods: ICP and a series of methods after it [10,18,19] control the target variable to be only affected by its direct variable by exploiting the heterogeneity within the data, but this method has strict requirements for the heterogeneity of the data and this approach has limited effectiveness in complex scenes. The invariant learning method represented by IRM [2,3,12,23] is different from the causal prediction method that assumes the original variable level. It generalizes the previous invariance assumption to the representation level and strives to find a classifier that is optimal in all environments. But this method usually requires dividing the data into different parts and extracting common features from the different parts. This data partitioning currently lacks constraints, which may lead to inaccurate causal feature extraction.

3   Methods

3.1   Overview

As shown in the Fig. 2, our model is roughly divided into three modules: the feature extraction module extracts the causal features F_c, the confounding features F_s, and the mixed features F_x from the input image x; the balanced division module uses the information in the confounding features to divide the dataset into data subsets of different environments through the balanced split generation algorithm; the causal inference module fuses the knowledge learned from the data subsets of different environments to distinguish the invariance across environments causal characteristics.

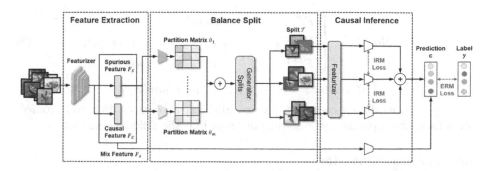

Fig. 2. Schematic diagram of the BP-Causal algorithm: the feature extraction module extracts features for subsequent computation; the balance split module divides the dataset into subsets with different environments in a balanced manner; the causal inference module uses IRM Loss and ERM Loss to constrain at the same time, training the ability to extract invariant features for prediction from different environments.

3.2 Feature Extraction Module

We use an attention module to separate causal and confounding features, In this module, we use F_c and F_s to denote causal features and confounding features, respectively. First, two samples are randomly selected from the training samples for a simple random weighted summation, and the labels of the samples also correspond to the weighted summation [27].

$$\tilde{x} = \lambda x_i + (1 - \lambda)x_j$$
$$\tilde{y} = \lambda y_i + (1 - \lambda)y_j \tag{1}$$

We use $\tilde{x}$ to obtain the feature z through an attention module Attention(x), and use the sigmoid function to disentangle the feature z to obtain the causal feature F_c and the confounding feature F_s:

$$Feature(x) = \begin{cases} z = Attention(\tilde{x}), \\ F_c = Sigmoid(z) \odot \tilde{x}, \\ F_s = Sigmoid(-z) \odot \tilde{x}, \end{cases} \tag{2}$$

where $z \in R^{w \times h \times c}$, Attention() is an attention module called CBAM [24], $\odot$ denotes the element-wise product and Sigmoid(-z) = 1 - Sigmoid(z). We add the module to the basicblock of ResNet to distinguish F_c and F_s. For the first block, the disentangling of features is a little different from the next blocks, just like the Eq. (2). For the next blocks, in D-Block, we input the mix features we got in the previous block and disentangle them to get the causal features and confounding features. In M-Block, the two input are fused to obtain mixed features to prepare for the calculation of the next block. Because we can have many blocks, the $j + 1^{th}$ D-Block and the jth M-Block are as follows:

$$D - Block^{j+1} : \begin{cases} \hat{F_c}^j, \hat{F_s}^j = Feature(\tilde{x}^j), \\ F_c^{j+1} = \hat{F_c}^{j+1} + F_c^j (skip - connection), \\ F_s^{j+1} = \hat{F_s}^{j+1} + F_s^j (skip - connection), \end{cases} \quad (3)$$

$$M - Block^j : F_x^j = Conv(F_c^j) + Conv(F_s^j) \quad (4)$$

Through this module, we extract disentangled causal, confounding and mix features from the input image, and output them into the following module.

3.3   Balance Split Module

In this module, we use the extracted confounding features F_s from the feature extraction module to train the partition matrix θ and update the data partition $\mathcal{T} = \{t_1, t_2, \cdots, t_m\}$. We first train a bias classifier h for each matrix and use h we get the prediction $c = h(F_s)$. We minimize the ERM Loss for it:

$$\mathcal{L}_{bias}^{erm} = E_{(x,y) \in \mathcal{D}} \ell(h(F_s), \tilde{y}) \quad (5)$$

where $\mathcal{D}$ is training data, h is a linear classifier, F_s is the confounding feature we got from the previous module, y is the label. Then using this classifier, under the constraint of an IRMloss [3], a partition matrix θ is trained to gradually update the partition of the dataset in a fine-grained way:

$$\mathcal{L}_{split}^{irm} = \sum_{t \in \mathcal{T}_i(\theta)} R^t(h) + \lambda \cdot \|\nabla_{w|w=1.0} R^t(w \cdot h)\|^2 \quad (6)$$

where $\mathcal{T} = \{t_1, t_2, \cdots, t_m\}$ is current data partition, $\mathcal{T}_i(\theta)$ denotes partition $\mathcal{T}_i$ is decided by $\theta \in R^{K \times m}$, K is the total number of training samples and m is the number of splits in a partition, $R^t(h) := E_{(x,y) \in t_i} \ell(h(F_s), y)$ is the risk under subset t_i, h is the bias classifier trained in the previous step, w = 1.0 is a scalar and fixed "dummy" classifier, the gradient norm penalty is used to measure the optimality of the dummy classifier at each subset t, and $\lambda \in [0, \infty]$ is a regularizer balancing between the ERM term and the invariance of the predictor $1 \cdot h$.

Training only one partition matrix θ may lead to a large imbalance in subsets. In order to alleviate the imbalance, we train multiple matrices, combine the probability distributions of multiple trainings, and then decide the final partition:

$$\theta_{final} = \sum_{i=0}^{m} \begin{pmatrix} p(k_1, m_1) & \cdots & p(k_1, m_j) \\ \vdots & \ddots & \vdots \\ p(k_n, m_1) & \cdots & p(k_n, m_j) \end{pmatrix}_i \quad (7)$$

where $p(k_m, m_n)$ denotes the probability that the nth image is divided into the jth partition. For $\theta_{final} \in R^{K \times m}$, the index of the split to be divided into is:

$$Idx = \underset{\theta}{argmax}(Softmax(\theta_{final})) \quad (8)$$

Then we can divide the K images into corresponding data subsets according to Eq. 8. Through this module, we divide the dataset into fine-grained subsets with different environments, which is more helpful for the model to extract causal features that are invariant across environments.

3.4   Causal Inference Module

Typically, we achieve causal inference by using backdoor adjustment:

$$P(Y|do(X)) = \sum_{t \in \mathcal{T}} P(Y|X,t)P(t) \tag{9}$$

where $P(Y|X,t)$ denotes the prediction of the classifier trained in split t and $P(t) := 1/m$. With do(X), we hope to exclude spurious correlation between the context and the prediction results, so we train the model on data from different environments that are balanced divided, so that the model can focus on the subject of the image in any environment to achieve causal inference.

We first use ERM Loss to constrain the feature extraction part and the classifier, so that the model can extract features accurately.

$$\mathcal{L}_{train}^{erm} = \frac{1}{m} \sum_{i=0}^{m} E_{(x,y) \in t_i} \ell(g_i(F_c), \tilde{y}) \tag{10}$$

where m is the number of splits in a partition, t_i represents a specific split, g_i is a linear classifier for t_i, F_c is causal feature. Then, by dividing and training multiple classifiers for the data of different environments, and using an IRM Loss to align these classifiers with constraints, a classifier that is optimal in all environments is obtained. With this classifier we can mitigate the context interference and make the model better focus on causal features.

$$\mathcal{L}_{invariance}^{irm} = \sum_{t \in \mathcal{T}_i(\theta)} R^t(g) + \lambda \cdot \|\nabla_{w|w=1.0} R^t(w \cdot g)\|^2 \tag{11}$$

After multiple partitions updating and training, we can gradually approach the backdoor adjustment formula 9 to achieve causal inference.

3.5   Training Strategy

There are multi-class loss constraints in BP-Causal, and a staged training method can be used. The extraction of training features in the first stage is jointly constrained by the empirical risk loss from different data subsets and the invariant risk loss of aligning the classifier weights under different environments. In order to make the model extract better features, we minimize these two losses:

$$min \, \mathcal{L}_{train}^{erm} + \mathcal{L}_{invariance}^{irm} \tag{12}$$

The second stage is training data partition. First we train a biased classifier using the empirical risk loss, then use that classifier to constrain the data partition by an invariant risk loss. We minimize the empirical loss to improve the model's ability to distinguish confounding features, but we maximize the invariant loss, so that the m splits are divided in different fine-grained confounding features, so as to achieve the purpose of dividing different environmental data subsets:

$$min \, \mathcal{L}_{bias}^{erm} + max \, \mathcal{L}_{split}^{irm} \tag{13}$$

4 Experiments

4.1 Datasets

NICO. [9] is a real-world dataset with 2 superclasses for a total of 19 classes, and 9 or 10 contexts under each class, accumulating a total of 188 (subject, context) combinations and collecting about 25,000 images. We follow the setting of [23], selecting 10 animal classes and 10 contexts. We make a challenging OOD setting consisting of three factors on context: 1) Long-tailed - The training context are long-tailed in each class; 2) ZeroShot - for each class, 7 of the 10 contexts are in the training images, the other 3 contexts only appear in the test; 3) Orthogonal - the head context for each class is set to be as unique as possible.

NICO++. [25] is an upgrade to the NICO dataset. Consistent with NICO, NICO++ decomposes images into (subject, context) combinations. NICO++ has included 80 classes, 10 public contexts, and 10 unique contexts for each class, with a total of 200,000 images. We picked 10 classes from the public context section, including animals, vehicles, and others. We follow the OOD settings [23], including long-tail, ZeroShot - 4 of the 6 context per class are in the training images, the other 2 labels only appear in test and orthogonal - as much as possible to ensure that each class' header context appears only once or twice.

4.2 Experimental Settings

Evaluation Protocol. We follow [23] and use the accuracy on the validation set and test set as the judging criterion. The formula is as follows:

$$Accuracy = \frac{TP + TN}{TP + TN + FP + FN} \tag{14}$$

where TP, TN, FP, FN are the number of true positive, false positive samples, true negative samples, and false negative samples.

Table 1. Recognition accuracies (%) based on ResNet18 on NICO and NICO++ dataset. "val" and "test" denote the accuracies on validation set and test set.

Method	Model	NICO		NICO++	
		val	test	val	test
Conv. method	ResNet-18	44.38	44.08	44.73	45.93
	Cutout	46.23	44.08	45.75	45.75
	Mixup	44.69	42.46	**49.00**	49.06
Causal method	CBAM	43.77	43.54	44.27	45.47
	CaaM	44.85	44.69	43.93	46.44
	BP-causal	**48.23**	**48.08**	48.38	**51.28**

Implementation Details. For NICO dataset, the optimizer was set to SGD with a learning rate of 0.05. We trained the model with 200 epochs and the learning rate was decreased by 5 at 120, 160 epoch. From 40 epoch, the data partition will be updated every 20 epochs, and we divide the dataset to 4 parts. For NICO++ dataset, the optimizer was set to SGD with a learning rate of 0.02. We trained the model with 200 epochs and the learning rate was decreased by 5 at 80, 120, 160 epoch. From 40 epoch, the data partition will be updated every 40 epochs, and we divide the dataset to 4 parts.

4.3   Performance Comparison

This section presents the performance comparison of BP-Causal with existing image classification methods, including the traditional Resnet-18 [8], two data augmentation methods [5,27], the CBAM attention mechanism [24] and a causal method CaaM [23]. We can observe the following Table 1:

- Simply adding the attention mechanism, in the OOD context, may cause the attention to focus on the wrong area, so that after adding attention module [24], the model performance is not as good as the baseline algorithm.
- The performance of the CaaM algorithm is better than that of the baseline algorithm, as well as the attention method. Because it learns causal features that are invariant across environments and stable in prediction from different environments by partitioning the dataset. However, there is a lack of constraints on the division of the dataset, which loses part of the performance.
- When BP-Causal divides the data set into different environment subsets, the balance between the subsets is enhanced by adding constraints to the division process. This method works better in the OOD case than baseline and using the attention mechanism alone, about 3%–5% performance improvement.

4.4   Ablation Study

In this section, we investigate the effectiveness of the proposed algorithm. The experiment selected resnet18 [8] as the baseline. As shown in the Table 2, adding the attention mechanism [24] directly will affect the performance, because the attention mechanism may capture spurious correlation as a basis for prediction in the OOD context. On the basis of CBAM [24], a causal method is added to alleviate the problem of paying attention to errors in OOD environments. However,there is no restriction on the partition of the data set, which leads to the problem of imbalance in the data partition. We try three balanced methods to constrain the partition. Loss Balance (LB) is to add a loss during training, Manual Balance (MB) is to balance images of different subsets by manual deletion and supplementation, Aggregation Balance (GB) is to alleviate the degree of imbalance by training multiple partition matrices. In the third way, the inference

Table 2. The influence of each module of the algorithm on the performance.

Model	NICO		NICO++	
	val	test	val	test
Baseline	44.38	44.08	44.73	45.93
+ CBAM	43.77	43.54	44.27	45.47
+ CBAM + Causal	44.85	44.69	43.93	46.44
+ CBAM + Causal + LB	45.23	45.85	46.04	47.24
+ CBAM + Causal + MB	46.46	46.62	44.05	47.41
+ CBAM + Causal + GB	45.62	46.85	46.38	47.46
+ CBAM + Causal + LB + mixup	48.08	47.38	**48.83**	49.74
+ CBAM + Causal + MB + mixup	45.62	47.92	48.55	51.00
+ CBAM + Causal + GB + mixup	**48.23**	**48.08**	48.38	**51.28**

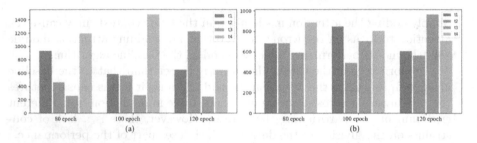

Fig. 3. Statistics on the number of subsets divided by different epochs. Where (a) is the result of using CAAM partition, (b) is the result of BP-Causal partition.

of the partition is minimal, but the imbalance of the partition is alleviated to a certain extent, so the best performance is obtained. In addition, we found that mixup [27], as an effective data augmentation method, also works well in OOD situations. We tested the effects of the three balancing methods after adding the mixup, and the Smooth Balance method is still the best than any other methods.

4.5   Analysis of Split Partition

In previous experiments we have demonstrated the positive effect of balanced partitioning on the generalization ability of the model, in this section we will show the practical effect of BP-Causal in balanced partitioning of subsets, as shown in Fig. 3. The division using the CAAM method has obvious imbalance between different splits, which largely restricts the ability of the model to learn invariant features from different subsets. The subset using BP-Causal division is relatively more balanced, and it is also very stable in different divisions, which effectively improves the effect of the model learning from the causal feature.

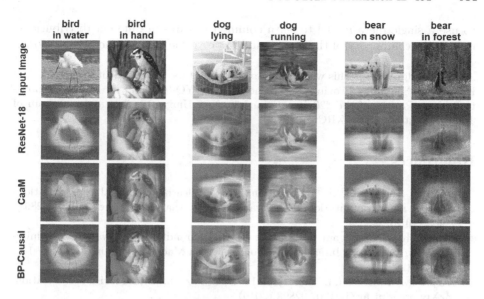

Fig. 4. Visualization of attention maps with base modal, CaaM, and BP-Causal.

4.6   Case Study

Figure 4 shows the qualitative attention map [20] comparison between our proposed BP-Causal algorithm, the traditional method ResNet18 and the causal method CaaM. We selected three categories of the NICO dataset, and each category selected two contexts for experiments. As can be seen from the figure, our method can focus more on the subject of the image rather than the surrounding environment and other objects compared to the other two methods. For different contexts of the same category, a large part of ResNet18's attention is focused on the surrounding environment, especially under the category of dogs, but our algorithm can pay attention to the characteristics of dogs in different environments. This improves the classification accuracy of the model.

5   Conclusion

This paper proposes a causal learning method BP-Causal based on balanced partition, which automatically generates balanced data subsets of different environments through training, extracts invariant causal features from different environments, and enhances the model's learning in OOD environments. Capabilities and generalization capabilities.

BP-Causal effectively alleviates the attention bias of the attention model and the interference of confounding factors in complex OOD scenarios. However, training multiple classifiers and then forcing the use of loss to align the weights of different classifiers may lead to difficulty in convergence and affect the performance of the model. We will try to use meta-learning and other means to use a single meta-model to learn common features of different distributions, reduce the complexity of the model, and improve the performance of the model.

Acknowledgments. This work is supported in part by the Excellent Youth Scholars Program of Shandong Province (Grant no. 2022HWYQ-048) and the Oversea Innovation Team Project of the "20 Regulations for New Universities" funding program of Jinan (Grant no. 2021GXRC073).

References

1. Achille, A., Soatto, S.: Information dropout: learning optimal representations through noisy computation. IEEE Trans. Pattern Anal. Mach. Intell. **40**(12), 2897–2905 (2018)
2. Ahuja, K., Shanmugam, K., Varshney, K., Dhurandhar, A.: Invariant risk minimization games. In: International Conference on Machine Learning, pp. 145–155. PMLR (2020)
3. Arjovsky, M., Bottou, L., Gulrajani, I., Lopez-Paz, D.: Invariant risk minimization. arXiv preprint arXiv:1907.02893 (2019)
4. Clark, C., Yatskar, M., Zettlemoyer, L.: Don't take the easy way out: Ensemble based methods for avoiding known dataset biases. arXiv preprint arXiv:1909.03683 (2019)
5. DeVries, T., Taylor, G.W.: Improved regularization of convolutional neural networks with cutout. arXiv preprint arXiv:1708.04552 (2017)
6. Geirhos, R., et al.: ImageNet-trained CNNs are biased towards texture; increasing shape bias improves accuracy and robustness. arXiv preprint arXiv:1811.12231 (2018)
7. Gong, M., et al.: Domain adaptation with conditional transferable components. In: International Conference on Machine Learning, pp. 2839–2848. PMLR (2016)
8. He, K., Zhang, X., Ren, S., Sun, J.: Deep residual learning for image recognition. In: Proceedings of the IEEE Conference on Computer Vision and Pattern Recognition, pp. 770–778 (2016)
9. He, Y., Shen, Z., Cui, P.: Towards Non-IID image classification: a dataset and baselines. Pattern Recognit. **110**, 107383 (2021)
10. Heinze-Deml, C., Peters, J., Meinshausen, N.: Invariant causal prediction for nonlinear models. J. Causal Inference **6**(2) (2018)
11. Hendrycks, D., Gimpel, K.: A baseline for detecting misclassified and out-of-distribution examples in neural networks. arXiv preprint arXiv:1610.02136 (2016)
12. Jin, W., Barzilay, R., Jaakkola, T.: Domain extrapolation via regret minimization. arXiv preprint arXiv:2006.03908 (2020)
13. Khan, S.H., Hayat, M., Bennamoun, M., Sohel, F.A., Togneri, R.: Cost-sensitive learning of deep feature representations from imbalanced data. IEEE Trans. Neural Netw. Learn. Syst. **29**(8), 3573–3587 (2017)
14. Kim, B., Kim, H., Kim, K., Kim, S., Kim, J.: Learning not to learn: training deep neural networks with biased data. In: Proceedings of the IEEE/CVF Conference on Computer Vision and Pattern Recognition, pp. 9012–9020 (2019)
15. Liang, S., Li, Y., Srikant, R.: Enhancing the reliability of out-of-distribution image detection in neural networks. arXiv preprint arXiv:1706.02690 (2017)

16. Mahajan, D., et al.: Exploring the limits of weakly supervised pretraining. In: Ferrari, V., Hebert, M., Sminchisescu, C., Weiss, Y. (eds.) ECCV 2018. LNCS, vol. 11206, pp. 185–201. Springer, Cham (2018). https://doi.org/10.1007/978-3-030-01216-8_12

17. Muandet, K., Balduzzi, D., Schölkopf, B.: Domain generalization via invariant feature representation. In: International Conference on Machine Learning, pp. 10–18. PMLR (2013)

18. Peters, J., Bühlmann, P., Meinshausen, N.: Causal inference by using invariant prediction: identification and confidence intervals. J. R. Stat. Soc. Ser. B (Stat. Methodol.) **78**(5), 947–1012 (2016)

19. Pfister, N., Bühlmann, P., Peters, J.: Invariant causal prediction for sequential data. J. Am. Stat. Assoc. **114**(527), 1264–1276 (2019)

20. Selvaraju, R.R., Cogswell, M., Das, A., Vedantam, R., Parikh, D., Batra, D.: Grad-CAM: visual explanations from deep networks via gradient-based localization. In: Proceedings of the IEEE International Conference on Computer Vision, pp. 618–626 (2017)

21. Shen, L., Lin, Z., Huang, Q.: Relay backpropagation for effective learning of deep convolutional neural networks. In: Leibe, B., Matas, J., Sebe, N., Welling, M. (eds.) ECCV 2016. LNCS, vol. 9911, pp. 467–482. Springer, Cham (2016). https://doi.org/10.1007/978-3-319-46478-7_29

22. Tzeng, E., Hoffman, J., Saenko, K., Darrell, T.: Adversarial discriminative domain adaptation. In: Proceedings of the IEEE Conference on Computer Vision and Pattern Recognition, pp. 7167–7176 (2017)

23. Wang, T., Zhou, C., Sun, Q., Zhang, H.: Causal attention for unbiased visual recognition. In: Proceedings of the IEEE/CVF International Conference on Computer Vision, pp. 3091–3100 (2021)

24. Woo, S., Park, J., Lee, J.-Y., Kweon, I.S.: CBAM: convolutional block attention module. In: Ferrari, V., Hebert, M., Sminchisescu, C., Weiss, Y. (eds.) ECCV 2018. LNCS, vol. 11211, pp. 3–19. Springer, Cham (2018). https://doi.org/10.1007/978-3-030-01234-2_1

25. Xu R., Yu, H., Shen, Z., Cui, P., Zhang, X., He, Y.: Nico++: towards better benchmarking for domain generalization (2022)

26. Yao, L., Chu, Z., Li, S., Li, Y., Gao, J., Zhang, A.: A survey on causal inference. ACM Trans. Knowl. Discov. Data (TKDD) **15**(5), 1–46 (2021)

27. Zhang, H., Cisse, M., Dauphin, Y.N., Lopez-Paz, D.: mixup: beyond empirical risk minimization. arXiv preprint arXiv:1710.09412 (2017)

Low-Light Image Enhancement Under Mixed Noise Model with Tensor Representation

Weipeng Yang[1,2], Hongxia Gao[1(✉)], Shasha Huang[1], Shicheng Niu[1], Hongsheng Chen[1], and Guoheng Liang[2]

[1] School of Automation Science and Engineering, South China University of Technology, Guangzhou, China
hxgao@scut.edu.cn
[2] Research and Development Center, Zhaoqing Honghua Electronic Technology Co., Ltd., Zhaoqing, China

Abstract. Compared with the traditional Retinex model, the robust Retinex model considers the influence of additive Gaussian noise to improve the performance of low-light image enhancement with strong noise. However, the real noise model is not so simple. In order to describe the noise model more accurately, this paper considers the enhancement of low-light images under the influence of Poisson and Gaussian mixture noise, so as to better model the noise model and suppress the noise amplification. In order to smooth the noise in the reflection component, the current methods generally decompose the V-channel of the image converted to HSV color space to obtain the illuminance component and the reflection component, and then constrain the reflection component a priori such as sparse, low rank or nonlocal self-similarity based on matrix or vector operations. The problem is that the conversion of color space may lead to color distortion, and the matrix operation and vectorization operation by channel may damage the structural relationship of channel and space respectively, and may occupy a high memory. In order to better maintain the correlation between RGB image channels, the RGB image is directly represented in the form of tensor, processed in the RGB color space as a whole, and the tensor nuclear norm is used to impose a low rank constraint on the reflection component to suppress the noise. Compared with the contrast method, the proposed method achieves good visual and quantitative results in low-light image enhancement tasks.

Keywords: Robust Retinex · Mixture noise · Tensor nuclear norm

1 Introduction

The Retinex theory developed by land and McCann [1] simulates the color perception of human vision in natural scenes. It can be regarded as the basic theory of internal image decomposition [2], and its purpose is to decompose the image into illuminance and reflectance components. Retinex has many applications, such as low-light image enhancement [3] and color correction [4].

L. Fang et al. (Eds.): CICAI 2022, LNAI 13604, pp. 584–596, 2022.
https://doi.org/10.1007/978-3-031-20497-5_48

Traditional Retinex methods roughly include center/surround methods [5, 6], partial differential equation (PDE)-based methods [7], and path-based methods [8, 9]. Center/surround methods include the commonly used Single-Scale Retinex (SSR) [6] and Multi-Scale Retinex with Color Restoration (MSRCR) [5]. These models lack reasonable structure-preserving constraints, only assume that the illuminance component is smooth and the reflection component is non-smooth, prone to halo artifacts around edges. The PDE method is based on the Retinex model whose solution satisfies the properties of the discrete Poisson equation, and the reflection component can be efficiently estimated using the Fast Fourier Transform. However, since gradients derived based on divergence-free vector fields generally ignore the patch-smooth prior, the illuminance component cannot be accurately estimated. Path-based methods assume that the reflection components can be computed by multiplying ratios along random paths. This method has poor self-adaptation, requires a lot of parameter adjustment, and consumes huge computing resources.

The idea of variational method is to decompose the image into illuminance and reflectance components based on Retinex model. [10] using smoothing prior to estimate the illuminance component, but this method is inefficient and ignores the regularization of reflectance. In [11], the image is transformed logarithmically to suppress the change of gradient amplitude in the bright area, but the reflectance component estimated based on logarithmic regularization is often too smooth, and the calculation in the logarithmic domain is easy to cause the amplification of noise. Therefore, the regularization terms of illuminance and reflectance are considered in the subsequent methods. A method based on total variation (TV) model is proposed in [12], but it is difficult to balance detail maintenance and noise smoothing. In order to reduce the detail loss in the reflectance component, [13] proposed a weighted variational model (WVM) to enhance the change of gradient amplitude in bright areas. However, the piecewise smoothness of the illuminance component is difficult to maintain. Based on the fact that there is often strong structural information where the illuminance changes, [3] proposed a joint inside-outside prior (JieP) decomposition model, but the model is easy to over smooth the illuminance and reflectance component. [14] adds power operation to the structure and texture a prior of [3] to improve the ability to distinguish between texture and structure, but the contrast of the image is not ideal. [14] proposed a robust Retinex method by considering the noise term, but it is easy to produce excessive smoothing at the details of the image.

In general, the above methods have the following problems. The current method based on Retinex model generally decomposes the V channel of the HSV color space to obtain the illuminance component and the reflection component, and then constrains the reflection component to be sparse, low-rank or non-local self-similar based on matrix or vector operations. The problem is that the matrix operation of sub-channels and vectorization operation may destroy the correlation between channels and spatial relations respectively, and may occupy a high amount of memory. In order to better maintain the correlation between RGB image channels, the RGB image is directly represented in the form of tensor, processed in the RGB color space as a whole, and the tensor nuclear norm is used to impose a low rank constraint on the reflection component to suppress the noise.

In addition, for distinguishing the light source from the white object more accurately, the initial value of the illuminance component is calculated based on the L0 norm, which is used to constrain the final illuminance component. Through extensive experiments on several datasets, our proposed method achieves good results both visually and quantitatively in low-light image enhancement tasks compared to contrastive methods.

2 Background

2.1 Intrinsic Prior on Shape and Texture

Although the illuminance component should be piecewise smooth, the illuminance component itself is unknown, so a priori should be used to constrain the shape of the illuminance component. One method is to detect the edge of the input low-light image and smooth out the detail information of small gradient. Because the edge corresponds to the point with sharp brightness change in the image, and the sharp brightness change in the image mainly includes discontinuity of depth, discontinuity of surface direction, different object materials (resulting in different reflection coefficient of light) and different illuminance in the scene.

Inspired by [3], this paper uses local variational deviation (LVD) to preserve the image, separate the edge and detail of the image, and smooth out the small gradient detail information. Unlike [3] which converts the sRGB image to HSV color space first and uses LVD to constrain the brightness Channel V, in order to better maintain the structural relationship of the three channels of sRGB image, this paper represents the sRGB image as a tensor, and uses LVD to constrain the three channels of R, G and B as a whole. The expression of $E_s(\mathcal{L})$ is as follows:

$$E_s(\mathcal{L}) = \sum_{c=1}^{3} E_{s,c}(\mathcal{L}) = \sum_{c=1}^{3} \left\| \frac{\nabla_h \mathcal{L}_c}{\frac{1}{|\Omega|} \sum_\Omega \nabla_h \mathcal{L}_c + \epsilon} \right\|_1 + \left\| \frac{\nabla_v \mathcal{L}_c}{\frac{1}{|\Omega|} \sum_\Omega \nabla_v \mathcal{L}_c + \epsilon} \right\|_1$$

where, $\nabla_{h/v}$ is the gradient operator in the horizontal and vertical directions, Ω is a local patch with the size of 3×3 in this paper. ϵ is a small number to avoid division by zero.

2.2 Initial Estimation of Illuminance Components

If the illuminance is limited to piecewise smoothing, the light source and white object cannot be estimated accurately. Methods [3, 17] constrained or optimized the illuminance component with the help of channel priors [18, 19], but the RGB image is estimated to be a brightness gray image based on channel priors, and some information of three channels was discarded, resulting in the inaccuracy of global illuminance estimation.

The calculation of the initial illuminance component $\mathcal{B}$ can simply and efficiently utilize the method of [20]. Unlike other edge-preserving methods, the method of [20] does not rely on local features, but locates important edges globally.

2.3 T-SVD

Definition 1. (Identity tensor). [24] Identity tensor $\mathcal{I} \in \mathbb{R}^{n \times n \times n_3}$ is the tensor whose first frontal slice being the $n \times n$ identity matrix, and other frontal slices are all zeros.

Definition 2. (Orthogonal Tensor). [24] A tensor $\mathcal{A} \in \mathbb{R}^{n \times n \times n_3}$ is orthogonal if it satisfies $\mathcal{A}^* \mathcal{A} = \mathcal{A} \mathcal{A}^* = \mathcal{I}$.

Definition 3. (F-diagonal). [24] A tensor is called f-diagonal if each of its frontal slices is diagonal matrix.

Theorem 1. (T-SVD). [15] Let $\mathcal{A} \in \mathbb{R}^{n_1 \times n_2 \times n_3}$. It can be factorized as
$$\mathcal{A} = \mathcal{U} * \mathcal{S} * \mathcal{V}^*$$
where $\mathcal{U} \in \mathbb{R}^{n_1 \times n_1 \times n_3}$, $\mathcal{V} \in \mathbb{R}^{n_2 \times n_2 \times n_3}$ are orthogonal, and $\mathcal{S} \in \mathbb{R}^{n_1 \times n_2 \times n_3}$ is an f-diagonal tensor.

2.4 Tensor Nuclear Norm (TNN)

Definition 4. (Tensor tubal rank). [26] Let $\mathcal{A} = \mathcal{U} * \mathcal{S} * \mathcal{V}^*$ be the t-SVD of $\mathcal{A} \in \mathbb{R}^{n_1 \times n_2 \times n_3}$. The tensor tubal rank, denoted as $rank_t(\mathcal{A})$, is defined as the number of nonzero singular tubes of $\mathcal{S}$.

$$rank_t(\mathcal{A}) = \#\{i, \mathcal{S}(i, i, :) \neq 0\}$$

According to [31], $rank_t(\mathcal{A})$ can be calculated by the following formula:

$$rank_t(\mathcal{A}) = \#\{i, \mathcal{S}(i, i, 1) \neq 0\}$$

Definition 5. (Tensor nuclear norm). [31] Let $\mathcal{A} = \mathcal{U} * \mathcal{S} * \mathcal{V}^*$ be the t-SVD of $\mathcal{A} \in \mathbb{R}^{n_1 \times n_2 \times n_3}$. The tensor nuclear norm of $\mathcal{A}$ is defined as
$$\|\mathcal{A}\|_* = \langle \mathcal{S}, \mathcal{I} \rangle = \sum_{i=1}^{r} \mathcal{S}(i, i, 1)$$
where $r = rank_t(\mathcal{A})$.

Theorem 2. [31] For any $\tau > 0$ and $\mathcal{Y} \in \mathbb{R}^{n_1 \times n_2 \times n_3}$, the proximal operator of TNN. $\min\limits_{\mathcal{X} \in \mathbb{R}^{n_1 \times n_2 \times n_3}} \tau \|\mathcal{X}\|_* + \frac{1}{2} \|\mathcal{X} - \mathcal{Y}\|_F^2$
$\mathcal{X}$ can be calculated by the tensor Singular Value Thresholding (t-SVT) operator as follows
$$\mathcal{D}_\tau(\mathcal{Y}) = \mathcal{U} * \mathcal{S}_\tau * \mathcal{V}^*$$
where, $\mathcal{Y} = \mathcal{U} * \mathcal{S} * \mathcal{V}^*$, and $\mathcal{S}_\tau = ifft\left(\left(\overline{\mathcal{S}} - \tau\right)_+, [], 3\right)$, $\overline{\mathcal{S}} = ifft(\mathcal{S})$, $t_+ = max(t, 0)$, $ifft()$ means inverse Fast Fourier transform (FFT) operator.

3 The Proposed Model

3.1 The Robust Retinex Model

The Robust Retinex model [21] decomposes images into reflectance, illuminance and additional noise term as:

$$\mathcal{Y} = \mathcal{L} \cdot \mathcal{R} + \mathcal{N} \tag{1}$$

where $\mathcal{Y}$ is the observed image, $\mathcal{L}$ and $\mathcal{R}$ represent the reflectance and the illuminance of the image. $\mathcal{N}$ is the additional noise term. The operator $\cdot$ denotes the element-wise multiplication.

The reflectance component $\mathcal{R}$ describes the internal properties of the captured object, which is considered to be consistent under any lighting conditions, and is full of structural details. Illuminance component $\mathcal{L}$ represents various brightness on the object. It is piecewise continuous and retains the main edges without small gradients [12].

In order to describe the noise model more accurately, we consider the enhancement of low-light images under the influence of Poisson and Gaussian mixture noise, as shown in (2), so as to better model the noise model and suppress the noise amplification.

$$\mathcal{Y} = P_{poisson}(\mathcal{L} \cdot \mathcal{R}) + \mathcal{N} \tag{2}$$

where $P_{poisson}()$ represents Poisson noise process and $\mathcal{N}$ represents additive Gaussian noise.

The probability density functions of Poisson and Gaussian noise are as follows:

$$P_{\text{poisson}}(\mathcal{Y}|\mathcal{U}) = \prod_{i=1}^{3*N} \frac{(\mathcal{U}_i)^{\mathcal{Y}_i} e^{-\mathcal{U}_i}}{\mathcal{Y}_i!}$$

$$P_{gaussian}(\mathcal{Y}|\mathcal{U}) = \frac{1}{\sqrt{2\pi\sigma^2}} e^{-\frac{\|\mathcal{Y}-\mathcal{U}\|_F^2}{2\sigma^2}}$$

where, $\mathcal{U} = \mathcal{L} \cdot \mathcal{R}$, N represents the number of pixels of a single channel.

Considering Gaussian noise and Poisson noise as uncorrelated, the probability density function of mixed noise has the following form:

$$P_{mixed}(\mathcal{Y}|\mathcal{U}) = \frac{1}{\sqrt{2\pi\sigma^2}} e^{-\frac{\|\mathcal{Y}-\mathcal{U}\|_F^2}{2\sigma^2}} \prod_{i=1}^{3*N} \frac{(\mathcal{U}_i)^{\mathcal{Y}_i} e^{-\mathcal{U}_i}}{\mathcal{Y}_i!}$$

Under the framework of Maximum a Posteriori probability (MAP), the negative logarithm of $P_{mixed}(\mathcal{Y}|\mathcal{U})$ is as follows:

$$-\log P_{mixed}(\mathcal{Y}|\mathcal{U}) = -\sum_{i=1}^{3*N} \log \frac{(\mathcal{U}_i)^{\mathcal{Y}_i} e^{-\mathcal{U}_i}}{\mathcal{Y}_i!} - \log \frac{1}{\sqrt{2\pi\sigma^2}} e^{-\frac{\|\mathcal{Y}-\mathcal{U}\|_F^2}{2\sigma^2}} =$$

$$\sum_{i=1}^{3*N} (\mathcal{U}_i - \mathcal{Y}_i \log \mathcal{U}_i + \log \mathcal{Y}_i!) + \frac{\|\mathcal{Y}-\mathcal{U}\|_F^2}{2\sigma^2} + \frac{1}{2}\log 2\pi\sigma^2$$

The following objective function can be obtained by removing irrelevant items:

$$\min_{\mathcal{U}} \sum_{i=1}^{3*N} (\mathcal{U}_i - \mathcal{Y}_i \log \mathcal{U}_i) + \frac{\|\mathcal{Y} - \mathcal{U}\|_F^2}{2\sigma^2}$$

In this paper, we try to improve the visibility of low-light images while mitigating the effect of noise in a joint optimization function based on the mixed noise model and tensor representation.

3.2 Baseline Decomposition

Estimating $\mathcal{R}$ and $\mathcal{L}$ from $\mathcal{Y}$ is an ill posed problem, so we construct an optimization function to solve the inverse problem of the Eq. (2) with regularization term:

$$\min_{\mathcal{U},\mathcal{L},\mathcal{R}} \sum_{i=1}^{3*N} (\mathcal{U}_i - \mathcal{Y}_i \log \mathcal{U}_i) + \frac{\lambda_1}{2\sigma^2}\|\mathcal{Y} - \mathcal{U}\|_F^2 + \lambda_2 E_s(\mathcal{L}) + \lambda_3 \|\mathcal{R}\|_* + \lambda_4 \|\mathcal{L} - \mathcal{B}\|_F^2 \tag{3}$$

$$s.t. \mathcal{U} = \mathcal{L} \cdot \mathcal{R}$$

where, $\|\mathcal{X}\|_F$ is Frobenius norm [15] of tensor $\mathcal{X}$, $\lambda_1, \lambda_2, \lambda_3 \lambda_4$ are tradeoff parameters. $E_s(\mathcal{L})$ is the constraint term for the piece-wise smoothness of the illuminance component, tensor nuclear norm $\|\mathcal{R}\|_*$ is used to constrain the low rank of $\mathcal{R}$ to suppress the noise in it. $\|\mathcal{L} - \mathcal{B}\|_F^2$ is used to limit the proximity of $\mathcal{L}$ to initial illuminance component $\mathcal{B}$.

3.3 Optimization Procedure

By introducing some auxiliary variables, we rewrite (3) into the following equivalent minimization problem:

$$\min_{\mathcal{U},\mathcal{L},\mathcal{R}} \sum_{i=1}^{3*N} (\mathcal{U}_i - \mathcal{Y}_i \log \mathcal{U}_i) + \frac{\lambda_1}{2\sigma^2}\|\mathcal{Y} - \mathcal{U}\|_F^2 + \lambda_2 E_s(\mathcal{L}) + \lambda_3 \|\mathcal{T}\|_* + \lambda_4 \|\mathcal{L} - \mathcal{B}\|_F^2 \tag{4}$$

$$s.t. \mathcal{U} = \mathcal{L} \cdot \mathcal{R}, \mathcal{R} = \mathcal{T}$$

Based on the ALM methodology, the above-mentioned problem (4) can be transformed into minimizing the following augmented Lagrangian function:

$$L\left\{\widehat{\mathcal{L}}, \widehat{\mathcal{R}}, \widehat{\mathcal{U}}, \widehat{\mathcal{T}}\right\} = \sum_{i=1}^{3*N} (\mathcal{U}_i - \mathcal{Y}_i \log \mathcal{U}_i) + \frac{\lambda_1}{2\sigma^2}\|\mathcal{Y} - \mathcal{U}\|_F^2 + \lambda_2 E_s(\mathcal{L}) + \lambda_3 \|\mathcal{T}\|_* \tag{5}$$

$$+ \lambda_4 \|\mathcal{L} - \mathcal{B}\|_F^2 + \frac{\rho}{2}\|\mathcal{U} - \mathcal{L} \cdot \mathcal{R} + \frac{\mathcal{J}}{\rho}\|_F^2 + \frac{\rho_1}{2}\|\mathcal{R} - \mathcal{T} + \frac{\mathcal{J}_1}{\rho_1}\|_F^2$$

ρ, ρ_1 is the penalty parameter, $\mathcal{J}$ and $\mathcal{J}_1$ are the Lagrange multipliers. Therefore, we can alternatively optimize the augmented Lagrangian function (5) over one variable while fixing the others. Specifically, variables involved in the model (5) can be updated as follows.

1) **Update $\mathcal{U}$:** Extracting all terms containing $\mathcal{U}$ from the augmented Lagrangian function (6), we need to solve:

$$\mathcal{U} = \arg\min_{\mathcal{U}} \sum_{i=1}^{3*N} (\mathcal{U}_i - \mathcal{Y}_i \log \mathcal{U}_i) + \frac{\lambda_1}{2\sigma^2}\|\mathcal{Y} - \mathcal{U}\|_F^2 + \frac{\rho}{2}\|\mathcal{U} - \mathcal{L} \cdot \mathcal{R} + \frac{\mathcal{J}}{\rho}\|_F^2$$

By introducing a column vector whose elements are all 1 and removing irrelevant items, the above problem can be converted to:

$$\underset{U_1}{argmin} I^T U_1 - I^T(Y_1 \cdot logU_1) + 2\left[\frac{\lambda_1}{2\sigma^2}Y_1 + \frac{\rho}{2}\left(\mathcal{L} \cdot \mathcal{R} - \frac{\mathcal{J}}{\rho}\right)\right]^T + U_1^T U_1$$

Calculate the derivative of the above formula, take the extreme value, and convert U_1 into the form of tensor to obtain the solution of $\mathcal{U}$ as:

$$\mathcal{U}_{k+1} = reshape(\frac{2M_k - 1}{4K} + \sqrt{\left(\frac{2M_k - 1}{4K}\right)^2 + \frac{Y_1}{4K\sigma^2}})$$

$$M_k = \frac{\lambda_1}{2\sigma^2} + \frac{\rho}{2}\left(\mathcal{L}_k \cdot \mathcal{R}_k - \frac{\mathcal{J}^k}{\rho}\right)$$

$$K = \frac{\lambda_1}{2\sigma^2} + \frac{\rho}{2}$$

2) Update $\mathcal{L}$: Extracting all terms containing $\mathcal{L}$ from the augmented Lagrangian function (5), we can deduce

$$\mathcal{L} = \underset{\mathcal{L}}{argmin} \lambda_2 E_s(\mathcal{L}) + \lambda_4\|\mathcal{L} - \mathcal{B}\|_F^2 + \frac{\rho}{2}\|\mathcal{U} - \mathcal{L} \cdot \mathcal{R} + \frac{\mathcal{J}}{\rho}\|_F^2$$

Since L1-norms in $E_s(\mathcal{L})$ cause non-smooth optimization, an iteratively re-weighted least square [22] method is introduced and $E_s(\mathcal{L})$ is rewritten as:

$$E_s(\mathcal{L}) = \sum_{c=1}^{3} E_{s,c}(\mathcal{L}) = \sum_{c=1}^{3} u_h\|\nabla_h \mathcal{L}_c\|_F^2 + u_v\|\nabla_v \mathcal{L}_c\|_F^2$$

where, $u_h = \left(\left|\frac{1}{|\Omega|}\sum_\Omega \nabla_h \mathcal{L}_c\right||\nabla_h \mathcal{L}_c| + \epsilon\right)^{-1}$, $u_v = \left(\left|\frac{1}{|\Omega|}\sum_\Omega \nabla_v \mathcal{L}_c\right||\nabla_v \mathcal{L}_c| + \epsilon\right)^{-1}$.

Thus, optimizing this problem can be treated as solving the following problem:

$$\mathcal{L} = \underset{\mathcal{L}}{argmin} \lambda_3 \sum_{c=1}^{3} u_h\|\nabla_h \mathcal{L}_c\|_F^2 + u_v\|\nabla_v \mathcal{L}_c\|_F^2 + \lambda_7\|\mathcal{L} - \mathcal{B}\|_F^2 + \frac{\rho}{2}\|\mathcal{U} - \mathcal{L} \cdot \mathcal{R} + \frac{\mathcal{J}}{\rho}\|_F^2$$

This problem can be transformed into the following equivalent problem:

$$\mathcal{L}_{k+1} = \underset{\mathcal{L}}{argmin} \mathcal{L}^T\left[\lambda_3 Q + \lambda_7 I + \frac{\rho}{2}\mathcal{R}_{diag,k}^T \mathcal{R}_{diag,k}\right]\mathcal{L} - 2\lambda_7 \mathcal{B}^T \mathcal{L} - \rho\left(\mathcal{U}_{k+1} + \frac{\mathcal{J}^k}{\rho}\right)^T \mathcal{R}_{diag,k}\mathcal{L}$$

where $Q = D_h^T U_h D_h + D_v^T U_v D_v$, D_h, D_v are the Toeplitz matrices of the gradient operator obtained by forward difference, U_h, U_v are the diagonal matrixed obtained by the expansion of the elements of u_h and u_v, respectively. Therefore, the problem can be transformed into the following linear system problem:

$$\left[\lambda_3 Q + \lambda_7 I + \frac{\rho}{2}\mathcal{R}_{diag,k}^T \mathcal{R}_{diag,k}\right]\mathcal{L}_{k+1} = \lambda_7 \mathcal{B} + \frac{\rho}{2}\mathcal{R}_{diag,k}^T\left(\mathcal{U}_{k+1} + \frac{\mathcal{J}^k}{\rho}\right)$$

3) Update $\mathcal{T}$: Extracting all terms containing $\mathcal{T}$ from the augmented Lagrangian function (5), we can deduce

$$\mathcal{T} = arg\min_{\mathcal{T}} \lambda_3 \|\mathcal{T}\|_* + \frac{\rho_1}{2} \left\| \mathcal{R} - \mathcal{T} + \frac{\mathcal{J}_1}{\rho_1} \right\|_F^2$$

This problem has a closed form solution and can be efficiently solved by the tensor Singular Value Thresholding (t-SVT) as follows:

$$\mathcal{T}_{k+1} = \mathcal{D}_{\frac{\lambda_3}{\rho_1}} \left(\mathcal{R}_k + \frac{\mathcal{J}_1^k}{\rho_1} \right)$$

4) Update $\mathcal{R}$: Extracting all terms containing $\mathcal{R}$ from the augmented Lagrangian function (5), we can deduce

$$\mathcal{R}_{k+1} = arg\min_{\mathcal{R}} \frac{\rho}{2} \left\| \mathcal{U} - \mathcal{L} \cdot \mathcal{R} + \frac{\mathcal{J}}{\rho} \right\|_F^2 + \frac{\rho_1}{2} \left\| \mathcal{R} - \mathcal{T} + \frac{\mathcal{J}_1}{\rho_1} \right\|_F^2$$

Therefore, the problem can be transformed into the following linear system problem:

$$\left(\rho \mathcal{L}_{diag,k+1}^T \mathcal{L}_{diag,k+1} + \rho_1 I \right) \mathcal{R}_{k+1} = \left[\rho \mathcal{L}_{diag,k+1}^T \left(\mathcal{U}_{k+1} + \frac{\mathcal{J}^k}{\rho} \right) + \rho_1 \left(\mathcal{T}_{k+1} - \frac{\mathcal{J}_1^k}{\rho_1} \right) \right]$$

$\mathcal{L}, \mathcal{R}$ are updated until $\|\mathcal{L}_{k+1} - \mathcal{L}_k\|_F^2 / \|\|\mathcal{L}_k\|_F^2\| \leq \varepsilon$ or $\|\mathcal{R}_{k+1} - \mathcal{R}_k\|_F^2 / \|\|\mathcal{R}_k\|_F^2\| \leq \varepsilon$, $\varepsilon = 1 \times 10^{-4}$. The preconditioned conjugate gradient (PCG) [23] method is used to speed up the solutions of the above three problems.

5) Update multipliers: According to the ALM algorithm, the multipliers number are updated by the following formulas:

$$\begin{cases} \mathcal{J}^{k+1} = \mathcal{J}^k + \rho(\mathcal{U}_{k+1} - \mathcal{L}_{k+1} \cdot \mathcal{R}_{k+1}) \\ \mathcal{J}_1^{k+1} = \mathcal{J}_1^k + \rho_1(\mathcal{R}_{k+1} - \mathcal{T}_{k+1}) \end{cases}$$

For parameter ρ and ρ_1, we first set the initial values as $\rho = 2$, $\rho_1 = 0.01 * \lambda_3$, and the update them as $\rho := \min(1.5\rho, 10^6)$, $\rho_1 := \min(1.5\rho_1, 10^6)$. This method of determining the values of the variables ρ and ρ_1 are widely used in ALM-based methods, which facilitates the convergence of the algorithm [25].

3.4 Illuminance Adjustment

After the illuminance component $\mathcal{L}$ and the reflection component $\mathcal{R}$ are estimated, the illuminance component $\mathcal{L}$ contains illuminance information, and an image with good visual effect can be obtained by adjusting the illuminance component for a low-light image. According to [13, 27], the illuminance components are adjusted using gamma correction, and the final enhancement result can be obtained by:

$$\hat{\mathcal{Y}} = \mathcal{R} \cdot \mathcal{L}^{\frac{1}{\gamma}}$$

where γ is empirically set as Sect. 2.2.

4   Experiments

In this section, we evaluate the proposed model based on Retinex decomposition and compared with existing state-of-the-art methods quantitatively and qualitatively. All these experiments are run on a computer with AMD Ryzen 5 3600 6-Core Processor and 16G memory using MATLAB 2018b. The experimental parameters are set as follows: $\lambda_1 = 0.01$, $\lambda_2 = 0.08$, $\lambda_3 = 0.003$, $\lambda_4 = 10$.

4.1   Datasets and Objective Metrics

In this paper, the proposed model and comparative methods are evaluated on two datasets: MEF [32] and LIME [17].

MEF: It contains 17 high-quality image sequences including natural sceneries, indoor and outdoor views and man-made architectures. Each image sequence has several multi-exposure images, we select one of poor-exposed images as input to perform evaluation.

LIME: The LIME dataset consists of 10 low-light images, one of which is heavily disturbed by noise.

4.2   Objective Metrics and Results Analysis

We evaluate these methods qualitatively and quantitatively from the subjective and objective quality indexes of enhanced images. The comparison method is evaluated according to two common indicators, one is the natural image quality evaluator (NIQE) [28] without reference image quality evaluation (IQA) index, and the other is the visual information fidelity (VIF) [29] of full reference IQA index. The lower the NIQE value, the better the image quality, and the higher the VIF value, the better the visual quality. The reason why we use VIF is that it is generally believed [3, 14], that VIF captures visual quality better than peak signal-to-noise ratio (PSNR) and structural similarity index (SSIM), which cannot be used in this task because there is no "ground truth" image available.

This paper uses NPE [30], WVM [13], Jiep [3], STAR [14] four methods to compare with the model in this paper, of which the last three comparison methods are based on the Retinex model.

For the image of the House, the color of the moon in the enhancement results of NPE method is distorted. The restoration results of WVM, Jiep and STAR methods do not sufficiently enhance the brightness, and the overall brightness is still low. The brightness enhancement of vegetation in dark areas by WVM method is particularly deficient. The method proposed in this paper can fully enhance the brightness without color distortion.

For the image of the Tower, the enhancement result of NEP method shows artifact at the flowers, the brightness of the image is still dark, and the contrast is low. The overall brightness of the enhancement results of WVM and Jiep methods is still very dark. The contrast of the enhanced result of STAR method is low. The method proposed in this paper can fully enhance the brightness, and the image contrast is better.

For the image of the Memorial, the enhancement result of NPE method shows serious color distortion in extremely dark areas. The overall brightness of the enhancement result of the WVM method is still very dark. The enhancement results of Jiep and Star methods show noise amplification in extremely dark areas, resulting in blurred images. The method proposed in this paper can not only fully enhance the brightness, but also suppress the amplification of noise.

Table 1. Comparison of the average results on the two datasets for the four methods based on the Retinex model (The red bold font corresponds to the optimal result, and the green bold font corresponds to the sub optimal result)

Dataset	Index	Input	WVM	Jiep	STAR	Proposed
MEF	NIQE	3.256	3.201	3.165	**3.14**	**2.8112**
	VIF	1	**1.7783**	**1.8578**	1.665	1.6381
LIME	NIQE	3.736	3.673	**3.61**	3.714	**3.590**
	VIF	1	2.055	**2.214**	2.212	**2.295**

The average indicator results of the two datasets as a whole are shown in Table 1, with the best ones in red bold and the second best in green bold. Among the four methods based on the Retinex model, the method proposed in this paper is the best for the NIQE indicators in the MEF dataset, the VIF and NIQE indicators are the best in the LIME datasets, which objectively proves the effectiveness of the method proposed in this paper (Fig. 1).

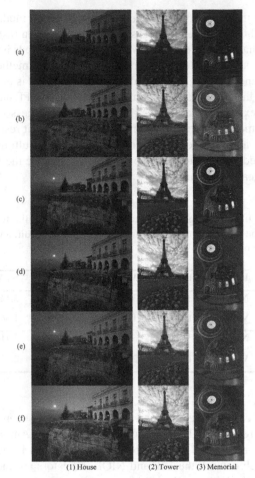

(1) House   (2) Tower   (3) Memorial

Fig. 1. Comparison of image enhancement results. (a) Input, (b) NPE, (c) WVM, (d) Jiep, (e) STAR, (f) The proposed method. Please zoom in for observation.

5   Conclusion

IN this paper, we consider the enhancement of low-light images under the influence of Poisson and Gaussian mixture noise, so as to better model the noise model and suppress the noise amplification. In order to better maintain the correlation between RGB image channels, the RGB image is directly represented in the form of tensor, processed in the RGB color space as a whole, and the tensor nuclear norm is used to impose a low rank constraint on the reflection component to suppress the noise. The experimental results show that the proposed method can not only enhance the brightness enough, but also suppress the noise amplification, and the contrast of the enhancement results is the best. In terms of quantitative indicators, the proposed method is almost the best.

Acknowledgments. This work was supported by the Guangdong Province Basic and Applied Basic Research Fund Project under Grant 2019A1515011041, Science and Technology Project of Guangzhou under Grant 202103010003, Science and Technology Project in key areas of Foshan under Grant 2020001006285, Xijiang Innovation Team of Zhaoqing under Grant XJCXTD3-2019-04B.

References

1. Land, E.H.: The retinex theory of color vision. Sci. Amer. **237**(6), 108–128 (1977)
2. Barrow, H., Tenenbaum, J., Hanson, A., Riseman, E.: Recovering intrinsic scene characteristics. Comput. Vis. Syst. **2**, 3–26 (1978)
3. Cai, B., Xu, X., Guo, K., Jia, K., Hu, B., Tao, D.: A joint intrinsic extrinsic prior model for retinex. In: Proceedings of IEEE International Conference on Computer Vision (ICCV), October 2017, pp. 4000–4009 (2017)
4. Ren, X., Li, M., Cheng, W.-H., Liu, J.: Joint enhancement and denoising method via sequential decomposition. In: IEEE International Symposium on Circuits and Systems (ISCAS) 2018, pp. 1–5 (2018)
5. Jobson, D.J., Rahman, Z., Woodell, G.A.: A multiscale retinex for bridging the gap between color images and the human observation of scenes. IEEE Trans. Image Process. **6**(7), 965–976 (1997)
6. Jobson, D.J., Rahman, Z., Woodell, G.A.: Properties and performance of a center/surround retinex. IEEE Trans. Image Process. **6**(3), 451–462 (1997)
7. Morel, J.M., Petro, A.B., Sbert, C.: A PDE formalization of retinex theory. IEEE Trans. Image Process. **19**(11), 2825–2837 (2010)
8. Land, E.H.: Recent advances in retinex theory and some implications for cortical computations: Color vision and the natural image. Proc. Nat. Acad. Sci. USA **80**(16), 5163–5169 (1983)
9. Brainard, D.H., Wandell, B.A.: Analysis of the retinex theory of color vision. J. Opt. Soc. Am. A. Opt. Image. Sci. **3**(10), 1651–1661 (1986)
10. Kimmel, R., Elad, M., Shaked, D., Keshet, R., Sobel, I.: A variational framework for Retinex. Int. J. Comput. Vis. **52**(1), 7–23 (2003)
11. Provenzi, E., Marini, D., De Carli, L., Rizzi, A.: Mathematical definition and analysis of the retinex algorithm. J. Opt. Soc. Am. A. Opt. Image. Sci. **22**(12), 2613–2621 (2005)
12. Ng, M.K., Wang, W.: A total variation model for retinex. SIAM J. Imag. Sci. **4**(1), 345–365 (2011)
13. Fu, X., Zeng, Huang, Y., Zhang, X.-P., Ding, X.: A weighted variational model for simultaneous reflectance and illuminance estimation. In: Proceedings of IEEE Conference on Computational Vision and Pattern Recognition (CVPR), June 2016
14. Xu, J., et al.: STAR: a structure and texture aware retinex model. IEEE Trans. Image Process. **29**, 5022–5037 (2020)
15. Kolda, T.: Tensor decompositions and applications. Siam. Rev. **51**, 455–500 (2009)
16. Peng, J., Xie, Q., Zhao, Q., Wang, Y., Yee, L., Meng, D.: Enhanced 3DTV regularization and its applications on HSI denoising and compressed sensing. IEEE Trans. Image Process. **29**, 7889–7903 (2020). https://doi.org/10.1109/TIP.2020.3007840
17. Guo, X.: LIME: a method for low-light image enhancement. In: ACM (2016)
18. He, K., Sun, J., Tang, X.: Single image haze removal using dark channel prior. IEEE Trans. Pattern Anal. Mach. Intell. **33**(12), 2341–2353 (2011)
19. Land, E.: The retinex theory of color vision. Sci. Am. **237**(6), 108–128 (1977)

20. Xu, L., Lu, C., Xu, Y., et al.: Image smoothing via L0 gradient minimization. In: SIGGRAPH Asia Conference. ACM (2011)
21. Li, M., Liu, J., Yang, W., Sun, X., Guo, Z.: Structure-revealing lowlight image enhancement via robust retinex model. IEEE Trans. Image Process. **27**(6), 2828–2841 (2018)
22. Candes, E.J., Wakin, M.B., Boyd, S.P.: Enhancing sparsity by reweighted L1 minimization. J. Fourier Anal. Appl. **14**(5–6), 877–905 (2008)
23. Barrett, R., et al.: Templates for the Solution of Linear Systems: Building Blocks for Iterative Methods. SIAM (1994)
24. Kilmer, M.E., Martin, C.D.: Factorization strategies for third-order tensors. Linear Algebra Appl. **435**(3), 641–658 (2011)
25. Lin, Z., Chen, M., Ma, Y.: The augmented Lagrange multiplier method for exact recovery of corrupted low-rank matrices. arXiv:1009.5055
26. Kilmer, M.E., Braman, K., Hao, N., Hoover, R.C.: Third-order tensors as operators on matrices: a theoretical and computational framework with applications in imaging. SIAM J. Matrix Anal. App. **34**(1), 148–172 (2013)
27. Fu, X., Liao, Y., Zeng, D., Huang, Y., Zhang, X.-P., Ding, X.: A probabilistic method for image enhancement with simultaneous illuminance and reflectance estimation. IEEE Trans. Image Process. **24**(12), 4965–4977 (2015)
28. Mittal, A., Soundararajan, R., Bovik, A.C.: Making a 'completely blind' image quality analyzer. IEEE Signal Process. Lett. **20**(3), 209–212 (2013)
29. Sheikh, H.R., Bovik, A.C.: Image information and visual quality. IEEE Trans. Image Process. **15**(2), 430–444 (2006)
30. Wang, S., Zheng, J., Hu, H.-M., Li, B.: Naturalness preserved enhancement algorithm for non-uniform illuminance images. IEEE Trans. Image Process. **22**(9), 3538–3548 (2013)
31. Lu, C., Feng, J., Chen, Y., Liu, W., Lin, Z., Yan, S.: Tensor Robust Principal Component Analysis with a New Tensor Nuclear Norm. IEEE Trans. Pattern Anal. Mach. Intell. **42**(4), 925–938 (2020)
32. Ma, K., Zeng, K., Wang, Z.: Perceptual quality assessment for multi-exposure image fusion. IEEE Trans. Image Process. **24**(11), 3345–3356 (2015)

Sequential Fusion of Multi-view Video Frames for 3D Scene Generation

Weilin Sun, Xiangxian Li, Manyi Li, Yuqing Wang, Yuze Zheng,
Xiangxu Meng, and Lei Meng[✉]

Shandong University, Jinan, Shandong, China
{sunweilin,xiangxian_lee,wang_yuqing,zhengyuze}@mail.sdu.edu.cn,
{manyili,mxx,lmeng}@sdu.edu.cn

Abstract. 3D scene understanding and generation are to reconstruct
the layout of the scene and each object from an RGB image, estimate its
semantic type in 3D space and generate a 3D scene. At present, the 3D
scene generation algorithm based on deep learning mainly recovers the
3D scene from a single image. Due to the complexity of the real environment, the information provided by a single image is limited, and there are
problems such as the lack of single-view information and the occlusion
of objects in the scene. In response to the above problems, we propose a
3D scene generation framework SGMT, which realizes multi-view position information fusion and reconstructs the 3D scene from multi-view
video time series data to compensate for the missing object position in
existing methods. We demonstrated the effectiveness of multi-view scene
generation of SGMT on the UrbanScene3D and SUNRGBD dataset and
studied the influence of SGCN and joint fine-tuning. In addition, we further explored the transfer ability of the SGMT between datasets and
discussed future improvements.

Keywords: 3D scene generation · Multi-view fusion · Multi-view time
series data

1 Introduction

3D scene generation is an important task in computer vision, which has a great
impact on many fields like augmented reality and virtual reality. The main idea
of the traditional 3D scene construction method is to manually process and fuse
the visual information, and reconstruct a 3D scene by scene rendering which
has high time and labor costs. To alleviate the above problems, end-to-end deep
learning methods are introduced into 3D scene generation, which avoids complex
manual processing through a data-driven manner.

The methods based on deep learning mainly divide the 3D scene generation
task into three sub-tasks: layout estimation, object detection, and shape recovery. Early works completed the three sub tasks separately [1,15,19]. Total3d [17]
bridged the gap between these three tasks and restored the 3D scene from the
perspective of the overall scene. On this basis, follow-up studies have proposed

© The Author(s), under exclusive license to Springer Nature Switzerland AG 2022
L. Fang et al. (Eds.): CICAI 2022, LNAI 13604, pp. 597–608, 2022.
https://doi.org/10.1007/978-3-031-20497-5_49

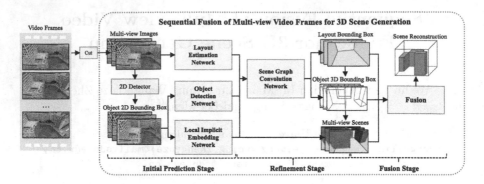

Fig. 1. The schematic diagram of SGMT, obtaining multi-view time series data from video frames as input, and finally realizing 3D scene recovery.

solutions to improve the accuracy of overall 3D scene restoration [23, 24]. However, most of the existing methods recover 3D scenes from a single image. Due to the complexity of the real environment, the information provided by a single image is limited, and there are some problems such as the lack of single-view information and the occlusion of objects in the scene.

To alleviate the aforementioned problems, we study to decouple and reorganize the existing deep learning-based 3D scene generation methods and explore the key factors affecting the performance. On this basis, we proposed a 3D scene generation framework SGMT, which recovers the overall 3D scene and compensates for the multi-view scene generation by fusing multi-angle position information. The overall framework of the model is shown in Fig. 1, which is mainly divided into three stages: the initial prediction stage, the refinement stage and the fusion stage. In the initial prediction stage, the geometric information in the visual input is extracted through the layout estimation network(LEN), the object detection network(ODN) and the local implicit embedding network(LIEN), and the initial prediction of the layout box, object box and object grid is realized.In the refinement stage, the scene graph convolution network(SGCN) is used to update the layout and object features and the refinement of the initial results is completed. In the fusion stage, the translation, rotation and fusion of the results from different perspectives are realized, so that the position information of the object can be adjusted and supplemented.

In order to explore the influence of the refinement stage in the proposed framework, we design comparative experiments to demonstrate its effectiveness in improving the generation result from both qualitative and quantitative perspectives. Further, we compare the result in the scene dataset SUNRGBD and UrbanScene3D multi-view video data, analyze it from the aspects of geometry and appearance, and discuss the transfer ability of 3D scene generation model and the problems in the transfer process in depth.

In summary, the main contributions of this paper include:

- On the basis of cutting-edge work in deep learning-based 3D scene reconstruction, we propose a multi-view 3D scene generation framework SGMT, which realizes the conversion from multi-view 2D video data to 3D scenes.
- The effectiveness of SGCN and joint fine-tuning in improving model performance is analyzed and verified, and the transfer ability of the model and the key problems in the process of model transfer are discussed.

2   Related Works

Layout estimation, object detection, and shape recovery are important components of 3D scene generation algorithms. **Layout Estimation.** Layout estimation can be divided into two types. One is to obtain the feature map of the layout based on the neural network, and then generate the parametric representation [2,15,19]. The other is a deep learning end-to-end method [5,6,11,12], which treats the layout estimation task as a regression of keypoints or a classification of spatial layout types, improving the accuracy of layout estimation. **Object Detection.** Object detection includes 2D object detection and 3D object detection. 2D object detection is to detect 2D bounding boxes and category information of objects in 2D images, such as Faster-RCNN [18] and YOLO series algorithms. 3D object detection often predicts the 3D bounding box based on the 2D bounding box [7], so as to obtain the information such as the length, width, height, offset angle and 3D space position of the object in the real 3D scene. **Shape Recovery.** Previous works of shape recovery have attempted to use point clouds and voxels to represent the 3D target object [1,10], or used retrieval methods to search for similar-looking models from the dataset [8]. The reconstruction results of these method have lower resolution and consume more memory. In order to alleviate the above problems, more methods begin to exploit the prior knowledge of shape, express the shape of an object as a feature vector or an implicit function, and finally recover its shape [3,4,16].

The above methods only consider independent geometries. In order to understand and reconstruct the scene from an overall perspective, a method of fusing the contextual information of the scene has emerged [17]. At the same time, the graph convolutional neural network is added to refine the model [23], and the structural implicit network is further used to improve the shape estimation of the object [24], which has become the most advanced method at present.

3   Method

The overall algorithm flow of SGMT is shown in Fig. 2, which includes five modules. We divide them into three stages, namely the initial prediction stage, the refinement stage, and the fusion stage. Their details are described below.

3.1   Initial Prediction Stage

The initial prediction stage adopts LEN, ODN, and LIEN in [17,24].

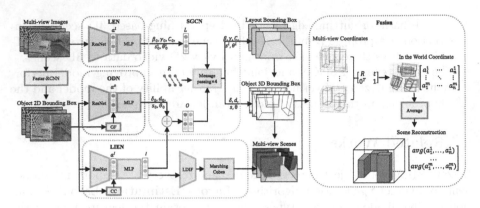

Fig. 2. Illustration of the algorithm flow of SGMT, enabling 3D scene recovery from multi-view time series data.

Layout Estimation Network. LEN is used for the initial prediction of the layout 3D bounding box $X_0^L \in \mathbb{R}^3$ and camera pose $R(\beta_0, \gamma_0) \in \mathbb{R}^2$, which is further parameterized by the method of [17,24] as,

$$X_0^L = h(C_0, s_0^l, \theta_0^l) \tag{1}$$

where $C_0 \in \mathbb{R}^3$ is the center of the layout box, $s_0^l \in \mathbb{R}^3$ is the space size, $\theta_0^l \in (-\pi, \pi)$ is the direction angle, and $h(\cdot)$ is the function that composes the 3D bounding box. The algorithm flow of LEN is shown in Fig. 2. First, the ResNet is used to extract the appearance features a_l, and then the two-layer MLP is used to predict $(\beta_0, \gamma_0, C_0, s_0^l, \theta_0^l)$.

Object Detection Network. ODN can predict 3D bounding boxes $X_0^O \in \mathbb{R}^3$ from 2D bounding boxes of objects. Using the method of [17,24], it is further parameterized as,

$$X_0^O = h(\delta_0, d_0, s_0, \theta_0) \tag{2}$$

where $\delta_0 \in \mathbb{R}^2$ is the offset between the center of the 2D bounding box and the 2D projection center of the 3D bounding box, $d_0 \in \mathbb{R}$ is the distance from the 2D projection center of the 3D bounding box to the center of the camera, $s_0 \in \mathbb{R}^3$ is the space size of the object, $\theta_0 \in (-\pi, \pi)$ is the orientation angle of the object. The algorithm flow of ODN is shown in Fig. 2. The appearance feature a_o is extracted from the 2D bounding box using ResNet, at the same time, the size and relative position of each object 2D bounding box are encoded as geometric features GF. GF and a_o are input into a two-layer MLP to predict $(\delta_0, d_0, s_0, \theta_0)$ of the object.

Local Implicit Embedding Network. LIEN is used to to recover the shape and pose of objects. The algorithm flow of this module is shown in Fig. 2. First, we input the 2D bounding box of the object to ResNet to extract the appearance feature a_I. In order to effectively learn the implicit shape features, the class code CC of the object is concatenated with its appearance feature a_I, and then the latent code I is obtained using a three-layer MLP. I is input into LDIF to obtain a 3D latent shape representation. Finally, we use the Marching Cubes [14] to get the point and surface information of the object.

3.2   Refinement Stage

In the refinement stage, SGCN is added to update the layout, object and relation nodes in the scene graph through the process of four message passing [24], as shown in the Fig. 2. We use the results of the initial stage to extract the feature vectors of layout and object nodes and then process them into feature matrices $M^o \in \mathbb{R}^{d \times (N+1)}$. The relation nodes are divided into two categories, one represents the relationship between the layout and the object, which is initialized with a constant value, and the other represents the relationship between the objects, which is initialized using the GT and bounding box coordinates, and then they are processed as feature matrices $M^r \in \mathbb{R}^{d \times (N+1)^2}$. The process of message passing can be expressed as

$$M^{o'} = \sigma(M^o + W^{sd} M^o + W^{rs} M^r A^{rs} + W^{rd} M^r A^{rd}) \tag{3}$$

$$M^{r'} = \sigma(M^r + W^{sr} M^o A^{sr} + W^{dr} M^o A^{dr}) \tag{4}$$

where s is the source object/layout node; d is the target object/layout node; r is the relation node; W and A are the linear transformation and adjacency matrix from the source node to the target node.

3.3   Fusion Stage

Multi-view scene fusion refers to the process of fusing objects from different perspectives into one scene. This process can be regarded as the transformation of the coordinate system of objects in the scene. Compared with generating a 3D scene from a single image, multi-view scene generation involves not only the rotation of the camera, but also but also the translation of the camera. For a point a on the object, the coordinate before transformation is $(a_1, a_2, a_3)^T$, the coordinate after transformation is $(a_1', a_2', a_3')^T$, and the rigid body transformation formula is

$$\begin{bmatrix} a_1' \\ a_2' \\ a_3' \end{bmatrix} = \begin{bmatrix} R & t \\ 0^T & 1 \end{bmatrix} \begin{bmatrix} a_1 \\ a_2 \\ a_3 \end{bmatrix} \tag{5}$$

where $R \in \mathbb{R}^{3 \times 3}$ is the rotation matrix of the camera, which can be predicted by LEN, and $t \in \mathbb{R}^{3 \times 1}$ is the translation matrix, which can be obtained by the aerial photography trajectory of the camera. We use the first scene graph as the world coordinate system, transform the 3D coordinates of objects from other perspectives into it, and then average the eight corner coordinates of the same object from different perspectives. Finally, the fusion of object position information is realized. The whole fusion process is shown in Fig. 2.

3.4   Loss Function

We refer to the method of [17,24] to define the loss function of the model in modules. When training LEN and ODN, we use classification and regression loss for every output parameter of LEN and ODN. When training LIEN, we weight shape element center loss L_c [3] and point sample loss L_p [24] to sum. In the initial prediction stage, the loss function is mainly optimized for the 3D bounding box parameters of the object and the layout, but not for the final prediction result. Therefore, when training SGCN, the cooperation loss L_{co} [7] is added, and the formula is as follows:

$$L_{co} = \lambda_{phy} L_{phy} + \lambda_{bdb2D} L_{bdb2D} + \lambda_{corner} L_{corner} \tag{6}$$

where L_{phy} is the mean square error loss, which is used to reduce the intersection between the layout and the object bounding box; L_{bdb2D} and L_{corner} are SmoothL1Loss, which is used to reduce the error of the 3D bounding box of the object and its 2D projection. In addition to L_{co}, $L_{ldifphy}$ [24] is also added in the joint fine-tuning to reduce the crossover between objects. The formula is as follows:

$$L_{ldifphy} = \frac{1}{N} \sum_{i=1}^{N} \frac{1}{|\mathbb{S}_i|} \sum_{x \in \mathbb{P}_i} ||relu(0.5 - sigmoid(\alpha LDIF_i(x)))|| \tag{7}$$

where N is the number of objects in the scene; $\mathbb{P}_i$ is the sampling point from each object; $\alpha LDIF_i(x)$ is the value of the obtained point on the LDIF decoder, and has been scaled by α. After the sigmoid and relu activation functions, the loss function only considers the points that intersect inside the object, that is, the points where $\alpha LDIF_i(x)$ is negative. Finally, we can get the loss function of the whole model, the formula is as follows:

$$L_{joint} = L_{LEN} + L_{ODN} + L_{co} + L_{ldifphy} \tag{8}$$

4   Experiments

4.1   Experiments Setup

Datasets. We use SUNRGBD [9,20–22] and UrbanScene3D [13] for model training, testing and transfer. The SUNRGBD dataset contains 10,335 RGBD images of indoor scenes, of which the 1–5050th images of the dataset are used for validation and testing; the 5051–10,335th images are used for training. The UrbanScene3D dataset contains 5 reconstructed real scenes. We intercepted the multi-view pictures of the scene from the aerial video of the Sci-Art, and got a total of 341 pictures. At the same time, annotations are established for each image, including the coordinates of the 2D bounding box of the object, the object category, the camera internal parameters, and the image ID. The processed UrbanScene3D dataset is used as multi-view time series data to complete the model testing and transfer.

Evaluation Measures. We use the mean of IoU to evaluate the accuracy of layout and object bounding box, the mean of camera radian error to evaluate the accuracy of camera pose, and Lg [17] to evaluate the accuracy of object triangular mesh. The formula is as follows:

$$IoU(G, E) = \frac{|G \cup E|}{|G \cap E|} \tag{9}$$

where G is the actual layout/object bounding box and E is the predicted layout/object bounding box;

$$Cam_{Err} = |\theta_g - \theta_e| \times \frac{180}{\pi} \tag{10}$$

where θ_g is the actual camera rotation angle, and θ_e is the predicted camera rotation angle;

$$Lg = \frac{1}{N} \sum_{i=1}^{N} \frac{1}{|\mathbb{S}_i|} \sum_{q \in \mathbb{S}_i, p \in \mathbb{M}_i} min\|p - q\|_2^2 \tag{11}$$

where N is the number of objects in the scene, q is a point on the ground-truth surface $\mathbb{S}_i$, p is a point on the predicted object grid $\mathbb{M}_i$, and $\|p - q\|_2^2$ represents the distance between the two points. To sum up, we set six evaluation metrics: $LayoutIoU$, $CamPitchErr$, $CamRollErr$, $Box3DIoU$, $Box2DIoU$, and Lg.

Implementation Details. For LEN, ODN and LIEN, we use pre-trained weight parameters [17,24]. SGCN is trained on the SUNRGBD dataset, using 30 epochs in total and Adam optimizer with a batch size of 32 and learning rate decaying from 2e–4 (scaled by 0.5 when the epoch reaches 18, 23, 28). When training SGCN individually, we use L_{joint} without $L_{ldifphy}$, and put it into the full model with pre-trained weights of other modules. Joint fine-tuning is similar to the training setup of SGCN, except that the batch size is 4, the learning rate decays from 1e–4 and L_{joint} with $L_{ldifphy}$ is used.

4.2 Comparative Experiment

In this section, we are going to analyse the effects of SGCN and joint fine-tuning in the refinement stage on improving SGMT performance from both quantitative and qualitative perspectives.

Quantitative Analysis. Six evaluation metrics are used to evaluate the performance change of the model before and after refinement and fine-tuning. As is shown in Table 1, from initial prediction to SGCN and then to joint fine-tuning, $LayoutIoU$, $Box3DIoU$ and $Box2DIoU$ are all improved, while $CamPitchErr$, $CamRollErr$ and Lg all decreases. This indicates that the performance of 3D scene generation improves, and possible reasons are as follows:

Table 1. Comparison of the SGMT performance before and after SGCN and joint fine-tuning in the SUNRGBD dataset. IP means Initial Prediction.

Evaluation metrics	IP	IP+SGCN	IP+SGCN+Joint fine-tuning
$Layout IoU$	0.61854	0.63649	0.67800
$Cam Pitch Err$	3.98966	3.04301	2.49251
$Cam Roll Err$	2.71317	2.18722	2.13512
$Box3D IoU$	0.13635	0.18991	0.29596
$Box2D IoU$	0.63158	0.67418	0.75534
Lg	1.20858	1.13047	1.10760

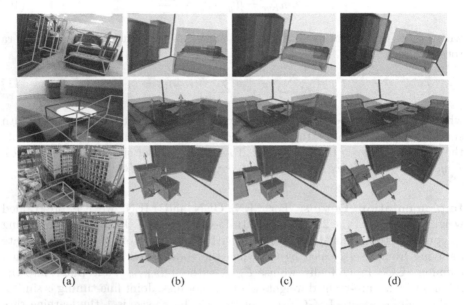

    (a)   (b)   (c)   (d)

Fig. 3. Comparison of model results before and after SGCN and joint fine-tuning: (a) input image and recognized objects; (b) initial prediction results; (c) results after SGCN; (d) results after joint fine-tuning.

(1) SGCN integrates scene context information, acquires important scene knowledge, and updates the features of objects and layouts, making the results more accurate. At the same time, L_{co} is added when training SGCN, which maintains the consistency between the 2D and 3D bounding boxes, and improves the accuracy of the model.

(2) During joint fine-tuning, some models that are frozen during SGCN training are unfrozen, and the weight parameters of the overall model are updated. At the same time, $L_{ldifphy}$ is added to reduce the intersection between objects, which further improves the accuracy of the model.

(a)   (b)

Fig. 4. Generation results of different datasets (a) SUNRGBD dataset; (b) Urban-Scene3D dataset.

Qualitative Analysis. According to the horizontal comparison of the results in Fig. 3, it can be found that: 1) The 3D reconstruction ability of initial prediction is relatively poor. As is shown in Fig. 3(b), although the approximate position and shape of objects in the scene can be predicted, there are lots of problems. For example, there are improper intersections between objects, between objects and layout boxes, and some objects floats in the air. Furthermore, some objects' orientation is different from the real one. 2) SGCN can solve some problems above. As is shown in Fig. 3(c), objects in the scene do not suspend in the air anymore and the position is more accurate. This indicates that after refinement by SGCN, the model can accurately predict the position and size of the object's 3D boundary box. 3) Joint fine-tuning can further improve the performance of the model. As is shown in Fig. 3(d), improper intersection between objects and between objects and layout boxes is reduced, and the orientation of objects is more accurate. 4) SGCN and joint fine-tuning can improve the transfer ability of the model. Comparing only the results on the UrbanScene3D dataset in Fig. 3, it can be found that the results are improved to same extent after adding SGCN and joint fine-tuning, but there are still many problems, which will be discussed in the following.

4.3 Deep Analysis of Model Transferability

As is shown in Fig. 4, we will show the generation effect of the model on the SUNRGBD and UrbanScene3D datasets, and the transfer ability of the model and the problems will be discussed.

Figure 4(b) shows that the model can accurately predict the location of objects in UrbanScene3D. However, comparing with Fig. 4(a) in SUNRGBD, there are still many shortcomings. For example, the reconstruction quality of details, shapes and textures of objects is poor, and the deviation of object's angle still exists. In addition, the category of reconstructed objects is relatively simple. Two main reasons are as follows:

(1) Different shooting methods. Most of SUNRGBD are head-up shots, while UrbanScene3D are mostly aerial shots and the camera position is not fixed.

Fig. 5. 3D scene generation visualization results from multi-view time series data.

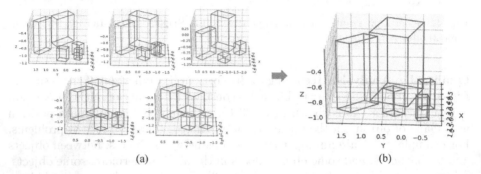

(a)   (b)

Fig. 6. Multi-view 3D scene fusion results. The left side is the 3D bounding box of the object generated by each frame of pictures before fusion, and the right side is the 3D bounding box of the fused object.

(2) Differences in object classes. SUNRGBD is meant for indoor scenes, and the objects are mostly furniture objects. However, UrbanScene3D is meant for outdoor scenes, and the objects are more complex and diverse.

4.4   Visualization and Fusion of Multi-view Scenes

We input multi-view time series data from UrbanScene3D to the model, and the results include 3D boundary boxes of layouts and objects, triangular mesh and rotation matrix. Based on those results, the geometries are created and rendered. The visualization results of two groups are shown in Fig. 5. It can be seen that the model can reconstruct 3D scenes from each frame of time series data. In this way, each frame has corresponding reconstruction result.

In order to fuse the boundary boxes of objects from different perspectives, the method in Sect. 3.3 is used. The results before and after the fusion of two groups are shown in Fig. 6. Comparing before and after the fusion, it can be found that the fusion makes up for the location information loss by the same object due to different shooting angles. In conclusion, the model can effectively recover the overall 3D scene from multi-view time series data and realize the fusion of multi-view location information.

5   Conclusion

In this paper, we design a framework SGMT, which can can recover the overall 3D scene from multi-view video data. However, there are still some problems remain to be further discussed. Firstly, what the framework can reconstruct is very dependent on the original dataset. When it was transferred to other datasets, the prediction of object categories, shape details and object position orientation is not accurate enough. Secondly, the method of multi-view scene fusion does not involve the fusion of object shape and texture features. Therefore, the next research will continue to train and optimize the model, improve the method of multi-perspective scene fusion, pay more attention to the fusion of object shape and texture features, and restore 3D scenes more completely.

Acknowledgments. This work is supported in part by the Excellent Youth Scholars Program of Shandong Province (Grant no. 2022HWYQ-048) and the Oversea Innovation Team Project of the "20 Regulations for New Universities" funding program of Jinan (Grant no. 2021GXRC073).

References

1. Achlioptas, P., Diamanti, O., Mitliagkas, I., Guibas, L.: Learning representations and generative models for 3D point clouds (2017)
2. Dasgupta, S., Fang, K., Chen, K., Savarese, S.: DeLay: robust spatial layout estimation for cluttered indoor scenes. In: Computer Vision Pattern Recognition (2016)
3. Genova, K., Cole, F., Sud, A., Sarna, A., Funkhouser, T.: Local deep implicit functions for 3D shape (2019)
4. Gkioxari, G., Malik, J., Johnson, J.: Mesh R-CNN (2019)
5. Hirzer, M., Roth, P.M., Lepetit, V.: Smart hypothesis generation for efficient and robust room layout estimation (2019)
6. Hsiao, C.W., Sun, C., Sun, M., Chen, H.T.: Flat2Layout: flat representation for estimating layout of general room types (2019)
7. Huang, S.: Cooperative holistic scene understanding: unifying 3D object, layout, and camera pose estimation (2018)
8. Huang, S., Qi, S., Zhu, Y., Xiao, Y., Xu, Y., Zhu, S.C.: Holistic 3D scene parsing and reconstruction from a single RGB image. In: European Conference on Computer Vision (2018)
9. Janoch, A., Karayev, S., Jia, Y., Barron, J.T., Darrell, T.: A category-level 3D object dataset: putting the kinect to work. In: IEEE International Conference on Computer Vision Workshops (2013)
10. Kulkarni, N., Misra, I., Tulsiani, S., Gupta, A.: 3D-RelNet: joint object and relational network for 3D prediction. In: 2019 IEEE/CVF International Conference on Computer Vision (ICCV) (2019)
11. Lee, C.Y., Badrinarayanan, V., Malisiewicz, T., Rabinovich, A.: RoomNet: end-to-end room layout estimation. In: 2017 IEEE International Conference on Computer Vision (ICCV) (2017)
12. Lin, H.J., Huang, S.W., Lai, S.H., Chiang, C.K.: Indoor scene layout estimation from a single image. In: 2018 24th International Conference on Pattern Recognition (ICPR) (2018)

13. Liu, Y., Xue, F., Huang, H.: UrbanScene3D: a large scale urban scene dataset and simulator (2021)
14. Lorensen, W.E., Cline, H.E.: Marching cubes: a high resolution 3D surface construction algorithm. In: ACM SIGGRAPH Computer Graphics, pp. 163–169 (1987)
15. Mallya, A., Lazebnik, S.: Learning informative edge maps for indoor scene layout prediction. In: 2015 IEEE International Conference on Computer Vision (ICCV) (2015)
16. Mescheder, L., Oechsle, M., Niemeyer, M., Nowozin, S., Geiger, A.: Occupancy networks: learning 3D reconstruction in function space. In: 2019 IEEE/CVF Conference on Computer Vision and Pattern Recognition (CVPR) (2019)
17. Nie, Y., Han, X., Guo, S., Zheng, Y., Zhang, J.J.: Total3DUnderstanding: joint layout, object pose and mesh reconstruction for indoor scenes from a single image. In: 2020 IEEE/CVF Conference on Computer Vision and Pattern Recognition (CVPR) (2020)
18. Ren, S., He, K., Girshick, R., Sun, J.: Faster R-CNN: towards real-time object detection with region proposal networks. IEEE Trans. Pattern Anal. Mach. Intell. **39**(6), 1137–1149 (2017)
19. Ren, Y., Li, S., Chen, C., Kuo, C.-C.J.: A Coarse-to-Fine Indoor Layout Estimation (CFILE) method. In: Lai, S.-H., Lepetit, V., Nishino, K., Sato, Y. (eds.) ACCV 2016. LNCS, vol. 10115, pp. 36–51. Springer, Cham (2017). https://doi.org/10.1007/978-3-319-54193-8_3
20. Silberman, N., Hoiem, D., Kohli, P., Fergus, R.: Indoor segmentation and support inference from RGBD images. In: Fitzgibbon, A., Lazebnik, S., Perona, P., Sato, Y., Schmid, C. (eds.) ECCV 2012. LNCS, vol. 7576, pp. 746–760. Springer, Heidelberg (2012). https://doi.org/10.1007/978-3-642-33715-4_54
21. Song, S., Lichtenberg, S.P., Xiao, J.: SUN RGP-D: a RGP-D scene understanding benchmark suite. In: IEEE Conference on Computer Vision Pattern Recognition, pp. 567–576 (2015)
22. Xiao, J., Owens, A.H., Torralba, A.: SUN3D: a database of big spaces reconstructed using SfM and object labels. In: 2013 IEEE International Conference on Computer Vision (ICCV) (2013)
23. Xiao, J., Wang, R., Chen, X.: Holistic pose graph: modeling geometric structure among objects in a scene using graph inference for 3D object prediction. In: Proceedings of the IEEE/CVF International Conference on Computer Vision (ICCV), pp. 12717–12726, (October 2021)
24. Zhang, C., Cui, Z., Zhang, Y., Zeng, B., Liu, S.: Holistic 3D scene understanding from a single image with implicit representation (2021)

Multi-model Lightweight Action Recognition with Group-Shuffle Graph Convolutional Network

Suguo Zhu[1](✉), Yibing Zhan[2], and Guo Zhao[1]

[1] Hangzhou Dianzi University, Hangzhou, China
zsg2016@hdu.edu.cn
[2] JD Explore Academy, Beijing, China
zhanyibing@jd.com

Abstract. Skeleton-based action recognition has attracted increasing attention in recent years. However, current skeleton-based action recognition models still exhausted huge parameters and computations to achieve superior accuracy. Despite effectiveness, the huge parameter/computation cost degrades the application of action recognition models on edge devices, such as mobile. How to obtain high accuracy while maintaining low computational/parameter efficiency remains a difficult yet significant challenge. In light of the above issues, we propose group-shuffle graph convolutional networks (GS-GCNs) for lightweight skeleton-based action recognition in videos. Specifically, GS-GCNs consist of two sequential modules: group-shuffle graph convolutional module (GSC) and depthwise-shuffle separable convolution module (DSC). GSC divides input features into several groups through feature channels, then shuffles the groups and sends each group into a discrete sub GCN to model relationships between each node in the skeleton. After that, DSC completes depthwise separable convolution on each group and shuffles each group. The final output is the concatenation of all group features. Essentially, through a shuffle-grouping strategy, GS-GCNs could significantly reduce the computational/parameter cost while obtaining competitive detection ability through an architecture of iterations. Extensive experiments show that GS-GCN achieves excellent performance on both NTU-RGB+D and NTU-RGB+D 120 datasets with an order of smaller model size than most previous works.

Keywords: Action recognition · Graph convolutional network · Lightweight model

1 Introduction

Human action recognition is popular and skeleton-based action recognition has attracted more and more attention especially. The skeleton-based action recognition approaches take skeleton data to input the recognition model. It is different between the skeleton-based features and the RGB features. Skeleton is a type

Supported by the National Natural Science Foundation of China under Grant 61902101.

L. Fang et al. (Eds.): CICAI 2022, LNAI 13604, pp. 609–621, 2022.
https://doi.org/10.1007/978-3-031-20497-5_50

of well structured data with each joint of the human body identified by a joint type, a frame index, and a 3D position.

Deep learning is widely used to model the spatio-temporal evolution of the skeleton sequence, such as, TCN [7], SynCNN [10]. On the other side, the skeleton nodes of human body can be used as graph structures, which extract the information between bone nodes well, and numerous approaches based on graph convolutional networks are emerging, such as AGCN [15] and DGNN [14],HPH [25], which all employs graph convolutional networks to aggregate information around the nodes, and achieve good results. However, these networks apply a single static graph structure for all layers of the networks, and the extracted features are too single to extract dynamic feature during human acting effectively. For example, the action of clapping. When clapping, the left and right hands generate relationships while there is not any edges to describe it in the single static graph structure. The relationships like "clapping","brushing teeth" are changing while the actions change. Consequently, it is not enough for skeleton-based action recognition algorithms to construct a single static graph structure.

Based on the above shortcomings, some researchers [1,22,23] consider dynamic graph convolutional network. ST-GCN [22] presents the learnable edge importance weighting matrix to be mutiplied by adjacency matrix, which may cause zero at some edges and there will be no more updated. Dyn-GCN [23] generates a dynamic graph through a series of transformations of input data, which produces good results, but this graph is only one for each sample, which is too single; AGCN [15] uses the non local method to establish the relationship between different nodes, and then adds this dynamic graph.However, the dynamic graph convolutional networks may loss the edges between some nodes, which are the inherent skeleton original structure in the static graph. And we will not be allowed to loss information during extracting feature arbitrarily.

In addition, these networks are stacked by layers, resulting in high parameter and computational complexity, and they cannot be effectively deployed to mobile devices. We analysis the parameters in the action recognition models and discover that it is more parameters in spatial modules than that in temporal modules.

To address the above mentioned limitations of current approaches, we propose a lightweight and excellent skeleton-based action recognition, which is the group-shuffle graph convolutional network. Figure 1 shows the overall framework. The extracted skeleton features are input into the group-shuffle graph convolutional network, including four streams, such as joint, bone, joint motion and bone motion. We cascade the GS-GCN to construct the action recognition framework and followed by the average pooling layer, full-connection layer and softmax function. In the GS-GCN, three modules are included, the group-shuffle GCN module (GSC) and the depthwise-shuffle separable convolution module (DSC). In the proposed model, we pay attention to the spatial features, such as dynamic graph and static graph are fused with the operation of addition, then we divide output into different groups and shuffle them for containing the global spatial features. For better performance and small number of parameters, we also seek to explore the temporal features with depthwise separable converlution module and shuffle the output.

The major contributions of this work lie in three aspects: 1) we propsed GS-GCN, a small action recognition model based on graph convolutional network, the results of which are also accurate on the public datasets. 2) We propose the group-shuffle GCN module for the spatial features, which employs dynamic graph to capture the motion between different joints. 3) we propose the depthwise-shuffle separable network for temporal features, which obtains high accuracy while maintains low computational and parameter efficiency.

2 Related Work

Action Recognition Based on Deep Learning. With the development of deep learning, numerous researches and applications begin to pay attention on deep learning. Action recognition is no exception (RNN-based [17], CNN-based [6,10] and GCN-based [4,8,22,27] action recognition). With the strong ability of representation of deep learning, action recognition based on deep learning achieved better performance compared with the traditional action recognition methods. [7] is the early approach in the action recognition based on deep learning. After it, lots of other deep learning methods emerged, such as action recognition with improved trajectories [20], dense trajectories [19], DSTA-NET [16], ST-TR [12].

Skeleton-Based Action Recognition. Action recognition is divided into the RGB-based and skeleton-based methods. RGB-based action recognition approaches always employ two-stream feature [7] or C3D feature [3]. It is a long time for the researches on RGB-based action [6,10] recognition compared with skeleton-based approaches. And the accuracy of RGB-base action recognition on the public datasets is very high while the accuracy of skeleton-based action recognition is not that high. For the characteristics of the skeleton structure itself, there are four streams which can be extracted, joint, bone, joint-motion and bone-motion. The researchers design different models to analysis the characteristics. Some force on two streams [21,26], including the adjacent matrix between joints and the motions. Others pay attention on four streams [2,12]. Influenced by the similarity between skeleton and graph, skeleton-based action recognition with graph convolutional network has been attracted the attention of people. From the static graph approaches at the beginning to now, more and more action recognition methods apply dynamic graph to design their models [1,21,23]. The lightweight models have been showed up, such as Shift-GCN [2], SG-GCN [26].

3 Methodology

3.1 Network Architecture

Skeleton based data can be obtained from motion-capture devices or pose estimation algorithms from videos. Usually the data is a sequence of frames, each

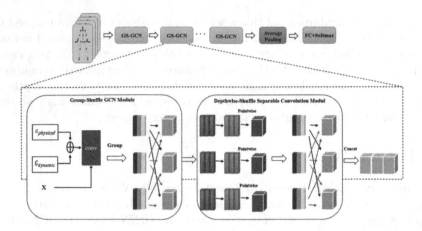

Fig. 1. The framework of the group-shuffle graph convolutional network (GS-GCN) for lightweight action recognition. We design the model with two parts: group-shuffle GCN module and depthwise-shuffle separable convolution module.

frame will have a set of joint coordinates. Graph convolutional networks (GCNs) have been successfully adopted to model skeleton data. Given the sequences of body joints in the form of 2D or 3D coordinates, we construct a spatial temporal graph with the joints as graph nodes and natural connectivities in both human body structures and time as graph edges.

3.2   Base Feature Network

A skeleton sequence is usually represented by 2D or 3D coordinates of each human joint in each frame. Previous work using convolution for skeleton action recognition concatenates coordinate vectors of all joints to form a single feature vector per frame. In our work, we utilize the spatial temporal graph to form hierarchical representation of the skeleton sequences. Particularly, let $G = \{V, E\}$ to be the skeleton-based graph, where V and E are the number of nodes and edges, respectivily. $A \in R^{V \times V}$ denotes the relationship of the nodes. The graph convolution is writted as:

$$Y = \sum_{k=1}^{K} \Lambda_k^{-\frac{1}{2}} A_k \Lambda_k^{-\frac{1}{2}} FW \qquad (1)$$

where K is the number of the kernel of spatial convolution, which is set followed by Yan et al. [22]. F is the input features, $F \in R^{C \times T \times V}$, C is the number of channles,and T is the temporal dimension. Y is the input the output features, W respects the parameter to be learned, A is the adjaccent matrix, and Λ is the degree matrix and the degree of every node is computed by $\Lambda^{ii} = \sum_j A^{ij} + \alpha$, A^{ij} is relationship of the i-th node and the j-th node. α is to avoid zero degree.

GCN-based models contain two parts: spatial graph convolution and temporal graph convolution. For the spatial graph convolution, the joint features of

300 frames are denoted by $Sequence = \{J^t\}_{t=1}^{300}$, and $J^t \in R^{3 \times N}$. Each edge is a vector node pointing to another vector node, then the edge feature is expressed as the difference between the target node and the starting node. The connectivities is $B^t = J^t_{t\,arg\,et} - J^t_{source}$. For the temporal graph convolution, given $M^t = J^{t+1} - J^t$ for the temporal displacement between two adjacent frames: the t-th frame and the $t + 1$-the frame. It is the same as for the motion of joints between two adjacent frames.

3.3 GS-GCN

As illustrated in Fig. 1, GS-GCN is composed of Group-shuffle Graph Convolution Module (GSC) and Depthwise-shuffle convolution module (DSC).

Group-Shuffle Graph Convolution Module (GSC): For seeking more spatial features, we design a group dynamic graph convolution module. Given the input feature $F \in R^{C \times T \times V}$ with C channels, each channel is conrresponding to one graph convolution. We divied the input features F into g groups, $F = CONCAT\{F_1, F_2, .., F_g\}$, and $F_i \in R^{c \times T \times V}$, $i = 1, 2, ..., g$, $c = C/g$. Specifically, the dynamic graph $G_{dynamic} \in R^{C \times V \times V}$ is divided into g groups, $G_{dynamic} = CONCAT\{G_1, G_2, ..., G_g\}$, $G_i \in R^{c \times V \times V}$, $i = 1, 2, ..., g$, $c = C/g$. The group dynamic graph convolution is formulated as:

$$Y_i = (G_i + G_{static})F_iW_i, i = 1, 2, ..., g \tag{2}$$

$$Y = CONCAT\{Y_1, Y_2, ..., Y_g\} \tag{3}$$

where W_i is the number of convolution kernels in i-th group, and the parameters of the graph convolution are shared int the same group. In this paper, we consider the static skeleton-based graph G_{static}, which is fused with the dynamic graph in each group. Dynamic graph can generate non-existent graph edges, which indicates the relationships between the actions and different joints, and extract more abundant information. In addition, the static graphs always keep the inherent connections between the human joints. And it is not to be dicarded. However, most of the previous work only considered one of dynamic graph and static graph in their action recognition algorithms.

Our dynamic group graph convolution keeps the static graph structure, groups the input features on the channel, and then each group will have a dynamic graph, so that each group will learn different information, which is equivalent to adding multi-scale information. And dynamic graph considers all nodes, so it is also a global operation. We know that global information is very important. Dynamic graph will dynamically generate global structure in the process of training, and it will extract global information in the process of graph convolution. Grouping increases the diversity of global information.

Before grouping, the amount of parameters and computational complexity are $C^2 + V^2$, $C^2TV + V^2C$, respectively. After grouping, the amount of parameters is reduced to $C^2/g + V^2g$, and the computational complexity is $(C^2TV + V^2C)/g$. It is obviously that both the amount of parameters and the computational complexity are greatly reduced, and the reduction is directly proportional to the number of groups.

As we carry out convolution operation on each group, different groups are isolated from each other, which will lead to poor information flow. For the purpose that each group is able to contain the information of other groups, we need to shuffle the channels of different groups. For g groups, we divide the channels in each group into c/g sub-groups, where c is the numbers of channels in each group. We shuffle the sub-group of each group to other groups. In this paper, we insert this "shuffle" module behind graph convolution. Cheng et al. [2] is similar to this step with their "shift" and the difference is that we shuffle all the channels of one node and Cheng et al. shift all the channels of all the nodes. And our performance is much better.

Depthwise-Shuffle Separable Convolutional Module (DWTCN): As the popular action recognition approaches, the temporal convolution module is always followed the spatial module. For better temporal performance, Liu et al. [11] established the connection between different nodes in different frames. However, the amounts of parameters and the computational complexity are both increased dramatically. In this paper, we analysis the parameters in the spatial module and the temporal module of the state-of-the-art approaches, and we find that the parameters of temporal convolution module account for more than two-thirds of the whole module.

Different from the stat-of-the-art approaches, we present the depthwise separable temporal convolution network (TCN) to capture robust motions with less parameter amounts and lower computational complexity. Depthwise separable network is a lightweight network which is often employed for the object recognition in images. If the traditional convolution kernel is $k \times k$ and the number of channels is C, the parameters are $k \times k \times C \times C$. However, if we employ depthwise separable network instead, the paremeters will be $k \times k \times C + 1 \times 1 \times C \times C$ compared with $k \times k + k \times k \times C \times C$ of traditional convolution kernel.

For the input features, the dimension is $C \times T \times V$. We set the convolution kernels in depthwise separable network is 9×9, and followed by the above computation, the parameters are $9 \times 9 \times C + 1 \times 1 \times C \times C$.

4   Experiments

We validate our GS-GCN on large skeleton-based action recognition benchmarks, NTU-RGB+D and NTU-RGB+D 120. We also conducted ablation experiments to verify the influence of different parts of the network on the experimental results. Finally, we compare the results of our method with the state-of-the-art methods.

4.1   Datasets

NTU-RGB+D. NTU-RGB+D [13] is the most widely used action recognition dataset. It contains 56880 skeleton fragments of 60 action categories. The clips were captured from three camera views in a laboratory environment. The annotation provides the 3D position (x, y, z) of each joint in the camera coordinate system. Each object has 25 joints. Each clip is guaranteed to contain up to 2 targets. We follow standard evaluation protocols, namely cross subject and cross view. In the C theme setting, 40320 clips from 20 themes are used for training, and the rest for testing. In the C-View setup, 37920 clips captured from cameras 2 and 3 are used for training, while clips captured from camera 1 are used for testing.

NTU-RGB+D 120. NTU-RGB+D 120 [9] is an extension of NTU-RGB+D, in which the number of categories is expanded to 120 and the number of samples is expanded to 114480. It is also recommended to use two evaluation protocols, namely cross subject and cross setup. In the c-subject setup, 63026 clips from 53 topics are used for training, and the rest are reserved for testing. In the c-subject setup, 54471 clips with even setup IDs are used for training, while the rest clips with odd setup IDs are used for testing.

Table 1. The results on different groups and parameters, different numbers of "shuffles" and different temporal convolution kernels.

Group	C-View	C-Subject	Params (M)
1	95.7	90	3.64
2	95.8	90	2.24
4	95.6	90	1.56
8	95.2	90.2	1.36
Shuffle	C-View	C-Subject	–
0	94.8	89.4	–
1	95	90.1	–
2	95.2	90.2	–
Temporal Kernel	C-View	C-Subject	–
9	95.1	89.9	–
11	95.2	90.2	–
13	95.2	89.6	–

4.2 Implementation Details

GS-GCN is trained in pytorch on NVIDA GeForce RTX2080. We use SGD with 0.9 nesterov momentum for optimization. The learning rate was set to 0.1 at the begining, and then it is reduced three times in the 35-th, 50-th and 60-th iteration with a coefficient of 0.1. A total of 65 epochs were trained. We divide the input feature channel and dynamic graph into 8 groups, and the dynamic graphs are initialized randomly. The temporal convolution kernel is 11. The input skeleton sequence is adjusted to a fixed length, 300 frames on NTU-RGB+D and NTU-RGB+D 120. We use a multi-stream mechanism, namely joint, bone, joint motion and bone motion. The four streams are trained separately, and the ensemble is performed during the test. In order to make a reasonable comparison with the baseline method SG-GCN [26], the number of space configurations is set to 3. To reduce over-fitting, we set the weight decay to 0.0004. Batch-size is 32 and cross entropy loss is used.

We set the number of GD module to be 10, and the number of output channels of each layer is 64, 64, 64, 64, 128, 256, 256, 256, respectively. We do not use group dynamic graph convolution in the first layer, the input channel of which is 3. We set the stride to 2 in layer 5 and layer 8, and the channel becomes twice of the original. We set the group number to 8 for each GD module.

Table 2. Performance comparison on the NTU-RGB+D dataset in both cross subject and cross view settings in terms of top-1 accuracy.

Methods	C-View	C-Subject	Methods	C-View	C-Subject
ST-GCN [22]	88.84	83.36	CA-GCN [28]	91.4	83.5
TS-GCN [5]	95.1	88.5	Shift-GCN [2]	96.5	90.7
TCN [24]	83.1	74.3	DC-GCN [1]	96.6	90.8
AS-GCN [8]	94.2	86.8	STIGCN [4]	96.1	90.1
DGNN [14]	96.1	89.9	Dyn-GCN [23]	96	91.5
PA-ResGCN [18]	96	90.9	SG-GCN [26]	94.5	89
AGC-LSTM [17]	95	89.2	MV-IGNet [21]	96.3	89.2
GS-GCN	**95.2**	**90.2**			

4.3 Ablation Studies

In order to verify the performance of our GS-GCN, we analyze the modules of the whole network. Firstly, we verify the affects of different numbers of dynamic graph convolution network. Secondly, we prove the different affects of "shuffles" with different numbers. Finally, we set the size of convolution kernel of depth-wise separable convolution to study the affect on parameters and computation complexity and the affect on temporal performance. Our ablation experiments are mainly conducted in NTU-RGB+D.

Group Dynamic Graph. In order to verify the effect of grouping dynamic graph convolution networks on the whole module, we analyze the number of groups. The output channels of the first four layers of our network are all 64, so in order to enable each sub-group to shuffle the information of other groups, the maximum number of sub-groups can only be set to 8, while the minimum number of sub-group is 1, which is that there are no sub-groups. In this case, the amount of parameters and computation is the largest.

As shown in Table 1, when the number of groups is 8, the parameter quantity is the smallest, only 1.36M, and the results on C-View and C-Subject are 95.2% and 90.2% respectively. As the number of groups decreases, the number of parameters increases. However, we can see that when the number of groups decreases, the result on C-View increases instead, reaching the maximum value of 95.8% when the number of groups is 2, while on C-Subject, it keeps at about 90, which is 0.2% less than that when the number of groups is 8. To sum up, it shows that increasing the number of parameters can help the model get better results when the number of groups decreases, but the decrease of dynamic graph convolution network groups will also bring performance loss. However, in C-View, the advantage of increasing the number of parameters is obvious, while in C-Subject, the performance does not increase when the number of parameters increases. It shows that the advantage of increasing the number of parameters and the performance loss of decreasing the number of dynamic graph groups offset each other. In addition, the number of parameters is 2.24M when the group is 2, and it is only 0.6% more in C-View when the group is 8, so it is reasonable to select the group as 8.

Table 3. Performance comparison on the NTU-RGB+D 120 dataset in both cross subject and cross view settings in terms of top-1 accuracy.(%)

Methods	C-Subject	C-Setup	Methods	C-Subject	C-Setup
MTCNN [6]	62.2	61.8	2s-ALSTM	61.2	63.3
Shift-GCN [2]	85.9	87.6	MV-IGNet [21]	83.9	85.6
MS-G3D [11]	86.9	88.4	Dyn-GCN [23]	87.3	88.6
PA-ResGCN [18]	87.3	88.3	DSTA-NET [16]	86.6	89
DC-GCN [1]	86.5	88.1	SG-GCN [26]	79.2	81.5
GS-GCN	**84.9**	**87.1**			

Shuffle. We analyze the effect of not adding shuffle, adding 1 shuffle and adding 2 shuffles on the results. Table 1 also shows the effect of the number of shuffles on the results. When the number of shuffles is 1, we put it between the convolution of group dynamic graph convolution layer and the temporal convolution layer. When the number of shuffles is 2, we implement the above and put the other after the temporal convolution layer. When the number of shuffle is 0, the results are 94.8 and 89.4 on C-View and C-Subject, respectively. As the number of shuffles increases, the performance also increases. It shows that shuffle plays an important role in GS-GCN.

Depthwise Separable TCN. Depthwise separable network plays a very important role in parameter quantity and computational complexity in GS-GCN. In the whole network, the parameter quantity of temporal module accounts for more than two-thirds of the whole network. For seeking the lightweight model, we employ depthwise separable convolution network to reduce the parameter quantity. Due to the limitation of the traditional convolution network, the convolution kernel can not be set too large, while it is generally 9. If we employ depthwise separable convolution network, the size of convolution kernel can be set larger, the model may increase the temporal dependence range and extract more abundant information, and the parameters of temporal module are greatly reduced. As can be seen from Table 1, the parameters of GS-GCN in temporal module are only 0.05M and in spatial module is 0.29M.

In order to confirm the proper size of the temporal convolution kernel, we have carried out the comparative experiments, and the experimental results are shown in Table 1. When the temporal convolution kernel is 11, the values of the C-View and C-Subject reach the maximum, which are 85.2% and 90.2%, respectively. When the convolution kernel is 9 and 13, the results decrease, indicating that the size of convolution kernel cannot be too large or too small. Compared with the traditional temporal convolution with the size of 9, GS-GCN can expand the size to 11, and the parameter quantity also decreases a lot, which shows that the deep separable convolution has generalization in the temporal domain.

4.4 Comparison with State-of-the-Art Methods

We compare our GS-GCN and the state-of-the-art methods on NTU-RGB+D and NTU-RGB+D 120 datasets, including approaches based on RNN, CNN and GCN framework. Tables 2 and 3 are describe the results on two datasets respectively.

Table 4. Comparison on the NTU-RGB+D in both Params and GFLOPs.(%)

Methods	Params (M)	FLOPs (G)	Methods	Params (M)	FLOPs (G)
ST-GCN [22]	3.1	–	TS-GCN [5]	7	37.3
AGC-LSTM [17]	–	54.4	AS-GCN [8]	–	27
DGNN [14]	4.09	35.56	Shift-GCN [2]	2.76	10
MS-G3D [11]	3.19	24.49	STIGCN [4]	1.6	4
SG-GCN [26]	**0.69**	–	MV-IGNet [21]	1.84	–
GS-GCN	1.36	4			

There are a lot of excellent works in action recognition basically using graph convolution network (GCN) in recent years, which show that approaches based on GCN have more advantages than RNN and CNN in action recognition to some extend. In Table 2, DC-GCN [1] achieves best on C-View in NTU-RGB+D dataset with the accuracy 96.6%, while on C-Subjext, MS-G3D [11] and DSTA-Net [16] achieve the best results with 91.5%. Our GS-GCN focuses on small models, and the accuracy is a little lower than the best one, however, GS-GCN is much better than the others. The C-View result of GS-GCN on NTU-RGB+D is

95.2%, and the C-Subject result is 90.1%, which is not more than 1.5% compared with the best result. Moreover, GS-GCN is better than some methods in 2020, such as CA-GCN [28] and SG-GCN [26]. GS-GCN has many advantages in terms of parameters and computational complexity.

We also demonstrate the GS-GCN on NTU-RGB+D 120 dataset and the results are shows in Table 3. Dyn-GCN [23] and PARESGCN [18] on NTU-RGB+D 120 c-subject and DSTA-Net [16] on C-Setup perform better than the others. The accuracy of GS-GCN is 84.9% on C-Subject and 87.1% on C-Setup. Although the accuracy of GS-GCN is not higher than the best, it is better than SG-GCN [26] and MVIG-Net [21],and the model of GS-GCN is much small. Furthermore, the performance of the approaches based on GCN are better than that based on RNN or CNN.

Table 4 shows calculation complexity and parameters of the models with input features of multiple streams (joint stream, bone stream, joint motion stream and bone motion stream). The calculation complexity and parameters in most of the previous methods are huge. The parameters in TS-GCN [5] is 7M and the calculation of 37.3GFLOPS compared with 1.36M and 4GFLOPS of GS-GCN. Although the parameters in GS-GCN is larger than SG-GCN [26], the accuracy in GS-GCN is better than SG-GCN. GS-GCN greatly reduces the size of the model while the performance is still competitive.

5   Conclusion

In this paper, we propose a novel lightweight skeleton-based action recognition with group-shuffle graph convolutional network. The proposed algorithm is composed of two modules: group-shuffle graph convolution module, which applies dynamic GCN and the features are divided into several groups and the sub-groups share the parameters; and depthwise-shuffle separable convolution module, which decreases the number of parameters and computation to a large extent. We verify the proposed method on two popular datasets NTU-RGB+D and NTU-RGB+D 120, and the performance is better and the parameters and computation are decreased.

References

1. Cheng, K., Zhang, Y., Cao, C., Shi, L., Cheng, J., Lu, H.: Decoupling GCN with dropgraph module for skeleton-based action recognition
2. Cheng, K., Zhang, Y., He, X., Chen, W., Cheng, J., Lu, H.: Skeleton-based action recognition with shift graph convolutional network. In: 2020 IEEE/CVF Conference on Computer Vision and Pattern Recognition (CVPR), pp. 183–192 (2020)
3. Dempsey, P.W., Allison, M.E., Akkaraju, S., Goodnow, C.C., Fearon, D.T.: C3d of complement as a molecular adjuvant: bridging innate and acquired immunity. Science **271**(5247), 348–350 (1996)
4. Huang, Z., Shen, X., Tian, X., Li, H., Huang, J., Hua, X.S.: Spatio-temporal inception graph convolutional networks for skeleton-based action recognition. In: ACM Multimedia, pp. 2122–2130 (2020)

5. Junyu, G., Tianzhu, Z., Changsheng, X.: I know the relationships: zero-shot action recognition via two-stream graph convolutional networks and knowledge graphs. In: AAAI (2019)
6. Ke, Q., Bennamoun, M., An, S., Sohel, F., Boussaid, F.: Learning clip representations for skeleton-based 3D action recognition. In TIP **27**, 2842–2855 (2018)
7. Kim, T., Reiter, A.: Interpretable 3D human action analysis with temporal convolutional networks. In: Conference on Computer Vision and Pattern Recognition CVPR, pp. 1623–1631 (2017)
8. Li, M., Chen, S., Chen, X., Zhang, Y., Wang, Y., Tian, Q.: Actional-structural graph convolutional networks for skeleton-based action recognition. In: 2019 IEEE/CVF Conference on Computer Vision and Pattern Recognition (CVPR), pp. 3595–3603 (2019)
9. Liu, J., Shahroudy, A., Perez, M., Wang, G., Duan, L.Y., Kot, A.C.: NTU RGB+D 120: a large-scale benchmark for 3D human activity understanding. IEEE Trans. Pattern Anal. Mach. Intell. **42**(10), 2684–2701 (2019)
10. Liu, M., Liu, H., Chen, C.: Enhanced skeleton visualization for view invariant human action recognition. Pattern Recognit. **68**, 346–362 (2017)
11. Liu, Z., Zhang, H., Chen, Z., Wang, Z., Ouyang, W.: Disentangling and unifying graph convolutions for skeleton-based action recognition. In: 2020 IEEE/CVF Conference on Computer Vision and Pattern Recognition (CVPR), pp. 143–152 (2020)
12. Plizzari, C., Cannici, M., Matteucci, M.: Spatial temporal transformer network for skeleton-based action recognition. arXiv preprint arXiv:2008.07404 (2020)
13. Shahroudy, A., Liu, J., Ng, T.T., Wang, G.: NTU RGB+D: a large scale dataset for 3D human activity analysis. In: Proceedings of the IEEE Conference on Computer Vision and Pattern Recognition, pp. 1010–1019 (2016)
14. Shi, L., Zhang, Y., Cheng, J., Lu, H.: Skeleton-based action recognition with directed graph neural networks. In: 2019 IEEE/CVF Conference on Computer Vision and Pattern Recognition (CVPR), pp. 7912–7921 (2019)
15. Shi, L., Zhang, Y., Cheng, J., Lu, H.: Two-stream adaptive graph convolutional networks for skeleton-based action recognition. In: 2019 IEEE/CVF Conference on Computer Vision and Pattern Recognition (CVPR), pp. 12026–12035 (2019)
16. Shi, L., Zhang, Y., Cheng, J., Lu, H.: Decoupled spatial-temporal attention network for skeleton-based action-gesture recognition. In: ACCV (2020)
17. Si, C., Chen, W., Wang, W., Wang, L., Tan, T.: An attention enhanced graph convolutional LSTM network for skeleton-based action recognition. In: 2019 IEEE/CVF Conference on Computer Vision and Pattern Recognition (CVPR), pp. 1227–1236 (2019)
18. Song, Y.F., Zhang, Z., Shan, C., Wang, L.: Stronger, faster and more explainable: a graph convolutional baseline for skeleton-based action recognition. In: ACM Multimedia, pp. 1625–1633 (2020)
19. Wang, H., Kläser, A., Schmid, C., Liu, C.L.: Dense trajectories and motion boundary descriptors for action recognition. Int. J. Comput. Vision **103**(1), 60–79 (2013)
20. Wang, H., Schmid, C.: Action recognition with improved trajectories. In: Proceedings of the IEEE International Conference on Computer Vision, pp. 3551–3558 (2013)
21. Wang, M., Ni, B., Yang, X.: Learning multi-view interactional skeleton graph for action recognition. IEEE Trans. Pattern Anal. Mach. Intell. **pp**, 1–1 (2020)
22. Yan, S., Xiong, Y., Lin, D.: Spatial temporal graph convolutional networks for skeleton-based action recognition. In: AAAI vol. 32 (2018)

23. Ye, F., Pu, S., Zhong, Q., Li, C., Xie, D., Tang, H.: Dynamic GCN: context-enriched topology learning for skeleton-based action recognition. In: ACM Multimedia, pp. 55–63 (2020)
24. Yuan, J., Ni, B., Yang, X., Kassim, A.A.: Temporal action localization with pyramid of score distribution features. In: Computer Vision Pattern Recognition (2016)
25. Zhang, J., Chen, Z., Tao, D.: Towards high performance human keypoint detection. Int. J. Comput. Vision **129**(9), 2639–2662 (2021)
26. Zhang, P., Lan, C., Zeng, W., Xing, J., Xue, J., Zheng, N.: Semantics-guided neural networks for efficient skeleton-based human action recognition. In: Proceedings of the IEEE/CVF Conference on Computer Vision and Pattern Recognition (CVPR), pp. 1112–1121 (2020)
27. Zhang, X., Zhou, X., Lin, M., Sun, J.: ShuffleNet: an extremely efficient convolutional neural network for mobile devices. In: 2018 IEEE/CVF Conference on Computer Vision and Pattern Recognition (CVPR), pp. 6848–6856 (2018)
28. Zhang, X., Xu, C., Tao, D.: Context aware graph convolution for skeleton-based action recognition. In: 2020 IEEE/CVF Conference on Computer Vision and Pattern Recognition (CVPR), pp. 14333–14342 (2020)

Global-View Re-identification Tracking with Transformer

Zhuangzhuang Gao and Zhangjin Huang[(✉)]

University of Science and Technology of China, Hefei 230026, Anhui, China
BryantGao@mail.ustc.edu.cn, zhuang@ustc.edu.cn

Abstract. Identity matching and trajectory association are the core of multi-object tracking (MOT) task. Recent works have also focused on the rich information contained in the trajectories, aiming to learn the strong connection between the long-term motion information and the inherent representation information of the target. However, in most current MOT trackers, trajectory update is sensitive. Once the detected object in the video frame is difficult to associate with the existing trajectories, the model quickly updates the target identity and the numbers of tracking trajectories. We propose a tracking framework named GRTrack based on fine-grained re-identification (ReID) feature extraction for reappeared targets in video from a global view. Our model not only preserves the long-term relationship between the global trajectory query and the tracking target motion, but also weakens the sensitivity to low-score updated trajectory. For reappeared targets in specific motion scenarios, we retain more long-term association, thus greatly improving the accuracy of identity matching. Our model performs well on the SportsMOT dataset and achieves satisfactory results.

Keywords: MOT · Transformer · Re-identification

1 Introduction

As a basic visual perception task, multi-object tracking (MOT) has been widely used in autonomous driving [13], video analysis [12], intelligent robots [11] and other fields. Its purpose is to detect and track all specific categories of objects frame by frame. In recent years, due to the rapid development of detection algorithm [4,6,15], the performance of detection and tracking paradigm has been greatly improved, so that researchers can focus more on the association matching of target identity. Recently, some work has solved the problem of frequent occlusion and short-term disappearance by establishing robust motion models to predict the trajectory of the target and generate the trajectory. Other works [20,25,26] focus on the appearance between past time frames [17,29] by introducing attention mechanism, and establish long-term spatial-temporal model based on position information and motion state, which has achieved good accuracy improvement (Fig. 1).

L. Fang et al. (Eds.): CICAI 2022, LNAI 13604, pp. 622–633, 2022.
https://doi.org/10.1007/978-3-031-20497-5_51

Fig. 1. The three pictures show the visualization of tracking results based on the GTR [29] model in the basketball game scenario. As shown in the figure, in the same video sequence, the number of trajectories is far from the total number of athletes in the video, and the ID representing the identity of athletes is updated frequently. And with the passage of the game time, the background image in the video frame is not fixed, but also will appear the phenomenon of mutual occlusion of athletes wearing similar clothes.

However, we observe that most of the target objects in the current MOT benchmark dataset have obvious distinguishable appearance, and the background of the video sequence is single and relatively static, and the target appears in a uniform or nearly linear motion mode. The proposed deep learning model can easily establish a robust target motion model or learn the appearance features with large discrimination. SportsMOT dataset is collected in sports competition scenes, the target objects are generally uniform, and the target tends to move at high speed and nonlinearly with frequent occlusion. In order to better capture the movements and images of athletes, the shooting of videos is often accompanied by rapid movement, which leads to the frequent identity switching of the target athletes to produce redundant trajectories in the tracking process.

For this reason, it is difficult to establish a simple motion prediction model which accurately associate the target with the corresponding tracking trajectory. Inspired by GTR [29] and TransReID [7], we leverage global ReID [28] features and global trajectory query features in our work. Specifically, our method uses a global tracking transformer to encode the detected object features in all frames. And we divide them into the corresponding tracking trajectory by trajectory queries. The trajectory query is the feature in the object detection box of the current frame. We associate global object features in temporal. In spatial, taking into account the generality of MOT and MTMCT in the representation model [5, 22], in a single video sequence, we set the appropriate interval to divide the sequence into several parts as multi-view. In order to learn the fine-grained and global ReID features, we flatten the features extracted by backbone and generate the ReID feature sequence by position embedding into transformer to learn the local spatial information and temporal connection of the target body.Based on this, we propose a global view ReID tracking called GRTrack, which learns a fine-grained ReID feature according to all detection objects, and generates a one-to-one correlation distribution between the existed trajectories and the detection object through global trajectory query.

We conducted tests on MOT and SportsMOT datasets, and compared the experimental results with the current excellent MOT trackers, which proved the effectiveness of our views and methods.

2   Related Work

2.1   Multi-object Tracking

The main task of MOT is to locate multiple interested targets in a given video at the same time, maintain their ID and record their trajectory . Models using traditional algorithms such as Kalman filter and Optical Flow [2] are usually associated by predicting the trajectory of the target in the next frame, such as Sort [1]. DeepSort [20] added detection and data association into Sort [1]. Affected by the rapid development of recent object detection technology, the latest tracker mainly adopts the paradigm of detection and tracking. Detection-based multi-target trackers such as ByteTrack [25] make full use of all low and high resolution detection boxes to establish strong detection association models.

2.2   Transformer in MOT

In recent years, Transformer [19] has made great achievements in the field of computer vision, and Detr has also brought a new target detection paradigm, which has inspired a lot of work. TransCenter [21] added a deformable DETR [31] on the basis of CenterTrack [27], abandoning bbox and using the heatmap of the target center to represent the target object, and overcoming the limitation of using only a small amount of query to query the decoder. Some embedding methods consider spatial-temporal correlations methods combined with appearance and motion information. Some learn trajectory embedding [14,30] by using the interaction between object, foreground and background, local and global information with relevance and attention. Inspired by GTR [29], our work sends the serial object features into the encoder through a global tracking transformer, and sends the trajectory query into the decoder [29]. The correlation score is generated between each query query and the object, and finally a global trajectory is generated. Based on this, we consider using transformer to help us establish global attention to trajectory query.

2.3   Re-identification of Person

In the existing benchmark datasets, the discrimination of objects are large, and most of the targets have obvious appearance differences. FairMOT [26] is based on CenterNet [28] and adds the ReID [28] branch. The feature map retains the high precision of two-step between target detection and ReID, and greatly reduces the time of model reasoning. Based on the same CenterNet [28], the method of multi-target tracking is extended to the monocular MOT task [22]. By establishing a multi-view trajectory comparison learning from the different motion information of the unified object in the historical frame, the trajectory center memory library is established to maintain the association between the trajectory center and the target detection in the current frame.

2.4   Multi-target Multi-camera Tracking

Multi-target multi-camera tracking (MTMCT) aims to track different identities through multiple cameras. A recent work [8] studied the intrinsic difference between MTMCT and ReID, and adapted the global ReID feature to the affinity measure suitable for local matching in MTMCT data association. Similar to MOT, MTMCT follow the detection-by-tracking paradigm. Most MTMCT methods are divided into tracklet-to-tracklet matching and tracklet-to-target mathing. The traditional methods [9] often use indirect association between trajectory and trajectory to match the local trajectory of a single camera in the whole cross-camera network. The work [10] forms the MTMCT problem as a direct correlation problem of trajectory targets. Local trajectories are allocated directly to each target by using network topology and global allocation matrix.

3   Methodology

3.1   Overview

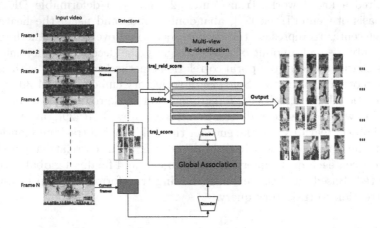

Fig. 2. Our Architecture of GRTrack. The input of the model is a video sequence. First, all targets are detected by a target detector. During training, the global trajectory storage is established according to ground truth. The object features are connected in series and sent to the encoder through the global correlation and the ReID feature extraction module under multi-view. During testing, the global association module generates association scores between each query trajectory and object, while the ReID The module extracts the ReID features of the nearest frame object in the query trajectory and the current detected object respectively, then calculates the association scores. Two associated fractional matrices jointly update trajectory storage.

Object Detection and Tracking. Assuming that an input image is defined as I. A target detector takes the image I as input and detects a set of objects $\{p_i\}_{i=1}^N$ and the corresponding bounding box $\{b_i\}_{i=1}^N, b_i \in R^4$ as output. For multi-class target detection, model learn classification features from the extracted object features, and then prediction head output a set of target category C and bounding box position $\tilde{b}_i$ and classification confidence score.

The input of a multi-target tracking task is a series of video sequences for T images in a video sequence $\{I^1, I^2, \ldots\ldots, I^T\}$. The target of the tracker is to predict the trajectory representation $\tau_k = [\tau_k^1, \ldots, \tau_k^T]$ of all targets over time. Each trajectory τ_k describes the position of the object over time. $\tau_k^t = \emptyset$ indicates that object k is not detected in time frame t.

3.2   Global View Trajectory ReID

Using a pre-trained ReID model directly for ReID feature extraction will bring huge time and space costs. During training, the ground truth result of the detection target n_i in the previous T frame of the current video sequence is taken as the location area under multiple-view.

In this module, we mainly train a model for person re-identification through monocular video sequences and use it to extract fine-grained re-identification features of athletes. Specifically, the Visual Transformer (ViT) [3] is used to construct the framework, as shown in Fig. 2, Given a video sequence V and athlete tracking trajectory identification IDs $\{n_1, n_2, ..., n_t\}$, each video V contains T athlete image I, $V = \{I_1, I_2, ..., I_T\}$. After convolution operation of the input image, the feature map $f \in R^{h \times w \times c}$ is obtained. Then the feature map is flattened to generate N features, where $N = h \cdot w$, the size of each feature is $1 \times c$. So each feature can be seen as the feature embedding of each image patch, and each image patch is the same size as the convolution kernel k. The feature embedding of each image block from image I is also called block token p. A class token ϕ_{cls} with a size of $1 \times c$ is also introduced to represent the feature embedding of the whole image. The class and patch labels are flattened into sequence $\{\phi_{cls}; p_1; ...; p_N\}$. As the patch labels lose the location information in the original athlete image,so the position information is preserved by embedding $\phi_{pos} \in R^{(N+1) \times c}$. A view embedding $\widehat{\phi}_{view}$ is also introduced to save view information. After these operations, the token sequence z^0 from athlete image I is calculated as follows [24]:

$$z^0 = [\phi_{cls}; p_1; ...; p_N] + \lambda_1 \phi_{pos} + \lambda_2 \phi_{view}$$
$$= [\phi_{cls}^0; p_1^0; ...; p_N^0]. \tag{1}$$

Query the ReID feature in the border box of each target appearing in the nearest frame of the current frame in the trajectory set $\{t_j\}_{j=1}^M$ as the matching set g_j. Extract ReID features of all detected objects in the current frame as query sets, and the traj-reid-score matrix is established to produce one-to-one matching results.

3.3   Global Association

In this section, we associate the object p_i^t in each frame I^t with a set of trajectory queries q_k. Each trajectory query q_k produces an object correlation score vector $g \in R^N$ that covers all frames. Then, this correlation fractional vector generates an object-level correlation $\alpha_k^t \in \{\emptyset, 1, ..., N_t\}$ for each frame, where $\alpha_k^t = \emptyset$ indicates no correlation, and N_t is the number of objects detected in frame I^t. The associated combination then generates a trajectory τ_k. The tracker accepts feature F and trajectory query $q_k \in R^D$, then generates a trajectory-specific association score $g(q_k, F) \in R^N$.

Formally, let $g_i^t(q_k, F) \in R$ be the score of the i object in frame t. A special output tag $g_\emptyset^t(q_k, F) = \emptyset$ indicates that there is no correlation at time t. Then, the tracking transformer predicts the correlation distribution of all objects n_i in the frame I for each trajectory τ_i, which is modeled as an independent soft start

---

Algorithm 1. trajectory memory update

Input: Image list $I = \{I_1, I_2, ..., I_N\}$;
Output: MOT trajectories results;
1: **for** each epoch **do**
2:      detect proposal bboxes;
3:      learn to extract reid feature;
4:      **while** first frame **do**
5:          Initialize trajectories;
6:      **end while**
7:      **for** each frame **do**
8:          compute traj-score of each existing trajectory with instances;
9:          find last bbox of all trajectories and extract reid feature;
10:          compute traj-reid-score of each existing trajectory with instances;
11:          **if** traj-score > thresh **then**
12:              update trajectories;
13:          **else**
14:              **if** traj-reid-score > reid-thresh **then**
15:                  update trajectories;
16:              **end if**
17:          **end if**
18:      **end for**
19: **end for**

---

for each time step t [29].

$$P_A(\alpha^t = i | q_k, F) = \frac{exp(g_i^t(q_k, F))}{\sum_{j \in \{\emptyset, 1, ..., N_t\}} exp(g_j^t(q_k, F))}. \tag{2}$$

During Training and Inference, we use the global trajectory correlation tracker to establish a trajectory correlation score matrix and a query target trajectory correlation score matrix respectively. According to the greedy algorithm, the correlation distribution P_A between the trajectory and all objects in the first frame is obtained. The ReID feature extractor obtained by ReID branch is used to obtain the ReID feature of all existing trajectories in the latest frame. The similarity score is calculated with the ReID feature of the detected target in the current frame, then a trajectory reid score matrix is obtained. Then a trajectory is also obtained with the ReID distribution R_A of all objects in frame I. When an object in the first frame is not associated with any trajectory, the trajectory τ_i is assigned to the object in the ReID distribution if there is a trajectory assignment for the object with higher scores and no duplication with the generated trajectory assignment. Trajectory assignment duplication that has not been associated with global trajectories

4 Experiments

4.1 Multi-object Tracking Datasets

MOT Datasets. MOT tracks pedestrians in crowd scenes. It contains seven training sequences and seven test sequences. These sequences contain 500 to 1500 frames, recorded and annotated at speeds of 25–30 FPS. We split each training sequence in half. We use the first half for training and the second half for validation.

SportsMOT. The existing pedestrian-tracking dataset mainly focuses on pedestrians in crowded street scenes (such as MOT17 or MOT20) or dancers in static scenes (DanceTrack [16]). However, in real sports scenes, there exists situations such as complex background images, uneven movement of athletes, and rapid movement of camera lens. The existing MOT dataset lacks such data and cannot cope with the increasing requirements of motion analysis. The SportsMOT dataset consists of 240 video clips with 3 categories (basketball, football and volleyball), which contains an average of 495 frames (19.8 s). Table 1 shows the total number of targets, trajectory length, fragment speed and the number of detection boxes in three different scenarios on SportsMOT dataset.

Table 1. Statistics of the annotations of 3 sports.

Categories	Track	Tracklen	Fragementlen	Speed	Density	Bboxsize	Defrate
Basketball	10	767	329	6	9	14305	2
Volleyball	12	335	115	9	11	8037	1
Football	20	442	160	6	12	2963	2

4.2 Implementation Details

For our MOT model, CenterNet [28] and DLA34 [23] backbone are used as object detectors. We use BiFPN [18] as the upper sampling layer. We use RoIAlign [6] to extract features for our global tracking transformer. We use a training size of 1280×1280 and a test size of 1280. We used two RTX3090 GPU cards to train the model. The training fragment of a video sequence was $T = 8$, but the test video sequence fragment was $T = 320$, mainly in order to retain the complete tracking trajectory. When reasoning, we set the output score threshold of MOT to 0.6 and the NMS threshold to 0.6. On SportsMOT dataset, the lengths of video sequences in training set, val set and test set are 40, 45, 150, respectively. We adopt a training strategy similar to MOT17 data set, and train and verify the training set and verification set separately, and the parameters set are consistent, and the initial weight is based on the pre-training model of GTR [29] on MOT17.

4.3 Evaluation Metrics

We use standard CLEAR-MOT measurement, including Multi-Object Tracking Accuracy (MOTA), Multi-Object Tracking Precision (MOTP), Identification F-Score (IDF1), Recall (Rcll) and ID Switch (IDs). Rcll (Recall): represents the number of detected targets correctly matched divided by the number of targets given by ground truth, the higher the value, the better, IDF1: the higher the value, the better the ratio of correct recognition detection to average true number and calculated detection number, IDs: represents the number of times the tracking trajectory switches the target label, the lower the value, the better, MOTA: represents the tracking accuracy (combined with the missing target, false alarm rate, accuracy after label conversion), MOTP: represents the tracking accuracy (the mismatch between the annotated and predicted bounding box), that is, the average border overlap rate for all tracking targets. The higher the values of MOTA and MOTP are, the better the tracking effect is.

Table 2. Comparison results with other the-state-of-art methods.

	Rcll(↑)	IDF1(↑)	IDS(↓)	MOTA(↑)	MOTP(↑)
	SportsMOT				
ByteTrack	96.7%	97.8%	3.1%	91.7%	0.210
FairMOT	95.4%	99.8%	1.6%	90.0%	0.186
GTR	94.2%	94.7%	0.4%	88.1%	**0.123**
TransTrack	85.3%	80.7%	2.7%	75.7%	0.136
GRTrack (Ours)	**96.9%**	**99.9%**	**0.3%**	**92.4%**	0.124
	MOT17				
ByteTarck	**83.1%**	**79.4%**	0.3%	**76.5%**	**0.155**
FairMOT	73.3%	78.2%	0.4%	72.8%	0.168
GTR	77.0%	72.6%	0.5%	67.9%	0.172
TransTrack	66.0%	62.9%	0.6%	61.9%	0.190
GRTrack (Ours)	82.3%	78.0%	**0.2%**	71.1%	0.166

4.4 Comparison Results with Other SOTA Methods

We tested the comparison with other trackers with excellent performance on the corresponding test set. Table 2 shows our test results on MOT17 and SportsMOT dataset, respectively. The test results on SportsMOT show that the performance of our model is almost optimal, especially for IDs. The smaller the proportion of IDs is, the less the number of target labels switched by the trajectory is in the MOT task. In this regard, the performance of our model is significantly better than ByteTrack [25], FairMOT [26] and TransTrack [17]. In view of the object detectors are using the existing detectors with excellent performance, so the difference in other indicators is not obvious. The test results on the MOT17 verification set show that although our model is not optimal in all the evaluation indexes, the IDs are still the smallest, mainly because of the different characteristics of the data set. In the MOT17 data set, the target does not produce obvious complex motion changes and frequent occlusions, disappear and reappear, and the motion speed is close to uniform and straight lines. To sum up, our model effectively overcomes the sensitive problem of MOT model trajectory update in complex motion scenes.

5   Conclusion

In this work, we believe that in real sports scenes, there are often situations such as complex background images, uneven movement of athletes, and rapid movement of camera lens. The existing deep learning model based on the benchmark MOT dataset ignores this problem. We believe that the fine-grained re-identification and extraction of the detected target are crucial for the MOT in sports scenes. We use the attention mechanism to establish the long-term attention of trajectory and appearance features, which effectively reduces the occurrence of target identity error correlation. But compared with the traditional model that adds ReID training branch, the training and inference speed of our model needs to be improved.

Acknowledgements. This work was supported in part by the National Natural Science Foundation of China (Nos. 71991464/71991460, and 61877056).

References

1. Bewley, A., Ge, Z., Ott, L., Ramos, F., Upcroft, B.: Simple online and realtime tracking. CoRR arXiv:abs/1602.00763 (2016)
2. Chen, Y., Zhao, D., Li, H.: Deep kalman filter with optical flow for multiple object tracking. In: 2019 IEEE International Conference on Systems, Man and Cybernetics, SMC 2019, Bari, Italy, 6–9 October 2019, pp. 3036–3041. IEEE (2019). https://doi.org/10.1109/SMC.2019.8914078
3. Dosovitskiy, A., et al.: An image is worth 16x16 words: transformers for image recognition at scale. In: 9th International Conference on Learning Representations, ICLR 2021, Virtual Event, Austria, 3–7 May 2021. OpenReview.net (2021). https://openreview.net/forum?id=YicbFdNTTy
4. Ge, Z., Liu, S., Wang, F., Li, Z., Sun, J.: YOLOX: exceeding YOLO series in 2021. CoRR arXiv:abs/2107.08430 (2021)
5. He, B., et al.: DeepCC: multi-agent deep reinforcement learning congestion control for multi-path TCP based on self-attention. IEEE Trans. Netw. Serv. Manag. **18**(4), 4770–4788 (2021). https://doi.org/10.1109/TNSM.2021.3093302
6. He, K., Gkioxari, G., Dollár, P., Girshick, R.B.: Mask R-CNN. CoRR arXiv:abs/1703.06870 (2017)

7. He, S., Luo, H., Wang, P., Wang, F., Li, H., Jiang, W.: TransReID: transformer-based object re-identification. In: 2021 IEEE/CVF International Conference on Computer Vision, ICCV 2021, Montreal, QC, Canada, October 10–17, pp. 14993–15002. IEEE (2021). https://doi.org/10.1109/ICCV48922.2021.01474

8. Hou, Y., Wang, Z., Wang, S., Zheng, L.: Adaptive affinity for associations in multi-target multi-camera tracking. IEEE Trans. Image Process. **31**, 612–622 (2022). https://doi.org/10.1109/TIP.2021.3131936

9. Hsu, H., Cai, J., Wang, Y., Hwang, J., Kim, K.: Multi-target multi-camera tracking of vehicles using metadata-aided RE-ID and trajectory-based camera link model. IEEE Trans. Image Process. **30**, 5198–5210 (2021). https://doi.org/10.1109/TIP.2021.3078124

10. Hsu, H., Cai, J., Wang, Y., Hwang, J., Kim, K.: Multi-target multi-camera tracking of vehicles using metadata-aided RE-ID and trajectory-based camera link model. CoRR arXiv:abs/2105.01213 (2021)

11. Kluge, B.: Tracking multiple moving objects in populated, public environments. In: Hager, G.D., Christensen, H.I., Bunke, H., Klein, R. (eds.) Sensor Based Intelligent Robots. LNCS, vol. 2238, pp. 25–38. Springer, Heidelberg (2002). https://doi.org/10.1007/3-540-45993-6_2

12. Liu, Y., Lian, Z., Ding, J., Guo, T.: Multiple objects tracking based vehicle speed analysis with gaussian filter from drone video. In: Cui, Z., Pan, J., Zhang, S., Xiao, L., Yang, J. (eds.) IScIDE 2019. LNCS, vol. 11935, pp. 362–373. Springer, Cham (2019). https://doi.org/10.1007/978-3-030-36189-1_30

13. Luo, C., Yang, X., Yuille, A.L.: Exploring simple 3D multi-object tracking for autonomous driving. In: 2021 IEEE/CVF International Conference on Computer Vision, ICCV 2021, Montreal, QC, Canada, October 10–17, pp. 10468–10477. IEEE (2021). https://doi.org/10.1109/ICCV48922.2021.01032

14. Meinhardt, T., Kirillov, A., Leal-Taixé, L., Feichtenhofer, C.: TrackFormer: multi-object tracking with transformers. CoRR arXiv:abs/2101.02702 (2021)

15. Ren, S., He, K., Girshick, R.B., Sun, J.: Faster R-CNN: towards real-time object detection with region proposal networks. IEEE Trans. Pattern Anal. Mach. Intell. **39**(6), 1137–1149 (2017). https://doi.org/10.1109/TPAMI.2016.2577031

16. Sun, P., et al.: DanceTrack: multi-object tracking in uniform appearance and diverse motion. CoRR arXiv:abs/2111.14690 (2021)

17. Sun, P., et al.: TransTrack: multiple-object tracking with transformer. CoRR arXiv:abs/2012.15460 (2020)

18. Tan, M., Pang, R., Le, Q.V.: EfficientDet: scalable and efficient object detection. CoRR arXiv:abs/1911.09070 (2019)

19. Vaswani, A., et al.: Attention is all you need. CoRR arXiv:1706.03762 (2017)

20. Wojke, N., Bewley, A., Paulus, D.: Simple online and realtime tracking with a deep association metric. CoRR arXiv:abs/1703.07402 (2017)

21. Xu, Y., Ban, Y., Delorme, G., Gan, C., Rus, D., Alameda-Pineda, X.: TransCenter: transformers with dense queries for multiple-object tracking. CoRR arXiv:abs/2103.15145 (2021)

22. Yu, E., Li, Z., Han, S.: Towards discriminative representation: multi-view trajectory contrastive learning for online multi-object tracking. CoRR arXiv:abs/2203.14208 (2022).

23. Yu, F., Wang, D., Darrell, T.: Deep layer aggregation. CoRR arXiv:abs/1707.06484 (2017)

24. Zang, X., Li, G., Gao, W.: Multi-direction and multi-scale pyramid in transformer for video-based pedestrian retrieval. CoRR arXiv:2202.06014 (2022)

25. Zhang, Y., et al.: ByteTrack: multi-object tracking by associating every detection box. CoRR arXiv:2110.06864 (2021)
26. Zhang, Y., Wang, C., Wang, X., Zeng, W., Liu, W.: FairMOT: on the fairness of detection and re-identification in multiple object tracking. Int. J. Comput. Vis. **129**(11), 3069–3087 (2021). https://doi.org/10.1007/s11263-021-01513-4
27. Zhou, X., Koltun, V., Krähenbühl, P.: Tracking objects as points. In: Vedaldi, A., Bischof, H., Brox, T., Frahm, J.-M. (eds.) ECCV 2020. LNCS, vol. 12349, pp. 474–490. Springer, Cham (2020). https://doi.org/10.1007/978-3-030-58548-8_28
28. Zhou, X., Wang, D., Krähenbühl, P.: Objects as points. CoRR arXiv:1904.07850 (2019)
29. Zhou, X., Yin, T., Koltun, V., Krähenbühl, P.: Global tracking transformers. CoRR arXiv:2203.13250 (2022).
30. Zhu, T., Hiller, M., Ehsanpour, M., Ma, R., Drummond, T., Rezatofighi, H.: Looking beyond two frames: end-to-end multi-object tracking using spatial and temporal transformers. CoRR arXiv:2103.14829 (2021)
31. Zhu, X., Su, W., Lu, L., Li, B., Wang, X., Dai, J.: Deformable DETR: deformable transformers for end-to-end object detection. In: 9th International Conference on Learning Representations, ICLR 2021, Virtual Event, Austria, 3–7 May 2021, OpenReview.net (2021). https://openreview.net/forum?id=gZ9hCDWe6ke

VERTEX: VEhicle Reconstruction and TEXture Estimation from a Single Image Using Deep Implicit Semantic Template Mapping

Xiaochen Zhao[1], Zerong Zheng[1], Chaonan Ji[1], Zhenyi Liu[2],
Siyou Lin[1], Tao Yu[1], Jinli Suo[1], and Yebin Liu[1(✉)]

[1] Tsinghua University, Beijing 100084, China
liuyebin@mail.tsinghua.edu.cn
[2] Jilin University, Changchun 130015, China

Abstract. We introduce VERTEX, an effective solution to recovering the 3D shape and texture of vehicles from uncalibrated monocular inputs under real-world street environments. To fully utilize the semantic prior of vehicles, we propose a novel geometry and texture joint representation based on implicit semantic template mapping. Compared to existing representations which infer 3D texture fields, our method explicitly constrains the texture distribution on the 2D surface of the template and avoids the limitation of fixed topology. Moreover, we propose a joint training strategy that leverages the texture distribution to learn a semantic-preserving mapping from vehicle instances to the canonical template. We also contribute a new synthetic dataset containing 830 elaborately textured car models labeled with key points and rendered using Physically Based Rendering (PBRT) system with measured HDRI skymaps to obtain highly realistic images. Experiments demonstrate the superior performance of our approach on both testing dataset and in-the-wild images. Furthermore, the presented technique enables additional applications such as 3D vehicle texture transfer and material identification, and can be generalized to other shape categories.

Keywords: Vehicle 3d reconstruction · Implicit representation

1 Introduction

Monocular visual scene understanding is a fundamental technology for many automatic applications, especially in the field of autonomous driving. Using only a single-view driving image, available vehicle parsing studies have covered popular topics starting from 2D vehicle detection, then 6D vehicle pose recovery,

Supplementary Information The online version contains supplementary material available at https://doi.org/10.1007/978-3-031-20497-5_52.

and finally vehicle shape reconstruction. However, much less efforts are devoted to vehicle texture estimation, even though both humans and autonomous cars heavily rely on the appearance of vehicles to perceive surroundings. Simultaneously recovering the geometry and texture of vehicles is also important for synthetic driving data generation [19], vehicle tracking [20], vehicle parsing [23] and so on.

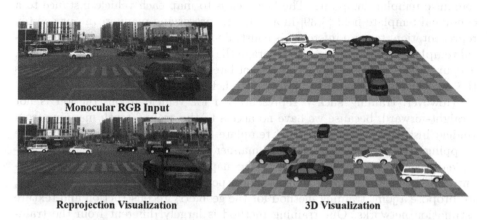

Fig. 1. We propose a method to recover realistic 3D textured models of vehicles from a single image (top left) under real street environments. Our approach can reconstruct the shape and texture with fine details. (We manually adjust the scale and layout of models for better visualization.)

Challenges for monocular geometry and texture recovery of vehicles mainly arise from the difficulties in inferring the invisible texture conditioned on only visible pixels while handling various vehicle shapes. Additionally, in real-world street environments, reconstruction methods are also expected to offset the adverse impact of complicated lighting conditions (e.g., strong sunlight and shadows) and diverse materials (e.g., transparent or reflective non-Lambertian surfaces). That said, the shape and appearance of vehicles are not completely arbitrary. Our key insight is that those challenges can be addressed with the prior knowledge from vehicle models, especially the part semantics. Therefore, we seek to find a method that is a) aware of the underlying semantics of vehicles, and b) flexible enough to recover various geometric structures and texture patterns.

Recently, deep implicit functions (DIFs), which model 3D shapes using continuous functions in 3D space, have been proven powerful in representing complex geometric structures [22,28]. Texture fields (TF) [26] and PIFu [31] took a step further by representing mesh texture with implicit functions and estimating point color conditioned on the input image. To do so, both TF and PIFu diffuse the surface color into the 3D space. However, it remains physically unclear how to define and interpret the color value off the surface. What's worse, geometry and texture are not fully disentangled in either PIFu or TF, as they rely on the location of surface to diffuse the color into the 3D space, making it difficult to incorporate semantic constraints.

In this paper, we explore a novel method, VERTEX, for VEhicle Reconstruction and TEXture estimation from a single image in real-world street environments. At its core is a novel implicit geo-tex representation that extends DIFs and jointly represents vehicle surface geometry and texture using implicit semantic template mapping. The key idea is to map each vehicle instance to a canonical template field [8,39] in a semantic-preserving manner. In our geo-tex representation, texture inference is constrained on the 2-manifold of the canonical template; in this way, we can leverage the semantic prior of vehicle template, encourage the model to learn a consistent latent space for all vehicles and bypass the unclear physical meaning of a texture field.

However, training such a representation for vehicle reconstruction is not straight-forward, because we have no access to the ground-truth mapping from vehicle instances to the canonical template field. [8,39] proposed to train the mapping network in an unsupervised manner, and the mapping follows the principle of shortest distance. As a result, the mapping in these methods is not guaranteed to preserve accurate semantic correspondences. To resolve this drawback, we propose a joint training method for the geometry reconstruction and texture estimation networks. Our training method is largely different from the training schedule of "first geometry then texture" adopted by typical reconstruction works [13,26,31]. This stems from the insight that the surface texture is closely related to its semantic labels; consider the appearance difference between different parts such as car bodies, windows, tires and lights as examples. The texture information can serve as the additional supervision to force the template mapping to be semantic-preserving.

Trained with our joint training method, our implicit geo-tex representation owns the advantages of both mesh templates and implicit functions: on one hand, it is expressive to represent various shapes, which is the main advantage of DIFs; on the other hand, it disentangles texture representation from geometry, thus supports many downstream tasks including material editing and texture transfer. Although it is initially designed for vehicles, our method can generalize to other objects such as bikes, planes and sofas.

To simulate real street environments and evaluate our method, we also contribute a synthetic dataset containing 830 elaborately textured car models rendered using Physically Based Rendering (PBRT) system with measured HDRI skymaps to obtain highly realistic images. Each instance is labeled with key points as semantic annotations and can be exploited for evaluation and future research.

In summary, our contributions include:

- a novel implicit geo-tex representation with semantic dense correspondences and latent space disentanglement, enabling fine-grained texture estimation, part-level understanding and vehicle editing;
- a joint training strategy leveraging the consistency between RGB color and part semantics for semantics-preserving template mapping;

– a new vehicle dataset, containing diverse detailed car CAD models, PBRT based rendered images and corresponding real-world HDRI skymaps.

2   Related Work

2.1   Monocular Vehicle Reconstruction

Recently, many works [1,10,13,16] concentrate on vehicle 3D texture recovery under real environments. Due to the lack of ground truth 3D data of real scenes, they mainly focus on the reconstruction from collections of 2D images utilizing unsupervised or self-supervised learning and build on mesh representation. Though eliminating the need for 3D annotations and generating meaningful vehicle textured models, these works still suffer from coarse reconstruction results and the limitation of fixed-topology representation. With large-scale synthetic datasets such as ShapeNet [4], many works [6,26,33] train deep neural networks to perform vehicle reconstruction from images. Based on volumentrically representation like 3D voxel [33] and implicit functions [26], these works generate plausible textured models in the synthetic dataset, but still struggle with low-quality texture. In contrast, our approach outperforms state-of-the-art methods in terms of visual fidelity and 3D consistency while representing topology-varying objects.

In addition, some works [3,9,25,27,38,40] focus on novel view synthesis, i.e., inferring texture in 2D domain. Although they can produce realistic images, they lack compact 3D representation, which is not in line with our goal.

2.2   Deep Implicit Representation

Traditionally, implicit functions represent shapes by constructing a continuous volumetric field and embed meshes as its iso-surface [2,32,34]. In recent years, implicit functions have been implemented with neural networks [5,11,22,28, 31,37] and have shown promising results. For example, DeepSDF [28] proposed to learn an implicit function where the network output represents the signed distance of the point to its nearest surface. Other approaches define the implicit functions as 3D occupancy probability functions and cast shape representation as a point classification problem [5,22,31,37].

As for texture inference, both TF [26] and PIFu [31] define texture implicitly as a function of 3D positions. The former uses global latent codes separately extracted from input the image and geometry whereas the latter leverages local pixel-aligned features. Compared with the above approaches [26,31] which predict texture distribution in the whole 3D space, our method explicitly constrains the texture distribution on the 2D manifold of the template surface with implicit semantic template mapping.

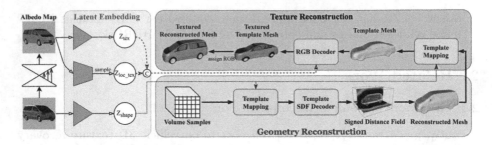

Fig. 2. The overview of our approach. Given the single RGB image, vehicle digitization is achieved by geometry and texture reconstruction. We first convert the original picture into an albedo map, and then extract multi-scale latent codes in Latent Embedding. Conditioned on these latent codes, our neural networks can infer SDF to reconstruct mesh surface and then regress RGB value for the surface.

3 Implicit Geo-Tex Representation

Our method for vehicle reconstruction and texture estimation is built upon a novel geo-tex joint representation, which is presented in this section.

3.1 Basic Formulation

We believe that an ideal geo-tex representation should disentangle texture representation from geometry as uv mapping does and should be accord with the physical fact that texture only attaches to the 2D surface of the object. In particular, observing that vehicles are a class of objects with a strong template prior, we extend DIT [39] and propose a *joint* geo-tex representation using deep implicit semantic templates. The key idea is to manipulate the implicit field of the vehicle template to represent vehicle geometry while embedding texture on the 2-manifold of the template surface. Mathematically, we denote the vehicle template surface with $\mathcal{S}_T$ as the level set of a signed distance function $F : \mathbb{R}^3 \mapsto \mathbb{R}$, i.e. $F(\boldsymbol{q}) = 0$, where $\boldsymbol{q} \in \mathbb{R}^3$ denotes a 3D point. Then our representation can be formulated as:

$$\begin{cases} \boldsymbol{p}_{tp} = W(\boldsymbol{p}, \boldsymbol{z}_{shape}) \\ s = F(\boldsymbol{p}_{tp}) \\ \boldsymbol{p}_{tp}^{(S)} = W(\boldsymbol{p}^{(S)}, \boldsymbol{z}_{shape}) \\ c = T(\boldsymbol{p}_{tp}^{(S)}, \boldsymbol{z}_{tex}) \end{cases} \quad (1)$$

where $W : \mathbb{R}^3 \times \mathcal{X}_{shape} \mapsto \mathbb{R}^3$ is a spatial warping function mapping the 3D point $\boldsymbol{p} \in \mathbb{R}^3$ to the corresponding location $\boldsymbol{p}_{tp}$ in the canonical template space conditioned on the shape latent code $\boldsymbol{z}_{shape}$, and F queries the signed distance value s at p_{tp}. $\boldsymbol{p}^{(S)} \in \mathcal{S} \subset \mathbb{R}^3$ is a 3D point on the vehicle surface $\mathcal{S}$, which is also mapped onto the template surface $\mathcal{S}_T$ using the warping function W, and $T : \mathcal{S}_T \times \mathcal{X}_{tex} \mapsto \mathbb{R}^3$ regresses the color value c of the template surface point $\boldsymbol{p}_{tp}^{(S)}$ conditioned on the texture latent code $\boldsymbol{z}_{tex}$. Intuitively, we map the vehicle surface to the template using warping function W and embed the surface texture of different vehicles onto one unified template. Therefore, in our representation, texture is only defined on the template surface (a 2D manifold), avoiding unclear physical meaning of a three-dimensional texture field.

3.2 Formulation for Image-based Reconstruction

For a specific instance, the shape information is defined by z_{shape}, while the texture information is encoded as z_{tex}, both of which can be extracted from the input image using CNN-based encoders. To further preserve fine details presented in the monocular observation, we fuse local texture information represented as $z_{loc\_tex}(p)$ at the pixel level. Not only the texture in visible region can benefit from local features, invisible regions can also be enhanced with the structure prior of the template. Formally, our formulation can be rewritten as:

$$\begin{cases} p_{tp} = \mathcal{W}(p, z_{shape}) \\ s = F(p_{tp}) \\ p_{tp}^{(S)} = W(p^{(S)}, z_{shape}) \\ c = T(p_{tp}^{(S)}, z_{tex}, z_{loc\_tex}(p)) \end{cases} \tag{2}$$

where $T : \mathcal{S}_T \times \mathcal{X}_{tex} \times \mathcal{X}_{loc\_tex} \mapsto \mathbb{R}^3$ is conditioned on the latent codes z_{tex} and z_{loc_tex}.

In summary, aiming at vehicle texture recovery, our representation is more expressive with less complexity. However, implementing and training our representation for textured vehicle reconstruction is not straight-forward. We will introduce how we achieve this goal in Sect. 4.

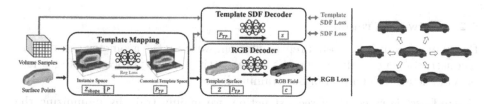

Fig. 3. To implement implicit semantic template mapping (right), we minimize both data terms of geometry (blue arrows) and texture (green arrows) reconstruction simultaneously. Besides, the regularization terms (orange and pink arrows) for specific network modules are applied to assist training. Note that Z in RGB Decoder is the concatenation of the global and local texture latent codes. (Color figure online)

4 Joint Geo-tex Training Method

4.1 Network Architecture

Figure 2 illustrates the overview of our network, consisting of three modules, i.e., Latent Embedding (yellow), Geometry Reconstruction (blue) and Texture

Estimation (green). Our network takes as input a single vehicle image and corresponding 2D silhouette, which can be produced by off-the-shelf 2D detectors [15], and generates a textured mesh.

Albedo Recovery: We empirically found that directly extracting texture latent codes from the input images leads to unsatisfactory results. Therefore, before feeding the input image to our network, we first infer the intrinsic color in 2D domain by means of image-to-image translation [30], and the recovered albedo image will be used as the input for texture encoders in Latent Embedding. We find this module effectively contributes to alleviating the noise effects of image illumination on consistent texture recovery.

Latent Embedding: The global shape and texture latent codes, z_{shape} & z_{tex}, are extracted from the input image and recovered albedo map using two separate ResNet-based [12] encoders respectively. The local texture feature, $z_{loc\_tex}(p)$, is sampled following the practice of PIFu [31]. Different with other texture inference works [26,31] which only utilize either global or local features for texture reconstruction, we fuse *multi-scale* texture features to recover robust and detailed texture.

Geometry Reconstruction and Texture Estimation: These two modules form the core of VERTEX. They consist of three main components: Template Mapping, Template SDF Decoder and RGB Decoder. Conditioned on z_{shape}, volume samples are sequentially fed to the Template Mapping and Template SDF Decoder to predict the continuous signed distance field. For texture estimation, surface points on reconstructed mesh are firstly warped to the template surface conditioned on z_{shape}, and then passed through the RGB Decoder with embedding latent codes z_{tex}, $z_{loc\_tex}(p)$ and z_{pose} to predict texture.

4.2 Network Training

Based on our implicit geo-tex representation, we train the geometry and texture reconstruction network jointly. We visualize the training process in Fig. 3 and provide detailed definition of our training losses.

Data Loss: For geometry reconstruction, we mainly train by minimizing the $\ell1$-loss between the predicted and the ground-truth point SDF values:

$$L_{geo} = \frac{1}{N_{sdf}} \sum_{i=1}^{N_{sdf}} \|T(W(p_i, z_{shape})) - s_i\|_1 \tag{3}$$

where N_{sdf} represents the number of input sample points, z_{shape} is the shape latent code corresponding to the volume sample point p_i, and s_i is the corresponding ground truth SDF value on the p_i.

To train the texture estimation network, we minimize the $\ell1$-loss between the regressed and the ground-truth intrinsic RGB value:

$$L_{tex} = \frac{1}{N_{sf}} \sum_{i=1}^{N_{sf}} \left\|T\left(W\left(p_i^{(S)}, z_{shape}\right), z_{tex}, z_{loc\_tex}(p_i^{(S)})\right) - c_i\right\|_1 \tag{4}$$

where N_{sf} represents the number of input surface points, c_i is the corresponding ground truth color value on the surface point p_i, and z_{shape}, z_{tex} and z_{loc_tex} are the latent codes corresponding to the $p_i^{(S)}$.

Regularization Loss: To establish continuous mapping between the instance space and the canonical template space, we introduce an additional regularization term to constrain position offsets of points after warping:

$$L_{reg} = \frac{1}{N_{sdf}} \sum_{i=1}^{N_{sdf}} \| W(p_i, z_{shape}) - p_i \|_2 \tag{5}$$

Template SDF Supervision: We supervise Template SDF Decoder directly using the sample points of the template car model. The loss is defined as:

$$L_{tp\_sdf} = \frac{1}{N_{tp\_sdf}} \sum_{i=1}^{N_{tp\_sdf}} \left\| T(p_i^{(tp)}) - s_i^{(tp)} \right\|_1 \tag{6}$$

where N_{tp_sdf} represents the number of input sample points, $p_i^{(tp)}$ represents the volume sample point around template model and $s_i^{(tp)}$ is the corresponding SDF value.

Overall, the total loss function is formulated as the weighted sum of above mentioned terms:

$$L = L_{tex} + w_g L_{geo} + w_{reg} L_{reg} + w_t L_{tp\_sdf} \tag{7}$$

4.3   Inference

As shown in the pipeline in Fig. 2, during inference, we first regress the signed distance field with the branch of geometry reconstruction, and then 3D points on the extracted surface are input to the branch of Texture Estimation to recover surface texture. However, because of the lack of ground truth camera intrinsic and extrinsic parameters, it is difficult for a 3D point to sample the correct local feature from feature map, which poses a significant challenge. We address the problem by setting a virtual camera and further optimizing the 6D pose under the render-and-compare optimization framework. See supplementary for details.

5   Experiments

In this section, we first introduce the new vehicle dataset in Sect. 5.1. In Sect. 5.2, we illustrate the reconstruction results under real environments and quantitative scores on our dataset compared with two state-of-art baselines. **The ablation studies and generalization to other object categories are presented in the supplementary.**

Fig. 4. Results on in-the-wild images. Monocular input images are shown in the top row. We compare 3D models reconstructed by ours and contrast works (PIFu and Onet+TF) retrained with our dataset. Two render views are provided to demonstrate reconstruction quality. Our results achieve great performance in terms of both robustness and accuracy.

5.1   Dataset

To generate synthetic dataset, we collect 83 industry-grade 3D CAD models covering common vehicle types, each of which is labeled with 23 semantic key points. We specifically select a commonly seen car as the vehicle template. To enrich the texture diversity of our dataset, we assign ten different texture for each model. We generate images with high visual fidelity using Physically Based Rendering (PBRT) [29] system and measured HDRI skymaps in the Laval HDR Sky Database [18]. Finally, we get a training set with 6300 instances and a testing set with 2000 instances in total. Please refer to supplementary for more details.

5.2   Results and Comparison

We compare our method with two state-of-the-art methods based on implicit functions. One is PIFu [31] which leverages pixel-aligned features to infer both occupied probabilities and texture distribution. The other one is Onet + Texture Field [22,26], of which Onet reconstructs shape from the monocular input image and TF infers the color for the surface points conditioned on the image and the geometry. For fair comparison, we retrain botth methods on our dataset by concatenating the RGB image and the instance mask image into a 4-channel RGB-M image as the new input. Specifically, for PIFu, instead of the stacked hourglass network [24] designed for human-related tasks, ResNet34 is set as the encoder backbone and we extract the features before every pooling layers in ResNet to obtain feature embeddings. For Onet and TF, we use the original encoder and decoder networks and adjust the dimensions of the corresponding latent codes to be equal to those in our method.

Qualitative Comparison. To prove that our method adapts to real-world images, we collect several images from Kitti [21], CityScapes [7], ApolloScape [35], CCPD[1], SCD [17] and Internet. As shown in Fig. 4, our approach generates more robust results when compared with PIFu, while recovering much more texture details than the combination of Onet and TextureField.

Table 1. Quantitative Evaluation using the FID and SSIM metrics on our dataset. For SSIM, larger is better; for FID, smaller is better. Our method achieves best in both two terms.

Method	FID ↓	SSIM ↑
PIFu*	215.8	0.6962
Onet+TF*	262.73	0.7002
Ours(w/o local feature fusion)	156.8	0.7057
Ours	**148.2**	**0.7208**
Ours(w/o joint training)	193.6	0.6902
Ours(MPV as the template)	173.2	0.6895
Ours(coupe as the template)	159.7	0.6983
Ours(sphere as the template)	187.4	0.6833

Quantitative Comparison. To quantitatively evaluate the reconstruction quality of different methods, we use two metrics: Structure similarity image metric (SSIM) [36] and Frechet inception distance (FID) [14]. These two metrics can respectively measure local and global quality of images. The SSIM is a local score that measures the distance between the rendered image and the ground truth on a per-instance basis (larger is better). FID is widely used in the GAN evaluation to evaluate perceptual distributions between a predicted image and ground truth. It is worth noting that both SSIM and FID can not evaluate the quality of generated texture of 3D objects directly. All textured 3D objects must be rendered into 2D images from the same viewpoints of ground truth. To get a more convincing result, for each generated 3D textured model, we render it from 10 different views and evaluate the scores between renderings and corresponding ground truth albedo images. As shown in Tab. 1, our method gives significantly better results in FID term and achieves state-of-the art result in SSIM term, proving that our 3D models preserve stable and fine details under multi-view observations. The quantitative results agree with the performance illustrated in qualitative comparison.

We also implement a variant of our method which does not fuse local features for the purpose of fair comparison. As shown in Tab. 1, our reconstruction conditioned on global latent codes still outperforms 'Onet+TF', demonstrating that our representation is more expressive in terms of inferring the texture on the vehicle surface.

---

[1] https://github.com/nicolas-gervais/predicting-car-price-from-scraped-data/tree/master/picture-scraper.

6   Conclusion

In this paper, we have introduced VERTEX, a novel method for monocular vehicle reconstruction in real-world traffic scenarios. Experiments demonstrate that our method can recover 3D vehicle models with robust and detailed texture from a monocular image. Based on the proposed implicit semantic template mapping, we have presented a new geometry-texture joint representation to constrain texture distribution on the template surface. We believe the proposed implicit geo-tex representation can further inspire 3D learning tasks on other classes of objects sharing a strong template prior.

Acknowledgements. This paper is supported by the National Key Research and Development Program of China [2018YFB2100500].

References

1. Beker, D., et al.: Monocular differentiable rendering for self-supervised 3D object detection (2020)
2. Carr, J.C., Beatson, R.K., Cherrie, J.B., Mitchell, T.J., Evans, T.R.: Reconstruction and representation of 3D objects with radial basis functions. In: Computer Graphics (2001)
3. Chan, E.R., Monteiro, M., Kellnhofer, P., Wu, J., Wetzstein, G.: pi-GAN: periodic implicit generative adversarial networks for 3D-aware image synthesis. In: Proceedings of the IEEE/CVF Conference on Computer Vision and Pattern Recognition, pp. 5799–5809 (2021)
4. Chang, A.X., et al.: An information-rich 3D model repository. Comput. Sci. (2015)
5. Chen, Z., Zhang, H.: Learning implicit fields for generative shape modeling. In: 2019 IEEE/CVF Conference on Computer Vision and Pattern Recognition (CVPR) (2019)
6. Choy, C.B., Xu, D., Gwak, J.Y., Chen, K., Savarese, S.: 3D-R2N2: A Unified Approach for Single and Multi-view 3D object reconstruction. In: Leibe, B., Matas, J., Sebe, N., Welling, M. (eds.) ECCV 2016. LNCS, vol. 9912, pp. 628–644. Springer, Cham (2016). https://doi.org/10.1007/978-3-319-46484-8_38
7. Cordts, M., et al.: The cityscapes dataset for semantic urban scene understanding. 2016 IEEE Conference on Computer Vision and Pattern Recognition (CVPR), pp. 3213–3223 (2016)
8. Deng, Y., Yang, J., Tong, X.: Deformed implicit field: Modeling 3D shapes with learned dense correspondence. In: Proceedings of the IEEE/CVF Conference on Computer Vision and Pattern Recognition, pp. 10286–10296 (2021)
9. Deng, Y., Yang, J., Xiang, J., Tong, X.: Gram: generative radiance manifolds for 3D-aware image generation. In: Proceedings of the IEEE/CVF Conference on Computer Vision and Pattern Recognition, pp. 10673–10683 (2022)
10. Goel, S., Kanazawa, A., Malik, J.: Shape and viewpoint without keypoints. In: Vedaldi, A., Bischof, H., Brox, T., Frahm, J.-M. (eds.) ECCV 2020. LNCS, vol. 12360, pp. 88–104. Springer, Cham (2020). https://doi.org/10.1007/978-3-030-58555-6_6

11. Gropp, A., Yariv, L., Haim, N., Atzmon, M., Lipman, Y.: Implicit geometric regularization for learning shapes. arXiv:2002.10099 (2020)
12. He, K., Zhang, X., Ren, S., Sun, J.: Deep residual learning for image recognition. In: Proceedings of the IEEE Conference on Computer Vision and Pattern Recognition, pp. 770–778 (2016)
13. Henderson, P., Tsiminaki, V., Lampert, C.: Leveraging 2D data to learn textured 3D mesh generation. In: IEEE Conference on Computer Vision and Pattern Recognition (CVPR) (2020)
14. Heusel, M., Ramsauer, H., Unterthiner, T., Nessler, B., Hochreiter, S.: GANs trained by a two time-scale update rule converge to a local NASH equilibrium. In: Advances in Neural Information Processing Systems, pp. 6626–6637 (2017)
15. Kaiming, H., Georgia, G., Piotr, D., Ross, G.: Mask R-CNN. IEEE Trans. Pattern Anal. Mach. Intell, pp. 1–1 (2017)
16. Kanazawa, A., Tulsiani, S., Efros, A.A., Malik, J.: Learning category-specific mesh reconstruction from image collections. In: Proceedings of the European Conference on Computer Vision (ECCV) (2018)
17. Krause, J., Stark, M., Deng, J., Fei-Fei, L.: 3D object representations for fine-grained categorization. In: 4th International IEEE Workshop on 3D Representation and Recognition (3dRR-13). Sydney, Australia (2013)
18. Lalonde, J.F,et al.: The Laval HDR sky database. http://sky.hdrdb.com (2016)
19. Li, W., et al.: AADS: Augmented autonomous driving simulation using data-driven algorithms. Science Robotics 4 (2019)
20. Meng, D., et al.: Parsing-based view-aware embedding network for vehicle re-identification. In: Proceedings of the IEEE/CVF Conference on Computer Vision and Pattern Recognition (CVPR) June 2020
21. Menze, M., Heipke, C., Geiger, A.: Object scene flow. ISPRS J. Photogrammetry Remote Sens.(JPRS) (2018)
22. Mescheder, L., Oechsle, M., Niemeyer, M., Nowozin, S., Geiger, A.: Occupancy networks: learning 3D reconstruction in function space. In: 2019 IEEE/CVF Conference on Computer Vision and Pattern Recognition (CVPR) (2019)
23. Miao, H., Lu, F., Liu, Z., Zhang, L., Manocha, D., Zhou, B.: Robust 2D/3D vehicle parsing in CVIS (2021)
24. Newell, A., Yang, K., Deng, J.: Stacked Hourglass Networks for Human Pose Estimation. In: Leibe, B., Matas, J., Sebe, N., Welling, M. (eds.) ECCV 2016. LNCS, vol. 9912, pp. 483–499. Springer, Cham (2016). https://doi.org/10.1007/978-3-319-46484-8_29
25. Niemeyer, M., Geiger, A.: Giraffe: representing scenes as compositional generative neural feature fields. In: Proceedings of the IEEE/CVF Conference on Computer Vision and Pattern Recognition, pp. 11453–11464 (2021)
26. Oechsle, M., Mescheder, L., Niemeyer, M., Strauss, T., Geiger, A.: Texture fields: learning texture representations in function space. In: Proceedings IEEE International Conf. on Computer Vision (ICCV) (2019)
27. Park, E., Yang, J., Yumer, E., Ceylan, D., Berg, A.C.: Transformation-grounded image generation network for novel 3D view synthesis. In: 2017 IEEE Conference on Computer Vision and Pattern Recognition (CVPR) (2017)
28. Park, J.J., Florence, P., Straub, J., Newcombe, R., Lovegrove, S.: DeepSDF: Learning continuous signed distance functions for shape representation. In: The IEEE Conference on Computer Vision and Pattern Recognition (CVPR) June 2019
29. Pharr, M., Jakob, W., Humphreys, G.: Physically based rendering: from theory to implementation. Morgan Kaufmann (2016)

30. Ronneberger, O., Fischer, P., Brox, T.: U-Net: Convolutional Networks for Biomedical Image Segmentation. In: Navab, N., Hornegger, J., Wells, W.M., Frangi, A.F. (eds.) MICCAI 2015. LNCS, vol. 9351, pp. 234–241. Springer, Cham (2015). https://doi.org/10.1007/978-3-319-24574-4_28

31. Saito, S., Huang, Z., Natsume, R., Morishima, S., Li, H., Kanazawa, A.: PIFU: pixel-aligned implicit function for high-resolution clothed human digitization. In: 2019 IEEE/CVF International Conference on Computer Vision (ICCV) (2019)

32. Shen, C., O"Brien, J.F., Shewchuk, J.R.: Interpolating and approximating implicit surfaces from polygon soup. ACM Trans. Graph. **23**(3), pp. 896–904 (2004)https://doi.org/10.1145/1186562.1015816

33. Sun, Y., Liu, Z., Wang, Y., Sarma, S.E.: Im2avatar: colorful 3D reconstruction from a single image (2018)

34. Turk, G., O'Brien, J.F.: Modelling with implicit surfaces that interpolate. ACM Trans. Graph. **21**(4), 855–873 (2002)

35. Wang, P., Huang, X., Cheng, X., Zhou, D., Geng, Q., Yang, R.: The apolloscape open dataset for autonomous driving and its application. IEEE Trans. pattern. Anal. Mach. Intell (2019)

36. Wang, Z., Bovik, A.C., Sheikh, H.R., Simoncelli, E.P.: Image quality assessment: from error visibility to structural similarity. IEEE Trans. Image Process. **13**(4), 600–612 (2004)

37. Xu, Q., Wang, W., Ceylan, D., Mech, R., Neumann, U.: DISN: Deep implicit surface network for high-quality single-view 3D reconstruction. In: Advances in Neural Information Processing Systems 32 (2019)

38. Xu, Y., Peng, S., Yang, C., Shen, Y., Zhou, B.: 3D-aware image synthesis via learning structural and textural representations. In: Proceedings of the IEEE/CVF Conference on Computer Vision and Pattern Recognition, pp. 18430–18439 (2022)

39. Zheng, Z., Yu, T., Dai, Q., Liu, Y.: Deep implicit templates for 3D shape representation (2020)

40. Zhu, J.Y., et al.: Visual object networks: Image generation with disentangled 3D representations. In: Advances in Neural Information Processing Systems 31 (2018)

TAR-Net: A Triple Attention Residual Network for Power Line Extraction from Infrared Aerial Images

Lei Yang[✉], Shuyi Kong, Hanyun Huang, and Heng Li

School of Electrical and Information Engineering, Zhengzhou University, Zhengzhou 450001, Henan, China
leiyang2019@zzu.edu.com

Abstract. Transmission line segmentation is of great significance for the intelligent power inspection, which could well serve the path planning and navigation of different inspection platforms. Combined with the strong context extraction ability, deep learning has provided an effective means for pixel-level image segmentation. However, the power lines are always against with complex natural environment, such as different lighting conditions, different visibility, different natural environment, etc, which will bring a great effect for accurate power line extraction from aerial images. Meanwhile, compared with the background environment, the image pixels of the power line account for a small proportion, which will lead to the problem of unbalanced pixel proportion, and it also will affect the whole segmentation performance. Faced with the above issues, with the encoder-decoder framework, a triple attention residual network, namely TAR-Net, is proposed in this paper for accurate power line extraction from aerial images. To realize effective feature extraction, a residual U-Net network is built to acquire strong contexts. Faced with the class imbalance issue, a triple attention block is proposed to make the segmentation network better focus on the power lines. Further, a dense convolution block is proposed for feature enhancement of local feature maps. Combined with public data sets on infrared aerial images, experiment results show that the proposed segmentation network could acquire a better segmentation performance on power lines against complex environments compared with other advanced segmentation models.

Keywords: Power lines · Deep learning · Residual network · Triple attention

1 Introduction

With the rapid development of smart grid, the market scale of power grid worldwide continues to expand, and various inspection technologies also have got rapid development. Because the traditional human detection technology is very dangerous and consumes a lot of time, manpower and material resources. Therefore,

© The Author(s), under exclusive license to Springer Nature Switzerland AG 2022
L. Fang et al. (Eds.): CICAI 2022, LNAI 13604, pp. 647–657, 2022.
https://doi.org/10.1007/978-3-031-20497-5_53

automatic inspection methods, such as unmanned aerial vehicles (UAVs) [12], line inspection robots [10], hybrid inspection robots [2] and other technologies, could well replace the traditional manual inspection methods to realize efficient and high-quality power inspection. For the above inspection platforms, the path planning and navigation rely on accurate power line extraction. However, the power lines are always against with complex natural environment, such as different lighting conditions, different visibility and different natural environment (lakes, hills, grasslands, forests, etc.), which will bring a great effect for accurate power line extraction from aerial images. Therefore, the accurate power line extraction is a meaningful but challenging task for smart grid.

To improve the detection efficiency and accuracy, researchers have proposed different detection schemes for automatic power line extraction. In order to extract features more effectively, Zhang *et al.* proposed a pixel statistical method based on the gray level co-occurrence matrix for image segmentation from insulator images [16]. Jaffari *et al.* proposed a focal phi loss to solve the problem of low segmentation accuracy caused by class imbalance issue, and introduced a convolution auxiliary classifier in vanilla U-net to improve the convergence speed of the model [5]. To make the segmentation network acquire more useful contexts, combined with a channel attention block and spatial attention block, Yang *et al.* proposed a power line extraction network, namely PLE-Net, for automatic and accurate power line segmentation [11]. Meanwhile, fused with the dilated convolution, a multi-branch network block was proposed for feature enhancement of local feature maps. Experiments had shown that it could acquire a better detection performance on power line extraction. Faced with multi-scale objects caused by shooting distances, to enhance the detection ability on multi-scale power lines, Yang *et al.* proposed a deep attention fusion network for power line extraction from aerial images [13]. Based on the different feature representation abilities, an attention fusion network block was proposed for effective feature aggregation of multi-scale features from the different network layers in attention U-net. To make the main segmentation network generate more accurate segmentation results, Chang *et al.* proposed a conditional generative adversarial network for over head ground wire segmentation [1]. Through the game learning of the generator and discriminator, the optimal segmentation results could be acquired. Combined with multi-scale feature fusion, Gao *et al.* proposed a parallel branch network for overhead power line segmentation [3]. Inspired by the above research work on power line extraction, based on the advantage of effective feature representation of deep convolution networks, a deep segmentation network is proposed in this paper for end-to-end power line extraction.

Based on the above discussion, this paper proposes a triple attention residual network, namely TAR-Net, for accurate power line extraction from aerial images. Combined with public data set on power line extraction, experimental results show that the proposed TAR-Net network could achieve a better segmentation performance compared with other classical segmentation networks, which further confirms the superiority and effectiveness of proposed TAR-Net network. The main contributions of this paper are as follows:

(1) In order to segment transmission lines more accurately, a deep segmentation network is proposed for end-to-end power line extraction.
(2) For effective feature representation, a residual U-Net network is built to act as the backbone network to acquire strong contexts.
(3) Faced with power line extraction with class imbalance issue, a triple attention block is proposed to make the segmentation network better focus on the power lines.
(4) A dense convolution block is proposed to embed into the bottleneck layer for feature enhancement to acquire multi-scale contexts.

The rest of this paper is arranged as follows. Section 2 gives the details about proposed TAR-Net and each network block in detail. Section 3 introduces the details of the experimental data set. Section 4 is about the experimental results and analysis. The conclusions of this paper are given in Sect. 5.

2 Proposed Method

In order to complete the accurate detection task of transmission lines, a deep segmentation network, namely TAR-Net, is proposed in this paper for automatic and accurate power line extraction. This section will describes the whole network framework and each network block in detail.

2.1 Overview of Proposed TAR-Net

To serve the path planning and navigation of intelligent inspection platforms, this paper proposes a TAR-Net network to provide an end-to-end power line detection scheme. Figure 1 shows the whole network structure of proposed TAR-Net network.

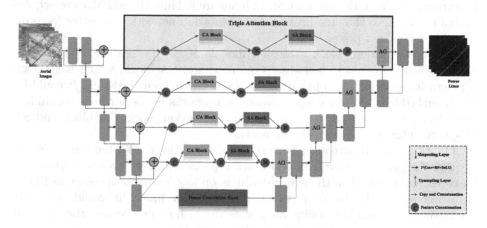

Fig. 1. Network framework of the proposed TAR-Net network.

As shown in Fig. 1, it includes three main parts: a backbone network, a triple attention block, and a dense convolution block. For effective feature representation, due to the success of residual network [4], a residual U-Net network is built in this paper to act as the backbone network to acquire strong contexts. On the basis, for feature enhancement of local feature maps, a dense convolution block is proposed to embed into the bottleneck layer to acquire multi-scale contexts.

Meanwhile, due to the ineffective processing of local feature maps by skip connections, it will cause the semantic gap issue. Here, a triple attention block is proposed to optimize the skip connections. And it could also address the class imbalance issue to make the segmentation network better focus on the power lines.

Further, multiple pooling operations could make the segmentation network acquire more complex and high-level contexts, but they will also cause the information loss on details. Faced with the information loss issue, a feature fusion scheme [14] is adopted to aggregate the high-level and low-level features.

2.2   Triple Attention Block

For the power line extraction from aerial images, compared with the background environment, the image pixels of the power lines only account for a small-scale proportion, which will lead to the problem of unbalanced pixel proportion, and it also will affect the whole segmentation performance. To make the segmentation network better focus on the power lines and suppress some unnecessary features, a triple attention block is proposed to optimize the skip connections for effective processing of local feature maps, as shown in Fig. 2 and 3, which is composed by a channel attention (CA) block, a spatial attention (SA) block and an attention gated (AG) block.

During the triple attention block, the input feature maps are first processed by a spatial attention block and a channel attention block to obtain the attention feature maps. Then, the output feature maps are fed into the AG block to acquire global contexts, so that the proposed segmentation network can better focus on the target pixels of power lines.

The convolutional block attention module (CBAM) (see Fig. 2) is a typical dual-attention block, including CA block and SA block, which has shown a promising performance optimization ability on different tasks [9]. It could be easily embedded into any deep convolution networks for performance optimization. Here, it is adopted to act as the dual-attention block: CA block and SA block, to optimize the raw skip connections.

On the basis of attention feature maps from the dual-attention block, to acquire the global contexts, an AG block is proposed to suppress the irrelevant features, and strengthen the learning ability on key features, as shown in Fig. 3.

Combined with the proposed triple attention block, it could not only strengthen the learning ability on key features, but also reduce the effect of the semantic gap issue caused by the skip connections.

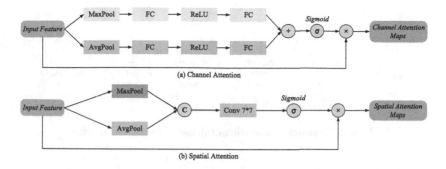

(a) Channel Attention

(b) Spatial Attention

Fig. 2. Network framework of channel attention block and spatial attention block.

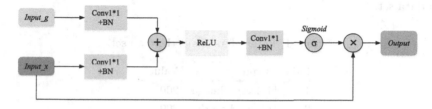

Fig. 3. Network framework of attention gated block.

2.3 Dense Convolution Block

Due to limited receptive field, the residual U-Net network exists a certain limitations on multi-scale feature representation. To address this issue, a dense convolution block is proposed to embed into the bottleneck layer for feature enhancement of local feature maps, as shown in Fig. 4.

As shown in Fig. 4, though the concatenation of multiple convolutions, different receptive fields could be acquired, which could be used for effective feature processing of local feature maps to acquire multi-scale contexts.

3 Experimental Data

The suitable dataset is the premise for the model evaluation. Here, a public infrared aerial image set collected by Turkish electric power company is used for model evaluation, which includes the infrared aerial images and their corresponding label images.

By observing this data set, all the aerial images have the characteristics of strong noise interference, poor contrast and class imbalance issue, which could be well used for model evaluation.

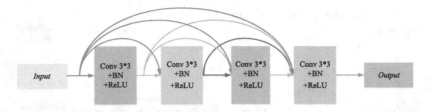

Fig. 4. Network framework of dense convolution block.

For the infrared aerial image set of power lines, there are 200 samples of infrared images and 200 corresponding ground truth. Table 1 gives the details of this data set.

Table 1. Parameters about the data set.

Index	Type	Value
1	Infrared images	200
2	Ground truth	200
3	Image size	512 * 512
4	Division ratio	8:2

4   Experimental Results and Analysis

In this part, the detection performance of proposed TAR-Net network on aerial images is tested in detail. Comparative experiments and ablation experiments are carried out to verify the effectiveness of proposed TAR-Net network.

First of all, the evaluation indicators are introduced in this paper for performance evaluation. Then, the implementation details of proposed TAR-Net network are briefly introduced. Finally, the ablation experiments and comparative experiments are carried out to verify the superiority of the proposed TAR-Net network in this paper.

4.1   Evaluation Index

In order to better evaluate the proposed TAR-Net network, some suitable evaluation indexes are introduced for performance analysis.

1. Accuracy: It is the proportion of correct predicted image pixels to the total image pixels, as shown in Eq. 1.

$$Accuracy = \frac{T_p + T_n}{T_p + T_n + F_p + F_n} \tag{1}$$

where T_p indicates true positive, T_n indicates true negative, F_p indicates false positive and F_n indicates false negative.

2. Dice Coefficient: It is used to calculate the similarity of predicted mask and ground truth.

$$Dice = \frac{2|P \bigcap G|}{|P| + |G|} \tag{2}$$

where P indicates the predicted mask, and G indicates the ground truth.

3. Mean Intersection over Union (mIOU): The average recognition accuracy of different categories is also an important index to measure the segmentation performance of different models.

$$mIOU = \frac{T_p}{T_p + F_p + F_n} \tag{3}$$

4.2   Implementation Details

For the proposed TAR-Net network, it is built with the PaddlePaddle framework. To speed up the model evaluation, the NVIDIA Tesla V100 GPU with 32 GB memory is selected for model training and test. It is embedded into a server with 4 cores CPU with 32 GB memory and 100 GB disk.

Here, the rmsprop optimizer is set the optimizer to guide the model training, and the initial learning rate is set as 0.001. Due to the advantage of the binary cross entropy loss function on classification tasks, it is set as the loss function. The training epoch is set as 100, and the batch size is set as 2.

4.3   Ablation Experiment

In order to test the influence of each network block to the whole segmentation performance of proposed TAR-Net network, the ablation experiments are carried out in this part to verify the effectiveness of each network block, such as residual network, triple attention block, and dense convolution block. Here, the typical U-Net [8] is set as the baseline network.

Here, for the ablation experiment, different network configurations are proposed, such as baseline network, baseline network with triple attention block (Baseline+TA), baseline network with dense convolution block (Baseline+Dense), and baseline network with residual network (Baseline+Res). Based on the public data set of infrared aerial images, the specific ablation experiment results are shown in Table 2.

Compared with the background environment, the image pixels of the power line account for a small proportion, which will lead to the problem of imbalanced pixel proportion. As shown in Table 2, due to the higher accuracy and lower Dice score and mIOU value, it is caused by the this class imbalanced issue.

Compared with the baseline, fused with these network blocks individually, such as residual network, triple attention block, and dense convolution block, the segmentation precision both has got improved which could prove the effectiveness of each network block on performance optimization.

Table 2. Ablation experiment results of proposed TAR-Net network.

Index	Method	Accuracy	Dice	mIOU
1	Baseline	0.9909	0.8271	0.8511
2	Baseline+TA	0.9962	0.8623	0.8770
3	Baseline+Dense	0.9969	0.8560	0.8725
4	Baseline+Res	0.9967	0.8538	0.8727
5	Proposed	0.9970	0.8809	0.8920

On the basis of baseline network, fused with the above network blocks to the baseline network, the proposed TAR-Net network has been built. As shown in Table 2, the proposed TAR-Net network could acquire the highest segmentation precision on the public data set of infrared aerial images, which could indicates the effectiveness of network configuration of proposed TAR-Net network.

4.4 Comparative Experiment

To better show the superiority of proposed TAR-Net network on power line extraction, some typical segmentation networks, including Deeplabv3 [15], PSPnet [6], U-Net [8], AttUNet [7], are selected for performance comparison. Combined with the public data set of infrared aerial images and introduced evaluation indexes, the specific experimental results are shown in Table 3.

Table 3. Comparative experiment on infrared aerial image set.

Index	Method	Accuracy	Dice	mIOU
1	AttUNet	0.9966	0.8658	0.8511
2	Deeplabv3	0.9936	0.7554	0.8770
3	PSPnet	0.9949	0.7173	0.7768
4	U-Net	0.9909	0.8271	0.8511
5	Proposed	0.9970	0.8809	0.8920

As shown in Table 3, the proposed TAR-Net network could acquire the highest value on each evaluation index, which could prove that the proposed TAR-Net network has shown a better segmentation performance on the infrared aerial images compared with other advanced segmentation models.

4.5 Qualitative Analysis

In order to better demonstrate the segmentation performance of proposed TAR-Net network, this subsection has carried out the visualization experiments on the infrared aerial images to directly show the segmentation results. Here, some sample images from test set are selected as experiment samples for performance visualization. Figure 5 shows the specific segmentation results of different samples.

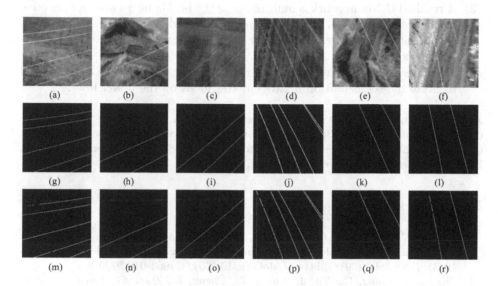

Fig. 5. Segmentation results of different samples. (a–f) Raw infrared aerial images; (g–l) Ground truth; (m–r) Predicted masks by proposed TAR-Net network.

As shown in Fig. 5, it could be seen that the proposed TAR-Net network can accurately extract the power lines from infrared aerial images against complex characteristics, such as strong noise interference, poor contrast and class imbalance issue, which could further prove the effectiveness of proposed TAR-Net network.

However, the proposed TAR-Net network also exists a ceratin shortcoming on high-precision power line extraction. As shown in Fig. 5, the above segmentation results by proposed TAR-Net network also exist some less segmentation areas due to poor contrast or similar texture. In the future work, we will continue this research work for further performance optimization to develop an effective and high-precision power line extraction model.

5   Conclusion

Faced with accurate segmentation task of power lines against complex characteristics, such as strong noise interference, poor contrast and class imbalance issue, a triple attention residual network, namely TAR-Net, is proposed for accurate power line extraction from infrared aerial images. Combined with the public data set of infrared aerial images, experiments have proven the effectiveness and superiority of proposed TAR-Net network on power line extraction. The main conclusions are drawn as follows.

(1) A deep TAR-Net network is proposed for end-to-end and accurate power line extraction from infrared aerial images.
(2) A residual U-Net network is built to act as the backbone network for effective feature representation. Meanwhile, a dense convolution block is proposed to embed into the bottleneck layer for feature enhancement to acquire multi-scale contexts.
(3) To address with the class imbalance issue, a triple attention block is proposed to make the segmentation network better focus on the power lines.

Acknowledgment. This work was supported by the National Natural Science Foundation of China (No. 62003309), the National Key Research & Development Project of China (2020YFB1313701) and Outstanding Foreign Scientist Support Project in Henan Province of China (No. GZS2019008).

References

1. Chang, W., Yang, G., Li, E., Liang, Z.: Toward a cluttered environment for learning-based multi-scale overhead ground wire recognition. Neural Process. Lett. **48**(3), 1789–1800 (2018). https://doi.org/10.1007/s11063-018-9799-3
2. Chang, W., Yang, G., Yu, J., Liang, Z., Cheng, L., Zhou, C.: Development of a power line inspection robot with hybrid operation modes. In: 2017 IEEE/RSJ International Conference on Intelligent Robots and Systems (IROS), pp. 973–978. IEEE (2017)
3. Gao, Z., Yang, G., Li, E., Liang, Z., Guo, R.: Efficient parallel branch network with multi-scale feature fusion for real-time overhead power line segmentation. IEEE Sens. J. **21**(10), 12220–12227 (2021)
4. He, K., Zhang, X., Ren, S., Sun, J.: Deep residual learning for image recognition. In: Proceedings of the IEEE Conference on Computer Vision and Pattern Recognition, pp. 770–778 (2016)
5. Jaffari, R., Hashmani, M.A., Reyes-Aldasoro, C.C.: A novel focal phi loss for power line segmentation with auxiliary classifier U-NET. Sensors **21**(8), 2803 (2021)
6. Li, Z., Guo, Y.: Semantic segmentation of landslide images in Nyingchi region based on PSPNet network. In: 2020 7th International Conference on Information Science and Control Engineering (ICISCE), pp. 1269–1273. IEEE (2020)
7. Oktay, O., et al.: Attention U-Net: learning where to look for the pancreas. arXiv preprint arXiv:1804.03999 (2018)
8. Ronneberger, O., Fischer, P., Brox, T.: U-Net: convolutional networks for biomedical image segmentation. In: Navab, N., Hornegger, J., Wells, W.M., Frangi, A.F. (eds.) MICCAI 2015. LNCS, vol. 9351, pp. 234–241. Springer, Cham (2015). https://doi.org/10.1007/978-3-319-24574-4_28
9. Woo, S., Park, J., Lee, J.-Y., Kweon, I.S.: CBAM: convolutional block attention module. In: Ferrari, V., Hebert, M., Sminchisescu, C., Weiss, Y. (eds.) ECCV 2018. LNCS, vol. 11211, pp. 3–19. Springer, Cham (2018). https://doi.org/10.1007/978-3-030-01234-2_1

10. Wu, G., Xiao, X., Xiao, H., Dai, J., Huang, Z.: Motion planning of non-collision obstacles overcoming for high-voltage power transmission-line inspection robot. In: Xiong, C., Huang, Y., Xiong, Y., Liu, H. (eds.) ICIRA 2008. LNCS (LNAI), vol. 5314, pp. 1195–1205. Springer, Heidelberg (2008). https://doi.org/10.1007/978-3-540-88513-9_127

11. Yang, L., Fan, J., Huo, B., Li, E., Liu, Y.: PLE-Net: automatic power line extraction method using deep learning from aerial images. Expert Syst. Appl. **198**, 116771 (2022)

12. Yang, L., Fan, J., Liu, Y., Li, E., Peng, J., Liang, Z.: A review on state-of-the-art power line inspection techniques. IEEE Trans. Instrum. Meas. **69**(12), 9350–9365 (2020)

13. Yang, L., Fan, J., Xu, S., Li, E., Liu, Y.: Vision-based power line segmentation with an attention fusion network. IEEE Sens. J. **22**(8), 8196–8205 (2022)

14. Yang, L., Wang, H., Huo, B., Li, F., Liu, Y.: An automatic welding defect location algorithm based on deep learning. NDT & E Int. **120**, 102435 (2021)

15. Yu, L., et al.: A lightweight complex-valued DeepLabv3+ for semantic segmentation of PolSAR image. IEEE J. Sel. Top. Appl. Earth Obs. Remote Sens. **15**, 930–943 (2022)

16. Zhang, L.P., Zhao, J.M., Ren, Y.F.: Research on multiple features extraction technology of insulator images. In: 2018 10th International Conference on Modelling, Identification and Control (ICMIC), pp. 1–6. IEEE (2018)

Deep Dynamic-Range Compression
of Infrared Video Camera

Bingcai Sun[1(✉)], Chengjia Wang[2], Jinrui Deng[1], Ying Zhang[2],
and Xueqi Wang[1]

[1] CNPC Research Institute of Safety and Environment Technology, Beijing, China
zkl2008826@163.com
[2] Nanjing Zhipu Technology Co., Ltd., Nanjing, China

Abstract. The visualization of infrared (IR) spectral videos in the high
dynamic range (HDR) is a great challenge for traditional display devices.
It is necessary to extend its display range of IR videos for user perception.
This research aims at leveraging the deep learning approach to adaptive
transform IR videos from the high data bits to the low data bits, which
is deep dynamic-range compression (DC). We propose a DC transformer
(IRDC-Former) to implement adaptive DC of IR video cameras. The
simplicity and feasibility of IRDC-Former are demonstrated by HDR
infrared videos in different scenes. The demo video is available at https://
v.youku.com/v_show/id_XNTg4MDIyNzQ5Mg==.html.

Keywords: Dynamic-range compression · Artificial intelligence ·
Infrared spectral camera

1 Introduction

Recent developments in various applications of the IR camera have heightened
the need for a HDR infrared videos [1]. The visualization of IR videos in the
HDR (14-bit), however, is extremely difficult on conventional display devices (8-
bit) [3]. It has become a pivotal bottleneck limiting the promotion of IR cameras
in practical applications [2,12,14,18,19].

The existing approaches of DC include statistics [7,13] and image transformation [4,11]. Statistics refers to the use of statistical information, such as mean,
variance, and histogram, for DC of IR cameras. The image transformation of IR
videos is a simple linear transformation of the data bits. However, all of these
previously mentioned methods are based on a certain mathematical model and
cannot handle a wide range of tasks.

The goal of our research is to explore a general technology [17] of artificial
intelligence to account for the visualization of IR spectral videos in the high
dynamic range. For this purpose, we demonstrate a deep learning-based approach, Dynamic-range Compression Transformer (IRDC-Former), which integrates the framework of U-Net [9] and Transformer [10] to implement adaptive
DC of IR spectral cameras.

This work was supported by the research project of CNPC (2020D-4626).

2   Framework Design

Our main goal is to apply DC to the IR RAW data with deep network adaptively. The input is the 14-bit RAW data and the output is the 8 bit images range from 0 to 255. The overall pipeline of our Dynamic-range Compression Transformer (IRDC-Former) is built on U-Net [9], and the loss function is L1-norm. As shown in Fig. 1, the left side is the encoder to extract features, The right side is the decoder which output the encoder features as images. The advantage of U-Net is providing the hierarchical multi-scale representation while remaining computationally efficient. The original U-Net is based on convolution operator which has local connectivity and translation equivariance. However, the convolution operator has limited receptive field and cannot adapt to the input content due to the static weights at inference. With the popularity of transformer structure [5,6,10] in recent two years, we replace the convolution operator with transformer to capture global dependencies.

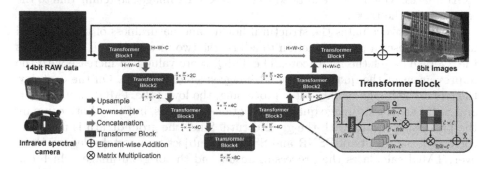

Fig. 1. The structure of Dynamic-range Compression Transformer (IRDC-Former).

First, We apply a convolution operator to the input RAW data $I \in R^{H \times W \times 3}$ to get the low-level feature embedding $F \in R^{H \times W \times C}$. Then we obtain the multi-level representation by U-Net, the encode features are concatenated with the decode features with skip connection. Each level of encoder-decoder adopts transformer block to extract features. For input feature map $X \in R^{\hat{H} \times \hat{W} \times \hat{C}}$, our IRDC-Former generates query (Q), key (K) and value (V) projections. We reshape query and key projections and generate the transposed-attention map A with dot-product interaction, the size of attention map A is $\hat{C} \times \hat{C}$. We get the feature map of $\hat{H}\hat{W} \times \hat{C}$ with the dot multiplication of attention map A and value (V) projection. The $\hat{H}\hat{W} \times \hat{C}$ feature map is reshaped to original size $\hat{H} \times \hat{W} \times \hat{C}$ and added with the input feature map X to get the he final output $\hat{X}$. Transformer block not only emphasizes the local context information, but also implicitly models the global context information relationship between pixels. The final refined features are added to the original image as a residual image to obtain an 8 bit stretched output image.

3   Experimental Evaluation

3.1   Experimental Setup

We use the handheld IR spectral camera to capture 10 dynamic video sequences in daily life scenes, including a total of 5615 pictures. The dataset contains some special scenes, containing high radiation objects such as soldering irons and engines, and low radiation objects such as the sky and iron sheets. To ensure rational experimental settings, all images are randomly divided into training and test sets at a ratio of 9:1. The input image in our experiment is the 14-bit original RAW data obtained by the handheld IR spectral camera, and the groundtruth image is the manually corrected image. The size of each image of is 288×384 with a batch size of 14 and the learning rate is set to $3e^{-4}$. The training and testing servers are equipped with two Nvidia GeForce RTX 3090s. For the accuracy of evaluation, the experimental evaluation criteria are selected as PSNR, SSIM [15] and TMQI [16]. TMQI is a metric used to evaluate the tone mapping result of RGB images, which can be applied to the task of IR image stretching due to the similarity of the tasks.

TMQI first evaluates the structural fidelity and naturalness of the stretched image, then uses a power function to adjust the two measures, and finally takes the average to get the final score. The TMQI score value will increase with the improvement of the quality of the IR image stretching result. On the contrary, the worse the image quality after processing, the lower the TMQI value. PSNR and SSIM are classic image quality evaluation indicators, but they both compare the processing results with the groundtruth. Since the groundtruth is manually corrected, the results of PSNR and SSIM are subject to a certain degree. However, TMQI calculates the processing result and the original image, which can reasonably analyze the fidelity and naturalness of the processed image. Therefore, the TMQI score is more convincing than other evaluation criteria.

3.2   Comparative Evaluation

Table 1. Average TMQI/SSIM/PSNR results of different methods.

Methods	CLAHE	LGT	ILGT	HE	Ours
TMQI ↑	0.82	0.83	0.86	0.91	0.92
SSIM ↑	0.64	0.63	0.74	0.75	0.86
PSNR ↑	14.59	14.64	19.28	17.44	21.97

We compare IRDC-Former with four classical methods: 1) Linear grayscale transformation (LGT): extend or compress the entire effective range of the image gray level into the required dynamic range according to a linear relationship; 2)

Improved linear grayscale transformation (ILGT) [4]: use histogram information to count a fixed number of points at the beginning and end to determine
a reasonable grayscale range to be processed. And the grayscale range to be
stretched to the required dynamic range according to the linear relationship; 3)
Histogram equalization (HE): The purpose of histogram equalization is to convert the input image into the output image whose each gray level has roughly
the same number of pixels. That is, the number of pixels in each gray level of
the output image is basically the same; 4) Contrast Limited Adaptive Histogram
Equalization (CLAHE [8]): based on histogram Image equalization, limiting the
height of the local histogram to limit the enhancement of the local contrast, and
realize the DC of the whole image (Fig. 2).

The results are all evaluated against the same test sets. Table 1 shows the
stretching results of each algorithm on IR images. IRDC-former achieves state-
of-the-art performance on all metrics, outperforming existing methods such as
LGT, ILGT, HE and CLAHE. The superiority of IRDC-Former in TMQI score
allows it to reasonably consider the whole and details of the image for IR image
stretching when it is applied to realistic scenarios (Figs. 3, 4, 5, 6, 7, 8, 9, 10, 11,
12, 13 and 14).

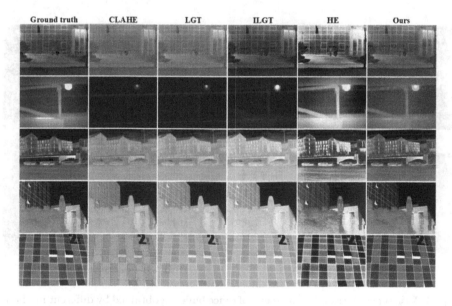

Fig. 2. Visual comparison for stretching results obtained by different methods.

Fig. 3. Visual comparison for the scene of chemical plant entrance obtained by different methods.

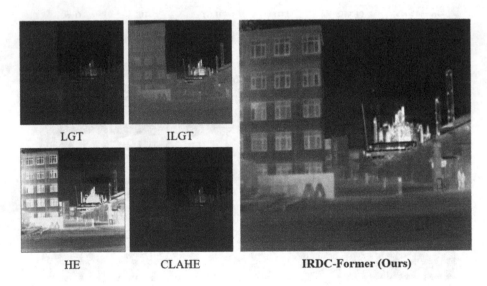

Fig. 4. Visual comparison for the scene of office building obtained by different methods.

Fig. 5. Visual comparison for the scene of pipeline area obtained by different methods.

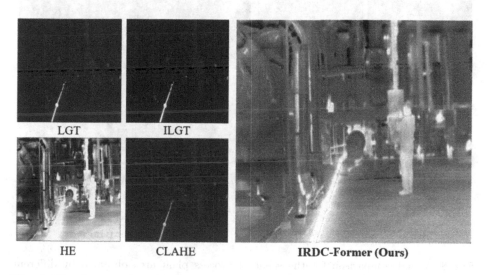

Fig. 6. Visual comparison for the scene of patrol inspection obtained by different methods.

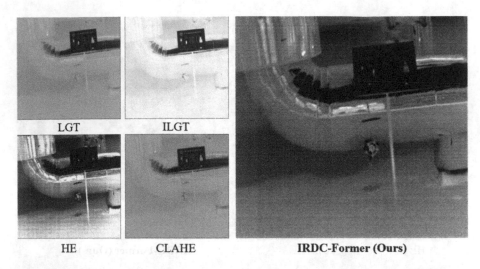

| LGT | ILGT | |
| HE | CLAHE | **IRDC-Former (Ours)** |

Fig. 7. Visual comparison for the scene of large air duct obtained by different methods.

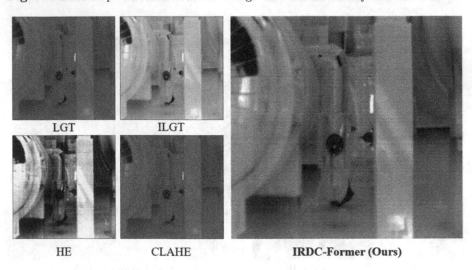

| LGT | ILGT | |
| HE | CLAHE | **IRDC-Former (Ours)** |

Fig. 8. Visual comparison for the scene of process plant area obtained by different methods.

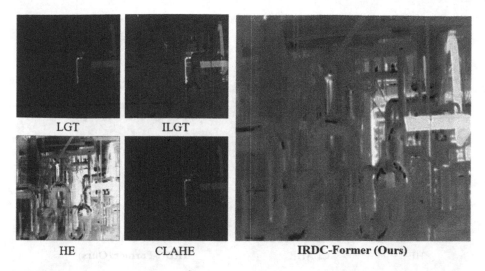

Fig. 9. Visual comparison for the scene of reaction zone obtained by different methods.

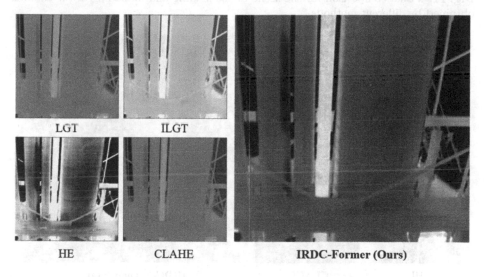

Fig. 10. Visual comparison for the scene of admission line obtained by different methods.

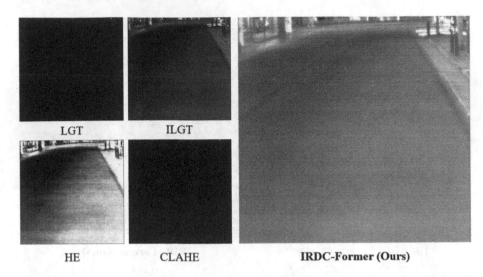

Fig. 11. Visual comparison for the scene of the loading and unloading of the channel obtained by different methods.

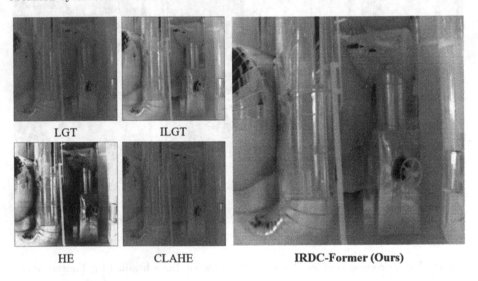

Fig. 12. Visual comparison for the scene of the output pipe obtained by different methods.

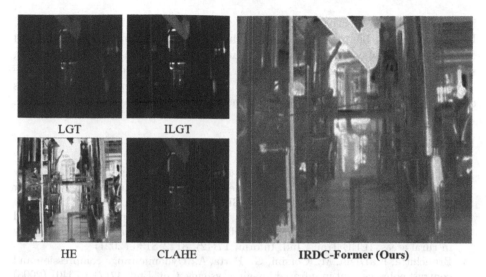

Fig. 13. Visual comparison for the scene of chemical reaction furnace obtained by different methods.

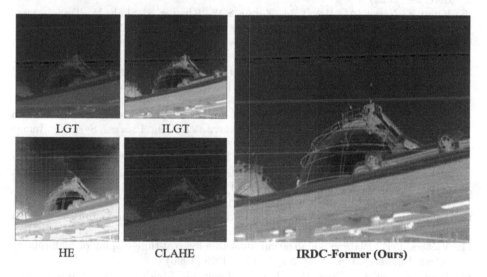

Fig. 14. Visual comparison for the scene of the exhaust gas outlet obtained by different methods.

4   Demonstration and Conclusion

This study proposes an innovative and efficient IR image stretching method. Compared with the results of classical methods, it can be seen that when there are high-radiation objects or low-radiation objects, the classical method will make the image tones appear black or gray to varying degrees, while IRDC-former can reasonably stretch the original image. The processing results are in line with the subjective perception of the human. Furthermore, the trained IRDC-former can be applied to the handheld IR spectral camera, which is used for real-time display. In applications that require IR image bandpass signals, such as gas leak monitoring, a reasonable visualization method will increase the contrast between the gas and the background, making it easier to find leaking gas during the inspection process, ensuring the safety of people's lives and property.

References

1. Beletic, J.W., et al.: Teledyne imaging sensors: infrared imaging technologies for astronomy and civil space. In: High Energy, Optical, and Infrared Detectors for Astronomy III, vol. 7021, pp. 161–174. SPIE (2008)
2. Bin, J., Rahman, C.A., Rogers, S., Liu, Z.: Tensor-based approach for liquefied natural gas leakage detection from surveillance thermal cameras: a feasibility study in rural areas. IEEE Trans. Ind. Inform. **17**(12), 8122–8130 (2021)
3. Branchitta, F., Diani, M., Corsini, G., Porta, A.: Dynamic-range compression and contrast enhancement in infrared imaging systems. Opt. Eng. **47**(7), 076401 (2008)
4. Cai, L., Zi, C., Chen, L.: Adaptive adjustment method and device for infrared detector (2022)
5. Khan, S., Naseer, M., Hayat, M., Zamir, S.W., Khan, F.S., Shah, M.: Transformers in vision: a survey. ACM Comput. Surv. (CSUR) **54**, 1–41 (2021)
6. Lin, T., Wang, Y., Liu, X., Qiu, X.: A survey of transformers. arXiv preprint arXiv:2106.04554 (2021)
7. Paul, A., Sutradhar, T., Bhattacharya, P., Maity, S.P.: Adaptive clip-limit-based bi-histogram equalization algorithm for infrared image enhancement. Appl. Opt. **59**(28), 9032–9041 (2020)
8. Reza, A.M.: Realization of the contrast limited adaptive histogram equalization (CLAHE) for real-time image enhancement. J. VLSI Sig. Process. Syst. Sig. Image Video Technol. **38**(1), 35–44 (2004)
9. Ronneberger, O., Fischer, P., Brox, T.: U-Net: convolutional networks for biomedical image segmentation. In: Navab, N., Hornegger, J., Wells, W.M., Frangi, A.F. (eds.) MICCAI 2015. LNCS, vol. 9351, pp. 234–241. Springer, Cham (2015). https://doi.org/10.1007/978-3-319-24574-4_28
10. Vaswani, A., et al.: Attention is all you need. In: Advances in Neural Information Processing Systems, vol. 30 (2017)
11. Vickers, V.E.: Plateau equalization algorithm for real-time display of high-quality infrared imagery. Opt. Eng. **35**(7), 1921–1926 (1996)
12. Wan, M., Gu, G., Qian, W., Ren, K., Chen, Q., Maldague, X.: Infrared image enhancement using adaptive histogram partition and brightness correction. Remote Sens. **10**(5), 682 (2018)
13. Wang, B.J., Liu, S.Q., Li, Q., Zhou, H.X.: A real-time contrast enhancement algorithm for infrared images based on plateau histogram. Infrared Phys. Technol. **48**(1), 77–82 (2006)
14. Wang, J., Ji, J., Ravikumar, A.P., Savarese, S., Brandt, A.R.: VideoGasNet: deep learning for natural gas methane leak classification using an infrared camera. Energy **238**, 121516 (2022)
15. Wang, Z., Bovik, A.C., Sheikh, H.R., Simoncelli, E.P.: Image quality assessment: from error visibility to structural similarity. IEEE Trans. Image Process. **13**(4), 600–612 (2004)

16. Yeganeh, H., Wang, Z.: Objective quality assessment of tone-mapped images. IEEE Trans. Image Process. **22**(2), 657–667 (2012)
17. Zamir, S.W., Arora, A., Khan, S., Hayat, M., Khan, F.S., Yang, M.H.: Restormer: efficient transformer for high-resolution image restoration. In: Proceedings of the IEEE/CVF Conference on Computer Vision and Pattern Recognition, pp. 5728–5739 (2022)
18. Zhang, T., Cao, S., Pu, T., Peng, Z.: AGPCNet: attention-guided pyramid context networks for infrared small target detection. arXiv preprint arXiv:2111.03580 (2021)
19. Zhou, K., et al.: Explore spatio-temporal aggregation for insubstantial object detection: benchmark dataset and baseline. In: Proceedings of the IEEE/CVF Conference on Computer Vision and Pattern Recognition, pp. 3104–3115 (2022)

Author Index

Printed in the United States
by Baker & Taylor Publisher Services